NORTHLAND

AUCKLAND • Auckland

THE CENTRAL
NORTH ISLAND

WELLINGTON
AND
THE SOUTH

• Wellington

0 kilometres   100

0 miles   100

D1510878

EYEWITNESS TRAVEL

NEW ZEALAND

EYEWITNESS TRAVEL

NEW ZEALAND

LONDON, NEW YORK,
MELBOURNE, MUNICH AND DELHI
www.dk.com

Produced by Editions Didier Millet, Kuala Lumpur

EDITORIAL DIRECTOR Timothy Auger
PROJECT MANAGER Noor Azlina Yunus
EDITORS Dianne Buerger, Zuraidah Omar
DESIGNERS Theivanai Nadaraju, Yong Yoke Lian

CONTRIBUTORS
Helen Corrigan, Roef Hopman, Gerard Hutching,
Rebecca Macfie, Geoff Mercer, Simon Noble, Peter Smith,
Michael Ward, Mark Wright

PHOTOGRAPHERS
Peter Bush, Gerald Lopez, Lloyd Park,
Ron Redfern

ILLUSTRATORS
Yeap Kok Chien, Tan Hong Yew, Denis Chai Kah Yune

MAPS
ERA-Maptec Ltd, Dublin, Ireland

Reproduced by Colourscan, Singapore
Printed and bound by South China Printing Co. Ltd., China

First published in Great Britain in 2001
by Dorling Kindersley Limited
80 Strand, London WC2R 0RL
A Penguin Company

Reprinted with revisions 2002, 2003, 2005, 2006, 2008, 2010

ISBN 978 1 40535 038 9

Front cover main image: Miter Peak, Milford Sound

We're trying to be cleaner and greener:

- we recycle waste and switch things off
- we use paper from responsibly managed forests whenever possible
- we ask our printers to actively reduce water and energy consumption
- we check out our suppliers' working conditions – they never use child labour

Find out more about our values and best practices at www.dk.com

---

**The information in this
DK Eyewitness Guide is checked regularly.**

Every effort has been made to ensure that this book is as up-to-date
as possible at the time of going to press. Some details, however,
such as telephone numbers, opening hours, prices, gallery hanging
arrangements and travel information are liable to change. The
publishers cannot accept responsibility for any consequences arising
from the use of this book, nor for any material on third party
websites, and cannot guarantee that any website address in this
book will be a suitable source of travel information. We value the
views and suggestions of our readers very highly. Please write to:
Publisher, DK Eyewitness Travel Guides, Dorling Kindersley, 80
Strand, London WC2R 0RL, Great Britain.

◁ Sheep and cattle grazing, Mount Hutt

CONTENTS

HOW TO USE THIS GUIDE 6

**Tamatekapua Maori meeting
house, Rotorua**

INTRODUCING NEW ZEALAND

DISCOVERING NEW ZEALAND 10

PUTTING NEW ZEALAND ON THE MAP: THE NORTH ISLAND 12

PUTTING NEW ZEALAND ON THE MAP: THE SOUTH ISLAND 14

A PORTRAIT OF NEW ZEALAND 16

NEW ZEALAND THROUGH THE YEAR 40

THE HISTORY OF NEW ZEALAND 44

**Pohutukawa in bloom at
Oriental Bay, Wellington**

Punting on the Avon River, Christchurch

Upmarket fish and chips

Club rugby match on the North Island's East Cape

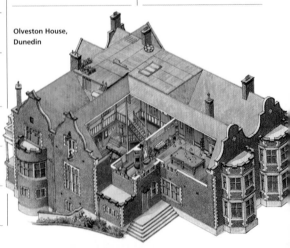
Olveston House, Dunedin

HOW TO USE THIS GUIDE

This guide helps you to get the most from your visit to New Zealand. *Introducing New Zealand* maps the country and sets it in its historical and cultural context. The seven area chapters in *New Zealand Area by Area* describe the main sights, with photographs, illustrations and maps. Features cover topics relating specifically to the North and South islands as well as subjects of regional interest. Restaurant and hotel recommendations can be found in *Travellers' Needs*. The *Survival Guide* has practical tips on everything from making a telephone call to transport.

NEW ZEALAND AREA BY AREA

New Zealand has been divided into seven main sightseeing areas, coded with a coloured thumb tab for quick reference. A map illustrating how the two main islands have been divided can be found on the inside front cover of this guide. The sights listed within the individual areas are plotted and numbered on a *Regional Map*.

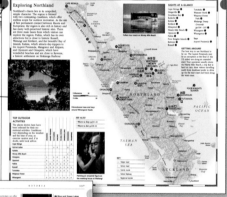

1 Introduction
The landscape, history and character of each region is described here, showing how the area has developed over the years and what it has to offer the visitor today.

A locator map shows the region in relation to the other areas of New Zealand.

Each area of New Zealand can be identified quickly by its colour coding.

2 Regional Map
This gives an illustrated overview of the whole area. All the sights covered in the chapter are numbered and there are useful tips on getting around by car and public transport.

3 Detailed Information
All the important towns and other places of interest are described individually. They are listed in order, following the numbering on the Regional Map. Within each entry there is detailed information on the important buildings and other major sights.

Features and story boxes highlight special or unique features of an area or sight.

4 Major Towns

*All the important towns are described individually.
Within each entry there is further detailed information
on interesting buildings and other sites. The Town Map
shows the location of the main sights.*

A Visitors' Checklist gives you
the practical details to plan your
visit, including transport
information, the address of the
tourist office and festivals.

The Town Map shows all major
and minor roads. The key sights
are plotted, along with train and
bus stations, parking areas and
tourist information offices.

5 Street-by-Street Map

*Towns or districts of
special interest to the visitor
are given a bird's-eye view in
detailed 3D with photographs
and descriptions of the most
important sights.*

A suggested route for
a walk covers the most
interesting streets in
the area.

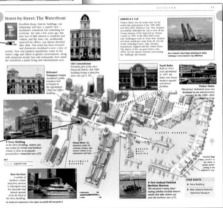

6 The Top Sights

*These are given two or
more pages. Historic buildings
are dissected to reveal their
interiors; national parks
have maps showing facilities
and trails; museums have
colour-coded floorplans.
Photographs highlight the
most interesting features.*

Opening hours, the telephone
number and transport details for
the sight are given in the
Visitors' Checklist.

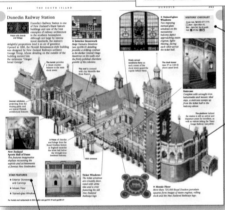

Stars indicate sights that
visitors should not miss.

INTRODUCING
NEW ZEALAND

DISCOVERING NEW ZEALAND

While most visitors are drawn to New Zealand by its natural splendours, the country offers a diverse spectrum of both land- and city-scapes, from the sub-tropical north to the sub-Antarctic south. Natural attractions include beaches, deep-water sounds, high

New Zealand wine

mountains, geothermal springs and forests. New Zealand's new-found cultural confidence can be sampled in the commercial, multi-cultural capital of Auckland and the capital Wellington, as well as in the "garden city" of Christchurch, and university town Dunedin and the vibrant provinces.

AUCKLAND

- Bohemian cafés and bars of Ponsonby
- Top art galleries and museums
- Waterfront action at the Viaduct Basin

Auckland *(see pp66–93)* is New Zealand's largest city and home to a quarter of its inhabitants. The cosmopolitan commercial capital has the largest Polynesian population anywhere. Auckland is the place to shop for New Zealand fashion and art, dine in trendy restaurants and hang out in cafés and bars. **Viaduct Basin** *(see p72)* has been the setting for America's Cup races and is a great place to watch boats and take a cruise. The city has superb entertainment, from SKYCITY casino to concerts at theatres and major sporting events. The nation's best Maori treasures and works by artists such as Colin McCahon and Ralph Hotere are on display in the city's museums and galleries. As an antidote to

Boats at Viaduct Basin, Auckland

The irregular coastline of the Bay of Islands, Northland

city life, the vineyards of **Henderson** *(see p87)* and the beaches at **Piha** and **Karekare** *(see pp86–7)* are close by.

NORTHLAND

- Cape Reinga, the country's rugged northernmost tip
- Stunning coves and inlets of the Bay of Islands
- Historic Kerikeri, Waitangi and Russell

Northland is the symbolic heartland of New Zealand, from **Cape Reinga** *(see p108)*, where Maori spirits depart for their homeland Hawaiki, to **Waitangi** *(see pp104–5)*, where the founding treaty of present-day New Zealand was signed in 1840. The west coast of this sub-tropical peninsula has long sandy beaches, while the east coast is broken up by stunning promontories and gulfs, studded with tiny islands.

The **Bay of Islands** *(see p103)* is an idyllic playground for messing about in boats, diving and deep-sea fishing; it's also the cradle of colonial

New Zealand, where missionaries first converted the Maori – a history which can be seen at the Mission Station in **Kerikeri** *(see p106)*, the quaint township of **Russell** *(see p102)* and the near sacrosanct **Waitangi Treaty Grounds** *(see pp104–5)*. Primeval New Zealand can still be seen in the form of the extraordinary Tane Mahuta, a 1,500-year-old kauri tree found in **Waipoua Forest Park** *(see p111)*.

CENTRAL NORTH ISLAND

- Hot mineral spas, bubbling mud and spouting geysers
- Sun-drenched vineyards and wineries of Hawke's Bay
- Surfers' paradise at Whale Bay, Raglan

The Central North Island offers numerous delights, from the geothermal wonderland of **Rotorua** *(see pp134–9)* and the volcanic ski-fields of **Mount Ruapehu** *(see p142)* to the hot and sunny vineyards of **Hawke's**

Bay *(see pp150–51)* and the famous left-hand surf break at Whale Bay, near **Raglan** *(see pp116–17)*. The best and least commercial Maori experiences are found on the remote **East Cape** *(see pp131–3)* and, to the west of the region, thrill-seekers can black-water raft through the glow-worm caves of **Waitomo** *(see pp120–21)*, while the **Coromandel Peninsula** *(see p124, p127)* offers a more relaxing seaside holiday amid alternative lifestylers and artisans.

A Hawke's Bay vineyard sheltered by mountains

Maori ceremony, Wellington

WELLINGTON AND THE SOUTH

- **Govett-Brewster Gallery in New Plymouth**
- **Boutique wineries of the Wairarapa**
- **Te Papa Tongarewa, the national heritage museum**

There are many lesser-known sights to be seen on the way to **Wellington** *(see pp153–67)*, **New Plymouth** *(see pp180–81)* has innovative, contemporary art shows at the **Govett-Brewster Gallery** *(see p180)* and the summer festival of lights. Or take a trip down the Whanganui River to **Wanganui** *(see pp178–9)*. Some of New Zealand's finest wines can be sampled in the wine area of **Martinborough** *(see p37, p172)*. **Te Papa Tongarewa** *(see pp166–7)*, the national heritage museum, is a must-see in Wellington. Also worth exploring is the historic district of **Thorndon** *(see p161)*, with its 19th-century villas clinging to the hillsides.

MARLBOROUGH AND NELSON

- **Arty, laid-back Nelson**
- **Whale-watching at Kaikoura**
- **Marlborough wines**

For gentle walking head to the **Abel Tasman National Park** *(see pp214–15)*, and for swimming and kayaking seek out the beaches near Golden Bay and vibrant, arty **Nelson** *(see pp210–11, p213)*. The east coast around **Kaikoura** *(see p208)* is famed for its whale-watching tours, while the renowned **Marlborough** wines *(see pp206–7)* round off a trip to the region nicely. For wildlife and secluded bays head to **Marlborough Sounds** *(see pp202–3)*.

CANTERBURY AND THE WEST COAST

- **"Garden city" Christchurch**
- **Lush West Coast rainforests**
- **Shimmering glaciers**

To the east of the Southern Alps lie the flat, dry plains of Canterbury and **Christchurch** *(see pp222–31)*, which bears the imprint of its Anglican founders with its leafy parks and gardens, and colonial-style buildings. To the west of two spectacular high alpine passes lies the **West Coast** *(see pp220–21)*, a strip of rain-forested land, punctuated by the blowholes at **Punakaiki** *(see p236)* and the **Fox** and **Franz-Josef glaciers** *(see p239)*. New Zealand's highest peak, **Aoraki/Mount Cook** *(see pp252–3)*, and the High Country offer great horse treks and walks.

OTAGO AND SOUTHLAND

- **Adrenaline rushes in Queenstown**
- **Primeval Fiordland**
- **Stewart Island birdlife**

For the ultimate outdoors experience, **Queenstown** *(see pp276–7)* and **Wanaka** *(see pp270–71)* are the capitals of white-water rafting, bungee-jumping, snow-boarding and skiing. This beautiful region also has the high peaks of the Remarkables, the primordial landscapes of **Fiordland** *(see pp280–83)*, the unspoilt native flora and fauna of **Stewart Island** *(see pp288–9)*, and the historic stone buildings of the main city, **Dunedin** *(see pp258–65)*.

A glacier walk

Putting New Zealand on The Map: The North Island

New Zealand lies in the South Pacific Ocean, 1,600 km (990 miles) to the east of Australia, 10,000 km (6,210 miles) from San Francisco and a similar distance from Tokyo. Comprising two large islands and a number of smaller ones, its total land area is 270,530 sq km (104,420 sq miles), making it comparable in size to Japan or the British Isles. The main North and South islands are separated by Cook Strait, 20 km (12 miles) wide at its narrowest point. Two-thirds of the country's 4.3 million people live in the North Island, and of these 1.2 million live in Auckland, the country's largest city and the world's most populous Polynesian centre. New Zealand's capital is Wellington, at the southernmost tip of the North Island.

NEW ZEALAND AND ITS ENVIRONS

PACIFIC OCEAN

VIETNAM PHILIPPINES

BRUNEI
MALAYSIA

MICRONESIA

INDONESIA

PAPUA NEW GUINEA

SOLOMON ISLANDS

VANUATU

INDIAN OCEAN

NEW CALEDONIA

AUSTRALIA

NEW ZEALAND

TASMAN SEA   Wellington

KEY TO COLOUR CODING

North Island

- Northland
- Auckland
- Central North Island
- Wellington and the South

North Cape
Cape Reinga

Kaitaia
Kerik
Kaikohe
Opononi
Dargaville

Tasman Sea

North Taranaki Bight

New Plymouth
Cape Egmont
Hawera
South Taranaki Bight
Wanga

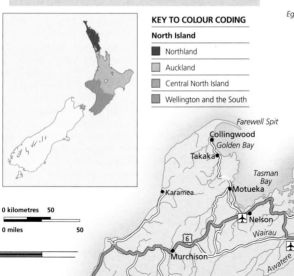

Farewell Spit
Collingwood
Golden Bay
Takaka
Tasman Bay
Marlborough Sounds
Kapiti Island
Paraparaumu
Karamea
Motueka
Nelson
Wairau
WELLINGTON
Blenheim
Murchison
Awatere
Cape Palliser

0 kilometres   50

0 miles   50

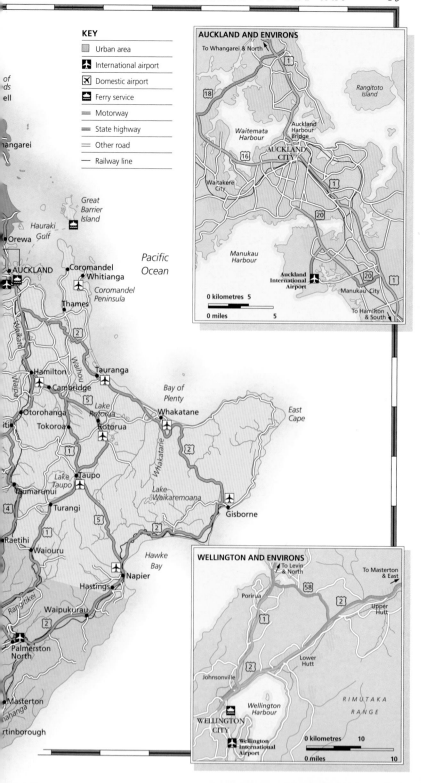

KEY

Urban area
International airport
Domestic airport
Ferry service
Motorway
State highway
Other road
Railway line

AUCKLAND AND ENVIRONS

To Whangarei & North

Rangitoto Island

18

Waitemata Harbour

Auckland Harbour Bridge

16

AUCKLAND CITY

1

Waitakere City

20

Manukau Harbour

Auckland International Airport

Manukau City

20

1

0 kilometres   5

0 miles   5

To Hamilton & South

of
ds
ell

hangarei

Great Barrier Island

Hauraki Gulf

Orewa

AUCKLAND

Coromandel
Whitianga

Coromandel Peninsula

Thames

Pacific Ocean

Whakatane

Waikato

Waipa

Hamilton
Cambridge

2

Otorohanga

5

Lake Rotorua

iti

Tokoroa

Rotorua

Tauranga

Bay of Plenty

Whakatane

East Cape

Whakatane

1

Lake Taupo

Taupo

Lake Waikaremoana

Gisborne

taumarunui

4

Turangi

Raetihi

5

1

Waiouru

2

Hawke Bay

Napier

Hastings

Rangitiki

Rangitiki

2

Waipukurau

Palmerston North

Masterton

mahanga

rtinborough

WELLINGTON AND ENVIRONS

To Levin & North

To Masterton & East

Porirua

58

2

Upper Hutt

1

Lower Hutt

Johnsonville

2

Wellington Harbour

RIMUTAKA

RANGE

WELLINGTON CITY

Wellington International Airport

0 kilometres   10

0 miles   10

Putting New Zealand on The Map:
The South Island

The South Island, 150,440 sq km (58,070 sq miles) in area, is slightly larger than the North Island. The Southern Alps mountain chain runs almost the length of the island, with 223 named peaks higher than 2,300 m (7,550 ft). The eastern side of the alps is dry and largely non-forested, while the West Coast has high rainfall and magnificent forests, mountains and glaciers. Christchurch, the largest city in the South Island, with 360,500 inhabitants, has good international travel links. To the south, Dunedin is an important university town. Stewart Island, south of Invercargill, is New Zealand's third largest island.

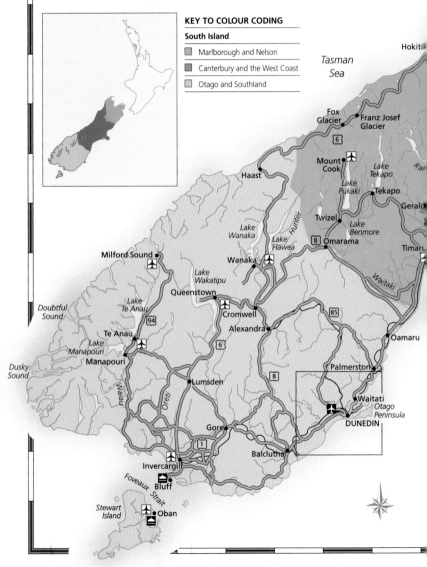

KEY TO COLOUR CODING

South Island

- Marlborough and Nelson
- Canterbury and the West Coast
- Otago and Southland

Tasman
Sea

Hokitik

Fox
Glacier
Franz Josef
Glacier

6

Mount
Cook
Lake
Tekapo

Haast
Lake
Pukaki
Tekapo

Ra

Gerald

Twizel
Lake
Benmore

Lake
Wanaka
Lake
Hawea
8 Omarama
Timaru

Milford Sound
Wanaka

Lake
Wakatipu
Waitaki

Queenstown

Doubtful
Sound
Lake
Te Anau
Cromwell
85

Te Anau
Alexandra
Oamaru

Lake
Manapouri
Manapouri
6

Dusky
Sound
Palmerston

Lumsden
8
Waitati
Otago
Peninsula
DUNEDIN

Gore
Balclutha

Invercargill

Bluff
Foveaux Strait

Stewart
Island
Oban

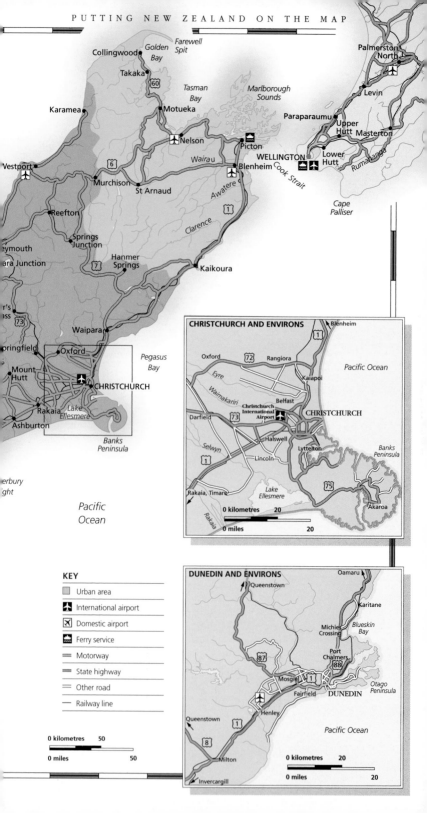

Collingwood
Golden Bay
Farewell Spit
Takaka
60
Tasman Bay
Marlborough Sounds
Motueka
Karamea
Nelson
Picton
WELLINGTON
Vestport
6
Murchison
St Arnaud
Wairau
Blenheim
Cook Strait
Reefton
Springs Junction
Awatere
eymouth
ara Junction
Hanmer Springs
7
Clarence
Kaikoura
Cape Palliser

Palmerston North
Levin
Paraparaumu
Upper Hutt
Masterton
Lower Hutt
Rumataranga

r's ass
73
Waipara
Oxford
pringfield
Mount Hutt
CHRISTCHURCH
Rakaia
Lake Ellesmere
Ashburton
Banks Peninsula
Pegasus Bay

erbury ght

Pacific Ocean

CHRISTCHURCH AND ENVIRONS

Blenheim
1
Oxford
72
Rangiora
Eyre
Kaiapoi
Pacific Ocean
Waimakariri
Belfast
Christchurch International Airport
73
CHRISTCHURCH
Darfield
Selwyn
Halswell
Lyttelton
Banks Peninsula
Lincoln
75
Lake Ellesmere
Rakaia, Timaru
Akaroa
Rakaia

0 kilometres   20
0 miles   20

DUNEDIN AND ENVIRONS

Oamaru
Queenstown
Karitane
Michies Crossing
Blueskin Bay
87
Port Chalmers
88
Mosgiel
1
Fairfield
DUNEDIN
Otago Peninsula
Queenstown
1
Henley
8
Pacific Ocean
Milton
Invercargill

0 kilometres   20
0 miles   20

KEY

Urban area
International airport
Domestic airport
Ferry service
Motorway
State highway
Other road
Railway line

0 kilometres   50
0 miles   50

A PORTRAIT OF NEW ZEALAND

New Zealand is one of the most isolated countries in the world. Maori, the first arrivals, called it Aotearoa, "the land of the long white cloud", the first indication to these canoe voyagers of the presence of the islands being the cloud lying above them. New Zealand's island location affects its climate, its history and its contemporary character.

Spanning latitudes 34 degrees and 47 degrees South, the islands of New Zealand are in the path of "the roaring forties", the winds that circle this lower part of the globe, and are separated from the nearest landmass, Australia, by 1,600 km (990 miles) of the Tasman Sea. On the International Date Line, opposite the Greenwich Meridian of zero degree, New Zealand claims to be the first country to see the sun rise.

Kiwi, a New Zealand icon

The climate ranges from subantarctic to subtropical. The maritime setting creates regular rainfall and abundant vegetation. There is extensive bird and fish life but other than two bat species, the only land mammals are those introduced by early Maori and Europeans. Comparatively a recent settlement, with a population of 4.3 million, New Zealand retains in many areas a clean, natural and untouched environment.

The snow-covered Southern Alps and glacial-formed lakes and fiords provide spectacular scenery, and there is extensive volcanic and thermal activity on the North Island central plateau. The country's coast-

The silver fern, one of New Zealand's symbols

◁ **Aerial view of the snow-capped Southern Alps**

The coastline as seen from Tunnel Beach, south of Dunedin

line provides both sheltered bays and harbours and superb beaches. New Zealand's tourism industry focuses upon this natural environment, the urban aspect being less significant by comparison.

SETTLEMENT

Captain James Cook's circumnavigation and charting of the main islands in 1769–70 paved the way for the sealing and whaling industry. The unruly conditions, the concerns of missionaries over friction with the Maori and pressure from Edward Gibbon's Colonising Society prompted the British to pursue a treaty with the Maori establishing sovereignty. At Waitangi in the Bay of Islands, a treaty was signed between the British Crown, represented by Captain William Hobson, and a number of Maori chiefs. Although the Treaty of Waitangi provided for protection of Maori and their natural resources, alienation of Maori land occurred well into the 20th century. Maori leaders pressed for justice and organized land marches. In 1975, the treaty was reconsidered, the Treaty of Waitangi Act passed by parliament set up the Waitangi Tribunal to consider Maori land claims.

Captain James Cook

Planned settlement in the 1840s was mainly by English and Scottish enterprises. Today the character of cities such as Christchurch and Dunedin still reflects those origins. Auckland, the country's former capital and now its commercial centre, remains more cosmopolitan. Wellington's early establishment as the capital contributes to its political character.

Maori leader Dame Whina Cooper setting out for a land march *(Hikoi)* in October 1975

Early settlers felled extensive areas of forest for the timber trade and for farmland. The independent spirit of New Zealanders can be said to derive from their determination to succeed in their new land. The people of New Zealand came from a cross section of English, Scottish and Irish society, and all were united in their desire to make their country prosper.

SOCIETY

New Zealand is an independent state. New Zealand's parliament, based on the Statute of Westminster, pays allegiance to the British sovereign through its governor-general. Proposals that New Zealand become a republic have some support in the country.

New Zealanders take pride in their history of social reform. The first in the world to give all women the vote in 1893, New Zealand had established compulsory, free primary schooling by 1877, and by 1938 a state-supported health system, universal superannuation and a liberal social welfare structure. The country declared its non-nuclear stance in 1986. This has resulted in non-alignment of its armed forces, though New Zealand troops are used in peace-keeping roles.

Although the Waitangi Tribunal has

The Beehive, part of the Parliament Buildings in Wellington, which houses the Ministers' offices

enabled substantial compensation for Maori whose land was confiscated, there are still some grievances to settle. Encouragement of the immigration of Pacific Islanders by the governments of the 1960s seeking to obtain a labour force has created ethnic diversity, as too has the influx of Asian immigrants.

Nevertheless, visitors comment on the friendliness and welcoming attitudes of New Zealanders, which may stem from a small population

Arts Centre weekend market in Christchurch

The New Zealand All Blacks before playing South Africa in Dunedin in 1999

living, by world standards, in good quality housing, in small cities that do not suffer from congestion or widespread crime. All have easy access to a superb natural environment. There is also a curiosity about the world and New Zealanders travel abroad a great deal. The great "OE" (overseas experience) is still popular with the young.

Although there is today evidence of a widening gap between rich and poor, New Zealand remains an egalitarian society. There are some social differences based upon wealth and occupation, but there is no class system in New Zealand based on birth and inheritance. Enterprise and energy can secure good employment

Maori youngsters on horseback

and quality of life. Almost 85 per cent of the population is urban, with 75 per cent resident in the North Island.

In the last 100 years or so the Maori population has increased and now makes up 16 per cent of the country's total. However, the social and economic status of some Maori is still below average, a situation that will hopefully be corrected in time by affirmative government education and employment policies.

WORK AND THE ECONOMY

Although agriculture is the major industry, with meat, dairy, fish and timber products predominating, a need to compete in the world markets has required diversification. A pioneer in agricultural research, New Zealand is a leader in animal and crop technology. Its wines, particularly whites, are now internationally recognized and its quality foodstuffs are exported to many countries. Tourism is important. Facilities, accommodation, restaurants and cafés cater for all tastes. Being a small nation that has to transport

Sheep droving on a state highway

its exports long distances to foreign markets, New Zealand is vulnerable to the international economy. It does not possess substantial mineral resources, although it has been able to utilize its own natural gas and oil. It also has no large manufacturing industry. However, signs of an export market in information technology, electronics and ship-building are encouraging.

Outdoor dining at Mapua, Nelson

The recession in the 1980s prompted a move from welfare state to "user pays" policies, with privatization of state-owned enterprises. The major political parties are Labour (centre left) and National (centre right), with minor parties influencing the balance of power.

Teacher and students studying in a park

of Pacific Island and Maori culture coincide with a resurgence of Maori and Pacific Island art and artists. New Zealanders can claim some notable firsts. Lord Rutherford from Brightwater was the first to split the atom and Sir Edmund Hillary, with Sherpa Tenzing, was the first to reach the summit of Mount Everest. Others of international repu-

SPORT AND CULTURE

New Zealand is a sportsperson's paradise. The successful defence of the America's Cup in 2000 attracted one of the world's largest gatherings of mega-yachts. Rugby is the most popular game, followed by netball and cricket. A wide range of international entertainers, musicians, artists and dance companies make frequent visits to the country. Festivals

tation are author Katherine Mansfield, opera diva Dame Kiri Te Kanawa, soprano Hayley Westenra, film director Peter Jackson and space scientist Sir William Pickering.

New Zealand is today a vibrant, hospitable, multicultural nation that has forged a unique identity derived from a combination of Maori heritage and colonial culture.

Street buskers providing entertainment in Auckland

New Zealand's Landscape

New Zealand is an old land with a young landscape: some of the rocks that underlie the country are, at 600 million years old, relatively ancient. However, the landforms that have been created from them are very young. The Southern Alps, for example, began to emerge only three million years ago and volcanic explosions and earthquakes continue to create new forms. The overriding feature of the landscape is its diversity: mountains, lakes, rivers, beaches, hills, plains, volcanoes, rainforests and fiords are all contained in a relatively small area.

Mount Ruapehu, *like other New Zealand cone volcanoes, erupts frequently. It sits astride one of the world's major volcanic centres (see pp64 –5).*

The foothills of the Southern Alps, the Great Divide between the west and east coasts, shelter the Canterbury Plains from prevailing westerly winds.

New Zealand's coastline *is 18,200 km (11,300 miles) long. About 80 per cent is exposed to open sea while 20 per cent borders sheltered waters. The coasts harbour marine life and are popular playgrounds for water sports.*

TECTONIC PLATE FORMATION

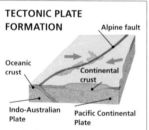

Alpine fault

Oceanic crust

Continental crust

Indo-Australian Plate

Pacific Continental Plate

For the last 20 –25 million years, New Zealand has been lying astride two of the world's 15 moving "plates". In the North Island, the Pacific Continental Plate pushes under the Indo-Australian Plate, forming volcanoes in between. In the South Island, the Indo-Australian Plate pushes under the Pacific one, forming an Alpine fault line.

SOUTH CANTERBURY AND SOUTHERN ALPS

Large-scale farming has transformed tussock plains into a landscape of grasslands dissected by rivers and dotted with livestock. The distant Southern Alps bear testimony to the powerful geological forces which have been shaping the country for the last 600 million years.

Tussock grasslands *cover about 10 per cent of New Zealand's land area. Much of this area was covered in forest or scrubland before the early Maori burned it while hunting for moa.*

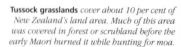

The Bay of Islands *comprises 144 offshore islands, all within 50 km (30 miles) of the coast. During glacial periods, when sea levels were lower, the islands were connected to the mainland.*

Braided rivers *(see p191)* transport rock and shingle from the Southern Alps to create fertile farmlands.

THE GONDWANALAND CONNECTION

Until about 80 million years ago, New Zealand formed part of the great super continent, Gondwanaland, which comprised present-day Antarctica, Australia, India, Africa and South America. Once New Zealand floated off into isolation, many of its plants and animals evolved into forms which were never seen on other landmasses.

180 million years ago, New Zealand occupied a corner of Gondwanaland, one of the world's two massive continents; the other is called Laurasia.

135 million years ago, Gondwanaland began to split apart into the present-day continents. At this time, New Zealand was still attached to Australia.

Today, the Tasman Sea separates New Zealand and Australia, and the continents continue to drift apart. New Zealand is moving northwards towards the equator at the rate of about 30 mm (1.2 inches) a year.

Sheep, farmed for both wool and meat, thrive on South Canterbury's hill country and rolling downs.

The fiords *of southwest New Zealand, carved out over millions of years by successive Ice Ages – the last 10,000 years ago – are among the most spectacular in the world (see pp280 –81). The coastline of the fiords extends 1,000 km (620 miles). Doubtful Sound, at 420 m (1,380 ft) is the deepest of the fiords, while Dusky Sound, which stretches 40 km (25 miles) inland, is the longest.*

Flora and Fauna

New Zealand has been a land apart for 80 million years, with the result that it is home to a collection of plants and animals found nowhere else in the world. It has only two land mammals (both bats), although seals, whales and dolphins are found around the coasts. Flightless birds, a diversity of lizards, giant snails, primitive frogs and plants that are as old as the dinosaurs combine to make New Zealand unique. Despite the impact of humans on flora and fauna over the last 1,000 years, much remains to fascinate the visitor.

Blue penguin

The tuatara *is the sole remaining species of an order of reptiles which evolved about 220 million years ago. The best place to see a tuatara is at the tuatarium in Invercargill (see p286).*

KAURI FORESTS

Northland's forests are dominated by massive, straight-trunked kauri trees interspersed with a mix of subtropical plants. So valuable was the timber for boat building, housing and carving that the forests have been depleted since the 1790s.

Kiwis *are found in forests on North, South and Stewart islands, where they use their long beaks to dig for food.*

Giant wetas, *flightless "crickets" as large as a person's hand, are harmless inhabitants of kauri forests.*

The silver fern *or ponga, widely adopted as a national symbol, takes its name from the silvery underside of the fronds.*

SHRUBLANDS

Shrublands consist of short, scrubby plants. They are home to many species of animals and are nurseries for mature forest. Widespread throughout the country, shrublands are often areas that were once logged and are now regenerating.

The green gecko *lives on the outer branches of shrubs and is a daytime hunter. It bears live young in contrast to other species which lay eggs.*

Kowhai, *sometimes described as New Zealand's national flower, has striking drooping yellow blooms in spring.*

Manuka *is a key pollen and nectar plant for bees.*

BIRDS OF NEW ZEALAND

New Zealand is famed for its unusual birds. Evolving without significant predators, such as rats, cats or dogs, to menace them, they lost any reason to fly. Some not only became flightless, but also developed into some of the largest birds ever to have lived. When Maori arrived, they discovered the huge moa, which stood more than 2 m (7 ft) tall. As a result of being hunted, the moa became extinct 300–500 years ago. Today, many of New Zealand's ancient bird species survive in limited numbers, among them the kiwi, kakapo, takahe, black robin and kea, and enormous efforts are being made to ensure their survival.

Kokakos are poor fliers but are noted for their singing abilities.

The kakapo is a large, flightless, nocturnal parrot.

ALPINE LANDSCAPE

New Zealand's alpine region begins at about 1,300 m (4,270 ft) above sea level in the North Island but drops to 900 m (2,950 ft) in the South Island. Intense cold, heat, dryness and wind combine to produce tussock and shrubs adapted to cope with the climate.

AROUND THE COAST

Rocky shores, sandy beaches and muddy estuaries provide a diversity of habitats for coastal flora and fauna. Many native plants thrive in the salty environment, thanks to adaptations such as tough leaves which retain moisture in dry conditons.

Keas are South Island mountain parrots. They have a reputation for play-fulness and intelligence.

The royal albatross breeds at Taiaroa Head on the Otago Peninsula (see p266) upon returning from its winter feeding grounds.

The vegetable sheep plant is a mass of thousands of small, separate plants which together resemble the wool of a sheep.

The pohutu-kawa's crimson flowers along the coasts of the North Island herald the arrival of Christmas.

Alpine plants climb above the competition to be noticed by pollinating alpine insects.

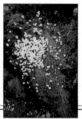

New Zealand fur seals are commonly seen lolling on rocks around the coasts.

New Zealand's National Parks and Reserves

Jewelled geckos

From the snow-capped volcanoes of Tongariro National Park to the sheer cliffs of Fiordland, New Zealand's national parks contain an awe-inspiring range of scenery, beautiful walking tracks, and numerous plants and animals found nowhere else in the world. The 14 national parks cover over 30,000 sq km (19,000 sq miles) or about 8 per cent of the country's land surface. There are also over 30 conservation and forest parks, thousands of reserves and over 30 marine reserves. Keep safe when tramping or hiking by being well prepared and equipped, and respect the natural environment by leaving the land undisturbed.

Abel Tasman National Park's *golden sand beaches fringe bush-clad cliffs. Inland, deep caves and underground rivers are a feature of the limestone landscape (see pp214–15).*

Aoraki/Mount Cook National Park *contains the highest mountain in Australasia, Mount Cook, known as Aoraki or "cloud piercer" by the Ngai Tahu tribe, as well as New Zealand's longest glacier (see pp252–3).*

Paparoa National Park's *limestone landscape gives this area its special flavour. Along the coast, constant pounding by the Tasman Sea has sculpted the limestone into the Pancake Rocks and blowholes (see p236).*

Fiordland National Park *is a vast, remote wilderness, with snow-capped mountains, fiords, glacial valleys and lakes, waterfalls, islands and dense temperate forest (see pp280–81).*

0 kilometres   100

0 miles   100

Abel Tas
National

Kahura
National

N

Nelson L
National

Paparoa
National
Park

Westland / Tai Poutini
National Park   Arthur's Pass
National Park

CHRISTCHU

Banks
Peninsula

Mount Aspiring
National Park   **Aoraki / Mount Cook National Park**

QUEENSTOWN

Fiordland
National Park

Otago
Peninsula

INVERCARGILL   DUNEDIN

Foveaux Strait

Rakiura
National Park

Stewart Island

KEY

☐ National parks

☐ Conservation parks

☐ Reserves

☐ Marine reserves

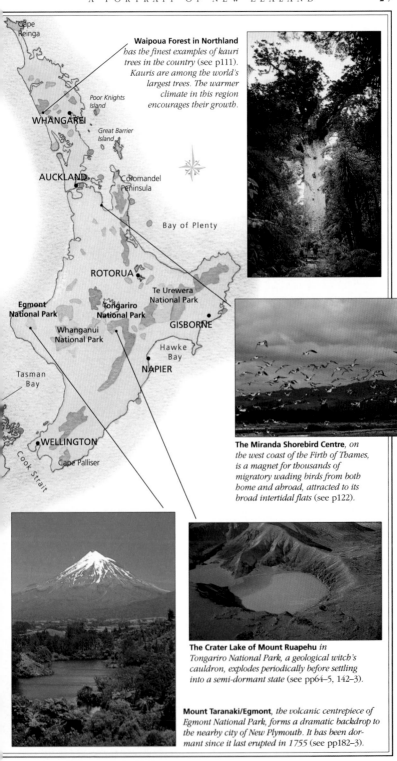

Waipoua Forest in Northland *has the finest examples of kauri trees in the country (see p111). Kauris are among the world's largest trees. The warmer climate in this region encourages their growth.*

The Miranda Shorebird Centre, *on the west coast of the Firth of Thames, is a magnet for thousands of migratory wading birds from both home and abroad, attracted to its broad intertidal flats (see p122).*

The Crater Lake of Mount Ruapehu *in Tongariro National Park, a geological witch's cauldron, explodes periodically before settling into a semi-dormant state (see pp64–5, 142–3).*

Mount Taranaki/Egmont, *the volcanic centrepiece of Egmont National Park, forms a dramatic backdrop to the nearby city of New Plymouth. It has been dormant since it last erupted in 1755 (see pp182–3).*

Architecture in New Zealand

Earthquake risk in New Zealand has limited the height and structure of buildings, giving towns and cities a somewhat uniform appearance, while abundant space has led to suburban sprawl. Interspersed with the country's ubiquitous wooden houses are gracious historic homes and buildings, well-preserved Maori meeting houses and impressive public and commercial buildings. The latter range from early European-style structures built in stone to modern glass and concrete towers. Contemporary architecture is an eclectic mix of "New Zealand" and imported styles.

Glass and concrete towers in Auckland

MAORI MEETING HOUSES

Communal meeting houses and storehouses have single gable roofs supported on posts sunk in the ground, and are elaborately carved. The porch bargeboards symbolize the arms of the ancestors, the ridgepole the tribal backbone, and the rafters the ribs of family lineage. Many older houses have been restored and new ones built of modern materials *(see p131).*

The figures on wall and roof posts represent ancestors and chieftains

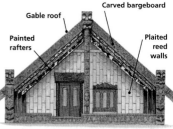

Carved bargeboard
Gable roof
Painted rafters
Plaited reed walls

Te Tokanganui-a-Noho *at Te Kuiti, a well-preserved meeting house built in 1872.*

HOMESTEADS

From the mid-1800s, wealthy sheep or cattle farmers and rich merchants demonstrated their affluence with substantial, architect-designed mansions to which they added rooms as they prospered. Stylistically varied, most mansions reflect a Victorian flavour, and some are romantically nostalgic and grandiose. The interiors are usually richly panelled, with elaborately carved stair rails, balusters, moulded ceilings and cornices *(see p265).*

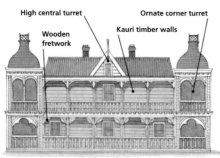

High central turret
Ornate corner turret
Kauri timber walls
Wooden fretwork

Alberton, *a two-storey residence built for farmer Allen Kerr in 1862, and later extended, now lies within Auckland city.*

PUBLIC BUILDINGS

By the 1860s, the construction of public buildings reinforced links with "home", reflecting, for example, the Gothic Revival style in Britain. Sometimes timber was substituted for the customary stone. The emphasis is on verticality and repeated ornamentation.

Otago University *(1878) in Dunedin, built in Gothic style after Scotland's Glasgow University (1870).*

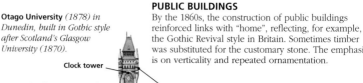

Clock tower
Local grey stonework
Lighter stone facings
Arched windows

BAY VILLAS

In the early 1900s, bay-fronted villas became the standard domestic house, with often a street at a time being built to a stock design. Usually constructed of timber weatherboard with corrugated iron or clay tile roofs, they ranged from single bay villas decorated with crude sawn fretwork to more sophisticated and elaborate multistorey homes for the affluent (see p161).

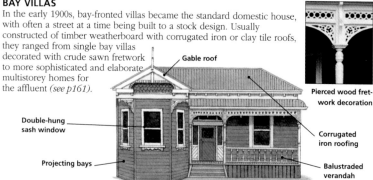

Pierced wood fret-
work decoration

Gable roof

Double-hung
sash window

Projecting bays

Corrugated
iron roofing

Balustraded
verandah

COMMERCIAL BUILDINGS

As New Zealand prospered in the early 1900s, more permanent commercial buildings replaced temporary shops and warehouses. A wide range of styles, including Classical Renaissance and Edwardian Baroque, demonstrated the substance and affluence of successful commercial enterprise. Although façades are often splendid, with Roman columns, the structure behind uses more modern techniques of steel framing and reinforced concrete. As such techniques allowed varied exterior treatment, there is little consistency of style in city buildings.

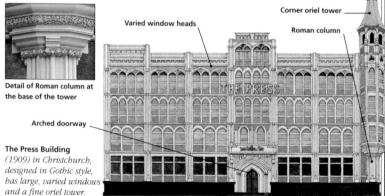

Detail of Roman column at
the base of the tower

Varied window heads

Corner oriel tower

Roman column

Arched doorway

The Press Building
(1909) in Christchurch,
designed in Gothic style,
has large, varied windows
and a fine oriel tower.

CONTEMPORARY NEW ZEALAND ARCHITECTURE

Although contemporary New Zealand architecture reflects international stylistic diversity, many architects are endeavouring to respond to the natural environment and to utilize ingredients from both Maori and European heritages.

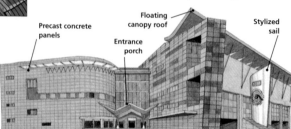

Abstract art design on
the exterior glazing

**The Museum of
New Zealand Te
Papa Tongarewa,**
opened in 1998,
incorporates
elements of the gable
forms of Maori
meeting houses.

Precast concrete
panels

Floating
canopy roof

Entrance
porch

Stylized
sail

Maori Culture and Art

Tiki pendant

Maori have developed a complex culture derived from their Pacific Island inheritance. Climatic and seasonal conditions that differed from their former home, and a more extensive land area, permitted independent tribal development and variations in language, customs and art forms. Forests enabled them to build large canoes for transport and warfare, as well as meeting houses. Maori excel in wood, bone and stone carving, and in plaiting and weaving. Oratory, chant, song and dance are the means of passing on ancestral knowledge, and form an essential dimension of the rituals of challenge, welcome and farewell.

Moko *(tattoo) involves incising lines into the skin and colouring them with pigment. The tradition has been revived and today, some Maori proudly wear moko.*

CARVING

The plentiful supply of large, straight-grained and durable timbers, and a variety of hard stones and obsidian that could be shaped into tools, enabled the early Maori to continue the Pacific tradition of carving. Today, an increasing awareness of Maori heritage has brought about a rebirth of traditional crafts. At Te Puia, a Maori arts and crafts centre in Rotorua, students learn to carve wood, bone and greenstone into exquisite and intricate \ Tiki pendants, combs and ceremonial objects *(see p138).*

Carving *in the Maori Affairs Select Committee Room of the Parliament Buildings in Wellington.*

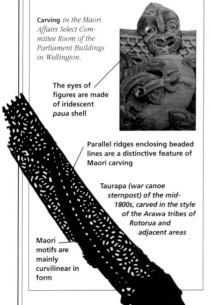

The eyes of figures are made of iridescent *paua* **shell**

Parallel ridges enclosing beaded lines are a distinctive feature of Maori carving

Taurapa (war canoe sternpost) of the mid-1800s, carved in the style of the Arawa tribes of Rotorua and adjacent areas

Maori motifs are mainly curvilinear in form

SONG AND DANCE

Singing and dancing are an important feature of Maori life. They are performed on various occasions by both men and women. The *poi* dance, with its graceful movements is, however, restricted to women.

The *haka* *is a war dance performed by men. Eyes and tongues protrude in a gesture of defiance.*

Plaiting and weaving, *using swamp flax, reeds or bird feathers, are women's arts. This 1880s* kete whakairo, *or decorated bag, was woven from flax.*

Cloaks and capes *are a feature of traditional Maori dress and are made of various materials, including flax, feathers and dogskin. This engraving by Sydney Parkinson (1745–71) depicts a cloaked warrior.*

Poi balls are stuffed with reeds and covered with woven flax fibre.

Songs are performed with the whole being; the body, hands, legs, arms and facial expressions all play their part.

Early Maori weapons *were made of wood, stone and bone. Close hand-to-hand fighting was the main characteristic of Maori warfare. This* wahaika, *or short wooden hand club, from the early 1800s, is an example of a weapon used for striking.*

Skirts consist of strips of flax hanging from a belt. The green leaves are scraped and dried so that they curl into tubes.

CONTEMPORARY MAORI ARTIST

Very much a part of the remarkable renaissance in contemporary Maori art, artist Cliff Whiting celebrates his ancestral inheritance in this interpretation of the legend of creation. Using a mixture of traditional and modern materials and processes, he depicts Tane Mahuta, God of the Forests, pushing apart Ranginui, his Sky Father, and Papatuanuku, his Earth Mother, to let light enter the world.

Mural by Cliff Whiting (1974), depicting the separation of Ranginui and Papatuanuku

New Zealand Artists and Writers

From the time of first contact, botanists, navigators, surveyors and amateur painters recorded aspects of New Zealand's flora and fauna, the Maori people and early settlements. There were also many reports, diaries and commentaries in the British press which provided interesting descriptions and accounts of the new land, such as Lady Barker's *Station Life in New Zealand* (1870). The poetry, novels and paintings of the late 19th century were very much in the European tradition, but by the 1900s distinctive national elements began to emerge in writing and art.

Lithograph of tuis (1888) by J G Kuelemans

Painting of a Maori chief by Charles Frederick Goldie

ARTISTS

The pioneer climate in New Zealand was not sympathetic to the arts. "Working class" settlers, struggling to survive in a strange and hostile land, had little knowledge of the arts. For the wealthy, the arts were largely a diversion for gentlewomen. Works of any substance were mainly by artists visiting New Zealand, such as William Hodges, whose work stylised the scenery into Romantic vistas. Italian Girolamo Pieri Nerli and Dutchman Petrus van der Velden, both also had a romantic European view of the untamed land.

A few New Zealanders sought training in European academies, such as Charles Frederick Goldie. By the 1900s art schools and societies had become established in New Zealand, but many artists, conscious of the Impressionist movement and other developments in Europe, escaped to that more exciting milieu. Frances Hodgkins left in 1901, and although some claim her as an eminent New Zealand artist, she achieved her reputation working in Britain and France.

In the 1920s, British-trained artists, such as Robert Field, Christopher Perkins and Roland Hipkins, came to teach and brought to their students the "radical" ideas of modernism, which were well established in Europe. Expressionist, Cubist and abstract influences began to appear in the works of John Weeks, Rhona Haszard and Louise Henderson, and by the 1940s a number of artists saw in modernism an opportunity to explore the "national" character of the land and its people. Much of the work of Eric Lee-Johnson, Sir Tosswill Woollaston, Russell Clark, Rita Angus and William Sutton seeks to define the substance or spirit of the land rather than give it superficial description.

In 1954 – late by world standards – the Auckland City Art Gallery presented New Zealand's first show of abstract paintings, "Object and Image", which caused a public outcry. However, artists such as Louise Henderson, Colin McCahon, Don Peebles and Rudy Gopas began to exhibit in the dealer galleries, which had become a feature of the larger cities.

Sculpture lagged behind painting, although Len Lye began his kinetic works as early as 1950. He moved to New York, but New Zealand is fortunate to have a substantial collection of his work at the Govett-Brewster Gallery in New Plymouth (*see p180*). From the 1960s, significant modern works were commissioned for public places from Jim Allen, Greer Twiss, Marte Szirmay, Terry Stringer, Neil Dawson and Paul Dibble.

Since the 1970s, there has been a substantial increase in the number of full-time professional artists, including outstanding Maori artists such as Ralph Hotere, Para Matchett, Fred Graham and Shona Rapira Davies.

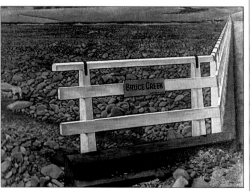

Dry September (1949), oil on canvas by William Sutton

Nga Morehu (The Survivors; 1988), a sculpture in mixed media by Shona Rapira Davies

WRITERS

New Zealand writing began to attract attention by the 1860s, but most of it was published in Britain as New Zealand lacked publishing houses. *Erewhon* (1872) by Samuel Butler is based upon his life in the high country of the South Island. *A History of New Zealand Birds* (1873) by Sir Walter Buller is still highly regarded for its careful documentation and illustrations. William Pember Reeves' *The Long White Cloud*, a romanticized version of New Zealand history, was published in 1898.

Jane Mander's *The Story of a New Zealand River* (1920) attracted some international attention for its depiction of colonial life. *Bliss*, Katherine Mansfield's first collection of short stories, marked the advent of New Zealand writing of originality and substance. Born in Wellington, Mansfield was sent to London to further her education. Although she returned briefly to New Zealand, she spent most of her life in France and England. Though produced abroad, her work, which reveals her sharp observation of human behaviour, is based upon her memories of a New Zealand childhood. Mansfield died in 1923 at the age of 34.

Katherine Mansfield

By the 1930s, there emerged a conscious determination by novelists and poets to shape a New Zealand style, using local idioms, references to the raw landscape, and characterization of its settler inhabitants. Time spent overseas in the armed forces during both world wars also gave writers a new perspective of their homeland and added more pungency to their writing. Typical is poet Allen Curnow's *Landfall in Unknown Seas*, a powerful evocation of the visitor confronted by an alien but compelling land.

By the 1950s, Denis Glover, Robin Hyde, Frank Sargeson and Ruth Dallas, among others, ushered in a period of substantial productivity. Novelists such as John Mulgan, Dan Davin, Roderick Finlayson, and poet

James K Baxter also cast a sharply critical eye upon what they saw as a conforming and conventional society that concealed disturbing undercurrents.

Historian and poet Keith Sinclair, in his *A History of New Zealand* (1961), was one of the first to question prevailing versions of New Zealand history, which promoted colonial supremacy over "native" primitivism and biased interpretations of land settlement and the subsequent land wars. Dick Scott's research in *Ask that Mountain* (1975) revealed to New Zealanders a truer account of early settlement and relations with Maori. Writers such as Fiona Kidman, C K Stead, Maurice Gee, Fleur Adcock and historian Michael King have demonstrated a new maturity in their commentary upon racial and social issues.

A number of Maori writers are a voice for their people, among them Witi Ihimaera, Patricia Grace and Hone Tuwhare. In 1985, Keri Hulme, of Maori and Pakeha descent, won the British Booker Prize with *The Bone People*. Maori writer Alan Duff's *Once Were Warriors*, later made into a film of the same name, is a powerful exposure of the turbulence within the urban Maori people. Sylvia Ashton-Warner's novel *Spinster*, on provincial attitudes in a rural community, was made into a film in the US, as was Ian Cross's *God Boy*, an insight into adolescence and religion.

Cover of *The Bone People*, a novel by Keri Hulme

James K Baxter

Farming and Horticulture

Cow on rural letter box

Despite being so urbanized (85 per cent of New Zealanders live in cities or large towns), the country still depends heavily on its agricultural economy. Farming industries utilize more than 62 per cent of the total land area of 165,000 sq km (63,700 sq miles) and produce more than half of all export earnings. Traditionally, pastoral farming has centred on sheep and cattle but other types of livestock, such as deer, goats, pigs and poultry, are gaining in importance. Pine trees cloak hills too steep to support livestock, while horticulture and other crops now dominate fertile coastal and inland areas.

Kiwifruit, *grown primarily in the Bay of Plenty (see p129), is successfully marketed in more than 50 countries. New Zealand supplies about a quarter of world production.*

Apples and pears, *New Zealand's main pip fruits, are grown mostly in Hawke's Bay and Marlborough/Nelson. About 18 million cartons are exported annually.*

Plastic sheeting protects rows of delicate berry fruits from frost.

Lines of trees between orchards serve as windbreaks.

Kiwifruit grow on vines supported by wooden trellises.

Peaches *and other stone fruit, such as apricots, nectarines, plums and cherries, are concentrated in Hawke's Bay and Central Otago.*

HORTICULTURE

Although pastoral farming is the major land use in New Zealand, large areas are now planted in crops. The mild, sunny climate and fertile soils of the coastal regions of the Bay of Plenty, Gisborne, Hawke's Bay, Nelson and Otago have created a stunning mosaic of orchards producing a variety of traditional pip and stone fruit as well as citrus, berry and subtropical varieties.

PASTORAL AGRICULTURE

New Zealand's 40 million sheep and nine million cattle are bred for their meat, wool, dairy produce and hides. Dairy herds are found on the fairly flat land, while sheep and beef cattle are farmed in the rougher hill country. Deer, goats and other livestock are scattered throughout both islands.

The Romney Cross *is the most common sheep in New Zealand and is bred for both meat and wool production.*

The black and white Holstein-Friesian *is the most common dairy cow, yielding more milk than other breeds.*

CEREAL AND OTHER CROPS

Fields of traditional cereal crops are found on the plains of the South Island, especially in Canterbury and Southland. Here, wheat and oats are grown for home consumption and for milling, and barley and oats for the manufacture of stock feed; barley is also grown for malting at New Zealand breweries. Large-scale vegetable production has made inroads into fertile coastal regions in both the North and South islands, while new and distinct plant varieties, such as sunflowers, lavender and garlic, add colour and variety to the country's agricultural landscape.

Sunflowers, grown for their seeds, near Palmerston North

Wheat and garlic in Marlborough

Sorting and packaging is done in packhouses.

Citrus trees are planted in long, straight lines.

Other fruits, *such as the citrus grapefruit and subtropical varieties like avocados, tamarillos, persimmons and pepinos (in addition to kiwifruit), are grown in warmer North Island orchards – Northland, around Auckland, the Bay of Plenty and Hawke's Bay — while berry fruits such as raspberries thrive in the cooler South Island.*

Grapefruit

Avocados

Pepinos

Persimmon

Tamarillos

Raspberries

Grapes *are grown mainly for wine production (see pp36–7). Marlborough, Canterbury, Gisborne and Hawke's Bay are the major grape producing areas. Few table grapes are grown.*

Deer *are bred on some 5,000 farms. Venison fetches premium prices worldwide, while deer velvet is popular in Asia.*

Goats *are farmed both domestically and commercially for their milk, meat and mohair as well as for weed control.*

Ostriches *(as shown here) and emus are among the new livestock breeds gaining in popularity.*

The Wines of New Zealand

Corbans Longridge labels

Although grapes were first planted in New Zealand as early as the 1830s, it was not until the 1980s when wine makers decided to concentrate on white wines, such as Sauvignon Blanc and Chardonnay, that the country's reputation as an excellent wine producer began. The number of wineries has since grown to almost 400, and export wine sales in 2006 reached 57 million litres (12 million gallons). In less than 20 years, the nation's wine makers have gone from producing wine of average quality to some of the best in the world. Wine drinking is popular in New Zealand. Many vineyards have restaurants, offer wine tastings and tours, and sell wine at the cellar door.

A visit to a vineyard *for wine tasting or a meal is a popular weekend leisure activity.*

JAMES BUSBY

Appointed by the British Government as Resident or government representative to New Zealand in 1833, James Busby (1800 –71) became the country's first recorded wine maker. He had earlier studied wine making in France and had also helped to establish a wine industry in the Hunter Valley in Australia. French explorer Dumont D'Urville confirmed the promise of viticulture in the country when he heaped praise on Busby's white wine, which he sampled during an 1840 visit to the Bay of Islands.

Marlborough *is New Zealand's largest wine-growing region (see pp206–7). The wide, flat Wairau Valley, dry, sunny climate and slow ripening conditions combine to produce the country's finest Sauvignon Blanc.*

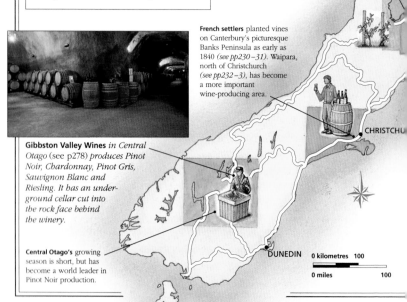

French settlers planted vines on Canterbury's picturesque Banks Peninsula as early as 1840 *(see pp230–31)*. Waipara, north of Christchurch *(see pp232–3)*, has become a more important wine-producing area.

Gibbston Valley Wines *in Central Otago (see p278) produces Pinot Noir, Chardonnay, Pinot Gris, Sauvignon Blanc and Riesling. It has an underground cellar cut into the rock face behind the winery.*

Central Otago's growing season is short, but has become a world leader in Pinot Noir production.

CHRISTCHU

DUNEDIN

0 kilometres 100

0 miles 100

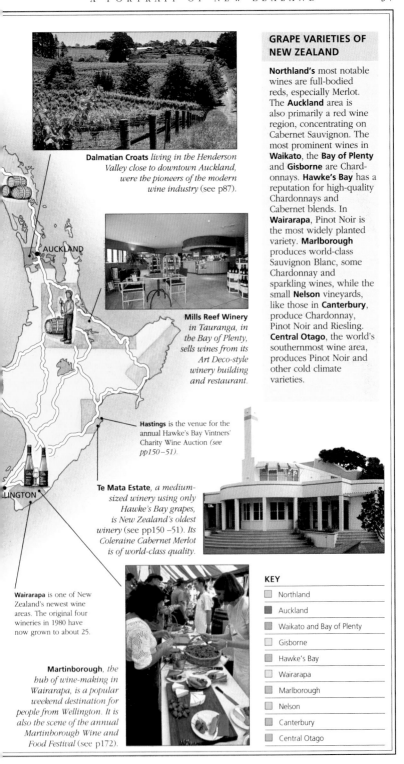

Dalmatian Croats *living in the Henderson Valley close to downtown Auckland, were the pioneers of the modern wine industry (see p87).*

GRAPE VARIETIES OF NEW ZEALAND

Northland's most notable wines are full-bodied reds, especially Merlot. The **Auckland** area is also primarily a red wine region, concentrating on Cabernet Sauvignon. The most prominent wines in **Waikato**, the **Bay of Plenty** and **Gisborne** are Chardonnays. **Hawke's Bay** has a reputation for high-quality Chardonnays and Cabernet blends. In **Wairarapa**, Pinot Noir is the most widely planted variety. **Marlborough** produces world-class Sauvignon Blanc, some Chardonnay and sparkling wines, while the small **Nelson** vineyards, like those in **Canterbury**, produce Chardonnay, Pinot Noir and Riesling. **Central Otago**, the world's southernmost wine area, produces Pinot Noir and other cold climate varieties.

AUCKLAND

Mills Reef Winery *in Tauranga, in the Bay of Plenty, sells wines from its Art Deco-style winery building and restaurant.*

Hastings is the venue for the annual Hawke's Bay Vintners' Charity Wine Auction *(see pp150–51).*

Te Mata Estate, *a medium-sized winery using only Hawke's Bay grapes, is New Zealand's oldest winery (see pp150–51). Its Coleraine Cabernet Merlot is of world-class quality.*

LINGTON

Wairarapa is one of New Zealand's newest wine areas. The original four wineries in 1980 have now grown to about 25.

Martinborough, *the hub of wine-making in Wairarapa, is a popular weekend destination for people from Wellington. It is also the scene of the annual Martinborough Wine and Food Festival (see p172).*

KEY

- ☐ Northland
- ◼ Auckland
- ◼ Waikato and Bay of Plenty
- ☐ Gisborne
- ☐ Hawke's Bay
- ☐ Wairarapa
- ☐ Marlborough
- ☐ Nelson
- ☐ Canterbury
- ☐ Central Otago

New Zealand's Sporting Year

Sport has always been an important part of New Zealand cultural life. Maori were fond of running races, wrestling, surfing and canoe competitions, although nothing was formalized. European settlers found the relatively easy climate gave them a chance to play a variety of sports, and sporting events brought together isolated farming communities. The national passion for an active recreational life has contributed to New Zealanders carving out an international reputation for their sporting prowess, producing numerous world-class champions out of all proportion to the size of the country's population.

The Lake Taupo International Trout Fishing Contest *attracts worldwide participation to this Mecca of trout fishing.*

The New Zealand Open Golf Championship, *held at a different golf course each year, attracts a world-class field.*

The New Zealand Winter Cup at Addington, Christchurch, is one of the important harness races on the racing calendar.

January	February	March	April	May	June

The Auckland Anniversary Regatta, in which more than 600 yachts take part, is one of the largest yachting events in the world.

The New Zealand Car Rally *attracts overseas competitors to race over some of the country's most difficult roads.*

The Wellington Cup, *like most of horse racing's premier events, is held during summer.*

The Dragon Boat Championships *take place on Wellington's Lambton Harbour.*

The Provincial Trophy *is cricket's premier event in New Zealand. Cricket is the most popular summer sport and attracts large numbers of spectators.*

The Adventure Racing World Championship, *a race for teams of three to five people, varies its course each year. Teams cycle and use kayaks and rafts to cross lakes and rivers.*

The Air New Zealand Cup, *rugby's top domestic prize, is the climax of the rugby season.*

The New Zealand Women's Amateur Golf Championship, *held at a different course each year, attracts keen players from around the world.*

y	August	September	October	November	December

The World Heli-Challenge, *at Wanaka, is just one of the many adventure sports events in New Zealand.*

KEY

	Cricket
	Golf
	Horse racing
	Lawn bowls
	Netball
	Rugby
	Skiing
	Surf life-saving

BLACK MAGIC

No sport has had such an effect on New Zealand life as rugby union. Imported from England in the 1870s, the sport was taken up with alacrity by New Zealanders, especially Maori and, recently, Polynesian Islanders. The standard bearers for rugby are the famous All Blacks, a name synonymous with the sport. In 1888, the Native team from New Zealand toured Britain, its uniform black with a silver fern on the chest. Known as the Blacks, they were the precursor to the first All Black team which conquered British teams in 1905.

Black attire was later adopted by other New Zealand sporting teams for international events. The national cricket team is dubbed the Black Caps and the basketball team, the Tall Blacks.

All Black Jonah Lomu

NEW ZEALAND THROUGH THE YEAR

Arts Festival poster

New Zealand's seasons are opposite to those in the northern hemisphere. Spring arrives in September and summer comes in December, autumn is from March to May and the winter months are June, July and August. The South Island's temperatures are slightly lower than those in the North Island. Rain falls heaviest in winter in most areas, with the summer months relatively dry. Visitors need to be prepared for sudden weather changes, a feature of the maritime climate. The country's latitudinal position opens it to prevailing westerly winds, ranging from gentle breezes to raging gales.

SPRING

With the onset of finer weather, the rugby posts come down from the playing fields and cricketers start to practise their strokes. Blossom and food festivals, garden and fashion shows begin, and the horse racing season swings into gear.

SEPTEMBER

Hastings Blossom Festival *(second week)*. The country's largest fruit-growing district ushers in a new season. Highlights include concerts and a blossom parade.
Air New Zealand Fashion Week *(mid-Sep)*, Auckland. The country's top fashion designers showcase their latest collections to local and international buyers, media and guests.

Cattle on parade at Showtime Canterbury

World of WearableArt Awards (WOW) *(late Sep)*, Wellington. A choreographed evening in which art designs are worn. The competition began in Nelson where there is a museum of past winners.

OCTOBER

Rotorua Trout Festival *(early Oct)*. The annual trout fishing tournament and festival open the trout season.
Dunedin Rhododendron Festival *(late Oct)*. Displays of rhododendrons set the Dunedin Botanic Garden and other gardens around Otago ablaze with colour in spring.
Taranaki Rhododendron Festival *(last week)*. More than 100 gardens are on view *(see p180)*.

NOVEMBER

Showtime Canterbury, Christchurch. Features the region's main Agricultural & Pastoral Show, horse races, concerts and a diverse range of events.
Adventure Racing World Championship *(mid-Nov)*, Buller. An adventure race through some of the toughest terrain in the South Island.
Toast Martinborough *(mid-Nov)*, Wairarapa. Showcases the best wine and food of the region, with entertainment by local artists.
Pohutakawa Festival *(end-Nov–mid-Dec)*, Coromandel. Kicking off summer, this month-long festival celebrates the music, arts and outdoor culture of the Coromandel.

Modelling designs in the World of WearableArt Awards

AVERAGE DAILY HOURS OF SUNSHINE

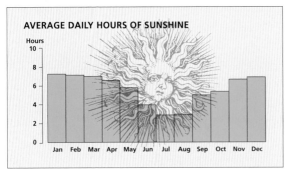

Sunshine Chart
The chart gives figures for Wellington, but these are similar to other main centres. Nelson and Blenheim in the South Island, and Tauranga, Napier and Gisborne in the North Island, enjoy more sunshine hours than any other places. The least sunny region is the southern part of the South Island.

SUMMER

Although many New Zealanders head off for their annual visit to the beach, lake or high country during the summer school break, shops no longer "shut down" apart from Christmas and New Year's days. Cities and towns have become increasingly lively places during the holiday season.

Maori performing at the Waitangi Day celebrations

DECEMBER

Kepler Challenge *(early Dec)*, Te Anau. An annual endurance run that follows the Kepler Track *(see p283)*, over mountain tops, swamps and river valleys, through magnificent scenery.
Festival of Lights *(Christmas to Feb)*, New Plymouth. Special festive lighting in Pukekura Park and city streets. There are music and dance performances in the park each evening *(see p181)*.
Nelson Jazz Festival *(early Jan)*. A week-long festival featuring local and overseas talent (as part of the Summer in Nelson festival).

JANUARY

Mainland New Zealand Kite Tour *(late Jan)*. Hosted by various regions, this festival attracts top kite flyers from all over New Zealand as well as overseas.
New Zealand Gliding Grand Prix *(late Jan)*, Omarama. The world's top glider pilots race head to head.

World Buskers Festival *(late Jan)*, Christchurch. Ten days of street entertainment.

FEBRUARY

Waitangi Day *(6 Feb)*, Waitangi National Trust. Commemorates the signing of the Treaty of Waitangi *(see pp104–5)*.

Anniversary Day Regatta in Auckland

Harvest Hawkes Bay *(first week)*. Wineries open their doors for this three-day food and wine festival.
Auckland Anniversary Regatta *(early Feb)*. Up to 600 yachts take part in one of the world's largest one-day regattas on Waitemata Harbour *(see p73)*.
Aotearoa Traditional Maori Performing Arts Festival *(early Feb, even years)*, Waikato. Festival of Maori culture and art by New Zealand's best groups.
Wine Marlborough *(second Sat)*, Blenheim. Wines and food under marquees in a vineyard setting *(see p208)*.
Art Deco Weekend *(third week)*, Napier. A celebration of Art Deco style with jazz-age dining and dancing, films, house tours, vintage cars and aeroplane rides.
Garden City Festival of Flowers *(third week)*, Christchurch. Prestigious festival celebrates the beauty of flowers.

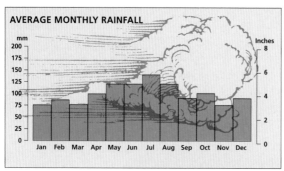

AVERAGE MONTHLY RAINFALL

| mm | | | | | | | | | | | | Inches |

200 — 175 — 150 — 125 — 100 — 75 — 50 — 25 — 0

Jan Feb Mar Apr May Jun Jul Aug Sep Oct Nov Dec

8 — 6 — 4 — 2 — 0

Rainfall Chart
Rainfall is not evenly distributed throughout New Zealand. The west coast of the North Island and South Island is wetter than the east coast. More rain falls in winter and spring than in summer and autumn, in most areas. The figures given here are only for Wellington.

AUTUMN

Autumn often brings the most settled weather of the year, a time of mild, calm days still warm enough for most summer activities. This is harvest season, a good time to experience wine and food festivals. Tramping, fishing and hunting are also popular autumnal pursuits.

MARCH

New Zealand International Arts Festival *(Feb to mid-Mar, even years)*, Wellington. This prestigious festival features some of the world's best talents *(see pp156–7)*.
Dragon Boat Championships *(Chinese New Year)*, Wellington. Crews race on Lambton Harbour.
Golden Shears *(first week)*, Masterton. The world's top shearers are in action at this popular event *(see p173)*.
Pasifika Festival *(second week)*, Auckland. Cultural events and displays by Pacific Islanders *(see p93)*.
Ellerslie Flower Show *(Mar)*, Christchurch. Large floral

Balloons Over Waikato Festival in Hamilton

exhibition located at Hagley Park *(see p227)*.
Wildfoods Festival *(mid-Mar)*, Hokitika. Possum stew and huhu grub are some of the delicacies on the menu.
Round the Bays Run *(end-Mar)*, Auckland. One of the world's largest fun runs with 60,000 people taking part.
Ngaruawahia Regatta *(late Mar)*, Ngaruawahia. Maori canoes compete on Waikato River in the hometown of the Maori monarch *(see p116)*.

APRIL

Rally of New Zealand *(early Apr)*, Greater Auckland. Part of the World Rally Championships, in which drivers battle it out on the back country roads.
Bluff Oyster & Seafood Festival *(mid-Apr)*. Features an array of seafood, fine wine and entertainment.

Royal Easter Show *(second week)*, Auckland. Livestock competitions, art and craft awards, wine awards and the largest equestrian show in the country.
Balloons Over Waikato Festival *(mid-Apr)*, Hamilton. More than 30 balloons drift over the city and surrounding areas. *(see p118)*.
Lake Taupo International Trout Fishing Contest *(third week)*. Fishermen vie at this fine trout fishing location *(see p141)*.
Warbirds Over Wanaka *(Easter weekend, even years)*. Classic vintage and veteran warplanes take to the skies in this world-class event *(see p270)*.

MAY

Rotorua Tagged Trout Competition *(May)*. Rotorua's premier fishing competition has a $10,000 trout waiting to be hooked.

Visitors at a food stall at the Hokitika Wildfoods Festival

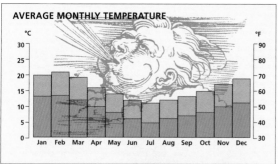

AVERAGE MONTHLY TEMPERATURE

Temperature Chart
The chart gives the average maximum and minimum temperatures for the city of Wellington. The North Island has mild winters and humid summers. The South Island experiences the country's hottest summer temperatures, but in winter these can plunge to below freezing point.

WINTER

Often the most spectacular time of the year to visit, winter also brings reduced rates on airfares, accommodation and activities. On the scenic west coast, rainfall is at its lowest and whales at Kaikoura can virtually be guaranteed to put in an appearance.

Spectators at the Rally of New Zealand in Auckland

JUNE

National Agricultural Fieldays *(mid-Jun)*, Mystery Creek, Hamilton. One of the world's largest agricultural events showcases the best of New Zealand's products, with emphasis on innovative technology *(see p118)*.

JULY

Queenstown Winter Festival *(mid-Jul)*. One of the highlights of the Queenstown calendar, this winter festival includes spectacular night skiing and firework displays.
World Heli-Challenge *(late Jul)*, Wanaka. International snowboarders and skiers take part in three days of heliskiing events.
Christchurch Arts Festival *(last week, odd years)*. A mid-winter festival of music, theatre, dance, film and the visual arts.

AUGUST

Bay of Islands Jazz and Blues Festival *(mid-Aug)*, Northland. One of the most popular events on the jazz calendar. More than 50 bands from New Zealand and overseas take part.
Crater to Lake Challenge *(late Aug)*, Taupo. Multi-sport event featuring skiing, cycling, kayaking, water-skiing and running from the slopes of Mount Ruapehu to Taupo.

PUBLIC HOLIDAYS
New Year's Day (1 Jan)
New Year Holiday (2 Jan)
Waitangi Day (6 Feb)
Good Friday (varies)
Easter Monday (varies)
Anzac Day (25 April)
Queen's Birthday
  (first Mon in Jun)
Labour Day (varies Oct)
Christmas Day (25 Dec)
Boxing Day (26 Dec)

Clydesdale horses and wagon at the National Agricultural Fieldays, Mystery Creek, Hamilton

THE HISTORY OF
NEW ZEALAND

T*he last of the world's significant landmasses to be colonized by people, New Zealand is a nation of immigrants. Maori settled in the country less than 1,000 years ago, while Europeans first arrived in 1642. Together, these two peoples have forged a unique identity out of their common experiences that reflects their Pacific environment.*

The date the first Maori arrived in New Zealand is shrouded in mystery. According to legend, the first explorer to discover New Zealand was the Polynesian Kupe, around AD 950. He then returned to his ancestral homeland, Hawaiki. Four centuries later, a fleet of canoes set sail for New Zealand, guided by Kupe's directions on how to find land.

**Coat of Arms of
New Zealand**

Basing their findings on radiocarbon dating of Maori middens, archaeologists believe that the first settlement was around AD 1300. Some scientists, however, believe that Maori arrived as long ago as 2,000 years, but these early settlers did not survive for long. Nonetheless, the rats that they brought with them went on to devastate the native bird, lizard and frog populations.

Regardless of when they did arrive, Maori are known to have carried a number of plants and animals with them. The *kiore*, the Polynesian rat, was considered a great delicacy when fattened up on berries. Also known to have survived the journey

was the native dog, the *kuri*. Root vegetables Maori brought with them were the yam, *kumara* and *taro*. The *kumara* grew more successfully in the colder climate than the other two, and proved important in the development of Maori culture, enabling permanent settlement.

ABEL TASMAN

Since Greek times, there had been talk of a Terra Australis, or "great southern continent", to counterbalance the lands of the northern hemisphere. Such a landmass was necessary, it was argued, to offset the weight of the continents in the north and to balance the Earth on its axis. The mathematician Pythagoras speculated about the existence of such a land, but it was not until almost 2,000 years later that 17th-century Dutch explorers finally sighted Australia.

In 1642, the Dutch East India Company, a trading firm anxious to explore prospects for commerce beyond the East Indies, sent Abel Tasman south from Java in Indonesia.

TIMELINE

Moa skeleton

Double canoe

1300	1400	1500	1600
	1400–1500 Maori hunting drives moa to extinction	**1500** Maori develop fortified sites *(pa)* to defend themselves	
1300 First Polynesian inhabitants arrive from Cook and Society islands	**1400** Great fires on the South Island east coast destroy swathes of forest	**1531** Map drawn with Terra Australis on it	**1642** Dutch explorer Abel Tasman sights New Zealand

◁ Detail from *The Signing of the Treaty of Waitangi* by Marcus King (1939)

Maori Exploration and Voyage

It is still debatable whether Polynesians, ancestors of Maori, made planned voyages to New Zealand or simply drifted there by chance. However, Polynesians were skilled navigators who sailed long distances between the islands in the Pacific in large craft. Driven out of an island by starvation or intertribal warfare, some groups would have deliberately sailed to a far-off land, especially if they had been given directions by someone like Kupe who had been there *(see p45)*. With their vessels laden with plants and small animals, they would have been guided by traditional navigation clues, such as the stars, migrating birds and cloud formations.

Stern of canoe

Kupe's Anchor Stone
A 1912 photograph of a Maori elder standing beside what may be Kupe's anchor stone.

Canoe Prow
The prows of Maori waka (canoes), carved in intricate patterns, had forward-thrusting prows to improve the canoes' performance.

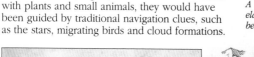

Fishing Net
Fish, a valuable part of Maori food supply, were caught using a variety of nets. This wood engraving (1840) by Joel Pollack is of a landing net.

Kuri
Maori brought the kuri (dog) with them on their migrations. It became extinct soon after European settlement.

Single Canoe
The single canoe was used as a coastal vessel. It had decking made of long rods. Thwarts, lashed from one top edge to the other, served as seats.

POLYNESIAN SETTLEMENT

Archaeological discoveries indicate that Polynesians came from Southeast Asia to the eastern Pacific islands, settling the lands from Hawaii to Easter Island. About 1,000 years ago, expeditions from the islands of central Polynesia reached New Zealand where they established coastal tribal settlements.

PERIODS OF SETTLEMENT

———	30,000 years ago
———	3,000 years ago
———	1,500–2,000 years ago
———	1,000 years ago
———	500 years ago

Double Canoes
The largest of these craft, depicted here by William Hodges, artist on Cook's 1773 voyage, were capable of carrying up to 200 passengers.

Taro Plant
Few plants taken from Polynesia survived the voyage to New Zealand. Taro grew, but because it was not productive, it became a luxury food.

PACIFIC OCEAN

HAWAII

NORTH AMERICA

SOLOMON ISLANDS

SAMOA

FIJI

TONGA

NEW CALEDONIA

TAHITI

COOK ISLANDS

EASTER ISLAND

NEW ZEALAND

0 kilometres 1,000

0 miles 1,000

Kiore
The kiore or rat was introduced from Polynesia. It was a source of food for the early Maori, but killed native birds.

Canoe Regatta
Maori today celebrate their heritage of exploration and voyage in the annual Ngaruawahia Regatta, held on the Waikato River (see p116).

Legend of Maui
An ink drawing (1907) by Wilhelm Dittmer depicts the legend of Maui, who created New Zealand by fishing the North Island out of the ocean.

Abel Tasman's ships, the *Heemskerck* and *Zeehaen*

After sailing past Tasmania (then known as Van Diemen's Land), Tasman reached a point off present-day Hokitika on 13 December 1642, noting "a large high elevated land". He and the crews of the *Heemskerck* and *Zeehaen* had sighted the Southern Alps. Tasman wanted to land, but the rolling swell off the coastline convinced him to head north, where he found a relatively calm anchorage in what is now called Golden Bay. However, hostile Maori rammed a sloop from the *Zeehaen*, and clubbed four of the Dutch sailors to death. The Dutch subsequently named the location Murderers' Bay. Tasman immediately set sail north and left New Zealand waters on 6 January 1643 without further investigation.

Abel Tasman

CAPTAIN JAMES COOK
There was a lull in European exploration of the New Zealand region for more than 100 years. No good commercial reason encouraged any visits; indeed, the reputation of the hostile Maori discouraged them. Then, in 1769, Englishman Captain James Cook set sail on a scientific expedition of discovery to the South Pacific, to observe the transit of the

sun by the planet Venus. After having observed the rare phenomenon at Tahiti, Cook sailed south until he sighted the east coast of New Zealand, on 9 October 1769.

Cook's ship, the *Endeavour*, was well equipped for its voyage, with botanists and artists on board. Besides documenting new scientific finds, Cook's mission was to assess the potential of the country as a colony. A master mariner, Cook mapped the coastline and the scientists on board made hundreds of discoveries. On this first of three visits to New Zealand, he claimed the country for England. Coincidentally, a French expedition led by explorer Jean de Surville sailed within a few kilometres of Cook at the end of 1769, but neither was aware of the other's presence.

Following Cook, Europeans trickled rather than flooded into New Zealand, working as whalers, sealers and timber traders. Seeking short-term profits, few became permanent immigrants, and as soon as the resource they sought disappeared, so did they. By the early 1800s it had become uneconomic to send sealing gangs to New Zealand because most of the easy prey had been taken; whale numbers, too, plummeted.

THE TREATY OF WAITANGI
The impact of these visitors on the traditional Maori way of life was enormous. Maori were exposed to a disastrous number of diseases, such as measles and smallpox, and their warlike instincts were incited by the purchase of guns. During the 1820s, at least 20,000 Maori were killed in

TIMELINE

	1791 First whaling ship sails into Doubtless Bay, Northland	1814 Samuel Marsden sets up first Anglican mission in the Bay of Islands	1821 Musket wars begin between Maori tribes	1831 Whaling stations established around Cook Strait	1833 James Busby appointed British Resident
1750	**1800**		**1820**	**1830**	**1840**
	1769 Captain Cook makes first of three visits to New Zealand	1815 First Pakeha child born in New Zealand	1835 Declaration of Independence signed by 34 northern chiefs		
HMS *Endeavour*			1840 British sovereignty proclaimed. Treaty of Waitangi signed by 50 chiefs		*Maori chief*

The Treaty House at Waitangi

Samuel Marsden established New Zealand's first mission station in the Bay of Islands in 1814, and although progress was slow in converting Maori to Christianity, the faith had a significant foothold by 1840.

By then Maori numbered about 115,000 and European settlers (Pakeha) 2,000. While some Maori benefitted by trading with the Europeans and growing crops for them, there was concern about increasing lawlessness, the buying up of land by Europeans and the intertribal warfare. Leading chiefs asked Queen Victoria to provide a framework of law and order. Eventually Captain William Hobson obtained the signatures of Maori chiefs on the 1840 Treaty of Waitangi, giving sovereignty to Britain. Although the Maori translation gave the chiefs a different understanding of the treaty.

intertribal "musket wars", which changed the political face of Maori New Zealand as tribes invaded neighbouring territories, sometimes taking them permanently.

Another major influence for change was Christianity. Anglican missionary

TREATY OF WAITANGI

The Treaty of Waitangi is New Zealand's founding document, an agreement between the British Government and Maori that is today the centrepiece of the country's race relations.

In return for giving Queen Victoria the right to buy land, Maori were granted all the rights and privileges of British subjects. A clause also gave them "full exclusive and undisturbed possession of their Lands and Estates Forests Fisheries and other properties". But misunderstanding arose because there were two different versions (Maori and English) which carried different meanings. The crucial difference was what was meant precisely by the word sovereignty, translated by many as *kawanatanga*, suggesting a distant figure of authority. Controversy over the Treaty continues to this day.

Signatures on the Treaty

THE NEW ZEALAND WARS
Unlike Australia, where some of the first immigrants were convicts, New Zealand settlers were freemen and many came in family groups. The New Zealand Company was set up in 1837 to transplant a cross-section of English society in the Antipodes. Planned settlements were established at Wellington, Wanganui, Nelson, New Plymouth, Christchurch and Dunedin.

Following the signing of the Treaty of Waitangi, Maori–Pakeha relations were relatively harmonious for some years. If there were conflicts, they were generally over land, and isolated skirmishes occurred until 1860, the year the New Zealand Wars began. The critical point was at Waitara, Taranaki. The cause was a land sale between the government and a minor

1844 Hone Heke chops down British flagpole and starts "War of the North"

1850 Canterbury settlement founded by genteel English emigrants

1860 New Zealand Wars begin between Maori and Europeans over land

Te Kooti

1867 Four Maori seats established in Parliament

1845	1850	1855	1860	1865

1848 Dunedin ttlement founded by Scottish pioneers

1854 First session of General Assembly (Parliament)

Gold nugget

1861 First New Zealand gold rush after discovery at Tuapeka, Central Otago

1865 Capital moves from Auckland to Wellington

chief of the Te Ati Awa tribe who did not have the tribe's permission to sell, a prerequisite for communal property under Maori custom. When the tribe refused to accept the bogus deal, the government retaliated by marching troops onto the land, seizing it by force.

In response, most central North Island tribes backed the Te Ati Awa, intensifying the rebellion. At the height of hostilities in the mid-1860s, British forces had increased to more than 20,000, against about 5,000 Maori warriors. On the British side were significant numbers of Maori who were either opportunists or had a score to settle with an enemy tribe.

United, Maori would have easily been a match for the Pakeha. Even divided, they came close to persuading many settlers to flee the colony. In 1868, two chiefs, Titikowarau in the west and Te Kooti in the east, won a series of significant battles, but internal squabbles saw them lose the support of the wider Maori population. By 1869, the New Zealand Wars came to a halt as Maori opposition fell away. Land sales escalated, many of them under duress. The wars resulted in the government confiscating 12,000

Passengers from the Cressy Landing at Port Lyttelton by **William Fox (1851)**

sq km (4,630 sq miles) of prime land. Most of it was given to "friendly" Maori tribes, while some was handed to Pakeha settlers. It was a legacy that came back to haunt the country more than a century later, as Maori pursued their legitimate grievances through the Waitangi Tribunal.

ECONOMIC EXPANSION

The 1861 discovery of gold in Otago, and subsequent finds on the West Coast, set the South Island on its industrial feet. Up until then, the North Island had been outstripping the South economically and in population terms; it was not until 1896 that the North Island reasserted itself.

The late 19th century saw a time of great economic expansion, thanks to large-scale government borrowing. The rail network was established, telegraph lines were installed and emigrants were assisted to the country. During the 1870s, the population doubled. Good export prices for wool (which proved to be the mainstay of the economy for the next 100 years) underpinned the frenzy of economic activity. Technological advances also played their part. The first shipload of

Te Henheu's Old Pa of Waitahanui at Lake Taupo by George F Angas (1847)

TIMELINE

1869 New Zealand Wars end because of Maori disunity

1882 First refrigerated ship leaves Otago for the UK

1893 First country in the world to extend the vote to all women

1907 New Zealand becomes a Dominion

| 1870 | 1880 | 1890 | 1900 | 1910 |

1879 Vote given to every male over 21

1887 Tongariro National Park, the first in New Zealand, established

Maori weapon

Early transport

frozen meat for Britain sailed from Otago in 1882; this technology was also vital later in shipping butter.

New Zealand soon gained a reputation for social innovation. In 1893, the Liberal Government granted the vote to all women, and in 1898 it introduced a means-tested old-age pension, both of which were the first in the world.

THE WAR YEARS

As New Zealand's population reached the one million mark in 1908, the country's status as a colony of Great Britain changed to that of the Dominion of New Zealand. In 1917, the title of governor (the representative of the Queen) became that of governor-general.

The Liberal Party, with its progressive tax policies, old-age pensions, votes for women and breaking up of large land holdings, was hailed domestically and externally for making New Zealand "the birthplace of the 20th century". Its hold on power lasted until 1912, by which time it had lost touch with the public. It was replaced by the Reform Party, which was led by Bill Massey and gained most of its suppport from the farmers. The Reform Party remained in power until 1928 and served in a coalition with the Liberals until 1935 when a Labour government was elected.

World War I was a defining moment for the fledgling nation. In 1915, New Zealanders and Australians combined to form the Australian and New Zealand Army Corps (ANZAC). Ordered by the British to attack well-armed and better-placed Turkish defenders on the Gallipoli Peninsula, thousands were killed in eight months of action. The 25th of April (Anzac Day) has since been set aside to remember the soldiers' sacrifice. For a small country, New Zealand suffered enormously during the war. Out of a total of 110,000 troops, 16,697 died and 41,262 were wounded – a massive casualty rate.

The period between the wars was one of mixed fortunes for New Zealand. While the 1920s were initially

World War I poster

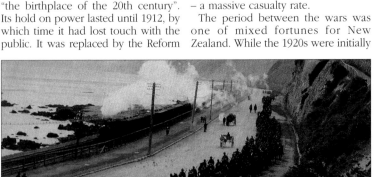

New Zealand Expeditionary Force on the Hutt Road near Petone, Wellington, 1914

1915 New Zealand troops suffer heavy losses in the Gallipoli campaign against Turkey	1920 First Anzac Day commemoration	*Elizabeth McCombs* 1933 Elizabeth McCombs first female MP		1936 New Zealand pilot Jean Batten flies from England to Australia in world record time
1915	**1920**	**1930**	**1935**	**1938**
1914 New Zealand enters World War I on the Allied side	1918 End of World War I	1935 First Labour Government elected	1936 40-hour week introduced	

Factory workers

Relief camp for unemployed workers at Akatarawa, Hutt Valley, in the 1930s

positive, the world's economic woes engulfed the country, and by 1932 it was in the depths of the Depression. The first Labour Government, elected in 1935, spent its way out of the Depression. New Zealand gained further accolades as the social laboratory of the world with its income-related health scheme and extended pension programme.

In 1939, for the second time in the century, New Zealand found itself embroiled in a world war. Prime Minister Michael Joseph Savage was in no doubt where the country's loyalty lay: "Where Britain goes we

go, where she stands we stand." New Zealand soldiers served in Greece, the Middle East and Italy, even though the most serious threat to the country came from Japan. After the attack on Pearl Harbour (1941), troops were increasingly deployed in the Pacific and links were forged with the US. American soldiers spent time in New Zealand during the war and took New Zealand wives back home with them. In 1951, military ties between the US, Australia and New Zealand were formalized with the signing of the ANZUS military pact.

MOVING AWAY FROM BRITAIN

After the war, while New Zealand looked to the US for its military security, its economy still remained firmly wedded to Britain. As Britain's "South Pacific farm", New Zealand had traditionally enjoyed easy access to UK's markets. As late as 1960, 55 per cent of its exports landed there. But the boom times came to an end once "the old country" joined the European Union (EU) in 1973 and its priorities shifted to the European continent.

Within 20 years of joining the EU, Britain took only 6 per cent of New Zealand's exports. New markets were found, and Asia became important. Hong Kong, China, Japan, Taiwan and South Korea are now among the top ten countries with which New Zealand trades.

Mirroring countries in the West, New Zealand went through great social changes during the 1960s, as baby-boomers reached adulthood and challenged conservative society. The

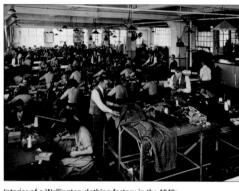

Interior of a Wellington clothing factory in the 1940s

TIMELINE

1939 New Zealand fights in World War II on Allied side		**1953** Sir Edmund Hillary climbs Mount Everest with Sherpa Tenzing	**1965** Combat force sent to Vietnam	**1981** First Maori language kindergarten opens **1981** Country divided by South African rugby tour with widespread protests
	Sir Edmund Hillary			

1940	**1950**	**1955**	**1960**	**1970**

| **1947** Statute of Westminster adopted by Parliament | **1948** Protest against exclusion of Maori from All Black rugby tour to South Africa | *Carving at Waitangi Marae* | **1961** Capital punishment abolished | **1973** Frigate sent to French Polynesia to protest French nuclear testing | **1975** Waitangi Tribunal established to investigate Maori land claims following confiscation and compensate where justified |

decision to support the US with a token force in the Vietnam War was vigorously opposed, and in 1972 conscription was dropped by the new Labour Government. A year later, the government sent a frigate to French Polynesia to protest against nuclear weapons testing there.

In the mid-1970s, as imported oil price hikes affected the population, New Zealanders returned to the conservative politics of the National Party under the combative Robert Muldoon. Finally, weary of his interventionist economic policies, the electorate voted in a socially leftist but economically rightist Labour Government in 1984, headed by David Lange.

For the next six years, the country experienced a whirlwind of change as Labour floated the exchange rate, deregulated industries, removed tariffs, sold off state assets and made thousands of civil servants redundant in a quest for greater efficiency. At the same time, foreign relations were in upheaval: New Zealand had always maintained a strong anti-nuclear weapons policy, and in 1985 the US was told that nuclear-armed or powered warships were no longer welcome in New Zealand ports. The

The *Rainbow Warrior*, sunk in Auckland Harbour in 1985

Americans suspended ANZUS. In that same year, French saboteurs sank the Greenpeace vessel, the *Rainbow Warrior*, in Auckland.

The National Government, which came to power in 1990 led by Jim Bolger (succeeded in 1997 by Jenny Shipley), continued with economic reforms, albeit at a slower pace. However, many New Zealanders, disillusioned over a succession of unresponsive administrations, voted in a Mixed Member Proportional electoral system based on the German model. The system was first tested in 1997, which resulted in a vastly more representative parliament than before, and the emergence of the country's first directly elected woman prime minister, Helen Clark of the Labour Party, in 1999.

New Zealand society today has changed significantly, from a period when an overwhelming majority of the population was Pakeha to a point where Auckland is now the largest Polynesian city in the world, and an increasing number of Asians have become citizens. With its increasingly diverse cultures, New Zealand is carving out a confident and independent identity as a Pacific nation in the international community.

Representatives of the Ngai Tahu tribe and the government signing the Deed of Settlement in 1997

	1985		1990		1995		2000		2005		2010

1985 *Rainbow Warrior* sunk

1987 New Zealand wins inaugural Rugby World Cup
1987 Maori becomes official language

1995 Team New Zealand wins America's Cup
1997 Jenny Shipley first woman prime minister

America's Cup yacht

2004 Peter Jackson's *Lord of the Rings* wins 11 Oscars

2008 National Party wins general election

1990 Dame Catherine Tizard first woman Governor-General
1990 National forms government

1997 First MMP Parliament elected

2000 Successful defence of America's Cup
1997 Government compensation to Ngai Tahu tribe for land confiscations

2006 Maori Queen Te Atairangikaahu dies aged 75, after a reign of 40 years

Jenny Shipley

84 Lange ernment es power

NEW ZEALAND AREA BY AREA

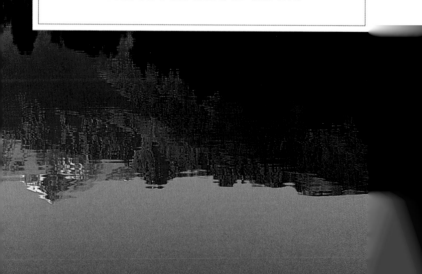

New Zealand at a Glance

Tucked away in the southwest corner of the Pacific
Ocean, New Zealand is one of the most isolated and
least populated countries in the world. It is also a
land of contrasts: between the subtropical north and
the colder south; the wet west and the drier east; the
volcanoes of the central North Island and the
mountains of the South Island. Powerful geological
forces have created a landscape that is dominated by
mountains, hills, lakes and rivers. These, in turn,
have allowed New Zealand to become a paradise for
nature lovers and outdoor enthusiasts. Sheep and
cattle farming still cover large areas of the country,
but more and more the accent is on diversity. The
more populated north is the centre of Maori and
Pacific Island culture.

One of the many vineyards in
Marlborough (see pp206–7)

The Pancake Rocks and blowholes at Punakaiki
in Paparoa National Park (see p236)

Christchurch Cathedral in the heart
of Christchurch (see p222)

**MARLBOROUGH
AND
NELSON**
(see pp196–21

0 kilometres   100

0 miles   100

**CANTERBURY
AND THE
WEST COAST**
(see pp218–253)

Christchurch

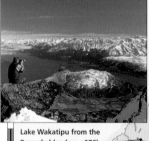

Lake Wakatipu from the
Remarkables (see p276)

**OTAGO
AND
SOUTHLAND**
(see pp254–291)

Dunedin

Larnach Castle, a century-old
stone mansion (see p266)

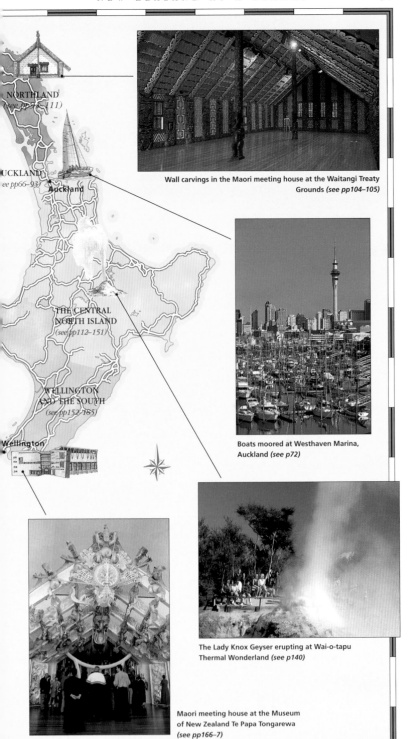

NORTHLAND
(see pp94–111)

AUCKLAND
(see pp66–93)
Auckland

THE CENTRAL
NORTH ISLAND
(see pp112–151)

WELLINGTON
AND THE SOUTH
(see pp152–185)

Wellington

Wall carvings in the Maori meeting house at the Waitangi Treaty Grounds (see pp104–105)

Boats moored at Westhaven Marina, Auckland (see p72)

The Lady Knox Geyser erupting at Wai-o-tapu Thermal Wonderland (see p140)

Maori meeting house at the Museum of New Zealand Te Papa Tongarewa (see pp166–7)

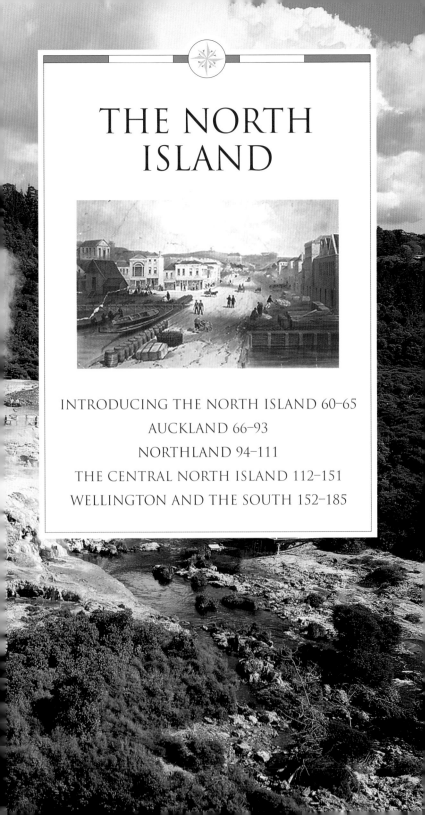

THE NORTH
ISLAND

Introducing the North Island

Blessed with a varied landscape, the North Island also offers a range of climates, from the "winterless" north to the snow-bound mountains of the Central Plateau and the blustery winds of the south. From the tip of Northland down to Taranaki on the west and Hawke's Bay on the east, the sea lends a distinct character to each coast. Although best known for its geothermal wonders around Rotorua and the Volcanic Plateau, the North Island is also a fertile land of lush dairy pastures, highly productive orchards and rolling sheep country. The country's largest city, Auckland, and its capital, Wellington, are both located in the North Island.

Bay of Islands marlin

NORTHLAND
(see pp94–111)

The Bay of Islands (see pp102–3) *is one of New Zealand's most beautiful and historic areas. The warm, sparkling, aquamarine waters, year-round sunshine, sandy beaches and quiet coves make the area a paradise for deep-sea fishing, underwater diving, swimming and sailing.*

Mount Taranaki/Egmont (see pp182–3), *a dormant, snow-capped volcanic peak, is the centrepiece of the agriculturally rich Taranaki region and the dominant feature of Egmont National Park.*

Climber on Mount Taranaki/Egmont

The Parliament buildings *in Wellington (see p158) are interesting for their varied architectural styles. The circular, copper-domed "Beehive", which houses Cabinet offices, is in complete contrast to the square marble Parliament Buildings, home to the House of Representatives.*

The "Beehive"

Sky Tower (see p75) *is Auckland city's dominant landmark. From its four observation decks, visitors enjoy 360-degree views of the city centre, its sprawling suburbs, harbours, and the Hauraki Gulf islands.*

LOCATOR MAP

0 kilometres 50

0 miles 50

Sky Tower

KLAND
(p64–91)

The Bath House in *Rotorua* (see p134), *an elegant Tudor-style building situated in the English-style Government Gardens, is the town's most frequently photographed building. Originally constructed as a thermal bath house in 1908, it is now home to the excellent Rotorua Museum of Art and History.*

Rotorua Museum exhibit

THE CENTRAL
NORTH ISLAND
(see pp110–149)

Rothmans Building

Napier's Art Deco buildings (see pp146–7), *such as the Rothmans Building, were constructed following a devastating earthquake in 1931.*

WELLINGTON
AND
THE SOUTH
(see pp150–183)

Martinborough
(see p172) *is the hub of wine growing in Wairarapa, and its wineries have gained a reputation as producers of red wines. A good way to experience the area's wineries is to join one of the many vineyard tours that leave from Wellington.*

Martinborough vineyard

Historic Northland

Between 700 and 1,000 years ago, the first Polynesian voyagers are believed to have come ashore on the northern coasts of the North Island. Northland is also sometimes referred to as "the birthplace of the nation". It was at Rangihoua in Northland that Samuel

Samuel Marsden

Marsden, the first missionary, set up an Anglican mission in 1814; at Waitangi that the Treaty of Waitangi was signed in 1840 *(see pp48–9)*; and at Russell that New Zealand's first capital was established in 1840 before shifting south. Here, too, were sown the first seeds of Maori rebellion against the British.

Kemp House
This Kerikeri Mission House, completed in 1822, is the oldest building in New Zealand. The house is associated with the Kemp family who lived in it for 142 years (see p106).

Waipoa Bay, Moturoa Island
Captain Cook (in 1769) and French explorer Marion du Fresne (in 1772) took water on board here. Du Fresne buried in the sand a bottle with a document claiming New Zealand for France.

Kauri trees are symbolic of Northland but much of the forest is now gone. Logging was at its height from 1870 to 1910.

LOGGING ON THE HOKIANGA
Charles Heaphy's painting *View of the Kahu-Kahu, Hokianga River* (1839) depicts the logging industry on the Hokianga River. The giant kauri trees made ideal ships' spars as well as timber for new settlements.

Hokianga Harbour
was one of the main points of early Maori settlement. Kupe *(see p45)* left for Hawaiki from here.

Russell, Bay of Islands
This whaling and sealing town was dubbed the "Hell-hole of the Pacific" in the lawless days of the early 1800s (see p102).

Hongi Hika
After Maori chief Hongi Hika met King George IV during a trip to England in 1820, he returned home determined to become king of New Zealand. In the 1820s, he led his Northland tribe, the Ngapuhi, in many conquests of other tribes.

Maori Kauri Gum

Gum from kauri trees, used in paints and polishes, was an important export product from Northland until World War II.

Pohutukawa
The pohutukawa has an important place in Maori mythology. Maori believe that the spirits of the dead descend down the roots of a pohutukawa tree at Cape Reinga on their way to the homeland on Hawaiki.

Kauri logs being towed to a waiting ship.

Warrior Chieftains
Hone Heke is shown here with his wife, Harriet, and another chieftain, Kawiti. Unhappy with the Treaty of Waitangi, he was one of the first chieftains to fight the British.

Pa Site at Ruapekapeka
This pa (fortification) site was one of the most complex ever built. In 1846, British troops stormed it on a Sunday morning, catching the Maori inside by surprise. They did not expect the British to fight on a day traditionally given to rest and prayer.

Volcanic Heartland

From White Island in the northeast of the North Island to Mount Ruapehu in the centre lies the Taupo Volcanic Zone, which also includes Rotorua's geothermal wonders. Here, where the Pacific "ring of fire" begins, the clash of the Pacific Continental Plate and the Indo-Australian Plate has created the conditions for one of the most active volcanic regions in the world *(see p22)*.

Skier on Mount Ruapehu

Beneath the Taupo Volcanic Zone, great slabs of crust are thrust down into the earth's mantle where they melt to form rhyolite magma. Every few thousand years, this magma reaches the surface, resulting in events like the Lake Taupo eruption of AD 186, when pumice was punched 50 km (30 miles) up into the air.

Mount Ruapehu
The North Island's tallest mountain is permanently snow-capped and cloaked by eight glaciers. Eruptions in 1995–6 emptied the crater of its lake and closed the mountain to skiers.

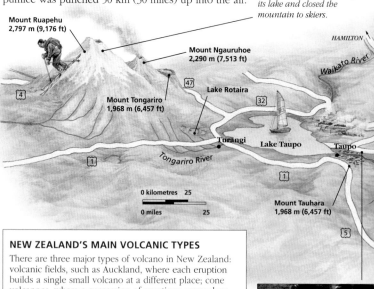

Mount Ruapehu
2,797 m (9,176 ft)

HAMILTON

Mount Ngauruhoe
2,290 m (7,513 ft)

Waikato River

[47]

Lake Rotaira

[32]

[4]

Mount Tongariro
1,968 m (6,457 ft)

Turangi

Lake Taupo

Taupo

Tongariro River

[1]

[1]

0 kilometres 25

0 miles 25

Mount Tauhara
1,968 m (6,457 ft)

[5]

NEW ZEALAND'S MAIN VOLCANIC TYPES

There are three major types of volcano in New Zealand: volcanic fields, such as Auckland, where each eruption builds a single small volcano at a different place; cone volcanoes, where a succession of eruptions occur close to a vent to form a large cone, which is the volcano itself; and caldera volcanoes, where eruptions are often so large that the ground surface collapses into the hole left behind. The Taupo Volcanic Zone contains three frequently active cone volcanoes (Ruapehu, Ngauruhoe and White Island) and the two most productive caldera in the world (Taupo and Tarawera). Mount Ngauruhoe is the vent for the adjacent Mount Tongariro.

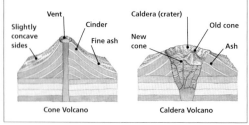

Vent

Slightly concave sides

Cinder

Fine ash

Caldera (crater)

New cone

Old cone

Ash

Cone Volcano

Caldera Volcano

Wairakei Geothermal Power Station
Almost 60 bores tap a vast underground water system, naturally heated by very hot rocks, to produce commercial quantities of steam.

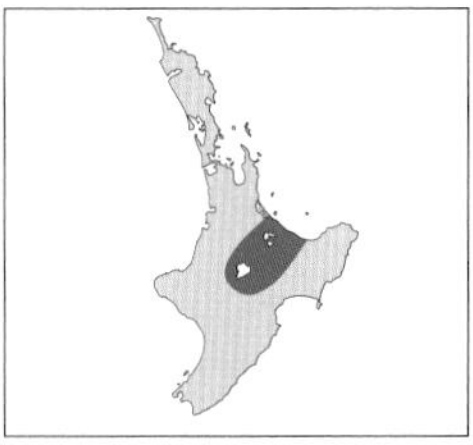

LOCATOR MAP

Pohutu Geyser
One of only 12 geysers in New Zealand, Pohutu Geyser thunders to a height of more than 30 m (98 ft) (see pp138–9).

White Island
This is an excellent active volcano to visit because of its intense thermal activity (see p130).

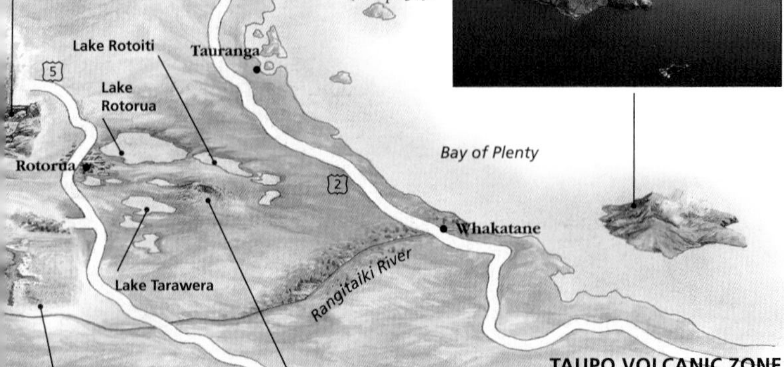
Lake Rotoiti
Tauranga
[5]
Lake Rotorua
Rotorua
Bay of Plenty
[2]
Whakatane
Rangitaiki River
Lake Tarawera

TAUPO VOLCANIC ZONE

The area from White Island to Ruapehu is by far the most frequently active of the North Island's five volcanic areas. Apart from its volcanoes, it has the greatest variety of volcanic features – geysers, cauldons, mineral pools, mud pools, silica terraces, lakes, rivers and waterfalls – making it one of New Zealand's most fascinating tourist destinations.

Wai-o-tapu
The bubbling, hissing Champagne Pool, with its beautiful ochre-coloured petrified edge, is one of the many colourful attractions at Wai-o-tapu (see p140).

Mount Tarawera
In a volcanic explosion in 1886, a 6-km (4-mile) long, 250-m (820-ft) deep chasm was formed and the nearby Pink and White Terraces were buried (see p137).

AUCKLAND

E very third New Zealander lives in the Auckland region, and the city, with its 1.2 million inhabitants, continues to expand faster than any other part of the country. Its population has increased by 20 per cent since 1991, almost double the national rate. Auckland is the place to enjoy city life, but quiet beaches and bush tracks are within an hour's drive of the central business district.

Maori had settled in the Auckland area as early as 1350. Tribal wars and epidemics brought about the destruction of their settlements, and the area was almost deserted when European settlers arrived in 1840. Because of its central position, good harbour and fine soil, the site was chosen as New Zealand's capital, to replace Russell in the north, after the signing of the Treaty of Waitangi in 1840 (see pp48–9). However, in 1865 the capital moved south to Wellington.

Although Auckland was initially not a prosperous settlement, a gold rush in the Coromandel region and increased agricultural production in the late 19th century helped to develop it into what it is today – the largest and fastest growing city in New Zealand. The inner city has become more vibrant since the mid-1990s, due to the trend among some Aucklanders to trade in the traditional suburban villa for an inner-city apartment. Places such as Vulcan Lane, Viaduct Basin, Parnell and Ponsonby have become gathering points with cafés, bistros and up-market restaurants. The retail trade and performing arts have reaped the benefits of this migration.

Auckland is also attractive to New Zealand's Pacific Island neighbours and it now is the largest Polynesian city in the world. With Europeans, Maori, Polynesians and Asians complementing one another, the city's cultural diversity gives it a very cosmopolitan atmosphere. This is reflected in the variety of ethnic shops and restaurants, and can be observed at the local markets, such as those in Otara and Avondale.

Surfing at Piha, on the coast west of Auckland

◁ Sky Tower viewed from Waitemata Harbour, Auckland

Exploring Auckland

Although the Auckland region is spread over more than 1,000 sq km (390 sq miles), many of its inner-city attractions are clustered near the waterfront and around the city's oldest parks. Panoramic views of the city, harbour and outer islands can be enjoyed from a number of extinct volcanic peaks, such as One Tree Hill *(see p84)*, and from the observation decks and restaurants of Sky Tower, the city's most distinctive landmark *(see p75)*. Queen Street, long known as Auckland's "golden mile", is a major business, entertainment and shopping area, complemented by Ponsonby, Parnell and Newmarket on the fringes of the city. Water is an important part of Auckland's magic, and no visit is complete without a trip to Rangitoto or one of the other islands in the Hauraki Gulf *(see pp88–9)*.

Yachts moored at Westhaven Marina, Auckland *(see p72)*

SIGHTS AT A GLANCE

Aotea Square and Aotea Centre at THE EDGE® 10
Auckland Art Gallery 15
Auckland Domain and Winter Gardens 16
Auckland Harbour Bridge 2
Auckland Town Hall 11
Auckland War Memorial Museum 17
Britomart Transport Centre 7
Ferry Building 6
New Zealand National Maritime Museum 5
Old Arts Building and Clock Tower 14
Old Customhouse 8
Old Government House 13
Sky Tower 12
SKYCITY Auckland 9
Viaduct Basin 4
Waitemata Harbour 1
Westhaven Marina 3

KEY

- Street-by-Street: The Waterfront *see pp70–71*
- Ferry terminal
- To Auckland International Airport
- Train station
- Coach station
- Tourist information
- [P] Parking
- Park
- Hospital

SEE ALSO

• ***Where to Stay*** pp298–300
• ***Where to Eat*** pp326–8

For additional map symbols *see back flap*

GETTING AROUND

Auckland's city centre is compact and most places of interest are within walking distance. Alternatively, visitors can take the Auckland Explorer Bus, which leaves the Ferry Building every 30 minutes from 9am (hourly from 10am in winter) and stops at 14 tourist destinations. The tour includes taped commentary in various languages. For drivers, good motorways and internal roads link the northern, southern and western suburbs, which are also serviced by buses. Regular ferry services take visitors to the islands in the Hauraki Gulf.

Rollerblading along Tamaki Drive (see p82)

Street-by-Street: The Waterfront

Maritime Museum sign

Excellent shops, historic buildings, top restaurants and bars, a superb view – Auckland's waterfront has something for everyone. Yet only 20 years ago, this area was of little interest to residents and visitors, and the inner city, traditionally reserved for offices, was almost deserted after dark. That trend has been reversed and downtown Auckland is now a hive of activity. New apartments, many on the water's edge and others in garden environments, along with numerous trendy bars and restaurants, have made the waterfront a prime living and entertainment area.

Old Customhouse
Formerly part of the city's financial district, this 1889 building houses a duty-free store (see pp73, 90).

Britomart Transport Centre
Auckland's public transport hub is housed in the refurbished Chief Post Office building.

CUSTOMS STREET EAST

LOWER ALBERT ST

QUAY STREET

QUAY STREET

★ Ferry Building
At the Ferry Building, visitors can buy tickets for ferries and harbour cruises or dine at its popular ground-floor restaurant (see p73).

QUEEN'S WHARF

Princes Wharf, the departure point for overseas cruises, also attracts visitors to its restaurants and bars.

KEY

– – – Suggested route

WAITEMATA HARBOUR

Boat Services
A variety of harbour cruises and ferry services to Devonport and the Hauraki Gulf islands operate from the back of the Ferry Building.

| 0 kilometres | 100 |
| 0 miles | 100 |

For hotels and restaurants in this region see pp298–300 and pp326–8

AMERICA'S CUP

Viaduct Basin was the home base for the yachts that participated in the 1999–2000 and 2002–2003 America's Cup. New Zealand successfully defended the cup it took off the Young America (USA) team led by Dennis Connor in 1995. In the 2002–2003 event nine challengers took on Team New Zealand and these syndicates came from all over the world, including France, Italy, Sweden, Switzerland, England and the United States. The history of the cup goes back to the 1850s, but the intense emotion surrounding the challenge still remains.

New Zealand's *Black Magic* defeating its Italian challenger in the America's Cup 2000 final

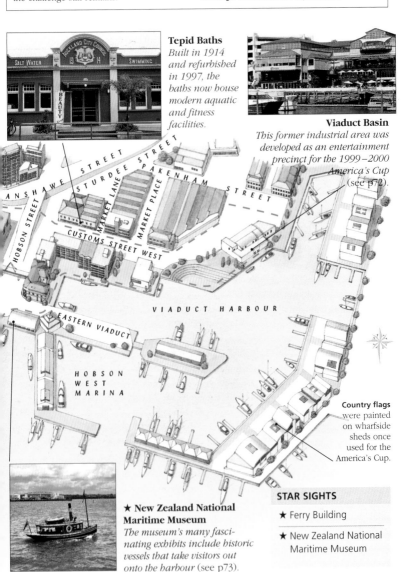

Tepid Baths
Built in 1914 and refurbished in 1997, the baths now house modern aquatic and fitness facilities.

Viaduct Basin
This former industrial area was developed as an entertainment precinct for the 1999–2000 America's Cup (see p72).

STURDEE STREET
SHORTLAND STREET
MARKET LANE
PAKENHAM STREET
MARKET PLACE
STREET

ANSHAWE STREET
HOBSON STREET
CUSTOMS STREET WEST

VIADUCT HARBOUR

EASTERN VIADUCT

HOBSON WEST MARINA

Country flags
were painted on wharfside sheds once used for the America's Cup.

★ **New Zealand National Maritime Museum**
The museum's many fascinating exhibits include historic vessels that take visitors out onto the harbour (see p73).

STAR SIGHTS

★ Ferry Building

★ New Zealand National Maritime Museum

A forest of masts at Westhaven Marina, viewed from the Auckland Harbour Bridge

Waitemata Harbour ❶

This sparkling harbour, with the green volcanic cone of Rangitoto Island in the background, is one of Auckland's most cherished sights. Not only does the harbour add to the city's scenic beauty, it also forms a natural barrier between the central business district and the populous North Shore. Ferries and cruise boats, as well as commercial ships, use the harbour daily.

Auckland Harbour Bridge ❷

State Hwy 1.

In the late 19th century, ferries began taking passengers across the water from Auckland City to the north. In 1959, the Auckland Harbour Bridge was built and ten years later, the 43-m (141-ft) high steel bridge was widened, increasing the number of lanes from four to eight. Peak hour traffic across the 1,020-m (3,350-ft) bridge is slow. Concrete barriers marking the traffic lanes are shifted twice daily by a custom-built machine to accommodate the morning flow into the city and the late afternoon return to the northern suburbs. An electronic traffic light system at both ends of the bridge clearly indicates which lanes are accessible to traffic. Despite the traffic jams, the Harbour Bridge offers some of the best views in the city.

The bridge does not only link two large areas of Auckland; State Highway 1 is also the main arterial route for northbound traffic. Southbound travellers driving across the bridge will notice a forest of masts on their left.

Westhaven Marina ❸

Westhaven Drive.

Westhaven Marina reflects Aucklanders' passion for yachting. Operating for more than 70 years, it is one of the largest marinas in the southern hemisphere, accommodating 1,950 vessels. Among the facilities are Pier Z (the home of several major charter boat companies), launching ramps for trailer craft and a mast gantry. The premises of prominent yacht clubs are on the northern side of the marina.

Viaduct Basin ❹

Cnr Halsey St and Viaduct Harbour.

Largely a legacy from the 1999–2000 America's Cup, the Viaduct Basin's up-market apartments, shops and restaurants overlook its mooring facilities. The basin is part of an extensive redevelopment of Auckland's waterfront, following the trend in cities such as Sydney, London and San Francisco. One of the best places to enjoy the precinct's vibrant atmosphere is Kermadec, a fish restaurant with a strong Pacific theme (*see p318*). The Loaded Hog is another popular meeting place for locals and visitors.

Café at Viaduct Basin

For hotels and restaurants in this region see pp298–300 and pp326–8

New Zealand National Maritime Museum ❺

Cnr Quay & Hobson sts. *Tel* (09) 373 0800 or 0800 7258 9726. ☐ daily. ● 25 Dec. 🖥 ♿ 🎫 🍴 ▯ ☐

www.nzmaritime.org

Boats have played a pivotal role in New Zealand's history, from those of the early Polynesian navigators who steered their canoes towards the country *(see pp46–7)*, to the whalers who made Russell *(see p102)* the centre of the whaling industry in the 1840s, and the thousands of immigrants who arrived in the 19th and 20th centuries. These aspects of the country's maritime past are highlighted in the museum. In Maori, the museum is called Te Huiteananui-a-Tangaroa, "the legendary house belonging to Tangaroa", god of the sea.

Even those with a limited interest in boats will enjoy the innovative exhibition galleries. One room is fitted out as a ship's interior, complete with a gently swaying floor and appropriate creaking noises. Several of the historic vessels berthed outside the museum take visitors for harbour trips.

Shore whaling exhibit at the National Maritime Museum

Ferry Building ❻

Quay St. 🚢 ☐ daily. 🍴 🖥

This 1912 Edwardian baroque building is the focal point for commuter ferries. A ten-minute ferry ride to Devonport leaves here, as do boats to Waiheke Island *(see p88)*. Designed by Alex Wiseman, the building is made of sandstone and brick,

The Ferry Building, a gateway to the harbour

with a base of Coromandel granite. Not just a transport centre, it is also home to Harbourside Restaurant *(see p327)*, a popular seafood restaurant with stunning views of the harbour.

Britomart Transport Centre ❼

Queen St.

The Britomart Transport Centre brings together Auckland's train, bus and ferry services in a single complex. The centre was the focus of an urban renewal project completed in 2009, which included the redevelopment of surrounding streets, creating new public spaces and a precinct of shops and restaurants.

Old Customhouse ❽

Cnr Albert & Customs sts. ☐ daily. ▯

The old Customhouse replaces a building that was burned down in the 1880s. Designed by Thomas Mahoney, the 1889 French Renaissance-style building is said to have been modelled on the present Selfridge's department store in Oxford Street, London. It features intricate plasterwork and kauri joinery.

The building used to house the Customs Department, Audit Inspector, Sheep Inspector and Native Land Court. It is now home to the city's largest duty-free shop *(see p90)*.

CITY OF SAILS

Auckland is purported to have the greatest number of pleasure boats per capita of any city in the world. The city's temperate climate also means that, on average, these are used more intensively than boats in Europe or on the east coast of America. Yachting has been a popular pastime in Auckland since the 1840s, when the first sailing regattas were held on Waitemata Harbour. Safe harbours and the nearby scenic islands make sailing attractive to overseas visitors as well. Charter company charges depend on the size of the yacht, the time of the year and whether a skipper is hired. The highlight of the nautical year is the Auckland Anniversary Regatta *(see p41)*.

Yacht racing on Waitemata Harbour

Casino in the SKYCITY complex

Imax (widescreen) Cinema (*see p93*), a games centre, cafés and shops. The Auckland Town Hall is situated on the other side of the square.

Collectively, the locations bordering Aotea Square – the Town Hall, Aotea Centre and Force Entertainment Centre – are known as THE EDGE®.

SKYCITY Auckland **❾**

Cnr Victoria & Federal sts. **Tel** *0800 759 2489, (09) 363 6000.* ☐ *daily.* 🚻 📶 📱 📷 **www**.skycityauckland.co.nz

Lucky punters can win luxury cars at SKYCITY Auckland, New Zealand's biggest casino. Open 24 hours a day, 7 days a week, the complex offers a wide variety of entertainment and leisure options. More than 1600 gaming machines feature all the latest stepper reel, video reel, poker and keno games offering both cash and car prizes. The complex boasts 4 casinos and over 100 gaming tables with traditional games such as Caribbean stud poker, craps, blackjack, baccarat, roulette and money wheel. Chinese favourites include tai sai, played with three dice in a clear glass dome, and pai gow, played with 32 domino pieces.

Entertainment at SKYCITY is not limited to gaming. The complex is best known for the Sky Tower, the country's tallest structure (*see p75*). There are also two hotels, the four-star SKYCITY Hotel, with 306 rooms and 38 suites, and the newly completed five-star Grand Hotel. In addition, there are a number

of bars, cafes and restaurants as well as conference facilities, and a 700-seat theatre.

Aotea Square and Aotea Centre at THE EDGE® **❿**

Queen St. **Tel** *(09) 309 2677.* **www**.the-edge.co.nz

In the late 1980s, several New Zealand souvenir shops began stocking a postcard that was entirely black except for a small heading, "Night Life in New Zealand". Things have since changed. Built in 1990, the Aotea Centre, was designed by New Zealand architect Ewen Wainscott and is a hub of vibrant night-

Sculpture at Aotea Square

life. On its opening night, the centre featured New Zealand-born Dame Kiri Te Kanawa, the world-renowned opera singer. It is a venue for dance, opera, classical music, theatre and shows. It is also used for festivals, such as the Aotearoa Hip Hop Summit.

Aotea Square, in front of the centre, houses a popular market as well as outdoor festivals. The wooden *waharoa* (gateway) at its entrance was created by Maori artist Selwyn Muru. The square is flanked on one side by the Force Entertainment Centre, which includes a 460-seat

Auckland Town Hall **⓫**

Queen St. **Tel** *(09) 309 2677.* ☐ *daily.* ⬤ *public hols.* 🚻

The wedge-shaped Edwardian Town Hall, built in 1911, is Auckland's prime historic building. It has been used extensively as an administrative and political centre, as well as a cultural venue. During work to re-store it to its original design, the building was gutted (non-original materials were removed) and strengthened structurally.

The Concert Chamber, Council Chamber and main street foyer were meticulously restored, a process which included using vintage glass to reconstruct windows that had disappeared over the years. The Great Hall, an excellent concert facility, is a replica of the Neues Gewandhaus in Leipzig, Germany, which was destroyed by Allied bombing during World War II.

Auckland Town Hall

For hotels and restaurants in this region see pp298–300 and pp326–8

Sky Tower ⑫

Opened in August 1997, Auckland's 328-m (1,076-ft) Sky Tower, a splendid tourist, broadcasting and telecommunications facility, has taken over from Sydney's AMP Tower as the tallest tower in the southern hemisphere. Part of SKYCITY Auckland, the tower is visited by almost one million people a year. Its four observation levels offer 82-km (50-mile) views while the tower's Sky Jump and 360° Skywalk provide the ultimate in adrenaline adventure.

VISITORS' CHECKLIST

Cnr Victoria & Federal sts. **Tel** 0800 759 2489. ◯ 8:30am till late daily. 🈸 ♿ 🍴 🛍 📷 🎁
www.skycity.co.nz

The **93-m (305-ft)** high spire weighs 150 tonnes and is the main telecommunications and broadcasting mast in the region. The Vertigo Climb, up the internal structure of the mast, leads to a 300-m (980-ft) high viewing platform.

The **sky deck** offers 360-degree views through seamless glass, and is the country's highest public viewing area.

The **outdoor observation level** features high-powered binoculars that offer a close-up view of Auckland and its surrounding areas.

Orbit, Sky Tower's revolving à la carte restaurant, makes a full revolution every 60 minutes.

Sky Jump is a 192-m (630-ft) cable controlled base jump.

The **structure** of the tower has been designed to withstand winds gusting to 200 km/h (125 mph) and earthquakes measuring 7.0 on the Richter Scale.

Observation Levels
Visitors enjoy fantastic views of the city of Auckland and its environs from the tower's indoor and outdoor observation levels.

The **floors** above and below the centre pod house telecommunications facilities.

The **Observatory**, a brasserie-style buffet restaurant, is New Zealand's highest dining location.

The **main observation level** offers free multilingual audio guides, live weather forecasts and touch-screen computers.

The **lower observation level** contains the Sky Lounge cafe.

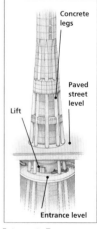

Concrete legs

Paved street level

Lift

Entrance level

Entrance to Tower
Entry to Sky Tower's lifts is through an underground gallery.

The Sky Tower at Night
The Sky Tower is an even more visible landmark at night. Over Christmas, it is lit in different colours that make its observation pod resemble a flying saucer.

Old Government House, New Zealand's first wooden mansion

Old Government House ⓭

Cnr Waterloo Quadrant and Princes St. *Closed to public.*

The classical Old Government House was the seat of government until 1865 when the capital was moved to Wellington. It was also the residence of New Zealand's governor-general until 1969. Royalty used to stay here, and Queen Elizabeth II broadcast her Christmas speech from upstairs in 1953. It is now a part of the University of Auckland, housing the staff common room, council reception suite and apartments for visiting academics.

Located within walking distance of the central business district, Old Government House, designed by William Mason and completed in 1856, appears from a distance to be made of stone. Like its British prefabricated predecessor, however, it is built from wood. A big coral tree and a Norfolk pine at the southern edge of the lawn are said to have been planted by Sir George Grey during his second term as governor from 1861 to 1867.

Old Arts Building and Clock Tower ⓮

Princes St. *Closed to public.*

Also part of the university buildings, the Old Arts Building and Clock Tower face Albert Park, a summer gathering place for students. Designed by Chicago-trained architect R A Lippincott, it was completed in 1926. Lippincott's brother-in-law, Walter Burley Griffin, was the designer of Canberra in Australia. The clock tower that crowns the building was inspired by the Tom Tower of Christ Church in Oxford, England, and has come to symbolize the university. The building's octagonal interior is vaulted and galleried with a mosaic floor and piers. A major reconstruction was undertaken between 1985 and 1988, which won an Institute of Architects award.

From the rear of the Old Arts Building, the Barracks Wall runs for 85 m (280 ft) to the back of the Old Choral Hall. Built in 1847, it is the only remnant of the wall which enclosed an area, including Albert Park, where British troops were stationed until 1870. The basalt stone wall was quarried from the slope of Mount Eden, now known as Eden Garden.

University of Auckland's Old Arts Building and Clock Tower

Auckland Art Gallery ⓯

Cnr Wellesley & Kitchener sts. *Tel (09) 307 7700.* ◯ *daily.* ● *25 December, Good Friday.* 🎟 *some exhibits.* ♿ 🚻 📷 🛍 www.aucklandartgallery.govt.nz

Visitors interested in art should add the Auckland Art Gallery (Toi o Tamaki) to their itinerary. Designing the 1887 French Renaissance-style building must have been a challenge to the architectural firm of Grainger and D'Ebro, as it occupies a rising corner site. The gallery originally housed civic offices and the public library, but today it is solely a gallery, mainly devoted to showcasing the development of New Zealand

Entrance to the New Gallery, Auckland Art Gallery

art. The collection of around 12,500 works includes international as well as national art. The gallery also organizes exhibitions on a regular basis. The New Zealand collection contains works from many of the nation's most prominent artists, including Frances Hodgkins, Colin McCahon and Ralph Hotere. The Mackelvie Collection, named after a self-made man who lived in Auckland between 1865 and 1871, is mainly of non-New Zealand paintings, as is the Grey Collection.

The New Gallery, almost next door to the Auckland Art Gallery, was a former telephone exchange. Refurbished by architect David Mitchell, it adds 30 per cent more space to the existing gallery and focuses on contemporary art. Wedged between these two is the commercially run Gow Langsford Gallery.

Auckland Domain and Winter Gardens ⓰

Auckland Domain ◯ daily.
Winter Gardens ◯ daily. ▣ (War Memorial Museum).

Central Auckland has been built around a number of extinct volcanoes, including 14 volcanic cones, many of which are now parks. The oldest park is the Auckland Domain, situated within walking distance of both the city centre and the Parnell area. Tuff rings created by volcanic activity thousands of years ago can still be seen in its contours.

Land for the city's 1.35-sq-km (0.50-sq-mile) park was set aside in 1840, in the early years of European settlement. In 1940, a carved Maori memorial palisade was installed around a totara tree on Pukekaroa knoll. This enclosure commemorates Maori leader Potatu Te Whero Whero, who made peace with the neighbouring tribes on the site a hundred years earlier.

Nearby is a sports field where the tuff rings form a natural amphitheatre. The

The Sky City Starlight Symphony playing at the Auckland Domain

field is used for free outdoor concerts over the summer that attract large crowds.

The large, shady Auckland Domain is also a popular place with walkers and picnickers. Several of the large trees in the park were seedlings from a nursery set up in 1841 to grow and distribute European plants and trees. The formal gardens feature many sculptures. The best known are the three bronze sculptures in the free-form pond. The central, male figure represents Auckland and the two females represent wisdom and fertility of the soil.

Statue at the Winter Gardens

The Winter Gardens, a legacy from the Auckland Exhibition of 1913, consist of two glasshouses joined by a

courtyard that contains a large water lily and lotus pool. The dome-roofed areas contain a wide variety of plants. In recent years, a scoria quarry behind the Winter Gardens has been converted into a fernery. Ferns are a dominant feature of the New Zealand landscape and there are more than 100 varieties in the fernery. The gardens are a popular venue for wedding and other photography.

The Domain's best-known structure is the Auckland War Memorial Museum (see pp78–9). Made of reinforced concrete and faced with Portland stone, the museum has bronze detailing. The façade contains plaques that list the battles of World War I, while at the rear of the building, added by RF and M K Draffin in 1960, there are lists of World War II battles.

One of the two glasshouses at the Winter Gardens

Auckland War Memorial Museum ⑰

Built in 1929 to commemorate the end of World War I, in which 16,697 New Zealanders died, the museum has a Neo-Classical façade that evokes the Greek temples that many servicemen saw from the decks of warships in the Mediterranean. The design of the cenotaph in front of the museum is based on newsreel footage, shown at the beginning of movies in the 1920s, of the tomb of the unknown soldier in London. Besides providing visitors with an introduction to New Zealand's history, people and landscape, the museum also contains a renowned collection of Maori treasures and Pacific artifacts and holds Maori cultural performances.

Museum cenotaph

Aerial view of the museum, located in the Auckland Domain

Museum Lobby
The lobby features tall columns reminiscent of the Parthenon in Greece. Light filters through the stained-glass ceiling above the lobby.

"Origins" features the skeletons of extinct animals, such as dinosaurs and moa, many of which were discovered in caves around the country.

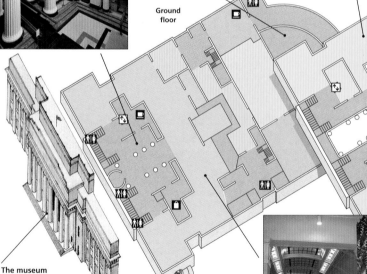

Garden

Ground floor

The museum **entrance** evokes the temples of Greece.

STAR EXHIBITS

★ Maori Treasures

★ World War I
   Sanctuary

★ **Maori Treasures**
This gallery showcases a superb collection of Maori artifacts, such as the waka *(canoe) in the foreground and a traditional carved meeting house.*

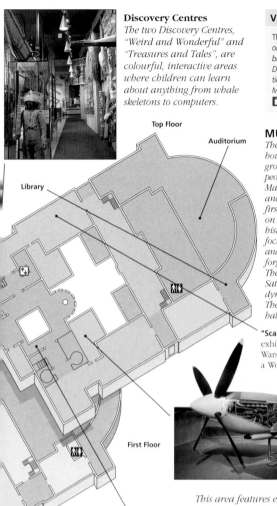

Discovery Centres

The two Discovery Centres, "Weird and Wonderful" and "Treasures and Tales", are colourful, interactive areas where children can learn about anything from whale skeletons to computers.

Top Floor

Auditorium

Library

First Floor

VISITORS' CHECKLIST

The Domain. *Tel* (09) 306 7067
or (09) 309 0443. Explorer
bus. 10am–5pm daily. 25
Dec, 25 Apr (am only). donation (none for war memorials);
Maori cultural show.
www.aucklandmuseum.com

MUSEUM GUIDE

The museum's collection is housed on three levels. The ground level is dedicated to the people of New Zealand, both of Maori and European descent, and the Pacific region. The first level provides information on the land and its natural history, while the top level focuses on New Zealand at war and how these experiences have forged the country's identity. The Library is open Monday to Saturday, 1–5pm, and offers a dynamic range of resources. The Atrium houses exhibition halls and retail space.

"Scars on the Heart" contains exhibits depicting the two World Wars, including a re-creation of a World War I front trench.

Spitfire Gallery

This area features early fighter planes. A high percentage of Royal Air Force pilots during World War II came from New Zealand, including its Supreme Commander, Keith Park.

"Oceans" helps visitors discover marine life with a rock pool and replicas of a beach and the Poor Knights Islands marine reserve.

★ World War I Sanctuary

The stained-glass ceiling above the entrance lobby shows the coat of arms of all British dominions and colonies during World War I. On the balcony are badges of the units, regiments and corps in which New Zealanders served.

TO FLOORPLAN

Natural History Galleries

Design & Decorative Arts

Exhibition Hall

Library

Maori and Pacific

Other exhibits

Discovery Centres

War exhibits

Further Afield

Beyond Auckland's city centre, visitors are offered a
range of places to visit and a variety of things to do.
Harbours, beaches and islands are prime attractions,
not only for their superb scenic views but also for sea
sports, such as kayaking, surfing and sailing. The city is
well known for its beautiful parks and gardens which
provide peaceful retreats; some offer visitors a chance
to walk through bush and wilderness. Families with
young children will find Kelly Tarlton's Antarctic
Encounter and Underwater World, Rainbow's End
Theme Park and the Auckland Zoological Gardens
enjoyable. Across the harbour, Devonport makes for a
pleasant outing for the day, with its many restaurants
and art and crafts shops.

A view of Auckland City from
Tamaki Drive

Tamaki Drive ❶

Tamaki Drive, east of the city,
shows Auckland at its best.
The road crosses Hobson Bay
and closely follows the
water's edge past Okahu Bay,
Mission Bay and St Heliers
Bay. The views across
Waitemata Harbour towards
Rangitoto Island and
Devonport are stunning and
should not be missed.

　Many of the city's most
prestigious homes are located
on the slopes behind Tamaki
Drive. Many tourist buses
make a small detour to go
through nearby Paritai Drive,
the most expensive real estate
in Auckland. Sandy beaches,
such as the one at Mission
Bay, are a major attraction
along Tamaki Drive. These
beaches serve as a base for
family outings, swimmers and
sunbathers.

　Mission Bay got its name
from the Melanesian Mission
House. Built in 1859, the
house was part of Bishop
Selwyn's Mission School.
When the school was
transferred to Norfolk Island
in 1867, the house was used
for different purposes. It is
now an up-market restaurant.

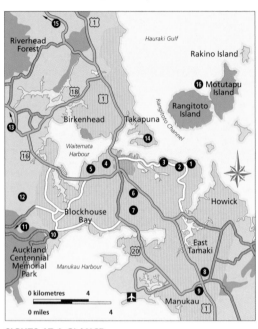

SIGHTS AT A GLANCE

KEY

▨	Central Auckland
▢	Auckland city
▨	Park, forest or reserve
▬	Motorway
▬	State highway
⋯	Other road
✈	Auckland International Airport

Cyclists enjoying the sun on
Tamaki Drive

For hotels and restaurants in this region see pp298–300 and pp326–8

Rangitoto Island, dominating Auckland's harbour horizon

Tamaki Drive ends at St Heliers Bay. Instead of turning right into St Heliers Bay Road, it is worthwhile to continue along Cliff Road, leading to Ladies Bay. The viewing platform at the top of the cliff offers a superb panorama of the Hauraki Gulf. Directly below the platform, but far enough from viewers not to be intrusive, is one of New Zealand's few nudist beaches. At other beaches along Tamaki Drive, nudity is prohibited.

Learning to windsurf

Savage Memorial Park ❷

Located off Tamaki Drive, the Savage Memorial Park was named after New Zealand's first Labour prime minister, Michael Joseph Savage (1871–1940). The gardens, which have formal arrangements, also contain concrete fortifications that date from World War II.

The area occupied by the gardens was originally a historic Maori *pa*, and its shoreline was renowned for its plentiful supply of mussels.

Originally named Tokapur-ewha, Maori for "mussel rocks", the area has since been renamed Bastion Point. It is best known for a Maori protest staged in 1977 after the government had razed a local Maori village to develop Bastion Point as a prime residential zone. A 506-day occupation was organized to protest against the appropriation of the site, followed by ten years of litigation. In 1990, the land was finally returned to the Ngati Whatua tribe. The nearby 900-sq-m (9,690-sq-ft) Orakei Marae is the tribe's meeting house. Smaller ones can be found around the Kaipara Harbour and at Helensville, on the North Shore.

Riding through the Plexiglas tube at Kelly Tarlton's Underwater World

Kelly Tarlton's Antarctic Encounter and Underwater World ❸

23 Tamaki Drive. **Tel** *(09) 528 0603 or 0800 805 050.* Downtown Centre, 757, 767, 769. daily. no flash. Antarctic Encounter.

Tamaki Drive's best-known tourist attraction is Kelly Tarlton's Underwater World and Antarctic Encounter. Visitors ride on a moving walkway through a Plexiglas tunnel inside a tank, with fish swimming around the sides. The tunnel winds past two marine aquariums, one devoted to reef fish and the other to sharks and stingrays. The Antarctic Encounter features a replica of the Cape Evans 1910 hut of South Pole explorer Robert F Scott (1868–1912), complete with ice and winds. A highlight is a ride in a heated Snow Cat through a typical subantarctic landscape, past a penguin colony, and under the ice to a subantarctic aquarium.

Museum of Transport and Technology ❹

Great North Rd, Western Springs. ▨ Customs St, 45. **Tel** (09) 815 5800, 0800 668 086. ◯ daily. ● 25 Dec. ▨ ☕ ▣ www.motat.org.nz

The Museum of Transport and Technology (MOTAT) has a collection of about 300,000 items, 20 per cent of which can be seen in various buildings and halls on two sites within walking distance of the Auckland Zoological Gardens. Exhibits vary from dental equipment and underwear to 19th-century houses.

The focal point is a collection of 30 rare and historic aircraft. These include a replica of a home-made plane by New Zealander Richard Pearse, believed by many to have preceded the Wright brothers in being the first person to fly (*see p248*). Also of interest is the Solent flying boat ZK-AMO *Aranui*, a luxurious aircraft that flew around the South Pacific from 1949 until 1960. An electric tram runs approximately every 20 minutes from the entrance of MOTAT to the zoo gates.

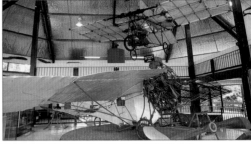

Early aircraft at the Museum of Transport and Technology

Auckland Zoological Gardens ❺

Motions Rd, Western Springs. ▨ Customs St, 45. **Tel** (09) 360 3800. ◯ daily. ● 25 Dec. ▨ ☕ ▮▮ ▣ ▢ www.aucklandzoo.co.nz

New Zealand's isolated geographical position means that its fauna has developed differently from that of most countries. A lack of predators, for example, has resulted in many flightless birds. With the exception of bats, there are no native mammals. There is no better place to learn about the country's varied and unusual wildlife than at Auckland Zoo. The zoo

Corrugated iron elephant at the zoo

houses saddlebacks, tui, kakas and kakarikis, besides the nocturnal kiwis.

The zoo's population, which is not limited to native animals, is presented in natural settings. Primates such as squirrel monkeys and macaques can be seen at close range in a rainforest. Zebras and giraffes roam on an African savanna with Zulu huts and interconnected habitats. A wetlands environment features baboons as well as hippopotamuses.

One Tree Hill ❻

Manukau Rd.

One Tree Hill (Maungakiekie), a dormant volcanic cone and once the site of the largest prehistoric Maori settlement in the region, was named after the solitary tree which

One Tree Hill (Maungakiekie), formerly the site of a large Maori fortification

was planted on its summit in 1640. Since then, a succession of single trees have stood on the summit. The last, a Monterey pine, was removed in October 2001 by city council workers as it was unstable (its replacement is still the subject of debate). Its most famous predecessor was a native totara tree, cut down in 1852 by a party of workmen angry at the non-arrival of rations.

Surrounding the hill is Cornwall Park, named after the Duke and Duchess of Cornwall, and donated to the city by Sir John Campbell during their royal tour in 1901.

Acacia Cottage, Auckland's oldest surviving wooden building, was built in 1841 by Sir John Campbell. It was relocated in 1920 from Shortland Street to Cornwall Park, where Sir John once had a farm.

Water ride at Rainbow's End Theme Park

Acacia Cottage, in Cornwall Park

At the base of the park, near the entrance, is the **Stardome Observatory**. It has telescopes for viewing the stars, and aspects of space and astronomy are shown at the Stardome Planetarium.

Acacia Cottage
Cornwall Park. *Tel* (09) 630 8485. ☐ daily. ● public hols. 🚌 302, 304, 305.

Stardome Observatory
One Tree Hill Domain. *Tel* (09) 624 1246. ☐ daily. ● public hols. 🚗 🦽 📷 Stardome and telescopes. 📷 www.stardome.org.nz

Highwic House ❼

40 Gillies Ave, Epsom. 🚌 Link bus. *Tel* (09) 524 5729. ☐ Wed–Sun. ● Good Fri, 25 Dec. 🦽

Built in 1862, Highwic was the home of Alfred Buckland, a stock and station owner. The house was built in stages, with the front part showing

more detail than the rest. The house, with its elaborate decoration and diamond pane windows, is an example of Carpenter Gothic Revival architecture. The extensive landscaped gardens are also worth a visit.

Auckland Regional Botanic Gardens ❽

Hill Rd, Manukau City. *Tel* (09) 267 1457. ☐ daily. 🦽 📷 📷 www.aucklandbotanicgardens.co.nz

These gardens, which sprawl over 640 sq km (250 sq miles), contain more than 10,000 species of New Zealand native and introduced plants, as well as a large collection of ornamental plants. Guided walks are held regularly. There is an award-winning visitor centre where the Ellerslie Flower Show is held each year.

Rainbow's End Theme Park ❾

Cnr Great South & Wiri Station rds, Manukau City. 🚌 *Central Auckland, 471, 472. Tel* (09) 262 2030. ☐ daily. ● 25 Dec. 🦽 🦽 📷 📷 📷 www.rainbowsend.co.nz

Lots of rides and entertainment are available at this large amusement park. The most popular attraction is a roller coaster that takes you up more than 30 m (98 ft) in the air, hurls you down through a complete loop, round a corner and through a double corkscrew. Other attractions include the Motion Master Virtual Theatre, featuring dinosaurs, an enchanted forest ride, a minigolf course, family go-karts, water rides and the Goldrush, which takes you on a thrilling ride through an abandoned gold mine in a runaway mining cart.

SIR JOHN LOGAN CAMPBELL

Sir John Logan Campbell (1817–1912) was one of New Zealand's pioneering entrepreneurs. On 21 December 1840, he set up a tent at the bottom of Shortland Street that served as Auckland's first shop. When he died at the age of 95, he was the city's most prominent businessman. Apart from trading and farming, he was involved in shipping, brewing, timber, the export of kauri gum, flax and manganese, news-paper publishing and banking. He was also a member of New Zealand's parliament, captain of the militia, and a founding member of the Mechanics Institute and the Northern Club. Today, "the father of Auckland" is best remembered for donating his farm, Cornwall Park (*see p85*), to the city.

Totem pole at the entrance to the Arataki Visitors Centre

Titirangi ⓾

Road map E2. 🚶 *3,400.* 🚌

Situated to the west of Auckland city, the small settlement of Titirangi offers superb views of the Waitakere Ranges and the 390-sq-km (150-sq-mile) Manukau Harbour to the south. The village, which is home to a number of artists and writers, has a reputation for being trendy. Its main street is lined with cafés and restaurants. The main landmark is the Spanish-style Lopdell House, opened in 1930, which houses an art gallery, small theatre and restaurant. The square in front of the nearby library is transformed into an art and crafts market on the last Sunday of the month from 9am to noon.

Titirangi is the gateway to the Auckland Centennial Memorial Park in the Waitakere Ranges. Formed by volcanic action about 1.7 million years ago, the park has about 250 km (155 miles) of walking tracks, suitable for people of all levels of fitness. It attracts over two million visitors a year.

The **Arataki Visitors Centre**, 5 km (3 miles) beyond Titirangi, has well-organized displays on the area's logging history and attractions, and also stocks detailed maps of the ranges, books, audio tapes and posters. Large timber decks around the building offers good views of the harbour. Across the road from the centre is the Arataki Nature Trail, a self-guided walk.

🏛 **Arataki Visitors Centre**
Scenic Drive. *Tel* (09) 817 0077.
⬜ *daily.* ⬤ *25 Dec.*

Piha ⓫

Road map E2. 🚶 *2,500.* 🚌

Prized by locals but not well known to tourists, Auckland's rugged, wind-swept west coast beaches are within easy reach of Auckland and are well worth visiting. Because they are exposed to the Tasman Sea, however, swimmers and surfers need to exercise care as the currents can be treacherous and conditions often change rapidly.

Piha is the most popular of the beaches because of its heavy surf. It is also the most gentrified. Here, many "baches", New Zealand's traditional ramshackle holiday homes, have made way for architect designed mansions. The Piha Surf Life Saving Club serves as a community centre over the summer.

Gannet at Muriwai

Environs
The bleakest, yet perhaps grandest, stretch of coast is at **Whatipu**, south of Piha at the entrance to the Manukau Harbour. A sand bar visible from the beach partly blocks the harbour. It was here that the HMS *Orpheus* was shipwrecked on 7 February 1863. Of the 259 officers and crew of the 1,727-tonne corvette, only 70 survived the disaster.

Just south of Piha, **Karekare** has several idyllic picnic spots and a swimming hole at the base of a waterfall. Its beach achieved some fame as the location for the award-winning film *The Piano*.

To the north of Piha is **Bethells Beach**, inhabited by Maoris for several centuries; some 75 sites have been recorded here by archaeologists. Ihumoana Island, just off the beach, is the area's best-preserved island *pa*. Although not as spectacular as Cape Kidnappers (*see p149*), a headland at **Muriwai Beach**, beyond Bethells, is home to a colony of around 2,000 Australasian gannets, which originally nested on offshore Motutara Island. Barriers and viewing platforms allow visitors to observe the birds without disturbing them. The best time to see the gannets is between December and March.

View of Piha from the lookout at the top of the road

Henderson ⑫

Road map E2. 🚶 *4,600.* 🚉

The vineyards at Henderson, an hour's drive from Auckland city, have become a popular weekend destination for Aucklanders and visitors alike. Many of the wineries sell food, ranging from a snack to a complete meal, and offer free wine tastings.

Family-owned Babich Wines has a picnic and *pétanque* area overlooking its vineyards. The winery has a reputation for award-winning vintages, such as Babich Patriarch, but also produces

Locally grown fruit and vegetables for sale at Kumeu

Outdoor eating area at Babich Wines in Henderson

inexpensive wines. New Zealand's second largest winery, Corbans Wine, established by Lebanese immigrants in 1902, is another popular destination, as is Montana Wines, which produces numerous varieties – half of the country's total output. Its Deutz Marlborough Cuvée, made under an arrangement with Champagne Deutz, won the 1998 Sparkling Wine of the Year award at the International Wine Challenge in London. Visitors can obtain details of Henderson's vineyards at the Auckland visitor centre.

Kumeu ⑬

Road map E2. 🚶 *1,800.* 🚉

Another popular weekend pursuit of Aucklanders is lunch at a vineyard restaurant followed by shopping for fresh fruit and vegetables from a roadside stall on the way home. At Kumeu, a wine as well as fruit growing district, where a high percentage of the people involved in the wineries and orchards are from Croatia, visitors are spoilt for choice. Kumeu River Wines

should be included in every wine safari. Specializing in regionally grown grapes, Kumeu River's Chardonnay has made the top 100 Wines of the World list of the United States *Wine Spectator* magazine five times. The House of Nobilo, with 4,000 tonnes of grapes crushed in 1998, is the country's fourth largest winery. It also sells wines from Selaks Wines, which it purchased in 1998.

Soljans Estate Winery features a pleasant picnic area and offers visitors tours. Its premium varieties include Chardonnay.

Matua Valley Wines produces a broad range of good quality wines. The winery also serves gourmet treats to accompany the wines. These may be enjoyed in the pleasant grounds, which have picnic and barbecue facilities, as well as a children's play area.

FILM MAKING IN NEW ZEALAND

New Zealand's coastal scenery has not escaped the notice of location finders in the movie industry. The beach scenes in Jane Campion's *The Piano*, winner of the 1994 Palme d'Or at Cannes and Oscars for Best Original Screenplay and Best Supporting Actress, were shot at Karekare. Bethells Beach features in *Xena: Warrior Princess* and *Hercules: The Legendary Journeys*. Numerous television series, such as *Black Beauty*, movies and commercials have also been filmed along the New Zealand coast. International interest has spawned a burgeoning domestic film industry. Over 120 feature films have been produced in the country since 1940. Lee Tamahori's *Once Were Warriors* was released in 1994 in cinemas around the world. Local director Peter Jackson's Oscar-winning *Lord of The Rings* trilogy eclipsed all previous New Zealand motion pictures in terms of scale and budget.

Shooting a film on a New Zealand beach

Well-preserved Victorian buildings on Devonport's waterfront

Devonport ⑭

Road map E2. 🚶 18,000. 🚃 ⛴

In comparison to Auckland's less affluent southern and western (except Titirangi) quadrants, the eastern and northern quadrants are seen to be prosperous. Although over-simplified, this view is not a completely inaccurate one. The North Shore, the suburban area north of the Harbour Bridge, is relatively wealthy and blessed with a string of beaches that also function as launching pads for sailing boats and dinghies.

Devonport is a ten-minute ferry ride from Auckland's Ferry Building (see p71). It is the only North Shore suburb with a distinctly historical flavour. With many of its villas found along the water-front, a stroll along King Edward Parade provides an impression of the suburb's Victorian architecture, as well as views of Auckland's central business district across Waitemata Harbour. From Victoria Wharf, where the ferries arrive, it is a five-minute walk to the cafés, res-taurants and book shops of Victoria Road. Mount Victoria and North Head, both extinct volcanoes, are accessible by car or by walking and offer good views.

Devonport has a long military history. Its association with the Royal New Zealand Navy dates back to 1841 and there are approximately 2,200 staff currently stationed at the local base. Devonport's naval heritage can be viewed at the **Navy Museum** which houses a collection of photographs, uniforms, weapons and other related memorabilia.

Further north, **Takapuna** has its own popular beach. Brasserie-style restaurants, cafés and shops are found along Hurstmere Road.

🏛 Navy Museum
Spring St. **Tel** (09) 445 5186.
◯ daily. ⬤ Good Fri, 25 & 26 Dec.
🖼 donation. 🎥 on request. 🛈

Orewa ⑮

Road map E2. 🚶 (including Hibiscus Coast) 28,000. 🚃 🛈 214A Hibiscus Coast Hwy, (09) 426 0076.

Beach houses and motels line the main road through this small seaside town, 40 minutes' drive north of Auck-land. Orewa's main attraction is its beach, a 3-km (2-mile) long stretch of sand. The beach is suitable for swim-ming, surfing and boating. Easterly winds from the sea also attract windsurfers.

Environs
Just north of Orewa, a small road off State Highway 1 leads to **Puhoi**, New Zealand's earliest Bohemian settlement. A tiny calvary shrine beside the road leading to the settlement is a reminder of the settlers' background. The local pub also doubles as a museum of the pioneers of the area. The Church of St Peter and St Paul, built in 1881, features a Bohemian painting.

About 48 km (30 miles) north of Auckland, Waiwera is best known for its thermal resort, **Waiwera Infinity Hot Pools**. The complex has nine indoor and outdoor pools, spas, water slides, beauty therapies and picnic areas. The natural springs deliver up to 1 million litres (0.2 million gallons) of water per day.

🏊 Waiwera Infinity Hot Pools
State Hwy 1. **Tel** 0800 924 937.
◯ daily. 🖼 🍴 🚻 🛈
www.waiwera.co.nz

Hauraki Gulf Islands ⑯

Road map E2. ⛴ 🛈 Department of Conservation, Ferry Building, Quay St, Auckland, (09) 379 6476.
www.doc.govt.nz

The Hauraki Gulf Islands are among the most beautiful in the world. Some of the 65 islands are popular spots for recreational activities. Others, with their rare bird sanctu-aries and unspoiled stands of native trees and plants, are protected for conservation. Waiheke is now home to many commuters, while Great Barrier and Kawau are preferred by those who enjoy a somewhat slower lifestyle.

The beach at Orewa, popular with swimmers and windsurfers

For hotels and restaurants in this region see pp298–300 and pp326–8

Sir George Grey's historic home, Mansion House, on Kawau Island, Hauraki Gulf

Waiheke Island has gained an "alternative" reputation because of its organic farms and artisans. Apart from its white sand beaches, its vineyards and olive groves are attractive to visitors.

Electricity on **Great Barrier Island**, the furthermost island in the Hauraki Gulf, is provided by windmills and diesel generators, while most refrigerators use kerosene. Drinking water comes from rain collected on roofs. The island is dominated by Mount Hobson, standing at 620 m (2,034 ft), and Ruahine, 410 m (1,345 ft). Visitors may spot a kaka, the New Zealand parrot, or a brown teal duck while on a tramping trip.

Regular boats to **Kawau Island** leave from Sandspit at Warkworth. The island is best known for Mansion House, built in 1846, the home of former New Zealand governor and prime minister Sir George Grey. Sir George imported a variety of animal species, such as kookaburras and peacocks. Several, such as the parma wallaby, thought to be extinct in Australia, can still be seen.

Rangitoto has a highly visible presence in the gulf.

Brown kiwi with egg

The now-extinct volcano erupted about 600–700 years ago to form an island. Now, the 260-m (850-ft) high lava slopes are covered in native trees and shrubs. Vegetation includes mosses, mangroves, ferns, tree daisies, orchids, coastal pohutukawa, manuka and rewa. There are good walks, including one to the summit. Alternatively, visitors can use a tractor-drawn train.

Rakino is popular with weekenders. A hotch-potch of houses sit perched on striking ridges. Its beaches are suitable for swimming and it is a favourite stop for yachts.

Little Barrier Island, a wildlife sanctuary, has 30 native and 19 introduced species of birds breeding on it. They include the brown kiwi, kaka and bellbird. Flora includes 370 native species, with 90 ferns. It is prohibited to land on Little Barrier but it is possible to visit the island with a permit obtained from Forest and Bird.

Gazetted in 1975, **Goat Island Marine** Reserve is also known as the Leigh Marine Reserve. The sheltered channel between Goat Island and the mainland provides an opportunity to see red moki, moray eel, snapper and blue cod, as well as marblefish and kelpfish.

The channel is only about 2 to 5 m (7 to 17 ft) deep and diving is possible straight from the beach. Underwater visibility fluctuates from 2 to 15 m (7 to 50 ft) and is at its best from January to June.

Waiheke Island
8,000. ⚓ ℹ Korora Rd, Oneroa, (09) 372 1234.
www.waiheke.co.nz

Great Barrier Island
1,000. ✈ ⚓ 🚌 ℹ Claris Airport, (09) 367 6009.
www.greatbarrier.co.nz

Kawau Island
200. ⚓

Visitors watching birds at the Leigh Marine Reserve

SHOPPING IN AUCKLAND

Shops in Auckland cater for the needs of most shoppers. However, the city is quite spread out and it pays to do some research first. Shops in downtown Auckland are predominantly European in character; in other areas they have a more Pacific or Asian flavour. Shoppers in search of local items should consider pure wool products, such as handknitted sweaters or cuddly toys made from possum fur. The New Zealand fashion scene is lively and creative, and local designers such as Zambesi, Karen Walker, Anne Mardell, and Trelise Cooper have outlets in all the smart shopping areas. Jewellery, pottery, glass and other crafts are of a high standard and are worth buying. Specialized retailers sell items such as crayfish, which they will package for outbound travellers.

Greenstone pendant

SHOPPING HOURS

Typical business hours are 9am to 6pm, with many stores open on Saturday and Sunday. Most large supermarkets are open until 9pm and some 24 hours. Dairies (convenience stores) are found throughout the suburbs and sell a wide range of groceries and other items, as do most gas stations.

DUTY-FREE SHOPPING

The New Zealand government adds 12.5 per cent Goods and Services Tax (GST) to sales items. Visitors to New Zealand can avoid paying this tax, as well as other government duty, by purchasing duty-free goods on arrival and departure at the airport or at the large duty-free shop, **DFS Galleria**, in the city. This results in savings of 30 per cent on average. Items purchased at the shop have to be collected at the airport. Besides the usual cigarettes and alcohol, sheepskin goods, *paua* shell jewellery, *paua* pearls, and finely crafted woodwork using local timbers are popular items with tourists.

SHOPPING AREAS

Queen Street is the major banking and commercial centre. However, the restoration of Charles Bohringer's Civic Theatre (1929), the Force Entertainment Centre and shopping complexes such as **Atrium on Elliott**,

Interior of a Rodd and Gunn outlet in the city

the **Tower Shopping Centre** and **Westfield Downtown Shopping Centre** have revitalized the central business district as a shopping and entertainment centre. Book stores such as **Whitcoulls**, **Dymocks** and **Unity Books**, CD and record shops such as **Marbecks Record Shop**, woollen clothing and couture boutiques, and many souvenir stores are also

The country's largest duty-free shop, DFS Galleria, located at the Old Customhouse

located downtown. Nautical-type clothing and souvenirs, sought after during the 2000 America's Cup Regatta, can be purchased at the **National Maritime Museum Shop**.

Newmarket is Auckland's prime shopping area. Shops along Broadway include **Country Road, Rodd and Gunn**, and **Living and Giving**. Parnell and Ponsonby retailers specialize in luxury goods, such as delicatessen food, clothing, art, ceramics and glassware.

Fresh fruit on sale at one of Auckland's markets

MARKETS

Shoppers who are more interested in typically New Zealand goods at lower prices should go to **Victoria Park Market**, a former rubbish destructor building built in 1905. Today, the site houses shops and stalls selling anything from souvenirs to snacks. There are also three licensed restaurants and a food court at the complex.

Saturday morning's **Otara Market**, open from 6am to noon, offers yams, green bananas, *hangi* (Maori food cooked on heated stones) and Pacific Island fashion.

DIRECTORY

SHOPPING CENTRES

Atrium on Elliott
21–25 Elliott St.
Tel (09) 375 4960.
www.atriumonelliott.co.nz

DFS Galleria
Old Customhouse,
Cnr of Albert &
Customs sts.
Tel 0800 388 937.

Dress-Smart Factory Outlet
151 Arthur St, Onehunga.
Tel (09) 622 2400.

Queens Arcade
34–40 Queen St.
Tel (09) 358 1777.

Tower Shopping Centre
125 Queen St.
Tel (09) 309 6949.

Westfield Downtown Shopping Centre
11–19 Custom St West.
Tel (09) 978 5265.

MARKETS

Otara Market
Newbury St & Te Puke,
Otara Community Hall.
Tel (09) 274 0830.

Victoria Park Market
210 Victoria St West.
Tel (09) 309 6911.
www.victoria-park-market.co.nz

FOOD AND WINE

Accent on Wine
347 Parnell Rd,
Parnell. *Tel (09) 358 2552.*

Pandoro Panetteria
427 Parnell Rd, Parnell.
Tel (09) 358 1962.

CLOTHES

Country Road
164 Queen St.
Tel (09) 309 6862.
157 Broadway,
Newmarket.
Tel (09) 529 1987.

Karen Walker
15 O'Connell St.
Tel (09) 309 6299.
6 Balm St, Newmarket.
Tel (09) 522 4286.

Living and Giving
277 Broadway,
Newmarket.
Tel (09) 522 1270.

National Maritime Museum Shop
Viaduct Basin.
Tel (09) 373 0800.

Rodd and Gunn
75 Queen St.
Tel (09) 309 6571.
277 Broadway,
Newmarket.
Tel (09) 522 0607.

Workshop
Cnr of Vulcan Lane and
High St.
Tel (09) 303 3735.
18 Morrow St,
Newmarket.
Tel (09) 524 6844.

BOOKS AND MUSIC

Borders
291–297 Queen St.
Tel (09) 309 3377.

Dymocks
246 Queen St.
Tel (09) 379 9919.

Marbecks Record Shop
25 Queen's Arcade.
Tel (09) 379 0444.
www.marbecks.co.nz

Real Groovy Records
438 Queen St.
Tel (09) 302 3940.

Unity Books
19 High St.
Tel (09) 307 0731.
www.unitybooks.co.nz

Whitcoulls
210 Queen St.
Tel (09) 984 5400.

Women's Bookshop
105 Ponsonby Rd.
Tel (09) 376 4399.
www.womensbookshop.co.nz

SOUVENIRS AND OTHERS

Breen's Sheepskin Specialists
Tower Centre,
6 Customs St.
Tel (09) 373 2788.

Höglund Art Glass Gallery
285 Parnell Rd, Parnell.
Tel (09) 300 6238.
www.hoglund.co.nz

OK Gift Shop
Downtown Shopping
Centre, Cnr of Albert &
Customs sts.
Tel (09) 303 1951.

Smith and Caughey's
253–261 Queen St.
Tel (09) 377 4770.
255 Broadway,
Newmarket.
Tel (09) 524 8049.

ENTERTAINMENT IN AUCKLAND

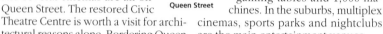

Reflecting Auckland's ethnic diversity, events staged in the city range from a Puccini opera to a Maori dance performance. Many of these take place at venues in the central business district. The Aotea Centre, Auckland Town Hall and several cinemas are all on Queen Street. The restored Civic Theatre Centre is worth a visit for architectural reasons alone. Bordering Queen

Busker in Queen Street

Street, Fort Street and Karangahape Road, commonly known as K-Road, offer alternative entertainment in the form of strip clubs and massage parlours. K-Road is also known for its funky atmosphere and its many nightclubs. SKYCITY Casino features more than 100 gaming tables and 1,000 machines. In the suburbs, multiplex cinemas, sports parks and nightclubs are the main entertainment venues.

Interior of the refurbished Civic Theatre Centre

INFORMATION

The entertainment section of *The New Zealand Herald* should be checked first for events in the city. It carries cinema listings and information about concerts, ballets and theatre performances. Several publications outlining what's on in Auckland are available from visitor information centres which can be found across the city. The country's two main booking agencies, **Ticketmaster** and **Ticketek**, list events on their websites. Reservations can be made online or by phone.

THEATRE

The two main venues, the **Aotea Centre** and the **Auckland Town Hall**, are part of the complex known as THE EDGE® *(see p74)* . This is where the biggest musicals and productions are staged. The renovated Great Hall in the Auckland Town Hall *(see p74)* is renowned for its acoustics. Other theatres include the Maidment Theatre at the university and the Silo in Grey's Avenue.

DANCE

New Zealand has a small dance community. Its leading contemporary dance choreographers are Mary Jane O'Reilly, Michael Parmenter, and Douglas Wright.

At present, the Footnote Dance Company is the country's only full-time contemporary dance company. Based in Wellington, the troupe regularly performs in Auckland, as does the classical Royal New Zealand Ballet, which also has its home in the capital. However, the Black Grace Dance Company is Auckland-based. There are regular tours by overseas dance and ballet companies.

Annabel Reid of the Royal New Zealand Ballet in *Raymonda*

MUSIC

For classical music, the New Zealand Symphony Orchestra (NZSO) and the Auckland Philharmonia Orchestra (APO) have a good reputation. The 33-member APO is unusual in that the musicians own the orchestra. Most concerts are held in the Auckland Town Hall. Both the NZSO and the APO also perform at the free "Symphony under the Stars" concert at Auckland Domain *(see p77)*. This event attracts huge crowds of more than 100,000 people.

Many pubs in Auckland have live bands which play most nights, including the Powerstation, King's Arms and The Dogs Bollix, a popular Irish pub.

Fireworks during a symphony performance at the Auckland Domain

A traditional show given by the Manaia Cultural Performance Group

CULTURAL PERFORMANCES

At the Auckland War Memorial Museum (see pp78–9), visitors are able to witness authentic Maori ceremonies and dances. During the shows, which are staged three to four times daily, talented singers and dancers from the Manaia Cultural Performance Group present the *haka*, the fierce war dance of the men, the *poi* dances of the women (see pp30–31), as well as various other traditional songs and dances. Each show lasts about 45 minutes.

Visitors can also get to see Pacific Island culture and events at the Pasifika Festival, held at Western Springs, in March every year (see p42). The festival features the traditional arts and culture of the various Pacific Island communities.

CLUBS

Although theatres throughout the country feature one-off performances by local and visiting comedians, the **Classic Comedy & Bar** claims to be the only venue in the whole of New Zealand that is dedicated to stand-up comedy.

The city's main nightclub strip is on Karangahape Road. Venues that are popular with young people include **Sinners Nightclub**, which can accommodate up to

1,000 people on busy nights, **Calibre**, a select nightclub that attracts a well-dressed crowd and foreign DJs on Friday nights, and **Kiss Bar**, a popular dance club playing mainly house music. Gay clubs include **Mea Culpa** on Ponsonby Road and **Flesh Nightclub & Lounge Bar** on O'Connell Street in the city which hosts drag acts and other entertainment evenings.

FILM

Multiplex cinemas are found throughout Auckland. The larger multiplexes, such as the **Village SKYCITY Cinemas**, show blockbuster movies, often before they are seen in Europe. Newmarket's refurbished **Rialto Cinema**, on the other hand, regularly screens foreign titles for more sophisticated movie buffs.

The highlight of the cinematographic year is the New Zealand Film Festival, held in July. Auckland filmgoers get to enjoy a wide selection of local and international films over several days.

Façade of the Village SKYCITY Cinemas

DIRECTORY

BOOKING TICKETS

Ticketek
Tel (09) 307 5000, 0800 TICKETEK. www.ticketek.com

Ticketmaster
Tel (09) 970 9700.
www.ticketmaster.co.nz

THEATRES

Aotea Centre
Queen St.
Tel (09) 309 2677.

Auckland Town Hall
Queen St.
Tel (09) 309 2677.

Civic Theatre Centre
Cnr Queen and Wellesley sts.

SKYCITY Theatre
Cnr Wellesley and Hobson sts.
Tel 0800 759 2489.

CLUBS

Boogie Wonderland
Cnr Custom & Queen sts.
Tel (09) 361 6093.

Calibre
179 Karangahape Rd.
Tel (09) 303 1673.

Classic Comedy & Bar
321 Queen St. *Tel (09) 373 4321.*

Khuja Lounge
536 Queen St. *Tel (09) 377 3711.*

Kiss Bar
309 Karangahape Rd.
Tel (09) 303 2726.

Mea Culpa
3/175 Ponsonby Rd.
Tel (09) 376 4460.

S P Q R
150 Ponsonby Rd.
Tel (09) 360 1710.

Spy Bar
204 Quay St, Viaduct Basin.
Tel (09) 377 7811.

CINEMAS

Rialto Cinema
169 Broadway, Newmarket.
Tel (09) 369 2417.

Village SKYCITY Cinemas
Tel (09) 972 2800.

NORTHLAND

*S*trong Maori roots, early European settlements, a subtropical climate and enchanting scenery – these make Northland both the cradle of the nation and one of its favourite playgrounds. Northland is where Europeans first made their presence felt in New Zealand. It is a region with a history of bloodshed and raw frontier emotions, but is today dominated by holiday fun.

The long history of Maori occupation in Northland is evident in the hillside *pa* sites and shellfishing grounds around the coast. Maori culture *(see pp30–31)* continues to be extensively practised in this region and many Maori tribes live here.

Early post-European history in Northland includes both the licentious whalers, who earned Russell its title of "hell-hole of the Pacific" *(see p102)*, and missionaries, who brought Christianity to the country. The brothels and taverns have now disappeared, but buildings like Pompallier House are reminders of early Christian influences.

Historically, Waitangi Treaty House, where the Treaty of Waitangi was signed *(see pp48–9, 104–5)*, is of prime importance. Cape Reinga *(see p108)* is a drawcard, because of its location at the top of the country where the Pacific Ocean and Tasman Sea merge, and also because of its significance in Maori mythology as the place from where the spirits of the dead depart for Hawaiki.

Visitors to Northland will be impressed by its natural beauty: gently rolling farmland, white sand beaches, massive sand dunes and rock formations. In a world where scenic spots are often spoiled due to countless visitors, Northland stands out. In its forests, with gigantic kauris that are around 2,000 years old, it is still possible to walk for hours without encountering a single fellow tramper. The region also offers other activities, such as fishing, diving, kayaking, tobogganing and horseback riding.

Diving near the wreck of the *Rainbow Warrior (see p53)* off Matauri Bay

◁ Wild flowers and rolling hills of the Northland landscape

Exploring Northland

Northland's charm lies in its unspoiled, simple character. The region is blessed with two contrasting coastlines, which offer endless scope for outdoor recreation. As the site of first permanent contact between Maoris and Europeans, the region is also rich in history and has many well-preserved historic sites. There are three main bases from which visitors can explore the region: Paihia, which has its own attractions but is close to historic Russell, Waitangi and Kerikeri, and the beautiful Bay of Islands; Kaitaia, which attracts day-trippers to the Aupori Peninsula, Mangonui and Ahipara; and Opononi and Omapere, which have wonderful beaches and are close to Rawene, a historic settlement on Hokianga Harbour.

CAPE REINGA
13
North Cape
Te Paki
AUPORI PENINSULA TOUR
Parengarenga Harbour
NINETY MILE BEACH
Te Kao
15
Great Exhibition Bay
Pukenui
14
Ka
Mohutar
Waipapakuri
A
Ahipara Bay
12 K
Tauroa Point
Ahipara
Broadv
Hok
Har
OPOR
Om

0 kilometres   20

0 miles   20

Pohutukawa trees and bays around Whangarei Heads

TOP OUTDOOR ACTIVITIES

The places shown here have been selected for their recreational activities. Conditions vary depending on the weather and the time of year, so exercise caution and, if in doubt, seek local advice.

	CRUISING	GAME FISHING	KAYAKING	SAILING	SCUBA DIVING	SNORKELLING	SWIMMING	TRAMPING
Cape Reinga								■
Kai-Iwi Lakes			●	■			●	
Kaitaia								■
Ninety Mile Beach							●	■
Omapere	●	■	●	■			●	
Opononi	●	■	●	■			●	
Paihia	●	■	●	■	●	■		
Russell	●	■	●	■	●	■	●	■
Tutukaka	●	■	●	■	●	■		
Waipoua Forest								■
Whangarei	●	■	●	■	●	■	●	■

SEE ALSO

- **Where to Stay** pp301–2
- **Where to Eat** pp328–30

Painting an ancestral figure on the meeting house at Waitangi

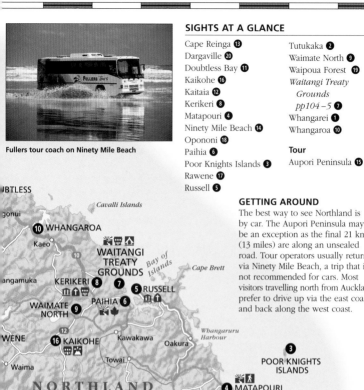

Fullers tour coach on Ninety Mile Beach

SIGHTS AT A GLANCE

Cape Reinga 13
Dargaville 20
Doubtless Bay 11
Kaikohe 16
Kaitaia 12
Kerikeri 8
Matapouri 4
Ninety Mile Beach 14
Opononi 18
Paihia 6
Poor Knights Islands 3
Rawene 17
Russell 5
Tutukaka 2
Waimate North 9
Waipoua Forest 19
Waitangi Treaty Grounds pp104–5 7
Whangarei 1
Whangaroa 10

Tour

Aupori Peninsula 15

GETTING AROUND

The best way to see Northland is by car. The Aupori Peninsula may be an exception as the final 21 km (13 miles) are along an unsealed road. Tour operators usually return via Ninety Mile Beach, a trip that is not recommended for cars. Most visitors travelling north from Auckland prefer to drive up via the east coast and back along the west coast.

Cavalli Islands
10 WHANGAROA
Kaeo
WAITANGI TREATY GROUNDS
Bay of Islands
Cape Brett
KERIKERI 8
7
5 RUSSELL
WAIMATE NORTH 9
PAIHIA 6
16 KAIKOHE
Kawakawa
Oakura
Whangaruru Harbour
Towai
Waima
3
POOR KNIGHTS ISLANDS
NORTHLAND
4 MATAPOURI
2 TUTUKAKA
Hikurangi
Purua
Tutamoe Range
Parakao
Maunu
1 WHANGAREI
PACIFIC OCEAN
Maungatapere
Kaihu
Kai-Iwi Lakes
Portland
McLeod Bay
Bream Head
Ruakaka
Bream Bay
DARGAVILLE 20
Waiotira
Waipu
Wairoa
Maungaturoto
Matakohe
Ruawai
Mangawhai
ASMAN SEA
Little Barrier Island
Kaipara Harbour
Wellsford
Leigh
North Head
Warkworth
Kawau Island
South Head
AUCKLAND
Hauraki Gulf
Orewa
Kaukapakapa
Helensville
Auckland
ajor road
inor road
enic route
inor railway
egional border
ll road

The Town Basin on the waterfront at Whangarei

Whangarei ❶

Road map E1. ⚏ 47,000. ✈ ⊟
⊞ ⓗ *Tarewa Park, 92 Otaika Rd, (09)
438 1079.* **www**.whangareinz.org.nz

The northernmost city in
New Zealand and the only
one in Northland, Whangarei
is a two-hour drive from
Auckland. The city lies between forested hills and a
deep harbour. The combination of fertile soil and temperate climate is reflected in
the city's lush gardens and
in the surrounding farmlands
and orchards.

Whangarei's historic Town
Basin, in the heart of the city,
has been redeveloped in a
colonial theme. Its cafés,
restaurants, art galleries,
museums and speciality shops
make it a popular gathering

The picturesque Whangarei Falls

place for locals and visitors. It
is also one of the most popular
destinations for yacht sailors
wandering the world, who
come here to avoid the
cyclonic storms common
in the South Pacific over
the summer. The Town
Basin and local marinas
are often full with visiting
yachts coming to refit.

A giant sundial marks
the location of the
Town Basin's **Clapham
Clock Museum**, which
houses more than
1,600 items donated
by A Clapham, who
made many of the
clocks himself. The
oldest, an English
lantern clock, dates from 1720.
The collection also includes
Biedermeier wall clocks,
grandfather and Black Forest
clocks, and a *staartklok*
(literally a "tail clock"
because of the shape of
its winding mechanism)
from Friesland in the
Netherlands. To avoid the
deafening sound of the
hundreds of time-pieces
marking the hour simul-
taneously, the clocks have
been set at different times.

Just to the west of
Whangarei is the **Quarry
Arts Centre**, offering
local arts and crafts for
sale. Set in a bush-clad
quarry the Trust is home
to a number of artists
who live on-site in adobe-
style dwellings. Further
out is the **Whangarei
Museum, Clarke
Homestead and Kiwi
House**. The museum
displays a fine range of

Clapham Clock
Museum exhibit

Maori artefacts, while the 1885
homestead remains as it was
when it was first built. The Kiwi
House provides the chance to
view one of the country's most
endangered birds.

For those looking for more
challenging activities, there are
many tramping opportunities
around Whangarei. The
Parahaki Scenic Reserve, on
the eastern side of the city,
has good bush walks. The war
memorial at the summit of
Parahaki Mountain can be
reached via Memorial Drive or
by two tracks from Mair Park
or Dundas Road, for a superb
panoramic view of the city
and harbour. There are Maori
pits and old gum-digging
workings on all the walks,
and a trail leads to a historic
Maori *pa* site nearby.

Whangarei Falls, known
as the most photogenic
waterfalls in New Zealand,
lie northeast of the Parahaki
Scenic Reserve in the
suburb of Tikipunga,
5 km (3 miles) north
of the town centre.
The 26-m (86-ft) high
waterfall drops over
basalt cliffs.
There are natural
pools and picnic spots,
plus two viewing plat-
forms that provide
excellent views of the falls.

🏛 **Clapham Clock Museum**
Town Basin, Quayside. *Tel (09)
438 3993.* ◯ *daily.* ⏺ *25 Dec.* ✎
♿ ✍ 🖼

🏛 **Quarry Arts Centre**
21 Selwyn Ave. *Tel (09) 438 1215.*
◯ *daily.* 🖼 ♿

🏛 **Whangarei Museum,
Clarke Homestead and Kiwi
House** State Hwy 14, Heritage
Park, Maunu. *Tel (09) 438 9630.*
◯ *daily.* ✎ ♿

Tutukaka ❷

Road map E1. ⚏ 520. ⊟ ⓗ *Dive!
Tutukaka, Marina Rd, (09) 434 3867.*

On the coastal loop road,
a short distance from
Whangarei, Tutukaka is a
well-known base for diving
trips to the Poor Knights
Islands and for big game
and deep-sea fishing. Several
diving companies are based
here and the sheltered,

Yachts moored at the marina in Tutukaka's sheltered harbour

natural harbour is alive with yachts and fishing boats.

One of the most popular diving sites off the coast between Tutukaka and Matapouri is an artificial reef created by the sinking of two former naval ships, the *Tui* and the *Waikato*. Several professional diving companies offer their services as guides to this underwater grave. For further information on diving trips available in the area, visit www.diving.co.nz.

Poor Knights Islands ❸

Road map E1. 🛈 *Tarewa Park, 92 Otaika Rd, Whangarei, (09) 438 1079.* **www**.whangareinz.org.nz

About 24 km (15 miles) from the coast at Tutukaka are the Poor Knights Islands. Once a favourite spot for fishermen, the area around these two islands was established as a marine reserve in 1981. Although landing on the islands is prohibited without a special permit from the Department of Conservation, the surrounding waters are accessible to divers. Well-known mariner Jacques Cousteau considered the reserve one of the world's top five diving sites because of its exceptional water

clarity and the variety of its sea life. The area benefits from a subtropical current that makes it warmer than the surrounding coastal waters, and promotes a profusion of tropical and temperate marine life. Eroded volcanic rock has created a seascape of tunnels, arches and caves where divers can view fish and sponges. Scuba diving in this haven can be enjoyed all year round. Boats leave daily from Tutukaka Marina.

Reptiles such as geckos and tuataras can be found on both islands, which are thought to be the world's only nesting spot for Buller's shearwaters.

Matapouri ❹

Road map E1.

Located a short distance north of Tutukawa on the coastal loop road, Matapouri has one of Northland's most beautiful beaches. Tucked between headlands and dotted with islets, Matapouri's calm waters and white sands make it a popular place for swimming and snorkelling.

A walking track connects the beach with Whale Bay, 2 km (1.2 miles) north. Look-out points on the track offer magnificent views of the coastline and ocean.

Diving in the marine reserve at Poor Knights Islands

Aerial view of the Bay of Islands ▷

The churchyard, Christ Church, Russell

Russell [5]

Road map E1. 👥 *1,000.* 🚌 ⛴ [i] *The Wharf, (09) 403 8020.*

At the turn of the 19th century, Russell, then known as Kororareka, served as a shore station for whalers. It became a lawless town, earning the title "Hell-hole of the Pacific". It was renamed Russell in 1844 in honour of the British colonial secretary of the day. Today, the quiet town is involved in tourism, fishing, oyster farming and cottage industries.

Formerly known as the Captain Cook Memorial Museum, the **Russell Museum** features a working model of Captain Cook's *Endeavour* and memorabilia from American author Zane Grey, who helped establish the Bay of Islands as a game fishing centre in the late 1920s. There is also a collection of early settlers' relics.

Christ Church, built in 1836, is the country's oldest surviving church. One of the contributors to the church was Charles Darwin, author of *The Origin of Species*, who visited New Zealand in 1835.

Stately **Pompallier Mission** was built on the waterfront between 1841 and 1842 to house the Marist mission's Gaveaux printing press. The building later became much neglected, until it passed to the New Zealand Historic Places Trust in 1968 and was restored to its original state in 1993. The country's oldest standing industrial building, it now houses a printing and bookbinding exhibition, which includes the original printing press.

Flagstaff Hill serves as a reminder of Russell's turbulent past. It was here that Hone Heke (1810–50) cut down the British shipping signal flagpole in 1844 *(see p63)*.

Paihia restaurant sign

🏛 Russell Museum

2 York St. ***Tel** (09) 403 7701.*
○ *daily.* ● *25 Dec.* 💲 ♿ 🛍

⛪ Christ Church

Church Rd. ***Tel** (09) 403 7707.*
✝ *10:30am Sun.*

🏠 Pompallier Mission

The Strand. ***Tel** (09) 403 9015.*
○ *daily.* ● *Good Fri, 25 Dec.*
💲 ♿ *garden only.* 📖 🛍

Paihia [6]

Road map E1. 👥 *1,850.* 🚌 ⛴ [i] *Marsden Rd, (09) 402 7345.*

Starting life as a mission post in 1823, Paihia now joins places such as Russell and Tutukaka as a base for deep-sea game fishing. To the north of Paihia, on the road to Kerikeri is the **Lily Pond Farm Park**. The park gives visitors the chance to interact with a whole range of farm animals including sheep, pigs and goats. There are also more exotic species of animal, such as eels, alpaca and emus. It is a working farm that will appeal to families with small children.

Located 3 km (2 miles) from Paihia, on the Waitangi River *(see pp104–5)*, are the **Haruru Falls**. The track from Waitangi to Haruru Falls was recently closed due to a devastating flood. Visitors can still walk to the mangroves, however, to see herons and nesting native shags. An alternative approach to the falls is by kayak along the river. Kayaks can be hired from **Coastal Kayakers**.

🐄 Lily Pond Farm Park

RD1 Puketona Rd.
***Tel** (09) 402 6099.* ○ *Fri–Tue.*
● *25 Dec.* 💲 ♿

🌊 Haruru Falls

Waitangi Treaty Grounds.
***Tel** (09) 402 7437.* ○ *9am–5pm daily.* ● *25 Dec.* 💲 📖
Coastal Kayakers Te Karuwha Pde, Waitangi. ***Tel** (09) 402 8105.*
www.coastalkayakers.co.nz

Leisure Activities in the Bay of Islands

A favourable climate, an irregular coastline lapped by the Pacific Ocean and some 150 islands dotted around its aquamarine waters combine to make the Bay of Islands one of New Zealand's most popular playgrounds. The region has been a favourite tourist destination since the 1930s when a road connecting Northland with Auckland to

Fishing club logo

the south was built. The Bay of Islands' reputation is based primarily on deep-sea fishing, but today visitors also have the opportunity to experience other water sports, such as swimming, kayaking, sailing, diving and water-skiing. Tour operators tempt visitors by adding new attractions, such as scenic flights, paragliding and horse trekking.

The Rowe family, keen anglers of the Bay of Islands Swordfish Club, with their prize catch

GAME FISHING

Deep-sea game fishing is a year-round activity in the Bay of Islands. The most prolific game fish is the striped marlin, which may weigh up to 120 kg (265 lb). Many other species, which can be caught using both heavy and light tackle, are abundant in the bay's waters. Deep-sea fishing charters usually include accommodation, food, tackle and bait. No licence is required for ocean fishing.

Anglers *increasingly are tagging and releasing the fish they catch, such as this striped marlin.*

Swimming with dolphins *in the bay's warm waters is a popular activity. Licensed tour operators ensure that human attention does not scare the dolphins.*

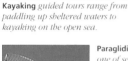

Kayaking *guided tours range from paddling up sheltered waters to kayaking on the open sea.*

Paragliding, *one of several airborne sports introduced in the Bay of Islands, is an excellent way to appreciate the beauty of the bay.*

Leisure cruises *include Paihia's Cream Trip. The boat used to collect cream from outlying dairy farms but now drops off mail and takes visitors on cruises.*

Waitangi Treaty Grounds ●

Waitangi earned its pivotal place in New Zealand's history on 6 February 1840 when the Treaty of Waitangi was signed *(see pp18, 48–9)* in front of the house of James Busby (1800–71), the British Resident. The Residency, renamed the Treaty House, became a national memorial in 1932. The house and grounds are a gathering point for Maoris and government leaders each year on 6 February, Waitangi Day. Visitors are recommended to take the guided tours.

Tatooed figure on meeting house

Aerial View of Waitangi Treaty Grounds
The grounds are surrounded by a beautiful coastline, tidal estuary, mangrove, forest and native bush.

Visitor Centre
An audiovisual presentation every half hour describes the events surrounding the signing of the Treaty of Waitangi. There are also displays on the major personalities involved and copies of the Treaty documents. A shop sells souvenirs, Maori carvings and books.

Waikokopu Café
(see p329)

Waitang

Te Tii Marae

Bay of Islands Yacht Club

PAIHIA

Tau Hemare Drive

Copthorne Hotel and Resort
(see p301)

A coastal walk takes visitors past unusual pillow lava rock, which fractured into hexagonal shapes as it erupted under water.

Car Park

Canoe House

HOBSON BEACH

| 0 metres | 200 |
| 0 yards | 200 |

★ Maori War Canoe
Carved from three kauri trees, this 35-m (114-ft) long canoe, named Ngatokimatawhaorua after the canoe in which Kupe discovered New Zealand (see p45), carries up to 120 warriors. It is launched each year on Waitangi Day.

STAR SIGHTS

★ Maori Meeting House

★ Maori War Canoe

★ Treaty House

For hotels and restaurants in this region see pp301–2 and pp328–30

VISITORS' CHECKLIST

Road map E1. ▥ from
Kerikeri. ▐ 1 Tau Henare
Drive, Waitangi, (09) 402 7437.
◯ 9am–5pm daily. ◯ 25
Dec. ▨ ☒ ☑ ☐ ☒
www.waitangi.net.nz

Mangrove Forest Boardwalk
*A boardwalk takes visitors
through a mature mangrove
forest to the Haruru Falls at the
end of the tidal Waitangi River.*

Hutia Creek

ver

★ **Treaty House**
*Prefabricated in
Australia, the Treaty
House (see p49), was
the home of the first
British Resident,
James Busby. It
was the venue for
important political
events up to 1840.*

Waitangi Golf
Course

Flagstaff

★ **Maori Meeting House**
*Opened on 6 February 1940 to
commemorate the centennial of the
Treaty, the meeting house
(Te Whare Runanga) contains
beautiful Maori wall carvings.*

Treaty Grounds
*A ceremonial celebration of the signing
of the Treaty of Waitangi is held each
year on the grounds in front of the
Treaty House.*

The Stone Store, St James Church and Kerikeri Mission House

Kerikeri ❽

Road map E1. 🏃 4,200. 🚗 🚆

The pretty town of Kerikeri is
noted for its subtropical
climate, citrus and kiwifruit
orchards, historic buildings,
and an art and craft trail.

The Kerikeri Basin is home
to **Kerikeri Mission Station**,
one of New Zealand's earliest
settlements. It was the second
European mission station to
be set up in New Zealand, in
1819, under the protection of
Maori chief Hongi Hika *(see
p63)*; the first mission was
established near the entrance
to the Bay of Islands five years
earlier. The mission station
includes Kerikeri Mission
House. Constructed in 1821,
the building belonged to the
Kemp family in 1832 and was
left to the New Zealand
Historic Places Trust in 1974.
Restored, it looks much as it
did in the 1840s. The mission
station also encompasses
New Zealand's oldest surviving stone building, the Stone
Store, built in 1835 as part of
the mission house. Intended
as a storehouse, it gradually
turned into a general store
and, from the 1960s, a souvenir shop. Its merchandise
includes hand-forged nails and
other products in keeping with
its history. On the slope
behind the mission house is
St James Church, constructed
in 1878 of native timbers
such as kauri and puriri.

Above the Basin are the
remnants of Kororipo Pa, a
Maori fortification. The
strategic base of Hongi Hika,
the *pa* is best known as an

assembly point for war parties
in the 1820s. Across the river
from the *pa* is **Rewa's Village**,
a reconstructed pre-European
Maori fishing village built from
native materials, those used
before the missionaries came.
It provides an introduction to
traditional buildings such as a
marae (gathering place) and
pataka (communal raised
storehouse). There are two
ancient canoes at the village
and a large, traditional garden.

🏛 **Kerikeri Mission Station**
The Basin. **Tel** (09) 407 9236.
⬜ daily. ● 25 Dec. 🎫 📷 by
prior arrangement. 🚻

🏠 **St James Church**
The Basin. 🚩 daily.

🏛 **Rewa's Village**
1 Landing Rd. **Tel** (09) 407 6454.
⬜ daily. ● Good Fri, 25 Dec.
♿ 📷 by arrangement. 🚻

Waimate North ❾

Road map E1. 🏃 700.

Not far from Kerikeri is
Waimate North, a missionary
community in the 1830s. It was
also the site of New Zealand's
first large English-style farm. It
is now best known for **Te**

Waimate Mission, the sole
survivor of three mission
houses built in 1832 and first
occupied by the Clarke family.
It is furnished with missionary
period furniture and early tools.

🏛 **Te Waimate Mission**
Te Ahu Ahu Rd. **Tel** (09) 405 9734.
⬜ May–Oct: Sat & Sun; Nov–Apr:
daily. ● 25 Dec. 🎫

Whangaroa ❿

Road map E1. 🏃 530. 🚆

A small, scenic settlement
with a beautiful harbour,
Whangaroa is best appreciated from the summit of St
Paul, a rock formation which
dominates the town. The
surrounding hills were once
covered in huge kauri trees,
which have long since been
turned into ship masts and
timber. Croatians worked the
Matauri Bay gumfields in the
late 19th century, extracting
resin *(see p110)*.

Today, Whangaroa Harbour
has become well known for
its big game fishing, cruises,
diving and snorkelling.

Doubtless Bay ⓫

Road map D1. 🚆

Said to be the first landfall for
the explorer Kupe *(see pp45
–6)*, Doubtless Bay was an
important base for whalers in
the early days of European
settlement. The bay encompasses a wide crescent of
golden beaches, including
Cable Bay and Cooper's
Beach, popular with swim-
mers and snorkellers. The
fishing village of Mangonui,
situated on the bay's estuary,
has many historic buildings.

Te Waimate Mission, one of New Zealand's oldest wooden buildings

Arts and Crafts

Art and crafts are well developed in Northland, often with a strong local flavour in the use of colours and motifs. Ironically, the best-known artist was not a New Zealander but Austrian architect and painter Hundertwasser, who spent much of his time in New Zealand until his death in March 2000. Visitors to Kawakawa, south of Paihia, and Russell can visit a grass-roofed Hundertwasser-designed toilet block.

Northland pottery

Local artist Chris Booth is known for sculptures that feature large stones – his best-known work is on the headland at Matauri Bay. There are many outlets in the area, however, that offer paintings, prints, bone carvings and traditional greenstone (jade) items. In Kerikeri, an art and craft trail leads visitors through shops selling a variety of individually handcrafted and decorated pieces of high quality.

SWAMP KAURI CARVING
Swamp kauri is turned by local artisans into items ranging from small bowls to dining sets. The timber is milled from the remnants of huge trees which fell into swamplands 30,000–50,000 years ago.

Part of a stone sculpture *by Northland artist Chris Booth, which forms the entrance to Auckland's Albert Park.*

Plaited floor mats, baskets and hats *made from flax, a swamp plant, are popular souvenirs. Flax weaving is a traditional Maori skill.*

Wood, bone or greenstone *are carved by crafts people like Hohepa Renata, who use their own designs or traditional Maori ones.*

Carved wooden mask

Pottery *is produced in a variety of techniques, including glazing methods from Japan.*

Kaitaia ⓬

Map D1. 👥 *5,300.* 🚌 ℹ *South Rd, (09) 408 0879.*

The largest town in the Far North, Kaitaia is a good base for day trips in the area. It is home to the **Far North Regional Museum**, which has the earliest authenticated European artifact left in New Zealand – a 1,500-kg (3,300-lb) wrought-iron anchor, lost in a storm in Doubtless Bay by J F M de Surville, the French explorer, in 1769.

> 🏛 **Far North Regional Museum**
> 6 South Rd. ***Tel** (09) 408 1403.* 🕐 *daily.* ⬤ *Good Fri, 25 Dec.* 🎟 📷 ♿ 🗣 *on request.* 🛍 **www.** farnorthmuseum.co.nz

Cape Reinga ⓭

Map D1.

Reinga, meaning "underworld", refers to the Maori belief that this is where the spirits of the dead leave for the journey to Hawaiki. The roots of an old pohutukawa tree at the tip of the cape are said to be the departure point for these spirits. Looking out from Cape Reinga over the Columbia Bank, visitors can see the Tasman Sea converge with the Pacific Ocean. The cape is not the very end of the country; the northernmost point is on North Cape.

Ninety Mile Beach ⓮

Map D1.

A misnomer, Ninety Mile Beach is, in fact, only 96 km (60 miles) long. The longest beach in the country, this area is almost like a desert, with sand dunes that can reach 143 m (470 ft) high fringing the beach. It was once a forested region, but the kauri trees were destroyed by inundations of water during successive Ice Ages. Pine trees have been planted to stabilize the dunes. Surf fishing and digging for shellfish are popular activities.

Aupori Peninsula Driving Tour

LAST
SERVICE
STATION
IN NZ ... BEFORE AUSTRALIA!

Gas station sign

Called "The Tail of The Fish" by Maori, Aupori Peninsula is a thin strip of land no more than 12 km (7 miles) wide between Ninety Mile Beach on the west coast and a number of beaches and bays along the east coast. The unspoilt beaches and coastline, together with high year-round temperatures, make this region an appealing holiday destination. The peninsula offers swimming, walking, sand tobogganing and fishing.

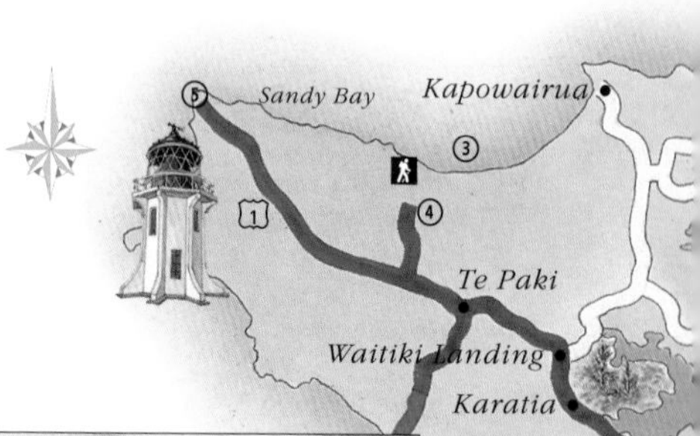
Sandy Bay
Kapowairua
1
Te Paki
Waitiki Landing
Karatia
The Bluff
0 kilometres 6
0 miles 6

Ninety Mile Beach ⑥
The hard sand on the beach makes it a popular area for farm biking and coach tours, as well as for cycling and marathons.

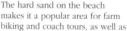

Cape Reinga Lighthouse ⑤
Visible from a distance of 48 km (26 nautical miles) offshore, the solitary, whitewashed Cape Reinga Lighthouse is New Zealand's northernmost lighthouse.

KEY

- ▬ Tour route
- ▬ Scenic route
- ═ Other roads
- 🚶 Walking track

Spirits Bay ③
This sacred Maori area is the starting point for the 28-km (17-mile) walking track to Cape Reinga.

North Cape

AIRAI 'NIC ERVE

Rarawa Beach ②
Sparkling white silica sand makes Rarawa Beach one of the most attractive beaches on the east coast.

Great Exhibition Bay

Gumdiggers Park ①
Take a walk around this park and learn about the ecology of the Manuka regrowth forest and its inhabitants.

Henderson Bay

Pukenui

Houbora Heads

Mohutangi

Hukatere

WAIPAPAKAURI BEACH

DIGGING FOR SHELLFISH

Gathering *kai moana* (seafood) is not just a Maori tradition. Many other New Zealanders fish from boats or the shore, dive for fish, or dig in the sand for shellfish to supplement their diet. At Ninety Mile Beach, people are likely to be searching for *tuatua*, a shellfish that occurs in large quantities in the area. The daily limit a person can collect is 150 and each shellfish must be at least 125 mm (5 inches) long. More difficult to find, *paua* (abalone) are also gathered along the beach. The daily limit per person is ten.

Digging for *tuatua* at Ninety Mile Beach

Te Paki Reserve ④
Tobogganing off the massive sand dunes is the main attraction here but there is also a pleasant 40-minute walk to the beach.

TIPS FOR DRIVERS

Length: 210 km (130 miles).
Stopping-off points: There are places to stay and eat between Kaitaia and Waitaki Landing. The final 21-km (13-mile) drive to the lighthouse follows an unsealed road. As an alternative to returning on State Hwy 1, 4WD vehicles can access Ninety Mile Beach at Te Paki, 16 km (10 miles) south of Cape Reinga Lighthouse, and exit near Waipapakauri Beach. Trips should be made two hours before or after high tide. Visitors are advised to take a coach tour, as rental cars are not allowed on the beach.

Boatshed Café and Gallery at Rawene

Kaikohe 16

Road map E1. 🚶 4,100. 🚌

A service centre for farms in the area, Kaikohe is best known for the **Ngawha Hot Springs** (Waiariki Pools). While such hot springs have been turned into major tourist attractions in places such as Rotorua *(see pp136–7)*, they are mainly a local feature in Kaikohe, where most visitors and the attendant are on first-name terms. Outsiders are welcome, and if they can accept the springs' unadorned character, they will enjoy the hot spring waters with temperatures between 32 and 42 °C (90 and 108 °F).

Kaikohe's **Pioneer Village** indoor and outdoor museum is a collection of houses and artifacts related to the district's early European history. A conducted tour takes visitors to attractions from the 1862 Old Courthouse to Maioha Cottage (1875), Utakura Settlers Hall (1891) and Alexander's Sawmill (1913). There are also vintage vehicles, a fire station, a bush railway and a small railway station. From a hillside monument to Chief Hone Heke (grand-nephew of the old chief), there are fine views of both coasts.

🏠 Ngawha Hot Springs
Off State Hwy 12. *Tel* (09) 405 2245. ⬜ daily. ⬤ public hols. 📷
⛪ Pioneer Village
Recreation Rd. *Tel* (09) 401 0816. ⬜ daily. ⬤ Good Fri, 25 Dec. 📷
♿ 📷 📷

Rawene 17

Road map D1. 🚶 520. 🚌
ℹ️ *Boatshed Café and Gallery, The Esplanade, (09) 405 7728.*

This quaint village, which has shops jutting out over the water, was home to James Reddy Clendon (1800–72), the first US Consul in New Zealand. He later became Hokianga's Resident Magistrate. **Clendon House**, now owned by the New Zealand Historic Places Trust, was probably built after 1866.

The ferry across Hokianga Harbour links with an alter-native route to Kaitaia, via Broadwood and Herekino.

⛪ Clendon House
Clendon Esplanade. *Tel* (09) 405 7874. ⬜ Sat–Mon. ⬤ May–Oct & 25 Dec. 📷 **www**.historic.org.nz

Opononi 18

Road map D1. 🚶 600. 🚌 🚢 ℹ️
Hokianga Information Centre, State Hwy 12, (09) 405 8869.

In the minds of many New Zealanders, the small beach town of Opononi is forever linked to that of its most famous visitor, Opo. This dolphin became a national celebrity when it spent the summer of 1955 playing with children and performing tricks with beach balls. Sadly, it was killed by unknown dynamite fishers. A sculpture by Christchurch artist Russell Clark marks the dolphin's grave outside Opononi's pub. A video of Opo can be viewed at the Hokianga Information Centre.

Diagonally across the road from Opo's statue is the wharf, which is the starting point for a short boat trip to see, at close range, the giant sand dunes on the far side of Hokianga Harbour.

Sculpture of Opo the dolphin at Opononi

THE EARLY KAURI GUM INDUSTRY

As the immigrants of the 19th century rapidly depleted the country's native forests of kauri trees, a new industry began to emerge. Resin, exuded by the trees, became a valuable commodity in the production of varnish. To reveal the location of lumps of resin, long rods were poked into the ground near dead trees, a job mostly carried out by Yugoslav immigrants. By 1885, 2,000 people were employ-ed in this trade. Many of these people later turned to grow-ing vegetables and to viticulture near Auckland.

Today, lumps of kauri gum, known as amber, are popular souvenir items. The gum is carved and polished and made into pendants and other small items. Sometimes insects or fern fragments can be seen trapped inside the finished items.

Polished kauri gum

Tane Mahuta, New Zealand's largest kauri tree

Waipoua Forest 🄳

Road map D1. 🄸 *Waipoua Forest, (09) 439 6445.* ⭕ *daily.*

Waipoua Forest is well worth a visit because of its magnificent kauri trees. Being in the presence of a tree that has entered its third millennium is a memorable experience, as photos seldom capture the grandeur of these trees. Local Maoris have christened the country's largest living kauri Tane Mahuta, "the god of the forest". Reached by an easy 5-minute walk from the road through the park, the tree is 51 m (168 ft) high, has a girth of 14 m (46 ft) and a volume of 244.5 cu m (8,635 cu ft). Department of Conservation experts estimate the tree to be about 1,500 years old. Four other known giant trees in the forest are at least 1,000 years old. The forest also contains around 300 species of trees, palms and ferns.

Dargaville 🄴

Road map E1. 🄸 *4,900.* 🚌 🄸 *67–69 Normanby St, (09) 439 0304.* **www**.kauricoast.co.nz

Dargaville is the nation's *kumara* capital and many road stalls with honesty boxes offer the opportunity to buy these sweet potatoes.
The **Dargaville Museum** is not just of interest to sailors. Apart from Maori canoes, ship models and other nautical items, the displays range from old photos of the local Yugoslav Social Club to memorabilia from the Northern Wairoa Scottish Society and a pig skull from New Mexico.

🏛 **Dargaville Museum**
Harding Park. **Tel** (09) 439 7555. ⭕ *daily.* ⭕ *25 Dec.* 🄸🄸🄸🄸

Environs
Located 45 km (28 miles) south of Dargaville, the **Kauri Museum** in Matakohe gives visitors an insight into kauri trees, especially after a trip through Waipoua Forest Park. The museum illustrates the role these mammoth trees played in New Zealand's pioneering history. A steam sawmill, with mannequins representing local settler families, shows how the logs were milled.
Within the main museum building there is also kauri furniture, carvings and timber panels as well as an extensive collection of carved and polished kauri gum. Outside is a kauri post office from 1909, a 6-room fully furnished early 20th-century home and an 1867 pioneer church.
The **Kai-Iwi Lakes**, 34 km (21 miles) north of Dargaville, may lack the excitement of west coast beaches, but they are well frequented by local families and visitors. Comprising the Waikere, Taharoa and Kai-Iwi, these brilliant blue lakes are popular with swimmers, water-skiers, fishermen, picnickers and campers.

🏛 **Kauri Museum**
5 Church Rd, Matakohe. **Tel** (09) 431 7417. ⭕ *daily.* ⭕ *25 Dec.* 🄸🄸 *by arrangement.* 🄸
www.kauri-museum.com

Boat exhibit in the Dargaville Museum

THE CENTRAL NORTH ISLAND

*S*tretching from Auckland down to Taranaki, Manawatu and Hawkes Bay, this area includes beautiful and varied natural and man-made sights: snow-capped volcanoes, geothermal features, trout-filled lakes and rivers, mountain ranges, sandy beaches, fertile farmlands, prolific orchards and vineyards, and extensive forests. It is also a major centre of Maori history and culture.

Cutting a swathe from White Island in the north to Mount Ruapehu in the south, the Taupo Volcanic Zone *(see pp64–5)*, is testimony to underground forces that have fashioned the central plateau. Rotorua has a range of thermal attractions: geysers, bubbling mud pools, multicoloured silica terraces, steaming lakes and streams and hot mineral pools. Lakes dotting the plateau offer excellent fishing, while rivers flowing from them are used for white-water rafting and jet-boating. In winter there is downhill skiing on the slopes of Mount Ruapehu in Tongariro National Park.

Steep, rugged, bush-clad ranges stretch 300 km (186 miles) from the volcanic plateau to the East Cape, separating the temperate area to the west from the warm, dry east coast region. Farming and forestry are well established in the Bay of Plenty, King Country and Waikato. Dairy farmers compete with horticulturists for the best land, while sheep, cattle and deer roam larger paddocks on hills clear-felled of their native forest in the 19th and early 20th centuries. The Coromandel Peninsula, gripped by gold fever in the latter half of the 19th century, is now home to alternative lifestylers and artists inspired by its natural beauty. The curving Bay of Plenty, the scenic East Cape and the beaches of Gisborne offer excellent swimming, fishing and surfing.

The entire region is rich in Maori history, and Rotorua is the main centre for Maori cultural experiences. The Waikato-based Maori King Movement *(see p117)* began here in 1858, shortly before battles waged between the government and Maori over land.

Maori cultural performance at Rotorua

◁ Kiwifruit orchard, Te Puke

Exploring the Central North Island

The Central North Island contains a wide range of landscapes and activities. Hamilton, the region's largest town, is set among lush farmland close to the western surf beaches of Raglan and the mysterious Waitomo Caves. North of Hamilton, the rugged Coromandel Peninsula flows into sandy, unspoilt Bay of Plenty beaches, the East Cape and the east coast, all popular spots for fishing and water sports. Hawke's Bay is famous for its Art Deco buildings, orchards and vineyards. Geothermal attractions stretch from lunar-landscaped White Island to the volcano Ruapehu, the North Island's best skiing location. At the bottom of the region, Tongariro National Park offers a wilderness experience.

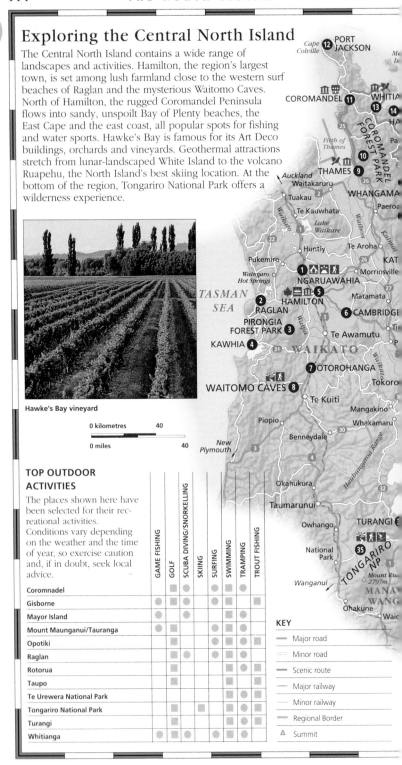

Hawke's Bay vineyard

0 kilometres   40

0 miles   40

TOP OUTDOOR ACTIVITIES

The places shown here have been selected for their recreational activities. Conditions vary depending on the weather and the time of year, so exercise caution and, if in doubt, seek local advice.

	GAME FISHING	GOLF	SCUBA DIVING/SNORKELLING	SKIING	SURFING	SWIMMING	TRAMPING	TROUT FISHING
Coromnadel		■	●		●	■	●	
Gisborne	●	■	●		●	■		■
Mayor Island	●		●			■	●	
Mount Maunganui/Tauranga	●	■			●	■	●	
Opotiki		■			●	■	●	■
Raglan		■	●		●	■	●	
Rotorua		■				■	●	■
Taupo		■				■	●	■
Te Urewera National Park						■	●	■
Tongariro National Park		■		■		■	●	■
Turangi		■				■	●	■
Whitianga	●	■	●		●	■	●	

KEY

— Major road

═ Minor road

— Scenic route

--- Major railway

— Minor railway

═ Regional Border

△ Summit

Map labels: Cape Colville, PORT JACKSON, COROMANDEL, WHITIA, CoROMANDEL FOREST PARK, Firth of Thames, THAMES, WHANGAMA, Auckland, Waitakaruru, Tuakau, Te Kauwhata, Lake Waikare, Huntly, Te Aroha, Pukemiro, Waingaro Hot Springs, NGARUAWAHIA, Morrinsville, KAT, HAMILTON, Matamata, RAGLAN, PIRONGIA FOREST PARK, Te Awamutu, CAMBRIDGE, KAWHIA, WAIKATO, OTOROHANGA, Tokoro, WAITOMO CAVES, Te Kuiti, Mangakino, Piopio, Whakamaru, Benneydale, New Plymouth, Okahukura, Taumarunui, Owhango, TURANGI, National Park, TONGARIRO NP, Wanganui, Mount Rua 2797m, MANA, WANG, Ohakune, Waic

SIGHTS AT A GLANCE

Cambridge 6
Cape Kidnappers 38
Coromandel 11
Coromandel Forest Park 10
Gisborne 27
Hahei 14
Hamilton 5
Hastings 37
Katikati 17
Kawhia 4
Mayor Island 20
Mount Maunganui 19
Napier pp146–9 36
Ngaruawahia 1
Opotiki 24
Orakei Korako Geyserland 31
Otorohanga 7
Pirongia Forest Park 3
Port Jackson 12
Raglan 2
Rotorua pp134–9 28
Taupo 33
Tauranga 18
Te Puke 21
Te Urewera National Park 26
Thames 9
Tongariro National Park pp142–3 35
Turangi 34
Waihi 16
Waimangu Volcanic Valley 29
Wai-o-tapu Thermal Wonderland 30
Wairakei Park 32
Waitomo Caves pp120–21 8
Whakatane 22
Whangamata 15
White Island 23
Whitianga 13

Tours

East Cape 25
Hawke's Bay Vineyards 39

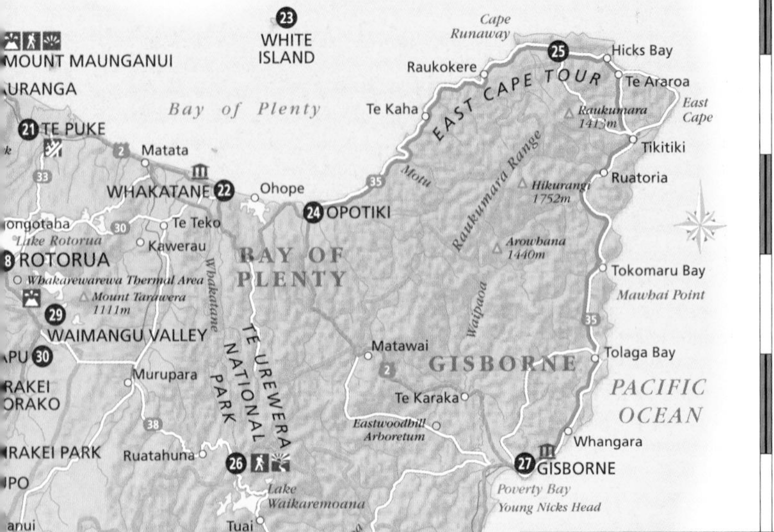

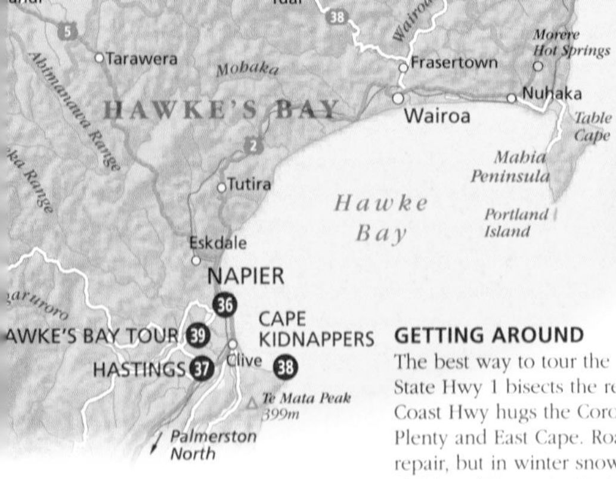

Maori meeting house at Te Kaha, Bay of Plenty

GETTING AROUND

The best way to tour the Central North Island is by car. State Hwy 1 bisects the region, while the scenic Pacific Coast Hwy hugs the Coromandel Peninsula, Bay of Plenty and East Cape. Roads are almost always in good repair, but in winter snow may close roads in the vicinity of Tongariro National Park. A passenger train service links Auckland with Wellington, with stops at Hamilton and other main towns. Local buses and tour companies operate throughout the region.

ALSO

ere to Stay pp302–7
ere to Eat pp330–34

Ngaruawahia ●

Road map E2. 🏘 6,500. 🚌 ℹ
*160 Great South Rd, Huntly, (07) 828
6406.* 🚣 *Ngaruawahia Regatta (Sat
closest to St Patrick's Day, 17 Mar).*
www.waikatodistrict.co.nz

Situated where the Waikato
and Waipa rivers meet at the
edge of the central Waikato
Basin, Ngaruawahia is one
of the oldest and most historic
settlements in Waikato and
an important centre of Maori
culture. On the northeastern
bank of the river, off River
Road, is one of the Maori
people's most important
locations – Turangawaewae
Marae, "the footstool" or home
of the Waikato Tainui tribe.
Turongo House, located within the *marae*, is the official
residence of the reigning
Maori monarch, Tuheitia Paki.
Although Turangawaewae
Marae is considered too sacred
for tourism, and visitors are
likely to be referred to Rotorua
where Maori cultural experiences are widely available,
the *marae* is open to the
public for the annual Ngaruawahia Regatta on the river,
which features *waka* (canoe)
racing, *iwi* dance competitions and other activities
(see p42).

Mount Taupiri, 6 km
(4 miles) north of Ngaruawahia, provides excellent
views of the Waikato Basin
for those who walk the loop
track to its summit. However,
care must be taken to avoid
a large sacred ancestral
burial ground situated on the

The single-plume Bridal Veil Falls southeast of Raglan

side of the hill facing State
Highway 1.

In the Hakarimata Reserve
on the slopes of the Hakarimata Range to the north of
Ngaruawahia, native rimu and
kauri trees grow beside three
well-marked tracks, which
offer excellent tramping and
views of the Waikato Basin.

Environs
Waingaro Hot Springs, 30 km
(19 miles) west of Ngaruawahia, features four open-air
mineral water pools ranging in
temperature from 32 to 42 °C
(89 to 107 °F) as well as private
spa pools. New Zealand's
longest hot water hydroslide
as well as bumper boats offer
plenty of excitement. A range
of accommodation options is
available at the springs.

🏠 **Waingaro Hot Springs**
Waingaro Rd. **Tel** *(07) 825 4761.*
⬜ *daily.* 🈺

Raglan ●

Road map E2. 🏘 3,100. 🚌 ℹ
4 Wallis St, (07) 825 0556. 🚣 *Raglan
Surf Classic (Nov).*

Waikato's only seaside resort
on the west coast, Raglan is a
small, pleasant town with
welcoming shady trees in the
main street. Raglan fills with
visitors during summer,
attracted to the water sports
available in its tranquil
harbour, its good swimming
beaches and its excellent
surfing. Te Kopua Beach and
Te Aro Aro Bay, close to
Raglan, are popular for
swimming, while Whale Bay,
a ten-minute drive south
along the coast, is famous
worldwide among surfers for
its left-hand break.

The 25-km (15-mile) drive
south along Raglan's narrow
coastal Whaanga Road pro-
vides breathtaking views of

Turangawaewae Marae, Ngaruawahia, home of the Maori king

For hotels and restaurants in this region see pp302–7 and pp330–34

the rugged coastline and the swells of the Tasman Sea.

About 21 km (13 miles) southeast of Raglan, on the road to Kawhia, an easy ten-minute walk through dense bush leads to the Bridal Veil Falls. The 55-m (180-ft) water-fall plunges in a single plume from a rock cleft to a deep pool below. A steep track continues to the base of the falls and an even more dramatic vantage point.

Mount Pirongia, an extinct volcanic peak

Whale Bay, Raglan, world famous for its surfing

Pirongia Forest Park ❸

Road map E3. 🚹 *798 Franklin St, Hamilton, (07) 871 9018.*

This park, comprising four separate forest areas south and southeast of Raglan, contains an extensive network of trails, from easy walks on the lower peaks to more strenuous hikes higher up. At 959 m

(3,146 ft), Mount Pirongia, an ancient volcano lying south-east of Raglan, is the most obvious landmark in the park; its dramatic skyline and dark green forest contrast strongly with the surrounding farm-land. Closer to Raglan, 756-m (2,480-ft) Mt Karioi rises sharply from the coastline. Tracks lead to both peaks.

During the summer months it is advisable to carry drink-ing water on the tracks as natural supplies are difficult to find. A number of native birds can be seen along the tracks and around the park's margins. Several native fish species and a huge variety of aquatic invertebrates can be found in the park's streams.

A hut on Mount Pirongia – Pahautea – sleeps six to eight people. Hut tickets are available from the Department of Conservation in Hamilton. There are picnic areas at the end of both Corcoran and Grey roads and a camping area alongside Kaniwhaniwha Stream, which is also an excellent trout fishing spot.

Kawhia ❹

Road map E3. 🚶 *550.* 🚹 *Kawhia Museum & Information Centre, Kaora St, (07) 871 0161.*

Located on the coast 55 km (34 miles) to the south of Raglan, along winding but scenic back roads, the small settlement of Kawhia com-prises a jumble of cottages on the north side of Kawhia Harbour, 5 km (3 miles) from the Tasman Sea. The harbour is remote, splendid and huge, its shoreline twisting and turning for 57 km (35 miles).

In former times, Maori prized the harbour and the fertile valleys running down to it and fought over rights to the area. The Maori migration canoe Tainui, which plied the coastline eight centuries ago, is buried on the slopes behind the Makatu meeting house. Stones placed 23 m (75 ft) apart above the bow and stern mark its position. The canoe was once moored to a pohutukawa tree, Tangi te Korowhiti, on the shore at the end of Karewa Street. Now a large clump of pohutukawas, the tree is still revered by the Tainui people as signifying the beginning of their associa-tion with Aotearoa.

The large Kawhia harbour on the west coast

MAORI KING MOVEMENT

Queen Te Atairangikaahu

This movement grew in the 1850s out of a realization among Maoris that intertribal feuding assisted the Pakeha (Europeans) to acquire Maori land. In 1858, several tribes chose a paramount king in the hope that the dignity and *mana* (respect) that would accrue to him would promote peaceful co-existence with the government and settle land conflicts. Instead, the govern-ment interpreted the Maori King Movement as a form of rebellion. Attitudes hardened and spawned the Waikato land wars of the 1860s *(see pp49–50)*. In 1966, Te Atairangikaahu was proclaimed queen. She was succeeded by King Tuheitia Paki in 2006, the seventh monarch. His role is mainly cultural and spiritual, though this is becoming more important as the place of Maori in New Zealand society is reassessed.

Hamilton 5

Road map E2. *118,000.* *10 km (6 miles) S of city.* *Cnr Bryce & Anglesea sts, (07) 839 3580.* *Balloons Over Waikato (Apr); National Agricultural Fieldays (Jun).* **www**.visithamilton.co.nz

New Zealand's fourth largest metropolitan area and largest inland city, Hamilton straddles a meandering section of the mighty Waikato River, at 425 km (264 miles) the longest in the country. The city has grown from a 19th-century military settlement into a bustling centre servicing the Waikato region, a huge undulating plain. Attractive parks and gardens, dissected by footpaths, border the river, and bridges connect the east and west banks. The **MV *Waipa Delta*** paddleboat cruises the river three times daily from its landing in central Hamilton, offering the best views of the area.

Perched on five levels above the river, the **Waikato Museum of Art and History** features a large collection of New Zealand art, Waikato history and history of the local Tainui people. On permanent display is an impressive war canoe, Te Winika.

The **Hamilton Gardens**, located at the southern end of the city, are Hamilton's most popular visitor attraction. Set along a scenic stretch of the Waikato River, they include pavilions showcasing Japanese, Chinese and English gardens as well as seasonal attractions.

Hamilton hosts Balloons Over Waikato, a fiesta which attracts balloonists from around the world, and the National Agricultural Fieldays at nearby Mystery Creek, one of Australasia's largest agricultural trade shows *(see p43)*.

MV *Waipa Delta*
Memorial Park Jetty, Memorial Drive. ***Tel*** *0800 472 3351.* *Thu–Sun.* **www**.waipadelta.co.nz

Waikato Museum of Art and History
1 Grantham St. ***Tel*** *(07) 838 6606.* *daily.* *25 Dec.* **www**.waikatomuseum.org.nz

Hamilton Gardens
Cobham Drive. ***Tel*** *(07) 856 3200.* *daily.*

Cambridge 6

Road map E3. *13,500.* *15 km (9 miles) E of city.* *Cnr Queen & Victoria sts, (07) 823 3456.*

Fifteen minutes' drive south of Hamilton, Cambridge lies amid farmland, home to New Zealand's thoroughbred horse industry. Known as "the town of trees" because of its avenues of oak and elm, the town has a charming village green and pretty gardens. The domain around Lake Koutu, fringed by exotic trees and native bush, is a popular place for walks and picnics.

Glassware at the Cambridge Country Store

Cambridge is also known for its contemporary art and crafts outlets; one, the large, award-winning **Cambridge Country Store**, is located in a church built in 1898. The town's numerous antique shops and galleries are another major attraction.

Items for sale at the Cambridge Country Store

Visitors can also view a potpourri of architectural styles at St. Andrew's church and the public buildings along and adjacent to Victoria Street.

Cambridge Country Store
92 Victoria St. ***Tel*** *(07) 827 8715.* *daily.* *25 Dec.* **www**.cambridgecountrystore.co.nz

Otorohanga 7

Road map E3. *2,600.* *21 Maniapoto St, (07) 873 8951.*

Fifty kilometres (31 miles) south of Hamilton lies Otorohanga, a small provincial town whose main attraction is the **Otorohanga Kiwi House**. Three kiwi species are bred at the zoological park and 300 birds, representing 29 species, can be viewed in a massive walk-through aviary. In addition to kiwis, these include native pigeons, tui, silvereyes, parakeets and saddlebacks. Geckos, wetas, and tuataras (an ancient reptile) are also on display.

Otorohanga is regarded as the gateway to the Waitomo Caves *(see pp120–21)*.

Otorohanga Kiwi House
20 Alex Telfer Drive. ***Tel*** *(07) 873 7391.* *daily.* *25 Dec.* *Nocturnal House.* **www**.kiwihouse.org.nz

The MV *Waipa Delta* cruising on the Waikato River

Stock-Stud Heartland

One of the most fascinating sights on the drive between Hamilton and Cambridge is the wooden-railed fences behind which young thoroughbred horses cavort, growing strong on the best pasture and supplementary feed their owners can provide. Set back from the road are signposted stud stables where the horses are

Holstein-Friesan cow

housed and trained. Another common sight is of black and white cows grazing on dappled green fields. New Zealand's thoroughbred racehorse and dairy cattle stud industries are concentrated in the Waikato region. Here a mild, wet climate produces lush cattle pasture and the rolling plains that are ideal for exercising and training racehorses.

THOROUGHBRED HORSES

Waikato is renowned internationally for its racing progeny, and the yearling export industry earns the country more than NZ$120 million annually. Some 60 stallions are available for breeding purposes at 18 Waikato commercial thoroughbred studs, the most sought after of these sires mating 100–150 mares.

Thoroughbred yearlings and foals on a Waikato stud farm

Cambridge Thoroughbred Lodge
VISITORS WELCOME OPEN TO 4.00 P.M. | HORSE MAGIC | A SPECIAL EXPERIENCE!

New Zealand Horse Magic, *6 km (4 miles) south of Cambridge, showcases a collection of horse breeds and features an informative hour-long show. Thoroughbred stud tours are also available at other stud farms in the area.*

Waikato-*bred horses have won Australia's Melbourne Cup, the pinnacle of the Australasian racing season, 18 times.*

New Zealand's main dairy breeds – *Holstein-Friesian, Jersey and Ayrshire – can be found in Waikato, although the Holstein-Friesian predominates. The average New Zealand cow produces 3,420 litres (752 imperial gallons) of milk a year.*

New Zealand's *thoroughbred industry is showcased to the world each February at the yearling sale held at Karaka on the southern outskirts of Auckland.*

Waitomo Caves

Glowworm Cave logo

The area known as Waitomo consists of a 45-km (28-mile) network of underground limestone caves and grottoes linked to the Waitomo River. A chamber of the Glowworm Cave was first explored in 1887, but most caves remain the domain of cavers and speleologists. Apart from touring the Glowworm and Aranui caves, famous for their glowworm grottoes and fantastic limestone formations, visitors can enjoy a range of cave-based adventure activities, including abseiling into a limestone shaft and cave system, and black-water rafting, an adventure sport unique to New Zealand. The 2.5 km (1.5 miles) of caves accessible to the public have superb lighting, good paths, handrails and informative local guides.

Waitomo Walkway
A 5-km (3-mile) walk over farmland and through native bush takes visitors past typical limestone karst features such as outcrops, small caves and sinkholes.

Black-water Rafting
Equipped with wet suits, lights and "cave rafts" (inner tubes), these black-water rafters drift in darkness, beneath millions of glowworms, along an underground river in the Ruakuri Cave.

KEY

══	Road
～	River
- -	Walking track

The Ruakuri Natural Tunnel, a large U-shaped tunnel eroded by the Waitomo Stream, is reached by a 30-minute walk up the Ruakuri Gorge. Guided tours of the Ruakuri Cave are available.

Te Anga Road

Waitomo Stream

Tumutumu Road

0 metres	500
0 yards	500

FORMATION OF THE WAITOMO CAVES

Caves are formed through the erosion of layers of limestone by water flowing underground. The cave systems in the Waitomo area have developed in fractured limestone, up to 100 m (330 ft) thick, along or adjacent to major fault lines *(see p20)* where percolation of groundwater is particularly high. Surface water flowing down cracks in the limestone created an underground drainage system which gradually increased in size and complexity. Inside the Waitomo caves, dripping water containing dissolved limestone has formed stalactites on the cave roofs, stalagmites on the floors, and other fascinating formations.

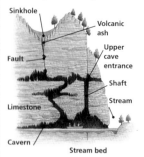

Sinkhole
Volcanic ash
Upper cave entrance
Fault
Shaft
Stream
Limestone
Cavern
Stream bed

★Aranui Cave
The high chambers, magnificent formations and pale brown, pink and white shades of the huge stalactites are the finest to be seen in Waitomo's caves.

Woodlyn Park
At the pioneer heritage show, visitors can help shear a sheep and train a farm dog.

The Tokikarpu meeting house, off Te Anga Road, serves the needs of the local Maori people.

The Waitomo Caves Hotel, built in 1908, nestles among trees on a hill above Waitomo village. It has rooms to suit every traveller *(see p304)*.

VISITORS' CHECKLIST

Road map E3. 21 Waitomo Caves Rd, (07) 878 7640. All sights: ◯ daily. ● 25 Dec. **Waitomo Museum of Caves Tel** (07) 878 7640. **Waitomo Glowworm Cave Tel** (07) 878 8227. 📷 except in Aranui Cave. **Woodlyn Park Tel** (07) 878 6666. Pioneer Show. **Black Water "Rafting" Tel** 0800 228 464. Lost World **Tel** 0800 924 866.

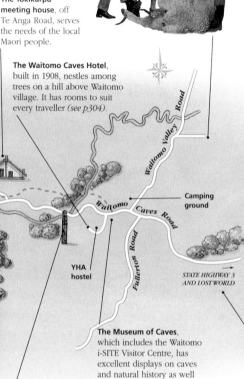

Waitomo Valley Road

Waitomo Caves Road

Camping ground

Fullerton Road

YHA hostel

STATE HIGHWAY 3 AND LOST WORLD

The Museum of Caves, which includes the Waitomo i-SITE Visitor Centre, has excellent displays on caves and natural history as well as a multi-media show about the New Zealand glowworms.

Lost World
The Lost World Adventure involves a 100-m (330-ft) abseil descent into a huge limestone shaft followed by an amazing caving expedition through the Mangapu Cave system.

★ Glowworm Cave
A walk through the three levels of the cave – the Banquet Chamber, Pipe Organ and Cathedral – is capped by a tranquil boat ride through the magical Glowworm Grotto.

STAR SIGHTS

★ Aranui Cave

★ Glowworm Cave

Karaka Bird Hide on the Firth of Thames

Thames ❾

Road Map E2. 🏘 *10,000.*
✈ *2 km (1.2 miles) S of town.* 🚌
ℹ *206 Pollen St, (07) 868 7284.*
🎭 *Pohutakawa Festival (Nov–Dec).*
www.thamesinfo.co.nz

Located at the southeastern
corner of the Firth of Thames,
against hills that 100 years
ago rang to the sound of
battery stamps pounding
quartz ore to extract gold,
Thames is the principal town
of the Coromandel region. It
services surrounding farmland
and a swelling coastal population. It is the gateway to the
Coromandel Peninsula and an
ideal base from which to explore the Coromandel Forest
Park wilderness area. Many
buildings in the town owe their
grandeur to wealth created
during the gold-mining era.

The **Thames Historical
Museum** features relics from
the town's past, including the
pioneering foundries that
sprang up to support the
mining industry, while the
**Thames School of Mines and
Mineralogical Museum**
features 5,000 mineral samples and equipment used to
process quartz ore and extract
gold. Mine managers were
taught in the school's
classroom from 1885 to 1954.

A large World War I memo-
rial, off Waiotahi Creek Road,
stands on a hill above the
town to the north, and affords
panoramic views of the town,
the Firth of Thames, and the
Hauraki Gulf beyond. At the

small Karaka Bird Hide, built
among mangroves off Brown
Street on the edge of town, a
variety of migratory wading
birds can be seen, especially
between high and low tides.

🏛 **Thames Historical Museum**
Cnr Pollen & Cochrane sts. **Tel** *(07)
868 8509.* ⬤ *1–4pm daily.* 🎫 ♿
♿ 📷

🏛 **Thames School of Mines
and Mineralogical Museum**
101 Cochrane St. **Tel** *(07) 868 6227.*
⬤ *daily.* ⬤ *Good Fri, 25 Dec.* 🎫
📷 📷

Environs
Along the Firth of Thames'
southern edge, 85 sq km (33
sq miles) of rich, intertidal
mud flats provide another
excellent habitat for migratory
wading birds, such as gulls,
shags, oystercatchers, and
pied stilts, and opportunities
to observe them. The
Miranda Shorebird Centre,

**Trampers in the Kauaeranga Valley,
Coromandel Forest Park**

established by the Miranda
Naturalists' Trust, can arrange
tours to see the birds as well
as accommodation. Nearby is
the Miranda Hot Springs, a
thermal pool complex.

🦜 **Miranda Shorebird Centre**
285 East Coast Rd, Pokeno. **Tel** *(09)
232 2781.* ⬤ *daily.* ⬤ *25 Dec.* 🎫
donation. ♿ 📷 **www**.miranda-
shorebird.org.nz

Coromandel Forest
Park ❿

Road map E2. ℹ *Kauaeranga Valley,
Thames, (07) 867 9080.*

This park stretches for 100
km (62 miles) along the
peninsula's interior, but the
most accessible portion is the
forested Kauaeranga Valley,
with its well-developed network of short walks, longer
tramps and picnic areas.

The valley was a major
source of kauri timber from
the 1870s to the 1920s. Remains of dams, trestle bridges
and river booms, used to
flush kauri logs into the Kauaeranga River, are evident.

Anglers can fish for trout in
the valley's streams where the
keen-eyed may also find gemstones. A rocky ridge known as
the Pinnacles offers fine views
of both coastlines. The Kauaeranga Visitor Centre, 13 km
(8 miles) northeast of Thames,
provides details of walks and
tramps that comprise the Kauaeranga Kauri Trail, a pack track
made by kauri bushmen, as
well as park accommodation.

Gold Fever in the Coromandel

The first significant gold find on the Coromandel Peninsula occurred in October 1852 near Coromandel Town. Three hundred diggers rushed to the area. Further discoveries near Thames in 1867 attracted 5,000 men into the surrounding hills. Soon Thames became a boom town and its population mushroomed to 18,000. Miners thronged the town on Saturdays, three live theatres were seldom closed, and more than 100 hotels sold

Gold nugget

liquor. But by the 1870s the Thames goldfields were in decline and interest had shifted southeast to Karangahake Mountain and to Waihi. By 1912, Waihi's Martha Mine had become one of the world's largest *(see p126)*. The mines all closed eventually, but new gold-bearing zones found within old fields prompted large-scale mining operations to begin once more at the open mining pit at Waihi from 1988 to 2007.

Candles provided light and indicated the presence of gas.

A mallet and pick were used to loosen gold-bearing rock.

GOLD-MINING RELICS
Old gold mines, shafts, mine dumps and abandoned mining machinery are dotted around Thames. The mining school and mineralogical museum, as well as the gold mine tours on offer, are further reminders of the town's gold-mining history. Coromandel gold had to be laboriously extracted from the ground with pick and shovel.

Canvas bags held any nuggets that were extracted.

Model of a miner at the Thames Gold Mine and Stamper Battery

Orange calcite

Goodlitite

Amethyst

Stitchtite

Pink tourmoline

Coromandel *is also rich in semi-precious gemstones. It is still possible to stumble across agate on some of the beaches north of Thames.*

This classroom *in the Thames School of Mines provided practical instruction for gold-miners working the quartz fields.*

Fossicking for gold *in the old gold mines is a popular pastime but care must be taken when entering old mines that they are structurally safe.*

The Imperial Hotel, *one of a number of fine colonial hotels in Thames built at the height of the town's gold-rush prosperity.*

Coromandel

Road map E2. 🏠 1,500. ✈ 3 km
(2 miles) S of town. 🚌 🅸 355
Kapanga Rd, (07) 866 8598.
www.coromandeltown.co.nz

Coromandel town, as it is
referred to by those wishing
to distinguish it from the
peninsula itself, is a quiet
fishing and crafts town about
an hour's drive north of
Thames. It owes its name to
the 1820 visit of HMS Coromandel, which called to load
kauri spars for the British
Royal Navy. Mining featured
prominently in the town's
formative years (see p123),
and fine examples of Victorian and colonial architecture
are a legacy of that era. The
laid-back atmosphere and
beauty of the area make it a
haven for artists and crafts
people, and an ideal place in
which to tramp, swim, fish,
sail or simply relax.

One of Coromandel's most
popular attractions is the
**Driving Creek Railway and
Potteries**, built by well-
known New Zealand potter
Barry Brickell to convey clay
and wood to his kiln, and to
service a kauri forest replant-
ing project. The narrow-
gauge mountain railway takes
visitors in specially designed
carriages on a one-hour
round trip through native
forest and tunnels and across
bridges to a viewpoint high
above Coromandel.

The **Coromandel Gold
Stamper Battery** and a 100-
year-old gold-processing
museum, featuring a large
working water wheel, lie at

**Water-powered bicycle at the
Waiau Waterworks**

the end of Buffalo Road to
the north of the town. The
**Coromandel School of Mines
and Historical Museum** has
displays of early gold-mining
and kauri logging, geological
specimens and an old jailhouse.

**🚉 Driving Creek Railway and
Potteries**
380 Driving Creek Rd. **Tel** (07) 866
8703. ⬜ daily. ⬤ 25 April, 25 Dec.
📷 ♿ 🅿
www.drivingcreekrailway.co.nz

**⚒ Coromandel Gold Stamper
Battery**
Buffalo Rd. **Tel** (07) 866 7933.
⬤ summer: daily; winter: Thu–Mon.
⬤ 25 Dec. 📷 ♿

**🏛 Coromandel School of
Mines and Historical Museum**
841 Rings Rd. **Tel** (07) 866 8039.
⬤ summer: daily; winter: Sat & Sun.
⬤ 25 Dec. 📷 ♿

Environs
The delightful **Waiau
Waterworks**, 9 km (5.5 miles)
from Coromandel Town,
showcases artist Chris
Ogilvie's genius for inventing

water-powered art forms and
gadgets that amaze both children and adults. One of Coromandel's most innovative
attractions, the waterworks is
set in park-like gardens.

Just east of the waterworks
is a turn-off to Castle Rock. At
525 m (1,722 ft), it is the core
of an old volcano on the
"backbone" of the peninsula.
A drive through pine forest
takes visitors to the start of a
45-minute walk. The last few
metres are a strenuous climb,
but panoramic views make it
worthwhile. Further along the
road is the Waiau Kauri Grove
where magnificent kauris,
protected for more than 100
years, can be seen ten
minutes' walk along a track
on the left side of the road.

🌿 Waiau Waterworks
471 The 309 Rd. **Tel** (07) 866 7191.
⬜ daily. 📷 ♿ 🅿
www.waiauwaterworks.co.nz

**Coastline between Coromandel
Town and Port Jackson**

Port Jackson

Road map E2. 🏠 10. 🅸 355
Kapanga Rd, Coromandel Town,
(07) 866 8598.

At the tip of the peninsula,
56 km (35 miles) north of
Coromandel, Port Jackson's
long, lupin-backed beach
comes as a surprise. The
road, which is unsealed from
the small settlement of Colville, the last supply point,
ends at Fletcher's Bay, 6 km
(4 miles) further on, a pretty
pohutukawa-shaded cove
with good fishing.

The Coromandel Walkway,
a 7-km (4.5-mile) track, leads
from Fletcher's Bay to Stony
Bay and takes about three
hours to complete. Port Jackson, Fletcher Bay and Stony
Bay all have camping grounds
with toilets, cold showers and
barbecue pits.

The unique Driving Creek Railway

For hotels and restaurants in this region see pp302–7 and pp330–34

Boats at sheltered Whitianga harbour

Whitianga ⑬

Road map E2. 🚶 *3,500.*
✈ *3 km (2 miles) SW of town.* 🚌
ℹ *66 Albert St, (07) 866 5555.*
www.whitianga.co.nz

Whitianga sits on the innermost recess of Mercury Bay which was named by Captain Cook *(see p48)* when he observed a transit of the planet Mercury on his 1769 visit to the area. Whitianga provides safe boat launching, ideal during the big game fishing season from November to April. Major fishing contests occur in February and March. The tiny Mercury Bay Boating Club, at the west end of Buffalo Beach, earned world fame when it spearheaded Auckland financier Michael Fay's unsuccessful 1988 challenge to the San Diego Yacht Club for the America's Cup.

The **Mercury Bay Museum** occupies a disused dairy factory opposite the wharf on The Esplanade. It documents

Boating club logo

the Polynesian chief Kupe *(see p46)*, whose descendants are said to have occupied the town for more than 1,000 years. A short ferry ride across the narrow harbour entrance takes visitors to Ferry Landing, the original site of Whitianga, where there are walks, lookouts and craft outlets. Whitianga Rock, upstream of Ferry Landing, was formerly a *pa* site of the Ngati Hei tribe. Whitianga's Buffalo Beach is named after an 1840 shipwreck. The British ship *Buffalo*, which had delivered convicts to Australia and was to return to Britain with kauri spars, was blown by a storm onto the beach and destroyed. A cannon from the ship is mounted at the RSA Memorial Park in Albert Street.

At the northeast tip of the headland, 1.5 km (1 mile) from Ferry Landing, is Shakespeare Lookout, named after the bard. Here also, a memorial to Cook stands above Lonely Bay and Cooks Beach. Wave action at Flaxmill Bay, at the

southwest end of Front Bay, has undercut the rock to form a natural soundshell.

The **Te Whanganui-A-Hei Marine Reserve** at Cathedral Cove covers 9 sq km (4 sq miles) and extends from Cooks Bluff to Hahei Beach. It was established in 1992 to restore the area's marine environment to its former rich and varied condition. No fishing or gathering of shellfish is allowed, although visitors may swim, dive and sail in the reserve.

🏛 **Mercury Bay Museum**
11 The Esplanade.
Tel (07) 866 0730. ◯ *daily.*
● *25 Dec.* 🎦 ⭑

Hahei ⑭

Road map E2. 🚶 *200.* 🚌 *General Store, Hahei Beach Rd.*

Hahei is the start of a two-hour return walk to Cathedral Cove, where a dramatic, cathedral-shaped cavern, accessible at low tide, cuts through a white headland. Reasonable fitness is required to reach the cove but panoramic cliff-top views make the effort worthwhile. Hahei's beach is sheltered by offshore islands and tinged pink with broken shells. The area is popular with divers.

At Hot Water Beach, 6 km (4 miles) south of Hahei, visitors can dig their own thermal spa in the sand between low and mid-tides. Spades are available for hire.

Visitors soaking in hot springs in the sand at Hot Water Beach, Hahei

Whangamata

Road map E2. 🏘 4,100. 🚌
🏛 616 Port Rd, (07) 865 8340.
www.whangamatainfo.co.nz

The town of Whangamata, meaning "obsidian harbour", was named after the dark, glass-like volcanic rock that has washed ashore from Mayor Island, 30 km (19 miles) from the mainland. The town is often referred to as "the surfing capital of New Zealand" because of the size of the waves in the area, particularly its sandbank surf break known as "the bar". Its surf is also popular with swimmers who enjoy large waves and with surf-fishers. Other superb surfing beaches in the vicinity include One-mana and Opoutere to the north of the town and Whiritoa on the coast to the south.

The hills and valleys behind Whangamata, a short drive

Whangamata Beach, one of New Zealand's best surf beaches

from the town, offer many outdoor activities. Within the Tairua Forest lie the Wentworth Valley, Taungatara Recreation Reserve and Parakiwai Valley. These are crisscrossed with walking tracks that make the most of stony streams and pockets of native bush. A popular walk takes in the "Luck at Last" gold mine and the remains of ore processors, water races, buildings and even a baker's oven. Walk details are available from the Whangamata information centre and forestry company Matariki Forests, which may close access when it is conducting forestry operations. Wharekawa Wildlife Refuge, 15 km (10 miles) north of Whangamata, is a conservation area based on the Opoutere sandspit. It is home to oyster-catchers and dotterels.

Martha Mine at Waihi

Waihi ⑯

Road map E2. 🏘 4,500. 🚌
🏛 Seddon St, (07) 863 6715.
www.waihi.org.nz

The history of Waihi has been linked with gold since Robert Lee and John McCrombie discovered a gold-bearing quartz reef in 1878. The **Martha Mine**, established on the site in 1882 and worked continuously until 1952, was the most important and successful of many in the district (see pp122–3). In 1988, it reopened, with concessions to operate until 2007, and substantial amounts of gold were extracted from the mine during this time. The mine is currently undergoing a rehabilitation project where, over a number of years, the site will be stabilised and transformed into a lake and the surrounding area revegetated.

The **Goldfields Railway** operates vintage diesel and steam trains on 7 km (4 miles) of track between Waihi and Waikino, gateway to the Karangahake gold fields. The

Karangahake Gorge Historic Walkway, a 5-km (3-mile) loop along the gorge past old bridges, abandoned mining equipment and mining shafts, is signposted from the road. Waihi Beach, 11 km (7 miles) east of the town, is one of the most popular along the coast.

🚂 **Goldfields Railway**
Wrigley St. **Tel** (07) 863 9020. 🕙 daily. ⬤ 25 Dec. 🎫 🛗 ⬤ 🍴 🏛

Katikati ⑰

Road map E2. 🏘 4,000.
🏛 34 Main Rd, (07) 549 1658.
www.katikati.co.nz

Enthusiastic Irish colonizer George Vesey Stewart bought Katikati and its surrounding land in the 1870s and sold it to 406 "refined and educated" Ulster families. Unfamiliar with the hard work needed to break in their land, these immigrants initially resented Stewart, but the district has since proved itself ideal for horticulture and dairy farming. Today, Katikati has earned a reputation as an open-air "art gallery". More than 30 murals and other art decorate its buildings, streets and parks, all produced by local artists. **Sapphire Springs**, set in a bush reserve 6 km (4 miles) from the town, has a number of freshwater thermal springs for swimming or soaking.

Street sculpture, Katikati

🏊 **Sapphire Springs**
Hot Springs Rd. **Tel** (07) 549 0768. 🕙 daily. 🎫 🏛

Mural on a building at Katikati

Coromandel's Artisan Lifestyle

The ever-changing sea, beautiful valleys and rugged forest interior of the Coromandel Peninsula not only offer a quiet alternative to city life but provide constant inspiration to a large number of artists and crafts people. Here painters farm, potters paint and raise silkworms, and weavers rear their own sheep for wool. Since their arrival in the early 1960s, many of these

Hand-blown glass bowl

"alternative lifestylers" have turned to art and crafts to support their nature-based lifestyle, honing their talents to produce a large number of attractive items for sale in retail outlets throughout New Zealand. The Coromandel Craft Trail leaflet, available at visitor centres, directs visitors to tucked-away studios where they can see artists at work and buy items direct at studio prices.

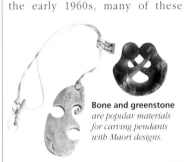

Bone and greenstone *are popular materials for carving pendants with Maori designs.*

Retail outlets *in Thames and Coromandel Town, such as Weta Art, sell a wide range of Coromandel and other New Zealand-made crafts.*

Barry Brickell at Driving Creek Potteries

Pottery items *are either thrown on a wheel or, like these pieces, hand-sculpted and glazed in a multitude of colours.*

COROMANDEL'S CRAFTS

Although the initial surge of artistic pursuits on the peninsula in the early 1960s focused on clay, crafts quickly diversified to include carving (in wood, bone and greenstone), kauri furniture, weaving, knitting, jewellery, leadlight glass work, hand-made knives and garden décor.

Alternative lifestylers *often choose to raise young children in supportive community environments where they grow organic produce, paint, sculpt and make crafts.*

Colville Store, *one of the peninsula's most unusual retail outlets, 26 km (16 miles) north of Coromandel Town, is owned by an 80-member co-operative.*

Tauranga 18

Road map E2. 🏔 *including Mount Maunganui, 100,000.* ✈ *3 km (2 miles) E of town.* 🚌 ℹ *95 Willow St, (07) 578 8103.* **www**.bayofplentynz.com

The largest city in the western Bay of Plenty and an important commercial centre and port, Tauranga lies along a section of the sprawling Tauranga Harbour, a plain thought to have been flooded at the end of the last Ice Age. On its seaward side, the city is sheltered by Matakana Island and to the west by the Kaimai Ranges.

In recent years, Tauranga has grown rapidly. Its benign climate and coastal location are attractive to retired New Zealanders and to anyone who enjoys year-round outdoor activities. Recreational and competitive boating, surfing and deep-sea fishing are among its major attractions. It is also a popular venue for jet-skiing, water-skiing, windsurfing, parasailing and diving. The Strand, in the centre of town, is the main shopping and restaurant area.

Originally a flax-trading and missionary town, Tauranga was the scene of fierce fighting during the New Zealand land wars in the 1860s *(see pp49–50)*. Many of the

troops involved in a significant battle at Gate Pa, 5 km (3 miles) south of the city, were stationed at Monmouth Redoubt, a military camp built by British troops in 1864 to stop supplies reaching the Waikato Maori King Movement *(see p117)*. Well-preserved earthworks and heavy artillery, are still in place.

The Elms Mission Station, built in stages between 1838 and 1847 by the Reverend Alfred Brown, is one of New Zealand's oldest homes. The grounds contain gardens and several buildings, including an 1839 free-standing library.

Tauranga's other attractions include 50 km (31 miles) of beach and foreshore reserve and 27 km (17 miles) of public walkways around the coast, estuary and inland reserves.

🏛 The Elms Mission Station
Cnr Mission & Chapel sts. **Tel** (07) 577 9772. ◻ *grounds: daily; house & library: 2–4pm Wed, Sat, Sun & public hols (tours by arrangement).* 🏠 *house & library.* **www**.theelms.org.nz

Environs
McLaren Falls Park, off State Highway 29 on the road to Hamilton, has walks through picturesque native bush interspersed with thousands of introduced trees. A river and Lake McLaren offer swimming. On scheduled days throughout

the year, top white-water action occurs downstream on the Wairoa River when floodgates on the hydro-controlled waterway are opened. The park has three backpacker hostels.

🌿 McLaren Falls Park
McLaren Falls Rd. **Tel** Tauranga District Council, (07) 577 7000. ◻ *daily.* ♿

Beach at Mount Maunganui from "The Mount"

Mount Maunganui 19

Road map E2. 🏔 *including Tauranga, 100,000.* ✈ *3 km (2 miles) S of town.* 🚌 ℹ *Salisbury Ave, (07) 575 5099.*

The town of Mount Maunganui, built on a narrow peninsula at the mouth of Tauranga Harbour, is the main port for the central North Island timber industry. Overshadowing the town is the 232-m (761-ft) cone-shaped Mount Maunganui. A walk to the summit and back takes 90 minutes and provides views of Maori fortifications dating from when "The Mount", as it is commonly called, was a *pa* site. At the top, unobstructed views up and down the coast can be seen. At the bottom are the **Mount Maunganui Hot Salt Water Pools**, which are heated by natural thermal water.

Magnificent Ocean Beach extends east from The Mount to Papamoa and beyond, creating an ideal summer playground for surfers and swimmers. In high seas, a blowhole at Moturiki Island, off Marine Parade, shoots spray skywards.

🏊 Mount Maunganui Hot Salt Water Pools
Adams Ave. **Tel** (07) 575 0868. ◻ *daily.* 📷 ♿ 🚻

Game fishing competition, Tauranga

Mayor Island 20

Road map F2. *35 km (22 miles) from Tauranga Harbour.* 🚢 *from Tauranga or Whangamata.* **Tel** *(07) 577 0531.*

Mayor Island (Tuhua) is rather hilly and bush-clad and there are very few landing places around its steep cliffs. The highest peak, Opauhau, reaches 354 m (1,161 ft) above a roughly circular island 4 km (3 miles) across. Two lakes, one green and the other black, lie within a crater crowning the summit of what is a dormant volcano rising from the sea floor.

The island's most striking feature is black obsidian, a natural glass formed by rapid cooling of silica-rich lava. In pre-European times, Maori prized obsidian and fought battles over the island.

An 18-km (11-mile) walking track circles the island while other paths cross the interior. All sea life is protected within a marine reserve on the northern coastline. A camping ground and cabins provide accommodation, but visitors must take adequate food and water as supplies on the island are limited. Game fish in the vicinity of the island include tuna, marlin, kingfish and mako sharks. Several companies run diving and sightseeing trips to the island.

Tour in kiwi-carts through Kiwi360

Te Puke 21

Road map F3. 👥 *6,800.* 🚌
ℹ️ *130 Jellicoe St, (07) 573 6772.*
www.tepuke.co.nz

Te Puke is another town originally settled with Irish folk by Ulsterman George Vesey Stewart *(see p126)* in the 1880s. Early farming of sheep and cattle in the area was hampered by "bush sickness," a cobalt deficiency that dogged farming in many central North Island regions until it was identified in the 1930s and corrected with cobaltized fertilizers.

Entrance to Kiwi360

With an ideal climate for sheep, cattle and dairy farming, these land uses predominated until interest in horticulture strengthened in the 1960s.

Pioneering horticulturists experimented with what was then known as the Chinese gooseberry, and developed an international market for it under a new name – kiwifruit. Since then Te Puke has been hailed as "the kiwifruit capital of the world". All aspects of the industry, from cultivation to processing, are displayed at the export kiwifruit orchard and horticultural park **Kiwi360**, 6 km (4 miles) southeast of Te Puke.

Spring Loaded Fun Park, 8 km (5 miles) south of Te Puke, is a large farm designed to show the diversity of New Zealand farming. There are sheep and pigs, as well as groves of avocado, kiwifruit and pine trees. Children can get up close to young animals and hand-feed 60-year-old eels. Visitors can also explore the stunning natural beauty of the bush-clad Kaituna River during a 30-minute jet-boat ride.

🏯 Kiwi360
35 Young Rd. **Tel** *(07) 573 6340.*
⭕ *daily.* ⚫ *25 Dec.* 🈲 ♿
⭕ *obligatory.* 🍴 📷 🅿️
www.kiwi360.com

🏯 Spring Loaded Fun Park
316 State Hwy 33, Te Puke. **Tel** *0800 867 386.* ⭕ *daily.* ⚫ *25 Dec.* 🈲
rides. ♿ 📷 *obligatory.* 📷 🅿️

KIWIFRUIT

Before kiwifruit *(Actinidia chinensis)* became an international marketing success, it was known in New Zealand as the Chinese gooseberry after its country of origin. The first plant was grown in Te Puke in 1918, but it was not until the mid-1930s that Te Puke grower Jim McLoughlin planted the first orchard and sold fruit on the local market. Offshore markets were sought as more kiwifruit were grown.

Kiwifruit from Te Puke

In the late 1960s, the industry was propelled to success by a combination of good marketing and the discovery that refrigerated kiwifruit remains in good condition for up to six months. In the late 1970s, many horticulturists became millionaires almost overnight. Since 1998, the yellow-fleshed, tropical-flavoured Zespri Gold variety has supplemented the traditional emerald green-centred Hayward variety.

Fishing at the mouth of the
Whakatane River

Whakatane ㉒

Road map F3. 🚶 *17,000.* 🚌
ℹ️ *Cnr Quay St & Kakahoroa Dr, (07)*
308 6058. **www**.whakatane.com

Resting in the coastal heart
of the eastern Bay of Plenty,
Whakatane is one of New
Zealand's sunniest
locations. The town enjoys
more than 2,500 sunshine
hours a year, making it ideal
for a wide range of marine
activities. These include
fishing and viewing and
swimming with dolphins.
Whales and Dolphin Watch
NZ takes visitors on a voyage
out into the Bay of Plenty to
swim with dolphins.
   The **Whakatane District
Museum and Gallery** gives an
insight into the lifestyles of
early Maori and European
settlers. It contains a pictorial
history of the district as well
as displays of Maori artifacts.
   There are several excellent
local walkways. One, the Nga
Tapuwae O Toi Walkway,
provides beautiful views of
the sea and coastal pohutukawa trees. Access to the

route, which takes seven
hours to complete, is from
Seaview Road above the
town. The first landmark is
Kapu te Rangi ("ridge of
heaven"), with some of the
country's oldest earthworks.

🏛 **Whakatane District
Museum and Gallery**
11 Boon St. **Tel** *(07) 307 9805.*
🕐 *Tue–Fri.* 🎟 *donation.* ♿
www.*whakatanemuseum.org.nz*

Environs
Whale Island, 10 km (6 miles)
north of the harbour entrance,
is a wild-life refuge. Excursions
are organized by the Wha-
katane Coastguard over the
Christmas–New Year period.
Bookings can be made at the
Whakatane Visitor Centre.
   East of Whakatane, idyllic
Ohope Beach stretches 12 km
(7.5 miles) from Otarawairere,
its western extremity, to the
mouth of tidal Ohiwa Harbour.
The harbour is an important
source of fish and shellfish.

White Island ㉓

Road map F2. *50 km (31 miles) from*
Whakatane.

New Zealand's most active
volcano, White Island lies at
the northern end of the
Taupo–Rotorua volcanic fault
line *(see pp64–5).* It can be
reached by boat or helicopter
or simply viewed from the air.
The island's terrain is likened
to that of the moon or Mars
and many visitors rate it as
one of the country's best
attractions. The island was
mined for sulphur until 1914,

when a night-time eruption
killed all the miners. Remains
of mining activities can be
seen. There is a large gannet
colony on the island and it
suffers no ill-effects from the
ash fall-out. The island also
offers excellent diving.

Old sulphur mining equipment
on White Island

Opotiki ㉔

Road map F3. 🚶 *4,150.* 🚌 ℹ️
Cnr St John & Elliott sts, (07) 315
3031. **www**.*opotikinz.com*

Situated at the confluence of
the Waioeka and Otara rivers,
Opotiki is the gateway to the
East Cape and the last major
town before Gisborne. In
1865, at Opotiki, the Reverend Carl Sylvius Völkner
was hanged and then decapi-
tated by Maori convinced he
passed information about their
movements and fortifications
to Governor George Grey
(see p76). Hiona St Stephen's
Anglican Church, where the
incident took place, lies at the
northern end of the Church
Street business area. A key is
held across the road at the
**Opotiki Heritage and Agricul-
tural Society Museum**, which
is full of early settlers' items.
   An excellent example of a
warm, temperate rainforest is
Hukutaia Domain, which can
be reached from the western
end of Waioeka Bridge along
Woodlands Road. The reserve
is home to more than 2,000
native tree species, including
a 2,000-year-old hollow puriri
(Vitex lucens) where the
bodies of important Maori
were once exposed.

🏛 **Opotiki Heritage and
Agricultural Society Museum**
123 Church St. **Tel** *(07) 315 5193.*
🕐 *Mon–Sat.* ● *Good Fri, 25 Dec.*
♿🅿🏪

Ohope Beach, Whakatane's best surf beach

For hotels and restaurants in this region see pp302–7 and pp330–34

Maori Migration and Settlement

According to legend, three migration canoes travelling from Hawaiki landed in the eastern Bay of Plenty in the 14th century *(see p45)*: the Mataatua at Whakatane, the Arawa at Maketu and Tainui at Whangaparaoa Bay, west of East Cape. Muriwai's Cave at Whakatane is testament to Muriwai's arrival on the Mataatua: she is believed to have had

Cave of Muriwai

supernatural powers and lived hermit-like in the cave. Mild weather and abundant seafood encouraged Maori to settle along the coastal margins. Maori continue to form a high proportion of the population in the Bay of Plenty area, and red-framed Maori meeting houses, important spiritually and as decision-making centres, dot the countryside.

MAORI ART AND CULTURE

The meeting houses and other Maori works of art seen along the coast reflect Maori history, belief in gods and ancestral spirits, and a hierarchical, tribal social structure. Maori culture was primarily a wood culture. Wood was crafted into objects for economic, social and religious purposes, and embellished with symbols and motifs *(see pp30–31)*.

Meeting houses, *like the beautifully carved Tukaki at Te Kaha, are usually symbolic of a male tribal ancestor. His head is represented by the mask below the gable figure, while the wide, sloping bargeboards represent his arms.*

Elements of Maori artistry *have been incorporated into Christian churches, such as the intricate woven panels, carved wooden wall panels and rafter patterns at St Mary's Church at Tikitiki.*

The haka, *a vigorous rhythmic posture dance formerly per-formed by warriors to steel their resolve for war, is taught in schools along the coast.*

This ornately carved gateway *guards the entrance to coastal Omaio Marae.*

A prominent carving *in the main street of Opotiki is indicative of a renaissance in Maori arts, culture and traditions that took hold in the 1980s and 1990s.*

East Cape Tour ㉕

Skirting the rugged hills of the East Cape peninsula, this section of the Pacific Coast Highway offers exceptional scenery. From Opotiki northeast to East Cape, the road clings to rocky coastline cloaked with pohutukawa trees. The second part of the route heads south to Gisborne along an inland farming route with secondary roads providing access to the coast. Most beaches and bays are suitable for swimming, fishing and diving. There are also opportunities for jet-boating, horse trekking and tramping. Maori *marae* and churches dot the route.

Pohutukawa flower

Te Araroa Pohutukawa ③
On the foreshore at Te Araroa grows Te Waha-o-Rerekohu ("the mouth of Rerekohu"), believed to be the largest pohutukawa tree in the country. It has 22 trunks.

Raukokore Church ②
Built in 1894, this small, wooden Anglican church, with its distinctive roofline, stands lonely sentinel between road and sea.

Motu River ①
The Motu River, banked by steep hills and forest, is a magnificent setting for rafting and jet-boating. There is also excellent fishing at its mouth.

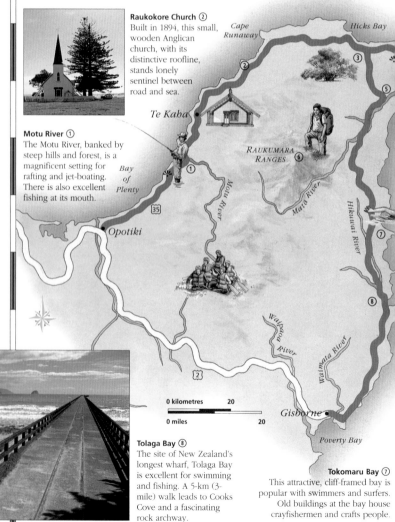

Tolaga Bay ⑧
The site of New Zealand's longest wharf, Tolaga Bay is excellent for swimming and fishing. A 5-km (3-mile) walk leads to Cooks Cove and a fascinating rock archway.

Tokomaru Bay ⑦
This attractive, cliff-framed bay is popular with swimmers and surfers. Old buildings at the bay house crayfishermen and crafts people.

'IPS FOR DRIVERS

.ength: 334 km (207 miles)
Stopping-off points: There is a pectacular view from the Maraenui Hill Lookout 36 km 22 miles) from Opotiki. Towns on the route are small, but most offer food. Accommodation is available at Hicks Bay. Permission o climb Mount Hikurangi must be obtained from Ngati Porou Outdoor Pursuits, Gisborne (06) 376 9960. Bookings for jet-boating on the Motu River can be made at the Opotiki nformation Centre (see p130).

East Cape Lighthouse ④
A gravel road along a picturesque coastline leads to New Zealand's most easterly lighthouse. The view from the lighthouse is well worth the climb up the 700 steps to reach it.

Tikitiki's St Mary's Church ⑤
Built in 1924 to commemorate Maori servicemen killed in World War I, St Mary's Church at Tikitiki is one of the most ornate Maori churches in the country *(see p131)*.

Mount Hikurangi ⑥
The first place in mainland New Zealand to see the sun each day, Mount Hikurangi is sacred to Maori and permission must be obtained to climb it.

KEY

- Tour route
- Other roads
- River
- Viewpoint

Star of Canada **wheelhouse, Gisborne Museum**

Te Urewera National Park ㉖

Road map F3. 🚌 ℹ *Aniwaniwa Visitor Centre, State Hwy 38, Wairoa, (06) 837 3803.* **www**.doc.govt.nz

This is New Zealand's fourth largest national park and the biggest tract of untouched native forest remaining in the North Island. For centuries its dense rainforest sheltered the industrious and resilient Tuhoe people. At the centre of Te Urewera lies the 243-m (797-ft) deep Lake Waikaremoana ("the lake of rippling waters"), formed 2,200 years ago by a landslide. A 46-km (28-mile) track around the lake, one of the country's Great Walks *(see p350)*, takes three to four days to complete. Booking through the Aniwaniwa Visitor Centre is essential. There are also many beautiful short walks into the park from the main road, which is partly gravel.

Gisborne ㉗

Road map F3. 👥 35,000. ✈ *4 km (2.5 miles) NW of town.* 🚌 ℹ *209 Grey St, (06) 868 6139.* 🎉 *Wine and Food Festival (last week of Oct).* **www**.gisbornenz.com

Gisborne is renowned for its warm summers, its farming, viticulture and horticulture, its surf beaches at Midway, Wainui and Makorori, and its history. A monument and reserve on Kaiti Hill are named in honour of Captain James Cook who made his first New Zealand landfall at Gisborne's Kaiti Beach *(see p48)* on 9 October 1769.

The **Gisborne Museum**, also known as the **Tairawhiti Museum and Arts Centre**, houses fine Maori and European artifacts and an extensive photographic collection. On the bank of the Taruheru River, but part of the museum complex, rests the salvaged wheelhouse from the *Star of Canada*, which sank off Kaiti Beach in 1912. Statues of Captain Cook and Young Nick, at the mouth of the Turanganui River, commemorate cabin boy Nicholas Young, the first crewman on board Cook's ship, the *Endeavour*, to sight New Zealand.

🏛 Gisborne/Tairawhiti Museum and Arts Centre
Kelvin Park, Stout St. ***Tel*** *(06) 867 3832.* ○ *daily.* ● *Good Fri, 25 & 26 Dec.* ♿ *except in Star of Canada.* 📖 🛍
www.tairawhitimuseum.org.nz

Environs
Eastwoodhill Arboretum, 35 km (22 miles) west of Gisborne, contains a world-renowned collection of exotic trees and shrubs in a rambling park setting. Set among lush native bush and abundant birdlife, **Morere Hot Springs**, 60 km (37 miles) south of Gisborne, has both hot and cold pools.

🍁 Eastwoodhill Arboretum
2392 Wharekopae Rd. ***Tel*** *(06) 863 9003.* ○ *daily.* ● *Good Fri, 25 Dec.* 🎟 ♿ 🚶 *by arrangement.*

Morere Hot Springs
State Hwy 2, Morere. ***Tel*** *(06) 837 8856.* ○ *daily.* 🎟 ♿ 🛍

Tall trees in the Eastwoodhill Arboretum, Gisborne

Rotorua

Situated on the southern shore of a lake of the same name, Rotorua is the North Island's most popular tourist destination. The city's hot and steamy thermal activity (evident from countless bores and fissures), healing mineral pools, adventure activities and surrounding lakes, rivers and crystal springs are major attractions. Rotorua is known as the heartland of Maori culture and offers visitors the chance to experience Maori art, architecture, song and dance and colourful evening entertainment to the visitor.

Government Gardens and the Rotorua Museum of Art and History

♣ Government Gardens
Queens Drive.
The formal Government Gardens are laid out in front of the stately Tudor-style Rotorua Museum of Art and History. They comprise a series of trimmed croquet and bowling greens and formal flower gardens dotted with steaming thermal pools. The 1927 Arawa Soldiers' Memorial, a short distance north of the museum, symbolizes the history of contact between Pakeha and local tribes. At its base is the Arawa migration canoe, from which Rotorua's Te Arawa people trace their descent.

🏛 Rotorua Museum of Art and History
Government Gardens, Queens Drive.
Tel (07) 349 4350. ☐ daily. ● 25 Dec. ⏣ ♿ ground level. 📷 🚻 ☐ 📷 www.rotoruamuseum.co.nz
Maori artifacts are plentiful in Rotorua's museum, situated within a magnificent building that opened as the Great Spa of the South Pacific in 1908. Some of the most important of these are bargeboards from Rotoiti's Houmaitawhiti meeting house, carved in 1860.

Also on display is 19th-century palisading from the Maori settlement of Ohinemutu and a female pumice figure, Pani, a *kumara* goddess depicted in the act of giving birth; most Maori fertility gods are male.

The story of the building itself is shown in "Taking the Cure", in a section of the building painstakingly restored to its original condition. History, mythology and geology are combined in a dramatic 15-minute film to explain Rotorua's geothermal activity and Maori history. The film also shows a re-enactment of the 1886 Tarawera eruption.

♣ The Blue Baths
Queens Drive. *Tel* (07) 350 2119.
☐ daily. ● 25 Dec. ⏣ ☐
These heated pools were built in the 1930s and offered the then-novel attraction of mixed bathing. Housed in a Spanish mission-style building, they were once a symbol of New Zealand's ambitions to become the premier spa of the British Empire. A museum documents the social history associated with the construction and use of the baths.

🔲 Polynesian Spa
Hinemoa St. *Tel* (07) 348 1328.
☐ daily. 📷 ♿ ☐
www.polynesianspa.co.nz
People from around the world visit the Polynesian Spa's mineral waters, which vary in temperature from 33 °C (92 °F) to 42 °C (107 °F). Radium and Priest waters, both acidic and cloudy, are sourced from an underground spring while alkaline Rachel water is piped to the spa from nearby. Adults have access to a mineral pool overlooking a large, heated, freshwater pool, with a shallow end for toddlers. Users can regulate the temperature in the spa's private pools. Aix massage (under jets of water) and other therapies are available in the luxury spa area.

SPA CITY

"Cripples throw away their crutches and the gouty man regains his health," a government report proclaimed in 1903, referring to Rotorua's mineral waters. Two mineral waters were used in a succession of 19th-century and early 20th-century spas, the largest being the Bath House, opened in 1908. The waters were considered "stimulating and tonic in reaction". Today, on the shores of Lake Rotorua, QE Health uses hot mineral waters to relieve pain, relax muscles and stimulate joint movement.

Mineral pool at Polynesian Spa complex

For hotels and restaurants in this region see pp302–7 and pp330–34

St Faith's Anglican Church

🕇 St Faith's Anglican Church

Ohinemutu. ◯ daily. 🕇 9am Sun; 10am.

Built in 1910, the Tudor-style St Faith's is the second church built at Ohinemutu, a Maori village on the shores of the lake around which Rotorua grew. An etched-glass window in the chapel at the far end of the church depicts Christ dressed in a *korowai* (chief's cloak) and appearing to walk on the waters of Lake Rotorua. The interior is richly embellished with Maori

carvings, woven wall panels and painted scrollwork. There are several graves of interest next to the church, including that of Seymour Mills Spencer (1810–98) who preached to the Arawa for 50 years, and Captain Gilbert Mair (1843–1923) of the Arawa Flying Column, a guerilla unit of local Maori who fought for the British army in the New Zealand wars.

⚠ Tamatekapua

Ohinemutu.

The magnificent Tamate-kapua meeting house, built in 1873, is the main gathering place of the Arawa tribe. Located opposite St Faith's, it was named for an earlier house that stood on Mokoia Island and the captain of the Arawa migration canoe. The figure at the base of the centre post is

Carving at Tamatekapua

Ngatoroirangi, the canoe's navigator, whom mythology credits with bringing thermal activity to the region.

⚠ Kuirau Park

Kuirau Rd.
Within Kuirau Park there are a number of boiling mud pools, steam vents and small geysers. Free thermal foot pools, picnic areas, well-kept gardens, a children's playground and a small, warm lake are other attractions within the domain.

Visitors will also appreciate a scented garden in the park.

VISITORS' CHECKLIST

Road map E3. 🏠 68,000.
✈ State Hwy 30, 10 km (6 miles) NE of city. 🚌 🚏 ℹ️
1167 Fenton St, (07) 348 5179.
◯ 8am–6pm daily. ◯ 25 Dec.
🎭 Biennial Rotorua Festival of the Arts (Jan/Feb, odd years); New Zealand International Two-Day Walk (Mar); Rotorua Marathon (May).
www.rotoruanz.com

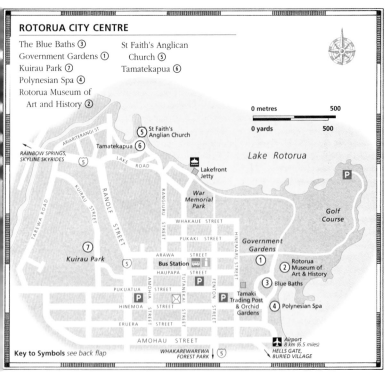

ROTORUA CITY CENTRE

The Blue Baths ③
Government Gardens ①
Kuirau Park ⑦
Polynesian Spa ④
Rotorua Museum of Art and History ②
St Faith's Anglican Church ⑤
Tamatekapua ⑥

0 metres 500
0 yards 500

⑤ St Faith's Anglican Church
Tamatekapua ⑥
ARIARITERANGI ST
RAINBOW SPRINGS, SKYLINE SKYRIDES ⑤
LAKE ROAD
KUIRAU STREET
RANOLF STREET
TAREWA ROAD
RANGIURU STREET
Lakefront Jetty
War Memorial Park
WHAKAUE STREET
PUKAKI STREET
ARAWA STREET
Bus Station
HAUPAPA STREET
HINEMARU STREET
Lake Rotorua
Golf Course
Government Gardens ①
② Rotorua Museum of Art & History
③ Blue Baths
④ Polynesian Spa
⑦ Kuirau Park ⑤
PUKUATUA STREET
AMOHIA STREET
TUTANEKAI STREET
FENTON STREET
Tamaki Trading Post & Orchid Gardens
HINEMOA STREET
ERUERA STREET
AMOHAU STREET
Key to Symbols *see back flap*
WHAKAREWAREWA FOREST PARK ⑤
✈ Airport 8 km (6.5 miles)
HELLS GATE, BURIED VILLAGE

Greater Rotorua

Figure at Tamaki Maori Village

Many of Rotorua's best attractions lie outside the city centre, around Lake Rotorua and the 15 other magnificent bush-fringed lakes that make up the Rotorua Lakes district. Complementing the lakes are geothermal wonders, bubbling springs, crystal-clear trout streams and unspoiled native forests. The rivers and lakes are renowned for their trout, and make a beautiful setting for boating, camping and tramping. Thrill-seekers can take four-wheel drive tours and ride horses to remote forest locations. Visitors can also enjoy Maori cultural experiences and observe the farming and livestock displays.

Visitors viewing trout at Rainbow Springs Nature Park

Lake Rotorua and Mokoia Island from Mount Ngongotaha

🌋 Lake Rotorua

This nearly circular lake is the largest of the lakes around Rotorua and is a popular venue for fishing, windsurfing and kayaking. It can be enjoyed by paddle steamer, kayak, jet-boat or water scooter. Mokoia Island, in the centre of the lake, is famous for the love story of Hinemoa, who defied her family's wishes and swam at night to the island to be with the chief Tutanekai, who played his flute to guide her. The island is rich in native bird life and offers 4 km (2.5 miles) of walking tracks as well as Hinemoa's thermal pool.

🚡 Skyline Skyrides

185 Fairy Springs Rd. *Tel (07) 347 0027.* ⬜ *daily.* 🏷️ 🛗 🍴 🏪
www.skylineskyrides.co.nz
Mount Ngongotaha towers 778 m (2,552 ft) above the city and lake. The Skyline lookout, at 487 m (1,598 ft), can be reached by gondola, and gives unmatched views of the city, lakes and country-

side. An exciting way to descend the mountain, by day or night, is by luge (a short, raised toboggan on wheels). A 2-km (1.2-mile) scenic ride suits most people, while two shorter and steeper rides provide an adrenalin rush. Chairlifts return riders to the start.

🌋 Rainbow Springs Nature Park

Fairy Springs Rd. *Tel (07) 350 0440.* ⬜ *daily.* 🏷️ 🛗 🏷️ 🍴 🏪 🏪
www.rainbownz.co.nz
Visitors can feed some of the thousands of rainbow, brown, brook and tiger trout in the crystal-clear freshwater streams and fern-fringed pools here, and view tuataras and kiwis in a walk-through aviary. Rainbow Springs is also home to Kiwi Encounter, a conservation-in-action attraction, combining natural history with wildlife conservation. Staff prepare, incubate and hand-raise kiwi chicks taken as eggs from the wild. Once at maximum weight, they are returned to the wild.

🍃 The Agrodome and Agroventures

Western Rd, Ngongotaha. *Tel (07) 357 1050.* ⬜ *daily.* 🏷️ 🛗 🏷️
🏪 🏪 **www**.agrodome.co.nz
Founded in 1972, this family business offers a broad range of farming-related as well as adventure activities. There are three live sheep shows daily, at which champion rams are introduced on stage, and sheep shearing and sheep dog trials are demonstrated. Visitors can also tour the organic farm, feeding and handling the animals. The souvenir shop specializes in quality woollen clothing and sheepskin rugs. Adventure activities on offer in the park include the Shweeb (the world's first human-powered monorail racetrack, consisting of two overhead rail circuits from

Live sheep show at the Agrodome Agricultural Theme Park

For hotels and restaurants in this region see pp302–7 and pp330–34

which hang high performance pedal-powered vehicles), bungy jumping, jet-boating and zorbing (rolling downhill inside a large plastic "ball").

Hell's Gate

State Hwy 33. *Tel* (07) 345 3151.
☐ daily. 🈂️ 👍 📷 🍴 📖 📷
www.hellsgate.co.nz
Sixteen km (10 miles) from Rotorua, at Tikitere, Hell's Gate is famous for its ferocious volcanic activity. Drifting, wraith-like mists part to reveal a fierce and spectacular thermal valley that includes the Kakahi Falls, the largest hot waterfall in the southern hemisphere, and New Zealand's largest boiling whirlpool. Another cauldron of water, the Sulphur Bath, is purported to cure septic cuts, bites and skin ailments. The area is well signposted, with good pathways and barriers. Traditional Maori massage is on offer at the Wai Ora Spa.

Whakarewarewa Forest Park

Off State Hwy 5.
This 40-sq km (15-sq mile) multipurpose forest adjoining the Whakarewarewa thermal area *(see pp138–9)* contains

Horse riding in Whakarewarewa Forest Park

majestic groves of redwoods, firs and other plantation trees. Forest walks can take from 30 minutes to all day. There are also mountain biking and horse tracks, a nature trail and picnic area.

Tamaki Maori Village

State Hwy 5. *Tel* (07) 349 2999. ☐
daily. ⬤ 25 Dec. 🈂️ 👍 📷 📖 📷
Visitors are introduced to Maori customs and traditions at this replica of a pre-European Maori village. Sampling a *hangi*, in which selected foods

A Maori "warrior" greets visitors at the Tamaki Maori Village

are cooked on hot rocks in an authentic earth oven, is part of the cultural experience. Overnight stays can be arranged during which visitors listen to Maori myths and legends. Education workshops are also held on traditional Maori carving and weaving, performing arts, weaponry and warfare, and Maori food and health.

Blue and Green Lakes

Tarawera Rd.
Eleven km (7 miles) southeast of Rotorua are the stunning Blue and Green Lakes (Tikitapu and Rotokakahi). The narrow isthmus that divides the lakes provides a good vantage point to compare their contrasting hues. Lake Rotokakahi is sacred to Maori and is not accessible, but Lake Tikitapu is the scene of many summer activities.

Buried Village

Tarawera Rd. *Tel* (07) 362 8287. ☐
daily. ⬤ 25 Dec. 🈂️ 👍 📷 📖 📷
www.buriedvillage.co.nz
Fifteen minutes' drive from Rotorua and 2.5 km (1.5 miles) from Lake Tarawera is what remains of the village of Te Wairoa, devastated by the eruption of Mount Tarawera in 1886. A walk through parkland takes in the excavations of several sites and an interactive museum explains the eruption. A bush walk leads to the Te Wairoa waterfalls.

TARAWERA ERUPTION

Months of underground rumbling culminated early in the morning of 10 June 1886 with the eruption of Mount Tarawera, which left a deep crater *(see pp64–5)*. Lasting about three hours, the blast spread along a 17-km (10-mile) rift and killed 153 people. The eruption hurled red-hot volcanic bombs and pieces of solidified lava 14 km (8.5 miles), and the Maori villages of Te Ariki, Te Wairoa and Moura were buried under 20 m (65 ft) of mud. The explosion's roar was heard in Christchurch and Auckland. The famous Pink and White Terraces, massive fan-like silica terraces, acknowledged as the eighth wonder of the world, were completely obliterated. Information on guided walks and 4WD tours to the crater, and on scenic flights over it, can be obtained from the Rotorua information centre *(see p135)*.

Painting by Charles Blomfield of the Pink Terraces, around 1890

Whakarewarewa Thermal Area

Maori carving

The geothermal area at Rotorua's southern edge, commonly referred to as Whaka, comprises two separate areas – Te Puia, once known as the New Zealand Maori Arts and Crafts Institute, and Whakarewarewa Thermal Village. Te Puia's attractions include Maori carving and weaving, cultural performances, examples of Maori buildings and fortifications, and the geysers Pohutu and Prince of Wales Feathers. At the Thermal Village, visitors can see a meeting house, cooking and bathing pools and a cemetery. At both venues, guides take visitors on an educational journey that unravels the mystery of Maori ways.

★ Te Aronui-a-Rua Meeting House
Visitors are greeted with a Maori "challenge" at Te Aronui-a-Rua meeting house at Te Puia.

★ Carving School
Ancient carving skills are passed to younger generations at Te Puia's carving school.

Kiwi House

Leaping Frog Mud Pool

HEMO ROAD

Te Puia

Cooking Pool

At the Weaving House, broad native flax is transformed into functional items.

0 kilometres 1

0 miles 1

Lake Waikaukau

Pataka
Storehouses like this were used by pre-European Maori to store food. However, kumara (sweet potato), their staple carbohydrate, was stored in pits in the ground.

STAR SIGHTS

★ Carving School

★ Pohutu Geyser

★ Te Aronui-a-Rua Meeting House

★ Wahiao Meeting House

★ Pohutu Geyser
Pohutu ("Big Splash") is the largest geyser and typically erupts 10–25 times a day up to 30 m (98 ft) high, depending on wind strength and direction.

At Puarenga Stream, village children dive for coins thrown from a bridge by tourists.

TRYON ST

Prince of Wales Feathers Geyser

Whakarewarewa Thermal Village

Geyser Flat, a 1-sq-km (0.4-sq-mile) silica terrace, is home to more than 500 thermal features, including seven geysers.

The Brainpot, a symmetrical silica basin, is said to have been used to cook the heads of enemies.

★ Wahiao Meeting House
Tourists, including children, join in a cultural performance outside Wahiao meeting house.

Above-ground Cemetery
At Whakarewarewa Thermal Village, the dead are buried above ground in vaults to keep the remains out of the steaming earth.

VOLCANIC FEATURES

The volcanic activity at Whakarewarewa is a reminder of how the earth is still changing and how the pressure of volcanic gases and heat below the surface can break through in spectacular and often dangerous ways. Here, superheated steam escapes from a vast chamber of boiling water through narrow vents in roaring towers of spray; mud pools boil and heave as gas and hot water seek to escape through the surface, and steam and gases are discharged in hot pools beside mineral-coloured silica flats.

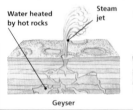

Water heated by hot rocks — Steam jet

Geyser

Hot water — Mud mixed with hot water

Mud pool

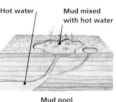

Steam — Superheated water

Fumarole

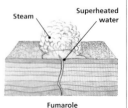

Waimangu Volcanic Valley ㉙

Road map E3. **Tel** (07) 366 6137.
☐ daily. ▨ & to bus stop &
boat cruise (assisted). 🍴 📷
www.waimangu.co.nz

Created on 10 June 1886 as
a result of the Tarawera
Eruption (see p137), Wai-
mangu is the only hydro-
thermal sytem in the world
wholly formed within historic
times. It offers an easy, mostly
downhill, 90-minute walk past
a succession of geothermal
features at the southern end
of the 17-km (10-mile) rift
created by the eruption.

The 38,000-sq-m (409,032-
sq-ft) Frying Pan Lake,
claimed to be the world's
largest hot water spring, emits
steam over its entire area and
is dominated by the red-
streaked Cathedral Rocks. The
lake was formed by an eruption in 1917 that buried a
nearby tourist hotel.

The pale blue steaming
water and delicate silica clay
terracing of the Inferno Crater
should not be missed, even
though it requires a short detour from the main path. The
water reaches 80 °C (176 °F)
in the lake and rises and falls
8 m (26 ft) over a 38-day cycle.

At the end of the walk lies
Lake Rotomahana, submerg-
ing what remains of the Pink
and White Terraces (see
p137). Across the water
stands Mount Tarawera. A
boat excursion follows a
shoreline scarred by craters,
fumaroles and geysers. Unusual thermal plants grow
along the lake's edge. Visitors
need to allow two to three
hours for the volcanic valley
walk and the boat cruise.

Champagne Pool at Wai-o-tapu Thermal Wonderland

Wai-o-tapu Thermal Wonderland ㉚

Road map E3. **Tel** (07) 366 6333.
☐ daily. ▨ & main area. ☑ 📷
📷 **www**.geyserland.co.nz

This is the country's most
colourful and diverse
geothermal area and is home
to the reliable Lady Knox
Geyser, named in 1904 after
Governor-General Lord Ran-
furly's daughter. The geyser
shoots water and steam
up to 21 m (69 ft) into the
air at 10:15am daily.

Other main attractions include the Artist's Palette, a
panorama of hot and cold
pools, boiling mud pools and
hissing fumaroles in a variety
of ever-changing colours, and
the Champagne Pool, with its
ochre-coloured petrified edge.
The Primrose Terraces are
also naturally tinted and have
delicately formed lacework
patterns. Walks through the
geothermal area, over boardwalks and along signposted
paths, take 30 to 75 minutes.

Orakei Korako Geyserland ㉛

Road map E3. **Tel** (07) 378 3131.
☐ daily. 📷 📷 📷 (includes boat
ride). **www**.orakeikorako.co.nz

Orakei Korako, or "The
Hidden Valley", as it is
known, lies at the southern
end of Lake Ohakuri, fed by
the Waikato River as it flows
northward from Lake Taupo.
Reaching the valley's geo-

thermal attractions requires a
boat trip across the lake to
the imposing Emerald Ter-
race, the largest silica feature
of its kind in the country.
Beyond is a 60-minute walk
taking in a geyser, more silica
terraces, hot springs, a cave
and mud pools. Cabin
accommodation is available
at the lake's edge.

Jet-boating rapids on
the Waikato River

Wairakei Park ㉜

Road map E3.

Ten kilometres (6 miles)
north of Taupo is the area
loosely referred to as Wairakei
Park. The star attraction is the
Huka ("foam") Falls, where
the Waikato River is channel-
led through a narrow rock
chute before hurtling over an
11-m (36-ft) bluff to a foam-
ing cauldron below. Access
down the Waikato River from
Taupo to the Huka Falls is
possible by jet-boat, or by the
more sedate paddlewheeler,

Inferno Crater at Waimangu
Volcanic Valley

built in 1908. A 7-km (4-mile) path leads from the falls down the right-hand side of the river to the Aratiatia Rapids, also accessible by road. Floodgates to the dam above the rapids are opened several times a day to allow kayaking and jet-boating.

At **Craters of the Moon**, at the end of Karapiti Road, 2 km (1.2 miles) south of Wairakei, steaming craters and boiling mud pits can be viewed free of charge among a bush-covered landscape.

The country's only prawn farm, off Huka Falls Road, uses geothermally heated river water to raise giant prawns for its restaurant, Prawn Farm Restaurant *(see p332)*. Tours of the farm are conducted hourly.

Taupo ㉝

Road map E3. ⚟ *21,300.* ✈ *8 km (5 miles) S of town.* 🚌 *Gascoigne St Travel Centre.* **Tel** *(07) 378 9005.* 🛈 *30 Tongariro St, (07) 376 0027.* ⚐ *Lake Taupo International Fishing Tournament (late Apr).* **www**.laketauponz.com

The town of Taupo lies at the northeastern end of Lake Taupo, New Zealand's largest lake, formed by a volcanic explosion in AD 186 *(see pp64–5)*. White pumice beaches and sheltered rocky coves surround the lake, which covers 619 sq km (239 sq miles). On a clear day, the distant volcanic peaks of Mounts Tongariro and Ngauruhoe and the snow-capped Ruapehu provide a spectacular backdrop to the lake.

Taupo services surrounding farms and forests and an important tourist industry. All year round the town attracts large numbers of holiday-makers who come for its excellent lake and river fishing, sailing and water sports, and local geothermal attractions. There is a wealth of accommodation in the town, much of it with lakeside views, and good dining and shopping. Many hotels have their own hot pools.

The wide selection of outdoor activities includes bungy jumping, boating and rafting, horse riding, mountain biking, tandem skydiving, flightseeing and golf. The bungy, set in majestic surroundings above the Waikato River off Spa Road, is a big draw. Details of the operators offering outdoor recreation may be obtained from the information centre in Taupo.

Turangi ㉞

Road map E3. ⚟ *5,500.* 🚌 🛈 *Ngwaka Place, (07) 386 8999.*

Located at the southeastern end of Lake Taupo on the banks of the Tongariro River, Turangi was a small fishing retreat until it was developed into a town in 1964 to accommodate workers for the Tongariro Hydro-Electricity Scheme. It remains an excellent resort area for anglers, and is also a popular base for trampers, white-water rafters, kayakers and skiers.

South of Turangi is the **Tongariro National Trout Centre**, a hatchery and research facility. Ova collected from wild female trout

Trimming pine trees in a pine forest near Turangi

are fertilized to breed trout for research purposes and to release into the lake. A self-guided 15-minute walk takes you through the hatchery and by a stream to an underwater viewing chamber to see trout in their natural environment.

🕊 **Tongariro National Trout Centre** State Hwy 1. **Tel** *(07) 386 8605.* ◑ *10am–3pm daily.* ● *1 Jan, 25 Dec.* ♿

TROUT FISHING PARADISE

World-famous Lake Taupo and its surrounding lakes – Kuratau, Hinemaia, Rotoaira and Otamangakau – are fed by numerous rivers and streams well-stocked with rainbow and brown trout. Fishermen frequently stand shoulder to shoulder at the mouth of the Waitahanui River to form the "picket fence" fishing phenomenon. Line fishing from boats on Lake Taupo or from the shore is effective from November until March, as trout feed upon smelt spawning close to shore. In late summer, trout congregate after dark where streams flow into the lake, providing excellent fly-fishing. River fishing is best from May till October. A special fishing licence, available from sports shops and information centres, is required in the Taupo Fishing District.

Fishing at the mouth of the Waitahanui River

Tongariro National Park

Bust of Tukino Te Heuheu IV

At the southern end of Lake Taupo lies the magnificent 7,600-sq-km (2,930-sq-mile) Tongariro National Park. The peaks of the three active volcanic mountains which form its nucleus, Ruapehu, Ngauruhoe and Tongariro *(see pp64–5)*, were a gift to the government in 1887 by Tukino Te Heuheu IV, a Ngati Tuwharetoa chief. The park, which is surrounded by access roads, is a winter playground for skiers and snowboarders and a year-round wilderness walking, tramping and mountain climbing area. The park was the first in the world to achieve UNESCO World Heritage status for both its natural (1990) and Maori spiritual and cultural (1993) value.

★ **Whakapapa Ski Area**
The largest developed ski area in New Zealand, Whakapapa has a sophisticated chairlift system and more than 30 groomed trails catering to all levels of skiers and snowboarders.

Bayview Chateau Tongariro
This luxury hotel, built in 1929 on the lower slopes of Mount Ruapehu, offers outstanding mountain and valley views (see p306).

★ **Mount Ruapehu**
In summer, visitors can climb to the crater of Mount Ruapehu, the North Island's tallest mountain, from the highest Whakapapa chairlift.

Round the Mountain is a four- to five-day tramp around Ruapehu for those seeking solitude, magnificent mountain views and a back-country experience.

Mountain biking is prohibited in the park but is allowed in the Rangataua, Erua and Tongariro Forest Areas.

The Turoa Ski Area is renowned for its expansive ski areas, long runs and vertical drops

KEY

▬▬	State highway
▬▬	Minor road
～～	River
_ ._	4 WD track
_ _	Walking track
▬ ▬	Park boundary
_ _	Restricted area
ℹ️	Tourist information
⚠️	Camp site
🏕	Picnic area
⛷	Skiing

Map labels: National Park · Mangare Road · 47 · 48 · 4 · Whakapapa Village · Makatote River · MOUNT RUAPEHU 2,797 m (9,176 ft) · Mangaturuturu River · Round the Mountain Track · Crater Lake · Mangawhero River · Ohakune Mountain Road · Mangawhero Falls · RANGATAUA FOREST · Ohakune · Dreadnought Road · 49

STAR SIGHTS

★ Emerald Lakes

★ Mount Ruapehu

★ Whakapapa Ski Area

0 kilometres 5
0 miles 5

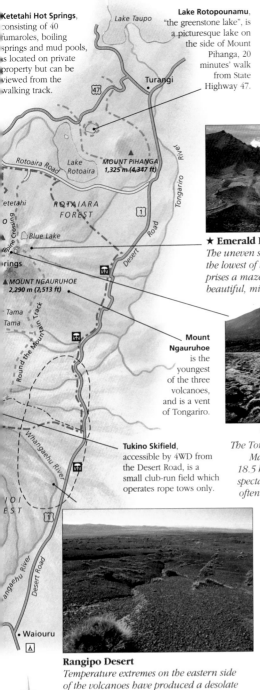

Ketetahi Hot Springs, consisting of 40 fumaroles, boiling springs and mud pools, is located on private property but can be viewed from the walking track.

Lake Taupo

Lake Rotoaira

Lake Rotopounamu, "the greenstone lake", is a picturesque lake on the side of Mount Pihanga, 20 minutes' walk from State Highway 47.

Turangi

47

Rotoaira Road

Lake Rotoaira

▲ **MOUNT PIHANGA** 1,325 m (4,347 ft)

Tongariro River

etetahi

ROTOAIRA FOREST

1

Blue Lake

Desert Road

rings

▲ **MOUNT NGAURUHOE** 2,290 m (7,513 ft)

Tama Tama

Round the Mountain Track

Whangaehu River

Whangaehu River

Desert Road

1

Waiouru

⚑

VISITORS' CHECKLIST

Road map E3. 🏔 National Park.
🛖 National Park Store, Carroll
St. **Ohakune** 🏠 54 Clyde St,
(06) 385 8427. ◯ daily, times
variable. **Whakapapa** 🏠 behind
Bayview Chateau Tongariro, (07)
892 3729. ◯ 8am–5pm daily.
www.doc.govt.nz

★ **Emerald Lakes**
*The uneven summit of Mount Tongariro,
the lowest of the three volcanoes, comprises a maze of craters, including the
beautiful, mineral-tinted Emerald Lakes.*

Mount Ngauruhoe
is the youngest of the three volcanoes, and is a vent of Tongariro.

Tongariro Alpine Crossing
*The Tongariro Alpine Crossing, from
Mangatepopo to Ketetahi, covers
18.5 km (11.5 miles) of varied and
spectacular volcanic terrain and is
often described as the best one-day
trek in New Zealand.*

Tukino Skifield,
accessible by 4WD from
the Desert Road, is a
small club-run field which
operates rope tows only.

VOLCANIC HAZARDS

*The volcanoes of Tongariro
National Park are unique because
of the frequency of eruptions,
their highly explosive nature and
the high density of active vents.
Volcanic activity can occur in the
park at any time and with little or
no warning. Anyone intending to
tramp or climb on the upper
slopes of the volcanoes needs to
check the current volcanic alert
status and exclusion zones with
the nearest visitor centre and
read any recommended safety
information for the area before
starting out.*

Rangipo Desert
*Temperature extremes on the eastern side
of the volcanoes have produced a desolate
landscape of gravel fields and hardy
alpine vegetation. The area is used mainly
for army training.*

Skiers at Whakapapa on Mount Ruapehu looking towards Mounts Ngauruhoe and Tongariro ▷

Street-by-Street: Napier ㊱

Wall panel,
Municipal
Theatre

Perched on the edge of the Pacific Ocean, this elegant city is a memorial to a 1931 earthquake and fire that destroyed most buildings and killed many people. The quake raised marshland and the harbour bed, providing new farmland and room for urban development. During rebuilding, an earthquake-proof building code was enforced and architects adopted the then fashionable Art Deco style. Today, the city's Art Deco buildings, with their pastel colours, bold lines and elaborate motifs, are internationally renowned.

Napier Mall
Traffic bollards and seats topped with Art Deco motifs enhance pedestrian-friendly Emerson Street.

★ Deco Centre
Purpose-built in 1922 as Napier's Central Fire Station, and refurbished in Art Deco style after the earthquake, it now houses the Art Deco Trust and Art Deco Shop.

The Municipal Theatre, built in 1938, is noted for its Egyptian-style columns and door lintels, and for the leaping nude wall panels flanking the stage in the auditorium.

The Public Trust Building's massive columns and internal oak fittings escaped earthquake damage.

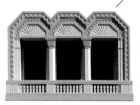

Countrywide Bank
This 1932 building has charming balcony windows framed by angular arches decorated with sunbursts and zigzags.

ART DECO TRUST

The Art Deco Trust is responsible for protecting, enhancing and promoting Napier's Art Deco buildings, keeping a register of them and maintaining worldwide links with other Art Deco groups. It also organizes Art Deco walks and publishes information on Art Deco tours. A highlight is the annual Art Deco Weekend, held in mid-February, a light-hearted celebration of the Art Deco style.

A couple dressed for an Art Deco Weekend

| 0 metres | 50 |
| 0 yards | 50 |

KEY

- - - Suggested route

STAR SIGHTS

★ The Dome

★ Deco Centre

The Napier Antique Centre, built in 1932, is one of four buildings in Napier ornamented with Maori designs.

VISITORS' CHECKLIST

Road map F4. 55,650. 5 km (3 miles) NW of city. Munro St. 100 Marine Pde, (06) 834 1911. 8:30am–5pm Mon–Fri; 9am–5pm Sat & Sun. 25 Dec. **Art Deco walks** Art Deco Trust, Deco Centre, 163 Tennyson St, (06) 835 0022. **www**.hawkesbaynz.com

Daily Telegraph Building
Built in 1932, this building is well endowed with Art Deco details – sunbursts, zigzags, ziggurats and fountain-like flowers.

Criterion Hotel
Leadlight glass was a favourite form of decoration in the 1930s, as shown in the window in the hotel's stairwell.

The ASB Bank's interior features fine examples of Maori carving and rafter patterns.

Masonic Hotel
Completed in 1932, the hotel features an unusual first-floor loggia built over the street.

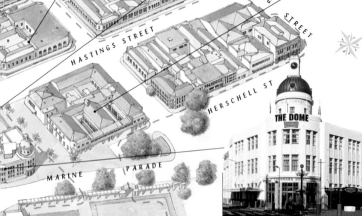

CATHEDRAL LANE

BROWNING STREET

HASTINGS STREET

HERSCHELL ST

THE DOME

MARINE PARADE

★ The Dome
This Napier landmark, built in 1936 to house the Silver Slipper Nightclub, has a beautifully restored elevator.

Exploring Napier

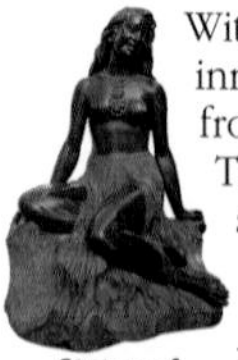

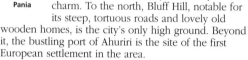

Statue of Pania

Within easy walking distance of Napier's inner-city Art Deco buildings is the ocean front Marine Parade, fringed by Norfolk pines. The floral clock, Tom Parker Fountain, statue of Pania (a maiden of local legend), Soundshell, Colonnade and Sunken Gardens, all on the seaward side of Marine Parade, add considerably to the city's charm. To the north, Bluff Hill, notable for its steep, tortuous roads and lovely old wooden homes, is the city's only high ground. Beyond it, the bustling port of Ahuriri is the site of the first European settlement in the area.

Ocean Spa

42 Marine Parade. **Tel** *(06) 835 8553.* ◯ *daily.* ● *25 Dec.* ♿
www.oceanspa.co.nz

This attractively landscaped open-air pool and spa complex has vast ocean views and is a great place to relax and recharge. Visitors can enjoy hot pools at various temperatures, a lap pool, two leisure pools, a toddler pool, outdoor and indoor private spas, as well as a sauna, steam room, gym and massage facility.

The National Aquarium of New Zealand

Marine Parade. **Tel** *(06) 834 1404.* ◯ *daily.* ● *25 Dec.*
www.nationalaquarium.co.nz

The aquarium is located in a stingray-shaped building on Napier's foreshore, and its proximity to the ocean means that fresh seawater can be pumped directly to its tanks and enclosures. The ground floor has native marine life and other species such as the tuatara (the New Zealand

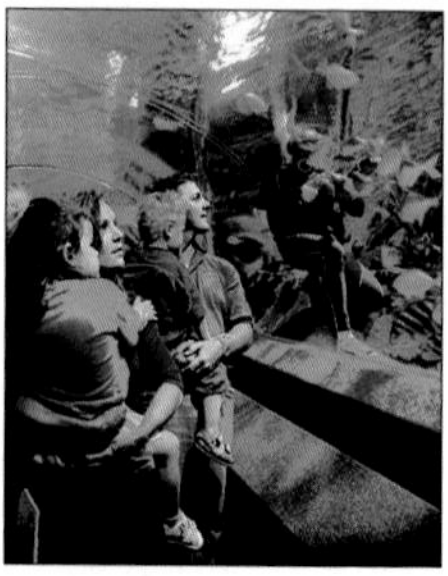

Visitors at the National Aquarium of New Zealand

lizard), while the upper floor is dedicated to creatures from different parts of the world.

The Oceanarium is viewed from an underwater tunnel, and is home to sharks, stingrays, seahorses and east coast native fish. Visitors can watch divers hand-feed the fish at 10am and 2pm every day, and there are even daily opportunities to take part in a supervised swim with the sharks. The aquarium is also involved in many conservation programmes and was the first to hatch a turtle egg in 1975.

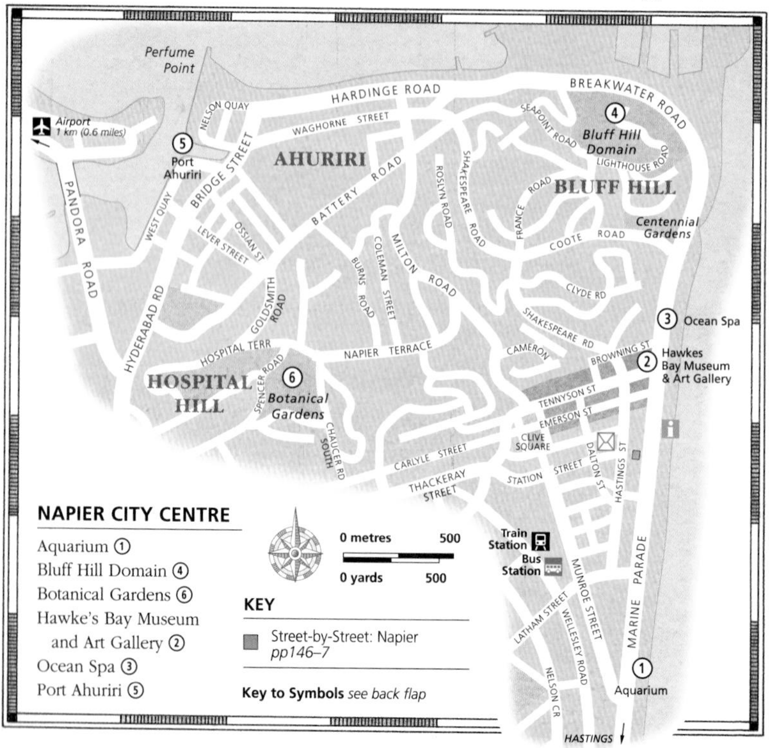

Perfume Point
Airport 1 km (0.6 miles)
NELSON QUAY
Port Ahuriri
PANDORA ROAD
WEST QUAY
BRIDGE STREET
HARDINGE ROAD
WAGHORNE STREET
AHURIRI
BATTERY ROAD
LEVER STREET
OSSIAN ST
HYDERABAD RD
GOLDSMITH ROAD
HOSPITAL TERR
HOSPITAL HILL
SPENCER ROAD
Botanical Gardens
CHAUCER RD SOUTH
BURNS ROAD
COLEMAN STREET
MILTON ROAD
ROSLYN ROAD
SHAKESPEARE ROAD
NAPIER TERRACE
BREAKWATER ROAD
SEAPOINT ROAD
Bluff Hill Domain
LIGHTHOUSE ROAD
BLUFF HILL
FRANCE ROAD
Centennial Gardens
COOTE ROAD
CLYDE RD
SHAKESPEARE RD
Ocean Spa
CAMERON
BROWNING ST
Hawkes Bay Museum & Art Gallery
TENNYSON ST
EMERSON ST
CLIVE SQUARE
DALTON ST
HASTINGS ST
CARLYLE STREET
THACKERAY STREET
STATION STREET
Train Station
Bus Station
MUNROE STREET
LATHAM STREET
WELLESLEY ROAD
NELSON CR
MARINE PARADE
Aquarium
HASTINGS
NAPIER CITY CENTRE
Aquarium 1
Bluff Hill Domain 4
Botanical Gardens 6
Hawke's Bay Museum and Art Gallery 2
Ocean Spa 3
Port Ahuriri 5
0 metres 500
0 yards 500
KEY
Street-by-Street: Napier pp146–7
Key to Symbols see back flap

🏛 Hawke's Bay Museum and Art Gallery

65 Marine Parade/9 Herschell St.
Tel (06) 835 7781. ⬭ daily.
⬤ 25 Dec. 📷 ♿ 📷 🛈

Housed in an Art Deco building, the museum has extensive collections of Maori treasures, fine art, applied and decorative arts and textiles, as well as artifacts relating to the daily lives of Hawke's Bay's early settlers. Through audiovisual displays and ephemera, visitors can also experience the devastation of the 1931 earthquake.

🌺 Bluff Hill Domain

Lighthouse Rd.
Prior to the 1931 earthquake, Napier comprised an oblong mass of hills (Scinde Island) surrounded almost entirely by water. A stroll or drive to the 102-m (335-ft) high lookout within Bluff Hill Domain will recreate this feeling if visitors imagine much of the low-lying area south of the hill covered in water. What were gun emplacements are now vantage points from which to view the Kaweka and Ruahine ranges to the west, the Mahia Peninsula to the northeast, and Cape Kidnappers to the southeast, as well as the spectacular sight of the commercial port below.

🏚 Port Ahuriri

At Port Ahuriri, 4 km (2.5 miles) from Napier's centre, visitors can watch boys fishing and fishing fleets being unloaded or enjoy the port's many lively bars and restaurants, which are among the finest in Napier. A beach boardwalk meanders to the harbour entrance at Perfume Point. The Rothmans Building, one of the most beautiful Art Deco buildings in Napier, is in nearby Ossian Street.

🌺 Botanical Gardens

Spencer Rd.
Located on a hill in the middle of the city, the gardens form a charming oasis. Apart from a spacious aviary, there are well-kept lawns bordered by flower beds, groves of stately trees, and a stream with ornamental bridges.

View north towards Napier from Te Mata Peak

Hastings ☰

Road map F4. 🏙 28,400.
✈ 25 km (15 miles) N of town. 🚉
🚌 Caroline Rd. 🛈 Russell St North, (06) 873 5526. 🎪 Harvest Hawke's Bay (first weekend of Feb); Hastings Blossom Festival (Sep).

Situated on the Heretaunga Plains, 20 km (12 miles) south of Napier, Hastings is the centre of a large fruit growing and processing industry, including wine making (see pp150–51). Rebuilt after the 1931 earthquake, it is the only city in New Zealand with streets laid out on the American block system. It has some fine Spanish Mission buildings, the most notable being the Hawke's Bay Opera House.

Hawke's Bay apples

Between Hastings and the eastern coastline, Te Mata Peak rises 399 m (1,309 ft). Maori legend describes the Te Mata ridgeline as the body of chief Te Mata O Rongokako, who choked and died eating his way through the hill, a task set him by the beautiful daughter of another chief. From Hastings the "bite" that killed him can be clearly seen, as can his body, which forms the skyline.

Cape Kidnappers ☰

Road map F4.

Maoris believe that the crescent-shaped bay and jagged promontory of Cape Kidnappers, 30 km (19 miles) south of Napier, represent the magical jawbone hook used by Maui to pull the North Island from the sea like a fish. In October 1769, Captain Cook anchored off the headland (see p48) naming it Cape Kidnappers after some Maoris attempted to carry off his Tahitian translator.

At the cape, up to 20,000 young and mature yellow-headed Australasian gannets surf wind currents metres from onlookers. The best time to see them is from early November to late February. Access is closed during the early nesting phase between July and October. At low tide, visitors can walk 8 km (5 miles) along the beach to the colony – check walking times with the local i-SITE Visitor Centre. Guided tours by coach and tractor-trailer are also available.

Australasian gannets at Cape Kidnappers Gannet Reserve

Hawke's Bay Vineyard Tour ㊴

Wine barrel race

Hawke's Bay's long sunshine hours, wide range of growing microclimates, and variety of soil types have allowed more than 40 wineries to develop all the classical grape varieties to a high standard. Traditionally a fruit-growing area, Hawke's Bay's fruit is sourced from varied vineyard and orchard sites, and wines are made using both modern and traditional techniques. The success of the region's wine is not only evident in its international awards, but in one of New Zealand's most important wine events, the annual Harvest Hawke's Bay, celebrated during the first weekend of February.

Mission Estate Winery ①
Established in 1851 by a group of French Catholic missionaries, early vintages were produced for sacramental purposes. Today, this historic winery, nestled on a hill overlooking sweeping vineyards, offers wine sales, winery tours, a gourmet restaurant and a craft gallery.

Clearview Estate Winery ⑨
Established in 1989 by Tim Turvey and Helma van den Berg, this gently sloping coastal vineyard produces small quantities of hand-made wines sold only from the winery, by mail order, or enjoyed at its seaside restaurant (see p331).

Te Mata Estate Winery ⑧
The oldest winery still operating in New Zealand (vines were planted on the lower slopes of Te Mata peak in 1892) and one of its most prestigious and successful, Te Mata produces mainly red wines, which can be purchased at its restored winery.

0 kilometres 4

0 miles 4

Vidal Wines ⑦
Anthony Vidal, an immigrant from Spain, established his winery in a stable in 1905. Urban development has encompassed the site but Vidals continues to produce good wines. Sales, tastings and a brasserie are available.

Sileni Estates ⑥
Located within an area of red-metal soils, massive investment has produced a showcase winery incorporating a gourmet food store, wine education centre and restaurant/café.

KEY

▬▬▬ Tour route

═══ Other roads

▬▬▬ River

Park Estate Winery ②

Formerly a traditional orchard, Park Estate has established niche markets for three very different beverages: grape wines, fruit wines from feijoa, boysenberry, kiwifruit and apple, and natural fruit juices. Orchard and winery tours, wine tasting and dining are available. A shop sells fresh fruit and homemade produce.

FRUITBOWL OF NEW ZEALAND

Hawke's Bay's warm, sunny summers and crisp winter frosts have been exploited by generations of horticulturists, who have earned the region its unofficial title of "fruitbowl of New Zealand". While apples are the largest crop, pears, kiwifruit, peaches and other stone fruits are also important. However, increased world production of apples and falling prices have begun to affect export levels. At Pernel Fruitworld, a large orchard on the outskirts of Hastings with its own packhouse, some 85 varieties of pip and stone fruits are grown. Tours are conducted hourly, fruit is available to taste, and a museum traces the history of the fruit industry.

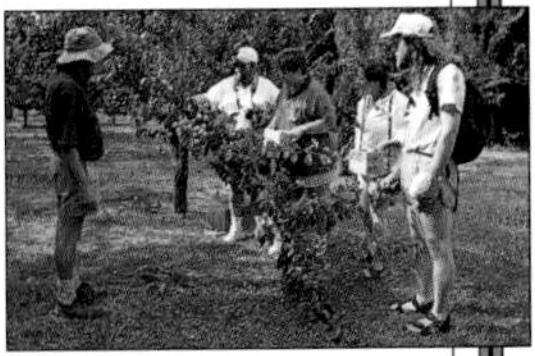

Orchard tour at Pernel Fruitworld

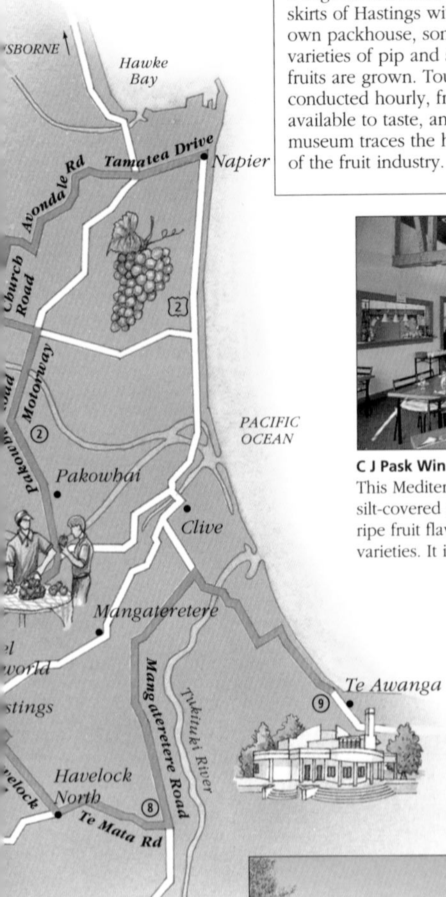
Hawke
Bay
Tamatea Drive
Napier
Avondale Rd
Church Road
2
Motorway
PACIFIC OCEAN
Pakowhai
Clive
Mangateretere
Mangateretere Road
Tukituki River
Te Awanga
Havelock North
Te Mata Rd

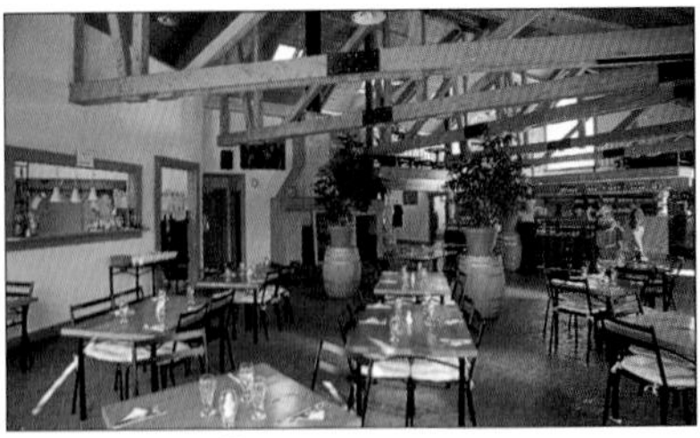

C J Pask Winery ③

This Mediterranean-style winery, located in a stony, silt-covered river bed, produces grapes with very ripe fruit flavours across a range of premium varieties. It is one of the region's best wineries.

Te Awa Winery ④

Named "River of God" for the enormous aquifer beneath the Hawke's Bay plains that is tapped to irrigate crops, Te Awa makes fine Bordeaux-blend red wines, which can be savoured at its restaurant.

TIPS FOR DRIVERS

Visiting three or four wineries in one day will allow time to taste and discuss the wines. Many wineries offer tours and most offer tastings and sales. Some have indoor and outdoor eating facilities, although booking is advisable. Information on the facilities at each listed winery can be obtained at the Napier Visitor Information centre *(see p147)**.*

Visitors planning to visit a greater number of wineries and make the most of tasting opportunities may prefer to take one of the many tours available.

Ngatarawa Wines ⑤

A large rectangular lily pond and stable buildings housing the winery make an attractive setting that is more than matched by Ngatarawa's wines. The vineyard also has a pleasant picnic area and a *pétanque* court.

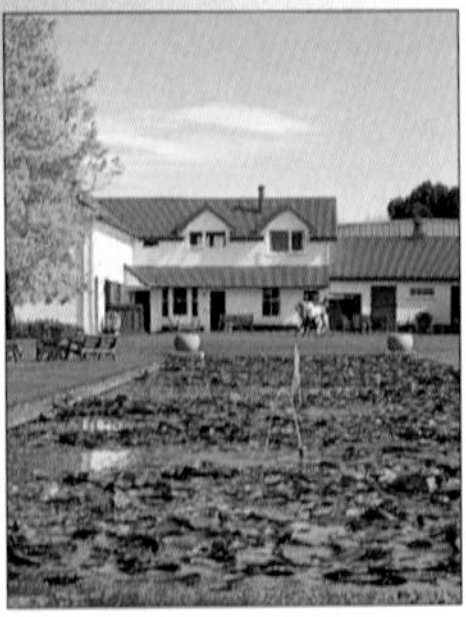

WELLINGTON AND THE SOUTH

uropean settlers arriving in the mid-1800s and making their way north of Wellington, New Zealand's capital city from 1865, quickly found themselves in the middle of virgin rainforest. The recent history of much of the area covered by Wellington and the South is linked to the massive clearance of the land through milling and burning of forest during the late 19th century.

In their thousands, ancient giant trees covered potentially rich pastoral land acquired from the Maori. Between the 1870s and 1910s, the area became the site of the country's biggest forest clearance programme as settlers poured in from overseas and demand for farmland grew. Sawmills, closely linked with the new rail network, sprang up throughout the district. Small towns along the railway enjoyed periods of importance before the sawmillers moved on. By 1907, however, milling output in the lower half of the North Island had passed its peak, to be superseded by the rich, rolling farmlands and rural lifestyles that have been a feature of the area ever since.

Although Taranaki, Wanganui and Manawatu are among the most productive and intensively farmed areas in New Zealand, these days diversity is the rule rather than the exception for the lower North Island. The exploitation of natural gas fields off the Taranaki coast, for example, has put an additional string to the region's economic bow.

Tourists are drawn to the compact lower North Island because of its mild climate, wild coastline, stunning beaches, scenic rivers, national parks, mountain ranges, ski fields, vineyards, and rich Maori heritage.

Harbour-fringed Wellington, situated at the bottom of the North Island, is the area's main city, and the centre of government, business, and the performing arts. The numerous small towns that radiate from it to the north, servicing local farms, are charming, friendly stopover points for travellers.

The Beehive and Parliament Buildings in Wellington, New Zealand's capital city

◁ Mount Taranaki, also known as Mount Egmont, in the centre of Egmont National Park

Exploring Wellington and the South

Wairarapa, the Kapiti Coast, Horowhenua, Manawatu, Wanganui and Taranaki are all within a day's drive of Wellington. The contrast between the arty, political capital city and the areas immediately to its north is striking. Within an hour, the country's rural heartland reveals itself with the numerous small, sleepy towns. Dairy and sheep farms continue to feature strongly in the region, but visitors can also see newer forms of land use, such as ostrich farms and vineyards. The Egmont and Whanganui national parks await the more adventurous.

Sheep farm near Martinborough

TOP OUTDOOR ACTIVITIES

The places shown here have been selected for their recreational activities. Conditions vary depending on the weather and the time of year, so exercise caution and, if in doubt, seek local advice.

	Golf	Jet-Boating	Kayaking	Sailing	Surfing	Swimming	Tramping	Windsurfing
Egmont National Park						●	●	
Manawatu Gorge			●				●	
Masterton	●		●			●	●	
New Plymouth	●	●	●	●	●	●	●	●
Oakura					●	●		●
Opunake					●	●		●
Palmerston North	●					●		
Paraparaumu	●	●	●	●	●	●	●	●
Sugarloaf Islands						●		
Waikanae	●	●	●			●	●	
Wanganui	●	●	●			●		
Wellington	●		●	●	●		●	●
Whanganui National Park			●			●	●	
Whanganui River		●	●	●		●	●	

KEY

▬▬ Motorway
──── Major road
═══ Minor road
┄┄┄ Major railway
──── Minor railway
▬▬ Regional border
△ Summit

Map labels: SUGAR LOAF ISLANDS ⑳, NEW PLYMOUTH ⑰, OAKURA ⑲, Egmont, Inglewood, CAPE EGMONT ㉑, Mount Taranaki 2518m, EGMONT NATIONAL PARK ⑱, STRATFORD ㉔, Oaonui, Eltham, OPUNAKE ㉒, TARANAKI, Manaia, HAWERA ㉓, Kakaramea, Patea, Te, Ur, Ur

GETTING AROUND

The area is well served by rail, bus and air services, and an extensive, well-maintained road network. The country's mild climate ensures roads in the region are usually passable throughout the year. Wellington's state-of-the-art airport serves both international and domestic travellers, while international cruise liners make use of the city's port. Several times a day, ferries, including those carrying cars, trucks and railway carriages, take travellers from Wellington across Cook Strait to the South Island and back again.

WHANGANUI NATIONAL PARK **16**

WHANGANUI NATIONAL PARK

WHANGANUI RIVER **15**

Taumarunui

Raetihi

Ohakune

Turangi

Pipiriki

Turangi **1**

Kakatahi

Taihape

Mangaweka

MANAWATU-WANGANUI

Napier **50**

Tikokino **2**

ANGANUI **14**
◆ 🏛 🎏

otara

Hunterville

Mangaweka 1733m

Ongaonga

Waipawa

Turakina

Takapau

Waipukurau

South Taranaki Bight

Marton **54**

Halcombe

HAWKE'S BAY

Bulls **3**

Wanstead

Feilding

Ashhurst

Dannevirke **52**

Manawatu Gorge

PALMERSTON NORTH **13**
🏛 ◆ 🍁

Woodville

Porangahau

Pahiatua

56

Manawatu

Foxton **1**

57

Konini

ASMAN SEA

Shannon

Eketahuna

Puketoi Range **52**

Ohau

8 LEVIN

Alfredton

Pongaroa

PITI ISLAND URE RESERVE **6**
🥾 🦅

7 OTAKI
🚣 🥾 🍁

12 MOUNT BRUCE NATIONAL WILDLIFE CENTRE

PACIFIC OCEAN

ARAUMU **4**
🏛 🥾

5 WAIKANAE

Tararua Forest Park

KARIKI **3**
◆ 🏛

WELLINGTON

11 MASTERTON
◆ 🏛

Castlepoint

ua

Upper Hutt

Greytown

Carterton

Lower Hutt

9 FEATHERSTON

Lake Wairarapa

🏛 🏛 🏛
WELLINGTON
⚓ ✈ 🚢

53

10 MARTINBOROUGH
🍷

RINE TOUR

Ruamahanga

urakirae Head

Palliser Bay

Aorangi Mountains

Putangirua Pinnacles

0 kilometres   20

0 miles   20

Cape Palliser

SEE ALSO

Chaffers Marina in Lambton Harbour, Wellington

Wellington: Cultural Capital

Poster for a comedy

Known primarily as the home of New Zealand's parliament and its public servant population, Wellington transformed itself during the 1980s and 1990s into a vibrant, culture-driven hot spot. Tucked around one of the world's most picturesque harbours, the capital city is intimate, sophisticated, arty and packed with national treasures. It is home to the Museum of New Zealand Te Papa Tongarewa *(see pp166–7)*, the Royal New Zealand Ballet, the New Zealand Symphony Orchestra, the National Business Review New Zealand Opera, the Chamber Music New Zealand and the New Zealand School of Dance. The city's strong arts scene combines an international flavour with an intrinsic Pacific identity.

Professional theatre, *strongly supported by Wellingtonians, can be enjoyed at several venues, including Downtown, Circa and Bats.*

The numerous public and private galleries *in Wellington are well patronized and exhibit local and international works of art. Dealer galleries, such as the Peter McLeavey Gallery, play a significant role in bringing the best of New Zealand art onto the market.*

The kiwi and the fern, *both symbols of New Zealand, form the logo for the New Zealand International Arts Festival.*

"WELLYWOOD"

Film making in New Zealand began on a large scale only in the 1960s and 1970s. Today, film production is a multimillion dollar industry in New Zealand. With much of the industry based in studios around Wellington, and international stars now often working there, the city has earned the nickname "Wellywood".

The city is also the home town of director Peter Jackson, whose international film credits include *Meet the Feebles, Brain Dead, The Frighteners* and *King Kong*. Much of the film work for these, as well as the making of J R R Tolkien's *The Lord of The Rings* trilogy, directed by Jackson, has been carried out in Wellington. The International Film Festival, held every July, attracts large crowds.

Film making at one of the many locations around the city

The New Zealand Symphony Orchestra, based in Wellington, performs regularly throughout the country. The orchestra accompanied New Zealand-born diva, Dame Kiri Te Kanawa, to welcome the dawn of the new millennium at Gisborne.

Percussion instruments, including assorted percussive junk, are drummed in a high-energy performance of rhythmic power.

BOOKS AND WRITERS

The emphasis on formal education, especially by Scottish immigrants who settled in Dunedin in the late 1800s, resulted in the demand that education in the new country be "free, secular and compulsory". Today, the early value placed on book learning by those settlers, many of them barely literate, has resulted in a national literacy rate of around 99 per cent. New Zealand-based reading programmes and books for children are exported around the world.

In Wellington, annual literary festivals, writers and readers programmes, and readings by local and visiting authors, are able to attract sponsorship as well as big audiences. Internationally recognized writers from Wellington include UK-based poet Fleur Adcock and novelists Maurice Gee, Elizabeth Knox and Vincent O'Sullivan *(see p33)*.

Author Linda Burgess at her book launch

— **A scaffold "cube"** formed the setting for the band's players and instruments.

INTERNATIONAL ARTS FESTIVAL
Held biennially in Wellington in early autumn, the New Zealand International Arts Festival is the country's largest performing arts festival. The New Zealand percussion group, Strike, is among the local and international artistes who have performed at the festival.

The Royal New Zealand Ballet *conducts national and international tours from its base in the capital city. Stephen Wellington and Nadine Tyson are shown here in a pas de deux from* Raymonda.

The Westpac Stadium *is the leading venue for one of the mainstays of New Zealand culture – sport. Rugby, cricket and soccer, as well as concerts, are held in the 40,000-seat state-of-the-art stadium.*

Wellington ❶

Wellington's compact central business district lies between the city's foothills and its mountain-encircled harbour. Partly built on land developed during reclamation projects begun in the mid-19th century, the area today is the working environment of the country's politicians and the national government infrastructure. Foreign embassies, the Court of Appeal, National Archives, National Library, Museum of New Zealand Te Papa Tongarewa and the head offices of local and international businesses are among the institutions and organizations in its precincts. The city is known for its stylish shops, café culture, restaurants and galleries, with an atmosphere that is both stimulating and unhurried.

Statue in Plimmers Lane

Lunching outdoors at Astoria Café on Lambton Quay

🏛 Lambton Quay

Wellington's premier shopping street, Lambton Quay runs through the heart of New Zealand's political and commercial life. Its lively 1,100-m (3,600-ft) route is lined with arcades, plazas and elevated walkways. Most of Lambton Quay and its seaward parts are sited on reclaimed land. Plaques set at intervals along its footpaths identify the lay of the shoreline before the mid-1800s. While steep steps lead up to the slopes on the west, side streets on the east offer flat access to the redeveloped harbourfront *(see pp162–5)*.

🏛 Cathedral Church of St Paul

34 Mulgrave St. **Tel** (04) 473 6722. ◯ *daily.* ● *to tourists Good Fri, 25 Dec.* 🚫 🚹 📷 *donation welcomed.* www.oldsaintpauls.co.nz
Known as Old St Paul's, the Cathedral Church of St Paul is an outstanding example of an early English Gothic-style cathedral adapted to colonial conditions and materials. Consecrated in 1866, it is made entirely of native timber, including its nails.

🏛 Wellington Cathedral of St Paul

Cnr Molesworth and Hill Sts. **Tel** (04) 472 0286. ◯ *daily.* 🚫 📷 *behind church.* 🚹
After a building programme spread over several decades, including a number of exterior and interior design changes and reversals, the Wellington Cathedral of St Paul was finally completed in 1998. Standing in the parliamentary precinct opposite the Law Courts and the National Library, the Romanesque-style cathedral houses unique etched and stained-glass windows, memorials to historic events, and a 4,000-pipe organ. The Lady Chapel, formerly a parish church on the Kapiti coast north of Wellington, was relocated to the site in 1998 to complete the cathedral complex.

Stained-glass window

🏛 Parliament Buildings

Molesworth St. **Tel** (04) 471 9503. ◯ *daily.* ● *1 & 2 Jan, 6 Feb, Good Fri, 25 & 26 Dec.* 🚫 🚹 📷 🚹 www.parliament.govt.nz
New Zealand's Parliament is made up of three main buildings: the Edwardian Neo-Classical style Parliament Building opened in 1922; the Parliamentary Library, completed in 1899; and the Beehive, occupied since 1979. Free guided tours take in all three buildings. They stand next to each other on the site that has housed the country's parliament since 1865, 400 m (1,300 ft) away from the earthquake fault line which runs through Wellington. Historic trees have been retained in the grounds, which also feature a rose garden.

Bolton Memorial
Lady Norwood Rose Garden
Begonia House
⑦ Wellington Botanic Gardens
Carter Observatory
Cable Car Museum
Kelburn Park
⑧ Victoria University

GLENMORE STREET
TIN
UPLAND RD
RAWHITI TERR
CENTRAL TERR
S. GLASGOW ST
KELBURN PARADE
SALAMANCA ROAD

Art in the Galleria of the Parliament Buildings

0 metres	500
0 yards	500

KEY

▢ Street-by-Street: The Harbourfront *pp162–3*

Key to Symbols *see back flap*

Old Government Buildings

VISITORS' CHECKLIST

Road map D5. 👥 494,000.
✈ 8 km (5 miles) S of city.
🚌 Bunny St (btw Featherston St
& Waterloo Quay). 🚉 🚆
Platform 9, Wellington Railway
Station, Waterloo Quay.
⚓ Aotea Quay Terminal.
ℹ Cnr of Wakefield and Victoria
sts, (04) 802 4860.
🎭 New Zealand International
Arts Festival (Feb–Mar).
www.wellingtonnz.com

🏛 Old Government Buildings

15 Lambton Quay. **Tel** (04) 472 7356.
⭘ daily. ⬤ 1 & 2 Jan, Easter Sun,
25 Apr, 25 & 26 Dec. 🚻 ▮ 🍴
🖥 📷

Across the street from the
Parliament Buildings are the
Old Government Buildings.
The largest wooden building
in the southern hemisphere,
and one of the largest such
buildings in the world, they
were built in the 1870s in a
style imitating stone. Used
in the early 20th century by
New Zealand's parliamentary
cabinet and then by various
government departments until
1990, the restored buildings
are now filled with students
of Victoria University's Law
School. The original cabinet
room on the first floor and
historic displays on the ground
floor are open to the public.

**Items for sale in the Katherine
Mansfield Birthplace**

🏛 Katherine Mansfield Birthplace

25 Tinakori Rd. **Tel** (04) 473 7268.
⭘ Tue–Sun. ⬤ Good Fri, 25 Dec.
🎫 🚫 📷 by arrangement. 📷
This 1888 villa is the birthplace and childhood home of
Katherine Mansfield (see p33),
possibly the country's most
famous author. It contains
period photographs, excerpts
from Mansfield's writing, and
antique furniture.

WELLINGTON CITY CENTRE

Exploring Wellington

Water lilies in Botanic Garden

A vibrant, inner-city area bordered to the north by a green belt, central Wellington encompasses late Victorian mansions, student flats, tiny former workers' cottages, the Prime Minister's residence, an historic cemetery and the main motorway in and out of the city.

At the end of the 19th century, as the number of overseas settlers increased, land near the foreshore became scarce, and steeper, less accessible land above the city was utilized for housing. Today, a walk around the suburb of Thorndon to higher points shows how a community has spread onwards and up-wards from its original concentration in the port area.

Cable car climbing to the top of the Botanic Garden

🚠 Wellington Cable Car
Cable Car Lane, 280 Lambton Quay. **Tel** (04) 472 2199.
Museum ⬜ daily. ⚫ 25 Dec. 🈂
www.wellingtoncablecar.co.nz
Opened in 1902 to link the hill suburbs with the city, the cable cars used on the route have been electrically powered since 1933. Stops on the way include Victoria University, with access to the Botanic Garden and Carter Observatory at the top. The Kelburn terminus has fine views over the city and harbour.

🌺 Wellington Botanic Garden
Tinakori Rd. **Tel** (04) 499 1400.
⬜ daily. 🈂 ▪ 🈂
www.wellington.govt.nz
Established in 1868, the garden is a mix of protected native forest, conifer plantings and plant collections. A major seasonal bedding programme includes a massed display of 30,000 tulips in spring and early summer. The Lady Norwood Rose Garden has 106 formal beds, including recent introductions and old favourites. The Begonia House features tropical and temperate plants, a lily pond, seasonal displays of orchids, and a collection of epiphytic and carnivorous plants. The garden's information hub, the Treehouse Visitor Centre, can be accessed via a tower lift. The more hardy can get to the centre via a steep path.

The **Carter Observatory**, New Zealand's national observatory, stands in the Botanic Garden complex near the terminus of the cable car. Astronomical displays, audio-visual shows and a planetarium are special features.

🏛 Carter Observatory
40 Salamanca Rd, Kelburn.
Tel (04) 472 8167. ⬜ daily. 🈂
www.carterobservatory.co.nz

The ivy-covered Hunter Building at Victoria University

🎓 Victoria University
Kelburn Parade. **Tel** (04) 472 1000.
With 21,000 students enrolled in over 50 departments and schools, Victoria University is the fourth largest of New Zealand's eight universities. Opened in 1897, Victoria University's main campus has occupied its Kelburn site overlooking downtown Wellington since 1904. The Faculties of Law and Commerce, as well as the School of Architecture and Design, are among the campuses located in the city.

Lady Norwood Rose Garden in the Wellington Botanic Garden

Suburban Hillside Villas

Often appearing to cling precariously to the sides of hills, accessible only by cable car or long flights of steep steps, hillside villas are a striking feature of Wellington's older city suburbs such as Oriental Bay, Mount Victoria, Thorndon and Kelburn. These ubiquitous New Zealand homes evolved during the late 19th and early 20th centuries from simple, flat-fronted single-storey colonial cottages with

Painted window surrounds

verandahs running across the front, to two-storey houses with projecting faceted bay windows. The villas were traditionally made of timber from New Zealand's kauri forests, roofed with corrugated iron, and decorated with mass-produced components ordered from catalogues. Other features included the use of stained glass, large double-hung sash windows and balustraded porches or verandahs.

Wooden villas on the hillside overlooking Oriental Bay

HARBOURFRONT SUBURBS

Wellington's early settlers were forced by a shortage of flat land to build on the hills bordering the harbour. Many original villas, as well as those restored and adapted as family homes, can be seen during a walk or drive through Wellington's harbourfront suburbs.

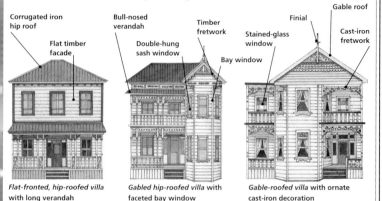

Corrugated iron hip roof

Flat timber facade

Bull-nosed verandah

Double-hung sash window

Timber fretwork

Stained-glass window

Bay window

Finial

Gable roof

Cast-iron fretwork

Flat-fronted, hip-roofed villa with long verandah

Gabled hip-roofed villa with faceted bay window

Gable-roofed villa with ornate cast-iron decoration

Late 19th-century villas *constructed for middle-income families usually had a living area (the "parlour"), three or four bedrooms and a central hallway, with a single bathroom and kitchen area to the rear. The toilet (often referred to as the "long drop") and laundry ("wash house") facilities were usually located at the back of the house.*

Parlour at the 1888 villa in Thorndon where Katherine Mansfield was born (see p159)

Street-by-Street: The Harbourfront

Silver fern globe, Civic Square

The area between Lambton Harbour and Clyde Quay Wharf on Wellington's harbourfront stands entirely on reclaimed land. It covers a site once central to Wellington's waterfront industry, and can be covered on foot within an hour. Echoes of the commercial sailing ships and liners that once dominated the area remain in the Museum of Wellington. In spring and summer, dragon boat competitions are held opposite the Museum of New Zealand Te Papa Tongarewa. The Civic Square, with its open spaces and nearby public buildings, such as the Town Hall, is a favourite meeting place for Wellingtonians and visitors alike.

Courtenay Place
Lined with bars, clubs, restaurants and theatres, Courtenay Place provides a taste of the city's nightlife (see p165).

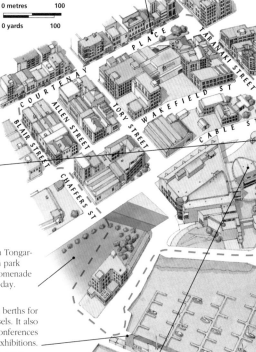

0 metres 100
0 yards 100

Circa Theatre
This refurbished building is one of the focal points of the city's contemporary theatre scene (see p156).

Waitangi Park, opposite Te Papa Tongarewa, is an award-winning urban park with a beach and boardwalk promenade - a popular spot on a summer's day.

The Overseas Terminal provides berths for yachts and other small vessels. It also houses facilities for conferences and exhibitions.

STAR SIGHTS

★ Museum of New Zealand Te Papa Tongarewa

★ Museum of Wellington

★ **Museum of New Zealand Te Papa Tongarewa**
The museum offers visitors interactive experiences of New Zealand's Maori heritage, national history and natural environment as well as art treasures (see pp166–7).

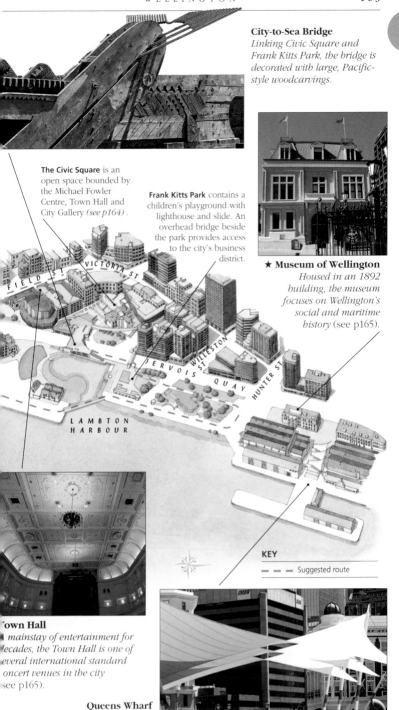

City-to-Sea Bridge
Linking Civic Square and Frank Kitts Park, the bridge is decorated with large, Pacific-style woodcarvings.

The Civic Square is an open space bounded by the Michael Fowler Centre, Town Hall and City Gallery *(see p164)* .

Frank Kitts Park contains a children's playground with lighthouse and slide. An overhead bridge beside the park provides access to the city's business district.

★ **Museum of Wellington**
Housed in an 1892 building, the museum focuses on Wellington's social and maritime history (see p165).

FIELD ST

VICTORIA ST

JERVOIS QUAY

WILLESTON ST

HUNTER ST

LAMBTON HARBOUR

KEY

- - - Suggested route

Town Hall
A mainstay of entertainment for decades, the Town Hall is one of several international standard concert venues in the city (see p165).

Queens Wharf
The complex of shops, cafés, restaurants and bars on Queens Wharf is a popular entertainment hub for nearby office workers.

The Harbourfront

Metal nikau palm

The Harbourfront is dominated by the City-to-Sea bridge, a pedestrian-only right of way above one of Wellington's main roads. Bordered on one side by Wellington's wharves and on the other by office blocks, the bridge leads from steps within the Civic Square complex to Frank Kitts Park and the waterfront, a lagoon and further on to the Museum of New Zealand Te Papa Tongarewa (*see pp166–7*). The bridge is a public art space in its own right, featuring works by leading New Zealand sculptors.

Contemporary exhibit at the City Gallery

♣ Civic Square

Wakefield St. **Tel** *(04) 802 4860.* ◻ *daily.* ♿ **www**.wellingtonnz.com
The heart of the city's cultural scene, this extensive paved, plaza-style courtyard was opened in the early 1990s, making use of an area that was previously a busy street. The pink and beige square is an open space that features various sculptures and provides a link to a number of institutions bordering it. These include the Public Library, Visitor Information Centre, City Council Buildings, City Gallery and the capital's main concert venues, the Town Hall and Michael Fowler Centre.

The square harkens back to its previous role as a thoroughfare. It brings together Wellington's central business district with the city's cultural and social side: the Museum of New Zealand Te Papa Tongarewa, the Opera House, theatres, cinemas and shops, as well as the bars and restaurants of the city's main night-time entertainment area, Courtenay Place. The square has become a well-used and central meeting place for Wellingtonians. Visitors to the square will often find themselves among street theatre performers and at outdoor concerts, exhibitions and rallies of all kinds.

🏛 City Gallery

Civic Square. **Tel** *(04) 801 3021.* ◻ *10am–5pm daily.* ● *25 Dec.* 📷 *international exhibitions.* ♿ ▢ **www**.citygallery.org.nz
Housed in a striking Art Deco building fitted with original kauri doors, marble finishes, handrails and steel windows, the building that for decades served as the city's Public Library is now home to the country's leading, and often most controversial, art gallery.

Primarily an exhibition space, with no permanent collection of its own, the gallery has nonetheless developed a distinctive character, specializing in bringing to Wellington the best contemporary art and design shows from within New Zealand and around the world. Exhibitions held at the gallery have covered a diverse range of media and subjects, including painting, sculpture, film and video, industrial and graphic design and architecture.

The building was redeveloped and expanded in 2009, with the addition of an auditorium, a gallery of Maori and Pacific art, and an enlarged Michael Hirschfield Gallery dedicated to exhibiting works by Wellington artists.

Neil Dawson's ferns sculpture suspended in the Civic Square

Michael Fowler Centre

Wakefield St. **Tel** (04) 801 4231.
daily. for concerts.
by arrangement.

Designed by Christchurch's
Sir Miles Warren and named
after a former mayor and
prominent architect, the
semicircular complex is internationally renowned for its
ability to distribute sound
throughout its 2,550-plus
seat concert chamber. Rock
concerts, conventions and
even political rallies are
staged in what has become
the city's premier concert hall.
Many events associated with
the increasingly popular
biennial New Zealand International Arts Festival *(see
pp42, 156–7)*, which
attracts thousands of local
and overseas visitors to
Wellington, are held here.

The Victorian-tiled lobby of the
Town Hall

Town Hall

Wakefield St. **Tel** (04) 801 4231.
daily. for concerts.
by arrangement.

Restoration of the Town Hall,
a sedate 1904 Edwardian
brick building with a Roman-
style portico, has returned
the hall to much of its former
glory. Restoration work
included seismic strengthen-
ing of the building, restoring
the floor's Victorian tiles,
uncovering wrought-iron
balustrades, manufacturing
lights and fittings from original samples, and repairing
the auditorium's pressed zinc
ceiling. The hall's magnificent
main staircase is now a major
attraction. The 2,000-seat
"shoe box" auditorium is regarded as one of the world's
leading venues for the performance of classical music.

Courtenay Place, a prime night-time entertainment area

Courtenay Place

Lined with a concentrated
strip of sophisticated nightclubs, trendy cafés and
restaurants, and professional
theatres, Courtenay Place and
the streets leading from it
form the night-time entertainment heart of the city.

With nearly every cuisine
style and price range available, from budget eating
outlets to award-winning
restaurants, Courtenay Place
is the venue to meet visitors,
mix with locals, and eat
and dance the night away.
Live music inside cafés and
bars is matched by a lively
street scene, where crowds
thread their way through
buskers and performers that
add to the area's relaxed
atmosphere.

Museum of Wellington

Queens Wharf. **Tel** (04) 472 8904.
10am–5pm daily. 25 Dec.
www.museumof
wellington.co.nz

Housed in the former
customs house which
was constructed in 1892,
the Museum of
Wellington gives an
insight into the capital's
rich cultural and social
history. The museum
uses model ships,
ships' instruments,
relics from wrecks,
maritime paintings, old
maps and sea journals,
as well as holographic
re-creations and videos
to tell the story of
Wellington in the
context of its harbour

and surrounding coast. One of
the most interesting exhibits
in the museum's collection of
ship models is the inter-island
ferry, the *Wahine*. This sank
off the Wellington suburb of
Seatoun in April 1968 during
a storm. A photograph exhibit
documents the tragedy. The
Plimmer's Ark Gallery displays
part of the excavated remains
of the ship *Inconstant* which
was built in 1848.

The museum also features a
12-minute show on Maori
creation legends and looks at
early Maori and European
settlement. A 20th century
gallery explores how the city
has changed in the last 100
years. There is also an
education room for children.

Façade of the Museum of Wellington
on the city's waterfront

Museum of New Zealand Te Papa Tongarewa

Museum logo

With exhibition space equivalent to three football fields, the Museum of New Zealand Te Papa Tongarewa ("Our Place") is one of the largest museums in the world. Committed to telling the stories of all cultures in New Zealand, home to the National Art Collection, and with ample gallery space for touring international exhibitions, the museum opened on its waterfront site in 1998. Te Papa's collections include a number of significant Maori works of art and treasures, as well as a unique 21st-century carved meeting house.

Mountains to Sea
The amazing variety of New Zealand's animals and plants, from kiwis to kauris are revealed in exhibits featuring the natural world

"Awesome Forces" help visitors experience the powerful forces shaping the country's landscape.

Earthquake House
In this simulation of the 1987 Edgecumbe earthquake, you can hear the roar of the earthquake and feel it shake the building.

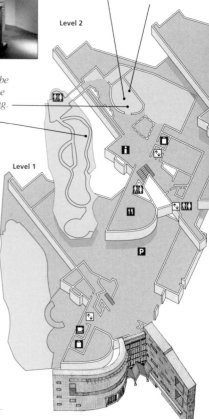

Level 2

Level 1

Bush City
Visitors step into the open air to experience native bush, wetlands, a volcanic landscape, a waterfall and a lagoon right in the centre of the city. They can also explore a glowworm cave.

STAR EXHIBITS

★ Mākōtukutuku
   Wharepuni

★ The Marae

VISITORS' CHECKLIST

Cable St. **Tel** (04) 381 7000.
🕐 10am–6pm daily (10am–9pm
Thu). 🏛 some temporary
exhibitions. ♿ 🎥 🍴 🛍 🎁
www.tepapa.govt.nz

★ Mākōtukutuku Wharepuni
*Go back 600 years on entering
this* wharepuni *(sleeping
house) reconstructed using
traditional methods and tools.*

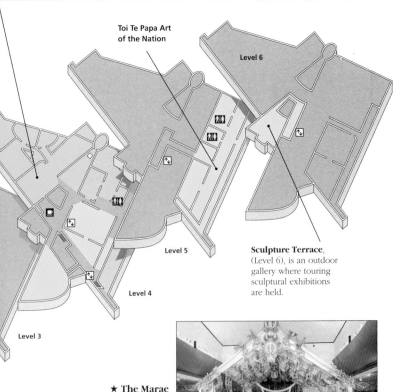

Toi Te Papa Art
of the Nation

Level 6

Level 5

Level 4

Level 3

Sculpture Terrace,
(Level 6), is an outdoor
gallery where touring
sculptural exhibitions
are held.

★ The Marae
*The contemporary meeting house is the
focal point of a Maori* marae*. Named Te
Hono ki Hawaiki ("the link back to
Hawaiki"), Te Papa's* marae *recalls the
ancestral land of Maori.*

KEY TO FLOORPLAN

- ☐ Art
- ☐ History
- ☐ Maori
- ☐ Nature

GALLERY GUIDE
*The first of the high-tech interactive exhibitions begins on
Level 2, which also provides access to Bush City. Level 3
features* Blood, Earth, Fire*, telling of the transformation of
New Zealand since human impact. Maori, Pacific Island
and European cultural exhibits are concentrated on Level 4.
Level 5 contains* Toi Te Papa Art of the Nation *as well as the
museum's library, reading room and research facilities. The
Sculpture Terrace and a small gallery are on Level 6. Works
from the National Art Collection are spread throughout
the museum.*

Marine Drive Tour ❷

Hugging the coastline from Oriental Bay, south-east of the city centre on the inner harbour, to Owhiro Bay on the outer shoreline facing Cook Strait, this route is one of New Zealand's great coastal drives. It is both picturesque on cloudless days and awe-inspiring when Wellington's famous southerly gales whip up pounding waves. The route takes visitors past numerous small bays and sheltered, sandy beaches. It also passes through several suburbs where wooden villas *(see p161)* perch on what seem precarious sites high above the road, and around steep, uninhabited hillsides covered with trees that come down to the water's edge.

Owhiro Bay ⑩
Tourers can turn right at this bay and return to the city via Happy Valley Road or continue onto the 4-km (2.5-mile) Red Rocks Coastal Walk, where a colony of 80–150 male seals takes up residence each year.

Island Bay ⑨
Descendants of Italian immigrants, who settled here in the early 20th century, are among those seen fishing in Cook Strait and beyond.

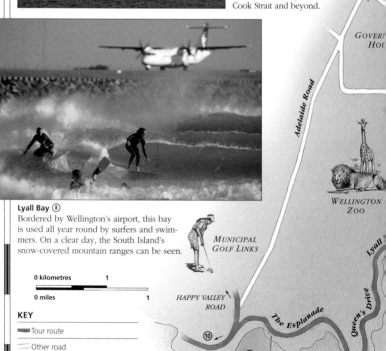

Lyall Bay ⑧
Bordered by Wellington's airport, this bay is used all year round by surfers and swimmers. On a clear day, the South Island's snow-covered mountain ranges can be seen.

CITY CENTRE

Cambridge

GOVERNMENT HOUSE

Adelaide Road

WELLINGTON ZOO

Lyall

MUNICIPAL GOLF LINKS

HAPPY VALLEY ROAD

The Esplanade

Queen's Drive

0 kilometres   1
0 miles   1

KEY

▬▬ Tour route
══ Other road
⁂ Viewpoint

Oriental Bay ①
This is an area of cafés and fashionable restaurants and a favourite spot for joggers and swimmers. Across from the sandy beach, stately Victorian villas share the hillside with modern apartment blocks.

TIPS FOR DRIVERS

Length: *30 km (19 miles).*
Stopping-off points:
There are glorious views at all points along the route. Several parking areas allow visitors to leave their cars and stroll along the bays. Eating places include Scorch-O-Rama at Scorching Bay, whose staff have permission to serve customers seated across the road on the waterfront.

Mahanga Bay ③
One of the smallest and most sheltered bays along the route, Mahanga Bay is fringed with pine trees.

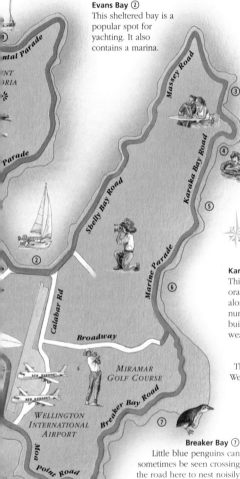

Evans Bay ②
This sheltered bay is a popular spot for yachting. It also contains a marina.

Scorching Bay ④
Popular with swimmers, this beach allows good views towards Somes and Ward islands and Cook Strait. The seaside suburb of Eastbourne is opposite.

Karaka Bay ⑤
This bay is named after the native orange-berried karaka trees found along its edge. It has a pier and a number of wooden summer houses built in the early 20th century by wealthy people from out of town.

Worser Bay ⑥
The eastern suburbs are the home of Wellington's thriving international film industry *(see p156)*.

Breaker Bay ⑦
Little blue penguins can sometimes be seen crossing the road here to nest noisily under nearby houses.

SLOW DOWN!
PENGUINS CROSSING
KIA TUPATO!
HE KORORĀ... WHITI ANA

Old trams at the Tram Museum, Paekakariki

Paekakariki ❸

Road map E4. 🏃 *1,700.* 🚉 🚌
🚌 ℹ *Coastlands, Paraparaumu,*
(04) 298 8195. **www**.kapiti.org.nz

Situated on the Kapiti
Coast, 40 minutes' drive
north of Wellington on
State Highway 1,
Paekakariki is the first
of four townships
spaced evenly along
40 km (25 miles) of
sweeping, sandy
coastline known as
the "nature coast". A
main attraction at
Paekakariki is Queen
Elizabeth Park, which
encompasses a stunning coastline, sand dunes, streams,
peat swamps and bush walks.
A tram ride from MacKays
Crossing north of Paekakariki
takes visitors through the 6.4-
sq km (2.5-sq mile) park.

At the **Wellington Tramway
Museum** in the park, visitors
can view displays of some of
the forerunners of the trolley
buses that still run on
Wellington's streets, and see
trams being refurbished.

🏛 **Wellington Tramway
Museum**
Queen Elizabeth Park. **Tel** *(04) 292
8361.* ◯ *summer: daily; winter: Sat
& Sun.* ◯ *25 Dec.* 🖼 ♿

Paraparaumu ❹

Road map E4. 🏃 *12,000.* 🚉
🚉 🚌 🚌 ℹ *Coastlands,*
(04) 298 8195.

The main centre on the
Kapiti Coast, Paraparaumu
has shorefront shops, cafés
and restaurants. It also has a
developed beach, with a park

and playgrounds. The town is
the departure point for boat
trips to Kapiti Island.

The area's major attraction
is the **Southward Car Museum**, which holds the largest
collection of vintage and
veteran vehicles in the
southern hemisphere.
The collection of bicycles
includes an 1863 bone
shaker. Marlene
Dietrich's limousine
is one of more than
250 classic and quirky
vehicles dating
from 1895. Racing
boats, home-made
vehicles, motor
cycles, early motoring
curios and traction engines
are also housed on the site. A
highlight is a 1950 Cadillac
Gangster Special, once owned

**Boy with calf
at Lindale**

by an employee of Al Capone
and Lucky Luciano. It boasts a
bomb-proof floor, armour-
plated doors, bulletproof
windows, and a hinged
windscreen to enable firing
from inside.

The **Lindale Tourist and
Agricultural Centre**, set
around a New Zealand farm,
is a good place to bring
children. The centre offers
sheep shearing demonstra-
tions as well as hands-on
opportunities to milk a cow,
bottle-feed lambs and goats,
play with chickens and baby
deer, and observe exotic
species like llama and emu.
There are farm walks and a
golf driving range for the
more active.

A shop showcasing the
award-winning gourmet
Kapiti Cheese and Kapiti Ice
Cream, is located on the site,
along with galleries, shops
and eating places.

🏛 **Southward Car Museum**
Otaihanga Rd, Paraparaumu. **Tel**
(04) 297 1221. ◯ *daily.* ◯ *Good
Fri, 25 Apr, 25 Dec.* 🖼 ♿ 🚻 🍴
🚻 ☕ **www**.southward.org.nz

🎿 **Lindale Tourist and
Agricultural Centre**
State Hwy 1, Paraparaumu. **Tel** *(04)
297 0916.* ◯ *daily.* ◯ *Good Fri, 25
Dec.* 🖼 ♿ 🚻 🍴 🚻 **www.**
lindale.co.nz

Vintage cars at the Southward Car Museum

For hotels and restaurants in this region see pp307–10 and pp334–6

Waikanae ❺

Road map E4. 🏃 8,600. 🚉 ✈
🚌 🛈 *Coastland, Paraparaumu, (04)
298 8195.* **www**.naturecoast.co.nz

Nestled between the foot-
hills of the Tararua Range
and the Kapiti Coast, Waikanae
is primarily a retirement centre,
known for its craft shops and
magnificent gardens. Burnard
Gardens, recognized as one of
New Zealand's most formally
designed English-style gardens,
is located here and viewings
can be arranged.

The **Waikanae Estuary
Scientific Reserve** is home to
over 63 species of birds
(though some of these are
migratory and so will not be
there all year), such as shags,
dabchicks, Caspian terns,
royal spoonbills and pukeko.
Fires, hunting and mountain
and trail biking are forbidden.

**View of Kapiti Island from
the mainland**

Kapiti Island Nature Reserve ❻

Road map E4. 🚌 *Paraparaumu.*
🛈 *Department of Conservation, 18–
32 Manners St, Wellington, (04) 471
0720.*

Kapiti Island, lying about 6 km
(4 miles) from the mainland,
dominates the Kapiti Coast.
The 10-km (6-mile) long
island has been a protected
wildlife reserve since 1897.
Access to the island is very
limited although a permit to
visit by charter boat can be
obtained from the Department
of Conservation in Wellington.
All parties are met by the
resident ranger. Trips around
the island, and diving or
fishing in the surrounding
waters can be done at any
time. Making their home on
the island are birds rare or

absent from the mainland,
such as saddlebacks and
takahe. Less rare, but twice
as cheeky, are the wekas,
which are likely to steal
anything unattended.

Otaki ❼

Road map E4. 🏃 7,600. 🚉 ✈ 🚌
🛈 *State Hwy 1, (06) 364 7620.*

Before the European settlers'
arrival in 1840, Otaki was
heavily populated by Maori.
It had the finest Maori church,
Rangiatea Church, in New
Zealand. Built in 1851, it was
destroyed by fire in 1995.
Construction of a replica of
the church on the site began
in 1998, and it opened in 2003.

Environs
Just south of Otaki is the **Hyde
Park Museum**. The museum
has Maori artifacts from pre-
European days, colonial
memorabilia and exhibits from
present-day New Zealand.
Included are a Royal Room
with displays from the 1953
visit of Queen Elizabeth and
Prince Phillip, old farm
machinery and a grocery
shop with over 3,000 items
marked at 1937 prices.

South of the town, the 19-
km (12-mile) Gorge Road
leads to Otaki Forks and the
Tararua Forest Park. Along the
way are walking tracks.

**Entrance to the Hyde Park Museum,
Otaki**

🏛 **Hyde Park Museum**
State Hwy 1, Te Horo. **Tel** (04)
298 4515. 🕐 *Tue–Sun.* 📷
donation. ♿

Levin ❽

Road map E4. 🏃 15,400.
🚉 ✈ 🚌

Levin sits on a fertile plain
that is one of the largest
vegetable-producing areas in
the country. Its main street,
lined with shops that service
its farming hinterland, epito-
mizes much of traditional
small town New Zealand.
Owner-operated outlets on
the outskirts of the town
offer "pick-your-own" freshly
grown produce direct from
the fields and orchards.

TE RAUPARAHA

Kapiti Island was once the base of Te
Rauparaha (1768–1849), chief of the Ngati
Toa tribe and one of the greatest Maori
generals of his era. After years of warfare
in the Waikato and Taranaki areas, he
moved to Kapiti Island in the 1820s,
dominating the southwestern part of the
North Island and the north of the South
Island until the 1840s. He is credited with
composing the well-known *haka* (war
chant) often performed by the All Blacks
before international rugby matches.

**Watercolour (1840)
by Isaac Coates**

Kamate. Kamate.
Ka Ora. Ka Ora.
Tenei te tangata
  puhuruhuru
Nana nei i tiki mai
I whakawhiti te ra.
Upane. Upane.
Whiti te ra.

It is death. It is death.
It is life. It is life.
This is the hairy person
Who caused the sun to
  shine.
Abreast. Keep abreast.
The rank. Hold fast.
Into the sun that shines.

Hay rolled into bales, ready for storing, on a farm near Martinborough

Featherston ⑨

Road map E4. 🏔 2,600. 🚌 🚆 🚐
ℹ️ Old Courthouse, Main St, (06)
308 8051, 10am–1pm. **www**.
wairarapanz.com

Situated at the foot of the
Rimutaka Range, Featherston
is the southern gateway to the
Wairarapa area for those
arriving from the Wellington
side of the divide. Known for
its antique shops and colonial
buildings, it also houses
several museums, including
the **Fell Engine Museum**, home
to the world's only surviving
Fell engine. Running on three
rails, these ingenious
locomotives used to climb up
and over the Rimutaka Range
in the district's early days.

🏛 **Fell Engine Museum**
Cnr Fitzherbert and Lyon sts. **Tel** (06)
308 9379. ◯ daily. ⬤ 25 & 26
Dec. 🈂️ 🚻 ♿

Environs
On the right side of the road
from Wellington, before
reaching Featherston, a
signpost points the way to a
lookout. This is the best spot
for visitors to get splendid
views across **Lake Wairarapa**
to the ranges of Haurangi
(Aorangi) Forest Park and
Palliser Bay. The lake is home
to internationally recognized
wetlands that are the third
largest in New Zealand. Both
native and migratory breeds
of bird gather at the lake.
   Southeast of the lake is **Cape
Palliser** where, next to a public
road, visitors can find one of

the country's largest breeding
colonies for the New Zealand
fur seal, one of nine fur seal
species found worldwide.
Seals can be seen throughout
the year, with breeding from
November to January.
   Another spectacular sight
in the area is the **Putangirua
Pinnacles**, formed in the past
120,000 years by heavy rain
eroding an ancient gravel
deposit. Some of the pinnacles
may be 1,000 years old.

Martinborough ⑩

Road map E5. 🏔 1,500. ℹ️ Kitchener St, (06) 306 9043. 🍞 Toast
Martinborough (Nov), Martinborough
Country Fair (Feb & Mar).
www.wairarapanz.com

Established in 1881 by Irish
immigrant John Martin,
Martinborough was once
reliant for its prosperity on

the surrounding farming
community. Since the late
1970s, the town has become
internationally known for
its grape growing and wine
making (see pp36–7). It is now
a fashionable weekend
destination for wine lovers
and those attracted by its
cafés, bars, restaurants and
thriving arts community. Most
of the area's 20 boutique
wineries are within walking
distance of Martinborough's
picturesque town square.

Environs
New Zealand's first commercial
wind farm, **Hau Nui Wind Farm**,
lies 21 km (13 miles) southeast
of Martinborough. Operated by
Wairarapa Electricity, the farm's
turbines are a surreal sight
ranged along a 540-m (1,770-ft)
ridge. Although on private
land, they can be seen from a
public viewing area.

Visitors enjoying the wine at the Grapevine in Martinborough

For hotels and restaurants in this region see pp307–10 and pp334–6

Masterton ⓫

Road map E4. 🏘 *22,800.* 🚃 🚌
🚌 ℹ *316 Queen St, (06) 370 0900.*
🎪 *Golden Shears (Mar).*
www.wairarapanz.com

Ninety minutes' drive from both Wellington and Palmerston North, Masterton is Wairarapa's largest town. It hosts a number of events during the summer, including an annual hot-air balloon fiesta, a biennial air show and also a traditional shearing competition known as the Golden Shears which is held every year.

Masterton is home to the **Shear Discovery Centre**, a museum dedicated to New Zealand's shearing heritage and also a recreation centre. The town also has the region's art and history musem, **Aratoi**, and a Farmers' Market on Saturday mornings. **Queen Elizabeth Park** has playgrounds, a boating lake, golf course and many other facilities.

🏛 **Shear Discovery Centre**
12 Dixon St. **Tel** *(06) 378 8008.* ◯
9am–5pm daily. ● *Anzac Day,
Good Friday, 25 Dec.* 📷 ♿ ▮

Environs

Masterton is close to the beach resorts of **Castlepoint** and **Riversdale**, which are popular for surfing, fishing and walking. State Highway 2 runs through the village of **Greytown**. Settled in 1854, it

Agricultural implements at the Cobblestone Museum

is the oldest town in Wairarapa and has a restored Victorian main street. It is home to the **Cobblestone Museum**. Located on the site of coach stables built in 1856 for the Wellington mail service, the museum houses colonial buildings, vehicles, agricultural equipment and a working saddlery. It has relocated and restored buildings, complete with memorabilia of the days of the early settlers.

The **Tararua Forest Park**, located within the rugged Tararua Range, can be accessed at Holdsworth, 15 km (9 miles) from State Highway 2, via Norfolk Road just south of

Masterton. The park has bush walks ranging from easy to difficult, while Grassy flats beside the Atiwhakatu Stream are ideal for picnics and barbecues.

🏛 **Cobblestone Museum**
169 Main St, Greytown. **Tel** *(06) 304 9687.* ◯ *daily.* 📷 ♿ ▮

Pukaha Mount Bruce National Wildlife Centre ⓬

Road map E4. **Tel** *(06) 375 8004.*
◯ *9am–4:30pm daily.* ● *25 Dec.*
📷 ♿ ▯ ▮ **www**.mtbruce.org.nz

Administered by the Department of Conservation, this centre, located 30 km (19 miles) north of Masterton, gives visitors the chance to get close to and learn about some of New Zealand's most threatened native birds.

Priority species, including the stitchbird, kokako and takahe, live in uncrowded aviaries. Bush walks to view ancient plant species lead through a last remnant of the forest once known as "Forty Mile Bush", containing native rimu, rata, kamahi, nocturnal kiwi and tuatara, while eels often sun themselves on the mud near the centre's river bridge.

Kokako at Mount Bruce

GOLDEN SHEARS COMPETITION

One of the biggest sheep shearing competitions in the world, the Golden Shears competition is held in Masterton from the Thursday to the first Saturday of March each year. Initiated by the Wairarapa District Young Farmers Club, the competition was originally envisaged to form part of the local Agricultural and Pastoral Show. Since the inaugural competition in 1961, the Golden Shears has become a national institution, attracting hundreds of competitors from around the world and thousands of observers. The competition reached its peak during the 1960s and 1970s when seats to the event were sold out 12 months in advance. Although several smaller shearing competitions are now held around the country, the Golden Shears remains the pre-eminent show in New Zealand. Sheep shearing has also entered the world of professionalism: prize money has risen over the years, corporate sponsorship has become the norm, and many shearers adopt fitness and training programmes not dreamed of in the early days of the event.

Sheep shearer in competition

Palmerston North ⓭

Institute of Rugby sign

From the mid-1960s, pastoral farming has been the stimulus for the development of Palmerston North, Manawatu's largest town. Lying in the centre of a broad, fertile coastal plain stretching from the Tasman Sea across to the Tararua and Ruahine ranges, the city is a major crossroad for the southern part of the North Island, with three main roads converging near it. New Zealand's largest university, Massey University, and several colleges and research institutes are based here, giving Palmerston North a pleasant university town atmosphere.

1926 poster in the New Zealand Rugby Museum

♣ The Square
ℹ (06) 350 1922.

Laid out in 1866, this tranquil, leafy garden zone at the heart of the city provides welcome relief to the busy commercial centre. Originally bisected by New Zealand's main trunk railway, The Square's clipped lawns, flower beds, trees and shrubs, ornamental ponds and fountains, war memorial and chiming clock tower attract large numbers of visitors all year round. The shops and buildings surrounding The Square reflect the diversity of styles in New Zealand's architectural history.

🏛 Te Manawa Art Gallery
326 Main St. **Tel** (06) 355 5000.
◐ daily. ● 25 Dec.
www.temanawa.co.nz

First opened in 1959 as the Palmerston North Art Gallery, the gallery was renamed and rehoused in a modern, spacious building near The

Square in 1977. Visitors are greeted at the entrance by local artist Paul Dibble's striking sculpture, *Pacific Monarch*, reputedly the largest bronze work cast in New Zealand.

The gallery's strength lies in its collection of recent art, particularly that from the 1970s, but it also houses a permanent collection of paintings, sculpture, prints, drawings, photographs and ceramics by prominent New Zealand artists. There is a regularly changing programme of exhibitions of New Zealand and international art and crafts. The gallery is part of the Te Manawa complex, which also includes a museum and science centre.

🏛 New Zealand Rugby Museum
87 Cuba St. **Tel** (06) 358 6947.
◐ 10am–4pm Mon–Sat, 1:30–4pm Sun. ● 25 Dec. 🦽 📷 📞 phone to book. www.rugbymuseum.co.nz

A turnstile previously installed at the gates of Wellington's famous Athletic Park allows visitors into the New Zealand Rugby Museum, located a few blocks from The Square. Founded in 1968, the museum contains exhibits and memorabilia relating to the history of rugby in New Zealand from the first game played in the country, at Nelson in 1870, to the present. There are also exhibits from other countries where rugby is played. The paraphernalia on

display includes caps, jerseys, trophies, badges, autographed balls, ties, posters and photographs. Famous international games can be watched on video. Also on display is a broken protestor's shield, a legacy of the bitter 1981 tour to New Zealand by the South African Springbok rugby team. The tour divided the country and caused demonstrations and bloody protests.

🏫 Massey University
Tennant Drive. **Tel** (06) 356 9099.
🦽 www.massey.ac.nz

Five km (3 miles) south of the city, the eclectic mixture of old homesteads and modern buildings that make up Massey University are set in superb countryside. On the Massey History Walk, part of the City Heritage Trail, visitors can look at these and some of the city's older sites and buildings. The world's first university-based Institute of Rugby and New Zealand's only university aviation school are both located here.

Environs
North of the city, the Manawatu River runs through the imposing **Manawatu Gorge**. The river defies geographical logic by rising on the eastern slopes of the Tararua Range, then turning back on itself to reach the Tasman Sea to the west. The gorge is popular with jet-boaters and kayakers.

There are a number of beautiful gardens around the city. One, the Cross Hill Gardens, a 45-minute drive north, has one of New Zealand's largest and most varied collections of rhododendrons.

Sculpture by Paul Dibble in front of Te Manawa Art Gallery

For hotels and restaurants in this region see pp307–310 and pp334–6

Te Manawa

At the heart of the Manawatu region, Te Manawa is the only institution of its kind in New Zealand to unite a museum, art gallery *(see p174)* and interactive science centre. The constantly changing exhibition programme features nationally significant collections as well as innovative hands-on shows. The museum forms the heart of the complex and recalls the long occupation of the region by Maori, as well as exploring the history of Te Manawa. The interactive science centre features changing exhibitions that are popular with children. From 2011 the New Zealand Rugby Museum *(see p174)* will also be located at the complex.

Reclining mermaid

VISITORS' CHECKLIST

326 Main St. **Tel** *(06) 355 5000.*
☐ *daily.* ● *1 Jan, Good Fri, 25, 26 Dec.* 🔲 *Science Galleries.* ♿
📧 www.temanawa.co.nz

Ivory Carving
Part of an exhibition, this exquisite carving features a Chinese mythological animal.

The Science Galleries have exhibits on the human body, light and communications.

Level 1

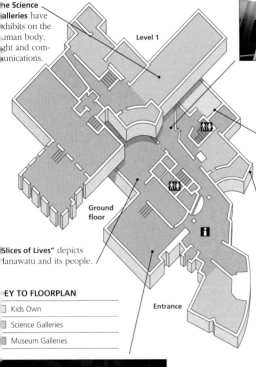

Ground floor

"Slices of Lives" depicts Manawatu and its people.

KEY TO FLOORPLAN

☐ Kids Own

☐ Science Galleries

☐ Museum Galleries

Entrance

★ **Hot Air Balloon**
Visitors can activate a blower inflating a balloon with heated air, to show how hot air causes lift.

"Kids Own" features tunnel adventures, a frozen shadows wall, and an ultraviolet room.

AgResearch Conservatory
This features samples of the plant kingdom, including New Zealand native and exotic species.

★ **Tangata Whenua Gallery**
These 19th-century carved palisade posts are among the Maori treasures exhibited in the gallery.

STAR SIGHTS

★ Hot Air Balloon
___
★ Tangata Whenua Gallery

The Pohangina River flowing through Manawatu's farmland ▷

Wanganui ⓮

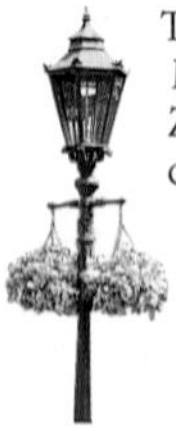

Hanging flower baskets

The area around Wanganui was first settled by Maori about AD 1100. By 1840 the New Zealand Company, unable to provide sufficient land in the Wellington district for the steady flow of new colonists, began to negotiate with Maori for land in Wanganui. The town became a distribution centre for the area extending to Waitotara in the west, Marton in the east and up the Whanganui River Valley in the north. Less than an hour by road to Palmerston North and only two and a half hours to Wellington, Wanganui's thriving arts scene sits alongside a variety of export-oriented industries.

🏠 Victoria Avenue

The preserved buildings, cinema, gaslights, wrought-iron street furniture and palm trees make Victoria Avenue, Wanganui's central city shopping area, a charming spot for visitors. From December to March, around 1,000 floral baskets are hung on streetlights and verandahs to celebrate the Wanganui in Bloom festival.

🏠 Durie Hill

Via Anzac Parade. ***Tel*** *(06) 345 8525.*
○ *daily.* 🎫

Located opposite the city bridge at the end of Victoria Avenue, Durie Hill is known for an historic elevator which rises 66 m (216 ft) inside the hill to the summit. Opened in 1919, it is one of several such elevators in the world. A pedestrian tunnel leads to the elevator. It takes about a minute to rise to the summit.

A climb up the spiral staircase inside the 34-m (110-ft) Durie Hill Memorial Tower, a short distance from the top of the elevator, allows panoramic views of Wanganui, Mount Taranaki/Egmont to the northwest *(see pp182–3)*, Mount Ruapehu to the east *(see pp143–3)*, and the Tasman Sea. The World War I memorial, opened in 1925, is constructed from blocks of fossilized seashell rock taken from quarries up the river.

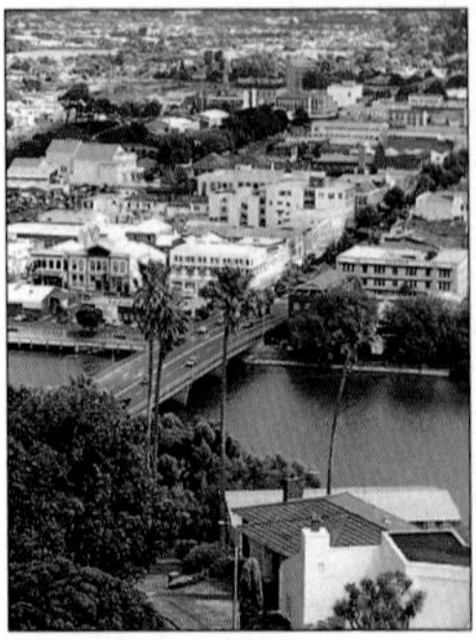

View of Wanganui and the city bridge from Durie Hill

🏛 Whanganui Regional Museum

Queens Park. ***Tel*** *(06) 349 1110.*
○ *daily.* ● *Good Fri, 25 Dec.* 🎫
📷 ♿ 🛍 **www**.wanganui-museum.org.nz

Among the treasures displayed in the Whanganui Regional Museum, visitors will find paintings of the Maori by Gottfried Lindauer (1839–1926), who managed to avoid service in the Austro-Hungarian army by settling in New Zealand, and Te Mata-o-Hoturoa, a *waka* (Maori war canoe) carved from a single totara tree. Established in 1895, the museum is concerned with the geology, natural and social history of the city and surrounding region.

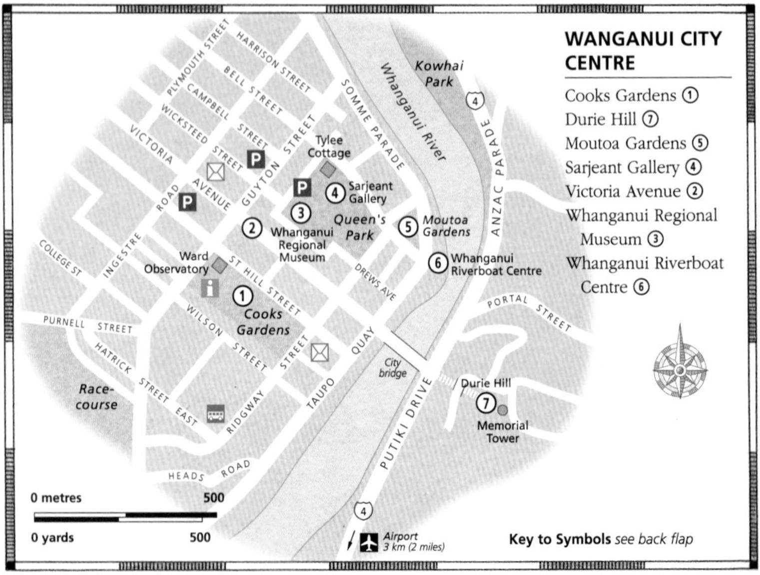

WANGANUI CITY CENTRE
Cooks Gardens ①
Durie Hill ⑦
Moutoa Gardens ⑤
Sarjeant Gallery ④
Victoria Avenue ②
Whanganui Regional Museum ③
Whanganui Riverboat Centre ⑥
Plymouth Street
Harrison Street
Bell Street
Campbell Street
Wicksteed Street
Victoria Avenue
Guyton Street
Somme Parade
Whanganui River
Kowhai Park
Anzac Parade
Tylee Cottage
Sarjeant Gallery
Queen's Park
Whanganui Regional Museum
Moutoa Gardens
Whanganui Riverboat Centre
Road
College St
Ingestre
Ward Observatory
St Hill Street
Drews Ave
Portal Street
Cooks Gardens
Purnell Street
Wilson Street
Hatrick Street East
Street
Quay
Taupo
City bridge
Putiki Drive
Durie Hill
Memorial Tower
Race-course
Ridgway
Heads Road
0 metres 500
0 yards 500
Airport 3 km (2 miles)
Key to Symbols see back flap

VISITORS' CHECKLIST

Road map E4. 🔢 44,000.
✈ 8 km (5 miles) SE of city.
🚉 165 Ridgway St. 🏛 101
Guyton St, (06) 349 0508. 🎭
Wanganui in Bloom (Dec–Mar).
www.wanganuinz.com

🏛 Sarjeant Gallery

Queens Park. **Tel** (06) 349 0506.
◯ daily. ⬤ Good Fri, 25 Dec.
♿ 🏛 www.sarjeant.org.nz
This gallery features a highly
regarded collection of New
Zealand oil paintings, watercolours and prints from the
19th and 20th centuries. It
houses the Denton photo-
graphy collection and World
War I posters and cartoons.

♣ Moutoa Gardens

Market Place.
Located at the site of the
settling of Wanganui as
a town, the beautiful
Moutoa Gardens
feature monuments
set within mature
specimen trees and
flower beds. In
recent years, the
gardens have been
a political rallying
point. In 1995,
Maori tribes
protesting about
land and river rights
occupied the
gardens for 79 days.

Moutoa
Gardens
statue

♣ Cooks Gardens

Maria Place.
A leading outdoor venue,
Cooks Gardens contain a
wooden velodrome and
an attractive old bell tower.
It was here, in 1962, that
New Zealander Peter Snell
ran the mile in under four
minutes, breaking the record
held by Roger Bannister
of Great Britain.

⬛ Whanganui Riverboat Centre

Taupo Quay. **Tel** (06) 347 1863.
◯ daily. 📷 🚫 inside. ♿ 🏛
www.riverboats.co.nz
This centre houses the salvaged and restored paddle
steamer *Waimarie*. Built in
London in 1899, it plied the
Whanganui River for 50 years.
Cruises on the restored
steamer leave from here.

The *Waimarie* on the Whanganui River

Whanganui River ⓫

Road map E3–E4. 🏛 Wanganui
Department of Conservation, cnr of
Ingestre and St Hill sts, (06) 345 2100.
www.whanganuiriver.co.nz

The Whanganui River is the
longest navigable and the
third longest river in New
Zealand. The 290-km (180-
mile) river begins its journey
high up on Mount Tongariro
in the centre of the North
Island, and meanders its way
down through the Whanganui
National Park to Wanganui
and the Tasman Sea.
Up until the 1920s there
was a regular river boat service carrying passengers, mail
and freight into the interior,
and a thriving tourist trade
operated between Mount
Ruapehu and Wanganui.
Today, the river, with its deep
gorges, sheer cliffs and 239
listed rapids, is New Zealand's
most canoed waterway.
The main entry and exit
points for journeys on
the river by canoe, raft
or jet-boat are
Taumarunui, Pipiriki
and Wanganui. The
145-km (90-mile) jour-
ney from Taumarunui
to Pipiriki takes about
five days by canoe.
From October to April,
visitors must obtain hut
and campsite passes
from the local Depart-
ment of Conservation
or other sales outlets.
The river can also be
followed by road from
Wanganui to Pipiriki.
Good side tracks lead
to historic sites, early
Maori villages, water-
falls and lookouts.

Whanganui National Park ⓬

Road map E3. 🏛 Department of
Conservation, 74 Ingestre St,
Wanganui, (06) 345 2100.

Established in 1987, the three
main sections of the park lie
within the catchment of the
Whanganui River. Broadleaf
podocarp forest surrounding
the river forms the heart of
the park. Tree ferns and
riverside plants are also a
feature, as is the birdlife. The
river is rich in fish.
Visitors can choose from a
variety of energetic activities,
including canoeing, kayaking,
rafting, jet-boating, and
tramping. There is also fishing
and hunting for deer and
goats. For a more leisurely
trip, visitors can enjoy a
cruise on the 19th-century
paddle steamer *Waimarie*.

The Whanganui River flowing through
Whanganui National Park

New Plymouth ⑰

Fountain in Pukekura Park

The principal centre of the Taranaki region, New Plymouth is situated around the only deep-water port on New Zealand's west coast, surrounded by surfing beaches along the North Taranaki Bight. The massive cone of Mount Taranaki/Egmont towers behind the city. Agriculture, with a strong emphasis on dairying, as well as heavy engineering, the marine industry and forestry are among the mainstays of the local economy. The area is also the base for the country's major oil, gas and petrochemical industries. New Plymouth is recognized for its many beautiful parks, gardens and reserves, and is an ideal base from which to explore Egmont National Park (see pp182–3).

Stained-glass windows in St Mary's Church

⛪ St Mary's Church

37 Vivian St. **Tel** (06) 758 3111.
◯ daily. ⛪ most days. ♿

Consecrated in 1848, St Mary's Anglican Church is the oldest stone church in New Zealand. It is a fine example of 19th-century architecture, and has some outstanding stained-glass windows. Headstones of children, settlers, soldiers and clergymen in the grounds of the church poignantly recall the difficulties faced by early settlers. Several Maori chiefs are also buried there.

🏛 Puke Ariki

1 Ariki St. **Tel** (06) 759 6060.
◯ daily. ♿🚻🅿️
www.pukeariki.com

Built on what was originally the most significant Maori site in Taranaki, Puke Ariki is an integrated library, museum and i-SITE. The centre provides a venue for the display of the museum's heritage collection, including 6000 nationally important Maori taonga (treasures). Puke Ariki overlooks a 7-km (4-mile) coastal walkway.

🏠 Richmond Cottage

Ariki St. **Tel** (06) 758 9583.
◯ 11am–3:30pm weekends and public hols. ♿🚻

Richmond Cottage, constructed in 1853 of stone instead of the customary timber, was the residence of the Richmond family. Many of the artifacts and furnishings on display in the beautifully restored cottage belonged to these former owners. During the 1880s, the cottage offered accommodation to seaside holiday-makers.

🌿 Pukeariki Landing

Ariki St. ◯ daily.

An oasis of green in the central city, Pukeariki Landing opened in 1990 when train tracks previously fronting the coastline were removed. This attractive park stands where surfboats, which carried people and supplies from ships, used to come ashore.

🏛 Govett-Brewster Art Gallery

40 Queen St. **Tel** (06) 759 6060.
◯ 10am–5pm daily.
● 25 Dec. ♿ specific exhibits.
♿🚻🅿️
www.govettbrewster.com

Opened in 1970 as a contemporary art museum – a novel concept in New Zealand and the Asia-Pacific region at the time – the Govett-Brewster Art Gallery was the gift of local benefactor Monica Brewster. She stipulated in her deed of gift that the gallery must always have a director of national standing and the ability to acquire art works with "minimal influence from local politicians".

Its main strengths lie in its collection of abstract art from the 1970s and 1980s, including works by Patrick Hanly, Michael Illingworth and Colin McCahon, and in its contemporary sculpture. The gallery is the site of the Len Lye Archive and contains the kinetic sculptures, paintings and films of this internationally renowned New Zealand artist, painter and film-maker (1901–80). The gallery also holds 20 exhibitions a year, conducts frequent art lectures and has a comprehensive research library.

TARANAKI'S GARDENS AND PARKS

Taranaki's parks, reserves and gardens are a highlight of the district and a drawcard for visitors. Long hours of sunshine, high rainfall, a mild climate, rich volcanic soils and shelter from prevailing winds combine to create ideal gardening conditions. Rhododendrons, azaleas and camellias suit Taranaki's conditions perfectly, and this is reflected in the large numbers of such species grown successfully throughout the region, along with roses, magnolias, irises and various native plants. From the end of October until the end of the first week of November, about 100 home gardens, both small and large, open their gates for public viewing in the annual Taranaki Rhododendron Festival. Visitors may enjoy tea at some of these gardens and buy plants. Visit www.gardens. org.nz for more information.

Rhododendrons in bloom

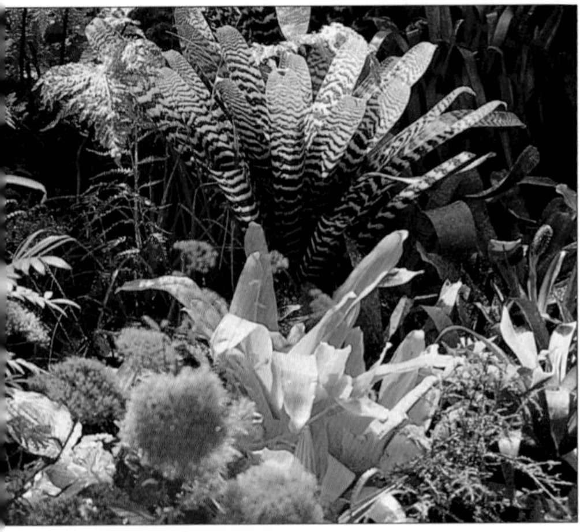

Fernery at Pukekura Park

Pukekura Park

Liardet St. ◯ *daily.* ♿

Opened in 1876 and only a ten-minute walk from the city centre, the dominant theme of Pukekura Park is water. Paths lead through dense native bushland, native and exotic trees, and fern gullies beside freshwater lakes and streams. A fernery, fountain, waterfall, water wheel, playground and boats for hire are other attractions. From the Tea House across the main lake there is a dramatic view of Mount Taranaki/Egmont.

During the Festival of Lights, held from Christmas to early February, Pukekura Park is transformed at night into a fairyland by thousands of coloured lights strung through its walkways and plantings.

VISITORS' CHECKLIST

Road map D3. 👥 *70,000.* ✈ *12 km (7.5 miles) NE of city.* 🚌 *Queen St.* ℹ *1 Ariki St (Puke Ariki foyer), (06) 759 6060.* 🎉 *Taranaki Rhododendron Festival (Oct–Nov), Festival of Lights (Dec–Feb).*
www.newplymouthnz.com
www.taranaki.info

Brooklands Park

Brooklands Park Drive. ◯ *daily.* ♿

Adjoining Pukekura Park, Brooklands is an English-style park with sweeping lawns and formal gardens. Originally a private family estate, it was bequeathed to the city in 1934. Highlights include an enormous 2,000-year-old puriri tree, 300 varieties of rhododendron, and a children's zoo. The Bowl of Brooklands, an outdoor soundshell in a bush and lake setting, is the site of concerts and other entertainment.

The park also contains a colonial hospital, the Gables, built in 1847. The beautiful beach stone building failed as a hospital, attracting only 55 patients, and is now an art gallery and medical museum.

NEW PLYMOUTH CITY CENTRE

Govett-Brewster Art Gallery ①
Puke Ariki ④
Pukeariki Landing ③
Pukekura Park ⑥
Richmond Cottage ②
St Mary's Church ⑤

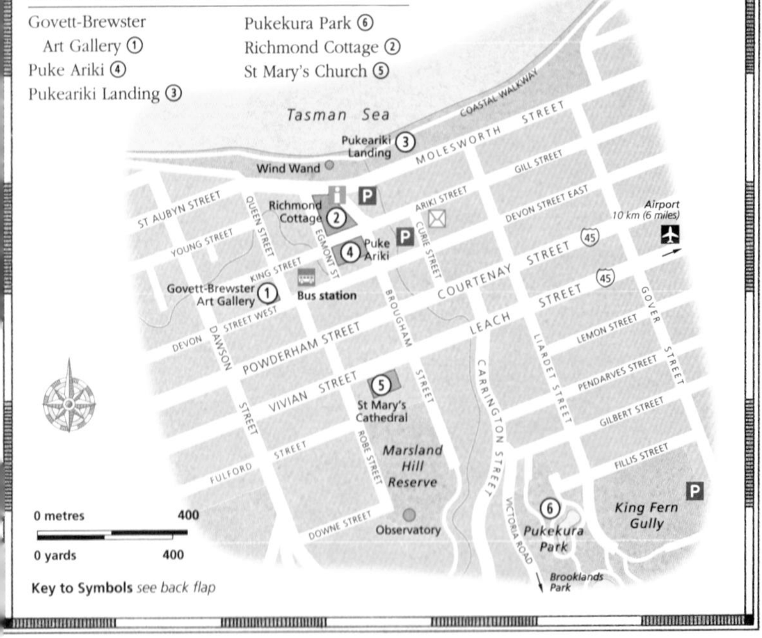
Tasman Sea
Coastal Walkway
Pukeariki Landing 3
Wind Wand
Moleswo rth Street
Gill Street
Ariki Street
Devon Street East
Airport 10 km (6 miles)
Richmond Cottage 2
St Aubyn Street
Queen Street
Young Street
Egmont St
Puke Ariki 4
Curie Street
King Street
Govett-Brewster Art Gallery 1
Bus station
Courtenay Street
45
Street West
Devon
Dawson
Brougham Street
Leach Street
Gover Street
Lemon Street
Powderham Street
Liardet Street
Carrington Street
Pendarves Street
Vivian Street
5
St Mary's Cathedral
Gilbert Street
Marsland Hill Reserve
Robe Street
Fulford Street
Fillis Street
King Fern Gully
Observatory
Downe Street
Victoria Road
6
Pukekura Park
Brooklands Park
0 metres 400
0 yards 400
Key to Symbols see back flap

Egmont National Park ⑱

Egmont National Park is one of the most easily accessed parks in New Zealand. The centrepiece is the solitary 2,518-m (8,261-ft) Mount Taranaki/Egmont, a dormant volcano. Ice and snow permanently cover the peak and upper slopes of this majestic and almost symmetrical mountain. Although weather conditions can change rapidly in the park, a 193-km (119-mile) network of tracks offers excellent climbing, skiing and tramping for the fit and well prepared. The park also has many tracks suitable for the average walker.

Tramper on the mount

Huts
Walking tracks link the huts in the park. Hut passes can be bought from information centres and Department of Conservation offices.

Native trees
The wet mountain climate, combined with periods of dry, hot weather, promote luxurious vegetation. Native trees are abundant on the lower slopes.

Oakura River

Dover Track

POUAKAI RANGE

Stony River

Puniho Track

▲ **Kahui**

Kahui Track

Oaonui Track

Waiaua Gorge ▲

Ihaia Track

Brames F

Waiaua River

Taungatara Track

0 kilometres 3

0 miles 3

WALKS IN EGMONT NATIONAL PARK

The park includes an extensive network of walking tracks leading to the summit or around the mountain. Shorter tracks start off from the three roads heading up the mountain. These range from easy to difficult and take from 30 minutes to several hours. The popular two-day Pouaki circuit offers walkers a taste of what Egmont has to offer: rainforest, tussock land, an alpine swamp and volcanic features. This track can be accessed from North Egmont. Vegetation in the park ranges from tall rimu and kamahi trees at lower altitudes, to dense subalpine shrubs and an alpine herbfield complete with plants unique to the park.

Tramper on one of the park's tracks

KEY

═══ Minor Road

∼∼∼ River

– ▪ – Park boundary

– – Walking track

ℹ️ Tourist information

▲ Hut

🏠 Picnic area

VISITORS' CHECKLIST

Road map D3. 🚉 *Stratford Depot.* ℹ️ *North Egmont Visitor Centre,(06) 756 0990; Dawson Falls Visitor Centre, (027) 443 0248;* @ *egmontvc@doc.govt.nz* **www**.doc.govt.nz

Mount Taranaki/Egmont
Mount Taranaki/Egmont is believed to have formed after a volcanic eruption more than 70,000 years ago. Sacred to local Maori, the mountain last erupted in 1775.

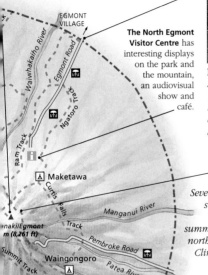

The North Egmont Visitor Centre has interesting displays on the park and the mountain, an audiovisual show and café.

Egmont Road
Signs at Egmont Village point to the 16-km (10-mile) Egmont Road which brings visitors into the northern area of the park. There are picnic areas along the way within the park.

Winter Climbing
Several ice and snow routes lead to the summit from the northern slopes. Climbers must always be properly equipped.

The Dawson Falls Visitor Centre has exhibits on the park's flora and fauna, and a model of its volcanic features.

Dawson Falls
Dropping 18 m (60 ft) down an ancient lava flow, the waterfall can be reached via a 20-minute walk from the Dawson Falls Visitor Centre.

View of one of the Sugar Loaf Islands

Oakura ❶⑨

Road map D3. 🏃 1,000.

Situated on a beautiful stretch of Taranaki coastline 15 km (9 miles) west of New Plymouth, Oakura is one of a number of small, scenic towns typifying the rural aspect of New Zealand. It has the traditional fixtures of such towns – the main street row of shops, service station, recreation grounds, churches, pubs and a war memorial. A train carriage restaurant in the main street is a novelty. The Crafty Fox, a neighbouring shop, sells works by the many artists and crafts people who live in the area.

The beach at Oakura is well known for its beautiful sunsets (in Maori, Oakura means "the place of flashing redness"). It is also a prime spot for swimming, windsurfing and surfboarding.

Sugar Loaf Islands Marine Park ❷⓪

Road map D3. 🚤 from Lee Breakwater, New Plymouth.

Established as a marine protected area in 1991, the Sugar Loaf Islands lie between 700 m (2,300 ft) and 1.5 km (1 mile) off New Plymouth's Port Taranaki breakwater. The stacks and reefs that make up the islands are the oldest volcanic features in Taranaki. They consist of eroded andesitic domes produced around 1.75 million years ago, lying at depths of between 5 m (16 ft) and 30 m

(98 ft). Of the eleven islands, or groupings of islands, the two largest are Motumahanga and Moturoa, located at the northern end of the park. They are often referred to as the "outer islands". Four rocky islets close to the mainland at Paritutu are known as the "inner islands".

The islands support a wealth of wildlife and plants. Among them are 80 recorded types of fish, at least 19 species of birdlife, rare and endangered native and introduced plants and 33 species of sponge. Fur seals are present on the islands all year round, with common and Maui's dolphins and killer, pilot and humpback whales also seen at times.

Although the best way to explore the islands is by charter boat, Round Rock, one of the "inner islands", can be accessed on foot from the beach during mid- to low tide. Snapper Rock, another "inner island", is accessible from the shore only when the spring tides are very low.

The relatively deep water, wide variety of marine life and spectacular underwater scenery make the park a popular venue for divers. Visibility often reaches 20 m (65 ft) during the summer and autumn months. Recreational fishing is also very popular in the park, although there are fishing restrictions. Blue cod, kingfish and snapper are among the most frequently caught species. Game fishing further offshore for tuna, marlin and mako shark usually takes place during summer and early autumn.

Cape Egmont ❷①

Road map D3.

Taranaki's most westerly point, Cape Egmont is characterized by strong wind and choppy seas. The solitary landmark is the Cape Egmont lighthouse, transferred from Mana Island near Wellington in 1881. Powered by diesel generators until 1951, it now operates on electricity.

Located 30 km (19 miles) offshore from the cape, the Maui field produces gas, which is processed at Oaonu 9 km (6 miles) northwest of the town of Opunake. At the site of the processing plant, a visitor centre provides details of the history of oil exploration in the Taranaki region. There are also scale models of ships and oil rigs. Visitors can use the binoculars at the centre to get a good view of one of the platforms, Maui A 35 km (21.5 miles) offshore.

Steps leading up to the Cape Egmont lighthouse

Opunake ❷②

Road map D3. 🏃 1,600. 🚌 🛈 Tasman St, (06) 761 8663. 🎭 Opunake Beach Carnival (Jan).

The thriving centre of a rich dairying district, Opunake is the largest town on the west side of Mount Taranaki/Egmont. The beach at Opunake, situated along the small, sheltered Middleton Bay, is regarded as Taranaki's best beach. It teems with tourists attracted to its safe swimming and its surfing during the summer months.

Opunake Beach, a picturesque swimming spot on the Taranaki coast

The Opunake Walkway takes visitors around the beautiful coastline and beach front, as well as around the nearby Opunake Lake, an excellent spot for canoeing, yachting and other water sports. Other points along the way include two old cemeteries. The 7-km (4-mile) route can be accessed from a number of points along the way.

Hawera ㉓

Road map D3. 👥 *9,000.* 🚌
🛈 *55 High St, (06) 278 8599.*

Part of Taranaki's rural heartland, Hawera boasts a number of interesting places for visitors. The 38,000-sq-m (409,000-sq-ft) **Hollard Gardens** were laid out in the late 1920s by farmer Bernard Hollard and presented to the Queen Elizabeth II National Trust in 1982. The gardens are at their most colourful from September to November.

Perhaps the best way to appreciate this beautiful region is from the air by taking one of the helicopter flights organized by **Heliview Taranaki**, a family-owned company specializing in passenger flights. They can pick up and drop off from any local hotel, motel and campsite using their mini bus. Fly over the city, the amazing coastline, over the summit of Mount Taranaki or the Pouakai Ranges. The best option is one of their 60-minute flights which can

include a landing to allow visitors to enjoy one of the sights close up, for example, Mount Damper Falls.

Near Hawera is the Fontera Dairy Factory, which is the largest single-site, multiproduct milk processing plant in the world. It is not open to the public.

Hawera and its surroundings can be viewed from the top of the town's water tower, built after a series of fires in the 1880s, one of which razed most of the main street. In 1914, a month after the tower was erected, an earthquake caused it to list 0.75 m (2.5 ft) to the south. The fault has now been reduced to 8 cm (3 inches).

The **Tawhiti Museum**, claimed to be the best private museum in the country, recreates many aspects of early life in South Taranaki. Housed in the town's former cheese factory, exhibits range from

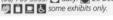

Cow statue outside Fontera Dairy

the early land wars to the development of the fledgling dairy industry. The life-like figures in the exhibits, modelled on the faces of local volunteers, were cast at the museum's on-site workshops. A bush railway takes passengers on a reconstruction of the logging railways that used to operate in Taranaki.

🌺 **Hollard Gardens**
Manaia Road, N of Kaponga. *Tel (06) 765 7127.* ⭘ *daily.* 🅿 *donation* ♿

🚁 **Heliview Taranaki**
Pouakai Heliport, 1291 Carrington Rd, New Plymouth. *Tel 0508 435 484. www.*heliview.co.nz

🏛 **Tawhiti Museum**
401 Ohangai Rd. *Tel (06) 278 6837.* ⭘ *variable.* 🅿 ♿ 📷 *by arrangement.* 🖥 🖼

Stratford ㉔

Road map D3. 👥 *5,700.* 🚌
🛈 *61–63 Miranda St, (06) 765 6708.*

Lying to the east of Mount Taranaki/Egmont, 40 km (25 miles) south of New Plymouth, Stratford is named after Shakespeare's birthplace, Stratford-upon-Avon, and many of its streets are named after Shakespearean characters. The **Taranaki Pioneer Village** in the town comprises restored or re-created buildings, including a school house, jail, railway station and about 50 other buildings that relate the area's local and provincial history.

🏚 **Taranaki Pioneer Village**
State Hwy 3, Stratford South. *Tel (06) 765 5399.* ⭘ *daily.* ⬤ *25 Dec.* 🖼 🖥 🖥 ♿ *some exhibits only.*

Life-size exhibits in the Tawhiti Museum, Hawera

THE SOUTH ISLAND

Introducing the South Island

Unparalleled scenic variety awaits the visitor to the
South Island. The snow-capped Southern Alps
dominate the island, dividing it in two and creating
a vast adventure playground of mountains, glaciers,
lakes, rivers and fiords. Golden sand beaches,
waterways and vineyards dominate the sun-soaked
north. Along the narrow West Coast, waves from the
Tasman Sea pound wild beaches. To the east is the
patchwork Canterbury Plains and the rich, rolling
farmland of Otago and Southland. Christchurch,
New Zealand's elegant "garden city", and Picton in
the picturesque Marlborough Sounds, are the two
main entry points to the South Island.

LOCATOR MAP

In Aoraki/Mount Cook National Park
(see pp252–3), *the highest peaks in New
Zealand soar above the crest of the
Southern Alps and over the surrounding
subalpine park. The park is one of the
country's most popular centres for walkers,
climbers and photographers.*

*Aoraki / Mount Cook
glacier landing*

Lake Te Anau (see p281),
*facing the glacier-carved
mountains of Fiordland
National Park, is one of the
longest lakes in New Zea-
land and is popular with
trout and salmon anglers.*

*Fishing in Lake
Te Anau*

OTAGO
AND
SOUTHLAND
(see pp254 -291)

*St Paul's Ca
in the Oc*

The Octagon (see pp258 & 261), *an attractive
eight-sided garden area in the centre of Dunedin,
is surrounded by imposing public buildings and a
statue of the Scottish poet Robert Burns.*

◁ A snow landing during a flight over Mount Cook

MARLBOROUGH
AND
NELSON
(see pp196 -217)

*Tramping in Nelson
Lakes National Park*

**Nelson Lakes
National Park**
*(see p212), at the
northern tip of the
Southern Alps, is
dominated by the twin
glacier-formed lakes,
Rotoiti and Rotoroa.*

CANTERBURY
AND THE
WEST COAST
(see pp218 -253)

*Whale on
the Kaikoura
coast*

Provincial
Council Buildings

0 kilometres   50

0 miles   50

The Kaikoura coast *(see pp208–9) is
the only place in New Zealand where
a pod of sperm whales can be seen
throughout the year. Eco-tourism
companies take visitors out to sea in
an open boat to spot the whales and
other marine life.*

*⟩eraki
⟩ulders*

The Provincial Council Buildings *in
Christchurch (see p226) are considered the
finest example of secular Gothic architecture in New Zealand and are the city's
most historic buildings.*

The Moeraki Boulders *(see p267), a group of perfectly
round, smooth, grey boulders of various sizes, are
scattered haphazardly along the seashore
and near the cliffs behind the beach.*

Southern Splendour

The overwhelming impression a visitor has of the South Island is its scenic diversity: the bush-clad inlets of the Marlborough Sounds, golden sand beaches of Nelson, sweeping plains of Canterbury, snow-covered mountains of the alpine chain, dripping rainforests of the West Coast, rugged tussocklands and rolling farmland of Otago and Southland and the fiords of the southwest. No less varied is the climate. Only three hours of driving separate the wetter west coast and the drier east coast.

Mitre Peak, *the centrepiece of Fiordland National Park, is the world's highest sea cliff.*

Abel Tasman National Park's *golden sand beaches contrast with the deep green of the forest (see pp214–15). The coastal walk in this park is one of the most popular in New Zealand.*

Sheep need supplementary feed, such as hay, during the coldest winter months.

SOUTHERN ALPS
Stretching almost the entire length of the South Island, the mighty Southern Alps and its various alpine environments were formed by the upward thrust of the Pacific Continental Plate *(see p22).*

The West Coast, *occupying a narrow strip of land between the Tasman Sea and the Southern Alps, has the highest rainfall in New Zealand. It also has some of the best examples of untouched rainforest, as shown here on the Milford Track (see p283).*

On Banks Peninsula, *the craters of past volcanoes, created by lava flows, are today's harbours of Lyttelton and Akaroa.*

The Marlborough Sounds, *in the north of the South Island, were produced by the drowning of an extensive river system* (see pp202–203).

Mountains and glaciers combine to produce spectacular scenery and numerous opportunites for outdoor activities.

The rocks of the Southern Alps, folded and raised by titanic forces, and eroded by wind, rain and ice, are a striking sight from the air or road.

The Sutherland Falls *in Fiordland, once thought to be the highest in the world, plunge 580 m (1,900 ft) in three cascades.*

The lakes on the eastern side of the Alps, such as Lake Ohau shown here, are the direct result of glacial gouging.

Lake Tekapo *and other eastern lakes are a milky blue, caused by ice rasping against rocks to produce fine powder.*

BRAIDED RIVERS

Weaving sinuous strands of water from the mountains to the sea, the braided rivers of the South Island's east coast are, globally, rare ecosystems. Over thousands of years the largest rivers, among them the Rakaia, Waimakariri, Rangitata and Waitaki, have carried rocks and shingle from the Southern Alps and deposited this debris to create the fertile Canterbury Plains. On the river flats lives the wrybill, the only bird in the world with a sideways turning beak. The world's rarest wader, the black stilt, breeds on shingle "islands" in the rivers of the Mackenzie Basin *(see p251)*.

The sinuous strands of the Waimakariri River cross the Canterbury Plains

Wildlife Colonies

Beware of wildlife sign

With a smaller population, there is less human pressure on wildlife in the South Island than in the North Island, and this is reflected in the number of wildlife colonies scattered around the mainland which are accessible to tourists. New Zealand has been described as "the seabird capital of the world" because of the number of species that either visit or breed along its coasts. A lack of predators has also led inland birds to be more fearless, and therefore more visible, than birds in most other countries. Marine mammals abound and tour operators guarantee an almost 100 per cent chance of seeing these animals in their natural habitat.

The white heron *breeds only in a coastal swamp near Okarito in September–October but is often seen in other estuaries along the coast.*

The royal albatross *has one of the greatest wingspans – up to 3 m (10 ft) – of any seabird. The world's only mainland breeding colony is at Taiaroa Head on the Otago Peninsula (see p266). Here a four-month-old chick is being weighed.*

The kaki/black stilt, an endangered wader, can be seen along the braided rivers of the Mackenzie Basin and at visitor hides *(see p251).*

The blue penguin, the smallest of all penguins, can survive near populated areas, such as Oamaru *(see p269)*, feeding on fish close to shore.

Bottlenose dolphins, known to swim as fast as 40 km/h (25 mph), prey on inshore bottom-dwelling species. A pod has taken up year-round residence in Doubtful Sound *(see p284).*

The Fiordland crested penguin, a rare native species, has a characteristic yellow crest over each eye. It comes ashore each June and makes its way to the Fiordland rainforest to breed.

The kiwi, *although primarily nocturnal, can be seen during twilight hours foraging in the forest on Stewart Island (see pp288–9).*

The yellow-eyed penguin, *the world's rarest species, is mostly concentrated on the Otago Peninsula (see p267). In the evening, they can be seen patrolling the beach.*

Okarito Lagoon

Haast

Milford Sound

Lake Wanaka

Lake Hawea

Doubtful Sound

Queenstown

Lake Wakatipu

Oam

Invercargill

STEWART ISLAND

Fur seals *haul out on rocky shorelines at several sites. At Cape Foulwind (see p234) there is a breeding colony where pups can be seen in spring and summer.*

Wading birds, *such as pied stilts (shown here), congregate in large numbers to methodically feed on rich tidal mud flats around the coastline.*

Farewell Spit

Marlborough Sounds

Nelson

Westport

Blenheim

ka

Kaikoura

Sperm whales, *which can be viewed off the Kaikoura coast (see p209), are specialized for hunting the deep sea, diving to depths of 1,000 m (3,280 ft) to feed mainly on large squid.*

RISTCHURCH

Akaroa

Banks Peninsula

Hector's dolphin, *a small species found exclusively in New Zealand, spends most of its time close to the shore, in pairs or small groups.*

kilometres 75

miles 75

KEY

	Kaki/Black stilt		Kiwi
	Blue penguin		Royal albatross
	Bottlenose dolphin		Sperm whale
	Fiordland crested penguin		Wading bird
	Fur seal		White heron
	Hector's dolphin		Yellow-eyed penguin

WILDLIFE WATCHING

It is important to cause as little disturbance as possible, especially when animals are breeding, and to be very patient. Seals can attack if people get between them and the sea, yellow-eyed penguins will not come ashore to feed their young if disturbed, and dolphins do not always welcome people swimming with them. It is best to view wildlife with an experienced guide who is well versed in wildlife etiquette, skilled at finding the animals and who can provide interesting and informative commentary.

Adventure Sports Paradise

Queenstown is tagged as New Zealand's top adventure tourism destination because of the many adrenaline-pumping sports on offer in and around the town. The area's mountains, lakes and rivers and generally dry climate combine to

Snowboarder

create conditions ideal for outdoor pursuits, while daredevil New Zealanders continue to pioneer ever more thrilling sports for the enjoyment of visitors. Strict regulations and highly trained operators reduce the risks involved in speeding through inches of water, leaping off bridges, skiing at remote sites and free-falling from airplanes, and explain New Zealand's excellent safety record.

Jet-boats – *propellerless power boats specially designed in New Zealand for use in 10-cm (4-inch) deep water – take visitors at breakneck speed down narrow river gorges.*

QUEENSTOWN AND SURROUNDINGS

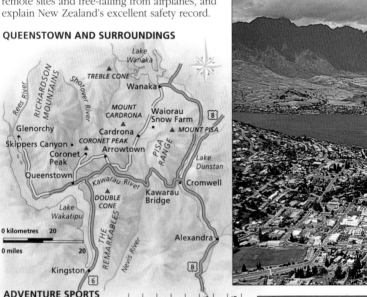

Lake Wanaka
TREBLE CONE
Wanaka
Rees River
RICHARDSON MOUNTAINS
Shotover River
MOUNT CARDRONA
Waiorau Snow Farm
8
MOUNT PISA
Glenorchy
Cardrona
Skippers Canyon
CORONET PEAK
Arrowtown
PISA RANGE
Coronet Peak
Lake Dunstan
Queenstown
Kawarau River
Cromwell
DOUBLE CONE
Kawarau Bridge
Lake Wakatipu
THE REMARKABLES
Nevis River
Alexandra
8
0 kilometres 20
0 miles 20
Kingston
6

ADVENTURE SPORTS AROUND QUEENSTOWN

These places are all within 115 km (70 miles) of Queenstown and offer a range of activities. Adventure sports tour operators provide transport, equipment and qualified instructors.

	BUNGY JUMPING	HANG-GLIDING	JET-BOATING	MOUNTAIN BIKING	SKIING	TANDEM PARAPENTING	TANDEM SKYDIVING	WHITE-WATER RAFTING
Cardrona Alpine Resort				▪	●			
Coronet Peak		▪		▪	●		●	
Kawarau Bridge			●					
Kawarau River			●					▪
Queenstown (see pp276–7)	●					▪	●	
Remarkables		▪		▪	●	▪	●	
Shotover River			●					▪
Skippers Canyon	●	●						
Treble Cone					●	▪		
Waiorau Snow Farm					●			
Wanaka (see pp270–71)				▪	●		●	▪

Downhill skiing *at the commercial ski fields near Queenstown is rated some of the best in the country.*

KEY

— State Highway

═ Minor road

≈ River

Mountain biking *allows riders, either independently or as part of a guided tour, to explore off-road routes that were traditionally walked.*

Queenstown, Lake Wakatipu and the Remarkables from the Skyline Gondola lookout on Bob's Peak.

White-water rafting *through the narrow gorges and thundering rapids of the Kawarau and Shotover rivers is a heart-pounding, exhilarating and drenching experience.*

The preparation area where ankles are strapped and adjustments made to the length of the cord to suit the weight of the bungy jumper.

BUNGY JUMPING

This was made famous by New Zealander A J Hackett, who dived from the Eiffel Tower in 1986 suspended by a rubber cord strapped to his ankles. Bungy jumping options now range from plummeting 134 m (440 ft) from a suspended "jump pod" over a gorge, dipping in at Kawarau Bridge, to hurtling earthward from "The Ledge" on Bob's Peak above Queenstown.

A jumper dives off the platform before soaring upwards again at the end of the bungy cord.

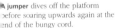

Cross-country skiing *is a speciality of the Waiorau Snow Farm in the Pisa Range near Wanaka, which also hosts cross-country racing and ski-jumping competitions during the ski season.*

Tandem parapenting *(or paragliding) – plunging off a hill with a guide, strapped to a rectangular parachute – is a safer option than the "ultimate" tandem activity, tandem skydiving – jumping out of an airplane with an instructor attached to one's back followed by a parachute descent to ground.*

MARLBOROUGH AND NELSON

*T*he warm climate of the Marlborough and Nelson region has always attracted visitors. Landscapes vary from wild coast, golden beaches, drowned valleys and dry inland mountains to lush, forested ranges. Known for its horticulture, the area is New Zealand's largest wine producer and a major source of fresh seafood. Along with heritage sites, its national parks are an added attraction.

Archaeological evidence dates Maori occupation of the region to at least AD 1200. Early Polynesian navigators, Kupe *(see p45)* and Rakaihautu, are also known to have spent time here. In 1642, Dutch explorer Abel Tasman sailed into Golden Bay *(see p48)*. A confused and ultimately fatal confrontation with Maori that left four of the crew dead, made the Dutch reluctant to revisit the area. James Cook's later visits to Queen Charlotte Sound in the 1770s fortunately proved more successful *(see p48)*.

Following the signing of the Treaty of Waitangi in 1840 *(see pp48–9)*, the New Zealand Company established its Nelson settlement in 1842 *(see pp210–11)*. In 1858, Nelson was declared New Zealand's second city, a year before Marlborough gained identity as a separate province. The region splits neatly into halves, Marlborough in the east and Nelson in the west. Marlborough's contrasts are perhaps greater, from the sinuous waterways of the Marlborough Sounds in the north, to the sheep farms and grape-growing region around Blenheim. Further south is the coastal area of Kaikoura.

In northern Nelson is the Golden Bay region, sheltered from the open sea by Farewell Spit and isolated behind the national parks of Abel Tasman and Kahurangi. Nelson city and Motueka sit on the shores of Tasman Bay. The rich hinterland, peopled by artists, vintners and horticulturists, extends south to the Southern Alps and the region's third national park, Nelson Lakes.

The weekend market at Nelson

◁ Golden sand beach at Totaranui in Abel Tasman National Park

Exploring Marlborough and Nelson

The northern region of the South Island beckons visitors with its sunny climate, inviting coastline, food, wines, marine reserves and three national parks: Nelson Lakes, Abel Tasman and Kahurangi. Marine life watching at Kaikoura *(see p209)*, winery tours *(see pp206–207)* and Nelson's Suter Art Gallery *(see p210)* are well-known attractions. Nelson is home to craft artisans and is an excellent base for boating and adventure tours. Walking, tramping and cycling tracks are spread throughout the national parks and other areas, including the Marlborough Sounds, a unique geographical feature of the region *(see pp202–203)*.

Kaiteriteri Beach near Motueka, a popular beach resort

SIGHTS AT A GLANCE

Abel Tasman National Park
   pp214–15 **14**
Blenheim **6**
Collingwood **18**
Farewell Spit **19**
Havelock **4**
Kahurangi National Park **13**
Kaikoura **7**
Marlborough
   Sounds pp202–203 **2**
Motueka **12**
Nelson pp210–211 **8**
Nelson Lakes National Park **11**
Picton **1**
Queen Charlotte Drive **3**
Richmond **9**
St Arnaud **10**
Takaka **16**
Takaka Hill **15**
Waikoropupu Springs
   Scenic Reserve **17**

Tour
Wairau Valley Vineyards **5**

Map labels

Cape Farewell
Puponga
FAREWELL SPIT **19**
COLLINGWOOD **18**
Golden Bay
WAIKOROPUPU SPRINGS RESERVE **17**
TAKAKA **16**
Tot
KAHURANGI
Aorere River
ABEL TASMAN NP
Marah
TAKAKA HILL **15**
Ka
MOTUEKA
13
Cobb Reservoir
Karamea
Karamea
Motueka River
Up
Mou
Woodstock
NATIONAL PARK
Mount Kendall 1810m
Tapawera
Bri
WEST COAST
Mount Owen 1875m
TASMAN
Owen River
Buller
Westport
Murchison
ST ARNAUD **10**
Inangahua
Lake Rotoroa
11
St Arnaud Range
Lake
Mawheraiti
NELSON LAKES NATIONAL PARK
Mount Travers 2338m
Mount Una 2301m
Springs Junction
Clarence
Hani
Spri

KEY

—	Major road
=	Minor road
—	Scenic route
⊢	Major railway
⊢	Minor railway
—	Regional border
△	Summit

SEE ALSO

• *Where to Stay* pp310–312

• *Where to Eat* pp336–8

GETTING AROUND

Beyond the highways of the Marlborough and Nelson region many roads are narrow and unsealed, particularly those into Marlborough Sounds and Molesworth Station *(see p208)*. A scenic journey by rail follows the east coast from Picton to Kaikoura and on to Christchurch, but there are no rail services to Nelson. Domestic airlines fly to Nelson city and Blenheim and private companies operate services from Wellington to Golden Bay and some locations in the Sounds. Bus and boat services at Nelson, Motueka, Marahau and Kaiteriteri provide access to all three national parks.

Vineyards at Blenheim in the Wairau Valley, New Zealand's largest wine producing area

TOP OUTDOOR ACTIVITIES

The places shown here have been selected for their recreational activities. Conditions vary depending on the weather and the time of year, so exercise caution and, if in doubt, seek local advice.

	BIRDWATCHING	BOATING	MARINE LIFE WATCHING	MOUNTAIN BIKING	SEA KAYAKING	SWIMMING	TRAMPING/WALKING
Abel Tasman National Park	●		●		●	●	●
Blenheim	●			●			●
Collingwood	●			●			●
Farewell Spit		●		●			●
Havelock		●			●		●
Kahurangi National Park	●						●
Kaikoura	●	●	●	●	●	●	●
Marlborough Sounds	●	●	●	●	●	●	●
Motueka	●					●	●
Nelson		●		●		●	●
Nelson Lakes National Park	●	●				●	●
Picton		●		●	●	●	●
Queen Charlotte Drive						●	●
St Arnaud	●	●		●	●	●	●

Picton ❶

Road map D4. 🏃 *4,000.*
✈ *Koromiko, 9 km (6 miles) S of town.* 🚆 🚌 🚢 ℹ *The Foreshore, (03) 520 3113.* www. destinationmarlborough.com

Set in the upper reaches of Queen Charlotte Sound, Picton is the South Island terminus for the ferries that cross Cook Strait. The buzz of port and railway activity dominates this pretty town nestled between the sea and the hills. Ferries and water taxis mingle with pleasure boats in the region, popular for its safe anchorages.

Picton's wide streets and historic buildings along the waterfront reflect the town's European beginnings. Formerly known as Waitohi, Picton was chosen to become the port for the Wairau district, and in 1859 became the capital of the newly formed province of Marlborough. That status shifted to Blenheim in 1866. An inter-island ferry service was first mooted in 1899 and the first rail and car ferry began operating in 1962.

Picton is a good base to explore the history of the Marlborough region. The **Picton Museum** tells stories of the whaling era, beginning in the 1820s, and of the 1770s visit of Captain James Cook to Queen Charlotte Sound.

At each end of the foreshore, the scow *Echo* and the sailing ship *Edwin Fox* provide a fascinating look at

Whaling exhibits at Picton Museum

New Zealand's shipping history. Built in 1905, the *Echo* is an old cargo scow that shipped around 14,000 tonnes of freight per year between Blenheim and Wellington. The *Edwin Fox*, the last Australian convict ship in existence, is an internationally significant link to the era of colonial settlement, having brought convicts to Australia and migrants to New Zealand. Built from teak in India in 1853, the ship is now being preserved in a dry dock beside a purpose-built museum. Along the Picton Waterfront is **EcoWorld Aquarium and Terrarium**, featuring the local species to be seen throughout Marlborough Sounds.

A number of walks and cycling tracks in Picton begin near the *Echo* or at Shelly Beach on Picton Harbour where a lookout affords excellent views of the town. A short uphill walk from the *Echo* leads to Victoria Domain, a bushy reserve named after Queen Victoria. A longer walk past Bob's Bay passes a panoramic view of Queen Charlotte Sound and leads to The Snout, the headland between Picton and Waikawa bays. Maori know the Snout as Te Ihumoeoneihu (nose of the sand worm). The Tirohanga and Essons Valley tracks allow exploration of the forest behind the town.

Maori club, Picton Museum

The *Edwin Fox*, formerly a convict transport ship

🐟 **EcoWorld Aquarium and Terrarium**
Picton Waterfront. **Tel** (03) 573 6030. ⬜ *daily.* ⬛ *25 Dec.* 🏷 🔲

🏛 **Picton Museum**
London Quay. **Tel** (03) 573 8283. ⬜ *daily.* ⬛ *25 Dec.* 🏷

🏛 **Echo**
Shelly Beach. **Tel** (03) 573 7498. ⬜ *summer: daily; winter: by appointment.* ⬛ *25 Dec.* 🏷 🔲 🔲

🏛 **Edwin Fox**
Dunbar Wharf. **Tel** (03) 573 6868. ⬜ *daily.* ⬛ *Good Fri, 25 Dec.* 🏷 🔲

Environs
A 20-minute drive northeast of Picton leads to Karaka Point, a narrow peninsula once occupied by a *pa*. A short walk leads down to the water with signs explaining the earthwork encountered on the way.

Marlborough Sounds ❷

See pp202–203.

Queen Charlotte Drive ❸

Road map D4.

The best-known road in the Marlborough Sounds, Queen Charlotte Drive is a scenic route connecting Picton and Havelock. With stopovers, it can take up to half a day to complete the 35-km (21.5-mile) journey on the sealed but narrow and winding road. Leaving Picton, the Queen Charlotte Drive passes lookout points above the town and at

Governors Bay, 8 km (5 miles) from Picton, with excellent views up and down Queen Charlotte Sound. Beaches and pleasant picnic and swimming areas can be found along the route that passes through the picturesque settlements of Ngakuta and Momorangi bays. At Ngakuta Bay, **Sirpa Alalääkkölä's Art Studio** showcases her large, bright paintings, many of them inspired by the Sounds.

Continuing west, a turn-off 12 km (8 miles) from Governors Bay leads to historic Anakiwa, where the Queen Charlotte Track begins *(see pp202–203)*. A shelter and picnic area are provided and an easy stroll along the track leads through beech forest to Davies Bay.

The Queen Charlotte Drive route continues through Linkwater with the road following the waters of the Mahakipawa Arm, the innermost reaches of Pelorus Sound. The walking tracks and viewpoint at Cullen Point provide another perspective on the waterways below, before the road's final descent into Havelock.

🏛 **Sirpa Alalääkkölä Art Studio**
Phillips Rd, Ngakuta Bay. *Tel (03) 573 7775.* ☐ by appointment.

Havelock ❹

Road map D4. 🚌 *500.* 🚗 🚌
🛈 *46 Main Rd, (03) 574 2104.*
www.havelockinfocentre.co.nz

The self-styled green lip mussel capital of the world, the village of Havelock receives a growing number of visitors attracted by its history and the success of its mussel farming industry. Havelock was established in the 1850s on the Nelson–Blenheim track near the uppermost navigable reaches of Pelorus Sound. Timber milling and gold mining were its first industries, while today fishing and aquaculture (the cultivation of shellfish) are major industries.

A restaurant in Havelock advertising green lip mussels

The main street still retains something of its pioneer character. Highlights of a walk around the waterfront are the stately 1880s home of timber miller William Brownlee, the stone St Peter's Church, and the old primary school (now a hostel) attended by Lord Ernest Rutherford *(see pp21, 212)* in the 1870s. A number of cafés can be found in the town along with many interesting shops selling antiques, jewellery, carvings, crafts, and Maori art.

Greenstone carved in Havelock

Tours and activities such as sea kayaking begin in Havelock, with the scenic mail run (where mail is delivered by boat) being perhaps the easiest and most popular way to get to the outer sounds. The **Havelock Museum** preserves relics from the pioneer era and Rutherford's time. The annual Mussel Festival takes place in March.

🏛 **Havelock Museum**
Main St. *Tel (03) 574 2176.*
☐ daily. 📷 donation.

Environs
Canvastown, 9 km (6 miles) west of Havelock, was established in 1864 following the region's first gold rush. A tent city grew here, attracting several thousand miners. Flood-prone fields and severe overcrowding

meant many miners left shortly after the gold fields in the West Coast were opened.

A further 11 km (7.5 miles) west, along State Highway 6, the road crosses the Pelorus River at **Pelorus Bridge Scenic Reserve**. Spared destruction after development of a town failed to proceed, the reserve is the last remnant of riverplain forest that formerly covered much of lowland Marlborough. A network of tracks allows visitors to explore the rich forest and river banks, with a suspension bridge, swimming holes and waterfalls. Other facilities include a shop, café, cabins and caravan park with electric powered sites. River cruises and nature tours are also available. Some of the walks are accessible by wheelchair.

Pelorus Bridge Scenic Reserve, a popular swimming and picnic area

Marlborough Sounds ❷

The Marlborough Sounds region is a mass of bays, inlets and hidden coves with numerous walking tracks, wildlife, historical sites and unsurpassed views. Picton and Havelock are the Sounds' main towns (see pp200–201). Launch services from these two towns provide the best access to the secluded bays and accommodation by the sea. The best ways to explore the Sounds are by bicycle, sea kayak, or on foot.

Mushroom on walking track

Cyclists on the road exploring the Sounds

D'Urville Island
Accessible by water taxi, the island was once an important source of argillite, a hard sandstone used in tool making by Maori. Today, farming is the main occupation with fishing, diving, kayaking and mountain biking popular pursuits.

French Pass
This picturesque fishing and farming village takes its name from the narrow and treacherous strait between the mainland and D'Urville Island.

| 0 km | 5 |
| 0 miles | 5 |

Tennyson Inlet is cloaked in native forest. Natural beauty abounds in this quiet inlet where picnic areas and campsites are found along the shoreline.

Main Road
Waitai Road
French Pass Road
Admiralty Bay
Pott Ligar Road
Maud Island
Nydia Sound
Pelorus Sound
Nydia Bay
Nydia Track
Kenepuru Road
NELSON
Havelock
Linkwater
Queen Charlotte Drive
6

HOW THE SOUNDS WERE FORMED

The Sounds region appears as a series of ridges rising above the water but is, in fact, a series of valleys drowned by the ocean. A combination of changing sea levels (due to world climate changes), movement along faults in the region, and tilting of the landmass downwards and towards the northeast has caused inundation by the sea. The last significant surge in sea level was at the end of an Ice Age about 12,000 years ago, and gives the area its current sinuous coastline.

Drowned valleys at Elaine Bay, Tennyson Inlet

STAR SIGHTS

★ Motuara Island

★ Outer Queen Charlotte Sound

★ Queen Charlotte Track

BLE

★ Queen Charlotte Track
This 71-km (44-mile) scenic walk (or mountain bike ride), begins at Ship Cove and ends at Anakiwa. A well-marked track, it is suitable for moderately fit people. Stout shoes are necessary.

Titirangi Bay, one of the few bays in the Sounds with a sandy beach, has a recreation reserve and farm park.

VISITORS' CHECKLIST

Road map D4. 🚌 *Picton to Anakiwa.* ⛴ *from Picton and Havelock.* 🛈 **Picton** *The Foreshore, (03) 520 3113;* **Havelock** *46 Main Rd, (03) 574 2104.* ◯ *daily.* ● *Good Fri, 25 Dec.* **www.doc.govt.nz**

★ Motuara Island
The open sanctuary of Motuara Island Scenic and Historic Reserve is host to myriad birdlife and can be explored on a walkway.

★ Outer Queen Charlotte Sound
The outer sound provides an enticing combination of open water, islands and wildlife. It is best visited by water taxi, sea kayak or wildlife tour.

Forsyth Island
Titi Island

Cape Lambert
Cape Jackson

Ship Cove

Titirangi Road

Long Island
East Bay

Queen Charlotte Track

Arapawa Island

Portage

Queen Charlotte Sound

Underwood Road

Whites Bay

KEY

▭▭	State highway
▭	Minor road
▬ ▬	Walking track
🛈	Tourist information
P	Parking
▲	Camp site
🏕	Picnic area
🚐	Water taxi
⚶	Viewpoint

Tory Channel was the site of New Zealand's first shore-based whaling stations, beginning in 1827. Closed in 1964, the remnants of the last station, Perano's, can still be seen.

Kenepuru Sound
Numerous accommodation styles are available in this quiet waterway where walking, fishing and camping are popular.

Port Underwood was a strategic whaling station in the 1830s. Today, its main attraction is White's Bay, with its swimming beach and old cable station.

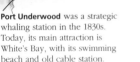

Sea kayaking at Abel Tasman National Park *(see pp214–15)* ▷

Wairau Valley Vineyard Tour ❺

Chardonnay grapes

Well known for its Sauvignon Blanc, the Wairau valley is New Zealand's largest and best known wine region. In the early 1970s, grape planting was begun by Montana Wines *(see p208)*. Now, nearly 70 wineries operate in the area. The wines of the Wairau are celebrated with the annual Wine Marlborough festival each February. South of Blenheim, at the Montana winery, is the Montana Brancott Visitor Centre covering all aspects of the wine experience.

Vineyards in the Blenheim region backed by the Richmond Range

Cloudy Bay ⑨
This is one of Marlborough's most successful exporting wineries, with a reputation for fine Sauvignon Blanc, Chardonnay and Pinot Noir. Tastings and sales are available daily.

Allan Scott Wines and Estates ⑧
One of the pioneers of grape growing in Marlborough, this vineyard offers wines characteristic of the region: Chardonnay, Sauvignon Blanc and Riesling.

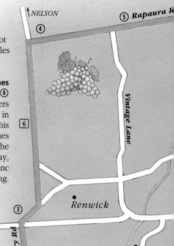

Stoneleigh Vineyards ⑦
Built on a former riverbed, the vineyard is named after the stones covering the area. Sunlight reflected from the stones speeds the ripening process of the grapes. Chardonnay, Riesling, Sauvignon Blanc and Pinot Noir wines are produced here.

Hunters Wines ⑥
This is one of the region's most awarded wineries. Red, white and sparkling wines are available, including Sauvignon Blanc, Pinot Noir, Cabernet/Merlot, sparkling Brut and Chardonnay.

KEY

▨	Tour route
⚊	Other roads
⚌	River

For additional map symbols *see back flap*

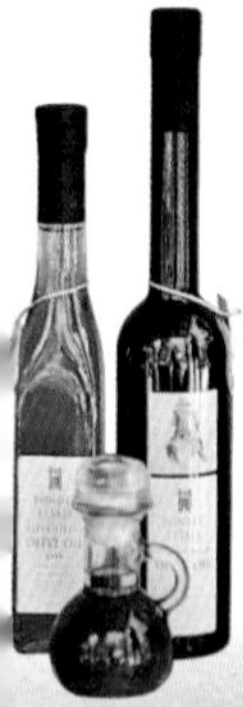

Ponder Estate ①
Producing award-winning Sauvignon Blanc and Chardonnay wines, the owners of Ponder Estate are also pioneers of olive growing in New Zealand. The white wines and olive oil are for sale in the estate's Shed Gallery. Mike Ponder's well-known works of art are also on display.

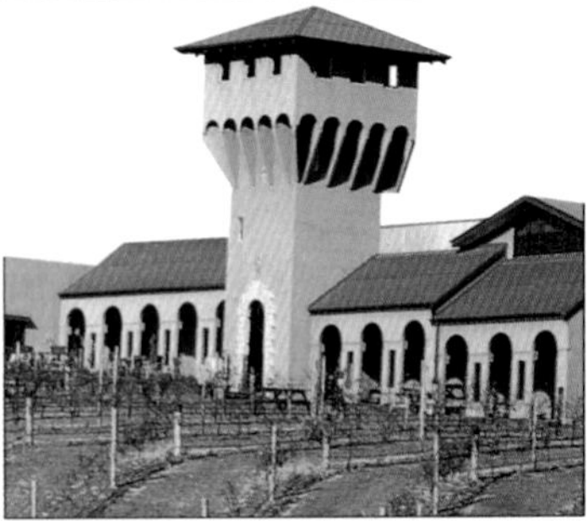

Highfield Estate ②
Visitors can get an excellent overview of the vineyard district from the Tuscan-styled tower of Highfield Estate. Tours of the winery and tastings are available.

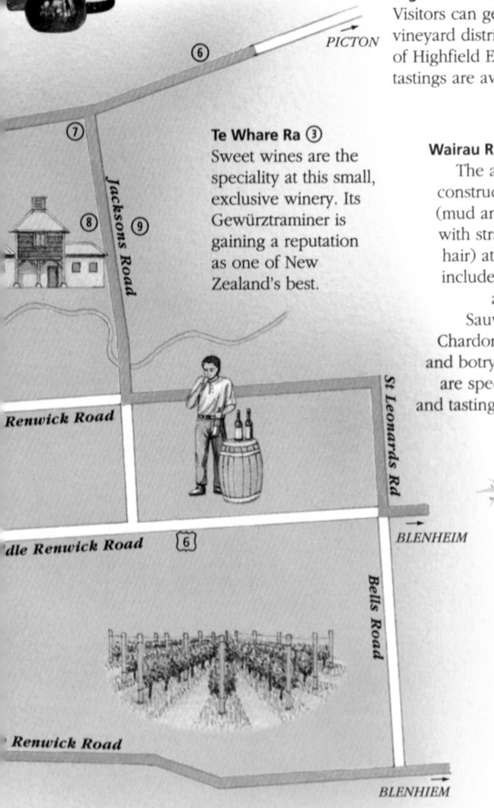

PICTON
⑥
⑦
⑧
⑨
Jacksons Road
Renwick Road
St Leonards Rd
BLENHEIM
dle Renwick Road
6
Bells Road
Renwick Road
BLENHIEM
0 kilometres 2
0 miles 2

Te Whare Ra ③
Sweet wines are the speciality at this small, exclusive winery. Its Gewürztraminer is gaining a reputation as one of New Zealand's best.

Wairau River Wines ④
The attractive cob-construction building (mud and clay mixed with straw and horse hair) at Wairau River includes a restaurant and gift shop. Sauvignon Blanc, Chardonnay, Riesling and botrytised Riesling are specialities. Sales and tastings are offered.

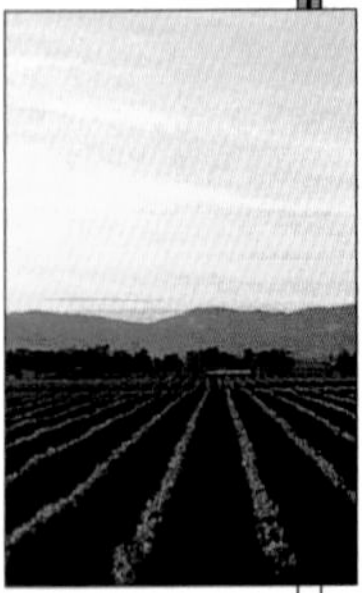

Cellier Le Brun ⑤
This winery specializes in *éthode traditionelle* sparkling wines. ours of the winery and underground cellar are available. Wine can be purchased at the wine shop.

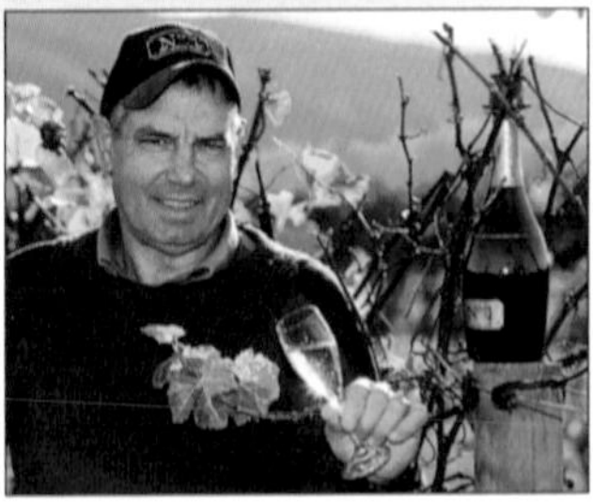

TIPS FOR DRIVERS

Tour length: *34 km (21 miles). Although a small area, more than one day is needed to taste the wines at a leisurely pace. Remember New Zealand's strict drink driving laws, something which makes a guided tour a wise choice. Enquire about these at the Blenheim Visitor Centre* *(see p208).*
Starting point: *Blenheim is a logical choice to begin and end the tour, which is a circle with a short side trip. Road conditions are good throughout.*
Stopping-off points: *Besides restaurants at the wineries, Renwick and Blenheim offer many eating choices. Fruit stalls abound in summer, with December a good time for cherries.*

The Clock Tower in Seymour Square, Blenheim

Blenheim ❻

Road map D5. 👥 20,500. ✈ 6 km (4 miles) W of city. 🚌 🚉 ℹ 2 High St, (03) 577 8080. 🎷 Wine Marlborough (second Sat of Feb); Classic Fighters Air Show (Easter); Hunters Garden Marlborough (second weekend of Nov).

The largest town in the Marlborough region, Blenheim's importance in the Wairau Valley has grown along with the development of the wine industry in Marlborough (see pp206–207). The annual food and wine festival is a major attraction. A number of art and crafts people also live and work in Blenheim and its environs.

In the city centre, Seymour Square has a fountain, pretty gardens and the Clock Tower. The **Millennium Art Gallery** houses works by local artists and sculptors, while the **Marlborough Museum** is set beside the heritage streetscape of Brayshaw Park on the southern edge of town. The park has a miniature railway, boating pond and reconstructed colonial village, giving some insight into the way of life in Blenheim during that period. Nearby is **Wither Hills Farm Park** where a network of foot and cycling tracks have been developed for visitors within the working farm. The tracks are well marked and require average fitness.

🏛 Millennium Art Gallery
Cnr Seymour and Alfred sts. **Tel** (03) 579 2001. ⬜ daily. ⬤ 1 Jan, 25 & 26 Dec. 📷 donation. ♿ 🚻

🏛 Marlborough Museum
Brayshaw Park, 26 Arthur Baker Place. **Tel** (03) 578 1712. ⬜ daily (archive Tue & Thu only). ⬤ 25 Dec. 📷 ♿

🌼 Wither Hills Farm Park
Redwood St. **Tel** Blenheim i-SITE Visitor Centre, (03) 577 8080. ⬜ daily.

Environs
South of Blenheim is the **Montana Brancott Visitor Centre**. One-hour tours include insights into the wine process, tastings, audio-visual shows, views of two barrel halls and an interactive "aroma wheel".

Further south, in the Awatere valley, **Molesworth Station**, New Zealand's largest farm, can be explored when the road through it opens each summer. The 59-km (37-mile) road journey through high country, passes historic cob houses, wide river valleys and mountains.

🎫 Montana Brancott Visitor Centre
State Hwy 1. **Tel** (03) 578 2099. ⬜ daily. ⬤ Good Fri, 25 Apr, 25 Dec. ♿ 🚻 📷 🍴 🛍

✂ Molesworth Station
ℹ Department of Conservation, (03) 572 9100. ⬜ Dec–Feb. 📷

Kaikoura ❼

Road map D5. 👥 3,700. 🚉 🚌 ℹ Westend, (03) 319 5641. 🎷 Kaikoura Seafest (first Sat in Oct); Kaikoura Races (Mon after Labour Day).

The name Kaikoura means "meal of crayfish" and reflects the importance of the sea throughout the area. Captain Cook sailed past the Kaikoura Peninsula in 1770,

naming the place "Lookers On" because of the reticence of local Maori.

The first European settlers and whalers arrived in 1842. The town's current tourism boom is also based on whales and other marine wildlife. The visitor centre has extensive displays and an audiovisual show. Whale tooth carvings can be seen at historic **Fyffe House**, a colonial cottage from the whaling days. Nearby, at the beach-front, is the Garden of Memories with a walkway encased with pairs of whale ribs.

Above town, Scarborough Street has a lookout point, a remnant *pa* and the Gold Gallery with wall sculptures gilded with gold leaf.

On the southern edge of town, guided tours can be taken at the **Kaikoura Winery** and at **Maori Leap Cave**, a limestone cave formed by the sea, full of stalagmites. Six km (4 miles) south of town is Fyffe Country Lodge which has pleasant gardens. Inland roads lead to Mount Fyffe, where superb views can be obtained from the walking tracks through the forest and mountains.

Whale tooth carving

🏮 Fyffe House
62 Avoca St. **Tel** (03) 319 5835. ⬜ summer: daily; winter: Thu–Mon. ⬤ Good Fri, 25 Dec. 📷 Adults.

🎫 Kaikoura Winery
State Hwy 1. **Tel** (03) 319 7966. ⬜ daily. ⬤ Good Fri, 25 Dec. 📷

🦴 Maori Leap Cave
State Hwy 1. **Tel** (03) 319 5023. ⬜ daily. ⬤ 25 Dec. 📷 obligatory. 🍴 🛍

Picnickers on the Kaikoura coast

Marine Life Watching at Kaikoura

In the late 1980s, the popularity of observing marine life in Kaikoura led to a tourism boom that transformed the town into one of New Zealand's premier visitor destinations. The main attraction is sperm whales, seen as they rest on the surface between dives, as well as orca and numerous dolphin species. Through the services of several eco-tourism companies in Kaikoura, the habits of whales and seals and the antics of the acrobatic

Stained-glass souvenir

dusky dolphins can be observed from the shore or air and both in and on the water. The special richness of Kaikoura's marine life is explained by the presence of very deep water and the mixing of warm and cold ocean currents there, which forces nutrients to the surface. Species of seabirds found in Kaikoura include the royal albatross, wandering albatross, grey petrel, Antarctic fulmer, and black-browed mollymawk.

Tourists get a close-up view from the Whale Watch® boat

WHALE WATCHING
Most whales seen at Kaikoura are toothed whales, quite often sperm whales. Unlike baleen whales, which feed by filtering plankton, toothed whales hunt their prey, including fish, krill and giant squid, sometimes at great depths.

Tour operators *offer opportunities to visitors to get close to the marine life.*

Swimming with dusky dolphins, *inquisitive, playful creatures, is a memorable experience.*

Fresh seafood *is a speciality of Kaikoura's restaurants. The abundance of scallops, fish, crayfish and prawns is celebrated annually in October with the Kaikoura Seafest.*

New Zealand fur seals *can be observed at a colony at Ohau Point, 23 km (14 miles) north of Kaikoura.*

Mollymawks *are one of the marine bird species to be seen within easy reach of the shores of Kaikoura.*

Nelson

Statue of Abel Tasman

Nelson was the second settlement developed by the New Zealand Company. The first settlers arrived in February 1842, but in 1844 the company failed. Some settlers persisted, and in 1853 Nelson became the capital of a province of the same name. A royal decree in 1858 made the small town New Zealand's second city. Today, Nelson is renowned as a vibrant art, crafts and festival centre with a superb climate. The compact city centre includes numerous galleries, craft shops and heritage attractions. A memorial to Dutch navigator Abel Tasman can be seen at Tahunanui, a popular swimming beach close to the centre of the city.

View of Nelson from Auckland Point

🍃 Anzac Park
Cnr Rutherford and Halifax sts.
The beautifully landscaped Anzac Park, with its pretty flowerbeds, tall palms and cenotaph, is Nelson's main war memorial. A horse-drawn passenger carriage ran alongside the park until 1901, using a section of New Zealand's first railway line. Auckland Point nearby was once the site of Matangi Awhio Pa, a fortification. The site is now being revegetated and a winding track to the summit provides excellent views over the city.

🏛 The Nelson Provincial Museum
Cnr Trafalgar & Hardy sts. *Tel (03)* 548 9588. ⬭ *daily.* ⬤ *Good Fri, 25 Dec.* 🖼 *donation.*
Two large galleries here focus on the natural and social history of the area, telling the stories and exploring the identity of the Nelson and Tasman region. Maori artifacts and *taonga* (treasures such as weapons

and ornaments) form a large part of the collection, along with historical photographs, ceramics, glass and silverware, and costumes and textiles from colonial times to the present.

🍃 Centre of New Zealand
Cnr Milton & Hardy sts.
An easy walk beginning at the Botanical Reserve – where the country's first rugby game was played in 1870 – leads up Botanical Hill to a lookout known locally as "the centre of New Zealand". The hill provides good views of the city, harbour, Maitai Valley and the Maitai River, which flows through the city into the harbour. A path follows the river downstream through a pleasant park and past Riverside Pool, a modern heated pool with a historic façade.

🏛 Suter Art Gallery
208 Bridge St. *Tel (03) 548 4699.* ⬭ *daily.* ⬤ *25 Dec.* 🖼 🕭 🚻 📷 **www.**thesuter.org.nz

One of New Zealand's oldest galleries (1899), the Suter Art Gallery holds a nationally important permanent collection, including paintings by Sir Tosswill Woollaston (one of the founders of New Zealand modern art), Frances Hodgkins, Colin McCahon, *(see p32)* and contemporary Nelson painter, Jane Evans. It also houses the collection of Andrew Suter, the city's bishop from 1866 to 1891. He donated early colonial paintings, including many by the colonial watercolourist John Gully, to the people of Nelson.

🍃 Queens Gardens and Albion Square
One of the city's heritage precincts, the main focus is the Queens Gardens. Some of the trees date back to the 1850s although the gardens were formally established in 1887. Albion Square borders the gardens and was once the political centre of Nelson when provincial government buildings dominated the square. Some historic buildings remain, such as a powder magazine, trout hatchery and fire station. A still-in-service 1864 post box and surveyors' test chain complete the picture.

🏫 Church Hill
Trafalgar Square.
Church Hill is dominated by the Anglican Christ Church Cathedral, the third church built on a site which has also been a survey base, *pa*, fort and immigration barracks. Church Hill is linked to Trafalgar Street by the impressive granite Cathedral

Christ Church Cathedral on Church Hill

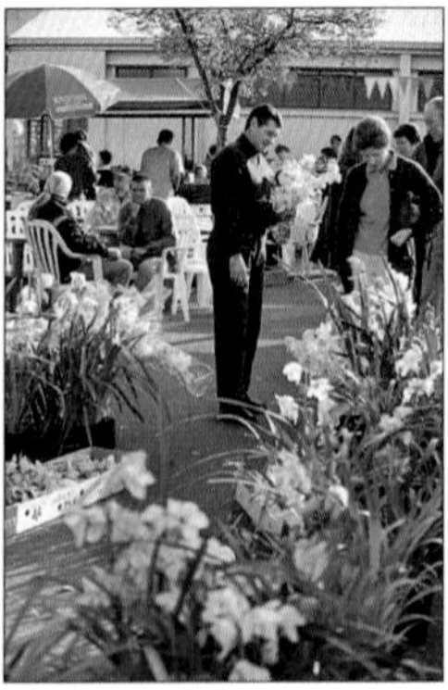

Fresh flowers at the Nelson weekend market

Steps, one of many gifts to the city by Thomas Cawthron, a noted philanthropist. Panels explain the history of Church Hill and some of its notable trees, while the remains of the old fort are visible near the cathedral entrance.

Nelson Market

Montgomery Square. ***Tel*** *(03) 546-6454.* *8am–1pm Sat, 9am–1pm Sun.* *1 Jan, 25 Dec.*

On weekends the car park at Montgomery Square is transformed into a colourful marketplace. Vendors of plants, toys, crafts, organic produce and foods, ranging from sushi to Dutch cheeses, set up their stalls. Shoppers and buskers bring the market to life, creating a busy spectacle that has become a key part of life in Nelson and of visits there.

Trafalgar Street South

Nelson's main street, Trafalgar, extends south of the cathedral to Trafalgar Street South. It leads to Fairfield Park and a small cemetery with graves of some early settlers.

Close by are two colonial era houses, Melrose and Fairfield. Melrose House (around 1878) is a truly grand home in the Italianate style. A feature of Fairfield House (1873) is its viewing tower, a replica of one used by its original owner, Arthur Atkinson, for astrological purposes. The garden contains some plantings made by the Dalai Lama during his 1996 visit to New Zealand.

VISITORS' CHECKLIST

Road map D4. *43,500.*
15 km (9 miles) SW of city.
27 Bridge St. *77 Trafalgar St, (03) 548 2304.*
Nelson Jazz Festival (Jan); School of Music Winter Festival (Jul); Nelson Arts Festival (Oct); Sealord Summer Festival (Dec–Jan). **www**.nelsonnz.com

South Street

To the west of Church Hill is the historic precinct of South Street comprising a collection of workers' cottages built between 1863 and about 1867. Sixteen cottages remain intact and many have been restored for use as accommodation or to house craft galleries.

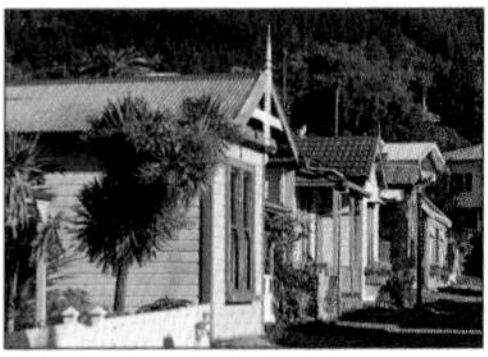

Former workers' cottages in the historic South Street precinct

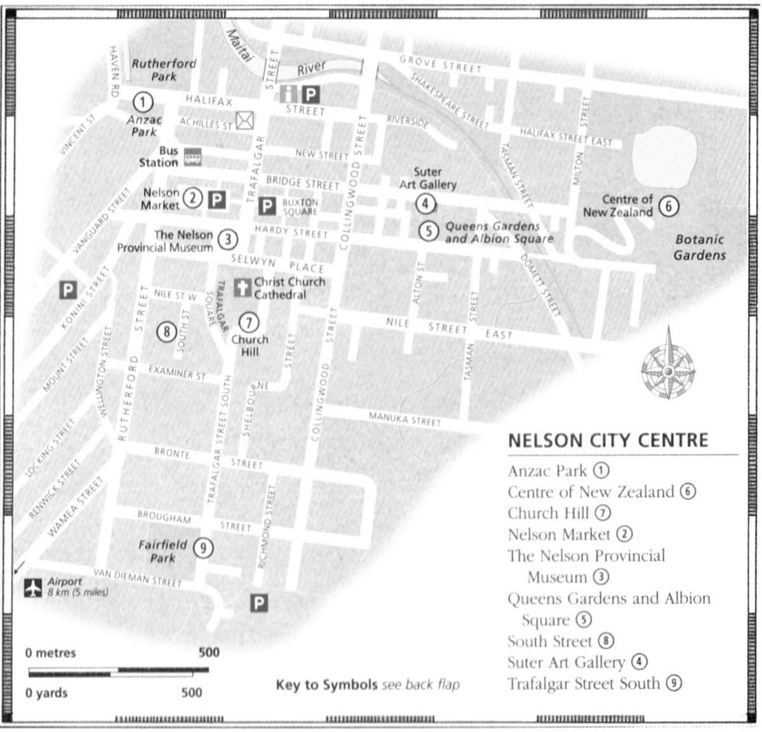

Rutherford Park
Anzac Park
Bus Station
Nelson Market
The Nelson Provincial Museum
Christ Church Cathedral
Church Hill
Suter Art Gallery
Queens Gardens and Albion Square
Centre of New Zealand
Botanic Gardens
Fairfield Park
Airport 8 km (5 miles)
Maitai River
HAVEN RD
HALIFAX STREET
ACHILLES ST
VINCENT ST
NEW STREET
BRIDGE STREET
BUXTON SQUARE
HARDY STREET
SELWYN PLACE
TRAFALGAR STREET
COLLINGWOOD STREET
GROVE STREET
SHAKESPEARE STREET
RIVERSIDE
HALIFAX STREET EAST
MILTON STREET
TASMAN STREET
DOMETT STREET
ALTON ST
NILE STREET EAST
NILE ST W
SOUTH ST
TRAFALGAR SQUARE
VANGUARD STREET
KONINI STREET
MOUNT STREET
WELLINGTON STREET
RUTHERFORD STREET
EXAMINER ST
TRAFALGAR STREET SOUTH
SHELBOURNE STREET
MANUKA STREET
LOCKING STREET
RENWICK STREET
WAMEA STREET
BRONTE STREET
BROUGHAM STREET
RICHMOND STREET
HARDY STREET
VAN DIEMAN STREET
0 metres 500
0 yards 500
Key to Symbols see back flap
NELSON CITY CENTRE
Anzac Park ①
Centre of New Zealand ⑥
Church Hill ⑦
Nelson Market ②
The Nelson Provincial Museum ③
Queens Gardens and Albion Square ⑤
South Street ⑧
Suter Art Gallery ④
Trafalgar Street South ⑨

Richmond ⑨

Road map D4. ⚒ 11,000.
✈ Nelson, 8 km (5 miles) W of town.
🚉 Gladstone Rd, (03) 543 9521.
🏵 Chelsea Flower and Garden
Show (Mar).

This busy town serves the
productive horticultural lands
to its south and west.
Highlights are the Wash-
bourne Gardens, complete
with 1862 jailhouse, and the
Redwood Stables restaurant,
built using bricks from New
Zealand's first racing stables.
Visitors can observe the art of
glass making at **Höglund Art
Glass** where Ola and Marie
Höglund create their re-
nowned glassware.

Environs
Six km (4 miles) southwest of
Richmond, at Brightwater, is a
memorial to New Zealand's
best known scientist, Lord
Ernest Rutherford (see p21),
born here in 1871. Also at
Brightwater is the **McGlashen
Pottery**. Continuing southwest
to Wakefield is a historic
church, St John's (1846).

🔷 **Höglund Art Glass**
Lansdowne Rd. **Tel** (03) 544 6500.
◯ daily. ⚫ Good Fri, 25 Dec. 🗹 🏠

🔷 **McGlashen Pottery**
128 Ellis St, Brightwater. **Tel** (03) 542
3585. ◯ daily. ⚫ Good Fri, 25
Apr, 25 Dec. 🏠

The South Island's oldest church, St
John's, at Wakefield

St Arnaud ⑩

Road map D5. ⚒ 200. 🚌 🚉
View Rd, (03) 521 1806. 🏵 Antique
& Classic Boat Show (Mar); Rainbow
Mountain Bike Race (Mar).

Approximately 90 minutes'
drive from Blenheim or
Nelson is the small town of St
Arnaud, nestled on the shore
of Lake Rotoiti, a trout fishing,

Lake Rotoiti in Nelson Lakes National Park

boating and water-skiing
paradise. The nearby Lake
Rotoroa also has good trout
fishing but is more secluded
and quiet. St Arnaud is the
gateway to Nelson Lakes
National Park and the closest
town to the **Rainbow Ski
Area**, where the terrain is
suitable for novice and inter-
mediate snowboarders and
skiers. In summer, the ski
field road continues through
to Hanmer Springs (see p233).

🔰 **Rainbow Ski Area**
Wairau Valley. **Tel** (03) 521 1861.
◯ June – Oct daily. 🗹 🖥

Nelson Lakes National Park ⑪

Road map C5. 🛶 🚌 🚉 View Rd,
(03) 521 1806.

The twin, glacier-formed
lakes Rotoiti and Rotoroa
dominate the 1017 hectares of
this park at the northern tip
of the Southern Alps. A water
taxi is the easiest form of
access to the area of high
passes, forests, valleys and
basins. The lakes and rivers
are popular for kayaking,
sailing, boating, swimming
and trout fishing. Winter
pastimes include ski touring.
There are many trails for
trampers and walkers, including the well-known 80-km (50-
mile) Travers–Sabine Circuit
that includes two major valleys,
an alpine pass, the wetland
Speargrass area and both main
lakes. The two-day return
walk along Robert Ridge to the
beautiful Lake Angelus is also
very pleasant but with high
altitudes, caution is advised.

Motueka ⑫

Road map D4. ⚒ 6,600. 🚌 🚉
20 Wallace St, (03) 528 6543.

Motueka has a diverse horticultural industry and is the
country's most prolific
orcharding area. Kiwifruit,
apples, berries, hops, pears,
and grapes are some of the
produce grown here. The
town is also a base for trips
to the Abel Tasman and
Kahurangi national parks.

Environs
Kaiteriteri, 14 km (9 miles)
north of Motueka, is known
for its stunning golden
beaches. South of Motueka
are the coastal villages of
Tasman and Mapua. Inland is
Upper Moutere village,
established in the 1840s by
German settlers. Each village
has its own artists, shops,
wineries, eating places and
boutique accommodation.

Kahurangi National Park ⑬

Road map C4. 🚉 20 Wallace St,
Motueka, (03) 528 6543.

A great variety of native
animals and plants live in the
4,510 sq-km (1,740 sq-mile)
park. A highlight is the
Heaphy Track, a four- to five-
day walking track. Kayaking,
hunting, caving, tramping, rafting and fishing are all popular
activities here. Alpine plants
can be seen growing near the
Cobb Reservoir. The major
gateway is Motueka, but access
is also possible from Karamea
(see p234).

The Nelson Arts Scene

A combination of a warm climate and a relaxed environment has attracted many artists to Nelson, making it one of New Zealand's most vibrant arts regions. Its history of artistic endeavour is long. Today, Nelson abounds with opportunities to explore art in the many galleries and studios of glass-blowers, painters, jewellers, textile artists, woodworkers and

Handblown glass vase

ceramic artists. The Suter Art Gallery *(see p210)* is noted for its extensive collection of historical and contemporary works. The Nelson region is also becoming known for music and performance events, such as the Nelson Jazz Festival and the Nelson School of Music Winter Festival. Nelson's Tasman Regional Museum houses a photographic display chronicling Nelson and New Zealand's early colonial beginnings.

CERAMICS

A variety of fine raw clays and glaze materials has long attracted ceramic artists to Nelson. A large number of pottery outlets showcase the work of talented potters, and many nationally recognized crafts people choose Nelson as a living and working base.

Handmade tiles adorn the doorway of a tile shop in Mapua

Ron McGlashen at work in his ceramic studio at Brightwater

Glassware in Nelson is made by combining modern design ideas with traditional glass-blowing methods (see p212). The result is colourful creations, each one hand-crafted and unique.

OPEN ESTUARY ARTS

Art and craft galleries are a common sight in the region

Artists *in Nelson have long been inspired by their surroundings. A nationally important collection can be seen at The Suter Art Gallery (see p210).*

Three-dimensional art, *designed to be viewed from many sides, is popular in Nelson. Some pieces are practical, others whimsical. Local sculptors have been commissioned to provide works for public areas.*

Abel Tasman National Park ⑭

Aerial view of Abel Tasman National Park

New Zealand's smallest national park, at 225 sq km (87 sq miles), Abel Tasman has a mild climate, golden beaches and sandy estuaries fringed by natural forest. The park is best known for its coast track which can be walked one way, with the return trip made on a launch or water taxi. There are huts and a large number of campsites on the coast track to break the journey. Due to the park's popularity, it is necessary to book walks and huts before visiting. Abel Tasman is also one of New Zealand's better sea kayaking destinations and a day spent drifting in a slowly filling estuary or watching seals, penguins, dolphins or birdlife from these quiet craft will not be forgotten.

Oystercatcher in the park

Pohara

Takaka

East Takaka

Uruwhenua

Abel Tasman Drive

Glenview Rd

Central Takaka Road

East Takaka Road

60

Wainui River

Wainui Track

Remaka Track

Harwoods Track

Canaan Road

★ **Wainui Falls**
Nelson's finest accessible falls are reached via an easy 30-minute walk from a small car park on the road to Totaranui.

★ **Harwoods Hole**
A 45-minute walk from Canaan car park (see p216) leads to the entrance of the 176-m (577-ft) vertical marble shaft known as Harwoods Hole. It is dangerous to get too close to the chasm as the sides may be unstable.

The Inland Track, more rugged than its coastal counterpart, is a three-day walk from Tinline Bay to Wainui Bay. Drinking water should be carried on the track.

STAR SIGHTS

★ Harwoods Hole

★ Totaranui

★ Wainui Falls

For hotels and restaurants in this region see pp310–12 and pp336–8

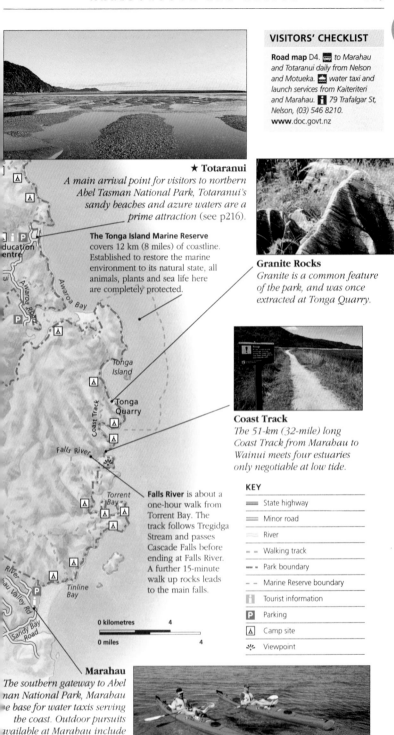

VISITORS' CHECKLIST

Road map D4. ▦ to Marahau and Totaranui daily from Nelson and Motueka. ▦ water taxi and launch services from Kaiteriteri and Marahau. ▐ 79 Trafalgar St, Nelson, (03) 546 8210.
www.doc.govt.nz

★ Totaranui
A main arrival point for visitors to northern Abel Tasman National Park, Totaranui's sandy beaches and azure waters are a prime attraction (see p216).

The Tonga Island Marine Reserve covers 12 km (8 miles) of coastline. Established to restore the marine environment to its natural state, all animals, plants and sea life here are completely protected.

Granite Rocks
Granite is a common feature of the park, and was once extracted at Tonga Quarry.

Coast Track
The 51-km (32-mile) long Coast Track from Marahau to Wainui meets four estuaries only negotiable at low tide.

Falls River is about a one-hour walk from Torrent Bay. The track follows Tregidga Stream and passes Cascade Falls before ending at Falls River. A further 15-minute walk up rocks leads to the main falls.

KEY

▬▬	State highway
▬▬	Minor road
▭▭	River
– –	Walking track
▬ ▬	Park boundary
- -	Marine Reserve boundary
▐	Tourist information
P	Parking
▲	Camp site
☀	Viewpoint

0 kilometres 4

0 miles 4

Marahau
The southern gateway to Abel [Tas]man National Park, Marahau [is th]e base for water taxis serving the coast. Outdoor pursuits [a]vailable at Marahau include sea kayaking, walking and swimming with seals.

View from Takaka Hill looking towards Motueka and Nelson

Takaka Hill ⓯

Road map D4.

Takaka Hill is commonly referred to as "the marble mountain" because of its large marble deposits that contrast sharply with the granite hills of adjoining Abel Tasman National Park. There are many caves and sinkholes to explore in the area, including **Ngarua Caves** near the summit of Takaka Hill, where a lookout offers views north to D'Urville Island and east towards Nelson city. Tours of the only cave open to visitors are available and bones of moa (see p25) can be seen. Visible below the caves is Marahau's golden beach (see p215), where marble from a local quarry was shipped to Wellington for use in New Zealand's Parliament Building.

To the west of Ngarua Caves, Canaan Road leads to Canaan car park, the starting point for walking tracks, including the Rameka Track, one of Nelson's better mountain bike rides. An easy walk leads to the impressive Harwoods Hole (see p214), a 176-m (577-ft) vertical shaft. A short steep side track leads to the Harwood Lookout with a fine viewpoint inland to the Tablelands in Kahurangi National Park (see p213).

To the east of Ngarua Caves is Hawkes Lookout. A short walk leads to a platform perched over a precipitous 500-m (1,640-ft) drop to the forest at Riwaka Resurgence.

🏚 **Ngarua Caves**
Tel (03) 528 8093. ◯ summer: daily; winter: school hols. 🧩 🅿 🚻

Takaka ⓰

Road map D4. 🏘 1,230. ✈ 6 km (4 miles) N of town. 🚌 🛈 Willow St, (03) 525 9136.
www.nelsonnz.com

Takaka is the main shopping and business area for the Golden Bay region and an access point to Abel Tasman National Park (see pp214–15). The townspeople are a mix of "alternative life-stylers" and farming folk. Dairy farming is one of the largest industries in the region. The **Golden Bay Museum** is

Painted gourd

excellent, and best known for its displays on Abel Tasman and the story of Golden Bay's many mining ventures. Several galleries operate in the area and many artists near Takaka show their work – painted gourds, pottery and wood or stone sculptures – to visitors.

At **Bencarri Farm Park & Café**, home to tame eels and farm animals, rare species such as yaks, llamas and alpacas are bred. Riverside walking and picnics in a valley at the park are other attractions.

🏛 **Golden Bay Museum**
Commercial St. **Tel** (03) 525 6268. ◯ 10am–4pm daily. ● Sun in winter, public hols. 🧩 🅰 🚻

🍴 **Bencarri Farm Park & Café**
McCallum's Rd. **Tel** (03) 525 8261. ◯ summer: daily. ● 25 Dec. 🅰 limited. 🖥 🚻

Environs

Beyond the beach at Pohara, 10 km (6 miles) from Takaka, is a memorial to Dutch navigator Abel Tasman, with a lookout platform and display. After the memorial, the road leads to **Wainui Bay**. Several coastal walks and one to Wainui Falls (see p214) begin there. Beyond Wainui Bay the road climbs to Abel Tasman National Park, descending finally to the sea and golden sands of Totaranui. A camp ground and visitor centre with a shop operate here over the summer

Llamas at Bencarri Farm Park

Waikoropupu Springs Scenic Reserve ⑰

Road map D4.

North of Takaka on State Highway 60, a turnoff leads to the Waikoropupu Springs Scenic Reserve. The waters here are exceptionally clear, coming from an underground cave system that is connected to the features encountered on Takaka Hill and at Riwaka Resurgence (see p216). In the past Waikoropupu was a place of ceremonial blessings for Maori.

Rivers in the ice cold, clear waters of Waikoropupu Springs

The springs are best viewed using a large fixed periscope set on a viewing platform. An easy walk through beautiful forest leads to the platform.

Beyond the springs (at the end of the road), the Pupu Walkway is a track that follows the line of a water race built to serve a gold mining claim. An impressive piece of engineering, the water race was later used (and still is) to generate electric power. The walk is about 3 km (2 miles) long.

Collingwood ⑱

Road map D4. 🏠 500. 🚌

A quiet village at the mouth of the Aorere River, Collingwood was designated a port of entry in the 1850s gold rush and was considered as the site for New Zealand's capital city. Despite several

devastating fires, the court-house, post office, original cemetery and Anglican St Cuthbert's Church remain to remind visitors of the town's fleeting moment of glory.

Collingwood acts as a base for tours to Farewell Spit and for buses serving the Heaphy Track in Kahurangi National Park (see p212).

Environs

Within 20 km (12 miles) of Collingwood is the beautiful Kaituna Track with river views and lush forest, the Te Anaroa Caves, a 350-m (1,148-ft) limestone cave system with glowworms and shellfish fossils, and the Aorere, New Zealand's first major gold field. Quartz, silver and gold were mined here. The workings can be explored by a walking track with views over the valley.

Farewell Spit ⑲

Road map D4. 🅸 Farewell Spit Information Centre (03) 524 8454.
⬜ daily. 🍴 📺 🚻

At the northern tip of the South Island, a 35-km (22-mile) sandspit sweeps eastward into the sea. Farewell Spit is a nature reserve with restricted access and has been designated a Wetland of International Importance.

In late spring, tens of thousands of migratory waders arrive from the northern hemisphere, joining the year-round residents before returning home in autumn to breed.

Early gold workings at Aorere, near Collingwood

Black swans, Canadian geese, Australasian gannets, Caspian terns, oystercatchers, black shags and eastern bartailed godwits are amongst the species to be seen in summer. As the region is a protected area, the only way to visit the spit is on a guided tour with one of the licensed tour operators based in Collingwood.

Environs

Immediately to the west of the spit is **Puponga Farm Park**, with walking tracks and viewpoints. Visitors can also participate in the activities on a working farm. A short walk from the Farewell Spit visitor centre and café leads to Fossil Point on the wild ocean beach. Further west is the easy climb to Pillar Point lighthouse and the Old Man Range, while at the end of the road a short track crosses a series of dunes to Wharariki Beach, with rock pools, birds, seals and the towering Archway Islands nearby.

Tourist bus at Farewell Spit

🐾 **Puponga Farm Park**
Collingwood–Puponga Main Rd.
Tel (03) 525 8026. ⬜ daily. 📺

Tourists climbing the sand dunes at Farewell Spit

CANTERBURY AND THE WEST COAST

anterbury and the West Coast, stretching from the Tasman Sea in the west to the Pacific Ocean in the east, is characterized by sharp and sudden distinctions of geology, flora and climate. The combined area contains four national parks and New Zealand's highest mountain. Christchurch, the largest city in the South Island, is an ideal base from which to explore the various subregions.

When large-scale European settlement of Canterbury began in 1850, both Canterbury and the West Coast were dominated by the Ngai Tahu tribe. By 1860, the bulk of the tribe's land had been acquired by the government in a series of dubious sales transactions, leaving the Ngai Tahu impoverished and unable to participate equally in the new settler economy. It was not until 1997 that the Ngai Tahu received compensation from the New Zealand Government.

While pastoral farming was the key to the development of Canterbury in the 1850s, it was the discovery of gold in the 1860s that brought European settlement to the West Coast. Today, "the Coast" retains a rustic mystique, a product of its mining heritage, powerful landscapes of rugged mountains and glaciers, lush rainforest, rushing rivers and sombre lakes, as well as its isolation from the rest of New Zealand.

The West Coast climate is wet, with prevailing westerly air-flows bringing frequent heavy rain as moisture-laden air is forced up and over the Southern Alps. By contrast, Canterbury is relatively dry, with warm, blustery winds commonly sweeping down the eastern side of the alps and over the Canterbury Plains.

The plains are carved into a patchwork of grazing and crop paddocks, backed by tussock vegetation and forest-covered mountain ranges. They merge to the north and south with rolling farmland, interspersed with wide, braided rivers. The inland region is a large, dry, open basin of austere beauty, over which New Zealand's highest mountains loom.

Climbers on the summit of Aoraki/Mount Cook

◁ The daffodil woodland in Hagley Park, Christchurch, a popular springtime rendezvous

Exploring Canterbury and the West Coast

Canterbury and the West Coast's distinctive landscapes are dominated by the Southern Alps through which there are only two roads and one railway line. To get the best out of the region, and particularly to appreciate the beauty of its varied geology, flora and fauna, a willingness to don sturdy shoes and set out on foot is necessary. For the independent outdoor enthusiast, the opportunities are enormous, and for those who prefer to be guided through the wilderness, commercially run adventure tourism activities are available at most key locations.

Inner-city tram in Christchurch

SIGHTS AT A GLANCE

TOP OUTDOOR ACTIVITIES

The places shown here have been selected for their recreational activities. Conditions vary depending on the weather and the time of year, so exercise caution and, if in doubt, seek local advice.

	Fishing	Golf	Mountain Biking	Mountain Climbing	Skiing/Heli-Skiing	Tramping	Walking	White-Water Rafting
Arthur's Pass National Park				■	●	■	●	
Banks Peninsula	●	■				■	●	
Franz Josef Glacier				■	●	■	●	
Hanmer Springs	●	■	●		●	■	●	■
Hokitika	●	■				■	●	
Karamea	●	■	●			■	●	●
Lake Ohau	●	■			●		●	
Lake Tekapo	●			■	●	■	●	
Lewis Pass			●	■	●	■	●	
Aoraki/Mount Cook		■			●	■	●	
Mount Hutt	●			■	●	■	●	
Paparoa National Park	●					■	●	
Port Hills			●				●	
Rakaia	●	■				●	●	■
Reefton	●		●			■	■	
Westport	●	■						

Abut Head
Ha

Whataroa

Franz Josef
Glacier

Fox Glacier

WESTLAND NATIONAL PARK

⑮

Mount Cook
3755m

AORAKI MT...
NATION...

Haast

Mount Ward
2644m

Mount Co

LAKE TEK...

Mount
Huxley
2499m

LAKE
PUKAKI
㉕
Te

Ben Ohau Range

Obau
Forest

LAKE
OHAU ㉗

TWIZE
㉖

8

Lak...
Ben...

Clay Cliffs
Omarama

Queenstown

83

Ku...

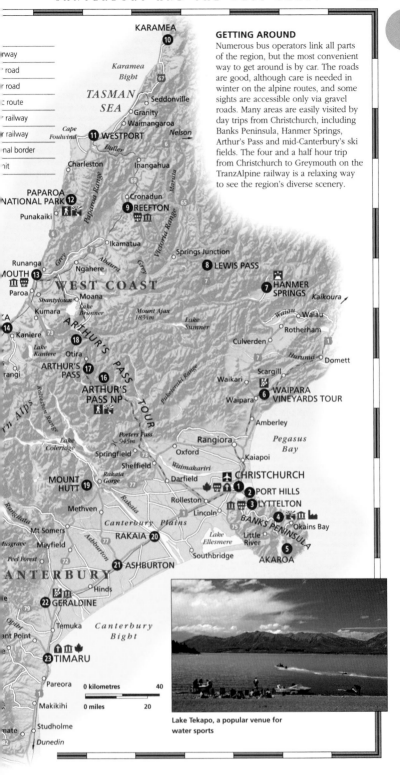

KARAMEA
10

Karamea Bight

rway

‑ road

‑ road

c route

‑ railway

‑ railway

nal border

hit

TASMAN SEA

Seddonville

Granity

Waimangaroa

Cape Foulwind

11 WESTPORT

Nelson

Buller

Charleston

Inangahua

PAPAROA
NATIONAL PARK **12**

Punakaiki

Paparoa Range

Cronadun

9 REEFTON

Victoria Range

Ikamatua

Grey

Ahaura

Springs Junction

8 LEWIS PASS

Runanga

Ngahere

MOUTH **13**

WEST COAST

Paroa

Shantytown

Moana

Kumara

Lake Brunner

Mount Ajax 1834m

Lake Sumner

7 HANMER SPRINGS

Kaikoura

Waiau

Waiau

Rotherham

Kaniere

Lake Kaniere

Otira

ARTHUR'S PASS **17**

rangi

18

ARTHUR'S PASS TOUR

ARTHUR'S PASS NP **16**

'n Alps

Rolleston Range

Puketeraki Range

Culverden

Waikari

Scargill

Waipara **6** WAIPARA VINEYARDS TOUR

Waikari

Waipara

Harunui

Domett

Lake Coleridge

Porters Pass 945m

Springfield

Sheffield

Oxford

Rangiora

Pegasus Bay

Kaiapoi

MOUNT HUTT **19**

Rakaia Gorge

Darfield

Waimakariri

CHRISTCHURCH

1

2 PORT HILLS

3 LYTTELTON

Methven

Rakaia

Rolleston

Lincoln

BANKS PENINSULA

4 Okains Bay

Mt Somers

Canterbury Plains

RAKAIA **20**

Lake Ellesmere

Little River

5

Mayfield

Ashburton

Southbridge

AKAROA

Peel Forest

21 ASHBURTON

ANTERBURY

Hinds

22 GERALDINE

Temuka

Canterbury Bight

ant Point

23 TIMARU

Pareora

Makikihi

nate

Studholme

Dunedin

0 kilometres 40

0 miles 20

GETTING AROUND

Numerous bus operators link all parts of the region, but the most convenient way to get around is by car. The roads are good, although care is needed in winter on the alpine routes, and some sights are accessible only via gravel roads. Many areas are easily visited by day trips from Christchurch, including Banks Peninsula, Hanmer Springs, Arthur's Pass and mid-Canterbury's ski fields. The four and a half hour trip from Christchurch to Greymouth on the TranzAlpine railway is a relaxing way to see the region's diverse scenery.

Lake Tekapo, a popular venue for water sports

Christchurch ❶

Christchurch's Wizard

Canterbury's provincial capital, Christchurch, is the largest city in the South Island and the principal gateway to its scenic wonders. Laid out as the capital of the Canterbury Settlement in 1850, the city has many notable buildings and monuments that recall its colonial heritage, as well as many parks and gardens. It is often thought of as a conservative city, a reflection of its origins as a Church of England settlement modelled on 19th-century English society. During the 19th century its economy was dominated by agriculture, but in the 20th century it became increasingly industrialized and is today a centre for IT. It has a sophisticated restaurant, café and arts scene.

Timber ceiling in Christchurch Cathedral

🏛 Cathedral Square

Lying in the heart of the city, Cathedral Square is dominated by the Anglican Christchurch Cathedral. Other historic buildings surround the square: the Renaissance-style Old Chief Post Office (built in 1879), the former Government Building (1911), the ornate Edwardian Regent Theatre (1905), and the Gothic Press Building (1909) *(see p29)*, which houses the city's daily newspaper. An 1867 statue of Canterbury's founder, John Robert Godley, faces the cathedral. The steps in front of the cathedral attract many eccentrics and street performers, including Christchurch's resident Wizard, who appears intermittently to cast "spells" and pontificate.

⛪ Christchurch Cathedral

Cathedral Square. **ℹ** *(03) 366 0046.* ◯ *daily.* 📷 *tower only.* ✝ *daily except Sat.* ♿ 🚻 📷 🎁

Begun in 1864 and completed in 1904, Christchurch Cathedral was built as the focal point of the new Anglican settlement of Canterbury. It remains the city's most important landmark. It was designed by English architect George Gilbert Scott in the Gothic Revival style. Noted local architect Benjamin Mountfort supervised the completion and also had considerable influence over the design. Built of Canterbury stone and native timbers, this impressive building has many notable features, including detailed wood and stone carvings around the high

altar and main pulpit. Other works of art depict the history of Canterbury's settlement, the city's connection with Antarctic exploration and military campaigns through the world wars. The tower's 134 steps can be climbed for an excellent view of the city, Port Hills, Canterbury Plains and distant Southern Alps.

GODLEY AND THE CANTERBURY SETTLEMENT

John Robert Godley (1814–61) is regarded as the founder of Canterbury although he spent only three years in the new province. With Edward Gibbon Wakefield, founder of the New Zealand Company *(see p49)*, he formed the Canterbury Association in 1848, which then purchased 1,210 sq km (470 sq miles) of land for the creation of a Church of England-dominated province in New Zealand. A slice of England was to be transplanted on Canterbury's far shores. English newspapers commented on the "respectability" of the so-called "Canterbury Pilgrims" who set sail on four ships, the *Randolph, Charlotte Jane, Cressy* and *Sir George Seymour*, in September 1850. Within three years of its founding, Canterbury was governing itself as one of New Zealand's six provinces. Godley returned to England in 1852.

Statue of Godley in Cathedral Square

(Map of central Christchurch showing Mona Vale, International Antarctic Centre, Victoria Lake, Conservatory Complex, Water Garden, Rose Garden, Cockayne Memorial Garden, Botanic Gardens, Avon, Hagley, RICCARTON AVENUE, Train Station)

Mona Vale
800m (880 yards)
⑮
International
Antarctic Centre

Hagley

Victoria Lake

Conservatory Com

Water Garden

Rose Garden

Cockayne Memorial Garden

Botanic Gardens ⑬

Avon

RICCARTON

AVENUE

Train Sta
1 km (0.6 r

0 metres	500
0 yards	500

KEY

▢ Street-by-Street: Christchurch *pp224–5*

-- Inner-city tram route

Key to Symbols *see back flap*

VISITORS' CHECKLIST

Road map C6. 🏙 *316,000*. ✈
10 km (6 miles) NW of city. 🚉
Troup Dr. 🚌 *123 Worcester St.*
🚏 *Cathedral Square.* ℹ
*Old Chief Post Office Building,
Cathedral Square, (03) 379 9629.*
🎭 *Showtime Canterbury (Nov);
Summertimes Festivals (Dec–
Mar).* **www**.christchurch.com

🐟 **Southern Encounter
Aquarium and Kiwi House**
3 Cathedral Square. **Tel** (03) 359 7169.
🕐 *daily.* ● *25 Dec.* ♿ 🚫 📷 ℹ
www.southernencounter.co.nz
This small aquarium, situated in
the old Regent Theatre building, specializes in the aquatic
life of the South Island. The fish
here are regularly returned to
the wild and replaced with
fresh stock. The rare North
Island kiwi is also on view.

Punting on the Avon River in Christchurch

🍁 **Avon River**
Cashel St & Oxford Terrace.
The Avon River, which gently
meanders through the city, is
Christchurch's greatest natural
asset and one of its main
attractions. Its grassy banks,
weeping willows, old oak
trees, ducks, and bridges linking the city's main streets lure
office workers and visitors

alike to its banks in summer.
A walk along the Avon River
bank from Victoria Square to
the Bridge of Remembrance
takes visitors past the Law
Courts, the Floral Clock, the
Provincial Council Buildings
and a 1917 statue of Antarctic
explorer Robert Scott sculpted
by his widow, Kathleen.

Another great way to
enjoy the river is to take a
boat trip. Punts operate from
various landings along the
river, including near the
Town Hall *(see p224)* and
Antigua Boatshed.

🍁 **Victoria Square**
Victoria Square is a beautifully
landscaped expanse of green
north of Cathedral Square.
Focal points are the Floral
Clock, statues of Queen
Victoria (1901) and James
Cook (1932), and the much
photographed Bowker and
Ferrier fountains. The Town
Hall, built in 1972, on the
banks of the Avon in Kilmore
Street, features a combination
of glass, marble, and still and
flowing water. A block away,
on Victoria Street, is the
Christchurch Casino, recog-
nizable by its stylized roulette
wheel façade.

CHRISTCHURCH CITY CENTRE

Victoria Square

Street-by-Street: Christchurch

Rose window,
Christchurch
Cathedral

The streets surrounding Cathedral Square are laid out in a grid pattern bordered by four broad avenues. The formality of the layout is broken by the quaint Avon River which winds serpentine through the inner city and adjacent parks. Christchurch's many Gothic Revival and Edwardian buildings, pretty parks and landscaped river bank support the oft-repeated description of Christchurch as the most English of cities outside England. The city is easily navigated on foot or bicycle. Yellow buses offer free inner-city transport and a tram route stops at the city's main historic and cultural attractions.

New Regent Street
This charming pedestrian-only area was built in the Spanish Mission style in 1932. The city tram regularly rumbles through.

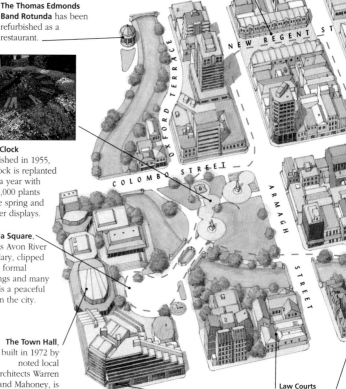

The Thomas Edmonds Band Rotunda has been refurbished as a restaurant.

Floral Clock
Established in 1955, the clock is replanted twice a year with over 5,000 plants to give spring and summer displays.

Victoria Square, with its Avon River boundary, clipped lawns, formal plantings and many trees, is a peaceful oasis in the city.

The Town Hall, built in 1972 by noted local architects Warren and Mahoney, is the city's principal venue for the performing arts.

Parkroyal Hotel

Law Courts

★ **Provincial Council Buildings**
These buildings, built between 1858 and 1865, feature fine stained-glass windows, a delicately stencilled ridge-and-furrow ceiling and mosaic tile work.

STAR SIGHTS

★ Christchurch Cathedral

★ Provincial Council Buildings

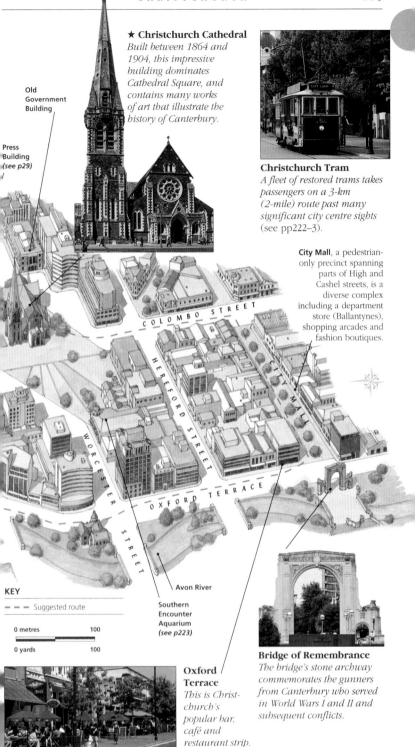

★ Christchurch Cathedral
Built between 1864 and 1904, this impressive building dominates Cathedral Square, and contains many works of art that illustrate the history of Canterbury.

Old Government Building

Press Building (see p29)

Christchurch Tram
A fleet of restored trams takes passengers on a 3-km (2-mile) route past many significant city centre sights (see pp222–3).

City Mall, a pedestrian-only precinct spanning parts of High and Cashel streets, is a diverse complex including a department store (Ballantynes), shopping arcades and fashion boutiques.

COLOMBO STREET

HEREFORD STREET

CITY MALL

WORCESTER STREET

OXFORD TERRACE

KEY

– – – Suggested route

0 metres 100
0 yards 100

Avon River

Southern Encounter Aquarium (see p223)

Oxford Terrace
This is Christchurch's popular bar, café and restaurant strip.

Bridge of Remembrance
The bridge's stone archway commemorates the gunners from Canterbury who served in World Wars I and II and subsequent conflicts.

Stone legislative chamber of the Provincial Council Buildings

🏛 Provincial Council Buildings

Cnr of Armagh & Durham sts. **Tel** *(03) 941 7680.*
○ *Mon–Sat.* ● *public hols.*
🚻 *limited.* 📷

Designed by Christchurch architect Benjamin Mountfort, the Provincial Council Buildings are claimed to be the finest example of secular Gothic Revival architecture in New Zealand. They are also the only council buildings to have survived from the period 1853–76 when the country was governed by elected provincial councils.

The buildings were constructed in three stages. The first two, from 1858 to 1861, saw the creation of a mainly wooden building. The third involved the construction of a stone council chamber, completed in 1865, the high point of this notable complex.

🏛 Bridge of Remembrance

Cnr of Cashel St & Oxford Terrace.

A commemoration of New Zealand soldiers who served in various arenas of war, the bridge stands at the head of City Mall, the city's central shopping area. The large stone archway over the bridge, built in 1923, underwent extensive refurbishment in the early 1990s.

🏛 Canterbury Museum

Rolleston Ave. **Tel** *(03) 366 5000.* ○
daily. ● *25 Dec.* 💷 *donation.* 🚻
www.canterburymuseum.com

Built between 1869 and 1876, Canterbury Museum is considered to be one of Mountfort's most successful adaptations of the Gothic style for secular purposes. The museum has a comprehensive selection of genuine Antarctic relics as well as one of the finest mounted bird displays in the southern hemisphere. Other halls feature oriental art, furniture and fashions through the ages, a reconstruction of a 19th-century Christchurch street, and a Maori cultural section, including displays of the extinct moa and the bird's early Polynesian hunters.

Moa skeleton, Canterbury Museum

🏛 Christ's College

Rolleston Ave. **Tel** *(03) 366 8705.*
○ *daily.* ● *buildings during school hols.* 📷 *by arrangement.*
🚻 *partial.*

At Christ's College, a modern-day reminder of Christchurch's English heritage, the sons of Canterbury's élite are educated in black and white striped blazers along English public school lines amid Gothic Revival buildings dating back to 1863. There are tours of the grounds and buildings.

🏛 Arts Centre

Cnr of Rolleston Ave & Worcester Boulevard. **Tel** *(03) 363 2836.*
○ *daily.* ● *Good Fri, 25 April (am), 25 Dec.* 🚻 *ground floor.* 📷
10am–4pm. 🍴 ▯ 🛍 *weekends.*
🎭 *World Buskers Festival (mid-Jan).*
www.artscentre.org.nz

Located in the old University of Canterbury buildings, the Arts Centre is Christchurch's art and crafts hub (*see p229*). The complex houses more than 40 galleries, studios and shops, as well as theatre, film and ballet venues and eateries. A bustling outdoor market is held every weekend throughout the year. Construction of the Gothic Revival-style buildings began in 1877. It was designed by a succession of architects, including Mountfort, who was responsible for the Clock Tower building, Great Hall and Classics block. Assembled piecemeal over 46 years, the buildings were linked by quadrangles and cloisters.

Weekend market at the Arts Centre in Christchurch

For hotels and restaurants in this region see pp312–16 and pp338–40

🏛 Christchurch Art Gallery (Te Puna o Waiwhetu)

Corner of Montreal St & Worcester Blvd. **Tel** (03) 941 7300. ◯ daily. ⬤ 25 Dec. 📷 for some exhibitions. ♿ 🅿 📷 🎁
www.christchurchartgallery.org.nz

Situated close to Cathedral Square, this is the city's principal art gallery. It houses a collection of 5,000 New Zealand and international works of art, which are complemented by touring exhibitions. The gallery's large, permanent display features Dutch, French, Italian and British paintings, drawings, prints, sculpture and ceramics.

The New Zealand collection, especially of Canterbury works, is one of the most comprehensive in the country. The collection displays works by Canterbury landscape artist William Sutton (see p32), as well as other prominent New Zealand painters, including Doris Lusk, Colin McCahon, Rita Angus, Charles Goldie, Frances Hodgkins, Dick Frizzell and Seraphine Pick.

🚣 Antigua Boat Sheds

2 Cambridge Terrace. **Tel** (03) 366 5885. ◯ daily. ⬤ 25 Dec. 📷 🖥
www.boatsheds.co.nz

The Antigua Boat Sheds, on the banks of the Avon River, have been providing people with river recreation since 1882. Here, canoes, punts and paddle boats can be hired for trips through the city or upstream to the Botanic Gardens. They are the only surviving commercial boat sheds of the five or six that once offered boats for hire.

⛲ Mona Vale

63 Fendalton Rd. **Tel** (03) 348 9660. ◯ daily. 🍴

Mona Vale, one of Christchurch's historic homes, built between 1899 and 1900, is situated among sweeping lawns, mature trees and landscaped gardens to the northwest of Hagley Park. The Avon River meanders through the property. Visitors are invited to stroll through the gardens and feed the ducks. The imposing homestead was almost demolished in the 1960s, but a public appeal for funds led to its purchase by

Mona Vale on the banks of the Avon River

the city. The gardens are open to the public, and morning and afternoon teas and lunches are available at the homestead.

🌳 Hagley Park

Tel (03) 941 6840. ◯ daily. ♿

Hagley Park, a vast green expanse in the heart of Christchurch, serves as the city's lungs. Within its boundaries are a golf course, sports grounds, tree-lined walking and cycling tracks, artificial lakes, and the Botanic Gardens (see pp228–9). When the early colonists laid out the site for their new town, they set aside 2 sq km (0.80 sq mile) for a public park, and in 1856 an ordinance was passed declaring it "reserved forever" for public recreation and enjoyment. By the early 1870s, the settlers had replaced the park's native flora with European plants, grasses and trees.

🏛 International Antarctic Centre

38 Orchard Rd. **Tel** (03) 353 7798. ◯ daily. 📷 ♿ 🖥 🎁
www.iceberg.co.nz

About 20 minutes from the city centre, near the airport to the west, is the International Antarctic Centre, the base for the New Zealand, United States and Italian Antarctic programmes. Its visitor centre has a range of exhibits on the exploration and geology of Antarctica. Visitors can also take rides on Antarctic vehicles.

🚠 Christchurch Gondola

10 Bridle Path Rd. **Tel** (03) 384 0700. ◯ daily. 📷 ♿ 🍴 🖥 🎁
www.gondola.co.nz

Southeast of the city, the Christchurch Gondola takes passengers from a terminal in the Heathcote Valley to the rim of an extinct volcano at the top of the Port Hills. From the top there are amazing 360-degree views of the city, Banks Peninsula, Canterbury Plains and the distant Southern Alps.

A boat operator offering punting in Hagley Park

Botanic Gardens

The Botanic Gardens, founded in 1863, contribute to Christchurch's reputation as New Zealand's garden city. The gardens' conservatories, rose and bulb beds, rock and water gardens, English lawns and woodland are largely enclosed in the loop of the Avon River, and the proximity of flowing water to all sections makes the gardens particularly tranquil. The area fringing the eastern side of the Botanic Gardens is Christchurch's creative and artistic heart. The city's museum, civic art gallery, ballet company, professional theatre and Arts Centre are located here.

Sculpted drinking fountain

★ Conservatory Complex
Of the complex's six glasshouses, one of the most notable is Cuningham House, built in 1923, which houses tropical plants.

Children's Playground

★ Water Garden
This is enclosed by herbaceous perennials and exotic trees and shrubs, creating a cool and tranquil setting.

The Cockayne Memorial Garden has specimen plantings of native trees and shrubs.

In the New Zealand Garden native plants are displayed in an authentic mixed forest setting.

Rose Garden
Roses, symbolic of the city's English heritage, are planted in a formal garden in front of the Conservatory Complex.

Daffodil Woodland and Bandsmen's Memorial Rotunda
The area surrounding the rotunda was planted with 16,000 bulbs in 1933, and in spring is a blaze of yellow.

STAR FEATURES

★ Conservatory Complex

★ Water Garden

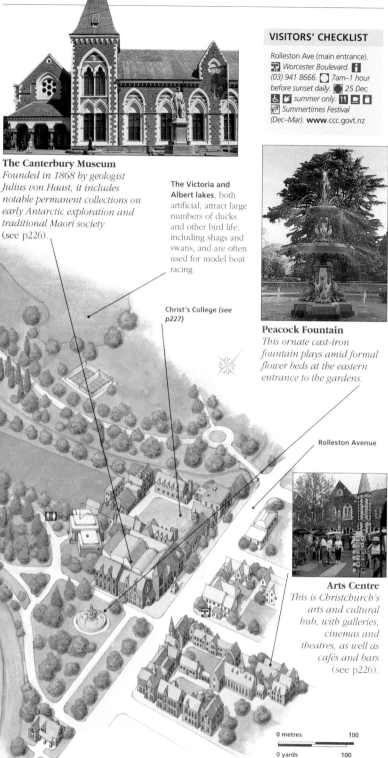

The Canterbury Museum
Founded in 1868 by geologist Julius von Haast, it includes notable permanent collections on early Antarctic exploration and traditional Maori society (see p226).

The Victoria and Albert lakes, both artificial, attract large numbers of ducks and other bird life, including shags and swans, and are often used for model boat racing.

Christ's College *(see p227)*

VISITORS' CHECKLIST

Rolleston Ave (main entrance).
🚌 Worcester Boulevard. ℹ️
(03) 941 8666. ⏰ 7am–1 hour before sunset daily. ⬤ 25 Dec.
♿ 📷 summer only. 🍴 🏪 🛍️
🎭 Summertimes Festival (Dec–Mar). www.ccc.govt.nz

Peacock Fountain
This ornate cast-iron fountain plays amid formal flower beds at the eastern entrance to the gardens.

Rolleston Avenue

Arts Centre
This is Christchurch's arts and cultural hub, with galleries, cinemas and theatres, as well as cafés and bars (see p226).

0 metres	100
0 yards	100

Sign of the Takahe, on Dyers Pass Road above Christchurch

Port Hills ❷

Road map C6. 🚌

The Port Hills separate Christchurch from Lyttelton Harbour, and were formed as the result of the eruption of the now extinct Lyttelton volcano. Their tussock-covered slopes and volcanic outcrops flank the southern part of the city. Because of their proximity to the city they are extremely popular with walkers, runners, rock climbers and mountain bikers.

The Port Hills are also easily accessed by car, thanks to the work of early 20th-century conservationist and politician Harry Ell, who strove for the creation of a road across the hills. The first stretch of the Summit Road was opened in 1938.

Ell's vision included the construction of a series of rest houses along the Port Hills, the most impressive of which is the Sign of the Takahe, completed in 1949. Nestled in the hill suburb of Cashmere, this imposing Gothic building was also the most cherished of his projects. Another Ell legacy, the Sign of the Kiwi, is a popular resting place for people travelling along the Summit Road.

The many tracks on the Port Hills provide striking views of Lyttelton Harbour, the Canterbury Plains and the Southern Alps. The rim of the crater can also be accessed via the Christchurch Gondola (see p227).

Lyttelton ❸

Road map C6. 🚶 4,000. 🚌 ℹ️
20 Oxford St, (03) 328 9093.

Lyttelton was the landing place of the Canterbury Pilgrims, brought out by the Canterbury Association to populate the new province in 1850, and was named after Lord Lyttelton, the chairman of the Association. In 1867, a rail tunnel was drilled through the volcanic rock of the Port Hills to provide a link between Lyttelton's port and Christchurch, and a road tunnel was completed in 1964. The town's port is one of the busiest in South Island.

Lyttelton Timeball Station

The **Lyttelton Museum** has interesting displays of local maritime history and relics from the colonial past, as well as a small section on Antarctic exploration.

The **Lyttelton Timeball Station** stands sentry over the town, as it has done since its construction in 1875. Each day

at 1pm the large black ball hanging from its tower is lowered to signal Greenwich Mean Time to the ships in the harbour. Its function was replaced by radios in 1934, but it remains in working order. A ferry service across the harbour to Quail and Ripapa islands and the small township of Diamond Harbour operates from the Lyttelton docks.

🏛️ **Lyttelton Museum**
Gladstone Quay. **Tel** (03) 328 8972.
⬤ Tue, Thu, Sat & Sun, pm only.
⬤ 25 Dec. 🏷️ donation.
♿ ground floor.

🏛️ **Lyttelton Timeball Station**
Reserve Terrace. **Tel** (03) 328 7311.
⬤ Oct–Apr: daily; May–Sep: Wed–Sun. ⬤ Good Fri, 25 Dec. 🏷️ 📷

Banks Peninsula ❹

Road map C6.

Formed by numerous eruptions of the Lyttelton and Akaroa volcanoes, Banks Peninsula was, until some 25,000 years ago, an island. Reminders of this dramatic geological past are everywhere, including rocky volcanic outcrops, craggy headlands, deep valleys and precipitous bluffs. The Summit Road allows excellent views of this striking scenery.

The peninsula has been settled by Maori for 1,000 years, and until the 1820s was a place of prosperity and security for the Ngai Tahu tribe. That changed as a result of internecine and intertribal fighting, conflict which contributed indirectly to the decision taken by the British

Maori and Colonial Museum and meeting house at Okains Bay

Laverick's Bay, Banks Peninsula

government to install a governor and sign the Treaty of Waitangi *(see pp48–9)*.

Among the peninsula's many attractions are its beautiful bays and picturesque villages, including Pigeon Bay, Okains Bay, Laverick's Bay and Le Bons Bay. There are many walking tracks, ranging from the five-hour Pigeon Bay Walkway to the two- to four-day Banks Peninsula Track, which traverses private farmland and the coastline of the remote eastern bays. These remote areas can also be visited on the **Eastern Bays Scenic Mail Run**, a mail delivery service that invites up to eight passengers to join its four-hour mail run.

At Okains Bay is the **Maori and Colonial Museum** which houses an extensive collection of Maori artifacts, including an 1867 Maori *waka* (canoe) used during the Waitangi Day celebrations in February *(see p41)*.

Also worth a visit is the boutique **Barry's Bay Cheese Factory**, which continues the peninsula's long tradition of cheese making. Just as popular for its good wine, food and picturesque rural setting is the French Farm Winery and Restaurant *(see p338)*.

✿ Maori and Colonial Museum
1146 Main Rd, Okains Bay. **Tel** (03) 304 8611. ◯ daily. ● 25 Dec. 📷

✿ Barry's Bay Cheese Factory
State Hwy 75. **Tel** (03) 304 5809. ◯ daily. ● 25 Dec.

✿ Eastern Bays Scenic Mail Run
19 Rue Renard. **Tel** (03) 304 7873. ◯ Mon–Sat. ● public hols.

Akaroa ❺

Road map C6. 580. 🚌
ℹ 80 Rue Lavaud, (03) 304 8600. www.akaroa.com

This attractive small town, nestled at the head of Akaroa Harbour, is the oldest town in Canterbury, and was founded by a small band of French settlers in 1840. The town boasts many French-influenced

historic buildings, narrow streets and a beautiful harbourfront location. Among the many reminders of Akaroa's French heritage is **Langlois-Eteveneaux House**, believed to have been prefabricated in France and erected in Akaroa in 1841. It is part of the **Akaroa Museum** complex, which also includes the town's old courthouse, opened in 1880. The museum exhibits cover natural and regional history and architecture. A self-guided walk through the town takes in 43 historic sites, including the 1880 **Akaroa Lighthouse**.

A good swimming beach lies at the centre of the town. Harbour cruises operate from the main wharf, and visitors may see Hector's dolphins, penguins and seal colonies. A number of walking tracks lead up to the surrounding volcanic saddles and peaks, affording panoramic views of the harbour. Akaroa also boasts an active art and crafts community, and many shops and galleries.

✿ Langlois-Eteveneaux House and Akaroa Museum
71 Rue Lavaud. **Tel** (03) 304 1013. ◯ daily. ● 25 Dec.

✿ Akaroa Lighthouse
Tel (03) 304 7325. ◯ weekends, public hols & by arrangement. ground floor.

JEAN FRANÇOIS LANGLOIS

The man primarily responsible for Akaroa's French heritage was whaler Jean François Langlois. In August 1838, he conceived the idea of a French colony and attempted to buy most of the peninsula from the local Ngai Tahu people. The following year he returned to France to gain support for

Langlois-Eteveneaux House

his plan, and formed the Nanto-Bordelaise Company as the vehicle for his colonizing ambitions.

French navy captain Charles Lavaud was dispatched to provide protection for the 57 colonists who landed at Akaroa in August 1840. However, French ambitions were thwarted by the British who, in the interim, had signed the Treaty of Waitangi and, upon hearing of the settlers' impending arrival, rushed to appoint two magistrates to Akaroa. Despite the assertion of British sovereignty, the settlers stayed, although by 1842 Langlois was back in France. The Nanto-Bordelaise Company was bought out by the New Zealand Company in 1849, opening the way for large-scale British migration to the settlement.

Waipara Vineyard Tour ➏

The Waipara district is a relatively new wine-growing region, with the first vineyards planted only in the 1980s. However, it has emerged quickly as a promising area, and many of its vineyards have won awards for their wines. Canterbury has over 30 vineyards, but Waipara, about 65 km (40 miles) north of Christchurch, is the area of most rapid development. Wine-tasting tours can be arranged through the Christchurch visitor information centre (see p223), including a tour in a Clydesdale-drawn wagon.

Cabernet grapes

Pegasus Bay ➀
This winery crushed its first grapes in 1991, but has already won many awards. Its wine-tasting venue has a charming garden setting overlooking the surrounding countryside.

Daniel Schuster Wines ➈
Established in 1988, this vineyard produces high-quality Chardonnay and Pinot Noir. It is open for wine tasting by appointment.

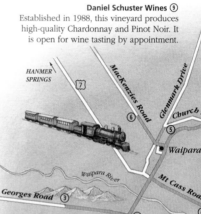

HANMER SPRINGS

Waipara

Mountford Vineyard ➇
Mountford produces top-of-the-range Chardonnay and Pinot Noir. A beautiful homestead overlooks the small vineyard.

Waipara Springs ➆
With its first vines planted in 1982, Waipara Springs is one of the oldest vineyards in the district, and has won many awards. Its popular wine-tasting venue is set in pleasant gardens.

0 kilometres   3

0 miless   3

CHRISTCHURCH

Mount Cass Vineyards
Formerly Chancellor Wines, th
vineyard, now owned by Alpi
Pacific Wine Company, off
tastings by appointment of Mou
Cass and Hanmer Junction wine

Glenmark Wines ➅
Glenmark's vines were planted in 1981, making it the district's first winery. Its wines have won many awards, and can be tasted in a pleasant, rustic setting.

Torlesse Wines ➄
Torlesse uses both Waipara and Marlborough grapes to produce a wide range of wines, including Gewürztraminer, Cabernet Sauvignon, Sauvignon Blanc and Chardonnay

TIPS FOR DRIVERS

Tour length: 170 km (105 miles) return from Christchurch. Most of the wineries are located on side roads or driveways off State Hwy 1, so it is important to be careful of fast-moving traffic when travelling between vineyards.
Stopping-off points:
Pegasus Bay, Canterbury House, Glenmark and Waipara Springs wineries have restaurants. Booking is advisable.

Mud House Winery ②

One of the newest additions to Waipara's wine industry, it is distinguished by a huge stone winery building next to State Highway 1.

Fiddlers Green ③

Producing its first vintage in 1998, this is another of Waipara's newcomers. However, its Riesling and Sauvignon Blanc wines have already won awards.

KEY

▬	Tour route
▬	Other roads
▬	River

Hot pool complex at Hanmer Springs

Hanmer Springs ❼

Road map C5. 🏠 *800.* 🚍
🛈 *42 Amuri Ave, (03) 315 7128.*
www.hurunui.com

This small alpine village, 385 m (1,260 ft) above sea level, is best known for the extensive **Hanmer Springs Thermal Reserve**. Although hot springs were first discovered in the area in 1859, they were officially opened only in 1883. Today, the complex has 12 thermal and freshwater pools of varying temperatures, as well as private pools and a children's water slide area.

Surrounding the hot pools is a 168-sq-km (65-sq-mile) forest park, which offers activities such as mountain biking and walks, ranging from the short Conical Hill walk (one hour return) to the longer Mount Isobel walk (five to six hours return). At the Waiau Ferry Bridge, 5 km (3 miles) from the village, tourist operators offer bungy jumping, jet-boating and rafting down the Waiau River.

📷 Hanmer Springs Thermal Reserve
42 Amuri Ave. Tel (03) 315 7511.
⭘ *daily.* ⬤ *25 Dec.* 🈺 🚻 ▯
www.hanmersprings.co.nz

Lewis Pass ❽

Road map C5.

Lewis Pass marks the crossing point on State Highway 7 over the South Island's Main Divide. The surrounding 183-sq-km (70-sq-mile) Lewis Pass National Reserve offers a range of unguided outdoor activities, including tramping, fishing and hunting.

Just over the pass, **Maruia Springs Thermal Resort** has a small complex of outdoor hot pools in a natural setting, with views of the surrounding bush and mountain peaks.

📷 Maruia Springs Thermal Resort
State Hwy 7. Tel (03) 523 8840.
⭘ *daily.* ⬤ *25 Dec.* 🈺 🚻 🍴

Reefton ❾

Road map C5. 🏠 *1,000.* 🚍
🛈 *67-69 Broadway, (03) 732 8391.*

Founded in 1872, Reefton takes its name from the gold-bearing quartz reefs in the area. The town's gold-mining heritage is evident in the many historic remains of the 1870s boom dotted around the region, especially in the beech forest-clad Victoria Forest Park. A network of tracks provides opportunity for exploration on foot or on mountain bike.

A heritage walk around Reefton takes in many historic buildings, including the **School of Mines**, which operated from 1887 to 1970 as part of a network of similar schools around New Zealand. Two km (1.2 miles) from Reefton, the **Black's Point Museum** exhibits relics from the gold-mining era.

🏫 School of Mines
Shiel St. Tel (03) 732 8391.
⭘ *by arrangement.* 🈺 🚻

🏛 Black's Point Museum
State Hwy 7. Tel (03) 732 8035.
⭘ *Wed–Sun.* ⬤ *25 Dec.* 🈺 🚻

Karamea ⑩

Road map C4. 🚶 700. 🚌 ℹ️
Market Cross, (03) 782 6652
📷 *Whitebaiters Ball (Oct).*
www.karameainfo.co.nz

Settled by Europeans in 1874, Karamea is an isolated farming community that lies at the northern end of the West Coast's State Highway 67. Nestled in a basin dominated by dairy farming and fringed by the Kahurangi National Park, Karamea is best known as the exit point for the Heaphy Track, which after following the coast from the Heaphy River ends 15 km (9 miles) to the north. Several short walking tracks are based around the Heaphy exit point, including the 40-minute Nikau Loop and the 90-minute Scotts Beach walk.

About 26 km (16 miles) to the northeast of Karamea is the **Oparara Basin**, featuring impressive limestone formations and a 15-km (9-mile) system of caves enveloped by dense forest. Much of the gravel road to the basin is narrow and winding, but can be undertaken in a 2WD vehicle. The highly fragile Honeycomb Caves system, first explored in 1980, is accessible only with a guide, and contains the remains of about 50 species, including the extinct moa and New Zealand eagle. Areas that can be explored without a guide are the

Cows, cabbage trees and beach near Karamea

Oparara Arch, 43 m (141 ft) high and 219 m (719 ft) long, which is reached after a 20-minute walk on a good track through the forest, and the Box Canyon and Crazy Paving caves. It is essential to carry a good torch. For the highly adventurous visitor, local tourist operators run grades four and five white-water rafting trips down the Karamea River.

Karamea is also a base for walkers using the popular three- to five-day Wangapeka Track. The Fenian Track is an historic gold-miners' route, and the four-hour return walk leads to the former mining settlement of Adams Flat.

🏞️ **Oparara Basin**
State Hwy 67. **Tel** (03) 782 6652.
📷 *Honeycomb Caves.* 📷
obligatory at Honeycomb Caves.

Westport ⑪

Road map C5. 🚶 5,000.
✈️ *5 km (3 miles) N of town.* 🚌
ℹ️ *1 Brougham St, (03) 789 6658.*
www.westport.org.nz

Although Westport's origins lie in the gold rush of the 1860s, coal has been its life-line for much of its history. Until 1954, coal from mines in the surrounding mountains was shipped out through the town's once busy port at the head of the Buller River, but today the bulk is taken by train to Lyttelton on the east coast *(see p230)*. The **Coal Town Museum** at Westport has extensive exhibits reconstructing aspects of the region's coal-mining heritage.

Westport is a base for a number of outdoor activities, including jet-boating and jet-skiing on the river. Among the most popular activities is underground rafting in the Nile River Canyon area. This can be done only with a guide and involves floating in inner tubes through glow-worm grottos and caverns before emerging into the open to float down the Waitakere River rapids and Nile River Canyon. The Metro Cave, which has dramatic limestone stalactite and stalagmite formations, can be explored on foot.

Seals at Tauranga Bay, near Westport

Westport's North Beach and Carter's Beach are both popular swimming and surfing spots, as is the scenic Tauranga Bay. On the Cape Foulwind Walkway at the edge of Tauranga Bay is a breeding colony of fur seals *(see p193)*. The walkway, which takes three hours return, crosses rocky granite bluffs, grassy downs, swampy streams and sandy beaches.

🏛️ **Coal Town Museum**
Queen St South. **Tel** (03) 789 8204.
⭕ *daily.* ⬤ *25 Dec.* 📷 ♿

Nikau Loop at the exit to the Heaphy Track

Coal-mining Heritage

Coal was first discovered on the West Coast by explorer Thomas Brunner in 1848. The largest of the early mines were on the Denniston and Stockton plateaus, north-east of Westport, where large-scale exploitation began in 1878. The task of extracting

Miner's Hall near Runanga, Greymouth

coal from the rugged, mountainous terrain was hazardous, and necessitated some striking feats of engineering. The most famous was the Denniston Incline, a gravity-powered rail system under which laden coal trucks were lowered 520 m (1,700 ft) down the mountainside on a steel cable. Empty wagons were pulled back up by the weight of full wagons. The incline closed in 1967, but during its 87 years of operation it carried 13 million tonnes of coal off the Denniston Plateau. The coal industry continues to be important to the West Coast economy, with over 2 million tonnes exported from the coalfields each year.

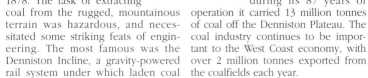

Coal wagon on steel tracks for transporting coal in and out of the mine

The entrance, carefully reinforced to prevent collapse

EARLY MINING TOWNS

Several mining settlements sprang up in the 19th century to support the coal industry, but they are little more than ghost towns today. The 120-km (75-mile) self-guided Buller Coalfields Heritage Trail leads through many mining relics, including the once thriving towns of Denniston, Stockton and Millerton. Information on the trail is available at the i-SITE Visitor Centre in Westport.

Coal miners at the entrance to the Rewanui coal mine

Coal wagons *like this one in the Coal Town Museum were used to bring coal down from the mountainous coalfields.*

This aerial ropeway *is used to lower coal from the opencast Stockton mine down to the coastal settlement of Ngakawau, where it is loaded onto trains bound for the port of Lyttelton on the east coast.*

Among the many *relics that remain at Denniston, the marshalling point for coal from all over the plateau, are retaining rock walls where coal would be screened before being lowered down the incline, and parts of machinery.*

Paparoa National Park ⑫

Road map C5. 🚐 🅸 *State Hwy 6, Punakaiki, (03) 731 1895.*

Founded in 1987, this 300-sq-km (115-sq-mile) park contains varied and dramatic scenery, most famously the Pancake Rocks and blowholes near the small coastal settlement of Punakaiki. Bands of limestone, separated by thin bands of softer mudstone, which has been worn away by thousands of years of rain, wind and sea spray, have created the layered formations of the Pancake Rocks. Over hundreds of thousands of years, caverns have also been formed as carbon dioxide-bearing rainwater has gradually eaten into cracks in the limestone. During high seas, these subterranean caverns become blowholes as the waves surge in under huge pressure and explode in a plume of spray. The Pancake Rocks and blowholes are easily accessible from the main highway via the short Dolomite Point walk. Wheelchair access, if assisted, is also possible.

Other short walks as well as longer tramps are available in the park, including the 15-minute Truman Track through subtropical forest to a wild coastline featuring caverns, a blowhole and waterfall, and the two-hour walk to a huge limestone structure known as "the ballroom overhang". A two- to three-day tramp through the heart of the park follows a pack track, built in 1867 to avoid dangerous travel along the isolated and rugged coastline.

Greymouth ⑬

Road map C5. 🚹 *13,500.* 🚌 🚕 🅸 *Cnr Herbert & Mackay sts, (03) 768 5101.* **www**.west-coast.co.nz

The largest town on the West Coast, Greymouth occupies the site of what was once Mawhera Pa. Although colonial government agents purchased the majority of the West Coast in 1860 for £300, the land under modern Greymouth remained a Maori reserve. Greymouth was laid out in 1865. Around this time, gold was being found in large quantities in the area, and coal had been discovered 17 years earlier. When the gold boom ended, coal mining ensured the district's continued survival. However, the Grey River mouth, which has served the town as a port, has also delivered misfortune. Repeatedly throughout its history, Greymouth has been submerged by flood waters, including twice in 1988. Since then a flood wall has been erected, popularly called "the great wall of Greymouth".

Greymouth's **History House Museum** has a large collection of historical photographs giving insight into the town's heritage. The **Left Bank Art Gallery** features an important greenstone collection, crafted in both contemporary and traditional designs, and hosts a major exhibition every two years. It also displays local art works.

Like other West Coast towns Greymouth offers a range of adventure tourism activities, including floating through the

Left Bank Art Gallery

Taniwha Caves on inflated tubes, and dolphin watching. The Grey River system is known for good fishing.

🏛 **History House Museum**
Gresson St. **Tel** *(03) 768 4028.*
◻ *summer: daily; winter: Mon–Fri.* ● *25 Dec.* 🅿 🅰

🏛 **Left Bank Art Gallery**
1 Tainui St. **Tel** *(03) 768 0038.*
◻ *summer: daily; winter: Tue–Sat.* ● *25 Dec, 1 Jan.* 🅿 🅰 🅲 *by arrangement.* 🅿

Pancake Rocks at Dolomite Point, Punakaiki

For hotels and restaurants in this region see pp312–16 and pp338–40

Street in Shantytown, a replica gold-mining town

Environs

One of Greymouth's most popular attractions is **Shantytown**, 11 km (7 miles) south. This elaborate replica gold-mining town includes a 1913 steam train which travels through native bush to a working sawmill and gold claim where visitors can try gold panning and perhaps strike it lucky and find a few specks of gold.

Lake Brunner, a restful, scenic spot surrounded by bush-clad mountains 42 km (26 miles) from Greymouth, is excellent for fishing, boating and water sports. The lake area is serviced by the small town of Moana, located at the northern end of Lake Brunner. There is a daily bus between Moana and Greymouth and the TranzAlpine scenic train, which leaves daily from Christchurch, is rated amongst the world's best scenic routes.

Shantytown
Rutherglen Rd. **Tel** (03) 762 6634.
◯ daily. ● 25 Dec. 🗺 🛗 🖵 🗖

Hokitika ⑭

Road map C5. 🏚 3,600. ✈ 2 km (1.2 miles) N of town. 🚌 🛈
Carnegie Building, Hamilton St, (03) 755 6166. 🎪 Wildfoods Festival (Mar). **www**.hokitika.org and www.wildfoods.co.nz

With its wide streets, notable historic buildings and excellent local craft studios, Hokitika is perhaps the West Coast's most attractive town. Little more than a shanty town in 1864, by 1866 Hokitika had become a thriving commercial centre thanks to gold. Its river port bustled with ships bearing miners flocking from the goldfields of Aus-

tralia, but it was a treacherous harbour where a ship went down every 10 weeks in the years 1865 and 1866. The wreck of one such ship is on the self-guided Hokitika Heritage Trail, which includes 22 historic buildings and sights. The most impressive of these is the 1908 Carnegie Library, now the home of the town's information centre and the **Historic Carnegie Complex and Museum**. The museum has displays on gold-mining and an audiovisual display of the town's history. It also houses a collection of rare books about the West Coast.

Jacquie Grant's Eco World is a small aquarium specializing in native fish species, including the adult version of the tiny whitebait for which the West Coast's rivers are renowned. The remarkable

Hokitika clock tower

Glowworm Dell, on the northern edge of the town, is worth a visit after dark. The best time to view the lights exuded by these carnivorous larvae is on a wet night.

🏛 Historic Carnegie Complex and Museum
Carnegie Centre, Cnr Tancred & Hamilton Sts. **Tel** (03) 755 6898.
◯ daily. ● 25 Dec. 🗺 🛗

🐟 Jacquie Grant's Eco World
64 Tancred St. **Tel** (03) 755 5251.
◯ daily. ● 1 Jan, 25 Dec. 🗺 🛗 🖵

Environs

There are a number of scenic areas around Hokitika. **Lake Mahinapua**, 10 km (6 miles) south, and **Lake Kaniere**, 20 km (12 miles) east of the town, are peaceful retreats, popular for boating, fishing, swimming and bush walking. The Lake Kaniere Walkway is 13 km (8 miles) and takes about four hours. **Ross** township, 28 km (17 miles) south of Hokitika, has a small local museum devoted to its colourful gold-mining history. Walks take visitors past old gold mine workings. New Zealand's biggest gold nugget was discovered here in 1909, and the area – said still to contain many millions of dollars worth of gold – is again being mined.

GREENSTONE

Nephrite jade *(pounamu)*, locally known as greenstone, is a hard, opaque, emerald stone. Formed in alpine fault lines under intense heat and pressure, greenstone boulders are eventually flushed from the eroding mountains into West Coast rivers. Greenstone holds great spiritual significance for Maori. Long before European colonization, tribes sent missions to search for the precious stone, later bartering it for food and other items. It was the hardest material known to Maori and was used for making tools, weapons and items of personal adornment. In 1997, ownership of the greenstone resource on the West Coast was handed back to the South Island Ngai Tahu tribe as part of a major Treaty of Waitangi settlement *(see p53)*.

Artisan at the Mountain Jade Greenstone Factory

Westland/Tai Poutini National Park ⑮

DANGER FALLING ICE

Warning sign, Fox Glacier

Stretching from the top of the Southern Alps in the east, where it shares a common boundary with Aoraki/Mount Cook National Park, to the Tasman Sea in the west, this 1,270-sq-km (490-sq-mile) national park is renowned for its mountain peaks (which reach a height of 3,500 m or 11,500 ft), dramatic glaciers, dense rainforest, coastal lagoons and beautiful lakes. Despite the intrusions of the West Coast gold rush of the 1860s and pastoral farming on the river flats, the area has remained largely unspoiled.

Ski touring
This is one of the best ways to experience the glaciers in the park. Ski-plane and helicopter tours also allow stunning views.

Gillespies Beach, a historic gold-mining settlement 20 km (12 miles) from Fox Glacier, offers walks along an early miners' track and to a fur seal colony along the beach.

TASMAN SEA

Gillespies Point

Gillespies Cook River Road

Cook River

Cook

KARANGARUA FOREST

Karangarua River

6

COPLAND RAN

Copland Track

Copland R

★ **Lake Matheson**
On clear, still mornings, Aoraki/Mount Cook and Mount Tasman are reflected in the lake, which is enveloped by forest.

KEY

▬▬	State highway
═══	Minor road
▬▬	River
‑ ‑	Walking track
▬•▬	Park boundary
ℹ	Tourist information
🏞	Picnic area

The Copland Valley Track, accessible from State Highway 6, is popular with trampers. For experienced climbers, the track continues over the Copland Pass and ends at Mount Cook village.

ROCKY RANGE

HOOKER

STAR SIGHTS

★ Fox Glacier

★ Franz Josef Glacier

★ Lake Matheson

Lowland rainforest
The park's extremely high rainfall (5,000 mm or 200 inches a year at Franz Josef village) supports lush, densely ferned lowland podocarp forest, featuring local species.

For hotels and restaurants in this region see pp312–16 and pp338–40

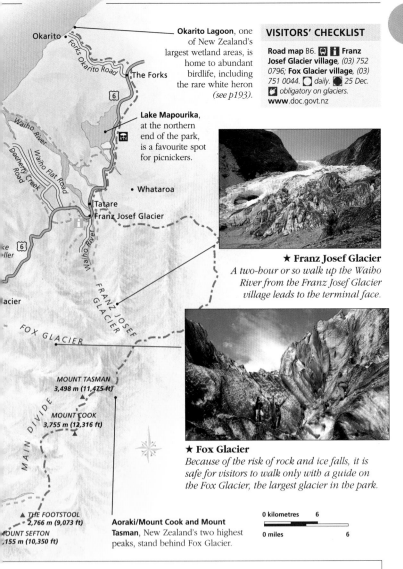

Okarito

Okarito Lagoon, one of New Zealand's largest wetland areas, is home to abundant birdlife, including the rare white heron *(see p193)*.

The Forks

Lake Mapourika, at the northern end of the park, is a favourite spot for picnickers.

• **Whataroa**

Tatare

Franz Josef Glacier

FRANZ JOSEF GLACIER

FOX GLACIER

MAIN DIVIDE

MOUNT TASMAN
3,498 m (11,475 ft)

MOUNT COOK
3,755 m (12,316 ft)

▲ **THE FOOTSTOOL**
2,766 m (9,073 ft)

MOUNT SEFTON
,155 m (10,350 ft)

Aoraki/Mount Cook and Mount Tasman, New Zealand's two highest peaks, stand behind Fox Glacier.

VISITORS' CHECKLIST

Road map B6. 🚉 🚌 **Franz Josef Glacier village**, *(03) 752 0796*; **Fox Glacier village**, *(03) 751 0044.* ⭘ *daily.* ⬤ *25 Dec.* 📷 *obligatory on glaciers.* www.doc.govt.nz

★ **Franz Josef Glacier**
A two-hour or so walk up the Waiho River from the Franz Josef Glacier village leads to the terminal face.

★ **Fox Glacier**
Because of the risk of rock and ice falls, it is safe for visitors to walk only with a guide on the Fox Glacier, the largest glacier in the park.

0 kilometres 6
0 miles 6

MOVEMENT OF A GLACIER

Snowline

Layers of snow and ice

Crevasses

Subglacial stream

Melted ice

Equilibrium line

Terminus

River gravel

A glacier is a large body of ice that forms on land and moves slowly downhill at a rate of about 1.5 m (5 ft) a day. Glaciers are fed by snow accumulating in high-altitude basins (névés) where it condenses to form bluish ice. This ice field flows downhill under its own weight, cracking into a jumble of deep crevasses and collecting moraine (debris) which scours the mountain sides to form U-shaped valleys. The glacier ends at a terminal where the ice melts. The Franz Josef Glacier 11 km (7 miles) long and Fox Glacier 13 km (8 miles) long, are unique in that they descend from regions of perpetual snow to rainforest close to the coast.

Hot-air ballooning on the Canterbury Plains ▷

Arthur's Pass Driving Tour ⑯

Arthur's Pass road is the highest and most spectacular highway across the Southern Alps. From Springfield, the road climbs steeply to the 945-m (3,100-ft) Porters Pass before travelling through wide, tussock-covered basins hemmed by mountains and past dramatic limestone outcrops. Entering the eastern flank of Arthur's Pass National Park, the road is enveloped by mountain beech forest. It then climbs to the 920-m (3,017-ft) Arthur's Pass summit, before descending steeply on the western side of the Southern Alps.

Porters Pass and Lake Lyndon ①
This area is characterized by distinctive dryland native fauna. Lake Lyndon is a good bird-watching spot in summer and a natural skating rink during the winter months.

Porters Ski field ②
This is the closest ski area to Christchurch and one of six ski fields along State Highway 73. Other than Porters, all are small fields run by local ski clubs where visitors are welcome.

Kumara Junction

Hokitika

Lake Brunner

Taramakau River

⑩

Otira

⑨

ARTHUR'S PASS NATIONAL PARK

Arthur's Pass

⑧

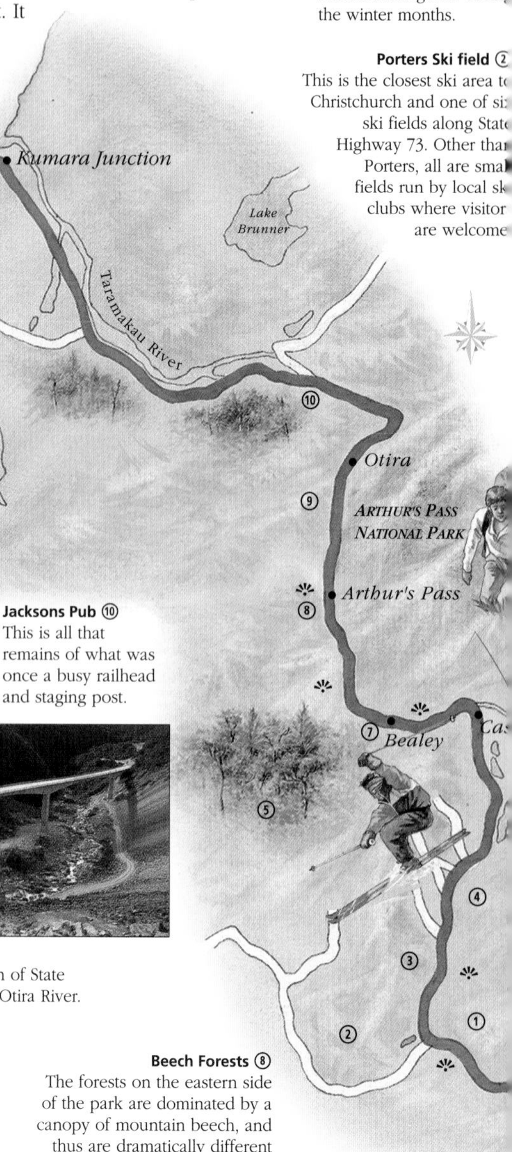

Jacksons Pub ⑩
This is all that remains of what was once a busy railhead and staging post.

⑦ **Bealey**

Cas

⑤

④

Otira Viaduct ⑨
Completed in 1999, this section of State Highway 73 spans the rugged Otira River.

③

①

KEY

▨	Tour route
--	Other roads
≈≈	River
🌿	Viewpoint

Beech Forests ⑧
The forests on the eastern side of the park are dominated by a canopy of mountain beech, and thus are dramatically different from the dense and varied forests on the western side.

②

For additional map symbols see back flap

astle Hill [3]
he large limestone rock form-tions of Castle Hill are eerily npressive, and very popular vith rock climbers. The area as historical significance to Iaori as a seasonal food-athering spot and as part of ne route used by Maori to each the West Coast.

TIPS FOR DRIVERS

Tour length from Springfield to Kumara Junction: *160 km (100 miles). This is an alpine route that is sometimes closed after snow, and drivers should check conditions.*
Stopping-off points: *There are many scenic viewpoints and lay-bys along the route. Arthur's Pass is the only township offering services between Kumara and Springfield, although there are hotels at Jacksons and Bealey.*

Cave Stream [4]
This 360-m (1,180-ft) limestone cave takes about two hours to navigate, and requires sturdy footwear, warm clothing and a good torch.

Craigieburn Forest Park [5]
The beech-covered hills in the park are popular spots for walking, picnicking and mountain biking.

Lake Pearson [6]
Lake Pearson and nearby Lake Grasmere are both good trout fishing spots. Lake Pearson is also known for its beautiful mountain reflections.

Bealey Spur [7]
A rustic cluster of holiday homes marks Bealey Spur, at the fringe of Arthur's Pass National Park.

ingfield

0 kilometres 20

0 miles 20

The road to Arthur's Pass

Arthur's Pass [17]

Road map C5. 👥 *50.* 🚆 🚌 🚍
ℹ *State Hwy 73, Arthur's Pass, (03) 318 9211.*

The tiny village of Arthur's Pass is nestled in a valley about 5 km (3 miles) east of the summit of Arthur's Pass. It was originally the camping site of contractors engaged to push the road through from Christchurch to the West Coast in 1865–6. In 1908, workers at Arthur's Pass village and at Otira, on the western side of the Main Divide, began construction of the 8-km (5-mile) Otira rail tunnel. In 1912, the population of Arthur's Pass had swelled to about 300, comprised mainly of tunnel workers. It took 10 years for the two ends of the tunnel to meet, and another 5 years before the first train travelled through it. A number of tunnellers' cottages remain in the village, now used as private holiday homes.

Since the 1920s, the village has been a base for day-trippers from Christchurch and Greymouth, walkers, trampers, and mountaineers, as well as skiers who enjoy the splendid views and low-key atmosphere of the nearby Temple Basin ski field. It is also the headquarters of Arthur's Pass National Park *(see pp244–5)*.

An original tunneller's cottage at Arthur's Pass village

Arthur's Pass National Park ⑱

Straddling the Southern Alps 153 km (95 miles) from Christchurch and 98 km (60 miles) from Greymouth, the 1,147-sq-km (443-sq-mile) Arthur's Pass National Park, the seventh largest in the country, is a place of huge geological and climatic contrasts. On the western side of

Alpine plant

the alps, where the rainfall is high, the park is clad in dense and varied rainforest through which steep, boulder-strewn rivers rush; on the drier eastern side, mountain beech forests and tussock-covered river flats predominate. Sixteen mountain peaks in the park exceed 2,000 m (6,560 ft). The park offers the well-equipped outdoor enthusiast superb mountain climbing and tramping opportunities, as well as many shorter walks suitable for people of all ages and fitness levels.

★ Dobson Nature Walk
This 30-minute walk on the Arthur's Pass summit gives an excellent introduction to the area's alpine and subalpine plants, which bloom from November to February.

Bealey Valley
A walking track leads from State Highway 73 through mountain beech forest to the beautiful Bealey Valley. It takes about three to four hours' return to complete the walk.

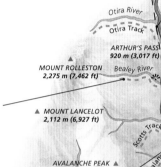

Otira River

Otira Track

ARTHUR'S PASS
920 m (3,017 ft)   Upper

▲
MOUNT ROLLESTON   *Bealey River*
2,275 m (7,462 ft)   Bridal
                                         Walk
▲ **MOUNT LANCELOT**   Cons
2,112 m (6,927 ft)   Pur
                         Scotts Track   Mt
AVALANCHE PEAK ▲   *Avalanche*
1,833 m (6,012 ft)   *Peak Track*   F

★ Devil's Punchbowl Waterfall
Although the top of this 131-m (430-ft) waterfall can be seen from the main road, a one-hour walk from Arthur's Pass village takes visitors to the base of the falls.

                              ▲
MOUNT BEALEY
1,836 m (6,022 ft)

Crow River

Waimakariri River

STAR SIGHTS

★ Devil's Punchbowl
  Waterfall

★ Dobson Nature
  Walk

Kea
These cheeky, inquisitive alpine parrots are sometimes seen in Arthur's Pass village, pecking the rubber from around car windscreens.

Temple Basin
Trampers can enjoy great views of Temple Basin's mountains and valleys. In winter, the ski field is accessible only by foot.

VISITORS' CHECKLIST

Road map C5. 🚗 🚌
ℹ️ Arthur's Pass village, (03) 318 9211. ⬭ daily. ⬤ 25 Dec.
♿ in village only; not on tracks.
🍴 🏕️ 📷
www.doc.govt.nz

MOUNT TEMPLE
1,913 m (6,274 ft)

FLORA AND FAUNA IN ARTHUR'S PASS NATIONAL PARK

As well as the impressive mountain beech forests in the east and mixed rainforest in the west, the park contains a wide variety of alpine and subalpine plant species, including tussock, snow grass, alpine daisies and herbs, sedge and ourisia. The park is also rich in birdlife, and species such as the paradise shelduck, bellbird, silvereye, fantail, kea and rifleman are often seen or heard. The area is home to a number of rare species, including the alpine rock wren, blue duck and great spotted kiwi.

Blue ducks

MOUNT AICKEN
1,859 m (6,097 ft)

MOUNT OATES
2,041 m (6,694 ft)

0 kilometres   5

0 miles   5

MOUNT WILLIAMS
1,718 m (5,635 ft)

Edwards River

KEY

▬▬	State highway
═══	Minor road
──	River
– –	Walking track
▬▬	Tranz Alpine Express route
– –	Tunnel
ℹ️	Tourist information
▲	Camp site
🏕️	Picnic area
🎿	Skiing
☆	Viewpoint

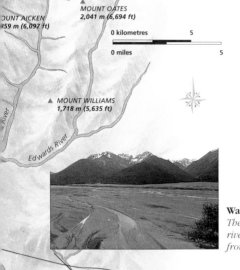

Waimakariri River
The sinuous strands of this mighty river transport rock and shingle from the Southern Alps (see p191).

Kyke Corner

Waimakariri River

BEALEY SPUR ▲
m (3,017 ft)   **Bealey Spur**

Bealey Spur Village
Tussock-covered valleys give way to tall, craggy hills as the road approaches Bealey Spur.

TIPS FOR WALKERS

The valleys, alpine passes and scree- and tussock-covered mountainsides of the park offer a range of graded walks, from short, easy strolls to demanding climbs. However, the climate in the park is highly changeable and many routes rudimentary, so it is important for tramping and climbing parties to register their intentions with the visitor centre at Arthur's Pass village.

Mount Hutt ski field with Lake Coleridge in the distance

Mount Hutt ⑲

Road map C6. 🚗 ℹ️ *121 Main St, Methven, (03) 302 8955.* 🎿 *New Zealand Walking Festival (Apr).*

Mount Hutt, in the foothills of the Southern Alps, is Canterbury's largest ski field, and claims to have the longest ski season in Australasia (early June to mid-October). The ski field is served by nine lifts and tows, as well as artificial snow-making facilities. From the 2,075-m (6,808-ft) mountain, there are excellent views over the Canterbury Plains.

Environs
The town of **Methven** serves as Mount Hutt's après-ski centre in winter, and reverts in summer to a typical New Zealand farming town. The 42-sq-km (16-sq-mile) Mount Hutt Conservation Area, 14 km (9 miles) west of the town, has a number of short walking tracks through native forest dominated by mountain beech. The Rakaia Gorge, about 16 km (10 miles) north of Methven, is popular for jet-boating. A 5-km (3-mile) walkway traverses its edge.

Rakaia ⑳

Road map C6. 🚶 *800.* 🚗 🎿 *Rakaia Salmon Fishing Competition (end Feb).*

Located on the southern bank of the Rakaia River, the small farming settlement of Rakaia claims to be "the salmon capital of New Zealand". A large fibreglass

fish in the middle of the township celebrates the excellent salmon and trout fishing to be had at various spots along the river.

Bridge over the Rakaia Gorge, a popular place for jet-boating

Ashburton ㉑

Road map C6. 🚶 *16,000.* 🚗 🚗 ℹ️ *The Green, East St, (03) 308 1050.* 🎿 *Wheels Week (May).*

Ashburton straddles the Ashburton River and is the principal town in the farming district of mid-Canterbury. The town was named after Lord Ashburton, a member of the Canterbury Association, which settled the province in the 1850s. Although originally dry and tussock covered, irrigation has allowed agriculture to flourish. The well-laid out town has historic brick buildings and many mature trees, including some in the Ashburton Domain. The **Ashford Craft Village** produces and sells a variety of high quality craft work and has a museum housing spinning wheels.

🧵 **Ashford Craft Village**
427 West St. **Tel** *(03) 308 9085.*
◯ *daily.* ● *Good Fri, 25 & 26 Dec.* 🚫 *in factory.* ♿ 📷 *required in factory.* 📖 📷

Geraldine ㉒

Road map C6. 🚶 *2,000.* 🚗 ℹ️ *Cnr of Cox & Talbot sts, (03) 693 1006.* 🎿 *Geraldine Arts and Plants Festival (Nov).*
www.southisland.org.nz

This attractive small farming town is a popular stopover for travellers heading south to the Mackenzie Country. First known as Talbot Forest, then Fitzgerald, and finally Geraldine, in 1866, it began as a sheep run and base for sawmillers. Talbot Forest now refers to the lowland podocarp forest which provides a backdrop to Geraldine. The town still has many historic buildings, such as the 1908 Post Office, which can be seen on a self-guided walking trail.
Locally produced juices and condiments can be sampled at **Barker's Berry Barn**. The **Vintage Car and Machinery Museum** has cars dating from 1907 to 1953 and tractors from 1874 as well as a large amount of early agricultural machinery.

🍓 **Barker's Berry Barn**
76 Talbot St. **Tel** *(03) 693 9727.*
◯ *daily.* ● *25 Dec.* ♿ 📷
🏛 **Vintage Car and Machinery Museum**
178 Talbot St. **Tel** *(03) 693 8756.*
◯ *daily in summer; weekends only in winter.* ● *1 Jan, 25 & 26 Dec.* 📖 ♿ 📷 *by arrangement.*

Environs
The town is a good base for exploring the forests and rivers of mid-Canterbury, including Peel Forest, 22 km (13 miles) north of Geraldine, the Mount Somers Conservation Area, 47 km (29 miles) north, and the Orari, Waihi and Te Moana gorges, 15 km (9 miles) north, which are good spots for swimming, rafting and picnicking.

The Post Office in Geraldine, built in 1908

High Country Farming

When the "Canterbury Pilgrims" arrived in 1850 to establish their new settlement, they quickly saw the potential of pastoral farming, and the runholders – the farmers who grazed Canterbury's extensive plains, downs and interior – soon became a powerful economic and political force. Although land reform in the late 19th century saw the great estates broken up, large high country stations, where much of the land is leased, have remained a feature of farming in New Zealand, particularly in Canterbury. Good roads and modern communications have reduced the isolation and harshness of station life, but it remains a unique existence defined by the climate and the topography of the high country and the annual cycle of farming.

The hardy merino

THE ANNUAL CYCLE

Stock graze the tussock-covered mountainsides over the summer, and are mustered down to lower ground before winter. This task takes several days and is carried out on horseback or on foot with the aid of teams of highly trained sheepdogs. As shearing, lambing and weaning are completed, stock are released back to the high country for the summer.

Mustering sheep

Selling and buying sheep *is a serious business at local livestock auctions as sheep farmers seek to buy stock that will improve the quantity and quality of their wool and meat production.*

Shearing *is done by skilled teams of contractors, often using manual blade shears which leave a protective layer of wool on the sheep's back. The dominant breed farmed on high county farms is the fine-woolled and hardy merino.*

Fodder crops, *such as hay and silage, are grown on the farms as supplementary feed for sheep during the cold winter months.*

Roast lamb *served with vegetables such as baked potatoes and beans remains a favourite traditional meal.*

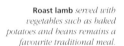

Merino wool *from the high country farms of the South Island is very fine, and is used to make luxury knitwear and fine suiting fabrics.*

Timaru ㉓

Painting by Goldie in the Aigantighe

About halfway between Christchurch to the north and Dunedin to the south is Timaru. It is built on rolling hills marking the edge of the Canterbury Plains and is the largest town in South Canterbury. Its name derives from Te Maru, meaning "a place of shelter", denoting its historical importance as a safe haven for Maori canoes travelling the coast. It was a whaling station from 1838. The town centre is built on 0.5 sq km (0.2 sq mile) of land acquired by early settlers George and Robert Rhodes, although settlement did not begin in earnest until 1859. Today, Timaru has the appearance of a sturdy and well-appointed provincial capital, with many notable buildings gracing its commercial heart.

Aigantighe gallery and grounds

⛱ Caroline Bay
♿ *not in piazza.*

From 1877, when Timaru's artificial port was first created, the white sand of Caroline Bay accumulated beside it to form a safe and popular swimming beach. The port flanks the southern end of the beach. Behind the beach is an extensive grassed area with a children's playground, an aviary, tennis courts and a mini-golf course. Large-scale redevelopment has added a seaside boardwalk, volleyball courts and other recreational facilities. The piazza, a series of staircases and platforms, links the bay with the central city on the hill above. To the north of the bay are the Benvenue Cliffs and the 1877 Timaru Lighthouse.

⛪ Basilica of the Sacred Heart
7 Craigie Ave. **Tel** (03) 684 4263.
◯ *daily.* ✝ *daily.* ♿

Arguably the most impressive of the many distinguished buildings in Timaru, Basilica of the Sacred Heart was designed by Francis William Petre and built in 1910–11. Its twin towers and large dome overlook the main route south through the city, and house an equally majestic interior featuring stencilled ceilings, large white pillars and stained-glass windows. Petre also designed the Catholic cathedrals in Christchurch and Dunedin.

🏛 Aigantighe
49 Wa-iti Rd. **Tel** (03) 688 4424.
◯ *Tue–Sun.* ● *1 & 2 Jan, 25 & 26 Dec.* 📷 ♿ 🛍 *by arrangement.*

This charming museum, pronounced "egg and tie" ("at home" in Scottish Gaelic) is housed in a 1908 building bequeathed to the city by Alexander and Helen Grant, Scottish immigrants who had farmed in the Mackenzie Country. It opened as an art museum in 1956, with much of its fascinating collection donated by the Grant family. Its permanent collection includes works by New Zealand and British painters, as well as English and continental china. The well laid out gallery sits amid a restful garden, which features a permanent exhibition of stone sculptures.

⛪ St Mary's Anglican Church
Church St. **Tel** (03) 688 8377.
◯ *Tue–Fri.* ● *Good Fri, 25 Dec.* ✝ *Wed, Fri, Sun.* ♿ 🛍

The foundation stone for St Mary's Anglican Church was laid in 1880, and its nave was consecrated in 1886. The interior of the church features high ribbed ceilings, many fine stained-glass windows, intricate wooden carvings and sturdy columns.

Many of the art pieces and plaques in the church bear the names of influential colonial families in South Canterbury. Steps in the tower can be climbed for an excellent view of the city.

RICHARD PEARSE

Inventor, aviator and farmer, Richard Pearse (1877–1953) has for decades been at the centre of debate about who was the first to achieve powered flight. Pearse was born near Temuka, north of Timaru, and although ridiculed in his lifetime, has been posthumously recognized as an inventive genius. In his farm workshop he constructed a monoplane of bamboo, aluminium, wire and canvas. His first flight in the aircraft is said to have covered 46–91 m (150–300 ft), ending with a crash into a hedge. No records were kept of the flight, but there is some eyewitness evidence that it occurred on 31 March 1903 – about nine months before the 13 December 1903 flight of Orville and Wilbur Wright, officially regarded as the first in the world. Some people even put the date at 1902.

Replica of Pearse's monoplane

Roses in the Timaru Botanic Gardens

Timaru Botanic Gardens

Queen St. **Tel** *(03) 684 8199.* ◯ *daily.* ♿

Set aside as a public park in 1864, the gardens have several notable features, including a 1913 statue of Scottish poet Robert Burns, a cabbage tree believed to date from pre-European times and a 1911 band rotunda. The gardens also boast a fine collection of rose species as well as many rare and endangered plants. The conservatory complex houses desert, tropical and subtropical collections.

South Canterbury Museum

Perth St. **Tel** *(03) 684 2212.* ◯ *Tue–Sun.* ● *1 Jan, 25 & 26 Dec.* 🚫📷 ♿

This octagonal-shaped museum, opened in 1966, is the main regional museum. Its collections cover the natural history of the area, local Maori history, the early whaling industry and European settlement. The development of the city is shown in a series of photographs. A highlight is a replica of the airplane built by Temuka farmer Richard Pearse, who is believed to have successfully flown in 1903, possibly before the Wright brothers in the US. The plane is suspended from the ceiling at about the height at which Pearse is thought to have flown.

Environs

Temuka, about 18 km (11 miles) north of Timaru, is the service centre for a rich farming hinterland, and is also the home of the well-known Temuka Homeware, which makes a wide range of high-quality household ceramics. Although the factory is not open to the public, there is a separate factory shop on the State Highway 1 bypass in Temuka.

State Highway 8 to Tekapo passes through the small township of Pleasant Point, where the **Pleasant Point Railway and Historical Museum** retains a 2-km (1.2-mile) section of the old Timaru to Fairlie line, built in 1875 and closed in 1968. Two steam locomotives ply the track on school and public holidays. The road winds through rolling green farmland and passes through the small towns of Cave, Fairlie and Kimbell, and the turn-off to Mount Dobson Ski Field, before reaching Burkes Pass, the entrance to the Mackenzie Country.

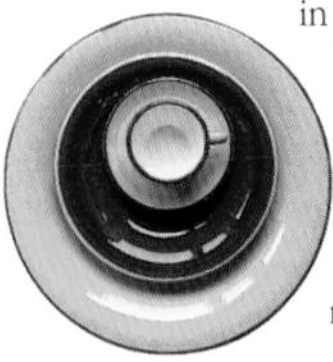

Temuka pottery

VISITORS' CHECKLIST

Road map C6. 👥 *27,500.* ✈ *12 km (7 miles) N of city.* 🚆 🚌 🚍 ℹ *2 George St, (03) 688 6163.* 🎉 *Caroline Bay Carnival (Dec–Jan).* **www**.southisland.org.nz

Pleasant Point Railway and Historical Museum

Main Rd. **Tel** *(03) 614 8323.* ◯ *variable.* 📷 ♿ 🛍

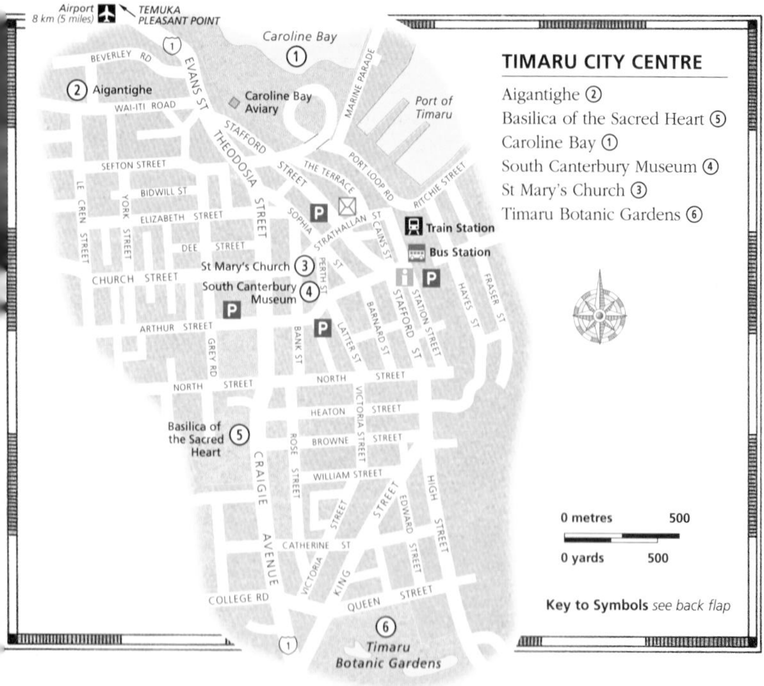

Airport 8 km (5 miles)
TEMUKA PLEASANT POINT
Caroline Bay
BEVERLEY RD
EVANS ST
Aigantighe
WAI-ITI ROAD
Caroline Bay Aviary
MARINE PARADE
Port of Timaru
STAFFORD
THEODOSIA
STREET
SEFTON STREET
THE TERRACE
PORT LOOP RD
RITCHIE STREET
BIDWELL ST
LE CREN STREET
YORK STREET
ELIZABETH STREET
SOPHIA
STRATHALLAN ST
CAINS ST
Train Station
Bus Station
DEE STREET
St Mary's Church
PERTH ST
CHURCH STREET
South Canterbury Museum
STATION STREET
STAFFORD ST
BARNARD ST
HAYES ST
FRASER ST
ARTHUR STREET
GREY RD
BANK ST
LATTER ST
NORTH STREET
NORTH STREET
HEATON STREET
VICTORIA STREET
Basilica of the Sacred Heart
BROWNE STREET
ROSE STREET
CRAIGIE AVENUE
WILLIAM STREET
EDWARD STREET
HIGH STREET
CATHERINE ST
VICTORIA
KING
COLLEGE RD
QUEEN STREET
Timaru Botanic Gardens
TIMARU CITY CENTRE
Aigantighe 2
Basilica of the Sacred Heart 5
Caroline Bay 1
South Canterbury Museum 4
St Mary's Church 3
Timaru Botanic Gardens 6
0 metres 500
0 yards 500
Key to Symbols see back flap

Lupins on the shores of Lake Tekapo

Lake Tekapo ㉔

Road map B6. 🚶 300. 🚌 ℹ️ *Kiwi Treasures, State Hwy 8, (03) 680 6686.* **www**.mountcooknz.com

Lake Tekapo is a place of exceptional beauty and clarity. The remarkable blue of the lake is caused by "rock flour" – finely ground particles of rock brought down by the glaciers at the head of the lake and held in suspension in the melt water. The lake is a very popular venue for fishing, boating, kayaking, swimming and hang-gliding.

On the lake front stands the Church of the Good Shepherd. The foundation stone of this stone-and-oak church was laid in 1935 by the Duke of Gloucester. The front window of the church creates a perfect frame for a view of the lake. Next to the church is a bronze statue of a sheep dog, erected in 1968 as a tribute to the important role played by these animals in the development of high country farming.

Because of the purity of the atmosphere above Lake Tekapo, the University of Canterbury has an observatory atop Mount John to the west of the township. There is a popular walkway to the top of the mountain (about three hours return). Cowan's Hill Track (about two hours) also provides good views of

the lake and mountains. Lake Tekapo town is a good base for skiing at Mount Dobson, about 30 km (18 miles) away, while the town's small tourist airport is also a base for scenic flights over Mount Cook. Lake Alexandrina, 10 km (6 miles) from Tekapo, is renowned for its trout fishing.

🏛 Church of the Good Shepherd
Pioneer Drive. **Tel** (03) 680 6871. ⬜ daily. ⬤ 25 Dec, weddings. 🏛 variable. 💰 donation. ♿ 📷

Lake Pukaki ㉕

Road map B6. ℹ️ *State Hwy 8, (03) 435 3280.* **www**.mountcooknz.com

Like Lake Tekapo, Lake Pukaki is a place of majestic scenery. State Highway 8 hugs the southern tip of the lake, and a large and popular lay-by

and picnic area allows stunning views of Mount Cook and the Southern Alps. The lake is fed by the Tasman River, which flows off the Tasman Glacier. It has been artificially raised as part of the Upper Waitaki hydroelectricity network and is linked by canals to Lake Tekapo and Lake Ohau. On a clear day, Mount Cook is reflected in the waters of the lake.

The **Mount Cook Salmon Farm** on the Pukaki–Tekapo canal sells fresh salmon and offers tours.

Glentanner Park Centre, about 20 km (12 miles) south of Mount Cook village, on the shores of Lake Pukaki, is a major base for flightseeing over Mount Cook. Other activites run from the centre include horse trekking, mountain biking, boat trips, hunting and fishing. The centre is set amid Glentanner Station, a 182-sq-km

Glentanner Park Centre, backed by the Southern Alps

(70-sq-mile) high country farm. Occasional short tours of the farm allow visitors to see sheep shearing and sheepdog demonstrations.

🐏 **Mount Cook Salmon Farm**
Canal Rd. **Tel** (03) 435 0085.
⬚ *daily.* 🖼 🚻 🚻 🛎

🍄 **Glentanner Park Centre**
State Hwy 80. **Tel** (03) 435 1855.
⬚ *daily.* 🖼 *for activities.* 🚻 *some activities.* **www**.glentanner.co.nz

Twizel ㉖

Road map B6. 🏃 *1,400.* 🚗 🏛
*Twizel Events Centre, Market Place,
(03) 435 3124.* **www**.twizel.com

Twizel was built in 1969 as a construction town for the Upper Waitaki hydro-electric development scheme. Once the hydro scheme was completed, the local people successfully fought to retain the town, and began to exploit its proximity to excellent fishing and boating lakes, and to Mount Cook 61 km (37 miles) away. Lake Ruataniwha, a man-made lake just south of Twizel, is popular for water sports. It has an international standard rowing course and is the site of national rowing events every year. From Lake Ruataniwha, a sealed back road leads to Lake Benmore, a 75-sq-km (29-sq-mile) hydroelectric dam that has also become a favourite boating destination.

Kaki/Black stilt

One of Twizel's most important attractions is the **Kakī Visitor Hide**. The kakī, or black stilt, is one of the rarest wading birds in the world, and the species has been subject to intensive conservation management since 1981 *(see p192).* Visitors can take tours to view captive breeding birds from specially designed hides.

🐦 **Kakī Visitor Hide**
Twizel Events Centre, Market Place.
Tel (03) 435 3124. 🗓 *daily (except 25 Dec).* 🖼 🚻

Clay cliffs at Omarama

Environs

South of Twizel, on State Highway 8, lies the small town of **Omarama**. The town has gained a worldwide reputation for gliding because of its strong northwest thermal updraughts.

About 10 km (6 miles) west of the town are the **Clay Cliffs**, a set of steep, high pinnacles separated by deep, narrow ravines. The cliffs are believed to have been frequented by early Maori travelling into the Mackenzie Country to hunt. Although privately owned, the cliffs are protected by covenant, and are accessible to the public.

📷 **Clay Cliffs**
Henburn Rd. **Tel** (03) 438 9780.
⬚ *daily.* 🖼

Lake Ohau ㉗

Road map B6.

About 30 km (18 miles) to the west of Twizel, Lake Ohau is a popular swimming, fishing, skiing and boating spot. The six native forests which surround the lake – the Ohau, Temple, Dobson, Huxley, Hopkins and Ahuriri – also provide excellent tramping and walking opportunities. Many huts are scattered in the forests for the use of more experienced trampers.

The Ohau ski field, overlooking the western side of the lake, is a commercial ski field serviced by basic facilities, such as a T-bar and platter lift.

UPPER WAITAKI HYDRO DEVELOPMENT SCHEME

The power stations of the Upper Waitaki and Mackenzie Country provide about one-third of New Zealand's hydro-electricity. The idea of harnessing the water resources of the region was first mooted in 1904, and today the vast scheme includes the Tekapo A and B power stations, Ohau A, B and C stations, and Benmore, Aviemore and Waitaki stations. An important feature of the scheme is 58 km (36 miles) of man-made canals, which pool the resources of Lakes Tekapo, Pukaki and Ohau, along which there is an attractive scenic drive. The lakes created by the hydro scheme have become popular venues for water sports.

Lake Benmore from the adjacent hills

Aoraki/Mount Cook National Park ㉘

Mount Cook lily

Aoraki/Mount Cook National Park takes its name from Aoraki/Mount Cook, which at 3,754 m (12,316 ft) is New Zealand's highest mountain. It is sacred to the Ngai Tahu tribe of the South Island, and Maori legend has it that the mountain and its companion peaks were formed when a boy named Aoraki and his three brothers came down from the heavens to visit Papatuanuku (Earth Mother) in a canoe. The canoe overturned, and as the brothers moved to the back of the boat they turned to stone. The 700-sq-km (270-sq-mile) area was designated a national park in 1953 and includes 19 peaks over 3,000 m (9,842 ft). Glaciers cover 40 per cent of the park.

Flightseeing
Scenic flights operate from Glentanner Park Centre and Mount Cook airstrip. They fly a range of routes over the park, and many include a landing on a glacier.

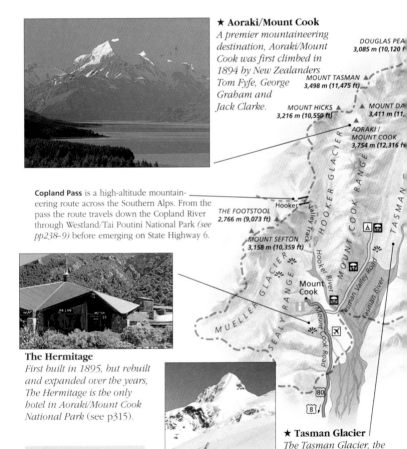

★ Aoraki/Mount Cook
A premier mountaineering destination, Aoraki/Mount Cook was first climbed in 1894 by New Zealanders Tom Fyfe, George Graham and Jack Clarke.

DOUGLAS PEA
3,085 m (10,120 f

MOUNT TASMAN ▲
3,498 m (11,475 ft)

MOUNT HICKS ▲
3,216 m (10,550 ft)

▲ MOUNT DA
3,411 m (11,

AORAKI /
MOUNT COOK
3,754 m (12,316 f

Copland Pass is a high-altitude mountaineering route across the Southern Alps. From the pass the route travels down the Copland River through Westland/Tai Poutini National Park *(see pp238–9)* before emerging on State Highway 6.

THE FOOTSTOOL
2,766 m (9,073 ft) ▲

Hooker

MOUNT SEFTON ▲
3,158 m (10,359 ft)

HOOKER GLACIER

HOOKER RANGE

MOUNT COOK RANGE

TASMAN

Valley Track

Hooker River

Mount Cook

MUELLER GLACIER

SEALY RANGE

Tasman Valley Road

Tasman River

Mount Cook Road

The Hermitage
First built in 1895, but rebuilt and expanded over the years, The Hermitage is the only hotel in Aoraki/Mount Cook National Park (see p315).

80

8

★ Tasman Glacier
The Tasman Glacier, the largest in New Zealand, is 29 km (18 miles) long and 1.6 km (1 mile) wide. Heli-skiing is a popular way to experience the glacier.

STAR SIGHTS

★ Aoraki/Mount Cook

★ Tasman Glacier

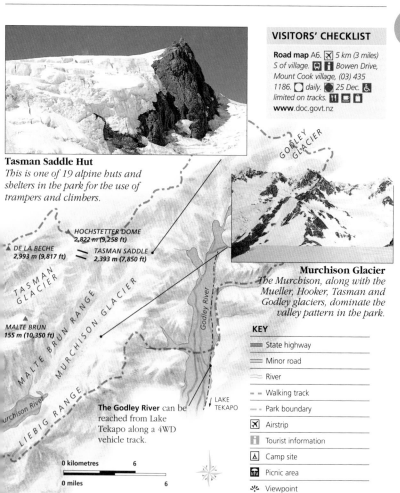

Tasman Saddle Hut
This is one of 19 alpine huts and shelters in the park for the use of trampers and climbers.

GODLEY GLACIER

Murchison Glacier
The Murchison, along with the Mueller, Hooker, Tasman and Godley glaciers, dominate the valley pattern in the park.

HOCHSTETTER DOME
2,822 m (9,258 ft)

▲ DE LA BECHE
2,993 m (9,817 ft)

TASMAN SADDLE
2,393 m (7,850 ft)

TASMAN GLACIER

MURCHISON GLACIER

MALTE BRUN RANGE

MALTE BRUN
155 m (10,350 ft)

Murchison River

LIEBIG RANGE

Godley River

LAKE TEKAPO

The Godley River can be reached from Lake Tekapo along a 4WD vehicle track.

0 kilometres   6
0 miles   6

KEY

▬▬▬	State highway
═══	Minor road
～～	River
- -	Walking track
---	Park boundary
☒	Airstrip
◱	Tourist information
⬛	Camp site
⬛	Picnic area
✳	Viewpoint

WALKS FROM MOUNT COOK VILLAGE

There are several walking tracks in the vicinity of Mount Cook village which are well formed and signposted. They are suitable for people who do not have any climbing experience.

Kea Point and Governors Bush are short walking trips which focus on the park's vegetation and birdlife. Longer walks from the village include the Sealey Tarns, Hooker Valley and Red Tarns tracks. Although these tracks are well marked, the ground is rough in places and it is advisable to wear stout shoes or boots and to carry a walking stick. A warm sweater or jacket is needed for places exposed to the wind, even during summer.

Brochures on the walks, giving descriptions and walking times, are available at the visitor centre in the village.

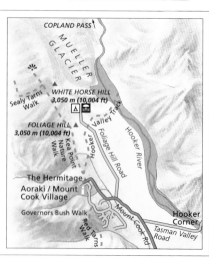

COPLAND PASS

MUELLER GLACIER

Sealey Tarns Walk

WHITE HORSE HILL
3,050 m (10,004 ft)

FOLIAGE HILL
3,050 m (10,004 ft)

Kea Point Nature Walk

Foliage Hill Road

Hooker River

Hooker Valley Track

The Hermitage
Aoraki / Mount Cook Village

Governors Bush Walk

Red Tarns Walk

Mount Cook Rd

Hooker Corner

Tasman Valley Road

OTAGO AND SOUTHLAND

With its high, snow-capped mountains, lush rainforests, dry tussocklands, deep glacial lakes, spectacular beaches and rugged coastlines, the Otago and Southland region is one of extreme natural beauty. Set among the area's untamed wilderness and historic settlements is Queenstown, a world centre for adventure sports and one of New Zealand's foremost tourist destinations.

Before the arrival of the first Europeans, Maori settled in coastal areas where seafood was plentiful, although they also hunted, and collected greenstone *(pounamu)*, in the rugged interior. The first Europeans also looked to coastal areas for an environment that would be easy to tame. Members of the Free Church of Scotland were the first to settle the area in an organized way, making Dunedin the centre of their new land. Hopes of an idyllic enclave were dashed in the early 1860s with the discovery of gold.

Gold-miners poured into the inhospitable lands of what is now known as Central Otago, in search of an elusive fortune. The money gold brought to the region saw it leap ahead, and for a time Dunedin became New Zealand's commercial capital. The legacy of the gold mining era lives on in the humblest of stone cottages on remote and rugged landscapes as well as in the splendid buildings that adorn the streets of Dunedin. The region's natural legacy also lives on in many areas, such as the Mount Aspiring and Fiordland national parks, which remain relatively untapped. They are beautifully complemented by other natural attractions, such as Stewart Island and the Catlins area on the southeast coast, while the farmlands that have been tamed provide an attractive contrast. Such is the variety on offer, that each corner of the region provides its own attractions, making exploration very rewarding.

The Octagon in the heart of Dunedin

◁ Reflections in the Mirror Lakes, Fiordland National Park

Exploring Otago and Southland

The geography, climate and scenery of the Otago and Southland region vary greatly over relatively short distances. To the west, the land rises steeply from the coast through thick rainforest to 3,000-m (9,900-ft) high mountain peaks in the space of only 40 km (25 miles) – features that make the Fiordland and Mount Aspiring national parks so spectacular. To the east of these peaks, the ranges and valleys of Central Otago provide a stark contrast. The interior is dry and rugged. Vivid blue lakes nestle among tussock-covered hills and snow-capped mountains to create the scenery and adventure playground that has made resorts such as Queenstown so popular. From the lakes, the land drops down to the eastern and southern coasts and hinterland where extra rainfall has produced fertile farmland to feed the cities of Dunedin and Invercargill.

White-water rafting, Shotover River, Queenstown

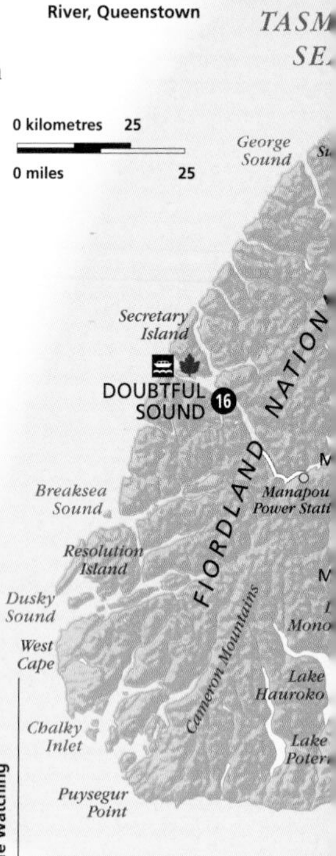

SIGHTS AT A GLANCE

TOP OUTDOOR ACTIVITIES

The places shown here have been selected for their recreational activities. Conditions vary depending on the weather and the time of year, so exercise caution and, if in doubt, seek local advice.

	Aerial Sightseeing	Bungy Jumping	Jet-boating	Paragliding	Skiing	Tramping/Walking	White-water Rafting	Wildlife Watching
Catlins						■		■
Dunedin	●					■		■
Fiordland National Park	●					■		■
Haast						■		■
Invercargill	●					■		■
Milford Sound	●					■		■
Mount Aspiring National Park	●					■		■
Oamaru						■		■
Otago Peninsula						■		■
Queenstown	●	■	●	■	●	■	■	
Stewart Island	●					■		■
Te Anau	●		●			■		■
Wanaka	●	■	●	■	●	■	■	

Map labels: TASMAN SEA · George Sound · Secretary Island · DOUBTFUL SOUND ⑯ · Breaksea Sound · Resolution Island · Dusky Sound · West Cape · Chalky Inlet · Puysegur Point · FIORDLAND NATIONAL PARK · Cameron Mountains · Manapouri Power Station · Lake Hauroko · Lake Poteriteri

0 kilometres 25
0 miles 25

KEY

═══	Motorway
▬▬▬	Major road
═ ═ ═	Minor road
▬▬	Scenic route
———	Minor railway
▬ ▬ ▬	Regional borders
△	Summit

The bright blue Lake Hawea, one of the largest southern lakes

SEE ALSO

• *Where to Stay* pp316–19

• *Where to Eat* pp340–41

GETTING AROUND

Road travel is the main means of getting around the region. There is a range of bus services along the main routes, and for those who choose to drive the state highways are good and generally not too busy, apart from peak holiday periods. Some roads, such as State Hwy 94 to Milford, require care because of the mountainous terrain. There are international airports at Dunedin and Queenstown, while the airport at Invercargill handles domestic flights.

Dunedin ❶

Bronze penguin

One of the joys of exploring Dunedin is that there is a great deal to see in a relatively small area. Its buildings are among the most interesting and architecturally diverse in the country. Many that have survived from Dunedin's heyday following the 1860s gold rush, when the city was the country's commercial centre, are within walking distance of the centre. Others are to the north of the city *(see pp264–5)* in proximity to Dunedin's many beautiful parks and gardens. The relatively flat central city, which remains the retail hub, is surrounded by hills, which afford a splendid view of the city and harbour below.

St Paul's Cathedral

♣ The Octagon

When the site of the settlement of "New Edinburgh" was first surveyed in 1846 by its Edinburgh-based surveyors, The Octagon was planned as the focal point. More than 150 years later, The Octagon continues to fulfil that role. It has watched over a passing parade of festivals, protests, parties and royal visits, as well as seeing sporting heroes waved off and welcomed.

This small oasis in the heart of the city – a popular lunchtime spot – is surrounded by a number of fine buildings. A large bronze statue of Scottish poet Robert Burns, erected in 1887, has a prime place in front of St Paul's Cathedral. Burns' nephew, the Reverend Thomas Burns, was the spiritual leader for the first group of Scottish settlers to arrive in Dunedin in 1848.

♨ Municipal Chambers

48 The Octagon. **Tel** (03) 477 4000.
◯ Mon–Fri. ● public hols. ⬤ inside. ♿ public areas.
Completed in 1880, the Municipal Chambers is an excellent example of the use of Oamaru stone *(see pp268–9)*. It has undergone considerable restoration and refurbishment both inside and out. It is home to the Council Chambers, where city councillors meet, and features a number of reception and meeting rooms. It also houses the Dunedin Visitor Centre. The Dunedin Convention Centre and the 2,800-seat Town Hall are located behind it.

♦ St Paul's Cathedral

The Octagon. **Tel** (03) 477 2336.
◯ daily. ✝ daily except Sat. ♿
📷 Summer.
Consecrated in 1919, the Anglican St Paul's stands high above The Octagon on an elevated site, with a broad staircase leading to its doors. It owes its prominent position in a predominantly Presbyterian settlement to the generosity of Johnny Jones, an early whaler and trader. The cathedral, which replaced a smaller church built on the site in 1863, has many fine architectural details, including a vaulted stone ceiling.

🏛 Dunedin Public Art Gallery

30 The Octagon. **Tel** (03) 477 4000.
◯ daily. ● Good Fri, 25 Dec. 📷 (special exhibitions only). ⬤ ♿ ▭
This modern gallery was designed to harmonize with The Octagon's historic buildings and has one of the best collections of European art in the country. It also has sections on early and contemporary New Zealand arts, including various works by the world-renowned artist Frances Hodgkins *(see p32)*.

Entrance foyer of the Dunedin Public Art Gallery

0 metres   300

0 yards   300

KEY

▢ Street-by-Street: Central Dunedin *pp260–61*

Key to Symbols *see back flap*

🏛 First Church

415 Moray Place. **Tel** (03) 477 7118.
⭕ daily. 🏛 Sunday only. 🚻 🏛

The flagship of the Presbyterian Church in Otago, First Church, consecrated in 1873, is considered to be architect Robert Lawson's greatest contribution to Dunedin's rich architectural heritage. Of note are its beautiful rose window, wooden ceiling and 56-m (184-ft) high spire. The church has undergone

The Law Courts in Central Dunedin

considerable restoration work to repair its exterior. Its history is told at the church's heritage centre. Bell Hill, on which First Church stands, was lowered by about 12 m (40 ft) to improve the city's traffic.

🏛 Law Courts

41 Stuart St.

These were completed in 1902 to a design by government architect John Campbell. The building is distinguished by its combination of local Port Chalmers bluestone and lighter Oamaru stone. Standing just around the corner in complete contrast is the former red brick Dunedin Prison, built to another Campbell design which mimics many aspects of London's New Scotland Yard, although on a smaller scale. Completed in 1895, it also served as the

Dunedin Police Station until a new building was built in the mid-1990s.

🏛 Otago Settlers Museum

31 Queens Gardens. **Tel** (03) 477 5052. ⭕ daily. ⬤ Good Fri, 25 Dec. 🗐 🚻 🖉 🏛

As its name suggests, this museum provides an opportunity to learn about the lives of the province's settlers from Southern Maori to Scottish pioneers and Chinese gold miners. The displays range from early photographs and household goods to implements and vehicles, including two large steam locomotives, one of which dates back to the 1870s. The museum is housed in two adjoining buildings, one a former art gallery, built in the early 1900s, the other a former bus station built in an Art Deco style.

ROBERT LAWSON

Many of Dunedin's finest Victorian and Scottish Edwardian-style buildings are attributed to architect Robert Lawson (1833–1902). The Scottish-born Lawson had trained as an architect in his home country before migrating to Melbourne, where he found little work, and instead made a living from gold-mining and journalism. He took up his profession again in 1861 and the following year won a competition for the design of First Church in Dunedin. Lawson moved to Dunedin and so began a successful association with the city. His list of credits includes the Municipal Chambers, Otago Boys High School (a handsome bluestone building completed in 1884) and Knox Church in George Street, which was consecrated in 1876. However, it was his initial Dunedin design, First Church, which many consider to be his masterpiece.

First Church

Street-by-Street: Central Dunedin

Statue of
Robert Burns

Dunedin has close historical links with the
Scottish city of Edinburgh. Not only is
Dunedin the old Gaelic name for Edin-
burgh, but many of its street names are
Scottish and several Scottish traditions
have been preserved since the first
Presbyterian settlers arrived in 1848.
The Octagon, so-called because of its
eight sides, gives the city a central focus.
Surrounding it, and within a few blocks,
are a number of Victorian and Edwardian public
buildings, which are among the finest in the country.
Visitors can also enjoy the many cafés and restaurants
dotted around the area.

St Paul's Cathedral
*St Paul's has the only
vaulted stone ceiling in
New Zealand (see p258).*

Stuart Street Terrace Houses
*Built around 1900 as town
residences for country folk, these
terrace houses are now popular
locations for restaurants, boutiques and professional offices.*

**Dunedin Public Art
Gallery** *(see p258)*

First Church *(see p259)*

Otago Settlers Museum
*This tells the story of Otago and its
settlers. One wing is dedicated to
old forms of transport (see p259).*

Queens
Gardens

STAR SIGHTS

★ Dunedin Railway
Station

★ The Octagon

0 metres 300

0 yards 300

KEY

– – – Suggested route

The Municipal Chambers

Built in 1880 at a time when Dunedin was revelling in the fortune brought by the gold rush, the building is topped by a 47-m (155-ft) high tower (see p258).

VISITORS' CHECKLIST

Road map B7. 120,000.
25 km (16 miles) S of city centre. Limited international flights to and from Australia.
Anzac Ave. Intercity, St Andrew St. 48 The Octagon, (03) 474 3300. Dunedin Summer Festival (3rd week of Feb); Rhododendron Festival (3rd week of Oct).
www.cityofdunedin.com

★ **The Octagon**
The Octagon is a popular gathering place for small groups who lunch under the trees, and for bigger crowds during festivals and exhibitions (see p258).

The Otago Daily Times Building, an interesting piece of 1930s Art Deco architecture, is the home of New Zealand's oldest newspaper.

Law Courts (see p259)

★ **Dunedin Railway Station**
Perhaps the finest stone structure in the country, the station has a 37-m (120-ft) high square tower, three huge clock faces and a covered carriageway (see pp262–3).

Dunedin Railway Station

Frieze with cherub and foliage

Dunedin's Railway Station is one of New Zealand's finest historic buildings and one of the best examples of railway architecture in the southern hemisphere. Although not large by international standards, the station's delightful proportions lend it an air of grandeur. Opened in 1906, the Flemish Renaissance-style building was designed by New Zealand Railways architect George Troup, whose detailing on the outside of the building earned him the nickname "Gingerbread George".

★ Exterior Stonework
Beige Oamaru limestone (see pp268–9) detailing provides a striking contrast to the darker Central Otago bluestone on the walls and the finely polished Aberdeen granite of the columns.

The turret provides a visual counterbalance to the main clock tower.

The roof is covered with clay Marseille tiles from France.

Dormer windows projecting from the sloping gable roof are typical Flemish architectural features.

New Zealand Sports Hall of Fame
This features imaginative displays recounting the exploits and achievements of famous New Zealanders.

A frieze of cherubs and foliage from the Royal Doulton factory in England encircles the ticket hall below the wrought-iron bordered balcony.

Main entrance

STAR FEATURES

- ★ Exterior Stonework and Carvings
- ★ Mosaic Floor
- ★ Stained-glass Windows

Ticket Windows
The ticket windows are ornately decorated with white tiles and a crest featuring the old New Zealand Railways logo.

★ Stained-glass Windows

Two imposing stained-glass windows on the mezzanine balcony depict approaching steam engines, lights blazing, facing each other across the ticket hall.

VISITORS' CHECKLIST

Anzac Ave. **Tel** *(03) 477 4449.*
◯ *8am–6pm Mon–Fri,*
9am–6pm Sat, Sun & public hols.
◉ *25 Dec.* ♿ 🅿

Finely carved sandstone lions on each corner of the clock tower guard the cupola behind them.

The clock tower rises 37 m (120 ft) above street level.

Staircase

Complete with wrought-iron balustrades and Royal Doulton mosaic tiled steps, a staircase sweeps up from the ticket hall to the balcony above.

The platform is the arrival and departure point for visitors taking the Taieri Gorge Railway *(see p264).*

★ Mosaic Floor

More than 725,000 Royal Doulton porcelain squares form images of steam engines, rolling stock and the New Zealand Railways logo.

North Dunedin and Environs

Dunedin's city centre is enclosed by hills to the north and west, and by water – the Otago Harbour and Pacific Ocean – to the east and south. In the north of the city are several green areas, most notably the Botanic Gardens at the foot of Signal Hill, and several historic buildings. A road along the narrow, scenic harbour leads to lookout points providing panoramic views of the city, harbour and peninsula.

🏞 Signal Hill
Signal Hill Rd via Opoho Rd.
◯ *daily.* ♿
To the north of the city, the road up Signal Hill leads to a monument built in 1940 to mark 100 years of British sovereignty in New Zealand. From here visitors can get excellent views of the central city, upper harbour and parts of the Otago Peninsula.

🌿 Dunedin Botanic Gardens
Opoho Rd. *Tel (03) 471 9275.*
◯ *daily.* ♿ 🍴 📷 🎁 📷
Rhododendron Festival (late Oct).
Dunedin's extensive Botanic Gardens were the first to be established in New Zealand, in 1868. The area's varied topography and microclimates are used to grow a diverse range of plants. The flat lower gardens are home to the more formal displays – lawns interspersed with trees and native bush and formal flower gardens – and to the Edwardian Winter Garden, first opened in 1908. On the hill, the upper gardens include more than 3,000 rhododendron varieties in the world-renowned Rhododendron Dell. These provide a spring-time feast for the eyes.

🏛 Otago Museum
419 Great King St. *Tel (03) 474 7474.* ◯ *daily.* ● *25 Dec.* 📷 *donation.* ♿ 🎫 *2pm Sat & Sun.* 📷 📷
www.otagomuseum.govt.nz
The displays in the large, Classical-style Otago Museum, opened in 1877, introduce visitors to the region's human and natural history. There are halls dealing with pre-European Maori life, Pacific culture, marine life, and archaeology of the ancient world. The museum also houses one of New Zealand's leading maritime exhibitions and an authentic Victorian "Animal Attic". The interactive Discovery World science centre includes a tropical forest with 1,000 butterflies.

🏞 Tunnel Beach Walkway
Blackhead Rd. ◯ *daily.* ● *Aug–Oct.*
Located 7 km (4 miles) south of the city, Tunnel Beach is named after the tunnel cut through sandstone cliffs in the 1870s by Edward Cargill so that his family could get down to the pretty beach below. The short but steep walkway to the beach gives breathtaking views of the sandstone cliffs which have been spectacularly sculpted by wind and sea.

University of Otago clock tower

🏛 University of Otago
Leith St. *Tel (03) 479 1100.* ◯ *Mon–Fri.* ● *public hols.* ♿ *ground & public areas.* **www**.otago.ac.nz
Founded in 1869, the University of Otago – New Zealand's oldest university – plays a crucial role in the life of the city. The bluestone clock tower registry building dates from 1878 *(see p28)*, while the semi-detached houses close to its northern end were built in 1879 to house the university's first four professors. The grounds are a pleasant place to wander.

🏞 The Organ Pipes
Mount Cargill Rd.
Strange multi-sided basalt columns, known as "the organ pipes", are a reminder of Dunedin's volcanic past. Reaching them requires a walk of at least an hour from a signpost on Mount Cargill Road, north of the city. The panoramic views are a bonus.

🚂 Taieri Gorge Railway
Anzac Avenue. *Tel (03) 477 4449.*
◯ *departs daily; additional departures during summer.*
● *25 Dec.* 📷 ♿ 📷 📷
www.taieri.co.nz
Departing from Dunedin Railway Station, the train takes passengers on a 77-km (48-mile) four-hour trip west of the city. Opened in 1879, the line passes through the greenery of Dunedin's coast, then climbs through a steep-sided river gorge to the arid grasslands and rocky outcrops of the Strath Taieri. It cuts through ten tunnels, crossing bridges and viaducts up to 47 m (155 ft) above the Taieri River.

Rhododendrons in bloom in the Dunedin Botanic Gardens

For hotels and restaurants in this region see pp316–19 and pp340–41

Olveston House

David Theomin

Olveston, a 35-room Jacobean-style mansion, was completed in 1906 for David and Marie Theomin and their children, Edward and Dorothy. Dorothy left the house and its contents to the city and it remains as it was when the family lived in it. Olveston's grand drawing room, dining room, library, billiard room and great hall contain fine furniture and many treasures collected by the Theomins, who were keen travellers.

VISITORS' CHECKLIST

42 Royal Terrace. **Tel** (03) 477 33 20. ☐ daily. ● 25 Dec.
♿ ground floor. 📷 obligatory; hourly 9:30am–4:00pm 📷
www.olveston.co.nz

The kitchen is dominated by a kauri dresser filled with blue and white Delft ware and a kauri table.

Library

Exterior Stonework
The double-brick house gets its warm exterior colour from a cladding of Moeraki pebbles with Oamaru stone highlights (see pp268–9).

★ Dining Room
Attractive features are the oak panelling, semicircular stained-glass windows and richly embossed wallpaper.

The Billard Room has a full-size table and adjustable overhead lights.

Main entrance

Card Room

Dutch gables and projecting windows add architectural interest to the exterior of Olveston.

The Drawing Room, used for entertaining and music, has the only decorated ceiling in the house.

★ Great Hall
A centre for receptions, the hall has oak joinery, printed hessian wall covering featuring acanthus leaves, and a collection of porcelain.

STAR FEATURES

★ Dining Room

★ Great Hall

Otago Peninsula ❷

Yellow-eyed penguin

The 24-km (15-mile) long Otago Peninsula offers a wide variety of attractions, including rare and unusual wildlife, historic buildings, woodland gardens and spectacular harbour and coastal scenery. The 64-km (40-mile) round trip, taking the "high" Highcliff Road, which runs over the top of the peninsula, on the outward journey, and returning via the "low" Portobello Road along the coast, can take a full day. The Highcliff Road offers the best views of the surrounding countryside and coastline.

🏰 Larnach Castle

145 Camp Rd. **Tel** (03) 476 1616.
◻ daily. ⬤ 25 Dec. ▨ ⬤ inside.
♿ ground floor. ⬤ by arrangement.
◻ ◻ www.larnachcastle.co.nz

Located 14 km (9 miles) from central Dunedin along the "high" road, Lanarch Castle is New Zealand's only castle. Built between 1871 and 1885 by financier, businessman and politician, William J M Larnach for his wife Eliza, the grand stone mansion, set in 2 sq km (0.8 sq mile) of bush and gardens, is built along Scottish baronial lines. It has many fine features, including elaborately carved and decorated ceilings and a large, hanging staircase. Its magnificent interior was created by English and Italian artisans brought to Dunedin to work on the building. There is also a ballroom, added as a complete wing as a birthday present for Larnach's daughter, Kate. Visitors can climb up the narrow stone steps for a view from the top of the tower. Accommodation is available next to the castle (*see p318*).

In 1967 the Barker family bought the castle which was by then derelict and spent many years restoring it to its former glory. Margaret Barker has worked particularly hard to restore the gardens and grounds, and they now contain a fine collection of native and exotic plants.

🐦 Royal Albatross Centre

Taiaroa Head. **Tel** (03) 478 0499.
◻ daily. ⬤ 25 Dec. ▨ ♿ visitor centre only. ⬤ except Tue am; tours obligatory; booking essential. ◻ ◻
www.albatrosses.org.nz

The prominent Taiaroa head-land at the mouth of Otago Harbour is home to the world's only mainland royal albatross colony. Opened in 1989, the centre contains excellent displays about these large birds. During the nesting period, guides take visitors to an observatory where the birds can be seen nesting and flying. A colony of Stewart Island shags is also visible from the observatory.

Black and white royal albatrosses at Taiaroa Head

Taiaroa Head's other main attraction is the Armstrong disappearing gun, a 15-cm (6-inch) diameter naval defence gun installed in 1886 during the "Russian scare". Designed to pop out of the ground, fire and then recoil back into its pit, it is the only one of its kind in the world still in working order in its original position.

Larnach Castle viewed from the gardens

Homestead in the Glenfalloch Woodland Gardens

🍂 Glenfalloch Woodland Gardens

430 Portobello Rd. *Tel (03) 478 0499.* ⬜ *daily.* 🎫 *donation.* ♿ *lower gardens.* 🚻 ⬛ *summer only.*

On the "low road", 10 km (6 miles) from Dunedin, the Glenfalloch Woodland Gardens – glenfalloch is Gaelic for "hidden glen" – have been attracting visitors since the 1870s. An elegant homestead, built in 1871, tearooms (open in summer), and a pottery, where pieces that are made on the spot are sold, are sheltered in grounds containing mature trees, shrubs, and a stream. The gardens are ablaze with rhododendrons and azaleas in spring, and during the summer months they are noted for their colourful displays of fuchsias.

Visitors to Glenfalloch can enjoy several short walking tracks through the trees and woodland gardens.

🐟 New Zealand Marine Studies Centre

Hatchery Rd, Portobello. *Tel (03) 479 5826.* ⬜ *daily.* ⬤ *25 Dec.* 🎫 ♿ 🚻 📷 www.marine.ac.nz

Portobello is a peaceful little harbourside settlement with shops and a tavern. Its main claim to fame is the Marine Studies Centre's aquarium, part of the University of Otago's marine research centre. Located at the end of a small peninsula near Portobello, the aquarium features the marine life of the region and a "touch tank" for children with starfish, crabs and sea anemones.

🏛 Otakou

Off Harrington Point Rd. ⬜ *daily.* 🚫 *inside.*

Otakou is the site of one of the earliest Maori settlements in the area, and it was this word which was anglicized to Otago to give the surrounding province its name. The local church and meeting house were built to commemorate the 1940 centenary of the signing of the Treaty of Waitangi (*see pp48–9*). What appear to be carvings are actually moulded concrete.

Maori church and meeting house at Otakau

🐧 Penguin Place

Harrington Point Rd. *Tel (03) 478 0286.* ⬜ *daily.* 🎫 🚗 *obligatory, bookings essential.* 📷

The road to Taiaroa Head passes Penguin Place, an award-winning venture to save the yellow-eyed penguin, the world's rarest species of penguin. Yellow-eyed penguins are found only on the Otago Peninsula and other isolated east coast areas of Otago and Southland. An ingenious system of camouflaged trenches at Penguin Place allows visitors to view nesting yellow-eyed penguins at close range without disturbing them. It is best to visit at dusk when the birds are most active.

Moeraki Boulders Scenic Reserve ❸

Road map B7.

The Moeraki Boulders, 78 km (49 miles) north of Dunedin on State Highway 1, have long been the subject of legend and curiosity. Almost perfectly spherical, with a circumference of up to 4 m (13 ft), the grey boulders lie scattered along a 50-m (164-ft) stretch of the beach. They were formed on the sea bed about 60 million years ago as lime salts gradually accumulated around a hard core.

Maori legend claims that the boulders were the food baskets or Te Kaihinaki of the Araiteuru canoe, one of the great ancestral canoes that brought Maori to New Zealand from Hawaiki. The canoe was wrecked while on a greenstone gathering trip. It is said that the *kumara* on board became rough rocks, the food baskets became smooth boulders, and the wreck turned into a reef.

It is not unusual to see small black and white Hector's dolphins playing in the surf near the boulders. A nearby café and restaurant service the flow of visitors.

The tiny, picturesque fishing village of Moeraki, a former whaling station established in 1836, is on the opposite side of the bay from the reserve.

Spherical boulders on the beach at Moeraki

Street-by-Street: Oamaru ❹

Warehouse window

The main town of north Otago and service centre for a rich agricultural hinterland, Oamaru is a pretty town with wide, tree-lined streets, well-kept gardens, galleries, beaches, colonies of rare penguins, and the best preserved collection of historic public and commercial buildings in New Zealand. The buildings were fashioned in the 1880s from Oamaru stone, a local cream-coloured limestone which is easily cut, carved and moulded. Oamaru was the childhood home of the novelist Janet Frame (1924–2004), who had an international reputation, and a walking tour takes visitors past sites featured in her writing.

★ Forrester Gallery
Ornately carved Corinthian columns distinguish this 1882 building, which formerly housed the Bank of New South Wales.

Courthouse
Built in 1883 and still in use, the Courthouse features a Neo-Classical portico with Corinthian columns.

Meeks Grain Elevator Building (1883)

National Bank (1871)

HUMBER ST

★ North Otago Museum
Exhibits in the museum, built in 1882, include displays on the quarrying and use of Oamaru stone.

THAMES ST

ITCHIN STREET

Oamaru's first Post Office, a small Italianate building with a squat clock tower, was built in 1864.

Colonial Bank (1878)

St Luke's Anglican Church (1865–1913) contains fine interior wood-carving

STAR SIGHTS

★ Forrester Gallery

★ New Zealand Loan and Mercantile Warehouse

★ North Otago Museum

Waitaki District Council
Originally Oamaru's second post office (1883), the building's 28-m (92-ft) clock tower was added in 1903.

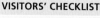

Criterion Hotel
Built in 1877, this hotel went "dry" in 1906 during prohibition. Now restored, it serves patrons in a Victorian pub atmosphere.

Harbour Board Office (1876)

Harbour Street
At the heart of the port area, this street is lined with 19th-century warehouses, commercial buildings and grain stores.

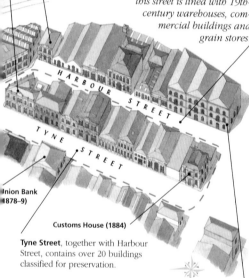

Union Bank (1878–9)

Customs House (1884)

Tyne Street, together with Harbour Street, contains over 20 buildings classified for preservation.

```
0 metres        100
0 yards         100
```

KEY

– – – Suggested route

★ New Zealand Loan and Mercantile Warehouse
This three-storey Victorian warehouse, built in 1882 for New Zealand's largest stock and station agency, was designed to hold up to 100,000 sacks of grain.

View of Oamaru and the harbour from Lookout Reserve

Exploring Oamaru
Apart from its historic harbour precinct which features a number of boutique businesses, Oamaru has several scenic and natural attractions. The 1-km (0.6-mile) South Hill Walkway above the harbour leads to Lookout Reserve. Further on is Bushy Beach where a viewing hide allows visitors to see blue and yellow-eyed penguins. Guided tours are available from November to February.

🐧 Oamaru Blue Penguin Colony
Waterfront Rd. **Tel** (03) 433 1195. ◯ daily. ⬤ 25 Apr, 25 & 26 Dec. 📷 🚫 no flash. ♿ 🏠
At Friendly Bay, an old quarry in Oamaru's harbour, visitors can see penguins leave at dawn to feed at sea, and return at dusk past a special viewing area. The colony was founded in 1992.

🌸 Oamaru Public Gardens
Chelmer St. ◯ daily, until sunset.
Established in 1876, these contain traditional features such as rose gardens, ponds, an azalea lawn and rhododendron dell. A band rotunda, summerhouse, aviary, peacock house and marble fountain are other attractions.

🏛 Totara Estate
State Hwy 1. ℹ️ (03) 434 7169. ◯ daily. ⬤ 25 Dec. 📷 ♿ 🏠
About 8 km (5 miles) south of Oamaru, this is where New Zealand's first shipment of frozen mutton to England in 1882 was processed, heralding the beginning of New Zealand's most important industry. Limestone buildings house displays on the history of the meat industry.

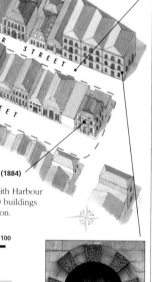

Stone woolshed at Morven Hills Station, Lindis Pass

Lindis Pass **❺**

Road map B6.

The main inland link between Otago and the Waitaki Basin, the Lindis Pass climbs through rocky gorges before reaching the tussock-covered hills of a Department of Conservation reserve near the summit. Early Maori, like today's holiday-makers, used the route in summer to get to Lakes Wanaka and Hawea.

In 1858, John McLean, the first European to settle in the area, established the 2,000-sq-km (772-sq-mile) Morven Hills Station. Many of the original buildings can still be seen about 15 km (9 miles) south of the summit. These include McLean's original homestead and a massive stone woolshed, built about 1880, which was capable of holding up to 1,500 sheep.

Lake Hawea **❻**

Road map B6. 🚶 1,100. 🎣 Hawea Picnic Day & Races (Dec).

Tucked among hills and mountains, the bright blue waters of Lake Hawea make it one of the most beautiful of the southern lakes. The lake, which is 410 m (1,345 ft) deep in places, is separated from the equally beautiful

Lake Wanaka by a narrow, 35-km (22-mile) isthmus, known as "the neck".

Lake Hawea is a popular holiday haven. There are many free camping spots around its shores. It is also well known for its excellent trout and land-locked salmon fishing and for various boating activities. The small town of Hawea on the lake's southern shores is the main base for outdoor activities.

Wanaka **❼**

Road map B6. 🚶 3,000. 🛈 100 Ardmore St, (03) 443 1233. 🎣 Wanakafest (Sep); Warbirds Over Wanaka (Easter, even-numbered years). **www**.lakewanaka.co.nz

Located at the southern end of the lake, Wanaka is one of the country's favourite holiday spots. The willow-lined shores and bays of Lake Wanaka are popular in summer for boating, fishing and water-skiing, while in winter skiers and snowboarders flock to the local ski areas. Snow-capped peaks provide a beautiful lake setting, and these natural attractions also bring hikers and walkers to the many breathtaking tracks in the nearby Mount Aspiring National Park *(see pp272–3)*.

Aside from the area's natural features, there is plenty to visit and see around the town. One of the chief attractions, the **New Zealand Fighter Pilots Museum**, located at Wanaka Airport, is home to a variety of World War II fighter aircraft, such as

a Hawker Hurricane, Tiger Moth, Vampire, Chipmunk, a replica of a SE5A and several rare Russian Polikar-povs. Illustrated displays explain the role of New Zealand fighter pilots and crews in several theatres of war. Visitors can also see aircraft being restored in the maintenance hangar. "Warbirds Over Wanaka", a major biennial airshow involving military aircraft, is held every second Easter in even-numbered years. It features aircraft from New Zealand as well as overseas in acrobatic displays and mock battles. Wanaka's open skies and dramatic alpine scenery provide a spectacular backdrop.

Next to Wanaka Airport is the **Wanaka Transport Museum**. Its large private collection of more than 13,000 items includes memo-rabilia, such as toys and

Stuart Landsborough's Puzzling World

models, as well as military vehicles and aircraft. A special exhibit is a huge Russian Antonov AN-2, the world's largest single engine biplane.

Stuart Landsborough's Puzzling World is based around "The Great Maze", 1.5 km (1 mile) of three-dimensional wooden passages and under- and overbridges. Other attractions include a Hologram Hall, the Tumbling Towers/Tilted House, and the Puzzle Centre where you can sit down with a cup of tea or coffee and try to solve one of the many challenging puzzles on display.

Like many other parts of Central Otago, Wanaka's climate is proving ideal for grape growing. **Rippon Vineyard**, established in 1974 just 4 km (2.5 miles) from the centre of town, is one of the

Fishing on the shores of Lake Hawea

Rippon Vineyard on the shores of Lake Wanaka

pioneering growers and wine makers of the region. The vineyard produces wines from a number of grape varieties.

🏛 New Zealand Fighter Pilots Museum
Wanaka Airport. **Tel** (03) 443 7010.
⬤ daily. ⬤ 25 Dec. 🖼 ♿ 🛍 ⬛
www.nzfpm.co.nz

🏛 Wanaka Transport and Toy Museum
State Hwy 6. **Tel** (03) 443 8765. ⬤
daily. ⬤ 25 Dec. 🖼 ♿ 🛍 ⬛ ⬛

🗺 Stuart Landsborough's Puzzling World
State Hwy 6. **Tel** (03) 443 7489.
⬤ daily. 🖼 ♿ 🛍 ⬛ ⬛
www.puzzlingworld.com

🏛 Rippon Vineyard
Mt Aspiring Rd. **Tel** (03) 443 8084.
⬤ daily. ⬤ May–June, 25 Dec.
🖼 wine tasting. ♿ 🛍 ⬛ Rippon Music Festival (biennial, even-numbered years in Feb).
www.rippon.co.nz

Environs
Twenty-five km (16 miles) south of Wanaka is the tiny township of Cardrona, consisting of a few cottages and a hotel dating back to 1863 (see p319).

The surrounding Cardrona Valley, a popular route for gold-miners in the 1860s, is now better known for the

Cardrona Ski Field on the southeastern slopes of Mount Cardrona, and for cross-country skiing at the nearby Waiorau Snow Farm (see pp194–5, 351).

The **Treble Cone Ski Area**, 20 km (12 miles) southwest of Wanaka, off Mount Aspiring Road, has uncrowded slopes which are great for skiers of all abilities (see pp194–5, 351). Guided back country heli-skiing over the Harris, Richardson and Buchanan mountains is another option, flying you to some of the best out-of-the-way ski spots in the area.

WANAKA'S OUTDOOR ATTRACTIONS

Wanaka is a recreational centre with a wide variety of outdoor pursuits in both summer and winter. Fishing is a popular activity on the lake shore, along rivers and from charter vessels. Waterborne adventures include kayaking, jet-boat and cruise boat trips, white-water sledging on small purpose-designed boards, and canyoning. There are several good walks which leave from or near the township, as well as longer hikes in the nearby Mount Aspiring National Park (see pp272–3) for more serious, well-equipped hikers. Horse riding, mountain biking and quad bike motorcycle tours are other ways of exploring Wanaka's back country areas.
Within easy distance of Wanaka lie two commercial downhill ski areas, Treble Cone and Cardrona, as well as the Waiorau Snow Farm cross-country ski area and heli-skiing in the surrounding mountains. From Wanaka Airport, flightseeing tours are available, or, for the more adventurous, acrobatic flights in Tiger Moths or World War II Mustangs.

Skiers on a chairlift at Treble Cone Ski Area, southwest of Wanaka

Mount Aspiring National Park ⑧

Alpine plant

New Zealand's third largest National Park after Fiordland and Kahurangi, Mount Aspiring National Park enjoys World Heritage status as part of the Te Wahipounamu/Southwest New Zealand World Heritage Area, which stretches from Aoraki/Mount Cook to the southern tip of Fiordland. Within the park's 3,500-sq km (1,350-sq mile) area, the scenery ranges from snow- and glacier-clad mountains to rugged rock faces, spectacular forested valleys and picturesque river flats. The park, close to the tourist centres of Queenstown and Wanaka, is a popular walking, tramping and climbing destination.

Exploring the park
Opportunities to explore the park on foot are varied, and range from short walks from the road to back country circuits for fit trampers.

The Olvine Wilderness Area, which constitutes the core of the park, is maintained in an undeveloped state for wilderness recreation and has no tracks or huts.

Okuru

Jackson Bay   Waiat

Arawhata River

HAAST RANGE

Waiatoto River

MAIN DIVIDE

*TITITEA /
MOUNT ASPIRING
3,033 m (9,950 ft)*

Aspiring Hut

ROB ROY GLACIE

Lake Wilmot

OLIVINE RANGE

Dart–Rees Track

Matukituki

Rob Roy Valley Walk

Valley Walk

▲ MOUNT EARNSLAW
2,820 m (9,252 ft)

★ **Mount Aspiring/Tititea**
Because of its pyramid shape, Mount Aspiring/Tititea is often described as New Zealand's "Matterhorn".

The Dart–Rees Track, a challenging four- to five-day loop track reached from the head of Lake Wakatipu, offers outstanding scenery but requires a high level of fitness and the proper equipment.

BIRDLIFE IN MOUNT ASPIRING NATIONAL PARK

Rock wren

This park is known for its abundant birdlife. Some 51 species, 38 of them native, inhabit the valley floors, riverbeds, forests, subalpine scrub and high alpine regions. Especially symbolic of the park are the kea, rock wren and blue duck. The kea, whose call may be heard echoing through the valleys, is an inquisitive bird well known for its interest in trampers' equipment and food. The hardy little rock wren lives high in the hills in one of the harshest environments in the park, while pairs of blue ducks can be seen feeding on vegetation and insects in the park's swift mountain streams, especially in the hanging valleys.

Matukituki Valley
A track up the west branch of the river from the end of the road takes trampers to the head of the valley and to some challenging climbing in the Mount Aspiring area.

★ **Gates of Haast**
At the Gates of Haast bridge, the Haast River roars down a steep-sided gorge strewn with boulders.

Mount Brewster
Accessible from State Highway 6, Mount Brewster is a popular climbing and camping spot.

★ **Thunder Creek Falls**
A short forest track from State Highway 6 leads to the 30-m (98-ft) falls which drop from a notch in a rock.

VISITORS' CHECKLIST

Road map A6. **Wanaka**
Ardmore St. **i** Department of Conservation, Ardmore St, (03) 443 7660. □ summer: daily, winter: Mon–Sat. ● 25 Dec. **i** **Makarora** **i** State Hwy 6, (03) 443 8365. □ summer: daily, winter: Mon–Sat. ● 1 Jan, 25 Dec. **i** www.doc.govt.nz

Haast ❾

Road map B6. 🚶 *300.* **i** *Cnr State Hwy 6 & Jackson Bay Rd, (03) 750 0809.*

A tiny community on the coast where the broad Haast River meets the sea, Haast is little more than a stopover and supply point for people travelling between the West Coast and the southern lakes, although it does offer good surf and river fishing. The visitor centre provides information on walks and tracks in the area, as well as maps, souvenirs and visitor publications. The staff can also advise on track and weather conditions in this high rainfall area. Fill up with fuel here before driving over the pass to Wanaka.

Environs
The road south to the fishing village of **Jackson Bay** provides a number of walking and sightseeing opportunities, such as the Hapuka Estuary Walk, the Cascade Viewpoint and the Smoothwater Bay track at Jackson Bay itself. The Wharekai Te Kau Walk leads to the Okahu Wildlife Refuge.

There are several places of interest north of Haast, such as the Dune Lake Walk through dense coastal forest stunted by wind at Ship Creek, and the stunning Knights Point viewpoint.

Further on, past **Lake Moeraki**, the Monro Beach Walk passes through luxuriant coastal forest to a remote beach where (from July to December) Fiordland crested penguins are sometimes seen. The road carries on to trout-filled **Lake Paringa** where a 15-minute walk passes through native trees such as silver beech, rimu and kahikatea.

KEY

▬▬	State highway
▭▭	Minor road
≋≋	River
‒ ‒	Walking track
▬ ▪	Park boundary
i	Tourist information
🅰	Camp site
⛟	Picnic area
⚘	Viewpoint

0 kilometres   10

0 miles   10

STAR SIGHTS

★ Gates of Haast

★ Mount Aspiring/Tititea

★ Thunder Creek Falls

Jackson Bay, surrounded by swamp, bush and mountains

Milford Sound in Fiordland National Park ▷

Queenstown

Bungy jumping
sign

Situated on the northeast shore of Lake Wakatipu, backed by the Remarkables range, Queenstown enjoys one of the most scenic settings in the world. Since the 1970s, it has developed from a sleepy lakeside town into a leading international resort and a world centre for adventure sports, including bungy jumping (see pp194–5). Like most towns in the area, Queenstown was established during the 1860s gold rushes. Although the pace of development in Queenstown has been dictated by the demands of tourism, it still has the feel of a small town and proudly maintains its links with the days of the gold boom.

TSS Earnslaw on Lake Wakatipu

Lake Wakatipu

There is no mistaking Lake Wakatipu's glacial origins, although Maori legend has it that the lake was formed by the imprint of a sleeping demon burnt to death by the lover of a beautiful Maori girl captured by the demon. Because his heart did not perish and still beats, the level of the lake rises and falls as much as 7 cm (3 inches) every five minutes. Lake Wakatipu, which is the second largest of the southern glacial lakes, after Te Anau, is up to 380 m (1,246 ft) deep in places.

The steep, rugged slopes of the Remarkables drop down to the lake's edge, leaving downtown Queenstown snuggled on one of the few pieces of relatively flat land in the area. Most private residences and many hotels have been banished to the surrounding hills. During the mining boom, the lake was the principal means of communication, but today it is a focus for recreational activities.

Queenstown Gardens

Park St. ◯ daily. &

Set on a glacial moraine peninsula, the Queenstown Gardens are within walking distance of the town centre. They are surrounded by stands of large fir trees and contain broad lawns and rose beds. The gardens provide a quiet oasis in an otherwise busy tourist town, and are particularly attractive in autumn. An ice skating rink, sporting greens, a children's park, and a walkway around the point are other attractions.

TSS Earnslaw

Steamer Wharf. **Tel** 0800 656 503.
◯ daily. 🎫 & main deck. ▣ ▢
The TSS (Twin Screw Steamer) Earnslaw is a wonderful relic of the mining boom when paddle steamers and other craft plied Lake Wakatipu, the principal means of communication. Launched in 1912, the 51-m (168-ft) vessel, affectionately known as "the lady of the lake", is still powered by its original twin 500-hp coal-fired steam engines. Its interior is finished with wood and brass.

A number of cruises depart from Queenstown all year round, from 90-minute cruises to four-hour dinner cruises in the warmer months. Visitors can also take daytime or evening excursions across the lake to the **Walter Peak High Country Farm**. Here they can enjoy refreshments at the Colonel's Homestead Restaurant, go horse trekking or watch displays of various aspects of high country life, such as sheep shearing and sheep dogs in action.

ADVENTURE CAPITAL OF NEW ZEALAND

Queenstown offers a range of adventures, from outdoor experiences to total adventure packages (see pp194–5, 350–55). Many activities are centred around the lake and on the several rivers nearby, in particular the Dart, Shotover and Kawarau, where jet-boat trips and white-water rafting offer

White-water rafting on the Shotover River

exciting rides through narrow, rocky canyons. In winter, two ranges within 30 km (19 miles) of Queenstown – the Remarkables and Coronet Peak – provide great skiing. The town's reputation as New Zealand's adventure capital, however, rests on its many airborne activities: bungy jumping, ranging from the 43-m (141-ft) high Kawarau Bridge to the 134-m (440-ft) high Nevis highwire bungy; hang-gliding from the area's mountainous terrain; tandem parapenting from Bob's Peak; and tandem skydiving.

➤ Underwater World

Maintown Pier. **Tel** (03) 442 8538.
◻ daily. 🖼 🏛
Built beneath the Maintown
Pier, Underwater World provides a unique opportunity to
see life below the surface of
the lake. From a viewing
lounge 5 m (16 ft) under the
water, visitors can observe
brown and rainbow trout
peacefully swimming
alongside enormous New
Zealand long-finned eels,
which are often visited by
diving black teal ducks.

🎫 The Mall

The best way to enjoy and get
to know Queenstown is on
foot and probably the best
place to start is at The Mall,
which is a popular meeting
place for visitors and a
pedestrian-only street
dominated by a variety of
restaurants and cafés, as well
as numerous souvenir shops.
The Mall leads directly down
to the Maintown Pier from
which boats and jetboats
regularly depart for cruises on
the lake.
A number of old colonial
buildings remain in The Mall.

🚠 Skyline Gondola

Brecon St. **Tel** (03) 441 0101.
◻ daily. 🖼 🛗 🏛 🏛
www.skyline.co.nz
The gondola up to Bob's
Peak is synonymous with
Queenstown. It rises 450 m
(1,476 ft) in just 730 m (2,400
ft) and provides breathtaking
panoramic views of the
Remarkables, Lake Wakatipu
and Queenstown from the
observation deck at the top.
Visitors can eat at the restaurant or café, take walks in the
area, watch parapenters float
down from the peak or take a
ride downhill on the luge – a
short, raised toboggan.

Skyline Gondola

🐦 Kiwi and Birdlife Park

Brecon St. **Tel** (03) 442 8059.
◻ daily. ● 25 Dec. 🖼 🛏 Kiwi
House. ♿ one house. 🏛 🏛
www.kiwibird.co.nz
Queenstown's Kiwi and Birdlife Park, below the gondola
terminal, is home to several
kiwis and other endangered
native birds. The birds are
either part of national breeding programmes, where young
birds are produced for release
into the wild, or are being
rehabilitated after injury.
A major attraction is the
nocturnal Kiwi House where
visitors can see this flightless
bird. Other species on view in
natural, parklike surroundings
include native owls, large
alpine parrots known as kea,
parakeets, and the black stilt
– a rare wader *(see p251).*

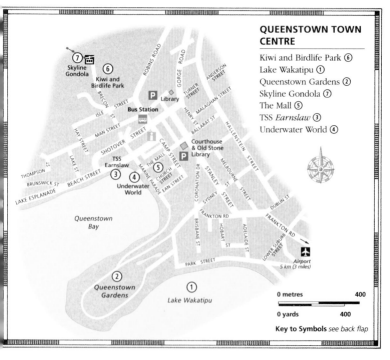

Key to Symbols *see back flap*

Glenorchy ⑪

Road map A6. 🏔 360. ℹ️ *Cnr Mull & Oban sts, (03) 441 0303.*

Glenorchy is a small, tranquil township at the head of Lake Wakatipu, 44 km (27 miles) or 40 minutes' drive from Queenstown. The town stands in the shadow of snow-capped peaks with names such as Mount Chaos and Mount Head which rise steeply above the Rees and Dart river valleys.

The town is the transit point for trampers entering the valleys, which are part of the Mount Aspiring National Park (*see pp272–3*), and which are among New Zealand's Great Walks. For the serious tramper, there is a 77-km (48-mile) loop track which connects both valleys via the 1,447-m (4,747-ft) Rees Saddle. Although it takes four to five days and requires proper equipment, it is possible to enjoy a few hours' return walk up either valley. A variety of outdoor activities are also available at Glenorchy.

Arrowtown ⑫

Road map B6. 🏔 2,000. ℹ️ *49 Buckingham St (in museum), (03) 442 1824.* 🎭 *Autumn Festival (Apr).*

Nestled at the foot of rugged hills 21 km (13 miles) from Queenstown, Arrowtown is the most picturesque and best preserved gold-mining town in the area. In 1862, a small band of miners, including William Fox and John O'Callaghan, discovered gold in the Fox River

Lake Hayes near Arrowtown

and within weeks they had recovered 113 kg (250 lb) of the precious metal. Arrowtown's population peaked at more than 7,000 and is one of the few boom towns not to have either become a ghost town or been overrun by more modern development. The main street, partly lined with deciduous trees, has many old colonial shops and buildings at one end and, at the other, tiny miners' stone cottages dating back to the 1860s and 1870s.

Chinese miners played a big part in Arrowtown's history after 1865, when they were invited to fill the vacuum created by European miners who had left for the West Coast gold rush. Their legacy is Arrowtown's **Chinese Settlement** with its preserved and restored stone buildings, including tiny cottages, an outhouse and a store.

Stone cottage at the Chinese settlement

The **Lakes District Museum** chronicles both Arrowtown and Queenstown's past, focusing on gold-miners and their innovations. It includes a

display on New Zealand's first hydroelectric plant, built in 1886 in what is now the ghost town of Bullendale. Other displays cover local geology, agriculture, sawmilling and domestic life of the gold rush period. The museum doubles as Arrowtown's visitor centre.

🏯 Chinese Settlement
Buckingham St. **Tel** (03) 442 1824. 🔾 *daily.* ♿ *assisted.*

🏛 Lakes District Museum
49 Buckingham St. **Tel** (03) 442 1824. 🔾 *daily.* ● *25 Dec.*

Environs

Near to Arrowtown is the much-photographed **Lake Hayes**, at its best in autumn. The road from Arrowtown to Queenstown passes the access road to Coronet Peak which heads 7 km (4 miles) up to great views from the ski area. **Macetown** is a popular destination for 4WD vehicles. A 26-km (16-mile) return journey from Arrowtown takes visitors up a steep, gold-bearing gorge. Ghost town relics include the remains of old stone building and a gold stamping battery.

Gibbston Valley Wines is a good example of vineyards in the area (*see pp36–7*). European varieties thrive in the hot summer days and cool evenings. Gibbston's wine is stored in a cool underground cave, and tours and wine tastings are available.

🍷 Gibbston Valley Wines
State Hwy 6. **Tel** (03) 442 6910. 🔾 *daily.* ● *most public hols.* ♿ 🍷 *cave.* 🏪 📷

The main street of Arrowtown

Cromwell ⓭

Road map B7. 🏠 3,300.
🛈 47 The Mall, (03) 445 0212.

Cromwell survived the gold era to become a service town in one of New Zealand's leading fruit growing areas. In the 1980s, an electricity generating dam built down river created nearby Lake Dunstan, flooding much of Cromwell's quaint and historic main street, although several of the more notable buildings were relocated stone by stone to a new site. Cromwell now makes its living from farming, horticulture, viticulture and tourism.

Environs

Gold-mining relics in the area include **Bendigo**, a ghost town 4 km (2 miles) off State Highway 8, the main road between Cromwell and Lindis Pass. By 1866 Bendigo was all but deserted until a rich gold-bearing quartz reef was found, and mined for more than 50 years.

A loop track above Bendigo leads to **Logantown** and **Welshtown**, two associated settlements deserted in the 1880s. It is wise to keep to the tracks because there are many old unmarked mine shafts throughout the area.

The **Goldfields Mining Centre** in the Kawarau Gorge, 5 km (3 miles) from Cromwell, offers visitors working exhibitions of gold-mining techniques.

🏛 Goldfields Mining Centre
Kawarau Gorge, State Hwy 6.
Tel (03) 445 1038. 🔾 daily.
🔴 25 Dec. 🖭 🔾 🔾 🔾 🔾

THE GOLD RUSH

The Otago gold rush began with the discovery of gold in Gabriel's Gully in 1861, near the present-day town of Lawrence, 92 km (57 miles) west of Dunedin. A tent town sprang up and prospectors soon began pushing further inland. Finds in the Dunstan area around Cromwell and Alexandra followed in 1862, with discoveries in the Wakatipu region soon after. Tens of thousands braved hot, dry summers, cold, harsh winters and starvation in search of a quick fortune. New discoveries were made in other corners of the province, but by the late 1860s the focus had shifted to the West Coast. With the main fields well picked over,

more sophisticated methods, such as sluicing, dredging and quartz reef mining, were needed to extract gold. Gold-mining continued well into the 1900s and, more recently, modern methods have led to large-scale mining operations in the area.

Arrowtown miners at their claim in the 1860s

Kingston ⓮

Road map A7. 🏠 65. 🔾 🚤 *Kingston to Queenstown Yacht Race (Jan).*

For a long time the little settlement of Kingston served as a railhead and steamer terminal for travellers heading towards Lake Wakatipu from the south. Nowadays, its main claim to fame is the **Kingston Flyer**, a restored vintage steam train with several coaches and staff in period costume which takes passengers on a 75-minute return trip.

🚂 Kingston Flyer
Kingston Railway Station. **Tel** (03) 248 8848. 🔾 Oct–Apr; daily.
🔴 25 Dec. 🖭 🔾 🔾

Environs

To the south of Kingston, on State Highway 6, is **Lumsden**, well known for the trout-filled rivers which crisscross the countryside surrounding the town. Just before Lumsden, State Highway 94 branches west to Te Anau, Manapouri and Fiordland National Park, and east to the farming area of Gore.

The vintage steam train Kingston Flyer on a short "flight" from Kingston

Fiordland National Park ⑮

Fiordland crested penguin

Fiordland National Park's 1.2 million hectares (2.9 million acres) make it the largest of New Zealand's National Parks, while its special geology, landscape, flora and fauna have earned it a place in the Te Wahipounamu – Southwest New Zealand World Heritage Area. It is a region dominated by forest and water. Its 14 fiords and 5 major lakes – the work of Ice Age glaciers – flanked by steep mountains clad with thick, temperate rainforest, make the interior virtually impenetrable except along its 500 km (310 miles) of tracks. The park is also known for its wildlife, especially its marine mammals and native birds, including the Fiordland crested penguin.

★ **Doubtful Sound**
This fiord extends 40 km (25 miles) from the foot of the main mountain divide to the open waters of the Tasman Sea (see pp284–5).

HOW THE FIORDS WERE FORMED

Although named otherwise, Milford Sound, Doubtful Sound and the other sounds are, in fact, fiords. Sounds are flooded river valleys whereas fiords are valleys carved by the tremendous pressure and power of glaciers during successive Ice Ages, then later flooded by the sea as the ice melts and sea levels rise.

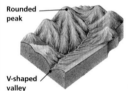

Rounded peak
V-shaped valley

10 million years ago, *intense pressure in the earth's crust caused the most recent uplift in the area, forming peaks and V-shaped valleys.*

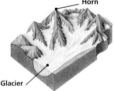

Horn
Glacier

2 million years ago, *the mountains were covered by glaciers. Ridges and peaks became sharper and valleys became U-shaped.*

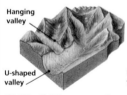

Hanging valley
U-shaped valley

20,000 – 12,000 years ago, *the ice melted as the Ice Age receded, leaving the tributaries of rivers as hanging valleys above the main valley.*

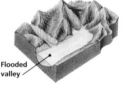

Flooded valley

6,000 years ago, *at the end of the last Ice Age, the sea reached its present levels, flooding the valleys and leaving the peaks exposed.*

DOUBTFUL SOUND

DUSKY SOUND

STAR SIGHTS

★ Cleddau Valley

★ Doubtful Sound

★ Mitre Peak

Dusky Sound
This sound can be reached by chartered cruise boat from Lake Manapouri via Doubtful Sound, or, for experienced climbers, via the 10-day Dusky Track.

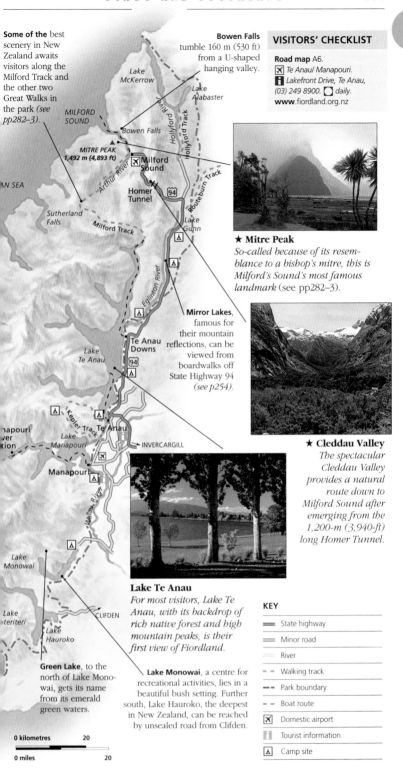

Some of the best scenery in New Zealand awaits visitors along the Milford Track and the other two Great Walks in the park (see pp282–3).

Bowen Falls tumble 160 m (530 ft) from a U-shaped hanging valley.

VISITORS' CHECKLIST

Road map A6.
Te Anau/ Manapouri.
Lakefront Drive, Te Anau, (03) 249 8900. daily.
www.fiordland.org.nz

★ **Mitre Peak**
So-called because of its resemblance to a bishop's mitre, this is Milford's Sound's most famous landmark (see pp282–3).

Mirror Lakes, famous for their mountain reflections, can be viewed from boardwalks off State Highway 94 (see p254).

★ **Cleddau Valley**
The spectacular Cleddau Valley provides a natural route down to Milford Sound after emerging from the 1,200-m (3,940-ft) long Homer Tunnel.

Lake Te Anau
For most visitors, Lake Te Anau, with its backdrop of rich native forest and high mountain peaks, is their first view of Fiordland.

Green Lake, to the north of Lake Monowai, gets its name from its emerald green waters.

Lake Monowai, a centre for recreational activities, lies in a beautiful bush setting. Further south, Lake Hauroko, the deepest in New Zealand, can be reached by unsealed road from Clifden.

KEY

State highway

Minor road

River

- - Walking track

-- Park boundary

- - Boat route

Domestic airport

Tourist information

Camp site

0 kilometres   20

0 miles   20

Exploring Fiordland National Park

With mountains rising 2,750 m (9,020 ft), sheer rock walls climbing 1,200 m (3,940 ft) from deep fiords, and waterfalls tumbling 160 m (530 ft), Fiordland's spectacular landscape attracts visitors from around the world. The Maori were the first to exploit the area's natural resources, then came sealers who from 1792 to the 1820s slaughtered

Church near Te Anau

hundreds of thousands of fur seals. Until 1953, when State Highway 94 (the Milford Road) was completed, the only way to Milford Sound was by boat or via the Milford Track. Today, visitors arrive by the busload, and those with the time, fitness and equipment can walk the famous tracks. Others visit the sound by boat or scenic flight.

Sheep drive on the road to Milford Sound

Te Anau
Road map A7. 🏠 *1,800.*
🚌 *Miro St.* 🛈 *Lakefront Drive,* *(03) 249 2924.*
Te Anau, on the southeastern shore of Lake Te Anau, is Fiordland's commercial centre (primarily tourism and deer farming) and a good base for exploring Fiordland National Park. The lake, the largest in the South Island, is 61 km (38 miles) long and 417 m (1,370 ft) deep, the result of glacial action. It is a popular venue for boating and fishing.

📷 Te Ana-au Caves
🛈 *Real Journeys Visitor Centre, Lakefront Drive, Te Anau.* **Tel** *(03) 249 7416.* ☐ *daily.* 📷 📷
At the Te Ana-au Caves, reached by a boat trip across Lake Te Anau, a combination of carefully formed walkways and small boats allow visitors

Te Ana-au Caves

to explore a series of magical limestone grottos. The caves are home to thousands of tiny New Zealand glowworms, which use their tiny light – the result of a chemical reaction – to attract insects for food. Return trips, which depart several times a day, take two and a half hours.

📷 The Milford Road
The 121-km (75-mile) road to Milford Sound from Te Anau has earned World Heritage Highway status for its beauty and scenic variety. This includes lush lakeside forest, rugged mountains, cascading alpine rivers and picturesque walks. Although Milford Sound can be reached by road in two hours, there are many side trips possible along the way to make the drive more memorable.

Te Anau Downs, 30 km (19 miles) from Te Anau, is the departure point for the boat to the Milford Track. From here there is a 45-minute forest walk to Lake Mistletoe. Further on, the Mirror Lakes are a short five-minute walk from the road across a boardwalk. On a calm day, beautiful reflections of the surrounding scenery are visible in the lakes *(see p254)*.

At Lake Gunn, about 46 km (29 miles) from Te Anau Downs, an easy 45-

NEXT 35 km

Sheep warning sign, Milford Road

minute loop through beech forest is suitable for all ages and for people in wheelchairs. The Divide, a short distance away, marks the start of the Routeburn Track, which leads overland to Lake Wakatipu (note that the track does not actually reach the lake, but ends at the road that then leads to the lake 10–15 km (6–9 miles) away). A three-hour return walk to Key Summit gives rewarding views. The nearby Hollyford Valley also makes a scenic trip.

Nineteen km (12 miles) east of Milford Sound is the 1,200-m (3,940-ft) long Homer Tunnel, started in 1935 but not completed until 1954. Leaving the tunnel, the road slopes very steeply downhill to the Milford side where there are spectacular views along the Cleddau Valley. The Chasm, a few kilometres from the tunnel, can be reached by a 20-minute walk to where the Cleddau River drops 22 m (72 ft) through a series of unusual rock formations.

📷 Milford Sound
Road map A6. 🏠 *170.*
Milford Sound, a 16-km (10-mile) long fiord, is Fiordland's best-known attraction. Its most famous landmark is Mitre Peak, a pyramid-shaped mountain rising 1,692 m (5,550 ft) straight from the deep fiord. Although scenic flights are available, the

grandeur of Milford Sound can be best appreciated by boat. Trips pass unusual geological features, such as Lion Mountain, the Elephant and Copper Point, as well as waterfalls: the Bowen Falls drop 160 m (530 ft) into the water, and the Stirling Falls 146 m (480 ft). Fur seals, dolphins, and the occasional Fiordland crested penguin can be seen along the way.

An Underwater Observatory at Milford Sound allows visitors to see the unusual black coral, red coral, anemones, starfish and fish that live in the fiord. High rainfall means there is a 3 – 4 m (10 –13 ft) layer of fresh water above the underlying salt water.

Fur seals at the entrance to Milford Sound

Apart from day trips in the Milford Sound, full-day and overnight cruises take visitors out of the sound to the open Tasman Sea, with stops at other sounds, such as Dusky Sound. Cruises often combine fishing and diving.

THE THREE GREAT WALKS

Trampers on the Milford Track

Fiordland National Park is considered by many to be the best place in New Zealand for trampers. Its three major walking tracks – the Milford, Routeburn and Kepler (*see pp280–81*) – can be walked independently, or on the Milford in a guided group, all year round. Advance booking is essential for the Milford and Routeburn tracks (*see pp350–51*) during the peak tramping season, while all tracks require advance purchase of hut or camp-site passes. All three walks are suitable only for experienced, well-equipped parties.

The spectacular 55-km (34-mile) **Milford Track**, which takes four days, climbs through the Clinton Valley to the Mackinnon Pass. It passes the Sutherland Falls before dropping down to Milford Sound. The 39-km (24-mile) **Routeburn Track** usually takes three days. It climbs through forest to spectacular subalpine terrain before crossing the Harris Saddle and descending the Routeburn Valley towards Lake Wakatipu. The **Kepler Track**, a three-to four-day 60-km (37-mile) loop, skirts Lake Te Anau, then climbs to panoramic views from Mount Luxmore before descending to Lake Manapouri.

Typical alpine plant

Aerial view of Milford Sound

A Trip to Doubtful Sound ⑯

Doubtful Sound was named by Captain James Cook in 1770, on his voyage to New Zealand when, looking at the narrow entrance to the sound, he was doubtful that he could safely get his vessel in and out. The 40-km (25-mile) long fiord is Fiordland's second largest and, at 421 m (1,380 ft), the deepest. It is a remote, unspoilt wilderness of mountain peaks, fiords and rainforest which supports a rich array of bird and marine life, including crested penguins, fur seals and bottlenose dolphins. Getting there is an adventure in itself, involving two boat trips and a coach ride over a mountain pass, with a side trip deep underground to the huge Manapouri Power Station generator hall.

Lake Manapouri ①
The trip to Doubtful Sound begins at the Pearl Harbour marina on the Waiau River, which feeds into Lake Manapouri. The lake, which is forested to the shoreline, covers 142 sq km (55 sq miles) and is dotted with 34 islands.

New Zealand Fur Seals ⑩
Colonies of New Zealand's most common seal can be seen on the islands dotting the entrance to Doubtful Sound.

TASMAN SEA

Secretary Island

Thompson Sound

Bradshaw Sound

Bauza Island

⑩

⑨

Malaspina Reach

Crooked Arm

⑧

Hall Arm

⑦

⑥

Bottlenose Dolphins ⑨
A resident pod of bottlenose dolphins may be seen playing in the waters at Malaspina Reach. They grow up to 4.5 m (15 ft).

Commander Peak ⑧
To the left at the head of Hall Arm Commander Peak is one of many awe-inspiring bush-clad peaks that visitors see during a cruise of Doubtful Sound's flooded glacial valleys *(see p280)*.

Deep Cove ⑦
The peaceful waters of Deep Cove hide the 10-km (6-mile tunnel under the mountains from the Manapouri Power Station

MANAPOURI POWER STATION

The Manapouri Power Station is a man-made wonder that takes advantage of the difference in height of the mountains between Lake Manapouri and Doubtful Sound to act as a natural dam. Water is chanelled through vertical penstocks into seven generators housed in a huge underground room. The water then flows out of a 10-km (6-mile) tunnel to Deep Cove. The electricity generated is used to power the Comalco Aluminium Smelter 171 km (106 miles) to the south, at Bluff.

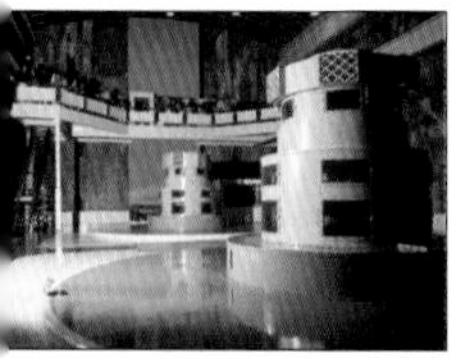

Underground machine hall

TIPS FOR TRAVELLERS

This trip takes eight hours and can only be undertaken with a commercial tour operator. Winter is the best time of the year for clear views and little rain, but the busiest time for tours is spring and summer. Visitors can order a picnic lunch or snack-pack when booking but it is advisable to take along something else to eat. Insect repellent, warm clothing and a waterproof jacket are also essential items. **Boat trips:** Real Journeys, *0800 65 65 01, (03) 249 7416,* **www**.realjourneys.co.nz; *Fiordland Explorer Charters, 0800 43 46 73,* **www**.doubtfulsoundcruise.com. *The Sound may also be explored by sea kayak.*

lanapouri Power Station ②
;oaches take visitors down a -km (1.2-mile) spiral access ınnel to the machine hall /hich is carved out of solid ;ranite 213 m (700 ft) under ıe mountains at West Arm.

Moss Gardens ④
Dozens of species of moss growing on a rock face show how plant life can get a foothold in all sorts of terrain in this high rainfall environment.

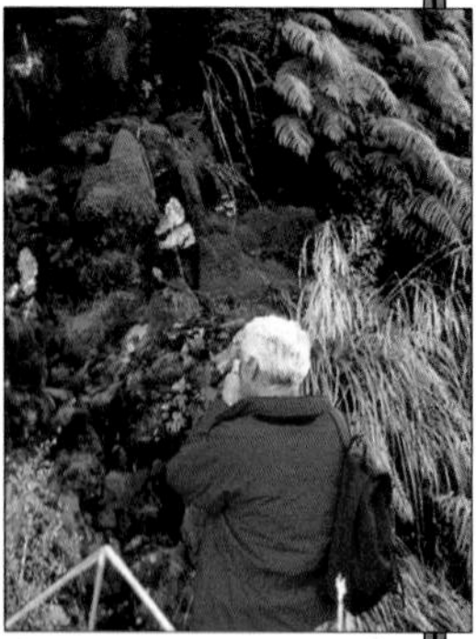

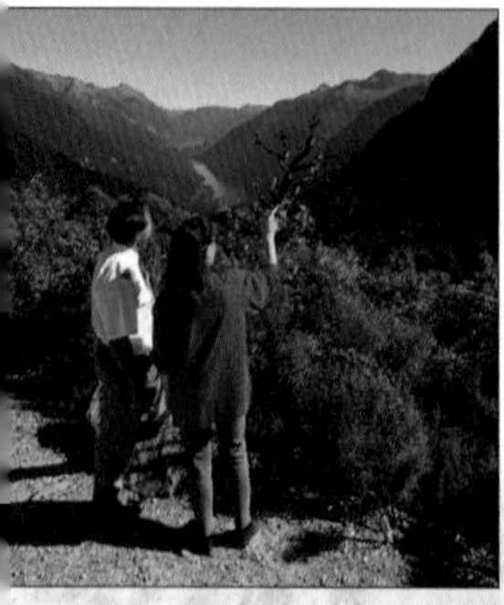

Wilmot Pass Road ③
The 22-km (13-mile) Wilmot Pass Road, completed in May 1965 to facilitate the building of the Manapouri Power Station tailrace at Deep Cove, cost more than $2 per cm ($5 per inch) to build.

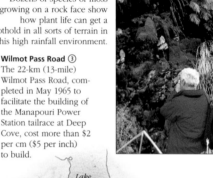

Cleve Garth Falls ⑤
The 365-m (1,200ft) high Cleve Garth Falls make a breathtaking entrance from a mountain ridge high above the Wilmott Pass Road.

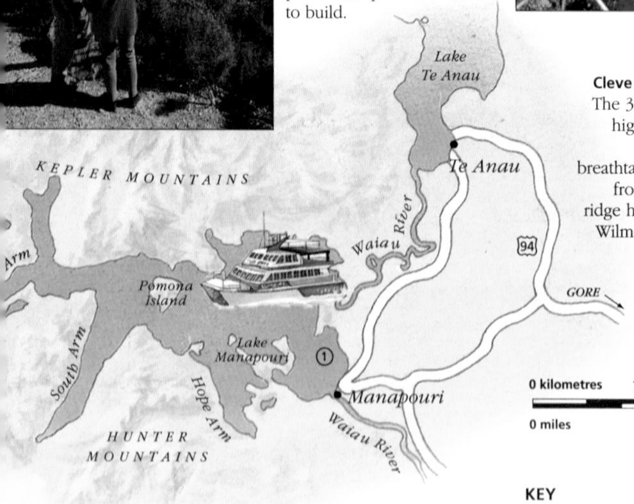
Lake Te Anau
Te Anau
Waiau River
94
GORE
KEPLER MOUNTAINS
Arm
Pomona Island
South Arm
Lake Manapouri
1
Manapouri
Hope Arm
Waiau River
HUNTER MOUNTAINS

0 kilometres 100

0 miles 100

KEY

- - Boat tour route

Coach tour route

Other roads

River

Wilmot Pass Summit ⑥
The 670-m (2,200-ft) summit is reached after a winding drive through cool temperate rainforest. The road then descends a one in five slope to Deep Cove.

Invercargill ⑰

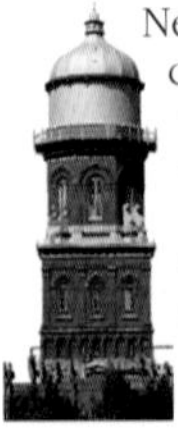

Water Tower

New Zealand's southernmost city, and the commercial hub of Southland, Invercargill is a well-planned city with wide, tree-lined streets and many parks and reserves. Settled in the 1850s and 1860s by Scottish immigrants, the city's cultural links with Scotland are reflected in the streets named after Scottish rivers and in its many historic buildings. To the west of the city are several sheltered beaches and walking tracks.

Queen's Park

Gala St **Tel** *(03) 214 6243.*

The best-known reserve in the city centre is the 0.8 sq km (0.3 sq mile) Queen's Park, a botanical reserve featuring formal gardens, including rose gardens and the extensive Steans Memorial Winter Garden. There is also a small wildlife park containing deer and wallabies, an aviary, and a challenging 18-hole golf course.

Southland Museum and Art Gallery

108 Gala St. **Tel** *(03) 219 9069.*
○ *daily.* ● *25 Dec.* ♿ 🚩 *by arrangement.* 📺 🔒 💰 *donation.*

Apart from its three art exhibition galleries, the Southland Museum and Art Gallery, housed in a pyramid-shaped building near the entrance to Queen's Park, contains displays outlining the area's human and natural history. It also features a tuatarium where visitors can see several of New Zealand's "living fossil" *(see p24)* at close range. The "Roaring Forties Experience" at the Subantarctic Islands Interpretive Centre provides an accessible introduction to New Zealand's five remote island reserves, which lie hundreds of kilometres to the south of Invercargill.

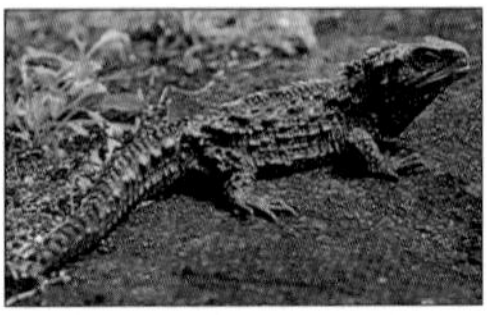

Tuatara at the Southland Museum and Art Gallery

VISITORS' CHECKLIST

Road map A7. 👥 *54,000.* ✈ *2 km (1.2 miles) W of city.* 🚆 *Leven St.* 🚌 ℹ *108 Gala St, (03) 214 6243.* ○ *daily.* ● *25 Dec.* 🎉 *Invercargill Summer Festival (early Feb); Garden Festival (Feb).* **www**.southlandnz.com

Water Tower

Leet St.

A distinctive landmark in the city, the 42-m (138-ft) high red brick water tower, completed in 1889 for the Public Works Department, is a fine example of Neo-Romanesqu industrial design of the time.

Dee and Tay Streets

Invercargill's early prosperity resulted in the construction c many fine commercial buildings and churches. At the no thern end of Dee Street lies the former Dee Street Hospital, the oldest public hospital buildings in New Zealand, and the quaint former Porter Lodge, built around 1866 an reputed to be the oldest house in Invercargill. Nearby is St Paul's Presbyterian Church, whose square tower houses a set of bells manufa tured in Italy from captured guns. Further down, the 190 red brick Alexander Building

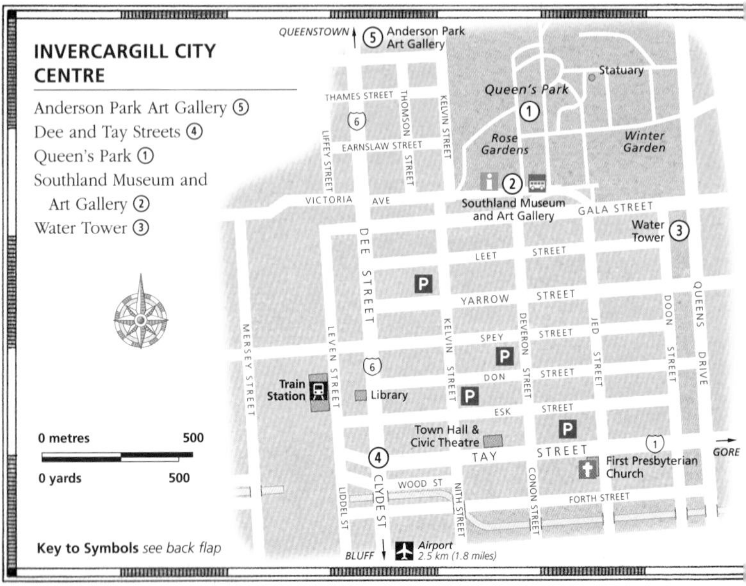

INVERCARGILL CITY CENTRE
Anderson Park Art Gallery [5]
Dee and Tay Streets [4]
Queen's Park [1]
Southland Museum and Art Gallery [2]
Water Tower [3]
0 metres 500
0 yards 500
Key to Symbols see back flap
QUEENSTOWN
Anderson Park Art Gallery
Statuary
Queen's Park
Rose Gardens
Winter Garden
Southland Museum and Art Gallery
Water Tower
THAMES STREET
THOMSON STREET
KELVIN STREET
LIFFEY STREET
EARNSLAW STREET
VICTORIA AVE
GALA STREET
LEET STREET
YARROW STREET
SPEY STREET
DON STREET
ESK STREET
TAY STREET
DEE STREET
MERSEY STREET
LEVEN STREET
DEVERON STREET
JED STREET
DOON STREET
QUEENS DRIVE
Train Station
Library
Town Hall & Civic Theatre
First Presbyterian Church
GORE
WOOD ST
LIDDEL ST
CLYDE ST
NITH STREET
CONON STREET
FORTH STREET
BLUFF
Airport 2.5 km (1.8 miles)

Anderson Park Art Gallery and gardens

is noted for its eclectic style, while the Grand Hotel opposite has fine iron balconies.

At the intersection of Dee Street and Tay Street (Invercargill's main street) stands the impressive Troopers' Memorial flanked by three elegant bank buildings, erected between 1876 and 1926. In Tay Street is the imposing Renaissance-style Civic Theatre, completed in 1906, and St John's Anglican Church, noted for its stained-glass windows and timber barrel-vaulted ceiling. The Lombardy-style First Presbyterian Church, also in Tay Street, features an unusual square 32-m (105-ft) tower.

🏛 Anderson Park and Art Gallery

91 McIvor Rd. *Tel* (03) 215 7432. 🕐 10:30am–5pm daily. 🔴 Good Fri, 25 Dec. 🈚 donation. 🚫 inside. 🚻 ground floor. 📷 by arrangement.
Five km (3 miles) north of the city centre, this beautiful Georgian-style house built in 1925, set in 0.2 sq km (0.08 sq mile) of gardens and native bush, houses a fine collection of New Zealand art.

First Presbyterian Church in Tay Street

Gore ⑱

Road map B7. 🏃 8,500. 🚉 Main St. 🚌 ℹ *Cnr Hokonui Drive & Norfolk St, (03) 203 9288.* 🎸 *New Zealand Gold Guitar Awards (May–Jun).* **www**.gorenz.com

Lying 66 km (41 miles) north of Invercargill, Gore has varied claims to fame: brown trout in the Mataura River and its tributaries (symbolized by a large trout statue in the middle of the town), sheep (the town is surrounded by fertile farmlands and thrives as an agricultural service town), moonshine whisky, and a reputation as the country music capital of New Zealand (country music devotees come each May for the New Zealand Gold Guitar Awards).

The Gore i-SITE Visitor Centre incorporates the **Gore Historical Museum** and the **Hokonui Moonshine Museum**. The latter covers the colourful period when whisky was made illegally in the Hokonui Hills behind Gore.

Fifteen km (9 miles) west of Gore on State Highway 94 is the **Croydon Aircraft Company** where they lovingly restore vintage aircraft, such as the Tiger Moth, and offer flights to visitors.

🏛 Gore Historical Museum and Hokonui Moonshine Museum

Cnr Hokonui Drive & Norfolk St. *Tel* (03) 203 9288. 🕐 daily. 🔴 1 Jan, Good Fri, 25 Dec. 🚻 📷

✈ Croydon Aircraft Company

Tel (03) 208 9755. 🕐 daily. 🔴 25 Dec. 🚻 📷 by arrangement.

Bluff ⑲

Road map A7. 🏃 2,000. 🚌 Gore St. 🚢 Stewart Island Wharf. 🎣 Bluff Oyster & Seafood Festival (May). **www**.bluff.co.nz

Bluff is New Zealand's southernmost export port and the departure point for ferries to Stewart Island. It is also the base for fishing fleets which cruise the south and west coasts for fish, cray-fish and rock lobsters as well as the famous "Bluff oysters". Unique to New Zealand, the oysters are harvested during a limited season from March to the end of August.

Bluff has a long history of human occupation, with Maori settlement dating back to the 13th century. The town is named after the 265-m (870-ft) high Bluff Hill which overlooks Foveaux Strait towards Stewart Island, which lies 32 km (20 miles) away. Beneath the hill is Stirling Point – the end of State Highway 1 – where there is a much photographed international signpost.

Boys with flounder

Several walks, including the Foveaux Walkway and the Glory Track, pass through native forest. A 45-minute climb up the hill gives panoramic views of the Foveaux Strait and inland areas.

The **Bluff Maritime Museum** traces the history of whaling, muttonbirding and oyster harvesting, as well as development of the port and the Stewart Island ferry.

🏛 Bluff Maritime Museum

241 Foreshore Rd. *Tel* (03) 212 7534. 🕐 daily. 🔴 25 Dec. 🈚 🚻 📷 by arrangement. 📷

International signpost at Stirling Point, Bluff

Stewart Island

New Zealand Fur Seal and pup

According to Maori legend, Stewart Island, New Zealand's third largest island, was the anchor of Maui's canoe (the South Island) when he pulled the great fish (the North Island) from the sea. Separated from the South Island by the 32-km (20-mile) Foveaux Strait, 85 per cent of Stewart Island became the Rakiura National Park in 2002. Its unspoilt inlets and beaches, bush-clad hills, rugged coastline and native birdlife combine to make the 1,746-sq-km (674-sq-mile) island a naturalist's paradise. First settled by Maori in the 13th century, Europeans arrived in the 1820s. Today's small population makes a living from fishing and tourism.

Paterson Inlet from Observation Rock

Oban

Oban, Stewart Island's only settlement, sits snugly around the picturesque, protected shores of Halfmoon Bay. It is easy to explore the town on foot but a 90-minute bus tour along Oban's 28 km (17 miles) of road takes visitors past the main points of interest in and around the town.

From Oban many short tracks lead through beautiful bush to places of scenic or historic interest, and to lookouts with stunning views, including Observation Rock, which provides splendid views over Paterson Inlet towards Ulva Island. On a clear, summer evening it is easy to see why Maori named Stewart Island "the land of the glowing skies". Several beautiful beaches also lie within walking distance to the north and east of the town.

The island offers a range of accommodation options, such as backpacker inns, beach houses, motels, bed and breakfasts, and the century-old South Sea Hotel.

The Rakiura Museum in Ayr Street, which is open daily, provides a fascinating insight into Stewart Island's past, such as its seafaring history and relics of whaling, sealing, tin mining and timber milling.

Boat charters are also available from Oban, catering for a whole range of interests, including fishing, sightseeing and wildlife spotting. On clear days, trips in glass-bottom boats allow visitors to see octopuses and crayfish and a variety of fish up close. For those that are more adventurous, diving, kayak hire and guided sea kayak excursions are among the many exciting activities which are on offer.

Paterson Inlet

Over the hill from Halfmoon Bay is the 16-km (10-mile) long Paterson Inlet, which extends deep into the hinterland. Charter boats and a water taxi can be hired in Oban for sightseers, divers and those wanting to catch their own fish. These trips are also a great opportunity to view various seabirds, including yellow-eyed and little blue penguins and mollymawks, as well as seals and dolphins. The remains of an old sawmill and whaling station are also accessible from the inlet.

Codfish Is Whenua

Ulva Island

Located in the centre of Paterson Inlet, Ulva Island is a 10-minute trip by water taxi from the wharf at Golden Bay. The island is predator-free, creating a sanctuary where visitors can get a close look at native New Zealand birds. Walks on the island range from 15 minutes to 3 hours.

Titī Islands

South Sea Hotel on the shores of Halfmoon Bay

For hotels and restaurants in this region see pp316–19 and pp340–41

Ocean Beach

"Kiwi spotting" (viewing kiwis at night in their natural habitat) is an experience unique to Stewart Island. Licensed tour operators take small groups by boat to the Neck in Little Glory Bay, then on foot through the bush to the Ocean Beach where the Stewart Island brown kiwi can be seen feeding as darkness falls.

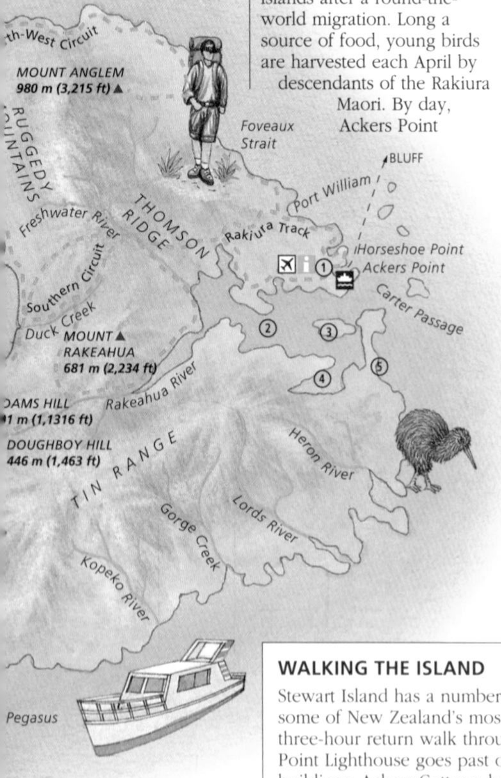

Big Glory Bay

Salmon and mussel farming have become important industries in Paterson Inlet. A boat trip takes visitors to a salmon farm at Big Glory Bay, past seal colonies and shag rookeries, with a stopover at Ulva Island on the way.

Titi Islands

Muttonbirds, or sooty shearwaters, breed on Stewart Island's many offshore islands after a round-the-world migration. Long a source of food, young birds are harvested each April by descendants of the Rakiura Maori. By day, Ackers Point

lighthouse gives panoramic views of the islands, and at night during the breeding season (October to April), visitors can hear the muttonbirds returning to land. Some tour operators are licenced to take visitors to the islands to view the birds from the boat.

Muttonbird (sooty shearwater) leaving its burrow

Codfish Island/Whenua Hou

Codfish Island, about 3 km (2 miles) off the northwest coast of Stewart Island, has been cleared of introduced fauna and is now a protected sanctuary for some 60 species of birds, including the rare and endangered kakapo, a large, flightless, nocturnal parrot. Visitors are not allowed to visit the island.

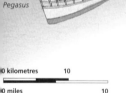

MOUNT ANGLEM
980 m (3,215 ft) ▲

North-West Circuit

RUGGEDY MOUNTAINS

Freshwater River

THOMSON RIDGE

Southern Circuit

Duck Creek

MOUNT RAKEAHUA
681 m (2,234 ft)

ADAMS HILL
401 m (1,1316 ft)

DOUGHBOY HILL
446 m (1,463 ft)

TIN RANGE

Rakeahua River

Gorge Creek

Kopeko River

Lords River

Heron River

Foveaux Strait

Port William

Rakiura Track

BLUFF

Ackers Point

Horseshoe Point

Ackers Point

Carter Passage

Pegasus

✈ ⅰ ①

② ③

④ ⑤

KEY

━━ River

- - Ferry route

- - Walking track

✈ Airstrip

🚢 Ferry

ⅰ Tourist information

0 kilometres   10

0 miles   10

WALKING THE ISLAND

Stewart Island has a number of tracks that take visitors into some of New Zealand's most beautiful bush. From Oban, a three-hour return walk through coastal forest to Ackers Point Lighthouse goes past one of New Zealand's oldest buildings, Ackers Cottage, built in 1835. The Ryan's Creek Track is a three- to four-hour loop through coastal forest above Paterson Inlet. For the fitter visitor, there is the Rakiura Track, which is a popular three-day circuit that climbs a high, forested ridge and traverses the sheltered Paterson Inlet.

There are also 10- to 14-day North-West and Southern Circuits, for which hut and camp passes must be obtained from the visitor centre in Oban. For further information on any of the walks call (03) 219 0002.

Tramper on the Rakiura Track, north of Oban

Tour of the Catlins 🄵

Gallery sign, Papatowai

Natural curiosities and beauty combine to make this southeastern corner of the South Island a scenic treasure. Fossilized trees, beautiful waterfalls, golden beaches, high cliffs and secret caves are all part of a unique mix of attractions in this area, commonly referred to as the Catlins after one of the early landowners of the 1840s. A varied coastline of cliffs and golden sand surf beaches provides a home to a wide range of wildlife, from rare Hector's dolphins to penguins, seals and sea lions. The area is made all the more spectacular by the ancient forests of rimu, matai, totara, beech and miro which reach almost to the sea, and which are filled with the sounds of native birds.

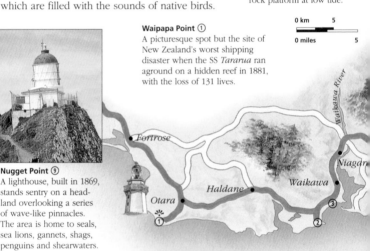

Curio Bay ②
The fossilized remains of a 160 million-year-old forest from the Jurassic period can be seen on a rock platform at low tide.

Waipapa Point ①
A picturesque spot but the site of New Zealand's worst shipping disaster when the SS *Tararua* ran aground on a hidden reef in 1881, with the loss of 131 lives.

Nugget Point ⑨
A lighthouse, built in 1869, stands sentry on a headland overlooking a series of wave-like pinnacles. The area is home to seals, sea lions, gannets, shags, penguins and shearwaters.

0 km   5
0 miles   5

Fortrose

Otara

Haldane

Waikawa

Niagar

Waikawa River

TIPS FOR DRIVERS

Tour length: 172 km (107 miles) from Invercargill to where the tour rejoins State Hwy 1 at Balclutha. It is well worth allowing at least a day to complete the journey because of the number of side tracks and walks taking visitors to the many sights

Stopping-off points: Most accommodation on this route is on a small scale. There are motels at Chaslands, Papatowai and Owaka, and camping grounds, backpackers hostels and homestays dotted around the area. If an overnight stay is planned, it is wise to book ahead. Food and refreshments are available at several places along the route.

Jack's Blowhole ⑧
Sea water surges through a subterranean tunnel before spraying out of this 60-m (197-ft) deep blowhole, located in the middle of cliff top pastures.

orpoise Bay ③
ittle black and white Hector's dolphins are often
een playing here in the surf as the waves break
long this long, curving beach.

McLean Falls ④
A 30-minute forest walk
leads to the McLean Falls
where the Tautuku River
makes an impressive drop
of 22 m (72 ft).

Cathedral Caves ⑤
The caves, accessible only at low tide, can be
reached after a 40-minute walk through forest
and along a beach. The opening of the
largest cave is 30 m (98 ft) high.

Lake Wilkie ⑥
This small forest lake is only a short
distance from the road but there is a
20-minute loop walk around it with
some good examples of the large tree
species found in the area.

Purakaunui Falls ②
A ten-minute walk through beech and podocarp
orest leads to a viewing platform overlooking
hese attractive waterfalls where the river drops
20 m (65 ft) over a series of wide terraces.

KEY

▬	Tour route
⋯	Other roads
≈	River
✲	Viewpoint

TRAVELLERS'
NEEDS

WHERE TO STAY

New Zealand offers a variety of accommodation to suit all budgets. At the top end of the range, five-star hotels and wilderness lodges provide luxury accommodation. Mid-range hotels, motels and motor lodges, self-catering apartments, country pubs, farmstays, and bed and breakfasts cater for travellers on a more modest budget. For those on a very tight budget, camping grounds and backpacker hostels offer good value. Away from the larger cities and resorts, the choice of accommodation can be limited, although there are motels and camping grounds in virtually all locations. The listings on pages 298–319 give full descriptions of different types of accommodation throughout New Zealand to suit all budgets.

Auckland hotel doorman

Crowne Plaza Hotel, Christchurch *(see p313)*

GRADINGS AND FACILITIES

New Zealand's accommodation grading system, Qualmark, was established in 1994 and now serves as New Zealand tourism's official quality mark. All businesses carrying the Qualmark have been independently assessed against a set of national quality standards. Accommodation is graded on a star system. One star indicates that the premises meet basic standards of cleanliness, comfort and hospitality, while five stars denote that the facility is among the best in New Zealand. In addition, three new categories have been established for visitor activities, transport and services. The Qualmark system is voluntary, however, and many establishments choose not to participate in it.

Many of the large chain hotels are air conditioned, but the New Zealand climate does not generally warrant air conditioning. Hot showers and heating are provided in all types of accommodation. Linen is also provided in hotels and motels. In back-packer hostels and camping grounds, linen is not always provided but can usually be hired for a reasonable fee.

PRICES

Prices vary according to the style of accommodation, facilities and services. Luxury lodges start at about NZ$650 a night, while a room in a back-packer hostel can be as low as NZ$30 a night. Most motels are in the range of NZ$80 to NZ$120 per unit, while bed and breakfast hotels cost between NZ$50 and NZ$100 per person. Off-season discounts are often available, and it is a good idea to ask about these when making bookings.

BOOKINGS

It is advisable to book accommodation in advance, especially at peak holiday times (December to February). During winter (June to August), hotels and motels in ski resort towns are often fully booked during school holidays (two weeks in both early July and in late September– early October). Bookings can be made directly to the accommodation provider, either by fax, telephone or via the Internet, through travel agents or at one of New Zealand's 100 visitor information centres.

In most cases, a credit card number will be requested when a booking is arranged. It is wise to ask about cancellation policies when

Edwardian façade of the Scenic Circle Southern Cross in Dunedin *(see p317)*

◁ An apple orchard in the Hawke's Bay area

Huka Lodge on the banks of the Waikato River *(see p305)*

making bookings as some premises will debit the credit card one night's accommodation if a cancellation is made at short notice. If additional services are required, such as children's cots, inform the accommodation provider when making a booking.

CHILDREN

Travelling with children in New Zealand is easy, with cots and baby-sitting services generally available on request. However, children are not welcome at some exclusive lodges and guesthouses. The definition of a "child" among hotels varies, ranging from under 2 to 17 years.

Children enjoy special rates only if they are the third or subsequent occupant of a room and do not request an extra bed. A useful website to look at is www.kidsnewzealand.com, which lists events as well as child-friendly places to visit, to eat and to stay.

DISABLED TRAVELLERS

New Zealand law stipulates that all new buildings as well as old buildings under-going major renovation must provide "reasonable and adequate" access for the disabled. Most facilities have wheelchair access. It is best to check in advance.

LUXURY LODGES

Often located near a lake, river or beach, such lodges provide breathtaking scenery, elegant surroundings and high quality service for a limited number of guests at any one time. Three New Zealand lodges that have won international acclaim are Huka Lodge located on the Waikato River near Taupo *(p305)*, Solitaire Lodge on a bush-covered peninsula of Lake Tarawera not far from Rotorua *(p305)*, and Wharekauhau Country Estate at Palliser Bay in Wairarapa *(p308)*.

Qualmark hotel grading sign

Many lodges specialize in fishing, hunting and other outdoor activities, and hosts often have extensive knowledge of the local environment. The tariff at the most exclusive lodges can be as high as NZ$1,900 a night, including meals and alcohol.

CHAIN HOTELS

Several international luxury hotel chains, including the **Hyatt**, **Millennium**, **Novotel** and **Sheraton**, are represented in New Zealand. Other chains include the **Copthorne**, **Scenic Circle** and **Best Western**, which offer a reliable standard of accommodation in the main cities and resorts of New Zealand. Chain hotels offer a full range of services,

including a television, telephone, minibar and bathroom *en suite* in all rooms, as well as room service and restaurants. Some also have sports, business and conference facilities. For hotel listings, see pp298–319.

COUNTRY PUBS

These are found throughout rural New Zealand and range in style from basic, inexpensive accommodation to "boutique" lodgings in renovated historic buildings. Prices vary greatly depending on the location and facilities, but can be as low as NZ$45 a night. Linen is provided and bathrooms may be private or shared. Some country pubs also provide backpacker accommodation and meals.

Typical wooden country pub accommodation

Last Resort backpacker lodge at Karamea *(see p315)*

SELF-CATERING APARTMENTS

This style of accommodation is not widely available in New Zealand, but can be found in the main cities and at major resort towns such as Queenstown. With spacious rooms and kitchen facilities, self-catering apartments are popular with corporate travellers seeking both comfort and independence. Prices vary depending on the length of stay.

For travellers wishing to spend a week or more in one location, a good option is to rent a holiday home. These can range in quality from a luxurious home to a tiny, rustic cottage known in New Zealand as a "bach" (pronounced "batch"). Check the availability of holiday homes at real estate agents in the area or information centres.

MOTELS AND MOTOR LODGES

Motels are the most common form of visitor accommodation in New Zealand, and even small towns have at least one. They are particularly suitable for large families or groups because they are spacious and have their own cooking facilities. They usually contain one or two bedrooms, a lounge, kitchen and bathroom, and have a television set, radio and telephone. Smaller units, where guests sleep in the lounge, are called studios. Larger motels and motor lodges are similar to hotels, with swimming pools,

laundry facilities, restaurants and room service.

Travellers can save money by purchasing a motel accommodation pass for one of the local chains, such as **Best Western** or **Golden Chain** *(see p297)*.

BACKPACKER HOSTELS AND YOUTH HOSTELS

New Zealand has more than 250 backpacker hostels in scenic locations around the country. These are clearly signposted along the main roads. Hostels offer clean, tidy and inexpensive accommodation, and are excellent places to meet other travellers and exchange up-to-date information as things change quickly. Prices can be as low as NZ$20 per person for a shared room and NZ$30 for a single room.

Another option for low-budget travellers is the **Youth Hostel Association** (YHA) *(see*

Accommodation sign in Marlborough

p297), which has a chain of 56 hostels in strategic locations. Despite the name, youth hostels cater for travellers of all ages. They usually offer separate male and female dormitories, as well as twin, double and family rooms for those wanting more privacy. Linen and blankets are provided. Youth hostels also have well-equipped communal kitchens and comfortable lounges for relaxation. However, bathroom facilities in most hostels are shared.

It is not necessary to be a member of the Youth Hostel Association to stay at a hostel, but non-members incur a surcharge of NZ$3–4 a night in addition to the regular fee.

FARMSTAYS AND HOMESTAYS

Farmstays offer visitors the chance to gain an insight into everyday farming life. Guests stay either in the farmhouse or in separate quarters, and may share meals with their hosts. Bathroom facilities may be either shared with the family or separate. In many cases, guests are able to participate in some farming activities.

Homestays are located in both urban and rural areas, and, like farmstays, guests stay in the family home or in adjacent quarters and often share meals with their hosts. Tariffs range from NZ$100 to NZ$400 a double per night.

Holiday-makers at a farmstay in Manawatu

Maui Rentals campervan on tour in the South Island

CAMPING GROUNDS

Camping grounds (also called holiday parks and motor camps) offer a cheap way of travelling. Some contain sites for tents and caravans only, while others have basic cabins fitted with bunk beds, or tourist flats with full cooking and bathroom facilities. Many have children's playgrounds and games rooms, and are located beside beaches, lakes or rivers in scenic locations.

Typical motor camp sign

Camping grounds have shared washing and laundry facilities, and fully equipped communal kitchens. At some, shops sell basic foodstuffs and supplies. It is wise to book during the main New Zealand holiday period, from Christmas until the end of January, but not necessary during off-peak periods. Most camping grounds charge about NZ$7 a night per person for a camp site and from about NZ$30 for a double cabin.

CAMPERVANS

A popular way to see the country is in a self-drive campervan. Two-, four- and six-berth vans are available, complete with amenities *(see p375)*. Rental charges vary according to the season.

Generally, campervan travellers stop at camping grounds for the night where they can hire a site with electric power. In remote locations, travellers can park in a rest area near the roadside. Many camping grounds have "dump stations" for the disposal of sewage effluent.

DIRECTORY

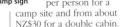

LUXURY HOTELS AND LODGES

Southern Crossings
Private Bag 93-236, Parnell, Auckland. *Tel (09) 309 5912.* @ nzdesign@southern-crossings.com

New Zealand Lodge Association
41 Towey St, Oamaru. *Tel (03) 434 7939.*
www.lodgesofnz.co.nz

CHAIN HOTELS

Best Western NZ
www.bestwestern.co.nz

Copthorne
www.mckhotels.co.nz

Hyatt
www.hyatt.com

Millennium
www.mckhotels.co.nz

Novotel
www.novotel.com

Scenic Circle
www.scenic-circle.co.nz

Sheraton
www.sheraton.com

MOTELS

Best Western NZ
PO Box 74-346, Auckland 5.
Tel 0800 237 893.
www.bestwestern.co.nz

Golden Chain NZ
PO Box 5341, Christchurch.
Tel (03) 358 0821, 0800 465 336.
www.goldenchain.co.nz

BACKPACKER AND YOUTH HOSTELS

Budget Backpacker Hostels New Zealand
208 Kilmore St, Christchurch.
Tel (03) 379 3014.
www.bbh.co.nz

VIP Backpacker Resorts New Zealand
PO Box 60177, Titirangi, Auckland.
Tel (09) 816 8903.
www.vip.co.nz

Youth Hostel Association of New Zealand
PO Box 436, Christchurch.
Tel (03) 379 9970, 0800 278 299. www.yha.co.nz

FARMSTAYS

New Zealand Farm Holidays
PO Box 74, Kumeu, Auckland.
Tel (09) 412 9649.
www.nzaccom.co.nz

HOLIDAY PARKS

Top 10 Holiday Parks
PO Box 9088, Tower Junction, Christchurch.
Tel 0800 867 836.
www.top10.co.nz

BED AND BREAKFAST HOTELS

New Zealand Federation of Bed & Breakfast Hotels
123 Grey St, Palmerston Nth. *Tel (06) 358 6928.*
www.nzbnbhotels.com

Choosing a Hotel

The hotels in this guide have been selected across a
wide price range for their good value, exceptional
location, comfort or style. Hostels in New Zealand are of
a particularly high standard and have therefore also been
included. The chart lists hotels by area. For map
references *see inside back cover.*

PRICE CATEGORIES
The following price ranges are for a
standard double room and taxes per
night during the high season. Breakfast
is not included unless specified.

$ under NZ$100
$$ NZ$100–NZ$150
$$$ NZ$150–NZ$200
$$$$ NZ$200–NZ$250
$$$$$ over NZ$250

AUCKLAND

CITY Auckland Central Backpackers (ACB) $

Cnr Queen and Darby streets **Tel** *(09) 358 4877, 0800 223 363* **Rooms** *74*   **Map** *E2*

This friendly modern hostel in a new high-rise building in downtown Auckland has won awards for its accommodation.
It is open 24 hours a day and has an internet café and a bar in the basement, as well as a travel centre to help
guests with planning their onward journeys. **www.staybase.com**

CITY Auckland City Hotel $

157 Hobson Street **Tel** *(09) 925 0777* **Fax** *(09) 925 0700* **Rooms** *138*   **Map** *E2*

Erected in 1912 in the heart of central Auckland, this former Trade Hall building has been transformed into a well
appointed boutique hotel, offering contemporary decor with satellite TV, the latest communications facilities
(including Internet access) and eco-friendly products. **www.aucklandcityhotel.co.nz**

CITY Auckland International YHA $

5 Turner Street **Tel** *(09) 302 8200* **Fax** *(09) 302 8205* **Rooms** *30*   **Map** *E2*

An outstanding five-star hostel with modern facilities within easy reach of the motorway. Downtown shops and
attractions are five minutes' walk away down Queen Street, while THE EDGE entertainment centre and the university
are close by. Some ensuite double rooms are available, as well as shared dorm rooms. **www.yha.co.nz**

CITY The Brown Kiwi $

7 Prosford Street, Ponsonby **Tel** *(09) 378 0191* **Fax** *(09) 378 0191* **Rooms** *8*   **Map** *E2*

Built in 1900, this two-storey refurbished colonial house has a pleasant garden and offers unusual warmth,
hospitality and character. A mere stroll from Ponsonby cafés, restaurants and nightclubs and the Link bus takes you
to all inner city suburbs and downtown. Book early, especially for doubles or twins. **www.brownkiwi.co.nz**

CITY Bavaria B&B Hotel $$

83 Valley Road, Mount Eden **Tel** *(09) 638 9641* **Fax** *(09) 638 9665* **Rooms** *11*   **Map** *E2*

A small, charming hotel in a 100-year-old kauri villa in a pleasant suburb of Victorian villas, 10 minutes' taxi ride from
city centre. Furnished with native timber furniture. Extra-long beds. German-style buffet breakfast. Near Eden Park
rugby stadium, Auckland Domain and Zoo. **www.bavariabandbhotel.co.nz**

CITY Baytree Cottage $$

42 Norfolk Street, Ponsonby **Tel** *(09) 360 1023* **Rooms** *4*   **Map** *E2*

Charming 100-year-old Colonial cottage in Ponsonby, close to boutiques, cafés and restaurants. Pleasantly refurbished
with stripped wooden floors. Sleeps up to seven people. An ideal solution for families wishing to spend a few days
exploring the attractions of Auckland. Not far from city-centre museums and art galleries. **www.baytree-cottage.com**

CITY City Towers Serviced Apartments $$

2 Maungawhau Road, Newmarket **Tel** *(09) 520 6186* **Fax** *(09) 524 6512* **Rooms** *33*   **Map** *E2*

Spacious apartments in the prime shopping district which are well priced considering the space and the central
location. A comfortable home from home and a good choice for families, or anyone planning a longer stay in
Auckland. **www.citytowers.co.nz**

CITY Ellerslie International Motor Inn $$

2 Wilkinson Road, Ellerslie **Tel** *(09) 525 1909, 0800 355 377* **Rooms** *36*   **Map** *E2*

Convenient, hassle-free location for travellers arriving from the airport or the south, just off the southern motorway
(take the Ellerslie Penrose off ramp). Close to racecourse and MT Smart Stadium, and a 10-minute drive to downtown
Auckland. Above average comfort and cleanliness, with a heated pool and lots of parking. **www.eimi.co.nz**

CITY Mercure Hotel Windsor Auckland $$

58–60 Queen Street **Tel** *(09) 309 9979* **Fax** *(09) 309 9978* **Rooms** *79*   **Map** *E2*

Mercure Hotel Windsor is located in the heart of Auckland's commercial district, near the waterfront and close to
Viaduct Harbour, ferry terminals and Vector Arena. This 1936 heritage-listed building is now a boutique hotel owned
by an international chain. Also has a spa, sauna and valet parking. **www.accorhotels.com**

Key to Symbols *see back cover flap*

CITY Parnell Inn   ⓈⓈ
320 Parnell Road, Parnell **Tel** *(09) 358 0642, 0800 00472* **Fax** *(09) 367 1032* **Rooms** *16*   **Map** *E2*

A small, quiet, personal hotel in the heart of Parnell, close to the restaurants, cafés, boutiques and art galleries of this classy inner-city suburb and adjoining Newmarket. Auckland Museum is a stroll away, and it is just a 20-minute walk to the waterfront, or you can hop on the Link bus, which passes by. **www.parnellinn.co.nz**

CITY Rydges Auckland   ⓈⓈ
Cnr Federal and Kingston streets **Tel** *(09) 375 5900, 0800 755 900* **Fax** *(09) 359 5901* **Rooms** *188*   **Map** *E2*

International hotel in the heart of the commercial district, close to Viaduct Basin, waterfront restaurants, Sky Tower and downtown shops. Upper storeys offer views of Auckland Harbour Bridge and Waitemata Harbour. Stylish, functional guestrooms and award-winning restaurant. **www.rydges.com**

CITY Amitee's on Ponsonby   ⓈⓈⓈⓈ
237 Ponsonby Road **Tel** *(09) 378 6325* **Fax** *(09) 378 6329* **Rooms** *7*   **Map** *E2*

Boutique hotel in the heart of Ponsonby, convenient for downtown and close to cafés, bars and restaurants. Each room has been individually themed (French provincial and nautical are two), with ensuite shower rooms and wireless Internet access. There is also a guest lounge with cosy fireplace. **www.amitees.com**

CITY Copthorne Hotel Auckland Harbour City   ⓈⓈⓈⓈ
196–200 Quay Street **Tel** *(09) 377 0349* **Fax** *(09) 307 8159* **Rooms** *187*   **Map** *E2*

Great location on the Waitemata Harbour. All rooms have a panoramic north-facing harbour view. Harbourfront shops, bars and restaurants are a stroll away, and it is just a 10-minute walk to the Sky Tower, a 20-minute ferry ride to Waiheke Island and a 5-minute taxi ride to Ponsonby cafés. **www.milleniumhotels.com**

CITY Crowne Plaza Auckland   ⓈⓈⓈⓈ
128 Albert Street **Tel** *(09) 302 1111, 0800 154 181* **Fax** *(09) 302 3111* **Rooms** *352*   **Map** *E2*

Conveniently located in the heart of the business district above the Elliott shopping complex and just a short walk from the Edge Entertainment Centre, SKYCITY complex and Queen Street. Amenities include bar, restaurant, gym, and conference and banquet rooms. The staff are multilingual and very friendly. **www.crowneplaza.com**

CITY Heritage Auckland   ⓈⓈⓈⓈ
35 Hobson Street **Tel** *(09) 379 8553, 0800 368 888* **Fax** *(09) 379 8554* **Rooms** *467*   **Map** *E2*

This is the largest hotel in Auckland and is set in a landmark building. Close to Viaduct Basin and within easy walking distance of Queen Street and Sky Tower, the facilities include a heated rooftop swimming pool, indoor lap pool, spa, sauna, gyms and tennis court. **www.heritagehotels.co.nz**

CITY Hyatt Regency Auckland   ⓈⓈⓈⓈ
Cnr Princes Street and Waterloo Quadrant **Tel** *(09) 366 1234* **Fax** *(09) 303 2932* **Rooms** *369*   **Map** *E2*

Excellent service and a reputation for good quality, innovative food. Apartments with kitchens available. Guests have access to the Spa at the Hyatt – a health club and fitness centre with a fully equipped gym, 25m heated pool, jacuzzi, steam room and sauna. Spa therapy treatments use local products. **www.auckland.regency.hyatt.com**

CITY Scenic Circle Airedale Hotel   ⓈⓈⓈⓈ
380 Queen Street **Tel** *(09) 374 1741* **Fax** *(09) 374 1740* **Rooms** *99*   **Map** *E2*

In a historic landmark building, completely renovated. Constructed in 1954, it was Auckland's first high-rise office building and is now protected by the NZ Historic Places Trust. Art deco details from the 1950s can be seen in the foyer. It is situated in the heart of the city, near THE EDGE and Auckland Town Hall.

CITY SKYCITY Grand Hotel   ⓈⓈⓈⓈ
90 Federal Street **Tel** *0800 759 248* **Rooms** *316*   **Map** *E2*

Luxury hotel with 316 rooms, right by the Sky Tower. The hotel itself has two restaurants, a cocktail lounge, terrace, lap pool, gym and spa, while the SKYCITY complex has 11 restaurants and bars, three casinos and live entertainment. Leave the kids with the hotel babysitter and relax. **www.skycity.co.nz**

CITY The Great Ponsonby B&B   ⓈⓈⓈⓈ
30 Ponsonby Terrace, Ponsonby **Tel** *(09) 376 5989, 0800 766 792* **Fax** *(09) 376 5527* **Rooms** *11*   **Map** *E2*

Small hotel in a restored 1898 villa in the fashionable suburb of Ponsonby. Two minutes' walk to cafés, restaurants and boutiques, five minutes' taxi ride to downtown. Colourful, understated modern décor, with 11 individually designed guestrooms displaying Pacific and New Zealand artworks. Courtyard and palm garden. **www.greatpons.co.nz**

CITY Aachen House   ⓈⓈⓈⓈⓈ
39 Market Road, Remuera **Tel** *(09) 520 2329* **Fax** *(09) 524 2898* **Rooms** *8*   **Map** *E2*

Winner of Leading Boutique Hotel in Australasia award at the 2005 World Travel Awards. Five-star luxury in a beautifully restored former grand residence, with a fine collection of Victorian and Edwardian antique furniture and porcelain. Close to Newmarket and Parnell shopping areas, and downtown attractions. **www.aachenhouse.co.nz**

CITY Cotter House Luxury Retreat   ⓈⓈⓈⓈⓈ
4 St Vincent Avenue, Remuera **Tel** *(09) 529 5156* **Fax** *(09) 529 5186* **Rooms** *4*   **Map** *E2*

A grandly renovated 1847 mansion in one of Auckland's smartest suburbs, 10 minutes' taxi ride from downtown. Rooms are decorated with antiques and contemporary art. Modern luxuries include underfloor heating in marble bathrooms, a heated swimming pool and an exercise pavilion for Pilates and yoga. **www.cotterhouse.com**

GREATER AUCKLAND The Stray Possum Lodge
Rooms 9   **Map** E2

Cape Barrier Road, Tryphena, Great Barrier Island **Tel** (09) 429 0109 **Fax** (09) 429 0680 **Rooms** 9   **Map** E2

Minutes from the ferry terminal, this sunny backpackers' hotel provides two self-contained chalets as well as bunk rooms, twins and doubles in a native bush setting. Community kitchen and dining room, sun deck and large grassed area for tents or play. Lively restaurant and bar popular with locals and travellers. **www.straypossum.co.nz**

GREATER AUCKLAND Crescent Valley Eco Lodge
50 Crescent Road East, Waiheke Island **Tel** (09) 372 4321 **Fax** (09) 372 4321 **Rooms** 4   **Map** E2

A rambling house and garden full of unpretentious charm and character, an easy stroll from Palm Beach. Delicious breakfasts can be eaten indoors or outside on sun-drenched decks. Other meals can be provided too – picnics to take to the beach, or dinners using organic home-grown vegetables. **www.waihekeecolodge.co.nz**

GREATER AUCKLAND Greenmead Farm Cottage
115 Bethells Road **Tel** (09) 810 9363 **Rooms** 2   **Map** E2

A well-maintained two-bedroom house that offers a rural alternative in Henderson (West Auckland). A good base from which to explore the Dalmatian wineries of the region, or to make excursions to Piha and the other spectacular west coast beaches (as featured in the film *The Piano*). Thirty-minute drive to inner-city Auckland. **www.greenmead.co.nz**

GREATER AUCKLAND Quality Inn
477 Great South Road, Papatoetoe **Tel** 0800 700 477 **Fax** (09) 277 8050 **Rooms** 68   **Map** E2

In the heart of Manukau City in South Auckland, 10 minutes' drive from the international and domestic airport terminals. This hotel offers a courtesy van to airports and is in a good location for the Botanic Gardens and Polynesian Saturday markets. Comfortable, family rooms at reasonable rates. **www.silveroaks.co.nz**

GREATER AUCKLAND Esplanade Hotel
1 Victoria Road, Devonport **Tel** (09) 445 1291 **Fax** (09) 445 1999 **Rooms** 17   **Map** E2

Slick, elegant luxury boutique hotel on the Devonport Village waterfront, a 10-minute ferry ride across the harbour from Auckland. Built in 1903 and meticulously restored with charm and character. Harbour and city views from tasteful rooms. Edwardian dining room open for lunch, dinner and weekend brunch. **www.esplanadehotel.co.nz**

GREATER AUCKLAND FitzRoy House
Port FitzRoy, Great Barrier Island **Tel** (09) 429 0091 **Fax** (09) 429 0492 **Rooms** 3   **Map** E2

A 1920s cottage in a beautiful location in a quiet cove surrounded by walkways through native bush. Sleeps five with a minimum two-night stay. Sea kayaks available, or the owners (a keen sailor and an artist) can arrange "tramp/sail" packages – walks with sailboat pick-ups. Otherwise bring mountain bikes and explore. **www.fitzroyhouse.co.nz**

GREATER AUCKLAND Villa Cambria Bed and Breakfast Inn
71 Vauxhall Road, Devonport **Tel** (09) 445 7899 **Fax** (09) 446 0508 **Rooms** 5   **Map** E2

An elegant B&B hotel, with a pleasant ambience. The beach is a short walk away. Close to the boutiques, bookshops and bijou bric-a-brac shops of Devonport. Stroll along the esplanade, or a courtesy car can pick you up or drop you off at the terminal for the ferry that links this suburb to central Auckland. **www.villacambria.co.nz**

GREATER AUCKLAND Rangiwai Lodge
29 Rangiwai Lodge **Tel** (09) 817 8990 **Fax** (09) 817 8990 **Rooms** 4   **Map** E2

A luxurious lodge well suited to visitors who want to combine visits to the city with walking in the Waitakere Ranges and the black sand surf beaches of the west coast at Karekare and Piha. Set in native rainforest at the 'fringe of heaven' (Titirangi), it is a good base for visiting West Auckland wineries, too. **www.accommodation-nz.com**

GREATER AUCKLAND The Boatshed
Cnr Tawa and Huia streets, Little Oneroa, Waiheke Island **Tel** (09) 372 3242 **Fax** (09) 372 3262 **Rooms** 5 **Map** E2

A boutique seaside hotel overlooking Oneroa Bay. Purpose-built suites resemble a lighthouse, boatsheds and the bridge of a ship. The three Boatshed suites are a nostalgic reminder of old-fashioned beach holidays, part beach hut, part boatshed, whitewashed and decorated with simple, stylish furnishings. **www.boatshed.co.nz**

AIRPORT Kiwi International Airport Hotel
150 McKenzie Road, Mangere **Tel** (09) 256 0046 **Fax** (09) 256 0047 **Rooms** 49   **Map** E2

One of several airport hotels offering similar services, the Kiwi International is more affordable than some of its competitors. It offers free 24-hour bus transfers to the airport, a garden for jet-lagged guests to acclimatize in, a spa pool to relax in, and a restaurant and bar to refuel in. **www.kiwihotel.co.nz**

AIRPORT Hotel Grand Chancellor Auckland Airport
Cnr Kirkbride and Ascot roads, Mangere **Tel** (09) 275 7029 **Fax** (09) 275 3322 **Rooms** 193   **Map** E2

Perhaps the ultimate place to recharge after a long flight, set in several acres of landscaped grounds with a swimming pool, gym and sauna to help you get the blood flowing again after sitting cramped on a plane for several hours. Restaurant, bar and shuttle to and from the airport. **www.ghihotels.com**

AIRPORT Jet Inn Airport Hotel
63 Westney Road, Mangere **Tel** (09) 275 4100 **Rooms** 128   **Map** E2

A family run hotel that is suitable for both business and tourist guests. There is an award-winning restaurant, a pool and an attractive garden. It is located close to the airport and there is a 24-hour complimentary shuttle service. **www.jetpark.co.nz**

Key to Price Guide *see p298* **Key to Symbols** *see back cover flap*

NORTHLAND

KAITAIA Historic Kaitaia Hotel 〒 👤 ⓢ
17 Commerce Street **Tel** *(09) 408 0360* **Fax** *(09) 408 0360* **Rooms** *36* **Map** *D1*

Low-cost, simple accommodation in central Kaitaia in a hotel built in 1837. There is a licensed restaurant and bar, and a casino and nightclub with Karaoke. Tours to Cape Reinga and Ninety Mile Beach can be organized here. This is a popular function venue so it may be occupied by large groups on courses.

KAITAIA Main Street Lodge 👤 ⓢ
235 Commerce Street **Tel** *(09) 408 1275* **Fax** *(09) 408 1100* **Rooms** *18* **Map** *D1*

A central location from which to explore Ninety Mile Beach, Cape Reinga and the kauris of Waipoua Forest. This Maori-run, backpacker-style accommodation in the Tuku Wairua Maori Cultural Centre has double and family rooms as well as shared dorms. Visitors can use sand and boogie boards, or learn bone carving. **www.mainstreetlodge.co.nz**

KAITAIA Northerner Motor Inn 〒 👤 📺 ⓢ
Cnr North Road and Kohuhu Street **Tel** *(09) 408 2800, 0800 33 44 22* **Fax** *(09) 408 0306* **Rooms** *75* **Map** *D1*

Mock Tudor motor inn a few minutes' drive from the centre of Kaitaia, refurbished in 2003. Hotel facilities bear the names of King Henry VIII and his wives. The licensed restaurant is one of the best places to eat in Kaitaia. Rooms range from studio units to family suites. Spa pool, gym and sauna. **www.northerner.co.nz**

KERIKERI Kerikeri Homestead Motel 〒 ≋ 👤 ⓢⓢ
17 Homestead Road **Tel** *(09) 407 7063, 0800 222 407* **Fax** *(09) 407 7656* **Rooms** *12* **Map** *E1*

This four-star motel is quiet but centrally located near the Kerikeri Mission Station and old town, overlooking the scenic golf course. It has 12 colonial-style units with balconies, some with spa bath, and an outdoor swimming pool and hot spa pool, as well as a restaurant and bar next door. **www.kerikerihomesteadmotel.co.nz**

KERIKERI Palm Grove Cottages 👤 ⓢⓢ
410 Kerikeri Road **Tel** *(09) 407 8484* **Fax** *(09) 407 8484* **Rooms** *6* **Map** *E1*

Self-contained cottages set in a large garden with water features. Each cottage has its own name (Robinia, Windrest, Mandalee), outdoor living space and garden, and faces a small lake. They are all hidden from one another in the five acres of subtropical valley gardens. A short drive from historic tourist sights. **www.palmgrove.co.nz**

MATAURI BAY Kauri Cliffs 〒 ≋ 📺 ⓢⓢⓢⓢ
Kauri Cliffs **Tel** *(09) 407 0010* **Fax** *(09) 407 0061* **Rooms** *22* **Map** *E1*

This American-owned, exclusive luxury lodge sits in a prime waterfront location, with panoramic ocean views from the cliffs. As if the 6,000-acre landscape and secluded beaches were not enough, the rolling green clifftops host a 72-par championship golf course, and the 22 guest suites share a pool, spa and gym. **www.kauricliffs.com**

OPUA Mako Lodge and Fishing Charters 👤 ⓢⓢⓢ
18 Point Veronica Drive **Tel** *(09) 402 7957* **Rooms** *5* **Map** *E1*

Close to Paihia, this lodge offers the option to go fishing or sightseeing on an 8m-long (27ft) vessel and free use of a sea kayak and dinghy to go paddling around the coves. There are lovely views of sailing boats in the channel, as well as an outdoor spa pool to relax in. Five minutes' walk to Opua Marina, and bay ferries. **www.makolodge.co.nz**

OPUA Harbour House Villa ⓢⓢⓢⓢⓢ
7 English Bay Road **Tel** *(09) 402 8087* **Fax** *(09) 402 8688* **Rooms** *6* **Map** *E1*

Stylish, weathered balcony furniture sets the tone for this charming villa, set in a subtropical garden amid native bush on a promontory overlooking Opua. A coastal walking path leads to the marina and Waitangi. Traditional or Japanese breakfasts are served in the well-appointed interior. **www.harbourhousevilla.co.nz**

PAIHIA Pickled Parrot Backpacker Lodge 〒 ⓢ
Greys Lane **Tel** *(09) 402 6222, 0508 727 768* **Fax** *(09) 402 6232* **Rooms** *12* **Map** *E1*

A small, personal hostel set around a courtyard in lush gardens where hammocks hang in the trees. Famous for its breakfast, café-style dining on a sunny deck and wood fires outdoors at night. Doubles, twins and singles, as well as dorms are available. It is close to the beach and they offer sports equipment for loan. **www.pickledparrot.co.nz**

PAIHIA Kingsgate Hotel Autolodge Paihia 〒 ≋ 👤 ⓢⓢⓢ
Marsden Road **Tel** *(09) 402 7416, 0800 652 929* **Fax** *(09) 402 8348* **Rooms** *77* **Map** *E1*

A business and leisure hotel on the waterfront in Paihia, 100m from the wharf. As well as offering an outdoor swimming pool, sauna and indoor spa pool, the hotel can lend you a bicycle to get around. Some rooms have kitchens, or guests can make use of the hotel's bar and restaurant. **www.kingsgateautolodge.co.nz**

PAIHIA Nautilus Resort ≋ 👤 ⓢⓢⓢ
9 Puketona Road **Tel** *(09) 402 8604, 0800 186 661* **Fax** *(09) 402 6247* **Rooms** *11* **Map** *E1*

Set in subtropical gardens amid native bush on the fringes of Paihia, close to the beach and a short walk from the town centre, the resort is well equipped for families, with a children's playground, tennis court and swimming pool. Two-bedroom and studio units are available, all with TV, and secure parking. **www.nautilusresort.co.nz**

PAIHIA Copthorne Hotel and Resort 🍴 🏊 👪 $$$$$

Tau Henare Drive **Tel** *(09) 402 7411* **Fax** *(09) 402 8200* **Rooms** *148* **Map** *E1*

This waterfront resort on a promontory within the Waitangi National Trust Reserve is surrounded by beautiful bush walks and is next to the golf course and wharf. Guests can relax in the pool, spa or bar. You can request a room with either a garden or sea view. **www.copthornebayofislands.co.nz**

PUKENUI Pukenui Lodge Motel 🏊 👪 $$

Cnr Wharf and Main roads **Tel** *(09) 409 8837* **Fax** *(09) 409 8704* **Rooms** *9* **Map** *D1*

New Zealand's northernmost motel, 42km north of Kaitaia in a waterfront setting on Hohoura Harbour and close to five beaches, overlooks the wharf where fishing boats tie up to unload their catch. There is a separate youth hostel next door. Horse trekking, boat charters, golf and Cape Reinga tours can be arranged. **www.pukenuilodge.co.nz**

RUSSELL Flagstaff Lodge $$$$$

17 Wellington Street **Tel** *(09) 403 7117, 0800 403 711* **Fax** *(09) 403 7817* **Rooms** *4* **Map** *E1*

This beautifully restored 1912 villa now offers boutique accommodation in four individually-styled waterfront rooms decorated in the latest fashions. Guests can take outdoor baths under the stars in the lodge garden, or book in for spa treatments. **www.flagstafflodge.co.nz**

TUTUKAKA Pacific Rendezvous Motel 🏊 👪 $$$

Motel Road, Tutukaka **Tel** *(09) 434 3847* **Fax** *(09) 434 3919* **Rooms** *30* **Map** *E1*

This moderately priced resort motel is set in 26 acres of coastal land on a promontory leading down to two secluded beaches. Tennis courts, swimming pool, spa, children's playground, car and boat wash and spectacular views of Tutukaka Harbour and Poor Knights Island are all part of the family-friendly package. **www.oceanresort.co.nz**

WAIPOUA FOREST Waipoua Lodge $$$$$

SH12, Katui **Tel** *(09) 439 0422* **Fax** *(09) 523 8081* **Rooms** *4* **Map** *D1*

This 120-year-old luxury lodge built of timber from the surrounding kauri forest has a sunny library, a cosy lounge with leather sofas by a crackling fire, and four apartments with balconies overlooking the forest. Night walks offer a rare chance to see nocturnal kiwi in their native habitat. **www.waipoualodge.co.nz**

WHANGAREI Mulryans 🏊 $$$$

Crane Road, Kauri **Tel** *(09) 435 0945* **Fax** *(09) 431 5146* **Rooms** *2* **Map** *E1*

A four-and-a-half-star romantic country retreat in a charming 100-year-old kauri villa with mature gardens, where guests can relax under the stars in an outdoor spa pool or take a cooling dip in the swimming pool on hot days. The two rooms have garden balconies, and beds are made up with quality bed linen. **www.mulryans.co.nz**

WHANGAREI Oceans Tutukaka 🍴 👪 $$$$

Marina Road, Tutukaka **Tel** *(09) 470 2000* **Fax** *(09) 470 2001* **Rooms** *40* **Map** *E1*

This hotel may not be much of a looker, but it is the home of the Dive! Tutukaka diving school. It offers luxury with a nautical flavour in its 28 rooms and 12 apartments, and a seafood restaurant whose produce assuredly does not come from the marine reserve. **www.oceanshotel.co.nz**

WHANGAROA Sunseeker Lodge 👪 $$

Old Hospital Road **Tel** *(09) 405 0496* **Fax** *(09) 405 1121* **Rooms** *5* **Map** *E1*

In a stunning location halfway between Kerikeri and Kaitaia, with views over Whangaroa Harbour, the lodge offers two motel units, one three-bedroom holiday home, backpacker accommodation and campsites. Motorboats and kayaks are available for hire. Children's playground and BBQ. **www.sunseekerlodge.co.nz**

CENTRAL NORTH ISLAND

CAMBRIDGE Number 1 Motels on Victoria 🍴 👪 $

85–9 Victoria Street **Tel** *(07) 823 1467* **Fax** *(07) 823 1468* **Rooms** *28* **Map** *E3*

This motor lodge at the top end of town, has pseudo-colonial frontage on the main street housing antique shops, book shops and art galleries. You can enjoy bar and brasserie dining in a glass-domed courtyard and it is close to a racecourse and a cricket club, just a short walk to town centre. **www.no1motels.co.nz**

CAMBRIDGE Riverside of Cambridge 🍴 👪 $$

7 Williamson Street **Tel** *(07) 827 6069* **Fax** *(07) 827 3068* **Rooms** *34* **Map** *E3*

Set in spacious grounds on the banks of the Waikato River at the point where navigation on the river ceased due to the narrowing of the river and start of many rapids. Lovely views and river walk. Golf club and jet-boat operator nearby. Warm, friendly, family-run business. **www.cambridgemotel.co.nz**

CAMBRIDGE Souter House 🍴 $$

19 Victoria Street **Tel** *(07) 827 3610* **Fax** *(07) 827 4885* **Rooms** *7* **Map** *E3*

Sophisticated, friendly atmosphere and charming setting, with beautiful rural views. There are seven suites in a rambling old colonial house (built in 1875 by Captain William Souter, it is one of the finest examples of Victorian architecture in the region). The elegant restaurant features award-winning cuisine. **www.souterhouse.co.nz**

COROMANDEL Admiral Arms Hotel 🍴 👪 [$]

146 Wharf Road ***Tel*** *(07) 866 8272* ***Fax*** *(07) 866 8272* ***Rooms*** *6* ***Map*** *E2*

A historic hotel, which gained its first liquor licence in the gold rush of 1872, refurbished to offer reasonably priced accommodation in an upstairs wing. Downstairs is a traditional sports bar, with a family garden. Good plain meals are served in a first-floor restaurant with a verandah overlooking the Harbour. **www.admiralsarms.co.nz**

COROMANDEL Coromandel Colonial Cottages Motel 🏊 👪 [$][$]

1737 Rings Road ***Tel*** *(07) 866 8857, 0508 222 688* ***Fax*** *(07) 866 8857* ***Rooms*** *8* ***Map*** *E2*

Eight Colonial cottage-style motel units are clustered around the original 1876 goldmine manager's homestead, in a park-like setting in native bush on the fringes of Coromandel town. The large swimming pool, BBQ area, children's playground, cots and highchairs are just some of the family-friendly features. **www.corocottagesmotel.co.nz**

COROMANDEL Jacaranda Lodge 👪 [$][$]

3195 Tiki Road (SH25) ***Tel*** *(07) 866 8002* ***Fax*** *(07) 866 8002* ***Rooms*** *6* ***Map*** *E2*

B&B located on a peaceful farm with delightful gardens with a great opportunity to see native birds and trees. There are kosher facilities and a guest kitchen. The host speaks Hebrew. Visit before Christmas when the jacaranda trees are in bloom. Home-made and, as much as possible, home-grown breakfasts. **www.jacarandalodge.co.nz**

COROMANDEL Anchor Lodge 🏊 👪 [$][$][$]

448 Wharf Road ***Tel*** *(07) 866 7992* ***Fax*** *(07) 866 7991* ***Rooms*** *16* ***Map*** *E2*

A motel, five minutes' stroll to town centre shops, cafés and restaurants. Self-contained studio and two-bedroom units are set among native bush, all with private balcony, harbour views and use of a heated swimming pool and spa. There is also a BBQ buffet and poolside bar. **www.anchorlodgecoromandel.co.nz**

COROMANDEL Celadon Motel Cottages [P] 👪 [$][$][$]

Cnr Alfred St & Oxford Terrace ***Tel*** *(07) 866 8058* ***Fax*** *(07) 866 8058* ***Rooms*** *4 cottages* ***Map*** *E2*

Four individual cottages in a secluded location, though still close to the town's attractions, restaurants, bars and cafés. The chalet is perfect for family groups of up to eight members. All the cottages have sundecks and are set in lovely gardens. **www.celadonmotel.com**

GISBORNE Chalet Surf Lodge [$]

62 Moana Road, Wainui Beach ***Tel*** *(06) 868 9612* ***Fax*** *(06) 868 4475* ***Rooms*** *5* ***Map*** *F3*

A few kilometres north of Gisborne overlooking the world-class surf at Wainui Beach, this lodge offers backpacker dorms, lodge rooms and self-contained apartments. Surf lessons and equipment hire can be arranged. You can even check wave conditions from your room. **www.chaletsurf.co.nz**

GISBORNE Blue Pacific Beachfront Motel 👪 [$][$]

90 Salisbury Road ***Tel*** *(06) 868 6099* ***Fax*** *(06) 867 0481* ***Rooms*** *13* ***Map*** *F3*

Right on Waikanae Beach, this authentic Kiwi motel has a spa and sauna and is next to an Olympic-size swimming pool and a children's adventure playground, as well as being close to a golf course. The absolute beachfront location of this family-friendly place is hard to beat so close to town. **www.seafront.co.nz**

GISBORNE Captain Cook Motor Lodge 🍴 👪 [$][$]

31 Awapuni Road, Waikanae Beach ***Tel*** *(06) 867 7002, 0800 227 826* ***Fax*** *(06) 867 7073* ***Rooms*** *21* ***Map*** *F3*

A 21-unit motel two minutes' walk from Gisborne's central city Waikanae Beach, which is patrolled by lifeguards and safe for children. Five minutes' walk from the city centre and the cafés and bars of the harbour district. Studio, one- and two-bedroom units all have private and sunny rear courtyards. **www.captaincook.co.nz**

GISBORNE Pacific Harbour Motor Inn 👪 [$][$]

Cnr of Reads Quay and Pitt Street ***Tel*** *(06) 867 8847* ***Fax*** *(06) 867 4586* ***Rooms*** *27* ***Map*** *F3*

Modern motor inn close to picturesque Gisborne Port, wharfside bars and restaurants and the town centre. Overlooks the Turanganui River and the inner harbour marina. Popular with government officials and business people as well as tourists. The design uses glass bricks and terracotta flagstones, tawa and steel. **www.pacific-harbour.co.nz**

GISBORNE Portside Hotel 🏊 👪 [$][$]

2 Reads Quay ***Tel*** *(06) 869 1000, 0800 767 874* ***Fax*** *(06) 869 1020* ***Rooms*** *64* ***Map*** *F3*

Sleek new hotel with elegant interiors overlooking Gisborne's inner harbour. Rooms and suites all have own bathroom and kitchen, harbour or city views and balcony. Each room has a broadband Internet connection in rooms and there is an inviting outdoor lap pool. An easy walk from city centre attractions and beach. **www.portsidegisborne.co.nz**

GISBORNE Wainui Beach Hideaway 👪 [$][$][$]

9B Cleary Road, Wainui Beach ***Tel*** *(06) 868 8114* ***Fax*** *(06) 868 8115* ***Rooms*** *3* ***Map*** *F3*

Homestay accommodation in two restored shearers' cottages, The Cottage and The Hideaway, set in a private native garden setting at Wainui Beach. Guests can soak in the hot spa pool. Home-cooked gourmet breakfasts are a speciality. It is a short stroll to the beach and local café/bar.

HAHEI The Church Accommodation and Dining 🍴 👪 [$][$]

87 Hahei Beach Road ***Tel*** *(07) 866 3533* ***Fax*** *(07) 866 3055* ***Rooms*** *11* ***Map*** *E2*

Character dining in the church building and accommodation in 11 cottages scattered around rambling gardens of flowers, NZ natives and exotic plants. Cosy, simple and charmingly furnished cottages with French windows opening onto sunny verandahs. Some have woodfires for winter. An easy walk to the beach and shops. **www.thechurchhahei.co.nz**

HAMILTON Le Grand Boutique Hotel   🟦🏃 $$$
Cnr Victoria and Collingwood sts **Tel** *(07) 839 1994* **Rooms** *38*   **Map** *E2*

Built in 1926 as an office block, this building was converted in 1994 into a 'European-style' hotel. Centrally located, close to Hamilton Gardens, Zoo and Waikato Museum of Art and History. Surprisingly warm, friendly atmosphere in a hotel which caters largely for business travellers. Good rates for tourists at weekends. **www.legrandhotel.co.nz**

HAMILTON Novotel Hamilton Tainui   🟦🏃🟫 $$$
7 Alma Street **Tel** *(07) 838 1366* **Fax** *(07) 838 1367* **Rooms** *177*   **Map** *E2*

In the heart of the city, on the banks of the Waikato River and adjacent to the Skycity Casino and entertainment complex. Award-winning restaurant, lobby bar and health club, with gym, sauna, spa and beauty therapies available. Easy access to shopping, dining and entertainment, or relaxing river walks nearby. **www.novotel.co.nz**

MAKETU BEACH Blue Tides Beachfront B&B and Seaview Unit   🏃 $$$
7 Te Awhe Road, Maketu Beach **Tel** *(07) 533 2023* **Fax** *(07) 533 2023* **Rooms** *4*   **Map** *F3*

Halfway between Mount Maunganui and Whakatane on the Pacific Coast Highway, overlooking the estuarine home of coastal and seabirds, where dolphins feed. Four good swimming beaches nearby. This large beach house in a friendly village – a million miles from the feverish development of Tauranga – has won tourism awards. **www.bluetides.co.nz**

MIRANDA Umoya Lodge $$$$$
30 Rataroa Road **Tel** *(09) 232 7636* **Rooms** *2*   **Map** *E2*

A luxury lodge set in 35 acres of native bush on Mount Rataroa, with views of the Coromandel Peninsula and Pacific Ocean. The South African owners named it Umoya after the Zulu for soul, spirit and breath. Terracotta-tiled floors and designer bathrooms are complemented by Persian carpets and antique furniture. **www.umoyalodge.co.nz**

MOUNT MAUNGANUI Beach House Motel   🟦🏃 $$$
224 Papamoa Beach Road, Papamoa **Tel** *(07) 572 1424, 0800 429 999* **Fax** *(07) 572 1423* **Rooms** *18*   **Map** *E2*

Architecturally distinguished motel a few kilometres down the coast from Mount Maunganui, midway between Bayfair and Palm Beach Plaza. The nautically themed corrugated metal buildings were erected in 1999, and won a prize for innovative design. It is just a short walk from the beach. **www.beachhousemotel.co.nz**

MOUNT MAUNGANUI Pacific Palms Resort $$$$
21 Gravatt Road, Papamoa **Tel** *(07) 572 0035, 0800 808 835* **Fax** *(07) 572 1135* **Rooms** *18*   **Map** *E2*

Family-style resort near Mount Maunganui, with five acres of landscaped grounds, a heated swimming pool with children's play area, spa pool, tennis courts, golf courses nearby, and a sandy beach within walking distance. Two- and three-bedroom apartments with balconies or patios. Next to shopping plaza. **www.pacificpalmsresort.co.nz**

NAPIER Napier Prison Backpackers $
55 Coote Road **Tel** *(06) 835 9933* **Rooms** *15*   **Map** *F4*

A chance to spend a night in a former prison without being taken there in a police car. The oldest prison in New Zealand (since 1862), which has also been an army barracks and a lunatic asylum, closed its doors to convicts in 1993 to reopen them as a hostel soon after. Close to town and Ocean Spa. **www.napierprison.com**

NAPIER Motel de la Mer $$
321 Marine Parade **Tel** *(06) 835 7001, 0800 335 263* **Fax** *(06) 835 7002* **Rooms** *11*   **Map** *F4*

A boutique motel on Napier's Marine Parade, with 11 ocean-view rooms, some with balconies. The shingly beach, ocean and a boardwalk leading to Napier's attractions are across the road, and city centre shops and cafés a short walk away. Superb children's playground and Marineland opposite. **www.moteldelamer.co.nz**

NAPIER Freemans on Clyde   🟦🏃 $$$
17 Clyde Road **Tel** *(06) 835 9124* **Fax** *(06) 835 9129* **Rooms** *3*   **Map** *F4*

One of several attractive B&Bs in Colonial buildings on Napier Hill, this one, in a historic farmhouse built in 1856, has been renovated with considerable attention to detail. A cosy Victorian-style lounge opens onto hidden, rambling gardens. Only a short walk from the shops, restaurants and bars.

NAPIER Scenic Circle   🟦 $$$
45 Marine Parade **Tel** *(06) 833 7735* **Fax** *(06) 833 7732* **Rooms** *109*   **Map** *F4*

The six-storey curved façade of Te Pania (named after a legendary Maori mermaid) overlooks Napier's beachfront boardwalk by the Ocean Spa pools, and is a stroll away from Hawke's Bay Museum, galleries, shops and cafés. The three-year-old hotel's crisp, international style has won it several architectural awards. **www.scenic-circle.co.nz**

NAPIER Mangapapa Petit Hotel   🟦🟫🟫 $$$$$
466 Napier Road (between Napier and Havelock North) **Tel** *(06) 878 3234* **Fax** *(06) 878 1214* **Rooms** *12*   **Map** *F4*

One of Hawke's Bay's most prestigious properties, this lodge was once the home of canned-food magnate Sir James Wattie. The gracious Colonial homestead has been fully refurbished in a style of understated elegance. Spa and beauty therapies are on offer. Food, wine and service are excellent. **www.mangapapa.co.nz**

NGARUAWAHIA Brooklands Country Estate   🟦🟫 $$$$$
Waingaro Road **Tel** *(07) 825 4756* **Fax** *(07) 825 4873* **Rooms** *10*   **Map** *E2*

A 19th-century villa hand-built using native timber as the homestead for a pioneering farm (now forested parkland). Rich, rustic elegance of antique country furniture, Persian rugs on kauri floors and New Zealand watercolours. Wide verandahs. Four-course dinners can be enjoyed around the communal oak table, or privately. **www.brooklands.net.nz**

OHOPE Surf's Reach Motels 👪 $$

52 West End ***Tel*** *(07) 312 4159* ***Fax*** *(07) 312 4995* ***Rooms*** *10* ***Map*** *F3*

A traditional beach motel a few minutes' drive down the coast from Whakatane, on the edge of the 11km-long safe, sandy, swimming beach at Ohope. Well-appointed units set in established grounds, with full kitchen facilities and TV. This is a good base for fishing, dolphin-watching, walking and golf. **www.surfsreachmotels.co.nz**

RAGLAN Solscape Accommodation Centre 👪 $$

Wainui Road ***Tel*** *(07) 825 8268* ***Rooms*** *19* ***Map*** *E2*

Unique accommodation in old railway carriages and cabooses near one of New Zealand's top surf beaches. Surfing lessons and surfboard hire available. Massage and organic garden for relaxation. Best known for the long peeling left-hand breaks, Raglan also offers ideal surf conditions for novice surfers. **www.solscape.co.nz**

ROTORUA Rotorua Treks Backpackers $

1278 Haupapa Street ***Tel*** *(07) 349 4088,* ***Fax*** *(07) 349 4086* ***Rooms*** *51* ***Map*** *E3*

A purpose-built backpackers' hostel two minutes' walk from shops, cafés and restaurants. Treks guarantees guests an "awesome" experience in its clean, modern, secure rooms. There are shared rooms (female only by request), twins and doubles, some ensuite, all with bed linen provided. Good kitchen and lots of bathrooms. **www.treks.co.nz**

ROTORUA Sudima Hotel Lake Rotorua ❄ 🍴 🏊 👪 $$$

1000 Ererua Street ***Tel*** *(07) 348 1174, 0800 783 462* ***Fax*** *(07) 346 0238* ***Rooms*** *250* ***Map*** *E3*

Rotorua's largest hotel is set on the lakefront next to the Polynesian Spa, Government Gardens and Rotorua Museum and offers in-house Maori cultural experiences at nightly hangi dinner, plus song and dance performance by an award-winning troupe. Heated pool and spas free for guests. Many rooms have lake views. **www.sudimarotorua.co.nz**

ROTORUA Regal Palms Motor Lodge 🏊 👪 🏋 $$$

350 Fenton Street ***Tel*** *(07) 350 3232, 0800 743 000* ***Fax*** *(07) 350 3233* ***Rooms*** *45* ***Map*** *E3*

This New Zealand Tourism award winner lies at the southern end of Fenton Street, in walking distance of geothermal attractions, shops and restaurants. Heated swimming pool, children's play area, gym, tennis court and nine-hole mini golf. Private spa pools in rooms. **www.regalpalmsml.co.nz**

ROTORUA Nicara Lakeside Lodge [P] 👪 $$$$$

30–32 Ranginui St ***Tel*** *(07) 357 2105* ***Fax*** *(07) 357 5385* ***Rooms*** *4* ***Map*** *E3*

This modern lodge was built in 2004 in a peaceful, secluded location on the shores of Lake Rotorua, away from the sulphur smells and close to many of the local tourist attractions. It is a superbly appointed hotel and the furnishings and decor are tasteful and luxurious. **www.nicaralodge.co.nz**

ROTORUA Solitaire Lodge 🍴 $$$$$

Lake Tarawera ***Tel*** *(07) 362 8208, 0800 765 482* ***Fax*** *(07) 362 8445* ***Rooms*** *9* ***Map*** *E3*

Award-winning resort with a stunning setting on a promontory of Lake Tarawera. Justly proud of its service, attention to detail and cuisine. Its nine suites enjoy panoramic lake views. Facilities include electronic safes and shower wands. Price includes four-course dinner and trout fishing. **www.solitairelodge.co.nz**

TAUPO Tiki Lodge $

104 Tuwharetoa Street ***Tel*** *(07) 377 4545* ***Fax*** *(07) 377 4585* ***Rooms*** *14* ***Map*** *E3*

Stylishly branded, "upmarket hostel" a short walk from both the town and lake. Bunk, family or double rooms, some with ensuite bathrooms, are available and bed linen is provided. There is also a kitchen, dining area, TV and DVD lounge, bike hire, spa pool, payphone and Internet café. **www.tikilodge.co.nz**

TAUPO Cypress Villas Motel 👪 $$

37 Rifle Range Road ***Tel*** *(07) 378 4322* ***Fax*** *(07) 378 4622* ***Rooms*** *6* ***Map*** *E3*

Modern, centrally located upmarket motel in a tranquil setting 200m from the lake edge and five minutes' from town centre shops and restaurants. Architecturally designed and simply decorated in a clean, crisp style. A good place for families, with two spacious two-bedroom villas. **www.cypressvillas.co.nz**

TAUPO Wairakei Resort 🍴 🏊 👪 🏋 $$$

SH1(Thermal Explorer Highway), Wairakei ***Tel*** *(07) 374 8021* ***Fax*** *(07) 374 8485* ***Rooms*** *137* ***Map*** *E3*

A top resort hotel, nestled in the 169-acre Wairakei Thermal Park 10km north of Taupo. A wide choice of suites and rooms with a range of facilities from kitchens to garden access. All guests can enjoy spa treatments, gym, golf course, outdoor heated swimming pools, tennis courts, restaurants and bar. **www.wairakei.co.nz**

TAUPO Huka Lodge 🍴 $$$$$

Huka Falls Road ***Tel*** *(07) 378 5791* ***Fax*** *(07) 378 0427* ***Rooms*** *24* ***Map*** *E3*

The queen of luxury retreats. On the banks of the Waikato River, a stroll from dramatic Huka Falls. Comfortable, stylish ambience, with rich, warm decor and spacious suites scattered along the riverbank. If you want to arrive in style, there is even a helipad. Dinner included. **www.hukalodge.co.nz**

TAUPO Point View Lodge ♿ 🏊 [P] $$$$$

20 Chesham Avenue, Botanical Heights ***Tel*** *(07) 377 4611* ***Fax*** *(07) 377 4610* ***Rooms*** *3* ***Map*** *E3*

This boutique guest lodge has spectacular views of the lake and the mountains. The rooms are luxurious and there is also a thermal pool. A gourmet breakfast is provided and dinner by arrangement. It is situated only five minutes from the airport and town centre. **www.pointview.co.nz**

TAURANGA Harbourside City Backpackers $

105 The Strand **Tel** *(07) 579 4066* **Fax** *(07) 579 4067* **Rooms** *24*   **Map** *E2*

In a prime location at backpacker prices, Harbourside City is very central and right on the waterfront among cafés and bars. Friendly and sociable, it has a bar of its own and a sunny deck overlooking the harbour. Dorms (including a female-only dorm), twins and doubles, some ensuite, are available. **www.backpacktauranga.co.nz**

TAURANGA Hotel on Devonport $$$

Devonport Towers, 72 Devonport Road **Tel** *(07) 578 2668* **Fax** *(07) 578 2669* **Rooms** *38*   **Map** *E2*

Smart business-type hotel in the centre of Tauranga offering surprisingly good value-for-money for its upmarket facilities. Comfortable, contemporary international-style rooms decorated in soothing neutrals and hush-glazed to keep out the noise. High-speed Internet and fresh air pumped into every room. **www.hotelondevonport.net.nz**

TE KUITI Tapanui Cottage $$$

1714 Oparure Road, Te Kuiti (near Oto) **Tel** *(07) 877 8498* **Fax** *(07) 877 8432* **Rooms** *2*   **Map** *E2*

Beautifully appointed home set in hill country amid stunning limestone outcrops. Panoramic views. "Country retreat" on a farm with pigs, goats and donkeys. Native rimu, soft-toned furnishings, NZ art, hand-crafted furniture and oriental carpets. Convenient for Waitomo Caves. No children. **www.tapanui.co.nz**

THAMES Seaspray Motel $

613 Thames Coast Road, Waiomu Bay **Tel** *(07) 868 2863* **Fax** *(07) 868 2863* **Rooms** *6*   **Map** *E2*

Right on a sandy beach in a small holiday village 10 minutes' drive north of Thames on the coast road. The six family-sized units have balconies overlooking the sea, from which to enjoy sunset views before firing up a seaside BBQ. A perfect base for fishing, beach and bush walks. **www.seaspraymotel.co.nz**

THAMES 33 Patui $$$$$

33 Patui Ave, Ngarimu Bay **Tel** *(07) 868 2272* **Rooms** *4*   **Map** *E2*

French-style 1950s villa restored to high standards in comfortable, neutral designer styles using natural materials, located above Ngarimu Bay, 10km north of Thames. In a mature garden setting surrounded by native bush, 33 Patui enjoys abundant native birdlife and seascapes. Five minutes' walk from the beach. **www.greatstays.co.nz**

TONGARIRO Bayview Chateau Tongariro $$$

SH48, Mount Ruapehu **Tel** *(07) 892 3809, 0800 CHATEAU (242 832)* **Fax** *(07) 892 3704* **Rooms** *115*   **Map** *E3*

At the foot of Mount Ruapehu, Chateau Tongariro (built in 1929) is one of New Zealand's historic hotels. Spa treatments, an indoor heated pool, golf course, tennis and petanque are on offer for guests, who also have a choice of luxury suites and family rooms. Café-style or fine dining. **www.chateau.co.nz**

TONGARIRO Powderhorn Chateau $$$

Mangawhero Terrace, Ohakune **Tel** *(06) 385 8888* **Fax** *(06) 385 8925* **Rooms** *32*   **Map** *E3*

Close to Turoa ski field, this hotel makes use of a natural timber finish to create a warm atmosphere. A perfect base from which to explore one of New Zealand's most magnificent alpine areas and only minutes away from breath-taking alpine scenery, native forest, volcanic landscapes, lakes and mountain streams. **www.powderhorn.co.nz**

TONGARIRO Skotel Alpine Resort $$$

Ngauruhoe Place, Whakapapa Village **Tel** *(07) 892 3719, 0800 756 835* **Fax** *(07) 892 3777* **Rooms** *48*   **Map** *E3*

New Zealand's highest hotel. On the edge of Whakapapa Village, it's a popular base for both winter skiing and summer walking holidays. Comfortable hotel rooms, small family cabins and shared backpacker rooms. Chalet-style wooden decor, friendly restaurant and bar, and relaxing spa pools. **www.skotel.co.nz**

WAITOMO Waitomo Caves Hotel $$$

RD7 Otorohanga **Tel** *(07) 878 8204* **Fax** *(07) 878 8205* **Rooms** *33*   **Map** *E3*

Historic hotel, built in 1909 in a New Zealand Victorian style inspired by Eastern European mountain chalets, and extended in Art Deco style in the 1920s. Sweeping staircases, large open fireplaces and a range of rooms from the honeymoon suite in a turret to bunk rooms for backpackers. **www.waitomocaveshotel.co.nz**

WHAKATANE Motuhora Rise B&B $$$

2 Motuhora Rise **Tel** *(07) 307 0224* **Fax** *(07) 307 0541* **Rooms** *2*   **Map** *F3*

A luxury B&B in the hills above Whakatane, just five minutes' drive from the town centre. Panoramic views of the Rangitaiki Plains and White Island or, if you get bored of the natural vista, a state-of-the-art entertainment centre. Outdoor spa pool and indoor fireplace. This B&B has a no children policy. **www.motuhora.co.nz**

WHAKATANE White Island Rendezvous $$$

15 The Strand East **Tel** *(07) 308 9500, 0800 242 299* **Fax** *(07) 308 0303* **Rooms** *25*   **Map** *F3*

The home of White Island Tours, and a good base if you plan to do the tour of the active marine volcano, this friendly new motel is close to shops, restaurants and cafés. Its own Peejay's Coffee House serves hearty breakfasts, lunches and all-day coffee and muffins. Tours depart wharf. **www.whiteisland.co.nz**

WHANGAMATA Whangamata Backpackers $

227 Beverley Terrace **Tel** *(07) 865 8323* **Fax** *(07) 865 8323* **Rooms** *16 beds*   **Map** *E2*

A small, friendly hostel by the beach and close to town. Forest walks, mountain biking, safe swimming and surf, horse-riding, windsurfing and canoeing are all nearby. Kitchen, laundry and other backpacker facilities are available. Shared dorms, single, double and triple rooms. **whangah@xtra.co.nz**

Key to Price Guide *see p298* **Key to Symbols** *see back cover flap*

WHANGAMATA Copsefield B&B

🖼 🏃 $$$

1055 SH25 **Tel** *(07) 865 9555* **Fax** *(07) 865 9510* **Rooms** *4* **Map** *E2*

Set in native bush near the riverbank, and a good base for walks and beaches. Guests can borrow bikes or canoes to reach Opoutere Beach 10 minutes away, or swim in the river swimming hole. Breakfast consists of home-made bread and yoghurt, and home-grown fruit and eggs. **www.copsefield.co.nz**

WHITIANGA Turtle Cove Accommodation

$

14 Bryce Street **Tel** *(07) 867 1517* **Fax** *(07) 867 1520* **Rooms** *7* **Map** *E2*

Budget and backpacker accommodation, two minutes' walk from all local amenities. Offers both dorms and private rooms, and there is a large shared kitchen and covered outdoor deck, sun deck and BBQ area. Free use of didgeridoo, drum and juggling balls, and mountain-bike loan. **www.turtlecove.co.nz**

WHITIANGA Beachfront Resort

🏖 🏃 $$$$

113 Buffalo Beach Road **Tel** *(07) 866 5637* **Fax** *(07) 866 4524* **Rooms** *8* **Map** *E2*

Pohutakawa-fringed gardens lead down from the resort to a sandy beach. Self-contained units with private decks all have ocean views and balcony or garden access. Free kayaks, boogie boards, dinghy and fishing rods are all available for loan. BBQ area and spa pool in the grounds. Close to Whitianga restaurants. **www.beachfrontresort.co.nz**

WHITIANGA Ferry Landing Lodge

🏖 🏃 $$$$

1169 Purangi Road, Cooks Beach **Tel** *(07) 866 0445* **Fax** *(07) 866 0792* **Rooms** *3* **Map** *E2*

A short ferry-ride across the harbour mouth from Whitianga, the lodge nestles above the ferry landing in native bush. Guests can walk in the bush, swim at nearby beaches or borrow their hosts' two-seater kayak. Breakfasts on the sundeck feature home-made preserves. **www.ferrylandinglodge.co.nz**

WELLINGTON AND THE SOUTH

KAPITI COAST Sand Castle Motel

🏃 $

20 Paetawa Road (off Peka Peka Road), Waikanae **Tel** *(04) 293 6072* **Fax** *(04) 293 3926* **Rooms** *8* **Map** *E4*

Set right in the dunes on Waikanae's safe, sandy beach, the cylinders, cones and blocks of this motel actually resemble a sand castle. Accommodation is in eight self-contained one-bedroom units, most of which face the sea and have private patios. An outdoor hot spa pool add to the appeal of this motel. **sandcastlemotel@clear.net.nz**

KAPITI COAST The Fantails Accommodation

🏃 $

40 MacArthur Street, Levin **Tel** *(06) 368 9011* **Fax** *(06) 368 9279* **Rooms** *5* **Map** *E4*

Bush surrounds this bed and breakfast, which also offers self-contained cottages. Evening meals and breakfasts feature organic food, much of it home-grown and all home-cooked. A peaceful haven in two acres of mature English-style gardens in the middle of town with a menagerie of animals in the back garden. **www.fantails.co.nz**

NEW PLYMOUTH B-K's Egmont Motor Lodge

🏃 $

115 Coronation Avenue **Tel** *(06) 758 5216, 0800 115 033* **Fax** *(06) 758 5215* **Rooms** *18* **Map** *D3*

All units have their own kitchen for self-catering in this friendly motor lodge at the lower end of the market. Opposite the racecourse, with views across the tracks to Mount Egmont, the restaurant has a chargeback scheme, and continental breakfasts are available. **www.egmontmotorlodge.co.nz**

NEW PLYMOUTH Egmont Eco Lodge

🍴 🏃 $

12 Clawton Street **Tel** *(06) 753 5720* **Rooms** *60* **Map** *D3*

Set in its own 7-acre secluded valley in central New Plymouth, amid native trees and by a bubbling brook. The lodge is 15 minutes' walk from the town along the riverbank. There is a free shuttle bus which takes you to 1,000 metres up Mount Egmont, the main base for walks in the National Park and summit climbs. **www.mttaranaki.co.nz**

NEW PLYMOUTH Landmark Manor Motel

🏃 $$

72 Leach Street **Tel** *(06) 769 9688* **Fax** *(06) 769 9689* **Rooms** *17* **Map** *D3*

This motel has well appointed units. A fairly central location, within walking distance of cafés, restaurants and shops, the coastal walkway and Pukekura Park, the venue for New Plymouth's annual summer Festival of Lights. Funky modern decor, with splashes of colour. **www.landmarkmanor.co.nz**

NEW PLYMOUTH Pukekura Lodge Motel

🏃 $$

52 Victoria Road **Tel** *(06) 758 2310, 0800 758 231* **Fax** *(06) 757 5408* **Rooms** *10* **Map** *D3*

On the edge of Pukekura Gardens, this family-owned motel has comfortable rooms and a friendly atmosphere. The place to be for the summer Festival of Lights (December to February), but you will need to book early for the high season. Self-contained one- and two-bedroom townhouses with own fenced gardens. **www.pukekuralodge.co.nz**

NEW PLYMOUTH Copthorne Hotel Grand Central

🏃 $$$

42 Powderham Street **Tel** *(06) 758 7495* **Fax** *(06) 758 7496* **Rooms** *60* **Map** *D3*

Smart business-type hotel in the centre of New Plymouth, within easy walking distance of the Puke Ariki museum, Govett-Brewster Gallery, coastal walkway and Pukekura Park, the venue for the annual summer Festival of Lights. Aquatic centre, golf courses and mineral pools are nearby. **www.millenniumhotels.com**

NEW PLYMOUTH Ahu Ahu Beach Villas $$$$$

321 Anu Anu Road, Oakura **Tel** *(06) 752 7370* **Rooms** *4*   **Map** *D3*

A 20-minute scenic drive down the coast from New Plymouth, set in farmland with sea views, these two cottage-style villas are built of recycled hardwood wharf piles, old French tiles, lattice windows and wooden doors, with stones, shells and fossils set into the floor, and have won sustainable architecture awards. **www.ahu.co.nz**

PALMERSTON NORTH Supreme Accommodation $

665 Pioneer Highway **Tel** *(06) 356 5265, 0800 112 211* **Fax** *(06) 356 5267* **Rooms** *25*   **Map** *E4*

One of New Zealand's largest motel complexes, 1km (an easy drive) from the city centre. Some units can sleep up to 10 people, and all have private bathrooms and kitchens. Large, heated indoor swimming pool and spa complex. Meals can be delivered to your room by one of five restaurants. **www.supremeaccom.co.nz**

PALMERSTON NORTH Palmerston North Motel $$

66 Linton Street **Tel** *(06) 358 0681, 0800 225 692* **Fax** *(06) 356 1753* **Rooms** *20*   **Map** *E4*

A range of units, some able to accommodate up to seven people, set in spacious, leafy grounds with playground and car parking. Three minutes' walk from The Square, Te Manawa Art Gallery and the groovy cafés and shops in George Street. The Rugby Museum is a few blocks further away. **www.pnm.co.nz**

PALMERSTON NORTH Hotel Coachman $$$

140 Fitzherbert Avenue **Tel** *(06) 356 5065, 0800 800 678* **Fax** *(06) 356 6692* **Rooms** *73*   **Map** *E4*

Palmerston North's classiest accommodation, in a surprisingly cosy upmarket business-type hotel. Central to The Square, Te Manawa and Rugby Museum, and only a few minutes' drive from Massey University. The hotel's La Patio café and bar, which opens onto The Avenue, is frequented by locals as well as hotel guests. **www.rydges.com**

PALMERSTON NORTH Plum Trees Lodge $$$

97 Russell Street **Tel** *(06) 358 7813* **Rooms** *1*   **Map** *E4*

Boutique accommodation in the centre of Palmerston North. Inner-city retreat, with mature garden and trees. Attractively designed to accommodate two people in luxury, with a breakfast hamper left for guests to enjoy on the sunny deck or in the cosy interior with its beamed roof. Close to all that Palmy has to offer. **www.plumtreeslodge.com**

WAIRARAPA Arbor Motel $

29–31 Main Street, Greytown **Tel** *(06) 304 9445* **Fax** *(06) 304 8445* **Rooms** *5*   **Map** *E4*

This clean motel in a picturesque garden setting on Greytown's historic main street is close to cafés, crafts and antiques shops. Less twee than most accommodation in the area, and less pricey too, this motel is child-friendly and has very accommodating hosts. **www.greytown.co.nz/accommodation**

WAIRARAPA Shadyvale $$

Hinakura Road **Tel** *(06) 306 9374* **Fax** *(06) 306 9374* **Rooms** *2*   **Map** *E5*

Two guest rooms at opposite ends of the pseudo-colonial main house, plus views of the Tararua Range, make rural Shadyvale a popular bed and breakfast destination in the rolling green countryside of the South Wairarapa. A short meander from Martinborough's wineries and restaurants, or a pleasant drive to the coast. **www.shadyvale.co.nz**

WAIRARAPA The White Swan $$

109 Main Street, Greytown **Tel** *(06) 304 8894* **Fax** *(06) 304 8824* **Rooms** *11*   **Map** *E4*

An old government building transported over Rimutaka Hill from Wellington (one half fell off the truck). Now renovated as an elegant country hotel, with rooms individually decorated in an eclectic range of styles from contemporary design to sumptuous Mughal. Excellent bar and restaurant, friendly service. **www.thewhiteswan.co.nz**

WAIRARAPA Peppers Martinborough Hotel $$$$$

The Square, Martinborough **Tel** *(06) 306 9350* **Fax** *(06) 306 9345* **Rooms** *16*   **Map** *E5*

Beautifully renovated hotel, built in 1882. Has its own library, whisky bar, bistro and courtyard garden. Choice of nine verandah rooms, overlooking The Square, or seven garden rooms, decorated with landscapes by Martinborough artist Scott Tulloch. **www.martinboroughhotel.co.nz**

WAIRARAPA Wharekauhau Country Estate $$$$$

Western Lake Road, Palliser Bay, Featherston **Tel** *(06) 307 7581* **Fax** *(06) 307 7799* **Rooms** *12*   **Map** *E5*

Exclusive luxury lodge set on a 5,000-acre working sheep station overlooking Palliser Bay. Outdoor activities from quad-biking to team-building are available and facilities include an indoor swimming pool, gym, tennis court and spa pool. Guests stay in individual cottages. Price includes dinner and breakfast, but lunch is extra. **www.wharekauhau.co.nz**

WANGANUI Anndion Lodge Accommodation $

143 Anzac Parade **Tel** *0800 343 056* **Fax** *(06) 343 3056* **Rooms** *12*   **Map** *E4*

Five-star, motorcycle-friendly accommodation hosted by owners Ann and Dion on the banks of the Whanganui River a few minutes' drive from the city centre at the start of the scenic Parapara Highway. For a treat ask for the ensuite super king room, or relax in the steamy spa and pool. Dion's a dab hand at barbecues. **www.anndionlodge.co.nz**

WANGANUI The Tamara Backpackers Lodge $

24 Somme Parade **Tel** *06 347 6300* **Fax** *06 345 8488* **Rooms** *16*   **Map** *E4*

Friendly, centrally located backpackers' lodge in Edwardian villa overlooking the Whanganui River, and with views of Mount Ruapehu. Large garden, pool table, bikes, BBQ, piano and guitar for guests' use. Spacious kitchen, dining an TV lounge areas. Shared, twin and double rooms, some ensuite. **www.tamaralodge.com**

Key to Price Guide *see p298*   **Key to Symbols** *see back cover flap*

WANGANUI Kingsgate Hotel The Avenue Wanganui
🍴🏊🏃 $$

379 Victoria Avenue **Tel** *(06) 349 0044* **Fax** *(06) 345 3250* **Rooms** *73*　　　　　　*Map E4*

On the main road into Wanganui, a 10-minute walk from shops, cafés and restaurants, and the city's historic, artistic and cultural attractions. A tidy business-type hotel, set in large grounds with an outdoor swimming pool. Award-winning, licensed restaurant offers New Zealand cuisine. Casual café-bar. **www.theavenuewanganui.com**

WANGANUI Rutland Arms Inn
🍴 $$

Cnr Victoria Avenue and Ridgway Street **Tel** *(06) 347 7677, 0800 788 5263* **Fax** *(06) 347 7345* **Rooms** *8* **Map** *E4*

Small bed and breakfast with excellent facilities, close to town centre. Friendly, convivial atmosphere with modern luxuries in this 'little piece of England' in Wanganui. Suites are individually decorated and bear surprising names (one is called the Goethe, or Gotty, suite). Large range of beer and whisky at the bar. **www.rutland-arms.co.nz**

WANGANUI Siena Motor Lodge
🏃 $$

335 Victoria Ave **Tel** *(06) 345 9009, 0800 888 802* **Fax** *(06) 345 9935* **Rooms** *10*　　　　　*Map E4*

Central, five-star motor lodge, within walking distance of restaurants, town-centre shops, the Sarjeant Gallery, Durie Hill Elevator and Memorial Tower, Cooks Gardens, Whanganui Riverboat Centre and the river itself. Spotlessly clean, fully equipped, comfortable rooms, many with spa bath. **www.siena.co.nz**

WANGANUI Arlesford House
$$$

202 SH3 **Tel** *(06) 347 7751* **Fax** *(06) 347 7561* **Rooms** *4*　　　　　　　　　*Map E4*

Country house B&B set in 6 acres of parklike gardens 7 km north of Wanganui. Arlesford House was designed by prominent Wanganui architect Bob Talboys and built by Joseph Gopperth in 1934, almost entirely of native heart rimu timber. It has been decorated in classic style with antiques and Persian carpets. **www.arlesfordhouse.co.nz**

WELLINGTON Cambridge Hotel and Backpackers
🍴 $

28 Cambridge Terrace **Tel** *(04) 385 8829, 0800 873 553* **Fax** *(04) 385 2503* **Rooms** *33*　　　*Map D5*

Budget hotel, in a restored old building. Within five minutes' walk of Te Papa museum, the waterfront, Courtenay Place bars and the shops, cafés and restaurants of the commercial district and Cuba Quarter. Family or group rooms with bunks are available. Luxurious backpacker wing with excellent showers. **www.cambridgehotel.co.nz**

WELLINGTON Comfort Hotel Wellington
$

213 Cuba Street **Tel** *(04) 385 2153* **Fax** *(04) 382 8873* **Rooms** *114*　　　　　　*Map D5*

Modern rooms in a completely renovated and earthquake-proofed 1908 building that was once a Salvation Army hotel known as the People's Palace. In the heart of the Cuba Quarter, surrounded by cafés, restaurants and boutiques, and a short walk from Courtenay Place nightlife and the waterfront. **www.comfortwellington.co.nz**

WELLINGTON Halswell Lodge
🛏🏃 $

21 Kent Terrace, Courtenay Place **Tel** *(04) 385 0196* **Fax** *(04) 385 0503* **Rooms** *36*　　　*Map D5*

Established hotel/motel close to Te Papa, Oriental Bay and downtown shops, restaurants and cafés. The lodge itself is in a lovingly restored villa on a quiet back street (rooms cost a bit more here), while the hotel may offer long-term rates. Self-catering two-bedroom motel units with car parking (critical in central Wellington). **www.halswell.co.nz**

WELLINGTON Holiday Inn Wellington
🛏♿🍴🏊🏃📺 $$

75 Featherston Street **Tel** *(04) 499 8686, 0800 154 181* **Fax** *(04) 798 3763* **Rooms** *280*　　　*Map D5*

A modern, well-run hotel as you would expect from this chain, with bright, clean rooms and professional service. It is close to Lambton Quay, Westpac Stadium, Victoria University and Wellington Railway Station. There are fantastic views of the harbour and city. **www.holidayinnwellington.co.nz**

WELLINGTON Hotel Willis
🏃 $$

318 Willis Street **Tel** *(04) 384 5955, 0800 249 467* **Fax** *(04) 384 5952* **Rooms** *25*　　　　*Map D5*

Small central-city hotel, close to the Cuba Quarter's boutiques and cafés, and a short walk from the Te Papa museum and waterfront, as well as many of Wellington's other tourist attractions. Clean, comfortable rooms make this hotel a good value option. Breakfast restaurant and bar serving drinks and snacks. **www.hotelwillis.co.nz**

WELLINGTON Kingsgate Hotel Portland Wellington
🛏🏃📺 $$

24 Hawkestone Street **Tel** *(04) 473 2208* **Fax** *(04) 473 3892* **Rooms** *123*　　　　　*Map D5*

Close to rail, bus and ferry terminals, and with easy motorway access, the Portland offers very good value for its comfortable, well-appointed ensuite rooms. Friendly atmosphere and personal service, free gym access and weekend bargains add to the appeal of this hotel. **www.portlandhotel.co.nz**

WELLINGTON Tinakori Lodge
$$

182 Tinakori Road, Thorndon **Tel** *(04) 939 3478, 0800 937 347* **Fax** *(04) 939 3475* **Rooms** *9*　　　*Map D5*

This characterful boutique hotel in a historic two-storey wooden building (1868) is located in the Victorian villa-studded neighbourhood of Thorndon. This enviable position offers access to the Botanic Gardens, Old St Paul's and the waterfront, as well as many delightful cafés and restaurants. **www.tinakorilodge.co.nz**

WELLINGTON Museum Hotel
🏃 $$$

90 Cable Street **Tel** *(04) 802 8900, 0800 994 335* **Fax** *(04) 802 8909* **Rooms** *47*　　　　*Map D5*

Across the road from Te Papa and the waterfront, the 5-storey, 3,500-tonne hotel was moved 120m on wheels along railway tracks from its original site to make way for the new museum – hence the name. It looks like a concrete bunker, but has comfortable rooms with harbour or city views. **www.museumhotel.co.nz**

WELLINGTON The Lighthouse and The Keep Bed and Breakfast $$$

326 and 116 The Esplanade, Island Bay **Tel** *(04) 472 4177* **Fax** *(04) 472 4177* **Rooms** *2*   **Map** *D5*

A short drive from the city centre in a seaside suburb with a historic Italian community which is now popular with young families. Well worth the drive to stay in the original lighthouse building or an unusual stone "keep". This B&B is well located, just a stone's throw from the beach, and near a café and pizzeria. **www.thelighthouse.net.nz**

WELLINGTON CityLife Wellington $$$

300 Lambton Quay, The Terrace **Tel** *(04) 922 2800, 0800 368 888* **Fax** *(04) 922 2803* **Rooms** *68*   **Map** *D5*

Modern hotel in the heart of the commercial district, close to shops, restaurants, cafés and the Beehive, and a short walk from other attractions. Tasteful, comfortable international-style decor. Standard rooms and suites with laundry and kitchen. Full-price rooms can be very expensive but deals are often available. **www.heritagehotels.co.nz**

WELLINGTON Hotel Intercontinental $$$$

2 Grey Street **Tel** *(04) 472 2722* **Fax** *(04) 472 4724* **Rooms** *233*   **Map** *D5*

Situated in the central business district, with all the conveniences and amenities you would expect of a large international hotel. A good selection of in-house restaurants and bars, room service, all imaginable business facilities and a swimming pool and gym. Comfortable rooms and highly professional service. **www.intercontinental.com**

WELLINGTON James Cook Hotel Grand Chancellor $$$$

147 The Terrace **Tel** *(04) 499 9500, 0800 275 337* **Fax** *(04) 499 9800* **Rooms** *260*   **Map** *D5*

At the heart of the commercial and retail districts, the James Cook Hotel is best known among locals for its elevator, which links The Terrace to Lambton Quay. Singapore-owned, it has won various awards for its re-development and hospitality, and holds a good reputation as a mid-range, modern, international hotel. **www.ghihotels.com**

WELLINGTON The Terrace Villas $$$$

202 The Terrace, **Tel** *(04) 920 2020* **Fax** *(04) 920 2030* **Rooms** *50*   **Map** *D5*

Centrally located, these self-contained apartments are set in restored late 19th-century villas dotted along The Terrace, one block up from Lambton Quay. Close to town and Victoria University, these are tastefully done up in turn-of-the-last-century style with an executive finish. Good for longer stays (weekly rates are lower). **www.terracevillas.co.nz**

MARLBOROUGH AND NELSON

ABEL TASMAN NATIONAL PARK Abel Tasman Marahau Lodge $$

Marahau Beach, Abel Tasman National Park **Tel** *(03) 527 8250* **Fax** *(03) 527 8258* **Rooms** *12*   **Map** *D4*

Five minutes' walk from the Abel Tasman National Park entrance. Beautiful accommodation in studios or self-contained chalets with private decks, nestled in native gardens. Sea kayaking, water taxis to beaches and coastal walks can be arranged, as can packed lunches. There is an outdoor spa pool. **www.abeltasmanmarahaulodge.co.nz**

ABEL TASMAN NATIONAL PARK Awaroa Lodge $$$$

Awaroa Bay, Abel Tasman National Park **Tel** *(03) 528 8758* **Fax** *(03) 528 6561* **Rooms** *26*   **Map** *D4*

Environmentally friendly, stylish, luxury lodge in Abel Tasman National Park. Creative organic cuisine. Despite remote wetland setting, the architecture is state-of-the-art and the facilities include a café, bar, lounge, decks, gallery and library. Accessible by helicopter, sea kayak, water taxi or on foot. **www.awaroalodge.co.nz**

ABEL TASMAN NATIONAL PARK Kanuka Hill Lodge $$$$$

The Anchorage, Abel Tasman National Park **Tel** *(03) 548 2863* **Fax** *(03) 548 2869* **Rooms** *3*   **Map** *D4*

Exquisite accommodation in the heart of the National Park, with stunning views of bush-covered hills sloping down to golden beaches and turquoise sea. Accessible by water taxi, kayak or on foot along the coastal track from Marahau. Full breakfasts, packed lunches and three-course dinners are available. **www.kanukalodge.co.nz**

BLENHEIM Copthorne Hotel $$

20 Nelson Street **Tel** *(03) 577 7333* **Fax** *(03) 577 7337* **Rooms** *28*   **Map** *D5*

Decorated in white and chocolate with dashes of red and exposed wood, leather sofas and chairs woven from water hyacinth reeds, this hotel boasts executive suites with spa baths, intimate doubles and family apartments with children's beds upstairs. Metal nikau palms flank the entranceway of this laidback hotel. **www.marlboroughhotel.co.nz**

BLENHEIM Olde Mill House B&B $$

9 Wilson St, Renwick **Tel** *(03) 572 8458, 0800 653 262* **Fax** *(03) 572 8458* **Rooms** *3*   **Map** *D5*

A 1920s villa on the site of the old Renwick Saw Mill, refurbished in "olde-worlde" style. Fifteen minutes' drive from Blenheim, two blocks from Renwick Village, where there are basic shops, and in the middle of the Marlborough wine growing district. Electric blankets and alarm clock radios are available to guests. **www.oldemillhouse.co.nz**

BLENHEIM Arwen Lodge $$$

62 Morven Lane, Fairhall **Tel** *(03) 579 2235* **Rooms** *3*   **Map** *D5*

On a ridge overlooking vineyards, a few minutes' drive from Blenheim and close to wineries, restaurants and a golf course, this is also a good base for the Sounds. Two well-appointed, self-contained cottages and an apartment make up the accommodation. Guests receive a welcoming bottle of wine and breakfast hamper. **www.arwenlodge.co.nz**

Key to Price Guide *see p298* **Key to Symbols** *see back cover flap*

BLENHEIM Château Marlborough ░░░░░ $$$
5–115 High Street **Tel** *(03) 578 0064, 0800 752 275* **Fax** *(03) 578 2661* **Rooms** *30* **Map** *D5*

Modern, comfortable motel overlooking the Seymour Square floral gardens, clock and fountain in the heart of Blenheim, which emulates European grandeur and elegance in its faux-château-style architecture. Swimming pool with poolside bar. Warm and welcoming bar, reception and breakfast room. **www.marlboroughnz.co.nz**

BLENHEIM Hotel D'Urville ░░ $$$$$
52 Queen Street **Tel** *(03) 577 9945* **Fax** *(03) 577 9946* **Rooms** *11* **Map** *D5*

Small hotel in the historic Public Trust building, with a neo-classical Art Deco façade. Rooms are stylishly decorated to individual themes. Personal service and an award-winning restaurant, which serves top-notch New Zealand cuisine add to the appeal and quality bar snacks are served in the funky contemporary bar too. **www.durville.com**

GOLDEN BAY Pohara Beachfront Motel ░ $$
Abel Tasman Drive, Pohara, Takaka **Tel** *(03) 525 9660, 0800 862 322* **Fax** *(03) 525 9660* **Rooms** *11* **Map** *D4*

Right on the beach in Pohara, a seafront settlement along the road to the Abel Tasman National Park from Takaka. Self-contained units are the perfect base for safe swimming, or expeditions further afield to the national park or any of the other stunning beaches, parks and reserves of Golden Bay. **www.poharamotel.co.nz**

GOLDEN BAY Twin Waters Lodge ░ $$$
10 Totara Avenue, Collingwood **Tel** *(03) 524 8014* **Fax** *(03) 524 8054* **Rooms** *3* **Map** *D4*

This attractively designed lodge sits between a calm estuary and a beach 10km north of Collingwood. Facilities include private decks with views of the water and a guest lounge. This is a peaceful place to hear the tuis sing in the pax. Dinner by arrangement. Breakfast included. No children or pets. **www.twinwaters.co.nz**

KAIKOURA The Old Convent ░░░ $$
Mt Fyffe Road **Tel** *(03) 319 6603, 0800 365 603* **Fax** *(03) 319 6690* **Rooms** *15* **Map** *D5*

A beautifully preserved convent built in 1911 for French nuns, set in farmland on Kaikoura's mountainous coastline. Now a B&B with a homely atmosphere, owned by three fifth-generation New Zealanders. The former chapel is now a lounge with a hearth. Petanque, croquet and bicycles are all available. **www.theoldconvent.co.nz**

KAIKOURA Anchor Inn Motel ░░ $$$
208 The Esplanade **Tel** *0800 720 033* **Fax** *(03) 319 5427* **Rooms** *15* **Map** *D5*

This award-winning motel is rightly trumpeted as a great value option with five-star facilities. It is located on the Kaikoura waterfront, with most of the comfortable, well-appointed rooms enjoying spectacular sea or mountain views. **www.anchorinn.co.nz**

KAIKOURA Fyffe Country Lodge ░ $$$$$
SH1 **Tel** *(03) 319 6869* **Fax** *(03) 319 6865* **Rooms** *6* **Map** *D5*

Luxury boutique lodge surrounded by English-style gardens with views of Mount Fyffe and the Kaikoura seaward ranges, 250m from the beach. Built with handmade mud blocks and recycled native New Zealand timbers, it boasts an award-winning restaurant. Fishing is available. No children under 12. **www.fyffecountrylodge.co.nz**

KAIKOURA Hapuku Lodge ░ $$$$$
SH1 at Hapuku Road **Tel** *(03) 319 6559, 0800 524 568* **Fax** *(03) 319 6557* **Rooms** *6* **Map** *D5*

Designed by the owner's architectural family, the lodge, in a spectacular location 12 km north of Kaikoura, also boasts an award-winning country kitchen and restaurant. Comforts include handcrafted furniture and granite or marble vanities in four luxury tree houses in a manuka grove. Wind garden and deer stud. **www.hapukulodge.com**

MARLBOROUGH SOUNDS Furneaux Lodge ░░ $$
Endeavour Inlet, Queen Charlotte Sound, Picton **Tel** *(03) 579 8259* **Fax** *(03) 579 8279* **Rooms** *16* **Map** *D4*

Built as a holiday home by the pioneering Howden family, who emigrated from Scotland to Wellington in the 1880s and fell in love with Endeavour Inlet and its backdrop of native bush. Accommodation is in self-contained chalets and backpacker dormitories, near the waterfront. Access by water taxi or on foot. **www.furneaux.co.nz**

MARLBOROUGH SOUNDS Te Mahia Bay Resort ░ $$
Tenepuru, Kenepuru Sound **Tel** *(03) 573 4089* **Fax** *(03) 573 4089* **Rooms** *13* **Map** *D4*

Waterfront units in a secluded bay surrounded by native bush, right on the edge of Kenepuru Sound. Personal, attentive service from the owners, who also lavish attention on the garden. Two spacious, modern apartments recently added. Freshly picked flowers are placed in the rooms. **www.temahia.co.nz**

MARLBOROUGH SOUNDS French Pass Sea Safaris and Beachfront Villas ░░ $$$
Rai Valley, French Pass **Tel** *(03) 576 5204* **Rooms** *3* **Map** *D4*

Self-contained waterfront villas in the French Pass coastal settlement, from where sea safaris can help you to touch the Mauri – a sense of unity between man and nature. Boat excursions to Kakaho Island, where you may see yellow crowned parakeets, bush robins, bellbirds, tuis, the rare king shag, seals and dolphins. **www.seasafaris.co.nz**

MARLBOROUGH SOUNDS Raetihi Lodge ░░ $$$$
Double Bay, Kenepuru Sound **Tel** *(03) 573 4300* **Fax** *(03) 573 4323* **Rooms** *14* **Map** *D4*

Off the beaten track, in its own bay which can only be reached by water taxi or private boat, this 1930s waterfront retreat is relaxing and comfortable. Award-winning architecture, with seaview, hillside and garden rooms. Massage therapist on hand to help you unwind. Alternatively, there are plenty of trips to go on. **www.raetihilodge.co.nz**

MARLBOROUGH SOUNDS Bay of Many Coves Resort   ⒒☲⋔ $$$$$

Queen Charlotte Sound, Picton **Tel** *(03) 579 9771, 0800 579 9771* **Fax** *(03) 579 9777* **Rooms** *40*   **Map** *D4*

A stunning setting in native bush on the bay of many coves. Fishing, walking, sailing and kayaking can be arranged, or guests can enjoy the freshwater pool and spa therapies. Stylish waterfront apartments and studios decorated in neutral sand, wood and stone tones. Access is by water taxi or private boat. **www.bayofmanycovesresort.co.nz**

MOTUEKA The Resurgence   ⒒☲⋔ $$$$$

Riwaka Valley Road, Riwaka **Tel** *(03) 528 4664* **Fax** *(03) 528 4605* **Rooms** *6*   **Map** *D4*

A luxurious lodge set in 50 acres of native bush near Abel Tasman and Kahurangi National Parks – a great place to chill out, or as a great base for sea kayaking, horse trekking and walking. Lodge rooms or self-contained cottages. Outdoor swimming and spa pool. Mediterranean-style home-cooked meal included. **www.resurgence.co.nz**

NELSON Nelson Central YHA   ⋔ $

59 Rutherford Street **Tel** *(03) 545 9988* **Fax** *(03) 545 9989* **Rooms** *92*   **Map** *D4*

The best of the backpacker hostels, this is centrally located by Nelson Market, which sells crafts, organic produce, plants and toys galore every weekend. It is just a short walk to galleries and gardens. Clean, new and modern, with sunny garden and dining area and well equipped kitchens. **www.yha.co.nz**

NELSON Rutherford Hotel Nelson   🅿⒒☲⋔🖵 $$$

Trafalgar Square **Tel** *(03) 548 2299, 0800 368 8888* **Fax** *(03) 546 3003* **Rooms** *113*   **Map** *D4*

Nelson's premier city-centre hotel has hosted royalty, film and sports stars and prime ministers, as well as ordinary tourists and business people, although it is not on record how many presidents have stayed in the presidential suite. Offers a buffet breakfast, sushi, café lunches and drinks at the bar. **www.rutherfordhotel.co.nz**

NELSON South Street Cottages   ⋔ $$$

1, 2B, 3, 12 South Street, Nelson **Tel** *(03) 540 2769* **Fax** *(03) 540 2769* **Rooms** *5*   **Map** *D4*

Luxury apartment and historic self-catering cottages in New Zealand's oldest preserved street. Experience 1860s colonial life in a quiet setting of character and charm. Log fires in all cottages, as well as more modern comforts such as kitchen and laundry. Enclosed garden courtyards. Close to city centre. **www.cottageaccommodation.co.nz**

NELSON Te Puna Wai Lodge   ⋔ $$$

24 Richardson St, Port Hills **Tel** *(03) 548 7621* **Fax** *(03) 548 7645* **Rooms** *3*   **Map** *D4*

Boutique B&B in a colonial villa on Nelson's Port Hills, with stunning views out to sea from the rooms which are charmingly furnished, with original wooden floors and antique furniture. Brand-new marble-tiled bathrooms with underfloor heating. Open fires and French doors opening onto verandahs and terraces. **www.tepunawai.co.nz**

NELSON The Honest Lawyer Hotel   ⒒ $$$

1 Point Road, Monaco **Tel** *(03) 547 8850, 0800 921 192* **Fax** *(03) 547 8868* **Rooms** *13*   **Map** *D4*

The stone architecture and Waimea Estuary setting make this hotel unique. The rooms are well appointed in English country style and there is a complimentary guest pantry. English country pub food with a Pacifica twist is served in the all-day restaurant. Ten minutes' drive from central Nelson. **www.honestlawyer.co.nz**

PICTON Americano Motor Inn   ⒒⋔ $$

32 High Street, Picton **Tel** *(03) 573 6398, 0800 104 104* **Fax** *(03) 573 7892* **Rooms** *26*   **Map** *D4*

A good base for the ferry terminal, town wharf and railway station, all of which are a short walk away, the Americano is as close as they come to cafés and shops. The motel's 26 units are on the ground and first floor; the upper ones have harbour views. **www.americano.co.nz**

ST ARNAUD Alpine Lodge   ⒒⋔ $$

Main Road **Tel** *(03) 521 1869, 0800 367 777* **Fax** *(03) 521 1855* **Rooms** *32*   **Map** *D4*

The Alpine Lodge offers comfortable, woody rooms with good facilities on the edge of the beech forest of Nelson Lakes National Park. Family units with mezzanine floor and budget chalets. It is a gateway to ski areas, lakes, forests, river adventures, gold-panning, nature tours, caving, hiking and mountain biking. **www.alpinelodge.co.nz**

CANTERBURY AND THE WEST COAST

AKAROA Akaroa Village Inn   ☲⋔ $$

81 Beach Road **Tel** *(03) 304 7421, 0800 695 2000* **Fax** *(03) 304 7423* **Rooms** *40*   **Map** *C6*

Waterfront units in the heart of the village beside the main wharf, ranging from luxury purpose-built self-catering apartments to courtyard cottages, accommodation in the old shipping office and comfortable suites with spa baths. Spectacular harbour views. Outdoor pool operates in summer. **www.akaroavillageinn.co.nz**

ARTHUR'S PASS Arthur's Pass Hotel   ⒒⋔ $$

SH73, Arthur's Pass **Tel** *(03) 318 9236* **Fax** *(03) 318 9276* **Rooms** *14*   **Map** *C5*

Spectacularly located at Arthur's Pass, in the middle of the Southern Alps, this rustic chalet-style accommodation is close to the winter ski-fields and the magnificent tramping and climbing areas of Arthur's Pass National Park. The attached bar and restaurant are also popular. **www.arthurspass.co.nz**

Key to Price Guide *see p298* **Key to Symbols** *see back cover flap*

ARTHUR'S PASS Wilderness Lodge Arthur's Pass   🍴🏃 $$$$$

SH73 (16km east of Arthur's Pass village) **Tel** *(03) 318 9246* **Fax** *(03) 318 9245* **Rooms** *24*   **Map** *C5*

Luxurious wilderness lodge in its own 2,500-hectare merino sheep station in the heart of the Southern Alps. Style, comfort, magnificent views and sheep shearing. Gourmet restaurant. Daily guided walks and canoe paddles offer the opportunity to explore mountain lakes, alpine flowers, glaciers, beech forests and birds. **www.wildernesslodge.co.nz**

ASHBURTON Hotel Ashburton   🍴🏊🏃 $$

Racecourse Road **Tel** *(03) 308 3059, 0800 330 880* **Fax** *(03) 307 1303* **Rooms** *54*   **Map** *C6*

Set in extensive landscaped grounds opposite a racecourse, the spacious hotel units have a garden outlook. Sauna, spa pools, indoor heated swimming pool, all weather tennis court, eight-hole pitch and putt golf course and mountain bike hire are available for guests. Also has bars, restaurants and a casino. **www.hotelash.co.nz**

CHRISTCHURCH Ashford Motor Lodge   🏊🏃 $$

35 Papanui Road **Tel** *(03) 355 3416, 0800 400 026* **Fax** *(03) 355 3414* **Rooms** *22*   **Map** *C6*

Ashford Motor Inn, with up-to-date furnishings and contemporary decor, is near Hagley Park with its attractive footpaths and cycleways, and a five-minute drive from the city centre. It offers guests a solar-heated pool and broadband access. **www.ashfordmotorlodge.co.nz**

CHRISTCHURCH Rydges   🍴🏃📺 $$

Cnr Worcester St and Oxford Terrace **Tel** *(03) 379 4700, 0800 446 187* **Fax** *(03) 365 5357* **Rooms** *208*   **Map** *C6*

One of few hotels overlooking the River Avon, near Cathedral Square and in easy walking distance of all city-centre sights and surrounded by shops, cafés and restaurants. This is an imposing, modern building with rooms for most budgets. Some have views of Southern Alps. **www.rydges.com**

CHRISTCHURCH Stonehurst   🍴🏊🏃 $$

241 Gloucester Street, Latimer Square **Tel** *(03) 379 4620, 0508 786 633* **Fax** *(03) 379 4647* **Rooms** *20*   **Map** *C6*

NZ Tourism award-winning motel and backpacker accommodation in central Christchurch, a short walk from Cathedral Square. Studio, one- and two-bedroom motel units with ensuite bathrooms. Pleasant outdoor deck, swimming pool and BBQ area. Pizzas and pasta can be ordered all day at the café. **www.stonehurst.co.nz**

CHRISTCHURCH Windsor Hotel B&B   🏃 $$

52 Armagh Street **Tel** *(03) 366 1503, 0800 366 1503* **Fax** *(03) 366 9796* **Rooms** *40*   **Map** *C6*

Central, family-run B&B hotel in a large Edwardian house. Rooms are individually decorated with watercolours by local artist Denise McCulloch. On the tram route and close to the Arts Centre, Canterbury Museum and Botanical Gardens. Full English breakfast included. Shared guest bathrooms. Free broadband. **www.windsorhotel.co.nz**

CHRISTCHURCH Château on the Park   🍴🏊🏃📺 $$$

189 Deans Ave **Tel** *(03) 348 8999, 0800 808 999* **Fax** *(03) 348 8990* **Rooms** *193*   **Map** *C6*

Christchurch's only resort-style hotel, set in five acres of gardens beside Hagley Park, and a short walk through the park from the city centre. Many of the lavish rooms open onto courtyard gardens. Live entertainment in the wood-panelled den bar, and good eating options at the airy garden court brasserie. **www.chateau-park.co.nz**

CHRISTCHURCH Hotel Grand Chancellor Christchurch   ♿🍴🏃 $$$

161 Cashel Street **Tel** *(03) 379 2999, 0800 275 337* **Fax** *(03) 379 9929* **Rooms** *176*   **Map** *C6*

This is the tallest hotel in Christchurch, set just beyond the City Mall. The rooms are spacious and have air-conditioning. Good restaurant and bar. Rooms, from the 15th floor up, feature sweeping views over Christchurch and the Canterbury Plains. **www.ghihotels.com**

CHRISTCHURCH Warner's Hotel   🍴🏃 $$$

50 Cathedral Square **Tel** *(03) 366 5159* **Fax** *(03) 379 5736* **Rooms** *34*   **Map** *C6*

Restored and comfortably furnished boutique accommodation in the heart of Christchurch, housed in a historic hotel built in 1863. It is situated in Cathedral Square and is close to all the city centre attractions. Meals are served in the Bailies Irish Bar and Restaurant. **www.warnershotel.com**

CHRISTCHURCH Crowne Plaza Christchurch   ♿🍴🏃📺 $$$$

Cnr Durham and Kilmore streets **Tel** *(03) 365 7799* **Fax** *(03) 365 0082* **Rooms** *298*   **Map** *C6*

Luxurious international business hotel with well-appointed air-conditioned rooms, atrium and several restaurants. Central location by Avon River and Victoria Square. Amenities include laundry pick-up, self-laundry and a health and fitness centre, as well as high-speed Internet access and full business facilities. **www.christchurch.crowneplaza.co.nz**

CHRISTCHURCH Hambledon $$$$

103 Bealey Ave **Tel** *(03) 379 0723* **Fax** *(03) 379 0758* **Rooms** *8*   **Map** *C6*

Luxury bed and breakfast in the gracious surroundings of a faithfully restored 1850s mansion house in the heart of Christchurch, decorated with heavy Victorian antiques including a carved mahogany four-poster bed. Guests can relax on the wisteria-clad verandah. Four suites, an apartment and three cottages. **www.hambledon.co.nz**

FOX GLACIER Fox Glacier Resort Hotel   🍴 $$

Cook Flat Road **Tel** *(03) 751 0839, 0800 273 767* **Fax** *(03) 751 0868* **Rooms** *61*   **Map** *B6*

A charming old wooden building, with accommodation in a wide price range, from low budget to fully serviced rooms. Built in 1928, it has been refurbished to offer suites, standard and superior rooms, as well as budget rooms. Guest lounges, bar and restaurant. **www.resorts.co.nz**

FOX GLACIER Scenic Circle Glacier Country Hotel $$$$

SH6 **Tel** *(03) 751 0847* **Fax** *(03) 751 0822* **Rooms** *51*   **Map** *B6*

Well placed for glacier skiing and hiking, rainforest and bush walks, alpine climbing, white heron, penguin or seal colony visits, fishing and hunting, the Scenic Circle is ideal for active travellers. Within Westland World Heritage Park, and close to information centres. It has a cosy bar with open fireplace and fully licensed restaurant. **www.scenic-circle.co.nz**

FRANZ JOSEF GLACIER Rainforest Retreat $$$

Cron Street **Tel** *(03) 752 0220* **Fax** *(03) 752 0003* **Rooms** *30*   **Map** *B6*

Deluxe tree houses, motel units, campervan sites and a backpacker hostel, spread over six acres of native rainforest a short walk from the centre of Franz Josef village. Travellers' comforts include a 'bubbling' spa pool and sauna, heating, laundry and drying facilities. Monsoon bar and restaurant. **www.rainforestretreat.co.nz**

FRANZ JOSEF GLACIER Scenic Circle Franz Josef Glacier Hotels $$$

SH6 **Tel** *03 752 0729* **Fax** *03 752 0709* **Rooms** *177*   **Map** *B6*

Three separate wings, two in the village and the third in landscaped grounds sloping down to the river just north of it. Several restaurants and bars to choose from, as well as comfortably appointed rooms. Popular venue for team-building events, which make the most of local sporting possibilities. Close to glaciers. **www.scenic-circle.co.nz**

FRANZ JOSEF GLACIER Terrace Motel $$$

1 Cowan Street **Tel** *(03) 752 0130, 0800 837 7223* **Fax** *(03) 752 0190* **Rooms** *10*   **Map** *B6*

This motel has spacious, modern and well-equipped rooms. The proprietors are friendly and helpful, and can assist with directions or planning of activities around Franz Josef Glacier and the West Coast region. Some rooms are painted an oddly soothing deep red colour. A short walk to restaurants, bars and shops. **www.terracemotel.co.nz**

GERALDINE The Crossing B&B $$$

124 Woodbury Road **Tel** *(03) 693 9689* **Fax** *(03) 693 9789* **Rooms** *3*   **Map** *C6*

Boutique English-style manor house nestled in a charming garden of roses and native plants, with views of Four Peaks mountain range. Built as a banker's retirement estate in 1908, it has been beautifully maintained and restored. The rooms are furnished with antiques and original furniture. **www.thecrossingbnb.co.nz**

GREYMOUTH Formerly the Blackball Hilton $

26 Hart Street, Blackball (28km inland from Greymouth) **Tel** *(03) 732 4705* **Fax** *(03) 732 4708* **Rooms** *18* **Map** *C5*

A historic West Coast hotel in a former gold-mining settlement. First settled around 1893, when a coal mine opened Blackball became synonymous with militancy when the miners went on strike in 1908, but since the 1960s has survived as a hippie enclave. The hotel serves food, wine and local beers. **www.blackballhilton.co.nz**

GREYMOUTH Revingtons Hotel $

47 Tainui Street **Tel** *(03) 768 7055* **Fax** *(03) 768 7605* **Rooms** *25*   **Map** *C5*

Historic hotel in the centre of Greytown since 1876, where Queen Elizabeth II and Prince Philip stayed during their 1954 Coronation Tour. Hotel rooms and a separate hostel. Irish bar, sports bar and licensed restaurant. Good base fo jade factory, replica 1880s gold-mining Shantytown and Monteith's Brewery tours. **www.revingtons.co.nz**

GREYMOUTH Paroa Hotel Motel $$

508 Main South Road, Paroa **Tel** *(03) 762 6860, 0800 762 6860* **Fax** *(03) 762 6865* **Rooms** *12*   **Map** *C5*

Authentic family-run West Coast motel hosted by the Monks for over 55 years. Close to the replica gold-mining settlement of Shantytown and rugged, driftwood-piled Paroa Beach, 8km south of Greymouth. The unusual stone-built motel has 12 units, recently refurbished, a bottle store, two bars and a restaurant. **www.paroa.co.nz**

GREYMOUTH The Ashley Hotel $$

74 Tasman Street **Tel** *(03) 768 5135, 0800 807 787* **Fax** *(03) 768 0319* **Rooms** *60*   **Map** *C5*

Greymouth's premier place to stay, with modern hotel and motel units. Its rooms – studios, apartments, suites and hotel rooms – cater for families, couples, groups, independent travellers and businesspeople alike. Heated pool, spa and gym. West Coast specialities served in formal à la carte dining room. **www.hotelashley.co.nz**

GREYMOUTH The Breakers B&B $$

Nine Mile Creek, SH6 (30km S of Punakaiki) **Tel** *(03) 762 7743* **Fax** *(03) 762 7733* **Rooms** *4*   **Map** *C5*

Friendly hospitality and great food in a stunning, secluded oceanside setting surrounded by native bush and rainforest. All rooms have balconies and sea views. Home-cooked dinner with advance notice. Good base for Pancake Rocks, Paparoa National Park walks, rafting, caving and dolphin-watching. **www.breakers.co.nz**

GREYMOUTH Rosewood Bed and Breakfast $$$

20 High Street **Tel** *(03) 768 4674, 0800 185 748* **Fax** *(03) 768 4694* **Rooms** *5*   **Map** *C5*

Pleasant, spacious, clean rooms in a tastefully renovated 1920s character home near the town centre, run by a friendly Kiwi-German couple who have recently returned from overseas. Free-range egg breakfasts. Hosts will pick u guests from railway station or bus terminal for free. **www.rosewoodnz.co.nz**

HANMER SPRINGS Drifters Inn $$

2 Harrogate Street **Tel** *(03) 315 7554, 0800 374 383* **Fax** *(03) 315 7235* **Rooms** *20*   **Map** *C5*

Right opposite the thermal pools, this has a cosy shared guest lounge, with TV, VCR and stereo, and blazing log fire in winter. Kitchen and dining facility with paved courtyard and outdoor BBQ area. Great base for skiing, white-water raftin trout and salmon fishing, bungy jumping, hunting, golf, walking and mountain bike trails. **www.driftersinn.co.nz**

Key to Price Guide *see p298* **Key to Symbols** *see back cover flap*

HANMER SPRINGS Forest Peak Motel

4 Torquay Terrace **Tel** *(03) 315 7132, 0508 224 678* **Fax** *(03) 315 7132* **Rooms** *10* **Map** *C5*

Wooden chalets and standard units set in a peaceful garden with children's playground, near forest walks and a short walk from village centre and thermal reserve. The freestanding chalets are a Fraemohs design and offer stunning views, space and privacy, while the standard units are in a block. **www.forestpeak.co.nz**

HANMER SPRINGS Hanmer Springs Scenic Views Motel

10 Amuri Road **Tel** *(03) 315 7419, 0800 843 974* **Fax** *(03) 315 7419* **Rooms** *16* **Map** *C5*

Spacious natural stone studio and two- to three-bedroom suites with underfloor heating and double-glazing to combat the winter chills. Built of natural dry stack stone and native timbers, with crisp, clean interiors. Less than 500m from thermal reserve and village centre. **www.hanmerscenicviews.co.nz**

HOKITIKA Beachfront Hotel

111 Revell Street **Tel** *(03) 755 8344, 0800 400 3461* **Fax** *(03) 755 8258* **Rooms** *23* **Map** *C5*

Owned and operated by the same family for years, the Southland offers a range of facilities on the beachfront. Views of Southern Alps or sea from all rooms. Restaurant serves excellent whitebait in season. Four bars take guests back to gold-mining days. Impressive range of New Zealand wines in the liquor store. **www.beachfronthotel.co.nz**

KARAMEA Karamea Village Hotel

Cnr Waverley Street and Wharf Road **Tel** *(03) 782 6800, 0800 826 800* **Rooms** *13* **Map** *C4*

A lovingly restored old hotel (built 1876) in quiet, remote Karamea, the first stop off the Heaphy Track. Family dining in the main building, and affordable accommodation in nine separate, modern units, three with their own kitchen. Winner of the New Zealand Wildfood Challenge in 2004. **karameahotel@xtra.co.nz**

KARAMEA Last Resort

71 Waverley Street **Tel** *(03) 782 6617, 0800 505 042* **Fax** *(03) 782 6820* **Rooms** *31* **Map** *C4*

From budget shared rooms to first-class self-contained cottages with two bedrooms. Largely hand-built in a cosy wooden style. Warm and friendly atmosphere. Licensed restaurant serves mussels, lamb shanks and its own 'little devil' cake. Also café-bar. Swimming, canoeing, fishing, walking, caving and rafting nearby. **www.lastresort.co.nz**

LAKE TEKAPO Godley Resort Hotel

SH8 **Tel** *(03) 680 6848, 0800 835 276* **Fax** *(03) 680 6873* **Rooms** *80* **Map** *B6*

In the centre of Tekapo village, a short walk from the Church of the Good Shepherd and the memorial to the working dog, with great views over spectacular Lake Tekapo, this is a comfortable hotel, with a wood fire heating the guest lounge in winter, and a swimming pool, gym and spa pool. **www.tekapo.co.nz**

LAKE TEKAPO Lake Tekapo Scenic Resort

SH8 **Tel** *(03) 680 6808, 0800 118 666* **Fax** *(03) 680 6806* **Rooms** *19* **Map** *B6*

This resort has views across stunning Lake Tekapo from its rooms, which open onto balconies or a large reserve. Lake Tekapo Tavern next door has a bistro and bar, and there are more restaurants and shops a short walk away. Lake Tekapo Budget Accommodation (for backpackers) is right there too. **www.laketekapo.com**

LAKE TEKAPO Lake Tekapo Lodge

24 Aorangi Crescent **Tel** *(03) 680 6566, 0800 525 383* **Fax** *(03) 680 6599* **Rooms** *4* **Map** *B6*

Small boutique lodge, purpose-built of adobe earth blocks that keep it warm in winter and cool in summer, which has sweeping views over the lake. Friendly, helpful hosts advise you where to eat, or help you to plan activities in the area during your stay. **www.laketekapolodge.co.nz**

METHVEN Methven Motels and Apartments

197 Main Street **Tel** *(03) 302 9200* **Fax** *(03) 302 9240* **Rooms** *N/A* **Map** *C6*

Offers a range of houses, cottages, apartments and motel units, or can even book you into a farmstay, homestay, lodge or hotel within reach of the Mt Hutt ski area. Options include the brand new Methven Motel, or The Hutt, a cosy cabin in the woods. All well located for outdoor activities. **www.methvenmotels.co.nz**

MOUNT COOK Glentanner Park Centre

Mount Cook **Tel** *(03) 435 1855* **Fax** *(03) 435 1854* **Rooms** *14* **Map** *B6*

The official camp site for the Mount Cook area also offers self-contained cabins and a backpacker hostel. Budget accommodation with great views of Mount Cook National Park. Walking, horse-trekking, heli-skiing, hunting, fishing and flightseeing trips depart from here. By Lake Pukaki, in the middle of a sheep station. **www.glentanner.co.nz**

MOUNT COOK The Hermitage

Mount Cook **Tel** *(03) 435 1809, 0800 686 800* **Fax** *(03) 435 1879* **Rooms** *214* **Map** *B6*

Established in 1884, the sprawling complex underwent a $20m upgrade in 2001, including a brand new accommodation wing. Motel units, chalets and luxurious hotel rooms, many of which have views of Mount Cook. **www.mount-cook.com**

PUNAKAIKI The Rocks Homestay B&B

33 Hartmount Place **Tel** *(03) 731 1141, 0800 272 164* **Rooms** *3* **Map** *C5*

A warm welcome in a superb wilderness setting with 360-degree views of the Tasman Sea, the rugged West Coast coastline, luxuriant Paparoa National Park, and limestone cliffs that rise steeply behind the house. Healthy breakfast and dinner by arrangement in good time; the nearest shops are 100 km (62 miles) away. **www.therockshomestay.com**

PUNAKAIKI Punakaiki Resort 🍴 👪 [$][$][$][$]

SH6 ***Tel*** *(03) 731 1168, 0800 786 2524* ***Fax*** *(03) 731 1163* ***Rooms*** *63* ***Map*** *C5*

Modern, award-winning hotel complex, architecturally designed to harmonise with the environment. Beachfront location, with spectacular views of the wild West Coast and Paparoa National Park rainforest. A short walk from the Pancake Rocks and Blowholes.Eco units feature energy efficient design and materials. **www.punakaiki-resort.co.n**

RAKAIA GORGE Terrace Downs 👪 [$][$][$][$][$]

Coleridge Road ***Tel*** *(03) 318 6943* ***Fax*** *(03) 317 9372* ***Rooms*** *130* ***Map*** *C6*

Luxury lodge and golfing resort in a beautiful high-country location, offering a choice of self-contained Fairway Chalets, with direct access to the fairway, and Terrace Villa Suites, with balcony views over the golf course to the Southern Alps. Restaurant with views. Guests get first refusal for the golf tee-times. **www.terracedowns.co.nz**

REEFTON Wilson's Hotel 🍴 👪 [$]

32 Broadway ***Tel*** *(03) 732 8800, 0800 468 351* ***Fax*** *(03) 732 8221* ***Rooms*** *7* ***Map*** *C5*

A warm, inviting hotel built in 1873 which is a relic of the gold-mining era in Reefton. A range of café-style food, including vegetarian, is served all day, accompanied by six beers on tap. Restaurant open seven days a week. There is a beer garden and often live music which can go on until late. **wilsons_hotel@hotmail.com**

TIMARU Grosvenor Hotel 🍴 👪 [$]

26 Cairns Terrace ***Tel*** *(03) 688 3129, 0800 106 102* ***Fax*** *(03) 684 8381* ***Rooms*** *48* ***Map*** *C6*

A grand hotel dating back to 1875, located in the commercial centre of Timaru, close to the waterfront and main shopping area. Known as the "Grand Old Lady of the South", the historic Grosvenor has ornate styling dating back to its 19th-century origins. Two bars and restaurants, one in cellar. **www.grosvenorhotel.co.nz**

TWIZEL Mountain Chalet Motels 👪 [$][$]

Wairepo Road ***Tel*** *(03) 435 0785, 0800 629 999* ***Fax*** *(03) 435 0551* ***Rooms*** *25* ***Map*** *B6*

A-frame chalets in a park-like setting with mountain views. In the heart of Mackenzie Country, halfway between Christchurch and Queenstown, and only 40 minutes' drive from Mount Cook. This is a great base for exploring the high country scenery, and nearby watersports. **www.mountainchalets.co.nz**

WESTPORT Westport Holiday Park and Motels 👪 [$]

31–37 Domett Street ***Tel*** *(03) 789 7043* ***Fax*** *(03) 789 7199* ***Rooms*** *25* ***Map*** *C5*

This family-friendly holiday park in the traditional Kiwi mould is an appropriate place to stay in a town keen to cash in on its authentic New Zealand image. Classic A-frame chalets with private decks in native bush, as well as motel-style units, apartments and bunkrooms. Children's playground and BBQ area. **www.westportholidaypark.co.nz**

OTAGO AND SOUTHLAND

BLUFF Foveaux Hotel 🍴 👪 [$]

40 Gore Street ***Tel*** *(03) 212 7196* ***Fax*** *(03) 212 7197* ***Rooms*** *7* ***Map*** *A7*

Historic building two minutes' walk from the ferry, this unique Art Deco hotel has been lovingly maintained in as near as possible original condition, with 1930s-style furniture, and offers cosy B&B accommodation. By the open fire is perfect place to snuggle up after over-indulging in Bluff oysters. **www.foveauxhotel.com**

CROMWELL Golden Gate Lodge 🍴 👪 [$]

Barry Avenue ***Tel*** *(03) 445 1777, 0800 104 451* ***Fax*** *(03) 445 1776* ***Rooms*** *47* ***Map*** *B7*

Well-appointed hotel, restaurant and conference complex in a central location midway between Wanaka and Queenstown. Great base from which to explore both areas, and enjoy the activities they have to offer, yet be away from the crowded streets and high prices of Queenstown itself. **www.goldengate.co.nz**

DUNEDIN Leviathan Heritage Hotel 🍴 [$][$]

27 Queens Gardens ***Tel*** *(03) 477 3160, 0800 773 773* ***Fax*** *(03) 477 2385* ***Rooms*** *80* ***Map*** *B7*

Cheap hotel and hostel not far from city centre. It is about 500m from The Octagon and 200m from the railway station. Courtesy coach to and from the intercity bus station. Pick-up and drop-off point for regional wildlife and sightseeing tours. Suitable for all budget travellers, from backpackers to families. **www.dunedinhotel.co.nz**

DUNEDIN Motel on York 👪 [$][$]

47 York Place ***Tel*** *(03) 477 6120, 0800 006 666* ***Fax*** *(03) 477 6122* ***Rooms*** *23* ***Map*** *B7*

Fairly new, five-star motel, close to city centre, with a range of suites and rooms from studios with or without balcony or terrace garden to one-bedroom suites which can interconnect to create larger family or group apartments. Many rooms boast underfloor heating and spa tubs in the bathroom. **www.motelonyork.co.nz**

DUNEDIN 97 Motel Moray Place 👪 [$][$]

97 Moray Place ***Tel*** *(03) 477 2050, 0800 909 797* ***Fax*** *(03) 477 1991* ***Rooms*** *40* ***Map*** *B7*

Good-value motel one block away from The Octagon, with famously comfortable beds. Close to St Paul's Cathedral, the Municipal Chambers, Dunedin Public Art Gallery and other city centre attractions, shops, theatres and restaurants – indeed, it claims there are over 50 eateries within five minutes' walk. **www.97motel.co.nz**

Key to Price Guide *see p298* **Key to Symbols** *see back cover flap*

DUNEDIN Pacific Park Hotel

↟ **$$**

22–23 Wallace Street **Tel** *(03) 477 3374, 0800 730 400* **Fax** *(03) 477 1434* **Rooms** *26* **Map** *B7*

On the edge of Dunedin's green belt, with great views over the city and harbour. Hotel rooms or motel units set in spacious gardens. Deluxe suites have spa baths. Kitchen facilities in most rooms. Room service, laundry room and tennis court. Brasserie and bar. Some rooms accommodate students in term time. **www.pacificparkdunedin.co.nz**

DUNEDIN Scenic Circle Southern Cross Hotel

↟ **$$$**

cnr Princes and High streets **Tel** *(03) 477 0752* **Fax** *(03) 477 5776* **Rooms** *178* **Map** *B7*

Dunedin's largest hotel, in the heart of the city, the Scenic Circle dates back to 1883, and has been fully modernized to 21st-century standards of comfort, with two restaurants, a bar, a café and a casino. A short walk to The Octagon, railway station, theatres, shops and Otago University. Good off-peak deals. **www.scenic-circle.co.nz**

DUNEDIN Corstorphine House

↟ **$$$$$**

Milburn Street, Caversham **Tel** *(03) 487 1000* **Fax** *(03) 487 6672* **Rooms** *8* **Map** *B7*

Grand home dating back to 1863 and beautifully restored as a boutique hotel, it is located in the heart of the city, surrounded by a 12-acre estate. Rooms are individually decorated, to themes such as Scandinavian, Indian and Art Deco, using rich textiles, antiques and a mix of subdued, vivid and warm colours. **www.corstorphine.co.nz**

GORE Scenic Circle Croydon Hotel

↟ **$$$**

Gore–Queenstown Highway **Tel** *(03) 208 9029* **Fax** *(03) 208 9252* **Rooms** *36* **Map** *B7*

In the heart of Southland, set in 13 acres of grounds which look towards the rolling Hokonui Hills. Nine-hole golf course with complimentary green fees for guests. Good base for brown trout fishing, Hokonui Pioneer Park and the Croydon Aircraft Company. Surrounded by bush, farmland, rivers, mountains and a lake. **www.scenic-circle.co.nz**

INVERCARGILL Queens Park Motels

↟ **$**

5 Alice Street **Tel** *(03) 214 4504, 0800 800 504* **Fax** *(03) 214 4503* **Rooms** *14* **Map** *B7*

In a tranquil setting off the road, this four-star motel is adjacent to Queens Park. A short walk through the park's rose gardens brings you to the city centre. Spacious, clean and tidy studio, one- and two-bedroom units in manicured grounds. Restaurants with chargeback facilities. **www.queensparkmotels.co.nz**

INVERCARGILL Victoria Railway Hotel

↟ **$$**

3 Leven Street **Tel** *(03) 218 1281, 0800 777 557* **Fax** *(03) 218 1283* **Rooms** *22* **Map** *B7*

Invercargill's Victorian railway hotel has had a complete upgrade, and now offers charming boutique accommodation in the centre of the city, near museums, parks and art galleries, the historic buildings of Dee and Tay streets. Comfortable rooms in a NZ Historic Places Trust building, with bar and restaurant. **www.hotelinvercargill.com**

MANAPOURI Murrell's Grand View House

$$$$$

Murrel Avenue **Tel** *(03) 249 6642* **Fax** *(03) 249 6966* **Rooms** *4* **Map** *A7*

In the Murrell family since 1860, when young Bob Murrell followed in his father's footsteps over the pass that old Bob had discovered from Lake Manapouri to Doubtful Sound, and built the guesthouse. The house has old Colonial furnishings and is set in spacious lawns and cottage gardens. There is a no children policy. **www.murrells.co.nz**

MILFORD AND DOUBTFUL SOUNDS Overnight Cruises

↟ **$$$$$**

Real Journeys, Lakefront Drive, Te Anau (for bookings) **Tel** *(03) 249 7416, 0800 656 501* **Rooms** *26* **Map** *A6*

The classy way to overnight in Fiordland is on a boat on Doubtful or Milford Sound. Cruises meander around hidden inlets before dropping anchor for the night. Choice of private, ensuite cabins or shared bunk rooms. Buffet-style dinner is served after sunset. Fur seals and bottlenose dolphins are often seen. **www.realjourneys.co.nz**

MILFORD SOUND Milford Sound Lodge

$

SH94 **Tel** *(03) 249 8071* **Fax** *(03) 249 8075* **Rooms** *16* **Map** *A6*

Possibly the best located hostel in the world, nestled in the ancient beech forest on the banks of the Cleddau River. One of only two places to overnight on Milford Sound, enjoying its tranquillity once the day trippers have left. A great base for walks, boat cruises and sea kayaking. **www.milfordlodge.com**

MOERAKI Moeraki Village Holiday Park

↟ **$**

114 Haven Street **Tel** *(03) 439 4759* **Rooms** *12* **Map** *B7*

This park is in the middle of Moeraki fishing village, just off SH1, 30 minutes' drive from Oamaru. It consists of five motels, three flats and three cabins. Two luxury motel units with spa baths have been added. It is only a short walk to a restaurant and a tavern. The owners speak German and Swiss German. **www.moerakivillageholidaypark.co.nz**

OAMARU Kingsgate Hotel Brydone

↟ **$$**

115 Thames Street **Tel** *(03) 434 0011* **Fax** *(03) 434 0010* **Rooms** *49* **Map** *B7*

The hotel was built of Oamaru stone in 1881. In the commercial district of Oamaru, it is close to historic buildings such as the Forrester Gallery, Courthouse and Waitaki District Council, the Blue Penguin Colony and Public Gardens. Attractive public areas, including a Victorian lantern glass bar, and comfortable rooms. **www.kingsgatehotels.co.nz**

OAMARU Tokarahi Homestead

$$$$

7 Dip Hill Road, Tokarahi **Tel** *(03) 431 2055* **Fax** *(03) 431 2551* **Rooms** *4* **Map** *B7*

Thirty-five minutes' drive inland from Oamaru, this exceptional homestead is well worth the detour. The unusual limestone house was built in 1878 by a wool baron, and its impressive front entrance hall and reception rooms added as a wedding present a few years later. Restored in Victorian style. Candlelit dining. **www.homestead.co.nz**

OAMARU Pen-y-bryn
11 $$$$$

41 Towey Street **Tel** *(03) 434 7939* **Fax** *(03) 434 9063* **Rooms** *5*   **Map** *B7*

Award-winning luxury heritage boutique lodge. An 1889 house featuring a billiard room, library and antiques. First-class cuisine using organic local produce, accompanied by New Zealand wines. Crisp, simple, charming country-style rooms. Tariff includes drinks, dinner and breakfast. **www.penybryn.co.nz**

OTAGO PENINSULA Larnach Lodge and Stablestay
11 ⅋ $$$

145 Camp Road **Tel** *(03) 476 1616* **Fax** *(03) 476 1574* **Rooms** *18*   **Map** *B7*

In the grounds of Larnach Castle, restored by the Barker family from a ruin since 1967, guests stay in a re-creation of a colonial farm building, with individually themed rooms, or in the converted stables. Lodge rooms have harbour views, while the stablestay is cheaper. **www.larnachcastle.co.nz**

QUEENSTOWN Discovery Lodge
11 $

49 Shotover Street **Tel** *(03) 441 1185, 0800 227 369* **Fax** *(03) 441 1187* **Rooms** *22*   **Map** *A6*

Backpacker accommodation in the heart of Queenstown, right on the main street near bars and restaurants. Funky café and groovy bar, as well as spacious lounge with open fire. Most rooms have balconies with lake or mountain views. Double, twin and shared rooms with clean, modern, white-tiled bathrooms. **www.dlq.co.nz**

QUEENSTOWN Alexis Motor Lodge & Apartments
⅋ $$

69 Frankton Road **Tel** *(03) 409 0052* **Fax** *(03) 409 0054* **Rooms** *16*   **Map** *A6*

All of the motel units are designed to take advantage of wonderful views of the Remarkable Mountains and Lake Wakatipu. Breakfast is delivered to your room, where it can be enjoyed on sunny lake-view patios. Five minutes' walk from central Queenstown. Secure ski storage and drying room. **www.alexisqueenstown.co.nz**

QUEENSTOWN Blue Peaks Lodge
⅋ $$

Cnr Stanley and Sydney streets **Tel** *(03) 442 9224, 0800 162 122* **Fax** *(03) 442 6847* **Rooms** *60*   **Map** *A6*

Nestled on a rise overlooking Queenstown, the motel is conveniently located five minutes' walk from the town centre, and close to Skyline gondola, jet boating, bungy jumping, parapenting, shopping, rafting, horse treks and walking tracks. Hexagonal design and blue peaked roof make it easy to find your way back to. **www.bluepeaks.co.n**

QUEENSTOWN Garden Court Suites and Apartments
⅋ $$$

41 Frankton Road **Tel** *(03) 442 9713, 0800 427 336* **Fax** *(03) 442 6468* **Rooms** *54*   **Map** *A6*

A choice of 54 suites or apartments in all shapes and sizes for families, groups or solo travellers. Rooms open onto balconies or private courtyard, and the more upmarket ones have solid oak furniture. Breakfast restaurant overlooks central garden court. Bar and spa. Skiing and outdoor activity planning is also on offer. **www.gardencourt.co.nz**

QUEENSTOWN Scenic Circle A-Line Hotel
11 ⅋ $$$$

27 Stanley Street **Tel** *(03) 442 7700* **Fax** *(03) 442 4715* **Rooms** *81*   **Map** *A6*

Refurbished Swiss-style 'chalet' in the hills, perched above the town centre. Close to the action, yet elevated enough to take advantage of spectacular views over Lake Wakatipu to the mountains. A-frame architecture helps create a traditional alpine atmosphere. Spa, sauna and bar. Linked to Scenic Circle Aurum Suites. **www.scenic-circle.co.nz**

QUEENSTOWN Villa del Lago
⅋ $$$$

249 Frankton Road **Tel** *(03) 442 5727, 0800 845 523* **Fax** *(03) 442 9498* **Rooms** *16*   **Map** *A6*

Five-star luxury one-, two- and three-bedroom apartments on the lakefront, with winter comforts such as gas log fires, double glazing and underfloor heating in bathrooms, and private terraces for summer. A few minutes' drive or an easy stroll along the Frankton Walkway to centre for shops, restaurants, bars and nightlife. **www.villadellago.co.nz**

QUEENSTOWN Heritage Hotel Queenstown
⌗⌧⌸⅋⌶ $$$$$

91 Fernhill Road **Tel** *(03) 442 4988, 0800 368 888* **Fax** *(03) 442 4989* **Rooms** *182*   **Map** *A6*

Award-winning, sophisticated European-style resort hotel overlooking Queenstown, situated above Lake Wakatipu with views of the Remarkables. Warm atmosphere, stone and cedar construction. A 10-minute walk along the lakefront to the town centre. **www.heritagehotels.co.nz**

STEWART ISLAND Bay Motel
⅋ $$$

9 Dundee Street, Halfmoon Bay **Tel** *(03) 219 1119* **Rooms** *12*   **Map** *A7*

Comfortable motel close to Rakiura National Park, with nine studio units, a one-bedroom unit and a popular two-bedroom family unit. Ten of the units have views over Halfmoon Bay. The Honeymoon Suite with spa bath has the best view and is quite private. Courtesy transfer to ferry or plane terminal. **www.baymotel.co.nz**

STEWART ISLAND Greenvale Bed & Breakfast
⅋ $$$$

Halfmoon Bay **Tel** *(03) 219 1357* **Rooms** *2*   **Map** *A7*

Five minutes' from Oban centre, with views of Foveaux Strait, Greenvale B&B is on the site of an original 1886 two-storey boarding house destroyed by fire in 1942. A hospitable base from which to explore the island's lush rainforest sweeping sand dunes and wetlands, home to native birds and mollymawks. **www.greenvalestewartisland.com**

STEWART ISLAND Stewart Island Lodge
11 $$$$$

Halfmoon Bay **Tel** *(03) 219 1085* **Rooms** *5*   **Map** *A7*

Luxurious lodge set in native bush overlooking Halfmoon Bay. Hear the rare native birds singing, and watch them from the terrace. Hosts Doug and Margaret will prepare you a gourmet meal using fresh local seafood and produce from their own herb garden and glasshouse, accompanied by fine New Zealand wines. **www.stewartislandlodge.co.nz**

Key to Price Guide *see p298* **Key to Symbols** *see back cover flap*

TE ANAU Te Anau Lakefront Backpackers

48–50 Lakefront Drive **Tel** *(03) 249 7713* **Fax** *(03) 249 8319* **Rooms** *14*

Map *A7*

Hostel on the lakefront, with plenty of communal spaces, including kitchen and dining area, TV and TV-free lounges with piano, guitar and log fire. Dorms and doubles, some ensuite. Can help with walking track planning, including going through your pack with you to check you have all essentials. **www.teanaubackpackers.co.nz**

TE ANAU Lakefront Lodge Te Anau

Cnr Lakefront Drive and Mokoroa Street **Tel** *(03) 249 7728* **Fax** *(03) 249 7124* **Rooms** *13*

Map *A7*

Upmarket modern motel on the lakefront, two minutes' walk to the small town centre for restaurants and cafés. Set in a charming cottage garden. Agent for Te Anau & Fiordland Sightseeing Trips and Tours so can advise on Fiordland activities. Clean, comfortable, tastefully decorated units with sound proofing. **www.lakefrontlodgeteanau.com**

TE ANAU Te Anau Top 10 Holiday Park

Te Anau Terrace **Tel** *(03) 249 7462, 0800 249 746* **Fax** *(03) 249 7262* **Rooms** *35*

Map *A7*

A five-star, NZ Tourism award-winning holiday park, by the lake and two minutes' walk from town. Luxurious lodge rooms, as well as cheaper self-contained motel units and tent sites. Matai Lodge has been designed to resemble the Milford Track lodges. Communal bathrooms have underfloor heating. **www.teanautop10.co.nz**

TE ANAU Kingsgate Hotel

20 Lakefront Drive **Tel** *(03) 249 7421* **Fax** *(03) 249 8037* **Rooms** *94*

Map *A7*

Spacious rooms, many with lake and mountain views, set amid manicured gardens on the lakeside. It's a pleasant 10-minute walk along the lakefront to town, information and main tourist departure points. Reasonably priced dinners and breakfasts make this a flexible option. **www.millenniumhotels.com**

TE ANAU Luxmore Hotel

Main Street **Tel** *(03) 249 7526, 0800 589 667* **Fax** *(03) 249 7272* **Rooms** *180*

Map *A7*

Comfortable, modern hotel in a carbuncular building with good facilities in the heart of Te Anau. Adjacent to main tourist departure points (several tour operators are based in the hotel). Bar and restaurant cater to all needs. **www.luxmorehotel.co.nz**

TE ANAU Te Anau Lodge

52 Howden Street **Tel** *(03) 249 7477* **Fax** *(03) 249 7487* **Rooms** *8*

Map *A7*

A former convent, which was shifted in 2003 from its original (1936) site in the mining village of Nightcaps. Breakfast made from home-grown ingredients is now served in the chapel. The restored interior and guest rooms are panelled in rimu, and furnished in a variety of native timbers. Mountain views. **www.teanaulodge.com**

WANAKA Cardrona Hotel

Crown Range Road **Tel** *(03) 443 8153, 0800 443 599* **Fax** *(03) 443 8163* **Rooms** *16*

Map *A7*

Gold-rush period hotel dating back to 1863, between Queenstown and Wanaka. Quaint restaurant and bar. Simple, stylishly decorated rooms enjoy cottage garden views. A spa is available for guest use. Close to five major ski areas. Transport to ski fields can be arranged. Drying room for gear. **www.cardronahotel.co.nz**

WANAKA Heritage Village Country Resort

Orchard Road **Tel** *(03) 443 5300* **Fax** *(03) 443 5307* **Rooms** *20*

Map *A7*

Ideal for longer family stays, in spacious grounds a few minutes' drive from Wanaka. Alpine-style wooden cottages and houses, decorated in comfortable taste for all seasons, with open gas fires, undertile heating and French windows opening onto private courtyards. Café, restaurant, spa and sandpit. **www.heritagevillage-wanaka.co.nz**

WANAKA Mount Aspiring Hotel

Lake Wanaka **Tel** *(03) 443 8216, 0800 688 688* **Fax** *(03) 443 9108* **Rooms** *48*

Map *B6*

Family-owned hotel, a short stroll from the lakeshore and Wanaka's Millennium Walkway, and 2 km (1.25 miles) from the heart of the village. Wood and stone Lockwood construction, with peaceful mountain outlook on tree-lined avenue. Restaurant serves Pacific Rim delicacies. **www.wanakanz.com**

WANAKA Te Wanaka Lodge

23 Brownston Street **Tel** *(03) 443 9224* **Fax** *(03) 443 9246* **Rooms** *13*

Map *A7*

Winter ski lodge and summer B&B hotel in Wanaka village, owned and operated by young outdoors enthusiasts. Fun and friendly place to stay, with a warm, alpine atmosphere. Library, outdoor spa and courtyard warmed by braziers. Located in the centre of the village, close to the lake, restaurants, shops and golf course. **www.tewanaka.co.nz**

WANAKA The Moorings

17 Lakeside Road **Tel** *(03) 443 8479, 0800 843 666* **Fax** *(03) 443 8489* **Rooms** *14*

Map *A7*

Self-contained studios with views of Lake Wanaka and the snow-capped mountains of Mount Aspiring National Park. An easy stroll from Wanaka's shops, restaurants and cafés, and 45 minutes' drive from the Cardrona and Treble Cone ski fields. Underfloor heating and ski drying room for winter, lakefront balconies for summer. **www.themoorings.co.nz**

WANAKA Edgewater Resort

Sargood Drive **Tel** *(03) 443 8311, 0800 108 311* **Fax** *(03) 443 8323* **Rooms** *106*

Map *A7*

Resort-style accommodation in sumptuous hotel rooms and fully appointed apartments. Sprawling lakeside complex with spa, sauna and tennis courts. Glorious views of lake and mountains. Excellent base for adventures roundabout. Award-winning restaurant serves seasonal New Zealand produce and NZ wines. **www.edgewater.co.nz**

WHERE TO EAT

New Zealand's restaurants and cuisine have both undergone a revolution in the past 30 years. Whereas eating in restaurants was once reserved for special occasions and usually included a traditional European meal, such as roast lamb and vegetables, New Zealand now has a wide variety of eating places to suit all tastes and all budgets. Although plainer fare is still available, the country's multicultural population has meant that restaurants serving traditional food sit alongside those offering cuisine from

Café sign, Martinborough

almost every corner of the world, especially in the larger towns. Influences from Asia and the Pacific have been particularly significant. New Zealand restaurants make good use of home-grown produce such as fresh fish, oysters, mussels, crayfish (rock lobsters), beef, lamb and venison, as well as vegetables and fruit. These can all be enjoyed with a glass of New Zealand wine *(see pp324–5)*. A popular tourist experience is a Maori hangi, where food is wrapped and cooked on heated rocks under the ground.

The lounge bar at Herzog restaurant in Blenheim *(see p337)*

TYPES OF RESTAURANTS

New Zealand's major cities have a vibrant restaurant scene ranging from formal dining to a multitude of casual cafés. Diners can experience haute cuisine or eat in a café offering cheaper, simpler food. Some eateries feature courtyard, garden or pavement seating. There is every type of ethnic restaurant imaginable, offering the cuisines of every continent, such as Chinese, Cambodian, Malaysian, Turkish and Greek. Some high-quality restaurants can be found in provincial and rural areas. Many vineyard restaurants serve ploughman's lunches with seating among the vines as well as more formal meals in picturesque restaurant settings. Pubs also offer food which can range

from cheap and basic fare to more sophisticated, restaurant-quality dishes. A typical and extremely popular pub meal is a roast.

A meal in a café or ethnic restaurant can cost as little as NZ$15 for a one-course meal. Restaurant prices range from NZ$25 to more than NZ$100 per person for a three-course meal. A range of fast-food chains, such as McDonalds, KFC and Burger King, have franchises in New Zealand, and there are the traditional, local fish and chip shops.

EATING HOURS AND RESERVATIONS

Many restaurants serve lunch from noon to 2pm and dinner from 6 to 10pm. Establishments may open earlier on the weekend for brunch. Some cafés are open

for breakfast and close later than restaurants, although those serving office and business workers close around 4pm. Late-night and 24-hour cafés are gaining in popularity.

Bookings are usually necessary at more formal restaurants. Cafés and bars vary in their booking policies, with some taking reservations and others operating on a casual basis. It pays to ring and check booking policies to avoid disappointment.

PAYING AND TIPPING

The majority of restaurants and cafés accept credit cards, though it is a good idea to check when booking. Most restaurants will not accept personal cheques or traveller's cheques. Government taxes are included in the menu prices and there are no service charges. New Zealand's egalitarian society

Chef preparing a seafood buffet at an Auckland hotel

Tables outside a café at Mount Maunganui

means tipping is not compulsory, although a tip will be appreciated for very good service and a quality meal. Patrons can leave tips in cash on the table or include them in credit card payments.

CHILDREN

Most restaurants cater for children. If travelling with very young children, it is best to check with the restaurant to ensure that children are welcome. An option in busy cafés is to book early before large numbers of adult diners arrive. Chinese, Greek and other ethnic restaurants tend to have more relaxed attitudes towards children. Fast-food chains can be found in most cities and towns, and children usually enjoy a takeaway meal at the park or beach. Families staying in motels with equipped kitchens may find that a trip to a local supermarket provides a break from having to take small children to eat out in restaurants.

WHEELCHAIR ACCESS

Government regulations require building owners to ensure that new and re-developed buildings are accessible by wheelchair. Facilities that comply with the code display an international symbol. Most restaurants also now provide toilet facilities for the disabled. However, as in most countries, it is wise to phone ahead to ensure facilities are accessible.

VEGETARIANS

Tourist offices should be able to provide details about vegetarian restaurants which are sprinkled throughout the cities and main towns, including resort areas. Many restaurants offer some vegetarian meals and will usually be happy to adapt menus, especially in areas where there is an abundance of home-grown produce. Most Asian restaurants also offer vegetarian food on their menus.

Vineyard café sign

ALCOHOL AND OTHER DRINKS

Licensed restaurants and bars serve a range of alcohol, including wine, beer and spirits. Most cafés are also fully licensed but may offer a more limited range of alcohol. Many restaurants and cafés highlight New Zealand wines and boutique beers. Restaurants in wine-growing areas usually specialize in wine from that region. BYO restaurants offer diners the opportunity to bring the wines they wish to drink with their meal. Tap water is safe everywhere. Bottled still or sparkling water and fresh fruit juices are also popular.

DRESS

Dress is informal compared to many other parts of the world. It is unlikely that a jacket or tie will be needed, although visitors may feel more comfortable formally dressed at the up-market restaurants. Informal but tidy dress is appreciated at less formal restaurants. Street fashion is the rule at most inner-city cafés.

SMOKING

Along with most other indoor workplaces, restaurants became smoke-free by law at the end of 2004. The ban does not apply to outdoor dining areas, and where possible, restaurateurs make every effort to satisfy a customer's requirements. It is a good idea to enquire about smoking arrangements when booking.

The Astoria at Lambton Quay, Wellington

BYO RESTAURANTS

BYO means to "bring your own" alcohol. Instead of a full liquor licence, restaurants may have a BYO licence that allows diners to bring their own alcohol. This is cheaper than purchasing alcohol on the premises, although a small fee may be charged for corkage. It is usual to bring bottled wine to a BYO restaurant, and acceptable to take along a few bottles of beer to a curry restaurant. Some fully licensed restaurants do allow diners to bring their own wine, but it is recommended to check when booking.

The Flavours of New Zealand

Cuisine in New Zealand is most likely to be characterized by its freshness and diversity and, as a relatively youthful nation, there is a willingness to experiment with food and flavours. Surrounded by clean ocean and with extremely fertile land, New Zealand offers food of the very highest standards, and many of its producers are certified organic, reinforcing its clean, green image. New Zealand's cuisine has been described as Pacific Rim, drawing inspiration from Europe, Asia, Polynesia and its indigenous people, the Maori. Chefs hailing from New Zealand are among the most sought-after in the world, due to their contemporary approach and passion for good ingredients.

Avocado oil

Flock of New Zealand's superb, pasture-fed sheep

MEAT

There are over 40 million sheep in New Zealand, all bred on natural, free-range pastureland. New Zealand lamb is world-famous and features on menus. It appears in a wide variety of dishes, ranging from a traditional rack of lamb to a Moroccan-style lamb tagine – and you can always expect to see more than a few chops on a barbecue. For a change from lamb, there are plenty of other meats available, such as beef, pork, chicken and cervena, which is a lighter, leaner style of farmed venison.

FISH & SEAFOOD

New Zealand has a plentiful supply of seafood, with many local varieties – in particular blue cod from the South Island and the Chatham Islands, oysters from Bluff, Southland, and the amazing green lip mussels of Havelock, Marlborough Sounds. Snapper, *tarakihi* and *hapuku* (the Maori name for grouper) are the most common saltwater fish. There is also wonderful farmed salmon (wild salmon cannot be sold commercially). Other popular fish include,

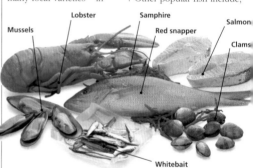

Lobster   Samphire   Salmon

Mussels   Red snapper   Clams

Whitebait

Selection of seafood found in the waters of New Zealand

NEW ZEALAND'S VARIED CUISINE

Cuisine in New Zealand is very diverse. Fine dining often has a French influence with a modern edge, and you will also find great bistros serving classics such as *boeuf bourginonne* and *tarte au citron*.

Cafés in New Zealand tend to have a more relaxed, Mediterranean approach. Most pubs serve a wide range of dishes, such as fish, salads, steaks and, of course, roast meats. There are increasing numbers of pubs serving restaurant-quality food. New Zealand is part of the Asia-Pacific region, and there is a vibrant Asian flavour to be found in

Manuka honey

many dishes. Look out for whitebait fritters on the West Coast from August to September, when the season is at its peak. Eating at one of the many wonderful vineyard restaurants is highly recommended, as is the chance to sample a genuine Maori *hangi*.

Kumara soup *Made with the native sweet potato, this soup is especially delicous topped with goat's cheese croutons.*

Basket of yams in a local farmers' market

John Dory, monkfish and blue warehau. As for shellfish, New Zealand has a native clam called *tuatua* and abalone called *paua*. Oysters, mussels and crayfish are also widely found.

Upmarket fish and chips, best enjoyed outdoors by the sea

FRUIT & VEGETABLES

The almost perfect farming conditions in New Zealand mean that the enormous variety of produce cultivated is of a consistently high quality. All common vegetables are farmed here, alongside some native varieties. Kumara is a local sweet potato, and a traditional Maori food. They are often baked in their jackets, and also boiled, roasted, fried or scalloped (sliced, seasoned, and slowly cooked in milk). Other common root vegetables are parsnips and yams. The tamarillo (tree tomato), kiwi fruit and feijoa are all local fruits. During harvest time, look out for roadside stalls near farms, selling fresh vegetables and fruit cheaply. Honey from the native

Manuka plant is popular worldwide for its woody, earthy aromas and supposed medicinal properties. Also gaining fame around the globe is the delicious and decadent avocado oil from the North Island.

DAIRY PRODUCE

The conditions in New Zealand are perfect for dairy farming. Wonderful cheeses, yoghurt and ice cream, made by small producers can be found all over the country. Hokey-pokey ice cream is a New Zealand speciality – delicious vanilla ice cream loaded with caramel chunks.

MAORI FOOD

New Zealand's abundant supply of food is explained in Maori legend as a gift from the gods. From Tane, god of the forest, come the game birds, from Tangaroa seafood, from Haumia wild plants, and from Rongo cultivated vegetables.

The main traditional method for feasting is the *hangi* (pronounced hung-ee). Men heat stones in a fire and dig an earth pit, while women prepare the meat and vegetables. The stones are placed in the pit with the food (covered in cloth), and earth is piled back into the pit. The food cooks slowly for up to four hours. The results of this laborious process are worth the wait – succulent, tender meat and smoky, delicious vegetables.

Pan fried hapuka *Roasted shallots, pancetta and rocket give this popular fish a Mediterranean flavour.*

Grilled lamb *Simple, fresh flavours, such as polenta and red pepper sauce, complement this superb meat.*

Pavlova *Aussies and Kiwis disagree over who invented this delicious meringue, cream and fruit dessert.*

What to Drink in New Zealand

Corbans Noble Riesling label

New Zealanders were until the 1960s a nation of beer drinkers and wine consumption was not that common. However, the meteoric rise of New Zealand's wine industry, which has scooped many international awards, means wine has enjoyed a dramatic rise in popularity over the last 40 years. New Zealand's temperate maritime climate is ideal for maximizing grape ripeness and the production of premium, intensely flavoured wines. There are about 300 wineries throughout the country, many near the coast (*see pp36–7*). In-depth guides on wines, vineyards and vineyard restaurants are available at larger book shops or can be found at www.nzwine.com.

Wine tasting at C J Pask Winery, Hastings (see pp150–51)

WHITE WINE

Huia Sauvignon Blanc

Palliser Sauvignon Blanc

Chardonnay and Sauvignon Blanc are regarded as New Zealand's most outstanding white wines, with critics naming New Zealand Sauvignon Blanc as the world's finest. New Zealand's white wines, produced by both modern and traditional methods, are known for their fruit flavours. There is also a fascinating range of Chardonnays to choose from: cheaper Chardonnays fermented in stainless steel tanks and bottled young to more expensive Chardonnays fermented and aged in oak barrels. Riesling is growing in popularity, with New Zealand Riesling often described as similar to the light and elegant German style. Pinot Gris is also increasingly popular.

SWEET WHITE WINE

New Zealand sweet wines are also winning international recognition and awards. The most interesting of these sweet wines are made from botrytis-affected grapes, with the Marlborough region emerging as a leading producer of the finest wines (*see pp206–7*). However, the weather conditions needed to produce botrytis-type wines occur irregularly in New Zealand, and therefore prices for these luscious dessert wines tend to be somewhat higher than other wine varieties.

Cave cellar at Gibbston Valley Wines (see p278)

WINE TYPE	REGIONS	RECOMMENDED PRODUCERS
Chardonnay	All key wine regions	Church Road, Clearview, Cloudy Bay, Corbans, Hunters, Morton Estate Wines, Vavasour
Chenin Blanc	Gisborne, Hawke's Bay	Collard Brothers, The Millton Vineyard
Gewürztraminer	Central Otago, Gisborne, Hawke's Bay, Marlborough	Brookfields, Chifney Wines, Dry River, Eskdale, Gatehouse, Lawson's Dry Hills, Stonecroft
Muller-Thurgau	Gisborne, Hawke's Bay, Marlborough	Corbans Gisborne Winery, Pleasant Valley Wines, Vidal of Hawke's Bay, Villa Maria
Pinot Gris	Canterbury, Marlborough	Brookfields, Dry River, Margrain, Martinborough Vineyard
Riesling	Canterbury, Central Otago, Hawke's Bay, Marlborough, Nelson, Wairarapa	Allan Scott Wines and Estates, Collards, Cooper's Creek, Corbans, Framingham Wine Company, Grove Mill, Martinborough Vineyard, Neudorf, Stoneleigh
Sauvignon Blanc	Canterbury, Gisborne, Hawke's Bay, Marlborough	Cloudy Bay, Grove Mill, Hunters, Jackson Estate, Nautilus, Palliser, Selaks, Villa Maria
Sémillon	Gisborne, Hawke's Bay, Marlborough	Collards, Huntaway, Kim Crawford, Pleasant Valley, Vidal of Hawke's Bay
Sweet wines	Central Otago, Gisborne, Hawke's Bay, Marlborough	Church Road, Cooper's Creek, Cottage Block, Dry River, Framingham Wine Company, Villa Maria

SPARKLING WINE

New Zealand sparkling wines are world class and have won a number of awards. Deutz Marlborough Cuvée was voted "Sparkling Wine of the Year" in the Great Wine Challenge held in Britain in 1998 and has been awarded numerous medals since. Visitors should be aware that there are two types of sparkling wine. At the bottom end of the market, "bubblies" are carbonated wines and tend to be rather sweet. However, the middle and top ends of the market feature *méthode traditionnelle* labels made by bottle fermentation methods. Marlborough is regarded as the country's top region for bottle-fermented *méthode traditionnelle*, although other regions in the country are now also gaining a reputation for producing high quality products.

Huia Marlborough Brut

WINE REGIONS OF NEW ZEALAND	
Auckland	Cabernet Sauvignon, Chardonnay, Merlot, Pinot Noir
Northland	Cabernet Sauvignon, Chardonnay, Merlot
Waikato and Bay of Plenty	Cabernet Sauvignon, Chardonnay, Chenin Blanc, Sauvignon Blanc
Gisborne	Chardonnay, Muller-Thurgau, Muscat, Sémillon
Hawke's Bay	Cabernet, Chardonnay, Chenin Blanc, Merlot, Sauvignon Blanc, Sémillon
Wairarapa	Chardonnay, Pinot Noir, Riesling, Sauvignon Blanc
Nelson	Chardonnay, Pinot Noir, Riesling, Sauvignon Blanc
Marlborough	Chardonnay, Pinot Noir, Riesling, Sauvignon Blanc
Canterbury	Chardonnay, Pinot Gris, Pinot Noir, Riesling
Otago	Chardonnay, Pinot Noir, Riesling, Sauvignon Blanc

RED WINE

Alana Estate Pinot Noir

Although New Zealand is still primarily known for its white wines, its red wines are gaining in importance as wine makers discover better sites, perfect their viticulture methods and as vines mature, making them more stable. Pinot Noir is the most widely planted red variety, but Cabernet Sauvignon, Merlot and Cabernet Franc are also well suited to New Zealand's soil and climatic conditions. Wine makers frequently blend red wines from different areas and provinces.

Clearview Estate's popular seaside restaurant, Hawke's Bay (see pp150–51)

WINE TYPE	REGIONS	RECOMMENDED PRODUCERS
Cabernet Sauvignon	Auckland, Hawke's Bay, Northland, Waikato	Benfield, Brookfields, Church Road, Delamere Esk Valley, Goldwater, Morton Estate, Villa Maria
Merlot	Auckland, Gisborne, Hawke's Bay, Marlborough	Arahura, Babich, Church Road, C J Pask, Clearview Estate, Corbans, Delegates, Esk Valley, Villa Maria
Pinotage	Auckland, Gisborne, Hawke's Bay, Marlborough	Cottle Hill Winery, Kerr Farm Vineyard, Landmark Estate Wines, Ohinemuri Estate Wine, Pleasant Valley
Pinot Noir	Canterbury, Central Otago, Hawke's Bay, Marlborough, Nelson, Wairarapa	Ata Rangi, Black Ridge, Cloudy Bay, Cooper's Creek, Dry River, Martinborough Vineyard, Palliser, Rippon Vineyard

BEER

Beer remains a popular drink in New Zealand and beers such as Steinlager and Kiwi Lager have won international recognition. There are about 64 breweries in the country producing styles that range from light lagers to draft beers and malt ales. Beer is usually served chilled and is available on tap in bars and hotels. Low-alcohol beers as well as overseas bottled and canned beers are available in supermarkets, bottle stores, bars and restaurants.

Steinlager

OTHER DRINKS

New Zealand's climate, which ranges from subtropical to alpine, allows the cultivation of a large variety of fresh fruit for juicing, including its famous kiwifruit (see p129). Its apples are made into cider. Other bottled drinks and mineral waters are also widely available. A speciality is Lemon and Paeroa, a lemon-flavoured mineral water originally from Paeroa on the Hauraki Plains. Coffee and tea are other popular drinks with New Zealanders.

Kiwifruit

Choosing a Restaurant

Restaurants have been selected across a wide price range for good value, facilities and location. Reservations are advisable in most restaurants. All restaurants, cafés and bars are now totally non-smoking indoors. Entries are arranged alphabetically within price categories by area. For Map references, *see inside back cover*.

PRICE CATEGORIES
The following price ranges are for a three-course meal for one, not including drinks, inclusive of goods and services tax (GST) charges of 12.5%.

$ under NZ$25
$$ NZ$25–NZ$35
$$$ NZ$35–NZ$50
$$$$ NZ$50–NZ$70
$$$$$ over NZ$70

AUCKLAND

CITY Dizengoff $
256 Ponsonby Road, Ponsonby **Tel** (09) 360 0108   **Map** E2

A popular lunching hole for the stylish Ponsonby lunch set, Dizengoff serves the sort of Jewish cuisine more commonly found in New York or the East End of London, with an interesting, healthy twist. The chopped liver is wonderfully rich and garlicky. Big breakfasts. Bagels and spirulina are all-day specialities.

CITY Grand Harbour Chinese Restaurant $
18–28 Customs Street West **Tel** (09) 357 6889   **Map** E2

A large, contemporary Hong Kong-style restaurant with a huge following in the Chinese community. The yum cha lunch is excellent, with plenty of choices, and there is a wide-ranging menu for dinner too. Bookings are essential, especially on weekends when there is always a queue – and you may still have to wait.

CITY Sheinkin $
3 Lorne Street **Tel** (09) 303 4301   **Map** E2

A consistently good downtown café-restaurant, with an Israeli-inspired breakfast and lunch menu. The various tasting plates are the best (the Israeli platter is highly recommended), and the beetroot salad, potato latkes and soups are also great. Good coffee, wines by the glass and a selection of teas to accompany your meal.

CITY Hees Garden Seafood Restaurant $$
599 Mount Eden Road, Mount Eden **Tel** (09) 630 0785   **Map** E2

An Auckland landmark, where authentic Chinese cuisine has been served in a traditional atmosphere for over 25 years, with a waterfall fishpond and live seafood tanks. There are over 70 dishes to choose from on the popular yum cha lunch menu (bookings essential), including BBQ pork and fish in lemon sauce.

CITY Karin $$
237 Parnell Road, Parnell **Tel** (09) 356 7101   **Map** E2

Auckland is an excellent place to eat Japanese food, especially sushi, combining the freshness of New Zealand fish with the culinary skills of the city's multi-cultural population. Karin's specialities include grilled eel rolls and udon noodles with wakame seaweed. Good set meals combine all the extras with a main dish.

CITY Oh Calcutta $$
151 Parnell Road, Parnell **Tel** (09) 377 9090   **Map** E2

Oh Calcutta has won numerous awards and citations. Try Meena's award-winning beef *shajahani*, a mild beef dish in a classical rich creamy almond sauce, finished with coriander, sliced almonds and spices with homemade cottage cheese – a royal treat – or *saag dhingari*, button mushrooms cooked in a lightly spiced purée of fresh spinach.

CITY Bolliwood $$$
110 Ponsonby Road, Ponsonby **Tel** (09) 376 6477   **Map** E2

Favourite Ponsonby Indian restaurant. Its large interior is ideal for groups, but nonetheless has some more intimate corners. Eclectic menu includes classics such as tandoori chicken, king prawn masala and vegetarian banquets, as well as garlic bread and $10 lunch special. Bolliwood has won Best Indian Restaurant in the New Zealand awards.

CITY Daikoku Teppan-Yaki $$$
148 Quay Street **Tel** (09) 302 2432   **Map** E2

One of six Daikokus dotted around Auckland, this one serves Japanese Teppan-Yaki cuisine, cooked by the chef at your table. The extravagant Daikoku Emperor platter includes crayfish and filet mignon (at a price). Separate bar with Japanese sake and beers. Ramen Daikoku, by the Britomart Transport Centre, serves noodle dishes.

CITY Mai Thai $$$
Cnr Victoria and Albert streets **Tel** (09) 366 6258   **Map** E2

Mai Thai's cuisine from the Five Great Siamese Kingdoms is a blend of tastes – hot, sour, salty, sweet and spicy, with the subtle addition of locally ground roots, grasses and aromatic herbs to enrich the traditional flavours and lessen the bite – served with a 'wai' (smile). Auckland's best Thai food.

Key to Symbols *see back cover flap*

CITY Mecca

$$$

85–7 Customs Street West, Viaduct Harbour **Tel** *(09) 358 1093*

Map E2

Mecca started out as one small café in Newmarket, but now has branches at the Viaduct Harbour, Chancery Centre, Bacons Lane and several other locations around the city. The food has mainly Middle Eastern flavours. At the Chancery Centre branch there are plenty of outdoor tables in a sheltered courtyard.

CITY Prego

$$$

226 Ponsonby Road, Ponsonby **Tel** *(09) 376 3095*

Map E2

Casual, friendly dining with delicious, straightforward pasta and wood-fired pizza and roasts. Large, noisy and usually crowded, Prego is a longstanding favourite of Aucklanders. No-bookings policy, so be prepared to wait at the bar. Freshly baked loaves from the oven stave off the hunger pangs meanwhile. Summer dining in courtyard.

CITY Rikka Newmarket

$$$

73 Davis Crescent, Newmarket **Tel** *(09) 522 5277*

Map E2

Stylish restaurant serving Japanese food including excellent sashimi in a smart setting. Funky decor by designer Richard Priest, with a chunky bar and rough-hewn floors. Traditional food is presented with flair and style, and service is attentive. An alternative is Sake Bar Rikka in Freeman's Bay above Victoria Park Market.

CITY The Occidental

$$$

6–8 Vulcan Lane **Tel** *(09) 300 6226*

Map E2

Belgian Beer Café in a building that has been the Occidental Hotel since 1870. Developed as a travellers' hotel, it housed a reading room, billiard room and café in addition to drinking space. Now it serves mussels and Flemish stew washed down with Lambic beers, Trappist ales and New Zealand wines.

CITY Traffic Bar and Kitchen

$$$

2 Queen Street (Cnr Queen and Quay streets) **Tel** *(09) 809 3559*

Map E2

In the Britomart building just opposite the harbour, this restaurant offers a range of options from bar snacks to full meals. Try the gourmet tapas or pizza, or opt for a meat dish. The specialized, temperature-controlled water bath used for cooking the meat ensures tender and flavoursome dishes every time.

CITY Wildfire Churrascaria

$$$

Princes Wharf, Quay Street **Tel** *(09) 353 7595*

Map E2

The Churrascaria (pronounced Shoo-has-ca-ria) is New Zealand's only Brazilian BBQ. A technique that apparently originated in the Rio Grande do Sul in the 18th century, it involves long skewers of beef, lamb, pork, chicken and fish marinated and roasted over red-hot coals. Fixed-price all you can eat. Fun for children, but touristy.

CITY Ariake

$$$$

Cnr Albert and Quay streets **Tel** *(09) 379 2377*

Map E2

Longstanding downtown Japanese restaurant, just behind the Ferry Building across from the waterfront. Simple, Japanese-style interior. Watch the sushi being made, or have other delicacies brought to your table by attentive waitresses in kimonos. As well as being the first, it is often voted the best Japanese restaurant in town.

CITY Bowmans

$$$$

597 Mount Eden Road, Mount Eden **Tel** *(09) 638 9676*

Map E2

Reliable, welcoming suburban restaurant which serves hearty portions of modern New Zealand food (European-Asian fusion) in a relaxed, informal setting. Renowned for its friendly service. Offering a good wine list and a large blackboard menu it has been awarded the NZ Lamb and Beef Hallmark of Excellence every year since 1998.

CITY Hammerheads Restaurant

$$$$

19 Tamaki Drive, Okahu Bay **Tel** *(09) 521 4400*

Map E2

One of the city's best-known restaurants, just five minutes' drive from downtown Auckland on the waterfront at Okahu Bay, with views of the harbour and skyline. It serves predominantly, but not solely, seafood prepared with a fusion of Asian and Mediterranean herbs and spices. The seafood platter is excellent, though at a price.

CITY Harbourside Restaurant

$$$$

1st Floor, Ferry Building, Quay Street **Tel** *(09) 307 0556*

Map E2

In a hard-to-beat location, Harbourside is perennially popular. The terracotta-tiled terrace has a stunning view of the ferry traffic, passenger liners and yachts coming and going in the harbour. Following a classy revamp, the large restaurant boasts new subtle décor and soft colours. Serves mainly fish, prepared in bold, uncomplicated ways.

CITY Kermadec

$$$$

Level 1 Viaduct Quay, Cnr Lower Hobson and Quay streets **Tel** *(09) 309 0412*

Map E2

Kermadec Ocean Fresh Restaurant dominates the Viaduct Harbour waterfront, with its two restaurants, three bars, one café and two private Japanese tatami rooms. It is all about fresh seafood prepared in unique Pacific Rim fashion. Its heyday was during the America's Cup regattas, but it remains a flagship of swanky style.

CITY O'Connell Street Bistro

$$$$

3 O'Connell Street **Tel** *(09) 377 1884*

Map E2

A small, intimate European-style bistro which has won many awards for its wine list and cuisine since it opened in 1999. Influences come from aboard the *QEII*, Terence Conran's Bluebird and Melbourne. Seasonal delicacies might include seared New Zealand scallops with grilled black pudding, red chard, potato crisps and champagne vanilla syrup.

CITY Rice 👪 ♿ $$$$

Cnr Federal and Wolfe streets ***Tel*** *(09) 359 9113* ***Map*** *E2*

As the name might suggest, Rice's menu features some variant of rice in every dish, with predominantly Asian flavours. Modern, stylish decor and personal, professional service. If you find it hard to choose, the tasting plate is a good starter. Bar serves infused sake (including vanilla, honey ginger and wasabi).

CITY Soul Bar and Bistro 👪 ♿ $$$$

Viaduct Harbour ***Tel*** *(09) 356 7249* ***Map*** *E2*

Hyper-trendy bar and restaurant on the waterfront at the Viaduct Harbour, with a large deck overlooking the yacht marina. Caters for the gamut of downtown Aucklanders, from corporate lunchers to after-work drinkers, relaxed diners, late-night groovers and Sunday brunchers. Light, mainly seafood menu. Excellent, friendly service.

CITY The French Café ♿ $$$$

210 Symonds Street ***Tel*** *(09) 377 1911* ***Map*** *E2*

Contemporary European cuisine in a sophisticated and intimate environment. Bar for drinks, conservatory and courtyard dining. Constantly nominated one of Auckland's top restaurants by dining and lifestyle magazines. Unusua seasonal offerings might include salt and pepper squid with chilli jam. New Zealand and French wines.

CITY Toto 👪 ♿ $$$$

53 Nelson Street ***Tel*** *(09) 302 2665* ***Map*** *E2*

Auckland's first Italian fusion restaurant, where tradition and modern Italian cuisine are combined in a light, unpretentious setting. Delicious variations on classic themes. In a country currently infatuated by its own wines, Toto is one place to offer top vintages from elsewhere, Italian Amarone, Brunello di Montalcino and Barolo among them.

CITY Antoine's Restaurant ♿ $$$$$

333 Parnell Road, Parnell ***Tel*** *(09) 379 8756* ***Map*** *E2*

Fine French-inspired New Zealand cuisine has been served at Antoine's since 1973, and the elegant restaurant has been booked out ever since. Chef Tony Astle, just 22 when it all started, travels the world annually to refresh his tastebuds. A 'nostalgia menu' features roast duckling, oxtail, and bread and butter pudding.

CITY Dine by Peter Gordon 👪 ♿ $$$$$

Level 3, SKYCITY Grand Hotel, 90 Federal Street ***Tel*** *(09) 363 7030* ***Map*** *E2*

A much-hyped restaurant bearing the insignia of New Zealand's top celebrity chef, Peter Gordon – the man behind the naissance of New Zealand cuisine, who founded the famous Sugar Club in Wellington in 1986. Dine, in the new SKYCITY Grand Hotel, serves his trademark fusion dishes in a slick, big-hotel ambience.

CITY Q Restaurant ♿ 👪 $$$$$

21 Viaduct Harbour Avenue ***Tel*** *(09) 909 8000* ***Map*** *E2*

One of the best and most luxurious restaurants in the city, offering superb European cuisine with a distinctive New Zealand twist. It is situated in the heart of Auckland, overlooking Viaduct Harbour. The decor is sumptuous and there is also outdoor seating available.

CITY Vinnies ♿ $$$$$

166 Jervois Road, Herne Bay ***Tel*** *(09) 376 5597* ***Map*** *E2*

A foodies' favourite, with a chef-owner who has revamped both the decor and the menu without deviating too far from the formula that has won countless accolades for cuisine and wines. Seasonal dishes might include black tiger prawn raviolo, swiss chard watercress and spiced carrot broth.

GREATER AUCKLAND Manuka 👪 ♿ $$

49 Victoria Road, Devonport ***Tel*** *(09) 445 7732* ***Map*** *E2*

A 12-minute ferry ride from downtown Auckland in the smart North Shore suburb of Devonport, Manuka is best known for the pizzas from its wood-fired oven. It also serves pasta, salads, seafood and steaks in an informal, friendly setting. Children's menu and crayons are on hand to keep the family happy.

NORTHLAND

DOUBTLESS BAY Mangonui Fish Shop ⛱ 👪 ♿ $

Beach Road, Mangonui ***Tel*** *(09) 406 0478* ***Map*** *D1*

Situated right over the water in Mangonui Harbour, with an all-weather deck. All fish are caught locally. Fish of the day may include snapper, terakihi, bluenose, gurnard or hapuka, and there are also scallops, mussels, oysters and kina (sea urchins), as well as smoked fish. Nowhere better for fresh fish.

HOKIANGA Boatshed Café and Gallery 👪 ♿ $

8 Clendon Esplanade, Rawene ***Tel*** *(09) 405 7728* ***Map*** *D1*

Arts and crafts, coffees and teas, cakes and muffins, breakfasts and lunches in an old storehouse jutting out over the water on Rawene beach. Friendly café ambience and home-baked food in this red-painted landmark, which doubles up as a tourist office for Hokianga Harbour.

Key to Price Guide *see p326* **Key to Symbols** *see back cover flap*

HOKIANGA Copthorne Hotel and Resort 🏃⚱ $$$$

SH12, OMapere **Tel** *(09) 405 8737* **Map** *D1*

Family-run hotel on the water's edge of Hokianga Harbour, where you are sure to meet the whole family, including the labrador, Bailey. Breakfast and hearty gourmet dinners are served in the quaint, elegant Colonial homestead, as well as drinks and bar snacks in the family-friendly pub, which is popular with locals too.

HOUHOURA Houhora Tavern 🏃⚱ $

Saleyard Road **Tel** *(09) 409 8806* **Map** *E1*

A 100-year-old historic hotel overlooking the tranquil harbour at Houhoura. Drinks are served on the verandah. Fresh snapper and seafood selection feature on the bistro menu, or lighter bar snacks can be prepared. Home-cooked meals at this, New Zealand's northernmost tavern make this your last chance for a good feed, beer and petrol, too.

KAIPARA Sahara Restaurant, Bar and Lounge 🏃⚱ $$$

Cnr Main and Franklin roads, Paparoa **Tel** *(09) 431 6833* **Map** *D1*

Housed in the old National Bank building, built in 1914 and lovingly restored down to an award-winning paint job, Sahara is an oasis on the Kaipara. Inspired by the Italian rural lifestyle, its owners, who have cheffed in Melbourne, London and Sardinia, use local pork, bacon, venison, vegetables, oysters and mussels.

KAITAIA Beachcomber Restaurant 🏃⚱ $$$

222 Commerce Street **Tel** *(09) 408 2010* **Map** *D1*

The slightly dated decor and location in the town plaza is more than compensated for by the friendly team here. Seafood, ostrich steak, vegetarian dishes and the salad bar are house specialities. Retro starters such as avocado and prawn cocktail are updated with chilli and lime juice, and Italian classics are also served. Good wines.

KAITAIA Bushman's Hut Steakhouse 🏃⚱ $$$

5 Bank Street **Tel** *(09) 408 4320* **Map** *D1*

The steakhouse offers prime New Zealand chargrilled beef steaks, alongside a variety of seafood dishes produced by an award-winning chef. Locally sourced produce and seafood matched with wines from top Northland vineyards. Rustic theme runs through the restaurant indoors and out. Warm atmosphere, friendly service.

KAITAIA Henry VIII Restaurant – Northerner Hotel 🏃⚱ $$$

Cnr North Road and Kohuhu Street **Tel** *(09) 408 2800* **Map** *D1*

Located in a mock Tudor building on the north side of Kaitaia for more than 20 years, the Henry VIII is part of the Northerner Motor Inn. It continues to serve reliable, hearty meals to satisfy more than just the inner gourmet, everyday from 4:30pm in its licensed restaurant.

KERIKERI Marsden Estate 🏃⚱ $$

Wiroa Road **Tel** *(09) 407 9398* **Map** *E1*

Named after Samuel Marsden, the early missionary who in 1819 planted the first New Zealand vines, Marsden Estate winery serves delicious, uncomplicated food (oxtail stew with baby onions on garlic and potato mash with rich bacon sauce) on a terrace overlooking the vineyard. Open for lunch seven days a week and for dinner Friday and Saturday.

PAIHIA Waikokopu Café 🏂🏃⚱ $

Waitangi Treaty Grounds **Tel** *(09) 402 6275* **Map** *E1*

An award-winning café which offers good coffee and an extensive range of food from breakfasts and snacks to serious beef, lamb and seafood dinners. A wide selection of vegetarian options available. Located in a shady garden at the entrance to the grounds (separate entrance). Children are welcome and catered for.

PAIHIA 35 Degrees South Aquarium Restaurant and Bar 🏃⚱ $$

The Wharf **Tel** *(09) 402 6220* **Map** *E1*

Breathtaking views encompass Waitangi, Russell and the stunning Bay of Islands from a restaurant over the water with a deck. Menu prepared by a well-travelled chef, who has brought plenty of influences home with him. Watch the fish in the saltwater aquarium as you tuck into your seafood dinner.

PAIHIA Only Seafood 🏃⚱ $$$

40 Marsden Road **Tel** *(09) 402 6066* **Map** *E1*

Situated on Paihia's waterfront in a Colonial-style building dating back to the late 1800s. New Zealand cuisine matched with an extensive selection of New Zealand wines. In summer, candlelit tables are scattered around the courtyard, with moonlit views of boats in the bay. Upstairs, Only Seafood offers a fish only menu.

PAIHIA The Sugar Boat 🏃⚱ $$$$

Waitangi Bridge **Tel** *(09) 402 7018* **Map** *E1*

Cocktail bar and restaurant on board an old sugar lighter in Paihia Harbour. Built in 1890, the boat was retired in the 1950s and became an artists' and potters' houseboat, a shipwreck museum and finally found its present incarnation. Drinks are served on deck, Mediterranean-inspired dinners in the elegant hold.

PAIHIA Pure Tastes 🏂⚱ $$$$$

116 Marsden Road, Paihia **Tel** *(09) 402 0003* **Map** *E1*

Situated in the Paihia Beach Resort and Spa, across the road from the beach, this restaurant by night and bistro by day offers contemporary cuisine with innovative flavours inspired from around the world. They use local ingredients as much as possible. It is open seven days a week.

RUSSELL Duke of Marlborough Hotel   🏃 ♿ $$$
35 The Strand **Tel** *(09) 403 7829*   **Map** *E1*

The historic Duke of Marlborough Hotel, holder of New Zealand's first liquor licence (1840), has been burned to the ground, rebuilt and refurbished many times over the past 150 years. It now offers bar, bistro or restaurant dining in its cosy interior or on the covered waterfront verandah. Seafood specialities.

RUSSELL Gannets Restaurant   🏃 ♿ $$$
Cnr York and Chapel streets **Tel** *(09) 403 7990*   **Map** *E1*

Award-winning restaurant with focus on fresh seafood. Changing daily menu of gamefish and fish of the day. Seasonal treats might include saffron seafood chowder or day's catch with white wine pernod sauce on mushroom risotto. Fusion cooking style influenced by European experience with Asian and Pacific flavours. Children's menu.

RUSSELL Sally's Restaurant   🌿 🏃 ♿ $$$$
25 The Strand **Tel** *(09) 403 7652*   **Map** *E1*

A well-established Northland restaurant situated on the beach front in Russell with a large outside patio area leading onto the beach and a fine view over the bay. The menu focuses on New Zealand cuisine and there is a great selection of New Zealand wines and beers. Reservations are recommended.

RUSSELL Kamakura   🏃 ♿ $$$$$
29 The Strand **Tel** *(09) 403 7771*   **Map** *E1*

An attractive mix of fine dining and stunning views of the bay. The menu is subtly inspired by Asian cuisine, with signature dishes such as crab, chilli and lime ravioli on a crayfish bisque, or try the five-course Northland Naturally Tasting menu which showcases local producers.

TUTUKAKA Schnappa Rock   🏃 ♿ $$$
Marina Road **Tel** *(09) 434 3774*   **Map** *E1*

Upbeat café, bar and restaurant on the beach, serving breakfast, lunch, drinks, dinner and more drinks, with a child-friendly sub-tropical garden. Serious meat and fish dinners with nursery desserts (rhubarb and custard), burgers and Caesar salads for lunch. Cocktails include a schnappa rocket (blue curaçao, bacardi and malibu). Hangover breakfast.

WAIPU COVE The Beach House Restaurant   🏃 ♿ $$$$
891 Cove Road, Waipu Cove, Bream Bay **Tel** *(09) 432 0877*   **Map** *E1*

This award-winning restaurant in Waipu Cove, which is on Bream Bay, south along the coast from Whangarei, offers superb contemporary New Zealand cuisine with subtle Mediterranean influences. It is attractively situated just 50 m from the white sands of the bay.

WHANGAREI Reva's on The Waterfront   🏃 ♿ $$
31 Quay Side, Town Basin Marina **Tel** *(09) 438 8969*   **Map** *E1*

Locally famous pizzeria which has been going at various locales around town since 1976 as a meeting place for local musicians, artists and travellers, and has now found a perfect home on the waterfront. As well as the substantial pizzas, Reva's serves Mexican dishes, hearty salads, pasta, fish and meat.

WHANGAREI à Deco   ♿ $$$$
70 Kamo Road **Tel** *(09) 459 4957*   **Map** *E1*

Modern New Zealand cuisine with an emphasis on fresh Northland produce served in the elegant setting of a 1939 Art Deco house. Highly recommended, award-winning restaurant. *NZ Cuisine* magazine has called it a 'not-to-be-missed dining experience', and it has received accolades from the New Zealand Beef and Lamb marketing board.

WHANGAREI Tonic Restaurant   🏃 ♿ $$$$
239A Kamo Road **Tel** *(09) 437 5558*   **Map** *E1*

Tonic serves some of the best food in Northland, as well as offering good service and value. Now considered one of the top two restaurants in Whangarei, it won all the good food awards in the region until à Deco came along and bumped it in the fine dining stakes.

CENTRAL NORTH ISLAND

COROMANDEL Pepper Tree Restaurant and Bar   🏃 ♿ $$$$$
31 Kapanga Road **Tel** *(07) 866 8211*   **Map** *E2*

In the heart of Coromandel township, in an old villa with sunny courtyard, shaded verandahs and cosy dining room. Award-winning modern New Zealand cuisine, with seafood a speciality. Try a Coro Sampler – crayfish, oysters, mussels and raw fish salad – or go all out with the Seafood Indulgence platter. Relaxed, friendly atmosphere.

GISBORNE The Works   🏃 ♿ $$
The Esplanade **Tel** *(06) 863 1285*   **Map** *F3*

Housed in the old freezing works built in 1906, The Works café offers a menu based on local produce – the abundant seafood, exotic vegetables, cheese and hill-country meats of the region. Relaxed and friendly. The same people make Works and Longbush wines (predominantly whites), which feature on the wine list.

Key to Price Guide *see p326* **Key to Symbols** *see back cover flap*

GISBORNE Poverty Bay Club

Cnr Childers Road and Customhouse Street **Tel** *(06) 863 2006*

$$\text{Map F3}$$

Once a private club for wealthy landowners, the Poverty Bay Club has opened its doors to the public for lunch, dinner, cocktails and tapas. This 'grand lady' turned restaurant is a fine example of late-19th-century provincial architecture, with its balcony, pillars and verandah ornamented with fretwork.

HAHEI Luna Café

1 Grange Road **Tel** *(07) 866 3016*

Map E2

Delicious home cooking in a warm, friendly atmosphere. All-day breakfasts, lunch and dinner. Famous for its muffins and Atomic coffee. Outdoor courtyard, with a playground next door. Bookings essential for dinner, especially over the summer holiday-making period when the Coromandel fills up with visitors. Reservations are preferred.

HAHEI The Church

91 Hahei Beach Road **Tel** *(07) 866 3797*

Map E2

Atmospheric dining in a restored 19th-century wooden church building, with high vaulted ceilings, arched windows and timber floors. Their Scottish-trained chef produces modern Scottish cuisine, such as fried breast of chicken stuffed with black pudding and wrapped in streaky bacon.

HAMILTON The Cazbar and Caffè Restaurant and Bar

The Marketplace, Hood Street **Tel** *(07) 838 0998*

Map E2

A warm, friendly restaurant and bar in Hamilton's Marketplace serving meals to excite your taste buds and wines to make them tingle in a wonderful atmosphere. Good breakfasts, long lunches and hearty dinners. Traditional fodder, from shrimp cocktails to steak and banoffee pie, plus Asian flavours all make an appearance on the menu.

HAMILTON Embargo

Ground Floor, 12 Garden Place **Tel** *(07) 834 1353*

Map E2

A striving-to-be-hip café and restaurant in the old New Zealand Herald building in Hamilton, opened by an Austrian-via-Sydney chef. Laidback Euro-style café by day, smart restaurant by night. Classical French cuisine melded with Pacific Rim flavours for dinner. Child-friendly Sunday brunches. Good New Zealand wines, with a couple of Alsatian options.

HAMILTON Tables on the River

12 Alma Street **Tel** *(07) 839 6555*

Map E2

The place to dine in the Waikato, Tables has been winner of best regional restaurant awards for the Waikato, has won the Beef and Lamb Award for many years, and has come first in best food and wine matches too. Excellent modern food, service and riverside location.

MOUNT MAUNGANUI Astrolabe

82 Maunganui Road **Tel** *(07) 574 8155*

Map E2

Concept dining on the Mount, with several distinct but interrelated areas (bar, café, courtyard, formal dining). Award-winning food, modern style and efficient service. Modern Pacific Rim cuisine using local produce and seafood. It is the sort of place that serves its organic bread with sea salt and extra virgin olive oil.

NAPIER Restaurant Indonesia

409 Marine Parade **Tel** *(06) 835 8303*

Map F4

In a region where good food is pricey, this longstanding family-owned restaurant is a good alternative – especially if you're tired of modern New Zealand cuisine. Centrally located on Marine Parade, near motels. Try the *rijsttafel* – an Indonesian banquet of many dishes including *babi pangang* (roast pork belly in a pineapple sauce).

NAPIER Clifton Bay Café

Clifton Road, Te Awanga **Tel** *(06) 875 0096*

Map F4

Rustic café in a building based on the original Clifton Station wool shed that once stood on the site. Superb location by the sea at the start (and finish) of walks to the gannet colony at Cape Kidnappers. Above average café food and local wines. Friendly staff welcome children.

NAPIER Pacifica Kaimoana

209 Marine Parade **Tel** *(06) 833 6335*

Map F2

Napier's best seafood restaurant. Famous for its grilled flounder, scattered with herb twigs, garlic and butter and crisped under the grill, and other varieties of fresh fish, simply served. Starters might include slivers of raw trevally or Nelson scallops. Woven mats, turquoise-painted exterior and courtyard braziers contribute to the Pacifica feel.

NAPIER Clearview Estate Winery and Restaurant

Clifton Road, Te Awanga **Tel** *(06) 875 0150*

Map F2

Award-winning boutique winery by the sea. The vineyard restaurant is in a delightful setting, with tables around a courtyard and among vines. Funky children's play area. Innovative use of local meat, seafood, cheese and seasonal produce, combined with fresh herbs, olives, citrus and avocados from the estate.

NAPIER Mission Estate Winery Restaurant

198 Church Road, Greenmeadows **Tel** *(06) 845 9354*

Map F2

One of the few winery restaurants to open in the evening, and pleasantly located on a hillside on the edge of town, Mission Estate Restaurant is housed in a restored French Marist seminary building with sweeping views of Napier and the ocean. European style of cuisine, with luscious desserts. Known for its annual concert.

NAPIER Provedore 👪 ♿ ♫ $$$$

60 West Quay, Port Ahuriri **Tel** *(06) 834 0189* **Map** *F2*

The place to hang out, eat well, drink and groove in Napier. Overlooking the fishing port, Provedore offers brunches, lunches, tapas-style bar snacks with a Cantonese twist and full-scale Mediterranean-Asian fusion cuisine at nights. Occasional live music/DJs. Head here for a glass of wine from the select list and a bite to eat. Open late.

NAPIER Te Awa Winery 👪 ♿ $$$$

2375 SH50 **Tel** *(06) 879 7602* **Map** *F2*

Another highly rated winery restaurant, this one in the prime Gimblett Gravels vineyard area – a beautiful 15-minute drive from Napier. Excellent European-inspired food without too many frills, served in a rustic setting under a pergola in summer. Fine estate wines. Lots of space for children to run around.

NAPIER Chambers Restaurant 👪 ♿ $$$$$

12 Browning Street **Tel** *(06) 835 7800* **Map** *F2*

Highly reputed fine dining restaurant. Although the cuisine is excellent, it is highly priced, and the ambience is a little on the staid side, especially when compared to some of the relaxed dine-among-the-vines alternatives around Hawke's Bay. On the other hand, it is open for dinner, and in the heart of Napier.

OTOROHANGA Be'Guinness 👪 ♿ $$

91 Maniapoto Street **Tel** *(07) 873 8010* **Map** *E3*

Traditional country food, with steak a speciality, plenty of other meat dishes on offer, and filling puddings. Guinness is available on tap, as well as other, locally produced beers such as Waikato Draught. The restaurant showcases landscape paintings by Waikato artists. Cosy, warm interior.

PAEROA Ohinemuri Estate Winery Restaurant 👪 ♿ $$$

Moresby St, Karangahake Gorge **Tel** *(07) 862 8874* **Map** *E3*

Attractively housed in what were once the estate's stables. The menu is strongly influenced by Mediterranean cuisine but with an emphatic New Zealand influence. The ingredients are sourced locally as much as possible and are always seasonal. There is an outside dining area in summer.

RAGLAN Marlin Café and Grill 👪 ♿ $$$

Raglan Wharf, 43 Rose Street **Tel** *(07) 825 0010* **Map** *E2*

Right beside the wharf, with a range of food for any occasion. Seafood is a speciality, but good meat grills are also on offer, and the owners will not mind if you just stop in for a quick drink. Views out to sea. Wooden, barn-like interior and sunny deck.

ROTORUA The Landing Café 👪 ♿ $$$

The Landing, Lake Tarawera **Tel** *(07) 362 8595* **Map** *E3*

Well worth the scenic half-hour drive from Rotorua, right by the wharf on beautiful Lake Tarawera. Not just a great location, it is a friendly, warm, relaxed place serving superb food. Lunch on the deck and watch the boats, or dine inside by the roaring fire in winter. Excellent mussel chowder.

ROTORUA Zanelli's Italian Cuisine 👪 ♿ $$$

1243 Amohia Street **Tel** *(07) 348 4908* **Map** *E3*

Italian restaurant which for 20 years has served a range of traditional pasta dishes, classic meat dishes such as veal in a white wine, lemon juice and parsley sauce, mouthwatering desserts including its famous gelato, tiramisù and zabaglione, and daily specials using seasonal ingredients. Quiet, central Rotorua location near sights.

ROTORUA Bistro 1284 ♿ $$$$

1284 Eruera Street **Tel** *(07) 346 1284* **Map** *E3*

Located in the geothermal heart of Rotorua, Bistro 1284 is regularly nominated the city's best restaurant, and winner of beef and lamb awards. Beautifully prepared, simple, European-inspired cuisine might include roast beef fillet with grilled mushrooms, chunky fries and Béarnaise sauce. Selective, reasonably priced New Zealand wine list. Unusual desserts.

TAUPO Beach Brasserie 👪 ♿ $$

Millennium Hotel & Resort Manuel's Taupo, 243 Lake Terrace **Tel** *(07) 378 5110* **Map** *E3*

Old-school decor, but it is right on the beach and low on pretention. Award-winning, affordable dining in a family-friendly environment with children's menu and family buffets at weekends. Desserts include verjuice and vanilla rhubarb pot topped with a ginger pound cake and finished with mascarpone and vanilla ice cream.

TAUPO Prawn Farm Restaurant 👪 ♿ $$

Huka Falls Road, Wairakei Park **Tel** *(07) 374 8474* **Map** *E3*

With the endearing motto "meet 'em, greet 'em, eat 'em", the prawn farm welcomes visitors on tours to see prawns being reared in geothermal water before tucking into a prawn-based meal. A prawn shell's throw from the Huka Falls, for those who cannot afford the more exclusive eatery at Huka Lodge.

TAUPO Huka Falls Restaurant 👪 ♿ $$$$

56 Huka Falls Road **Tel** *(07) 376 0260* **Map** *E3*

Fresh seafood and other seasonal fare dominates the menu at this relaxed restaurant with sweeping views over the Huka Falls Winery and out to Mount Tauhara. It is located at Huka Falls Resort along the Waikato river, and there is the opportunity to dine outside in summer.

Key to Price Guide *see p326* **Key to Symbols** *see back cover flap*

TAURANGA Café Bravo
$$$

Red Square **Tel** *(07) 578 4700* **Map** E2

Clean, modern lines set the tone for this stylish downtown café. Hearty breakfasts (lamb's fry and black sausage on the menu), chunky sandwiches, pizzas and light lunches which might include smoked salmon potato cakes with caper aioli.

TAURANGA Harbourside Bar and Brasserie
$$$$

Old Yacht Club building, south end of the Strand **Tel** *(07) 571 0520* **Map** E2

In a prime location over the water overlooking the boats in the harbour, with a bright, spacious interior and covered deck. Mainly seafood, prepared in Asian and European styles – fettucine and hokkien noodles sit side by side on the menu with fish and chips, bouillabaisse and pepper-encrusted venison. Good wines.

TAURANGA The Lobster Club
$$$$

Tauranga Bridge Marina **Tel** *(07) 574 4147* **Map** E2

Waterfront dining on the port of Tauranga, offering New Zealand and Asian cuisine from lamb shanks to tempura tarakihi. The seafood platter serves up not only salmon, market fish, scallops, squid, oysters, prawns and shrimp, but also Scotch fillet. Salads, omelettes, pizza, pasta and other lighter meals are available too.

TE KUITI Bosco Café
$$

57 Te Kumi Road, Te Kuiti **Tel** *(07) 878 3633* **Map** E3

A somewhat surprising experience in this quaint country town is this bustling café attracting customers from all over the world with its hip menu and fast and friendly service. Dishes include curries, homemade pasta, meatballs and a range of fresh gourmet sandwiches.

THAMES Sola Café
$

720B Pollen Street **Tel** *(07) 868 8781* **Map** E2

Elegant little café serving vegetarian cuisine and excellent coffee, recommended by carnivores. Delicious, carefully prepared food might include an assortment of grilled breads served with Marlborough olive oil, or a salad of chickpeas, red onion and warm sautéed haloumi, followed by a ginger crème brulée. Good value. Open daily.

TONGARIRO NATIONAL PARK Beef & Beer Steakhouse
$$

72 Clyde Street, Ohakune **Tel** *(06) 385 8268* **Map** E3

Not one but two open fires warm this modern, relaxed restaurant, which features a wooden horseshoe-shaped bar. Specializes in steaks of all sorts. Welcoming, family-friendly atmosphere in this popular, cosy après-ski bar. Filling avant-ski brunches served up at the weekend in winter.

TONGARIRO NATIONAL PARK Fat Pigeon Garden Café
$$

2 Tyne Street, Ohakune **Tel** *(06) 385 9423* **Map** E3

Diners may eat outside in the picturesque garden at the bottom of the mountain road, where the kereru, the native (fat) pigeon, coos in the trees, or cosy up in front of the wood fire after a day on the mountain. Fillet steak and fresh fish specialities. Extensive wine list.

TONGARIRO NATIONAL PARK The Station Café Bar and Restaurant
$$$

Findlay Street, National Park Village **Tel** *(07) 892 2881* **Map** E2

The tastefully redecorated historic railway station in National Park Village, built in 1908, is still a fully operational railway station, serving the Auckland–Wellington trains that pass through a couple of times daily, but also offers café-style food, and full dinners in the evenings. Cosy, warm atmosphere conducive to lingering.

TONGARIRO NATIONAL PARK Bayview Château Tongariro
$$$$

Whakapapa Village **Tel** *(07) 892 3809* **Map** E3

Lamb and venison specialities are served in the Ruapehu Room at this famous hotel. Formal dress is required, in an endeavour to resurrect the elegant standards of the hotel's 1920s heyday. Asian cuisine is available at the Pihanga Café, one of the more casual dining options in the hotel complex.

WAITOMO Waitomo Tavern
$

Waitomo Caves Road **Tel** *(07) 878 8448* **Map** E3

Good, cheap food in a fun atmosphere, largely devoted to drinking. The tavern is a popular spot in the evenings for both locals and those relaxing after a hard day's adventure. Live music on Saturdays and some other nights. Bar meals. Located between the caves, YHA and Waitomo Caves Hotel.

WAITOMO Huhu Café
$$$

Waitomo 10, Caves Road **Tel** *(07) 878 6674* **Map** E3

A stunning modern café/restaurant which is surrounded by a terrace balcony overlooking Waitomo Valley. They offer a wide range of snacks and meals, and the provision of à la carte dining rather than the standard café style of ordering over the counter sets this place apart from the rest. It is open daily and most evenings.

WHAKATANE Fig Bar and Eatery
$$

93 The Strand **Tel** *(07) 308 6549* **Map** F3

Delicious, affordable Mediterranean-style cuisine, with excellent "fusion" coffee, bar and a relaxed friendly atmosphere. Good venue for brunch or lunch. Outside courtyard tables. Delicious classic Middle Eastern dishes and variants such as chicken served on fruit and nut couscous with peach, ginger and fig sauce. Closed Monday.

WHAKATANE Global Thai Restaurant and Bar ⬛⬛⬛ $$

Cnr Commerce Street and The Strand **Tel** *(07) 308 9000*   **Map** *F3*

Popular Whakatane restaurant, with menu offering global and Thai cuisine. Coq au vin, penne, seared scallops or lamb shanks, teriyaki beef, ostrich or steak pommes frites. Extensive range of New Zealand and international wines, or BYO, and fully licensed bar offering a range of beers and cocktails.

WHAKATANE Wharf Shed ⬛⬛⬛ $$$

Strand East **Tel** *(07) 308 5698*   **Map** *F3*

Nautical restaurant in the former cream and butter store on the quayside, with views of boats in the harbour. Outdoor seating on the deck or sunny wharf. Extensive menu offers everything from chowder, sushi and seafood to steaks and vegetarian meals. Friendly and relaxed. Winner of beef and lamb awards. Bookings essential.

WHITIANGA Salt Restaurant ⬛⬛ $$$$

1 Blacksmith Lane **Tel** *(09) 866 5818*   **Map** *E2*

A great location right by the water's edge with spectacular views of the marina. The menu offers a huge range of dishes but the emphasis is very much on seafood and fish. They also have an impressive wine list. Open seven days a week for lunch and dinner.

WHITIANGA The Fire Place Restaurant ⬛⬛ $$$$

9 The Esplanade **Tel** *(07) 866 4546*   **Map** *E2*

Off the rocks and into the fire place – competition is fierce along Whitianga's esplanade. This is the place for gourmet wood-fired pizzas, rotisserie chicken and lamb and interesting appetisers such as chilled bloody mary oyster soup. Cosy, cheerful rustic-style interior and spacious decks overlooking the bay. Good New Zealand wines.

WELLINGTON AND THE SOUTH

KAPITI COAST Brown Sugar Café ⬛⬛⬛ $

SH1, Otaki **Tel** *(06) 364 6359*   **Map** *E4*

Charming roadside café in a historic cottage built around a leafy courtyard, which started life as a racing stables in the 1920s. Fresh, café-style food, good coffee and pleasant, friendly service. It plays an important role in the social life of Otaki residents as well as travellers along the highway.

KAPITI COAST The Fisherman's Table ⬛⬛ $

Main Road South, Paekakariki **Tel** *(04) 292 8125*   **Map** *E4*

One of a chain, this Fisherman's Table has a stunning seafront location at Paekakariki, one of the Kapiti Coast's less suburbanized beach settlements. Large, family-orientated, budget-priced restaurant. An all-you-can-eat salad bar features on the menu, as well as plenty of fried fish and chips. Great stop-off with the kids.

NEW PLYMOUTH Bella Vita ⬛ $$$

37 Gover Street **Tel** *(06) 758 3393*   **Map** *D3*

Bella Vita dishes up classic Italian cuisine without too many frills in an intimate setting. Good, reliable pasta dishes, as well as meat and fish courses making the most of New Zealand produce, and delicious desserts such as tiramisù and pannacotta. Steps to restaurant make disabled access difficult.

NEW PLYMOUTH The Salt Restaurant ⬛ $$$

1 Egmont Street **Tel** *(06) 769 5304*   **Map** *D3*

Salt, upstairs in New Plymouth's newest, most stylish hotel, is open all day every day for breakfast, lunch, dinner and all-day light meals, snacks and drinks. Watch the waves roll in from all the tables, whether inside or on the balcony. Seafood predominates on the full dinner menu.

NEW PLYMOUTH Albert's ⬛⬛ $$$$

161 Courtney Street **Tel** *(06) 759 1348*   **Map** *D3*

Classic, contemporary European-style restaurant in the heart of New Plymouth. Chic setting with white linen tablecloths and fine crystal glasses, and good service. Brings together fine food and wine in a meat-heavy menu. Wine list features mainly New Zealand wines.

PALMERSTON NORTH Bella's Café ⬛⬛ $$

2 The Square **Tel** *(06) 357 8616*   **Map** *E4*

In a bright Mediterranean-café-style setting on Palmerston North's Square, Bella's offers inventive Italian- and Asian-inspired cuisine. The menu features "classics" and a constantly changing selection of dishes such as Maple-glazed kumara, crispy bacon and toasted pine-nuts with spinach, drizzled in a balsamic and kikorangi blue cheese olive oil.

PALMERSTON NORTH Barista ⬛⬛ $$$

59 George Street **Tel** *(06) 357 2614*   **Map** *E4*

In Palmerston North's grooviest street, near Te Manawa and the Square, Barista takes its food and wine as seriously as its coffee, serving delicious, sophisticated but simple New Zealand staples with a fusion twist. Known as the espresso bar, it also serves wine, classic breakfasts, café-style lunches and delicious, unfussy dinners.

Key to Price Guide *see p326* **Key to Symbols** *see back cover flap*

PALMERSTON NORTH Aberdeen Restaurant and Bar $$$$

161 Broadway Avenue **Tel** *(06) 952 5570*

Map E4

Housed in a former Turkish sauna, this restaurant and bar still has a warm ambience, with a brick fireplace in the centre, and a sunny, covered courtyard at the rear. Standard brunches (eggs benedict), light lunches and robust fusion dinners. Wines by the glass. Live music on Thursday and Friday.

PALMERSTON NORTH Déjeuner $$$$

159 Broadway Avenue **Tel** *(06) 952 5581*

Map E4

Palmerston North's veteran fine-dining restaurant. Situated in an old house built by one of the city's founding fathers, which functioned for years as a doctor's surgery, it is now decorated in establishment style with rich, dark colours. Signature dish is slow roasted lamb or veal shanks on a flavoured mash.

WAIRARAPA Wild Oats Café $

127 High Street, Carterton **Tel** *(06) 379 5580*

Map E4

Opened recently by the family that has run the Dixon Street Deli in Wellington since 1930, this is a great place to stop for a light lunch or to stock up on coffee and the enormous range of sandwiches, baps, rolls, baguettes and pastries on the drive north from Wellington.

WAIRARAPA Café Cecille $$

Queen Elizabeth Park, Masterton **Tel** *(06) 370 1166*

Map E4

Conveniently located near Masterton's fantastic new museum, Aratoi, and just off the main north-south road. There are plenty of outdoor seats at this café in the park, whose other attractions include an aviary, playground, gardens, deer park and mini golf. Views of cricket matches in summer a bonus. BYO Tuesdays.

WAIRARAPA Saluté $$$

83 Main Street, Greytown **Tel** *(06) 304 9825*

Map E4

A surprising place to find one of New Zealand's top Middle Eastern and Mediterranean restaurants, which has won many awards. Authentic shady courtyard with fountain, warmed by fire in winter. Range of dishes from eggs Florentine and French toast to *Harira*, a Moroccan lamb, chickpea, lentil, lemon and herb soup.

WAIRARAPA Est Wine Bar and Eatery $$$$

The Square, Martinborough **Tel** *(06) 306 9665*

Map E4

In the 19th-century post office building on Martinborough's main square. The former bank vault now houses the restaurant's cellars. Dining is by an open fire in the lounge, or in one of two courtyards. Full contemporary New Zealand menus, bar menu or platters to go with not only Martinborough wines.

WANGANUI Amadeus Riverbank Café $

69 Taupo Quay **Tel** *(06) 345 1538*

Map E4

Longstanding, popular café on the riverbank. Serves interesting versions of classic breakfast and lunch dishes, such as New Zealand smoked salmon and scrambled eggs on toasted bagel, guacamole with corn chips or a sandwich known as a hot babe – bacon, avocado and banana – washed down with coffee, juice, beer, wine or spirits.

WELLINGTON Dixon Street Deli $

45 Dixon Street **Tel** *(04) 384 2436*

Map D5

In the same family since it was opened in 1930 by Russian immigrants, Dixon Street Deli has grown from deli to café in its third generation. Just off Cuba Street, it offers breakfasts and lunches such as pumpkin risotto alongside offerings from the deli counter. Try the Dixon Deli Platter.

WELLINGTON Café Istanbul $$

156 Cuba Street **Tel** *(04) 385 4998*

Map D5

Meze platters, shish kebab and sticky baklava as well as lesser-known delicacies are among the Turkish treats on offer in a cosy Turkish-style setting – carpets on the walls, Turkish lanterns hanging from the ceilings and huge open fireplace right in the middle. Good place to go with a large group.

WELLINGTON Floriditas Café and Restaurant $$

16 Cuba Street **Tel** *(04) 381 2212*

Map D5

In Cuba Street in the heart of Wellington, this stylish, modern restaurant and café serves simple but delicious, seasonal food such as pasta dishes and risotto, with all ingredients sourced from the local region or from New Zealand. There's also an extensive wine list and an assortment of cocktails to choose between.

WELLINGTON Roti Chenai $$

5/120 Victoria Street **Tel** *(04) 382 9807*

Map D5

Wellington has plenty of Malaysian restaurants, but this one is consistently rated one of the best by Wellingtonians and food critics alike. It specializes in the gentler, milder flavours of southern Indian cuisine and the mixed Chinese, Indian and Malay styles of Malaysian cuisine. An affordable family restaurant. Very central.

WELLINGTON Chow $$$

45 Tory Street **Tel** *(04) 382 8585*

Map D5

Fresh flavours of Asia in a casual modern setting. Pick and choose from an extensive menu which might include manuka smoked eel rolls or banana leaf chicken. All main dishes served with jasmine rice. Live music and cabaret. Open seven days a week.

WELLINGTON Monsoon Poon
12 Blair Street **Tel** *(04) 803 3555*

$$$ **Map** *D5*

A melting pot of Southeast Asian cuisine – South Indian, South Chinese, Malay, Thai, Vietnamese and Philippine – in a cheerful, relaxed setting. Plenty of favourites such as mee goreng, nasi goreng, laksa and beef rendang galore, washed down by cocktails, beers, wines or lassi. Dial-a-rickshaw to get you home.

WELLINGTON Arbitrageur Wine Room and Restaurant
125 Featherston Street **Tel** *(04) 499 5530*

$$$$ **Map** *D5*

Arbitrageur's menu is European with an emphasis on French and Italian, serving light, bistro-type meals. Located in a high-ceilinged 1950s building in the heart of downtown Wellington, it is known for its lengthy wine list (over 600 wines). As well as vintages, many good wines are available by the glass.

WELLINGTON Boulcott Street Bistro
99 Boulcott Street **Tel** *(04) 499 4199*

$$$$ **Map** *D5*

Regarded as one of Wellington's finest restaurants since it opened in 1991. Award-winning food, lively atmosphere and slick, friendly service. Housed in an 1876 Victorian house, with chic, elegant décor. Classic and modern dishes such as lamb shanks and crème brulée. Good wines by the glass. No reservations for dinner.

WELLINGTON Citron Restaurant
270 Willis Street **Tel** *(04) 801 6263*

$$$$ **Map** *D5*

A well-known restaurant which specializes in three- and eight-course set menus. The style of cuisine combines chef Rex Morgan's classical training with ideas picked up on his travels – dishes such as lightly spiced chicken thigh and Maori potato salad with mango and kawakawa salsa. The restaurant has won many awards and accolades.

WELLINGTON Ford's Café
342 Tinakori Road **Tel** *(04) 472 6238*

$$$$ **Map** *D5*

Ford's is located in the heart of Thorndon, in a historic cottage which has always been famous for its food. A well established Wellington icon, the perfect place for cake and coffee, weekend brunch, a light lunch or a cosy dinner (try the antipasto platter). Sheltered, sunny courtyard. Casual service.

WELLINGTON Matterhorn
106 Cuba Street **Tel** *(04) 384 3359*

$$$$ **Map** *D5*

The Matterhorn is a Wellington institution on Cuba Street. Established in 1963 as an immigrant Swiss pastry shop, Matterhorn now prides itself on offering the finest and freshest of New Zealand's music, dining, drink, design and culture. Original cocktails and new and old world wine list. Open until 3am daily.

WELLINGTON Café Bastille
16 Majoribanks Street, Mount Victoria **Tel** *(04) 382 9559*

$$$$$ **Map** *D5*

Award-winning Bastille is a traditional French bistro serving delicious food. In contrast to the myriad influences and flavours of contemporary New Zealand cuisine, it offers French classics such as coq au vin, onion soup, Provençal bouillabaisse and steak pommes frites. A good selection of French wines. Children's menu. No bookings.

WELLINGTON Martin Bosley's Yacht Club Restaurant
103 Oriental Parade **Tel** *(04) 920 8502*

$$$$$ **Map** *D5*

Open to all, but located in the Royal Port Nicholson Yacht Club building, with a fabulous waterfront location offering panoramic views of Wellington and the harbour. Delicious menu that focuses on seafood, and lots of daily specials. The wine list is particularly strong on Martinborough and Marlborough wines.

WELLINGTON Shed 5 Restaurant and Bar
Queens Wharf **Tel** *(04) 499 9069*

$$$$$ **Map** *D5*

Built in 1888 as a woolshed, Shed 5 is one of the oldest remaining wharf stores in Lambton Harbour. Situated right on Queens Wharf close to the city centre, the painstakingly restored historic wooden building now houses one of Wellington's best-known seafood restaurants. Wide range of wines, beers and cocktails.

MARLBOROUGH AND NELSON

BLENHEIM Bacchus
3 Main Street **Tel** *(03) 578 8099*

$$$ **Map** *D5*

Consistently good value for money, this licensed restaurant serves mainly seafood in a cosy interior with a fireplace, or outdoors in summer. Intimate dining, very good menu and service. Good selection of local produce. Extensive wine list, featuring mainly some excellent wines from the Marlborough region. Open for dinner only.

BLENHEIM Bellafico Restaurant and Wine Bar
17 Maxwell Road **Tel** *(03) 577 6072*

$$$ **Map** *D5*

A Blenheim institution, Bellafico is owned by two Germans, Dietmar and Volker, who have maintained its warm ambience and friendly service while taking its cuisine to new heights. Unusual German-influenced menu includes rösti potatoes and bratwurst and sophisticated dinners. Extensive Marlborough wine list.

Key to Price Guide *see p326* **Key to Symbols** *see back cover flap*

BLENHEIM Herzog Winery Restaurant ♿ $$$$$

81 Jeffries Road ***Tel*** *(03) 572 8770* ***Map*** *D5*

Gourmet restaurant in a boutique vineyard, highly praised for the wines, its cuisine and the highly professional service. Mediterranean-inspired food, best enjoyed as part of a gourmet set menu. Jacket and tie required. Cooking workshops on the first Saturday of the month, which in the past have been shown on TV. Bistro serves cheaper lunch menu.

BLENHEIM Twelve Trees Restaurant 🚸 ♿ $$$$$

Allan Scott Wines & Estates Ltd, Jacksons Road ***Tel*** *(03) 572 7123* ***Map*** *D5*

Named after the walnut trees that line the entrance to the winery, Twelve Trees is one of Marlborough's longest-standing winery restaurants. Beautiful indoor/outdoor garden restaurant among the vineyards. Wines recommended to accompany dishes such as venison medallions with raspberry jus. Lunch only.

GOLDEN BAY Wholemeal Café 🚸 ♿ $

60 Commercial Street, Takaka ***Tel*** *(03) 525 9426* ***Map*** *D4*

Another Golden Bay hippie institution, the Wholemeal Café is a hub of the local alternative lifestyle community (check out the noticeboard). Soy lattes, spirulina, cakes, muffins and baked savouries, salads and an interesting range of hot and cold vegetarian meals with a high fibre content. It also has a gallery.

GOLDEN BAY Mussel Inn 🚸 ♿ ♫ $$

SH60, Onekaka ***Tel*** *(03) 525 9241* ***Map*** *D4*

The place to go in Golden Bay (17km north of Takaka) for home-brewed beers, ales, ciders, lemonade or ginger ale, wines, food and music, the Mussel Inn is a much loved local haunt. Large garden. Regular live music nights with a folky bent. Food features steamed mussels and mussel chowder. Be prepared to wait in summer.

HAVELOCK Mussel Pot 🚸 ♿ $$$

73 Main Road ***Tel*** *(03) 574 2824* ***Map*** *D4*

A fun, family-friendly eatery showcasing local green-lipped mussels with the slogan 'clean, green and mussel orientated'. Options include mussel chowder, mussel steamers, grilled mussels and mussel baskets. Marlborough white wines. Look out for trademark dancing mussels on the roof as you approach.

KAIKOURA The Craypot Café and Bar 🚸 ♿ $$$$

70 Westend Road ***Tel*** *(03) 319 6027* ***Map*** *D5*

Cheerful, friendly place to sample crayfish thermidor, mussel chowder, battered fish and other seafood delights. Good selection of light lunch dishes and a heavy-duty chocolate brownie cake to sink you. Relaxed, family-friendly atmosphere in a hard-to-miss location across the road from the seafront, village green, carpark and dolphin tours.

MOTUEKA Hot Mamas Café 🚸 ♿ ♫ $

105 High Street ***Tel*** *(03) 528 7039* ***Map*** *D4*

Tune in to the hippie vibes at Hot Mamas Café in Motueka before heading over Takaka Hill to Golden Bay. Blackboard menu features soups, vegetarian dishes, pizzas and snacks like nachos, or check the cabinet for cakes and muffins. Outlandish murals. Fire in winter, opens onto street in summer. Live music.

NELSON Morrison Street Café 🚸 ♿ $

244 Hardy Street ***Tel*** *(03) 548 8110* ***Map*** *D4*

Seasonal cuisine and excellent coffee in a friendly, buzzing atmosphere in the heart of Nelson. Local art exhibited indoors, and seating in a courtyard outdoors. Has won many best café and hospitality awards for its congenial ambience and delicious food. A popular hangout for Nelson locals and travellers alike.

NELSON Miyazu Japanese Restaurant 🚸 ♿ $$$

Rutherford Hotel, Trafalgar Square ***Tel*** *(03) 548 2299* ***Map*** *D4*

The Miyazu Japanese Restaurant has won the Best International Restaurant category in the Taste Nelson awards for several years in a row. Dining options range from raw fish at the sushi and sashimi bar to a traditional Japanese barbecue at the Teppan Yaki bar, or Japanese cuisine à la carte.

NELSON Seifried's Vineyard Restaurant 🚸 ♿ $$$

Cnr Redwood Road and SH60, Appleby ***Tel*** *(03) 544 1555* ***Map*** *D4*

Affordable dining in a vineyard setting with a children's play area. Fresh local produce. Art by Nelson artists on display indoors. Warmed by an open fire in winter, with seating amid the vines in summer. Twenty minutes' drive from Nelson towards Abel Tasman National Park. Look for the Rabbit Island turnoff.

NELSON Waimea Estates Café in the Vineyard 🚸 ♿ ♫ $$$

Appleby Highway, Hope ***Tel*** *(03) 544 4963* ***Map*** *D4*

Indoor and heated outdoor dining in the middle of the Waimea Estates vineyards. Live music at weekends in summer. Cuisine based where possible on fresh, locally sourced ingredients might include grilled Motueka Valley venison steak served with Moroccan carrot salad and roasted potatoes or the vineyard platter of mixed antipasti.

NELSON Bardelicious 🚸 ♿ $$$$

276 Trafalgar Street ***Tel*** *(03) 546 9400* ***Map*** *D4*

This is a New York-style eatery with a dark-wood interior, candles and a distinctive ambience. It has tables upstairs and downstairs, as well as a street frontage courtyard. The menu offers Italian cuisine. It is situated in the historic area of the town.

NELSON Boat Shed Café
350 Wakefield Quay **Tel** *(03) 546 9783*   **Map** *D4*

Seafood restaurant in a prime harbourside setting on wharf piles over the water, consistently voted one of Nelson's best. Be prepared to pay more for crayfish, paua and other New Zealand seafood, or go all out with the seafood extravaganza – a selection for around $230 for two.

NELSON Three Rooms Rest
294 Queen Street, Richmond **Tel** *(03) 544 0610*   **Map** *D4*

Universally recommended, Three Rooms Rest is on the waterfront 15 minutes' drive from the centre of Nelson. A good selection of seafood and excellent New Zealand beef and lamb, prepared in a fresh, contemporary style. Has won awards for fish, meat and mushroom cuisine. Small, selective wine list, featuring local wines.

CANTERBURY AND THE WEST COAST

AKAROA By The Green
37 Rue Lavaud **Tel** *(03) 304 7717*   **Map** *C6*

Located in the historic quarter of Akaroa, a licensed café which serves breakfast, lunch and all-day deli food based on local seasonal produce, such as gurnard with lemon aioli and salad. Enjoy good coffee, a glass of local wine or a cocktail while watching the comings and goings of Akaroa. Currently closed Mondays and Tuesdays.

AKAROA French Farm Winery and Restaurant
12 Winery Road **Tel** *(03) 304 5784*   **Map** *C6*

Vineyards and sweeping lawns surround this delightful restaurant, which has roaring fires in winter. French provincial cuisine incorporating fresh local produce. The unpretentious food might include grilled Akaroa salmon with Provençal vegetable *pithivière* or grilled rack of Canterbury lamb with potato gratin and minted jus. Estate wines. Also pizzeria.

AKAROA Harbour 71
71 Beach Road **Tel** *(03) 304 7656*   **Map** *C6*

Akaroa is famous for its (farmed) salmon, and Harbour 71's award-winning chef Darren Wright concocts some fabulous dishes from it, such as cold smoked salmon mousse and salmon caviar on hot smoked salmon. Alternatives from scallops and groper to lamb and venison. Fine wines. Located in a historic two-storey harbourfront store.

CHRISTCHURCH Belgian Beer Café
88 Armagh Street **Tel** *(03) 377 1007*   **Map** *C6*

You will find traditional Belgian cuisine here, including Flemish stew, cheese croquettes and, of course, steak frites with creamy mayo. Centrally located in an historic 100-year old building, it has a terrace area looking out over the beautiful Avon River.

CHRISTCHURCH Indochine
209 Cambridge Terrace **Tel** *(03) 365 7323*   **Map** *C6*

An exceptional dining experience, celebrating the opulence, flavours and colours of the East. The interior is stunning and the food is as equally impressive, and can be described as Euro-Asian cuisine. There is also a cocktail bar. It is centrally located close to the Town Hall and convention centre.

CHRISTCHURCH Annie's Wine Bar and Restaurant
Cnr Rolleston Avenue and Hereford Street **Tel** *(03) 365 0566*   **Map** *C6*

Popular restaurant with a wonderful location in the South Quad of the Arts Centre, in the former sculpture room of the old stone Gothic Revival university buildings. Good, uncluttered Mediterranean-Pacific cuisine with excellent wines and superb breads. Native timbers, recycled brick and stained-glass windows exude warmth and rustic charm.

CHRISTCHURCH Cook 'n' with Gas
23 Worcester Blvd **Tel** *(03) 377 9166*   **Map** *C6*

This upbeat bistro offers cutting edge New Zealand cuisine and extensive wine and beer lists, including 40 national and international beers. Centrally located right opposite the Arts Centre and housed in a 19th-century colonial villa. Reservations recommended.

CHRISTCHURCH Sala Sala
184–6 Oxford Terrace **Tel** *(03) 366 6755*   **Map** *C6*

Japanese Teppan Yaki and sushi bar, with a wide variety of authentic dishes, expertly prepared and presented by the chefs, for a taste of fine Japanese cuisine. Sushi and sashimi specialities. A large range of New Zealand wines, Japanese sake and beers. Another Sala Sala is located in Arrowtown.

CHRISTCHURCH Pescatore
50 Park Terrace **Tel** *(03) 371 0257*   **Map** *C6*

This excellent restaurant is in the luxurious The George Hotel and provides an outstanding fine dining experience. Pescatore has gained international recognition for its Pacific Rim cuisine and its wine list is equally highly acclaimed. The sumptuous dining room overlooks Hagley Park.

Key to Price Guide *see p326* **Key to Symbols** *see back cover flap*

FAIRLIE The Old Library Café

🎎 & $$$

6 Allandale Road **Tel** *(03) 685 8999*

Map C6

Built in 1914, the old Fairlie Library has been tastefully renovated to create a pleasant restaurant which serves award-winning cuisine from snacks to full gourmet meals. Rich, delicious desserts. Warm atmosphere, friendly service and great coffee to speed you on your way from Christchurch to Queenstown (or vice versa). Indoor and outdoor tables.

FOX GLACIER Cook Saddle Café and Saloon

🎎 & 🎵 $$$

SH6 **Tel** *(03) 751 0700*

Map B6

A large stone open fire place makes this pleasant restaurant inviting even on the wettest West Coast day. Variety of well-cooked American themed dishes at reasonable prices in a relaxed comfortable setting. Keas play in the trees by the verandah. Family-friendly and packed with local history. Serves excellent local beers.

FRANZ JOSEF Beeches Restaurant

🎎 & $$$

SH6 **Tel** *(03) 752 0721*

Map B6

Café, restaurant and bar, open for breakfast, lunch and dinner. Extensive selection of food including whitebait (in season), salmon and venison. Generous portions. Good wine list. You can eat indoors, or outside when it is not raining. Staff tend to be seasonal working holiday-makers, and service can be a bit erratic.

GREYMOUTH Café 124 on Mackay

🎎 & $

124 Mackay Street **Tel** *(03) 768 7503*

Map C5

Relaxed indoor and outdoor café-style dining in newly built premises alongside a gift emporium. Great food, excellent coffee and warm friendly atmosphere with great service. Some of the best food in town (beef and lamb notable), and the only place here where you can sit out at a pavement table.

GREYMOUTH Waterline Restaurant

🎎 & $$$$

State Highway 6, Punakaiki **Tel** *(09) 731 1168*

Map C5

An award-winning restaurant with floor-to-ceiling windows that really allow you to enjoy the spectacular beach-front location. Outside dining on the balcony is also available only metres from the water. The cuisine is simple, uses local produce and naturally specializes in seafood.

HAAST The Craypot

🍴 📷 🎎 $

Jackson Bay **Tel** *(03) 750 0035*

Map C6

A mobile restaurant in remote wilderness with ocean views. At Jackson Bay, as far south as the road will go from Haast, an ominous but beautiful spot which has been settled and abandoned many times over. Fresh fish and chips, whitebait patties and hamburgers. Some seating in the tiny caravan.

HOKITIKA Café de Paris

🎎 & $$$

19 Tancred Street **Tel** *(03) 755 8933*

Map C5

Founded by a French chef 20 years ago, award-winning Café de Paris has an excellent reputation on the West Coast and beyond for its French- and Italian-inspired cuisine. Classics such as *soupe à l'oignon*, *carré d'agneau* and *scaloppine di vitello ai funghi* on the menu.

KARAMEA The Last Resort

📷 🎎 & $$

71 Waverley Street **Tel** *(03) 782 6617*

Map C4

Part of the sprawling, low-key hotel complex at Karamea, the Last Resort café and bar offers pizza, burgers, salads, nachos, fish and chips, desserts, cakes, tea, coffee, juices, wines, and beers on tap. The Last Resort restaurant offers a selection of good seafood and some meat dishes in the evening.

KARAMEA Karamea Bight Restaurant

🎎 & $$$

Cnr Waverley Street and Wharf Road **Tel** *(03) 782 6800*

Map C4

Friendly proprietors offer a wide range of cheap bar meals as well as full meals in the old-fashioned pub setting of the Karamea Village Hotel. Regional and national winner of the Wild Food Challenge, with dishes such as local whitebait in a seaweed basket or wild rabbit with feijoa chutney.

MOUNT COOK Old Mountaineers' Café Bar and Restaurant

🎎 & $$

Larch Grove **Tel** *(03) 435 1890*

Map B6

Next door to the DOC visitor centre in the Aoraki/Mount Cook National Park, the Old Mountaineers' was officially opened by Sir Edmund Hillary in 2003. Offers warming soups, Mediterranean-style snacks, and good old-fashioned New Zealand cuisine (grilled steak or fish and chips) followed by warm puddings, pies and crumbles.

MOUNT COOK Alpine Restaurant

🎎 & $$$$

The Hermitage **Tel** *(03) 435 1809*

Map B6

The main restaurant at Aoraki/Mount Cook, in The Hermitage resort complex. Sumptuous buffets for breakfast, lunch and dinner with views of Aoraki/Mount Cook from every table. A range of fare including soup, salads, seafood, meats and desserts. Open year round, offering cheaper meals than its sister restaurant, the Panorama.

MOUNT COOK Panorama Restaurant

& $$$$

The Hermitage **Tel** *(03) 435 1809*

Map B6

Upmarket restaurant in The Hermitage resort complex at Mount Cook, where you can watch the sun set on Aoraki/Mount Cook while you dine. Venison, hare and New Zealand meats, such as lamb and beef, a speciality, followed by mouthwatering desserts. It has gone from strength to strength in its 40 years, winning many awards.

WAIPARA VALLEY Pegasus Bay Winery Restaurant ⛓ ♿ $$$$$

Stockgrove Road, Amberley, Waipara **Tel** *(03) 314 6869*   **Map** C6

Voted New Zealand's best casual dining restaurant by prestigious Cuisine magazine, the restaurant is part of the family-run Pegasus Bay boutique winery, where the Donaldson parents, children and partners produce top wines and fine food. Contemporary New Zealand art in warm rimu interior, and breathtaking gardens. Fresh, seasonal cuisine.

WESTPORT The Bay House Café and Art Gallery ⛓ ♿ $$$$

Tauranga Bay **Tel** *(03) 789 7133*   **Map** C5

With a superb setting among coastal flaxes, and sweeping views across Tauranga Bay near the seal colony at Cape Foulwind, the Bay House is a great place for lunch, dinner or coffee. Innovative use of locally sourced produce including black passionfruit. Local seafood is a speciality, especially the seafood chowder.

OTAGO AND SOUTHLAND

ARROWTOWN Pesto ⛓ ♿ $$$

18 Buckingham Street **Tel** *(03) 442 0885*   **Map** B6

The younger sibling of Saffron (see below) Pesto offers family-friendly pizza and pasta down a cobbled alleyway lit by braziers on cold nights in quaint Arrowtown. There is nothing twee about the restaurant's decor, which is all recycled timbers, exposed aggregate concrete and copper ceilings.

ARROWTOWN Saffron ♿ $$$$$

18 Buckingham Street **Tel** *(03) 442 0131*   **Map** B6

South Island game features on Saffron's diverse menu, which is complemented by a wine list showcasing pinot noirs from Central Otago. Located in Arrowtown's main street, the corrugated iron building belies the seriously sophisticated cooking inside. Interesting combinations such as roast duck and crabmeat soup with tapioca.

BLUFF Lands End ⛓ ♿ $$$

10 Ward Parade **Tel** *(03) 212 7575*   **Map** A7

A superb location at Stirling Point overlooking Stewart Island, at the southern tip of mainland New Zealand where SH1 ends. Fresh, locally caught fish a speciality. Known for local blue cod, salmon and Bluff oysters (in season). Excellent choice of New Zealand wines. Local crafts and souvenirs are on sale next door.

CLYDE Oliver's ♿ $$$

34 Sunderland Street **Tel** *(03) 449 2860*   **Map** B6

A restaurant with a reputation in the original Victoria Stores complex in Clyde, built in 1863 and lovingly restored. Unusually for New Zealand, it has schist stone walls and has been floored with red brick, creating the deceptively simple atmosphere of a rustic French restaurant. Simple, delicious food and wines.

DUNEDIN Nova ⛓ ♿ $$

29 The Octagon **Tel** *(03) 479 0808*   **Map** B7

This central café (beside Dunedin Public Art Gallery) is a previous winner of the Nobilo café of the year award. It is impeccably child-friendly, and open seven days for breakfast, lunch and dinner until late. All-day menu makes use of fresh local produce from breakfast classics to Italian and Asian dinner dishes.

DUNEDIN Plato Café ⛓ ♿ $$$

2 Birch Street **Tel** *(03) 477 4235*   **Map** B7

Relaxed café dining on Dunedin's harbourfront, Plato occupies a former hostel for seafarers. Menu emphasizes seafood, but also showcases a wide range of local produce from organic salad greens to eye fillet. Good, uncomplicated home-style food served with Central Otago wines and local beers. Friendly service and great coffee.

DUNEDIN Bell Pepper Blues ⛓ ♿ $$$$

474 Princes Street **Tel** *(03) 474 0973*   **Map** B7

Modern New Zealand cuisine with more than a hint of Asian flavours (the pan-seared beef sirloin is rubbed with Asian aromatics, and the mahi-mahi is grilled with a dust of dukkah spice), although there are strong European influences too (roast pumpkin gnocchi with wilted baby spinach, and chicken supreme reinvented). $10 corkage.

GORE The Moth ⛓ ♿ $$

SH94, Mandeville **Tel** *(03) 208 9662*   **Map** B7

Adjacent to the old Mandeville airfield, The Moth was originally the Old Railway Hotel, famous in prohibition days as the closest 'wet' area for the town of Gore. It has been totally renovated in a nostalgic aviation theme, and has featured in New Zealand's *Home and Garden* magazine. Delicious vegetarian dishes.

INVERCARGILL The Cabbage Tree ⛓ ♿ $$$

379 Dunns Road **Tel** *(03) 213 1443*   **Map** A7

Ten minutes' drive south of Invercargill towards Oreti Beach, The Cabbage Tree has been assembled from a relocated community hall, semi-derelict beach store, windows from an old hospital, old power poles, church pews galore. The garden is planted with natives. Gourmet café food (venison focaccia).

Key to Price Guide *see p326* **Key to Symbols** *see back cover flap*

MOERAKI Fleur's Place
🏃 ♿ $$$$$
169 Haven Street **Tel** *(03) 439 4480* **Map** *B7*

Restaurant on the waterfront by Moeraki's old jetty, built on the site of an early whaling station in 2002, from recycled materials. Offers fish of the day from the Moeraki boats simply cooked with a choice of sauces including caper and lime butter or coconut and coriander. Famous blue cod. Bookings essential.

OAMARU Whitestone Cheese Café
🏃 ♿ $
3 Torridge Street **Tel** *(03) 434 8098* **Map** *B7*

An innovative cheese-based blackboard menu accompanied by Central Otago wines at this award-winning handmade cheese factory. The Make Room can be viewed from an exterior platform before cheese tastings. Excellent sheeps' milk cheeses, fetas and cows' milk blues, bries and camemberts.

OAMARU Casa Nova House
♿ $$$$
1 Alt Street **Tel** *(03) 437 1782* **Map** *B7*

In a grand mansion built in 1861 for an Englishman along the lines of his ancestral home in Leicestershire, who, within 10 years had abandoned the two-storey Gothic house to fight in the Land Wars and never returned. Now it is coastal Otago's finest dining restaurant, with intimate dining room.

QUEENSTOWN Vesta
🏃 ♿ $
Williams Cottage, Marine Parade **Tel** *(03) 442 5687* **Map** *A6*

Fun café with unparalleled views of Lake Wakatipu, Vesta is also an innovative store showcasing contemporary New Zealand-made homeware, design and gifts. Situated in Williams Cottage, a historic building, which has retained its original 1800s fittings and wallpaper. Cosy lounge and funky lakeside garden.

QUEENSTOWN Vudu Café
♿ $
23 Beach Street **Tel** *(03) 442 5357* **Map** *A6*

Groovy Internet café and hangout, open daily from 8am until late. Make friends in Queenstown (and elsewhere) before you go, through the 24-hour Internet chat room, and make real friends once you get there in the Vudu Café. Buy the T-shirt and take home a bag of freshly roasted coffee.

QUEENSTOWN Amisfield Winery Bistro
🏃 ♿ $$
10 Lake Hayes Road **Tel** *(03) 442 0556* **Map** *A6*

Country-style bistro offering fresh, simple local food to complement estate-grown wines. Delicious fare might include the likes of salmon with lemon and capers, duck with quince paste or roast pork with pea purée. Sample the chef's daily whims with the 'trust the chef' menu. Superb location overlooking Lake Hayes. Courtyard or fireside eating.

QUEENSTOWN Finz Down Under Queenstown
🏃 ♿ $$
Steamer Wharf **Tel** *(03) 442 7405* **Map** *A6*

Fun, friendly and affordable, Finz Down Under Queenstown is a new seafood and rotisserie restaurant on the Steamer Wharf. With its wide-ranging menu, extensive wine list, retro decor and funky atmosphere, Finz is the place to go for a noisy meal out with a big group of friends.

QUEENSTOWN Gibbston Valley Winery Restaurant
🏃 ♿ $$$
SH6, Gibbston **Tel** *(03) 442 6910* **Map** *A6*

The winery pulls in the hordes between bungy jumping and Arrowtown with its cave cellar tours. Its cuisine is a little over-complicated for some tastes (Milford Sound crayfish and pumpkin fritters with lemon aioli and a scampi, rhubarb and cucumber salad), but it is of a very high quality and the wines are excellent.

QUEENSTOWN Roaring Megs
🏃 ♿ $$$
53 Shotover Street **Tel** *(03) 442 9676* **Map** *A6*

The place to go for beef and lamb in Queenstown. Although it kow tows to Asian fusion trends, the cuisine here is a little more robust than elsewhere. Try the hors d'oeuvre platter, featuring smoked fish, duck liver and orange terrine, hot smoked salmon, venison salami and New Zealand cheeses.

QUEENSTOWN Boardwalk Seafood Restaurant
🏃 ♿ $$$$
Steamer Wharf **Tel** *(03) 442 5630* **Map** *A6*

On the shores of Queenstown Bay by the bustling Steamer Wharf, with stunning views of the lake and mountains. Specialises in fresh seafood flown in daily from North and South islands – oysters, kingfish, yellow-fin tuna, snapper, john dory, scallops, crayfish, blue cod and groper, Akaroa salmon and whitebait (in season).

QUEENSTOWN The Bathhouse
🏃 ♿ $$$$$
28 Marine Parade **Tel** *(03) 442 5625* **Map** *A6*

The King George V Bathhouse, built on the shores of Lake Wakatipu to commemorate the coronation, has been restored as a charming waterfront restaurant and café with views across the lake to Walter Peak. Offers coffee, wine or top-notch three-course meals in the conservatory-style sunroom. Great meals for children.

STEWART ISLAND Church Hill Café Bar and Restaurant
♿ $$$$
36 Kamahi Road, Half Moon Bay **Tel** *(03) 219 1323* **Map** *A7*

Enjoy breathtaking views over Half Moon Bay while dining on locally caught, innovatively prepared New Zealand seafood here. Scampi and seafood salad may feature on the menu alongside the catch of the day. Muttonbird, a sea bird traditionally eaten by Maori, is another rare treat here. Friendly service. You must make a reservation for dinner.

SHOPPING IN NEW ZEALAND

New Zealand has a lot to offer the visiting shopper, including goods not available in most

Out of New Zealand

Craft shop sign in Auckland

other countries. Such items range from traditional Maori bone and greenstone carvings to sheepskin rugs and handmade wool sweaters. Many small towns in popular tourist areas have galleries where local crafts people sell their goods, and Auckland, Wellington and Christchurch have major markets where artisans sell unique products. Because New Zealand is one of the most open economies in the world, with few tariffs and no import licensing, goods such as cameras and audio equipment are very reasonably priced. New Zealand's wines *(see pp324–5)*, meats, seafoods, dairy products and fruits are also well worth sampling.

Kirkcaldie and Stains, Wellington's leading department store

SHOPPING HOURS

Most shops in New Zealand are open from 9am to 5pm or 5:30pm, Monday to Saturday. Most stores are open on Sundays also for shorter hours. In big cities, late night shopping is usually available on Thursdays or Fridays, when stores stay open until 9pm.

Supermarkets and shopping malls in urban areas are open seven days a week, and many supermarkets stay open until 8pm or 9pm and some offer a 24-hour service. In towns, suburbs and rural areas, dairies stay open long hours.

HOW TO PAY

Credit and debit cards are accepted by most stores, usually with a minimum purchase limit. If your card is encoded with a PIN number, you can withdraw cash from one of the many automatic teller machines at banks and shopping centres. Identification, such as a passport or driver's licence, is required when presenting traveller's cheques. Personal cheques may also be accepted, but shops prefer credit cards. New Zealand shopkeepers are not accustomed to bargaining and many also prefer cash transactions.

All goods sold in New Zealand are levied a Goods and Service Tax (GST) of 12.5 per cent, which is included in the purchase price. GST is not refunded when you leave New Zealand.

RIGHTS AND REFUNDS

The **Consumers' Institute** ((04) 384 7963) can provide detailed information about your rights as a buyer. If the goods purchased are defective, you are entitled to a refund. If you decide you do not like an item, many shops will allow you to return or exchange it for something else. If you want to return or exchange an item, you will need to present the receipt.

DEPARTMENT STORES

Each of the four main cities has a major department store selling high quality goods. In Auckland, it is **Smith and Caughey's**; in Wellington, **Kirkcaldie and Stains**; in Dunedin, **Arthur Barnett**, and in Christchurch, **Ballantynes**.

Farmers, Kmart and The Warehouse sell a wide range of lower priced goods, and have numerous branches throughout the country.

SHOPPING MALLS

Large indoor shopping malls are a feature of cities and larger towns. Most are located in the suburbs rather then central city areas, and usually include at least one supermarket plus a range of shops selling items such as clothing, sports equipment, household appliances and books. Many also have food halls selling a variety of inexpensive meals.

Shop assistant arranging a display of Zambesi fashion clothes

DAIRIES

Dairies are small convenience stores that can be found in most towns and suburbs (though they are slowly disappearing). Hours of opening vary, but most are open seven days a week from about 7am until 8pm. They sell basic food supplies, snacks, drinks, newspapers and cigarettes.

ROADSIDE STALLS

Roadside stalls selling fruit and vegetables are common in major horticultural areas such as the Bay of Plenty, Marlborough and Central Otago. Many orchards encourage people to "pick their own", and may also sell the produce at a reduced price. Strawberries can be found everywhere in late spring and summer; cherries in Marlborough at Christmas; apricots, nectarines and peaches in Otago around January–February, and kiwifruit in the Bay of Plenty from April to September. Visitors should also look out for the many cheese factories in Waikato, Taranaki, Marlborough and Canterbury which sell delicious, locally made dairy products.

Roadside stall sign

MARKETS

Most New Zealand markets specialize in crafts rather than foods, although Otara Market in South Auckland (see p91) specializes in Pacific foods. Farmers' markets, such as at Hastings and Dunedin, are also increasingly popular. Auckland, Christchurch and Nelson have craft markets. Opening times vary: in Auckland, the Victoria Park Market (see p91) is open daily; while Christchurch's Arts Centre market (see p224) and Nelson Market (see p211) are open at the weekend.

New Zealand-made crafts and souvenirs for sale in Blenheim

HANDICRAFTS

A wide variety of shops selling locally made crafts and souvenirs can be found in New Zealand's main cities, tourist towns and resorts. In areas where the local craft industry is particularly strong, such as Coromandel (see p127) and Nelson (see p213), small galleries maintained by individual artists and crafts people are dotted along the roadsides. Museum shops, such as at the **Museum of New Zealand Te Papa Tongarewa**, Wellington (see 166–7), and **Auckland War Memorial Museum** (see pp78–9) also sell top-of-the-range handcrafted products.

The variety and quality of New Zealand handicrafts is continually improving. Products worth buying are traditional Maori flax baskets, bone and greenstone jewellery and ornaments, *paua* (abalone) shell jewellery, ceramics, hand-blown glassware, wood products made from New Zealand's native timbers, and sheepskin and wool items (see pp344–5).

Colourful crafts for sale at Nelson's weekend market

DESIGNER LABELS

New Zealand has a number of internationally successful fashion designers, whose clothing can be bought in boutiques in the main cities. Labels to look for are Trelise Cooper, Karen Walker, World, Zambesi and NomD. Top quality casual wool clothing is available under several labels, including Untouched World.

Quality outdoor clothing and equipment is available under the Canterbury, Heritage and Macpac brands (see p345). Arthur Ellis manufactures high quality Fairydown equipment, as well as the less pricey Great Outdoors brand.

What to Buy in New Zealand

Woven flax basket

New Zealand offers a wide range of unique goods. Some, such as bone and greenstone carvings and jewellery, and plaited flax items, are reflective of the country's Maori heritage, while others, such as sheepskin rugs and wool garments, reflect its strong agricultural base. Other good buys are wood products made from New Zealand's native timbers, ceramics, outdoor equipment, and food and wine. Hundreds of gift and craft shops, as well as department stores and museum shops, make it easy to find New Zealand-made products to suit every budget.

Sheepskin floor rug with thick, combed wool

Hand-knitted sweater

Sheepskin slippers

Wool and sheepskin *products from New Zealand are major shopping attractions. Although most New Zealand wool is exported for use in carpets, merino wool is used locally for fine knitwear and suiting fabrics. Hand-knitted sweaters made from hand-spun, hand-dyed wool are widely available in department stores and souvenir shops, as are sheepskin rugs, car seat covers, jackets, boots, slippers, gloves, and souvenir items.*

Lamb's wool muff

Woollen gloves

Bowl made from the trunk of a tree

Woodcrafts *fashioned from native timbers are well known for their attractive grains and fine workmanship. The most commonly used woods are rimu, kauri, matai and beech. Many crafts people also use recycled timber as well as exotic species such as macrocarpa.*

Wooden coasters with *paua* **shell inlay**

Kauri timber trinket box

Carved Maori figure with *paua* **shell eyes**

Finely carved traditional Maori club

Pendant with perforated spiral design

Greenstone *(or jade) is New Zealand's most precious stone. Artisans craft it into a wide range of jewellery and ornaments using both traditional Maori and contemporary designs (see p237).*

Bone, *originally used by Maori to fashion fish-hooks, is now used mainly for decorative items. Stylized fish-hook pendants, embellished with delicate tracery, are popular purchases.*

Paua *(abalone) is a shellfish found around the New Zealand coastline, but it is treasured more for its iridescent inner shell than for its meat. It is used primarily to make pendants and earrings, and for inlays in woodcrafts and traditional Maori carvings.*

Paua shell and silver pendants and necklace

Box with inset *paua* **shell**

Hand-painted dish

Wine goblet

Red glass vase

Perfume bottle

Ceramics and glassware *are the most widely available craft items in New Zealand. Ceramics range from rustic earthenware pieces to delicate ornamental works and top quality tableware. Hand-blown glassware is of high quality, and many artisans are happy to allow visitors to watch them at their work (see p 213).*

Earthenware coffee mug

Cat-shaped coffee pot

Outdoor equipment *made in New Zealand is among the best in the world. The leading brand is Macpac, which regularly tests its own equipment in the mountains of the South Island. The best places to buy such goods are specialist outdoor equipment shops in the main cities.*

Tent in bag

Windcheater

Backpack

Food and drink, *products of New Zealand's extensive farmlands, include excellent meats, fruit, dairy produce and wines. As well as lamb and beef, speciality meats such as ostrich and venison are available. Cheeses made by small boutique factories are worth trying, as is New Zealand's delicious ice cream and its honey from native plants. New Zealand wines have also gained a strong international reputation (see pp36–7, 324–5).*

Selection of Kapiti cheeses

Kiwifruit flavoured chocolates

Jars of local honey

Sauvignon Blanc from Marlborough

ENTERTAINMENT IN NEW ZEALAND

From professional theatre, opera and ballet to Maori and Pacific Island culture, music and dance and "Down Under" rock music, New Zealand has a diverse entertainment scene. The liveliest places are the main cities, but even small provincial towns boast their own local bands and amateur performance societies.

Entertainer at Auckland market

New Zealand is on the itinerary of many international performers, although some of these venture no further than Auckland and Wellington. Maori culture is an important theme in New Zealand art, and is showcased at festivals and specialist venues, such Te Puia, a Maori arts and crafts centre situated in Rotorua.

INFORMATION SOURCES

Tourism New Zealand posts a yearly calendar of events around the country on its website (see p347). Daily newspapers and magazines such as *North and South*, *The Listener* and *Metro* also provide details about current and upcoming performances.

THE EDGE®, Auckland's main entertainment complex

MAJOR VENUES

The major entertainment venues for the performing arts are located in New Zealand's four main cities. They include Auckland's **THE EDGE®**, which comprises the Aotea Centre, Town Hall and Civic Theatre; Wellington's **Michael Fowler Centre**; Christchurch's **Town Hall** and **Isaac Theatre Royal**, and Dunedin's **Town Hall**.

BOOKING TICKETS

It is wise to book in advance for most live performances. The easiest way is to use the nationwide **Ticketek** and **Ticketmaster** systems, either via the Internet or by telephone through their many

agencies around the country. In many cases, tickets can also be purchased at the venue.

THEATRE

Professional theatre companies are restricted to the main cities, while the smaller provincial towns are served by amateur troupes. Wellington has the most vibrant theatre scene, with three professional theatre companies (see pp156–7): **Downstage**; **Circa**, a co-operative established in the 1970s, known for its consistently excellent plays; and **Bats**, best known for experimental theatre performances. New Zealand's only national Maori theatre company, **Taki Rua**, specializes in indigenous ethnic drama and is based in Wellington, but also tours the country regularly with new productions.

Other professional theatre groups are the **Auckland Theatre Company**, which performs at the Maidment, Herald and Sky City theatres; the **Court Theatre** in Christchurch's historic Arts Centre; and the **Fortune Theatre**, located in Dunedin in an historic inner-city church.

CLASSICAL MUSIC, OPERA AND DANCE

The **New Zealand Symphony Orchestra** is based in Wellington (see pp156–7) but tours the country regularly, covering about 50,000 km (31,000 miles) a year, making it one of the most travelled orchestras in the world. It sometimes performs outdoor city concerts in summer.

New Zealand's regional professional orchestra companies are of a high standard and

New Zealand Symphony Orchestra at the Town Hall, Wellington

Saxcess, New Zealand's premier saxophone quartet

perform regularly. The principal opera company is the **National Business Review New Zealand Opera**, which performs mainly at the Aotea Centre in Auckland and in Wellington. Canterbury is home to Southern Opera.

The **Royal New Zealand Ballet** is the oldest professional dance company in Australasia. It tours the country frequently with a wide range of work (*see pp156–7*). **Footnote Dance**, New Zealand's only national contemporary dance troupe, also tours the country regularly, presenting productions created by New Zealand's own choreographers and composers.

Entertainment posters

ROCK, JAZZ AND COUNTRY

Kiwi rock music has a quirky charm that attracts fans worldwide. The Muttonbirds, Dave Dobbyn, Neil Finn and The Datsuns are among New Zealand's most internationally successful rock performers, and they occasionally perform in the country. Many local bands perform in pubs and popular venues such as Auckland's **THE EDGE**®.

Events such as Wellington's International Arts Festival attract both local and international jazz performers (*see pp156–7*), as do regional festivals such as the Bay of Islands Jazz and Blues Festival each August.

Country and Western has a strong following in New Zealand and there are a number of excellent singers and bands. Lovers of traditional country music should make their way to Gore in Southland during May and June to watch the Gold Guitar Awards.

MAORI MUSIC AND DANCE

Traditional Maori performing arts are showcased at a number of venues, including **Te Puia**, a Maori arts and crafts centre, at Rotorua (*see pp138–9*), and at the **Auckland War Memorial Museum** (*see pp78–9*), both staging daily concerts. The biennial three-day Aotearoa Traditional Maori Performing Arts Festival, held at different locations, features Maori culture, music and dance from around New Zealand. Tourist operators specializing in Maori heritage include music and dance in their programmes (*see p355*).

Maori cultural performance at an arts festival in Wellington

DIRECTORY

INFORMATION SOURCES

Ticketek
Tel (09) 307 5000.
www.ticketek.nz

Ticketmaster
Tel (09) 970 9700.
www.ticketmaster.co.nz

Tourism New Zealand
Tel (04) 917 5400.

MAJOR VENUES

Isaac Theatre Royal, Christchurch
Tel (03) 366 6326.

Michael Fowler Centre, Wellington
Tel (04) 801 4231.

Town Hall, Christchurch
Tel (03) 366 8899.

Town Hall, Dunedin
Tel (03) 474 3614.

THE EDGE®
Tel (09) 309 2677.

Wellington Town Hall
Tel 0800 202 324.

THEATRE

Auckland Theatre Company
Tel (09) 309 0390.

Bats Theatre
Tel (04) 802 4175.

Circa Theatre
Tel (04) 801 7992.

Court Theatre
Tel 0800 333 100.

Downstage Theatre
Tel (04) 801 6946.

Fortune Theatre
Tel (03) 477 8323.

Taki Rua
Tel (04) 385 3110.

CLASSICAL MUSIC, OPERA AND DANCE

Footnote Dance
Tel (04) 384 7285.

National Business Review New

Zealand Opera
Tel (09) 379 4068.

New Zealand Symphony Orchestra
Tel (04) 801 3890.

Royal New Zealand Ballet
Tel (04) 381 9000.

MAORI MUSIC AND DANCE

Auckland War Memorial Museum
Tel (09) 309 0443.

Te Puia, Rotorua
Tel (07) 348 9047.

Film and Popular Music

New Zealand arts and entertainment are in the midst of a mini renaissance, buoyed up by government investment in the country's culture. Local music has benefited from a music commission that helps to market the industry both at home and overseas, so more New Zealand bands are now heard on the radio. The big theatres and cinema chains are found in the main centres (see p92), but many smaller towns also have vibrant entertainment venues, many of which play host during the international festivals.

FILM AND FESTIVALS

Although major New Zealand productions such as the *Lord of the Rings* trilogy have been making the headlines in recent years, for every Peter Jackson there are countless other filmmakers working on short films and digital feature films. New Zealanders love going to the cinema and advances in digital projection have prompted the revival of boutique suburban cinemas and an explosion of "small" big screen theatres that seat about 50 moviegoers in comfortable surroundings.

Alongside the growth in screen numbers there has been an explosion in the number of specialist film festivals. The biggest of them all is the **International Film Festival**, now in its 35th year. It presents a programme of critically acclaimed films from the international festival circuit alongside classics and director showcases, and includes world premieres of works by new and established New Zealand filmmakers. The festival travels the country starting in the main centres in July and takes in the provinces until the end of the year. The magnificently refurbished **Embassy Theatre** in Wellington is one beneficiary of the festival's popularity. Dunedin's arthouse cinema **Metro** and the **Academy** in Christchurch also host festival showings.

Out Takes is a festival for gay and lesbian film that takes place in May and June in Auckland, Wellington and Christchurch, while The Date Palm Film Festival in September focuses on film from the Middle East. Also in September and October is the International Documentary Film Festival, with showings at Auckland's independent **Academy Cinema**. The Italian Film Festival takes place in the main centres and provincial towns during October and November.

POPULAR MUSIC

There is no definitive New Zealand sound, but artists who are able to instil a local flavour to whatever genre they work in stand out from the crowd. The Wellington-based dub/soul/funksters Fat Freddy's Drop picked up all the major New Zealand Music awards in 2005 for their album *Based on a True Story.*

New Zealand hip hop is popular, with producer P Money leading the way, and MCs such as Scribe and Ladi 6 topping the charts. Local hip hop often fuses American gangster styles with Pacific Island rhythms and tales. Dub, roots and reggae are also popular, especially at summer festivals; The Black Seeds, Katchafire and Kora are leaders in these genres.

The Datsuns are a three-piece rock band from the provincial town of Cambridge who have exported their AC/DC style power chords to the rest of the world. Led Zeppelin bass player John Paul Jones produced their second album. Bands such as the Sneaks and the Checks are following in their wake. Stereogram, Pluto and Elemeno P are mainstream pop rockers who have benefited from commercial radio's current inclusive approach to local music.

Most of the live music action takes place in pubs and clubs, but established artists such as Neil Finn, Dave Dobbyn and Bic Runga now also play seated concerts in larger theatres such as the Opera House in Wellington and The Edge® (see p74) in Auckland.

Jazz festivals are held in Wellington, Nelson and on Waiheke Island, and the national country music awards are held annually at the bottom of the South Island in Gore.

CLUBS, BARS AND CAFES

The traditional New Zealand pub with at least three bars and accommodation is alive in the provinces, but in the cities it is rapidly being replaced by smaller bars and cafés offering good food and live entertainment as well as drinks. Many bars and cafés turn the lights down and the music up later in the evening, however, with the entertainment starting when the food stops. It is worth checking whether food is still being served when you arrive. Irish-themed bars, with Guinness on tap and Irish music, can be found in most reasonable sized towns.

It is often said Wellington has more bars, cafés and restaurants per head then New York City. That may or may not be true, but the most vibrant areas are in and around Courtenay Place and on Cuba Street. Bars cater for most musical tastes with **San Francisco Bathhouse**, **Mighty Mighty** and **Bar Bodega** flying the flag for live music while clubs like **The Garden Club** and **Sandwiches** cater for the dance crowd. **The Matterhorn**, **Good Luck** and **Lagerfield** are some of the many that offer good food and an eclectic selection of DJs.

Auckland's nightlife is more dispersed. Viaduct Basin (see p72) was developed in the late 1990s to cater for followers of the Americas Cup yachting regatta. The cup may have gone but bars such as **Float** and **Chic** remain. The city's dance clubs are mainly found on High Street, Ponsonby Road and Karangahape Road.

Rakinos restaurant hosts live bands and DJs, and among the bars on High Street is **Cube**. **Occidental Belgian Beer Café** is an institution and Queen Street's **Khuja Lounge** is heading that way. Also on Queen Street are Auckland's home of underground dance music **Fu Bar** and jazz pub, **London Bar**. Two main band venues are the **Kings Arms** and **Dogs Bollix**. **Galatos** has long been associated with reggae and dub. Karangahape Road is home to such clubs as **K'Road Ballroom**, **Eden's** and **Rising Sun**.

Christchurch is the home of New Zealand drum 'n' bass music. The premiere venue for live music is undoubtedly **Dux de Lux**, but **Zebedees**, **Creation** and **Foam Lounge** also play host to local and touring bands. **Ministry Nightclub** offers dance sounds and **Wunderbar** in nearby Lyttleton has live music.

Dunedin was the birthplace of some of New Zealand's more influential guitar bands such as The Chills and the Bats. **Arc Café** has carried on the tradition and often books guitar bands. The café is also the home of a record label that began recording Dunedin bands, but has since branched out and takes on acts from elsewhere in the country.

Chicks Hotel is a well-known haunt of a number of iconic Dunedin artists. It has a great atmosphere with locals and students converging to watch Dunedin music being performed. **Bath St**, a club named after its address, regularly hosts reggae and hip hop nights. The **Crown Hotel** and **10 Bar** both host DJs and live music.

DIRECTORY

SPECIALIST HOLIDAYS AND ACTIVITIES

DOC logo

Lovers of the outdoors will find New Zealand an ideal place to pursue their interests, or to experience something they have never tried before. From quick thrills, such as bungy jumping, jet-boating and helicopter rides to mountain climbing, abseiling, white-water rafting and skiing, New Zealand offers a huge range of activities for outdoor enthusiasts. The best places to find out what is available are at the Department of Conservation (DOC) offices, visitor information centres (i-SITES) and travel agents.

TRAMPING AND WALKING

With its 14 national parks, as well as many forest parks and protected natural areas, New Zealand offers immense opportunities for walking and tramping at all levels; tramping is the term New Zealanders use for trekking or hiking. A national network of walkways, ranging from short, well-graded paths to rudimentary alpine routes, thread their way throughout New Zealand, and every location boasts tracks and trails that allow visitors to experience the locality's finest aspects.

The best tramping routes are in the national parks, which are serviced by basic but comfortable huts costing between NZ$10 and NZ$45 per night. Three of these tracks – world famous for their beauty – have been designated "Great Walks".

Tramping can be done with a guide or independently. In the latter case, trampers are required to be self-sufficient in food, clothing and sleeping gear. Tramping huts vary in size and facilities, and it is wise to check with the DOC before setting off. It is also vital to check track and weather conditions with the DOC. Always sign in at the local DOC office or in intentions books provided at the beginning of major tracks. Although New Zealand has a sophisticated search and rescue system, it cannot operate if trampers do not leave a record of their whereabouts and expected date of return. On popular routes, such as the Abel Tasman Coastal Track and the Routeburn and Milford tracks, advance booking is essential.

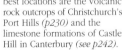

Walkway signpost

MOUNTAINEERING AND ROCK CLIMBING

With 30 peaks at heights over 3,000 m (9,840 ft), the South Island's Southern Alps provide climbers many opportunities for technically demanding mountain climbing. The principal climbing regions are the Aoraki/Mount Cook, Westland/Tai Poutini, Tititea/Mount Aspiring, Arthur's Pass and Fiordland national parks, while in the North Island the Central Plateau offers the best climbing. The main season is from November to March. Weather in the mountains can change extremely rapidly, and it is important that climbers get an up-to-date weather forecast, are adequately equipped, and post their intentions with the DOC before setting off. Experienced mountain guides, such as Aoraki/Mount Cook's **Alpine Guides (Aoraki) Ltd**, are available in many of the major climbing regions.

There is also plenty of scope for rock climbing. Among the best locations are the volcanic rock outcrops of Christchurch's Port Hills *(p230)* and the limestone formations of Castle Hill in Canterbury *(see p242).*

CAVING AND ABSEILING

New Zealand has extensive cave systems, among the most notable being the Waitomo Caves in the central North Island *(see pp120–21)* and the Takaka region in northwest

Guided walk on Franz Josef Glacier *(see pp238–9)*

Abseiling in the Mangapu Cave system, Waitomo *(see pp120–21)*

Nelson *(see p216)*. Some caves are easily accessed, while others are more suited to experienced cavers. Black-water rafting, in which participants float in rubber tubes through extensive cave systems illuminated by glowworms, is a popular way of experiencing New Zealand's cave formations. Two of the best locations for this activity are Waitomo *(see p120–21)* and Westport *(see p234)*, where rafting operators run tours.

Both the North and South islands offer exhilarating abseiling. In the Waitomo area, tourists can descend down a 100-m (330-ft) hole into the "Lost World" *(see p121)* Mangapu Cave system with **Waitomo Adventures**.

CYCLING

Cycle touring on New Zealand's highways and back roads is a popular way of seeing the country. Among the many scenic roads suited to cycling are the Queen Charlotte Drive in the Marlborough Sounds *(see p202)* and State Highway 6 on the West Coast. The **Otago Central Rail Trail**

Mountain biking in Rangataua Forest *(see p142)*

offers three to five days cycling along a 150-km (93-mile) old rail line, upgraded specifically for cyclists. An extensive network of off-road tracks is also available for mountain bikers. Hanmer Springs *(see p233)* and Victoria Forest Park *(see p233)* are among the best mountain biking destinations.

SKIING

New Zealand has numerous ski fields, ranging from highly commercialized fields to small fields owned by local ski clubs. Major fields are **Whakapapa Ski Area** and **Turoa Ski Resort** on the slopes of the North Island's Mount Ruapehu *(see pp142–3)*, the **Mount Hutt Ski Area** in Canterbury *(see p246)*, and **Coronet Peak**, the **Remarkables Ski Area**, **Cardrona Alpine Resort** and **Treble Cone** in Central Otago *(see pp194–5)*.

The ski season runs from mid-June to September. In the South Island, heli-skiing operators take skiers to untouched powder snow. Ski touring and cross-country skiing take place in many locations, including the **Waiorau Snow Farm** near Wanaka *(see pp194–5)*.

DIRECTORY

Surfing at Whale Bay, Raglan
(see pp116 – 17)

WATER SPORTS

With a coastline 18,200 km (11,300 miles) long and an abundance of lakes and rivers, New Zealand offers plenty of opportunities for visitors to participate in water sports. From Auckland's Hauraki Gulf northwards is a yachting paradise where experienced sailors can hire boats for "bareboat" cruising *(see pp88–9)*. Skippered sailing is more common, however, as the country's gusty winds can test even the most capable "boaties".

Surfing is popular, especially in the North Island at beaches like Piha *(see p86)*, Raglan *(see pp116–17)* and in the Bay of Plenty *(see pp126, 128)*. The calm waters of the country's harbours and lakes are suitable for windsurfing, and boards can be hired at many waterfront locations.

The Bay of Islands, Auckland's Hauraki Gulf, Nelson, the Marlborough Sounds, Fiordland and Stewart Island are prime venues for sea kayaking. Tours can take as long as a week. Kayaks can also be hired for a few hours' paddling around the harbours of Auckland, Wellington and other coastal cities.

New Zealand's fast-flowing rivers are excellent for white-water rafting and kayaking. Among the most challenging rivers are the Motu *(see p132)*, Rangitikei and Tongariro in the North Island, while the South Island has dozens of rivers, from the Buller on the West Coast to the Clarence in Canterbury. Among the rivers suitable for the inexperienced is the Whanganui River, the North Island's second longest river, which winds through the historic Whanganui National Park *(see p179)*.

There are many good dive spots, including the network of marine reserves around the New Zealand coastline *(see pp26–7)*. Near Whangarei, the dramatic underwater caves of the Poor Knights Islands are rated as one of the world's top diving destinations *(see p99)*. Further north, the Greenpeace boat, the *Rainbow Warrior*, is a well-known underwater wreck. In Fiordland, a unique marine ecosystem, tempered by huge quantities of freshwater run-off, attracts species nearer to the surface than in other areas.

HUNTING

Because many of the animals introduced into New Zealand by Europeans have no natural predators, they have become pests, and therefore hunting of big game is encouraged by the authorities. No licence is required, there is no restriction on the numbers killed and the season is generally open all year round.

Professional guiding companies operate throughout the country, many with access to extensive tracts of private land. Seven species of deer, wild pigs and goats are common in forests, while chamois and thar can be found in mountain areas of the South Island. The duck shooting season starts at the beginning of May and lasts eight weeks.

FISHING

New Zealand is justly renowned for the quality of its sea and freshwater fishing. Lake Taupo and the rivers surrounding it (especially the famed Tongariro) are internationally regarded as the Mecca of trout fishing *(see p141)*, although there are good rivers throughout the country. The trout fishing season runs from October to May. The main salmon rivers are on the east coast of the South Island. A licence is compulsory in order to fish for trout and salmon, and tackle is readily available.

The Bay of Islands is the centre of deep-sea marlin fishing *(see pp102–103)*. The

Kayaking over rapids on the Tongariro River

Fishing in the Waikato River near Huka Lodge *(see p295)*

best deep-sea angling is found on the North Island's east coast, northwards from the Bay of Plenty. The best fishing months are from January to May and licences are not necessary.

ECOTOURS

A long tradition of environmental activism in New Zealand has led to numerous ecotourism developments. There are many specialist nature tour operators to choose from, and guides

working in the adventure tourism area, such as blackwater rafting *(see p120)*, often have a good knowledge of local flora and fauna.

There are numerous opportunities for bird watching *(see pp192–3)*, including at the Royal Albatross colony on Otago Peninsula, ocean birds at Kaikoura *(see p209)*, the white heron colony at Okarito and the immense birdlife of Farewell Spit *(see p217)*.

Kaikoura is synonomous with whale watching *(see p209)*. During winter there is

nearly a 100 per cent chance of seeing sperm whales. Dolphin watching tours operate from many areas, including Banks Peninsula, the Bay of Islands and Southland.

Whale Watch® tour at Kaikoura
(see p209)

DIRECTORY

RAFTING

Queenstown Rafting
35 Shotover St, Queenstown. **Tel** *(03) 442 9792, 0800 723 8464.*
www.rafting.co.nz

Wet 'n' Wild Rafting Company
2 White St, Rotorua.
Tel *(07) 348 3191, 0800 462 7238.* **www**.
wetnwildrafting. co.nz

KAYAKING

Fiordland Wilderness Experiences
66 Quintin Drive, Te Anau.
Tel *(03) 249 7700.* **www**.
fiordlandseakayak.co.nz

Abel Tasman Kayaks
RD2, Marahau.
Tel *(03) 527 8022.*

www.abeltasmankayaks.
co.nz

Abel Tasman Wilson's Experiences
265 High St, Motueka.
Tel *(03) 528 2027.*
www.abeltasman.co.nz

DIVING

Dive! Tutukaka
Marina Rd, Tutukaka, Whangarei. **Tel** *(09) 434 3867.* **www**.diving.co.nz

Splash Gordon
432 The Esplanade, Island Bay, Wellington.
Tel *(04) 939 3483.*
www.splashgordon.co.nz

HUNTING AND FISHING

Chris Jolly Outdoors
PO Box 1020, Lake Taupo.

Tel *(07) 378 0623.*
www.chrisjolly.co.nz

Fly Fishing New Zealand Limited
PO Box 106, Queenstown.
Tel *(03) 442 5363.*
www.wakatipu.co.nz

Mountain High Adventure Company
C/- Snow and Stream Lodge, 5/7 Farquhar Place, Methven.
Tel *(03) 302 8733.*
www.fishandhunt.co.nz

ECO TOURS

Albatross Encounter
96 Esplanade, Kaikoura.
Tel *(03) 319 6777.*
www.oceanwings.co.nz

Catlins Wildlife Trackers Ecotours

5 Mirren St, Papatowai, RD2, Owaka, South Otago. **Tel** *(03) 415 8613, 0800 228 546.*
www.catlins-ecotours.nz

Dolphin Discoveries
PO Box 400, Cnr Marsden & Williams rds, Paihia, Bay of Islands. **Tel** *(09) 402 8234.* @ enquiries@
dolphinz. co.nz
www.dolphinz.co.nz

Heritage Expeditions
53b Montreal St, Christchurch. **Tel** *(03) 365 3500.* **www**.heritage-expeditions.co.nz

Whale Watch® Kaikoura Ltd
PO Box 89, Kaikoura.
Tel *(03) 319 6767, 0800 655 121.*
www.whalewatch.co.nz

Tandem skydiving over Hawke's Bay

AERIAL ADVENTURES

Hot-air ballooning, tandem parapenting (paragliding) and tandem skydiving are more adventurous ways of taking to the air than flying *(see p195)*. Commercial operators offering all three types of aerial thrill exist in the main cities and major resorts *(see p355)*. A hot-air balloon ride is a spectacular way to view the extensive Southern Alps and Canterbury Plains, while parapenting from Te Mata Peak in Hawke's Bay *(see p149)* and the Remarkables near Queenstown is a unique experience *(see pp194–5)*. Check with local visitor centres or travel agents for details of available services.

Aerial sightseeing is also popular throughout the country, either in small planes, helicopters or float planes. Highlights in the North Island include flights over the volcanically active White Island *(see p130)* and volcanic Tongariro National Park *(pp142–3)*. In the South Island, flights over Mount Cook, the Fox and Franz Josef glaciers *(see*

Flightseeing over Fiordland National Park *(pp280–3)*

pp252–3) and Fiordland *(see pp280–81)* are popular and readily available. Many flights touch down in spectacular locations, such as White Island and the glaciers of the Southern Alps.

Bungy jumping from the Kawarau Bridge, Queenstown *(see p276)*

BUNGY JUMPING

Ever since A J Hackett used an historic bridge over the Kawarau River in Queenstown *(see pp194–5)* to launch the bungy jumping phenomenon in 1988, tourism operators have set up bungy jump sites in picturesque locations, usually on bridges above river gorges, in both the North and South islands.

Safety is a key issue in bungy jumping. Jumpers are weighed so that the correct length of bungy cord can be calculated for their jump. The cord is securely attached to their ankles before the jump from a bridge or platform.

JET-BOATING

Bill Hamilton, a local engineer and farmer, perfected the design of the jet-boat so it is no coincidence that these highly manoeuvrable craft are so popular on the nation's waterways. In locations such as Waikato *(see p140)* and Queenstown *(see pp194–5)*, jet-boat operators take tourists through narrow canyons, across the shallowest of water and whirl 360 degrees "on a sixpence". Some operators offer jet-boat safaris, taking visitors on longer trips into the scenic back country. Mandatory life jackets are supplied.

GOLF

There are more than 400 golf courses in New Zealand, more per head of population than virtually any other country. Green fees can be as low as NZ$5 for a club in rural areas. Even the more exclusive city courses charge no more than NZ$50. Weekends are often reserved for members, although a number of clubs have reciprocal membership with overseas clubs, allowing visitors to play at any time. Major clubs have carts and clubs for hire.

FOUR-WHEEL DRIVE TOURING

In the high country and rural areas of New Zealand are hundreds of rough tracks, many of which were created to provide access to farms, timber mills, gold mines and mining settlements. A four-wheel drive vehicle is a physically undemanding way to explore these locations. Numerous tour operators exist throughout the country, offering both day trips and longer safaris through varied terrain.

HORSE TREKKING

The wide open spaces of the country encourage horse riding and there are many operators who offer horse trekking through forests, high country trails or along one of the many beaches. Options

Horse trekking at Hanmer, North Canterbury

range from half-day or all-day treks to multi-day camping safaris. Some operations are conveniently located close to cities. Most operators cater for a range of riding abilities and provide all equipment.

SPECTATOR SPORTS

New Zealanders are passionate about rugby. It is worth visiting a match during the rugby season from March to October (*see pp38–9*). The Super 14 and Air New Zealand Cup are the major competitions. Matches

generally attract large crowds, as do one-day cricket test matches. Highly entertaining, the atmosphere is best at the day–night matches which begin in the afternoon and are played through the evening under lights.

Horse racing is a national passion, and a number of big race meetings are held between November and April (*see pp38–9*). Netball also has a large following, with the most exciting games often involving the national team, the Silver Ferns.

Tickets for sports events can be obtained from Ticketek (*see p347*).

MAORI HERITAGE TOURS

Tour companies offering genuine encounters with Maori heritage operate in a number of locations. Tours may include a visit to a *marae*, where participants share a *hangi* (a traditional feast) and learn about Maori protocol, myths and legends, dance and art. One such operator, **Te Urewera Adventures**, offers horse trekking and a stay on a *marae* in the Urewera country, spiritual home to the Tuhoe people.

Waikato supporters at a provincial rugby match

DIRECTORY

AERIAL ADVENTURES

Air Safaris
PO Box 71, Lake Tekapo.
Tel (03) 680 6880.
www.airsafaris.co.nz

Aoraki Hot Air Balloon Safaris
PO Box 75, Methven.
Tel (03) 302 8172, 0800 256 837.
www.nzballooning.com

Fiordland Helicopters
PO Box 180, Te Anau Airport. *Tel* (03) 249 7575.
www.fiordland
helicopters.co.nz

New Zealand Paragliding Ltd
6 Sumnervale Drive, Christchurch.
Tel (03) 326 7634, 0800 111 6111.
www.paragliding.co.nz

Sky Trek
PO Box 2406, Whakatipu, Queenstown. *Tel* (03) 409 0625. www.skytrek.co.nz

BUNGY JUMPING

A J Hackett Bungy
PO Box 488, Queenstown.
Tel (03) 442 4007.
www.ajhackett.com

Taupo Bungy
202 Spa Rd, Taupo.
Tel (07) 377 1135, 0800 888 408.
www.taupobungy.com

FOUR-WHEEL DRIVING

Edgewater Adventures
59A Brownston St, Wanaka.
Tel (03) 443 2869.
www.adventure.net.nz

JET-BOATING

Huka Jet
Wairakei Park, Taupo.
Tel (07) 374 8572.
www.hukajet.co.nz

Shotover Jet
PO Box 189, Queenstown.
Tel (03) 442 8570.
www.shotoverjet.co.nz

HORSE TREKKING

Alpine Horse Safaris
Waitohi Downs, Hawarden, Canterbury.
Tel (07) 314 4293.
www.alpinehorse.co.nz

Dart Stables
PO Box 47, Glenorchy.
Tel (03) 442 5688.
www.dartstables.com

Hurunui Horse Treks
757 The Peaks Rd, Hawarden, Canterbury.
Tel (03) 314 4204.
www.hurunui.co.nz

Pakiri Beach Horse Rides
Rahuikiri Rd, Pakiri, RD 2, Wellsford.
Tel (09) 422 6275.
www.horseride-nz.co.nz

MAORI HERITAGE TOURS

Red Feather (Tia Raukura) Expeditions
PO Box 60243, Titirangi, Auckland.
Tel (09) 818 7770.
www.ecotoursnz.com

Tamaki Tours
PO Box 1492, 1220 Hinemaru St, Rotorua.
Tel (07) 346 2999.
www.maoriculture.co.nz

Te Urewera Adventures of NZ
Matuatua Rd, Rotorua.
Tel (07) 366 3969.

SURVIVAL
GUIDE

PRACTICAL INFORMATION

Tourism is one of New Zealand's most important industries, attracting over 2.4 million overseas visitors a year. As the industry has grown, services and facilities have improved to keep pace with demand. Visitors are well served by a wide range of accommodation and restaurants *(see pp294–319, 320–41)*. There is easy and free access to good quality information through the many i-SITE

i-SITE Visitor Centre logo

visitor centres which are co-ordinated by Tourism New Zealand. Many of the best attractions in New Zealand are free – particularly the national parks, beaches, lakes and rivers. New Zealanders are very friendly people who are willing to offer assistance, although it is highly advisable for visitors to have at least a basic grasp of English as relatively few New Zealanders are fluent in other languages.

Visitor information centre, Viaduct Basin, Auckland *(see p72)*

WHEN TO GO

Spring, summer and autumn (from September to April) are the most popular seasons for travellers, although the ski season is a major attraction during the winter months (June to September).

One word sums up the New Zealand climate: changeable. The north of the North Island is subtropical, while the remainder of the country is temperate. However, all regions are subject to sudden changes in the weather. In the South Island, it is not unusual for a hot summer day of 30 °C (86 °F) to be followed by temperatures as low as 15 to 20 °C (60 to 68 °F). Average summer temperatures range between 20 and 30 °C (68 and 86 °F), and winter between 10 and 15 °C (50 and 60 °F). The greatest climatic extremes are experienced in the inland Central Otago region, where summer temperatures often soar above 30 °C (86 °F) and in

winter often fall to below 0 °C (32 °F). New Zealand has a pronounced west–east climate variation: the west coasts of both main islands are in the path of westerly winds, which sweep rain in from the Tasman Sea. Although the east is much drier and sunnier, the wet, humid climate of the west sustains dense and varied rainforests.

Spring is generally unsettled throughout the country, with more rain and wind than in other seasons. People crowd the coastlines, lakes and rivers during summer when water temperatures are pleasant for swimming in most regions. From February to late April, the weather tends to be warm and settled. Snow in winter falls mainly in the mountains, although the inland and coastal parts of the southern South Island occasionally experience heavy falls. Winter is not as cold nor as long in New Zealand as in the northern hemisphere.

TIME DIFFERENCES

New Zealand is 12 hours ahead of Greenwich Mean Time and two hours ahead of Sydney. Clocks are put forward one hour each October for daylight saving, which lasts until March.

PASSPORTS AND VISAS

Visitors to New Zealand must have a passport valid for at least three months longer than the intended period of stay. Visas are not required for Australian citizens or holders of a current Australian resident return visa, nor for visits of up to three months by residents of any of the 50 countries with which New Zealand has a visa waiver agreement. For a list of those countries, visit the website of the New Zealand immigration service at www.immigration.govt.nz

Newmans tour coach on the Milford Road in autumn

◁ **Trampers at Green Lake, Fiordland National Park *(see p281)***

Department of Conservation information centre, Totaranui *(see p215)*

and various animal products, including ivory, turtle shell, clam shells and whalebone.

Visitors can buy duty-free goods on arrival (alcohol is bought on arrival), departure and at duty-free stores in cities *(see p90)*. For travellers over 17 years old, the customs allowances are: 200 cigarettes, 250 grams of tobacco or 50 cigars, or a mixture of all three weighing no more than 250 grams; 4.5 litres of beer or wine and one 1,125 ml (40 oz) bottle of spirits or other beverages.

British citizens who have permanent UK residency also do not need a visa and are issued with a six-month visitor permit on arrival. Visas for tourists from other countries can be obtained through the nearest New Zealand embassy. When entering the country or when applying for a visa, visitors must give proof of a return air ticket and show they have sufficient funds for the duration of their stay – about NZ$1,000 per person per month. All visitors should check visa requirements prior to travelling.

To obtain a work permit for New Zealand, applicants must, in the first instance, show they have an offer of employment.

Resort signboard

However, such an offer is not, in itself, a sufficient condition for obtaining a permit since the employer must also satisfy certain requirements. Another option is the reciprocal working holiday scheme, maintained between New Zealand and a number of other countries. This scheme allows visitors to work in the country temporarily without first obtaining an offer of employment. However, it is only open to those aged between 18 and 30.

Vaccinations are not required for visitors entering New Zealand.

DEPARTURE FEE

An airport user fee is levied on passengers aged 12 and above departing from New Zealand's international airports. The fee from Auckland, Wellington and Christchurch airports is NZ$25.

AGRICULTURAL RESTRICTIONS AND CUSTOMS ALLOWANCES

New Zealand relies heavily on its agricultural industries, and great effort is made to keep the country free of introduced pests and diseases that could affect the productivity of its farms and orchards. All fruit, meat, plant material and animals must be declared on arrival. Failure to declare quarantine items can lead to a fine of NZ$100,000 or five years in jail. If in doubt about an item, declare it to the Ministry of Agriculture and Forestry inspectors on arrival; they will advise you whether it is permitted. In many cases, items will be inspected, treated if necessary, and then returned to you. Tents or shoes that have been used recently in the countryside should be declared.

Class A drugs are prohibited, as are firearms and weapons unless a permit is obtained from the New Zealand Police on arrival. The country is also party to an international convention designed to prevent trade in endangered species,

TOURIST INFORMATION

The central tourism body is Tourism New Zealand but the official information service that most visitors have contact with is the **i-SITE** Visitor Centre Network. Independently owned but coordinated by Tourism New Zealand, there are over 80 i-SITE centres scattered throughout New Zealand, sporting a distinctive green and black logo. Open daily, they provide abundant information on local attractions and activities, sell maps and guidebooks, and arrange bookings for accommodation, tours, travel and activities. Most centres sell souvenirs and have internet facilities.

Department of Conservation visitor centres in the national parks are the best source of detailed information on activities and attractions in the parks, and many have excellent displays, audiovisual programmes and lectures on the natural history of the area. They also provide up-to-date weather forecasts and information about the condition of roads, rivers and tracks.

Enjoying the sun at Scorching Bay, Wellington *(see p169)*

Entry is free to the Te Papa Museum
(see pp166–7)

OPENING HOURS AND ADMISSION PRICES

At the height of the season, most major tourist sites are open seven days a week, but it is best to check in advance. Admission prices to attractions vary: in some cases, entry is free, while many galleries and museums request a donation or modest entry charge. Entry into the national parks is free, although access to certain areas is possible only with an approved guiding company. There is also a charge for overnight stays in huts. Private companies run New Zealand's many adventure tourism ventures, and charges vary according to the activity.

For opening hours of retail outlets, see p342.

ETIQUETTE

Like Australia, New Zealand is a relatively informal society. On the whole, the people are relaxed and open,

enjoy sharing their country with overseas visitors, and are happy to assist tourists needing information or help. Dress standards vary depending on the venue, but most restaurants and cafés are happy with tidy casual wear.

Smoking is banned in offices, shops, airplanes, public transport and taxis, as well as in bars, cafes, restaurants and casinos. It is not acceptable to smoke in private homes without first asking the permission of the host. If invited to a New Zealander's home for a meal, it is appropriate to take a bottle of wine or an item of food to share, but most New Zealanders will be uncomfortable with ostentatious gifts.

Tipping in restaurants and hotels is not obligatory, although it has become more widespread with the increase in overseas tourists. Many New Zealanders do not approve of tipping and do not tip taxi drivers, bartenders and porters, but it is not inappropriate to reward particularly good service in a restaurant (about ten per cent of the bill).

DISABLED TRAVELLERS

Disabled travellers are well catered for in New Zealand. Every new or substantially renovated building is required by law to have adequate access for people with disabilities. As a result, most hotels, restaurants, tourist sites, cinemas, airports and shopping centres have wheelchair facilities, and

guide dogs for the blind are always welcome.

Airports provide ground staff to assist with boarding and disembarking disabled passengers, although trains and buses are often inaccessible without assistance. Avis has cars available with hand controls, but 14 days' notice must be given *(see p377)*. All major cities and towns have taxis which carry wheelchairs.

Some tourism adventure activities may be difficult to access for the disabled, although operators are usually keen to assist provided sufficient notice is given.

TRAVELLING WITH CHILDREN

New Zealand, with its wide, open spaces, lack of dangerous animals and low crime statistics is a safe place to take children for a holiday. Children are well catered for in most types of accommodation, but motels are particularly suitable for families, with family rooms and self-catering facilities. Restaurants often have children's menus or small portions, and many have high chairs. Major international fast food chains are represented in New Zealand, along with a wide selection of local takeaway services. Large department stores and shopping malls have nappy changing facilities and feeding rooms.

Many of New Zealand's top attractions appeal equally to children as to adults, such as the Museum of New Zealand Te Papa Tongarewa *(see pp166–7)*, the International Antarctic Centre *(see p227)*, and the national parks.

Air, coach, train and boat operators offer a range of discounted prices for children, which makes holidaying with families affordable. Children under five are required by law to be restrained in an infant car seat. Car hire firms will rent these out for a small fee, but they should be given advance notice if possible.

WHAREPAKU
WAHINE **TĀNE**
WOMEN **MEN**

Maori/English
toilet sign

Spectators dressed casually at a cricket match in Wellington

STUDENT TRAVELLERS

Students with a valid ISIC (International Students Identity Card) can obtain substantial discounts on travel, especially on internal flights. Students are also entitled to reduced charges in cinemas, theatres, art galleries and museums. To find out what special deals are available, students should contact their local student travel office in their country of origin. The card can be purchased only by students who are studying courses at a school, university or a polytechnic.

NEWSPAPERS, MAGAZINES, RADIO AND TELEVISION

Each of the main cities has its own morning newspaper, while many provincial cities and towns have afternoon newspapers. *The New Zealand Herald*, the country's largest, is published in Auckland. The Christchurch *Press* is the South Island's largest newspaper. The *Otago Daily Times* is published in Dunedin, *The Dominion Post* in Wellington and the *Southland Times* in Invercargill. Excellent weekend reading is contained in *The Sunday Star Times*, which is published nationally. The best current

A selection of daily newspapers

affairs magazines are *The Listener* and *North and South*, and for specialized business news *The National Business Review, Independent Business Weekly* and *Unlimited Magazine*. Overseas magazines and newspapers, such as *Time* and *The Economist*, are available in book stores and newsstands in larger towns.

The state-owned, non-commercial Radio New Zealand and the Concert programme are renowned for the quality of their broadcasting. The three main free-to-air television channels are TV1 and TV3, which screen mostly local programmes, and TV2, which relies more heavily on US programmes. Pay channel Sky offers specialist channels, such as CNN and National Geographic.

CONVERSION CHART

Imperial to metric
1 inch = 2.54 centimetres
1 foot = 30 centimetres
1 mile = 1.6 kilometres
1 ounce = 28 grams
1 pound = 454 grams
1 pint = 0.6 litres
1 gallon = 4.6 litres

Metric to Imperial
1 centimetre = 0.4 inches
1 metre = 3 feet, 3 inches
1 kilometre = 0.6 miles
1 gram = 0.04 ounces
1 kilogram = 2.2 pounds
1 litre = 1.8 pints

ELECTRICAL SUPPLY

New Zealand's electrical current is 230/240 volts 50 hertz, although most hotels and motels provide 110 volt AC sockets for electric razors. For all other equipment, an adaptor is necessary, as power outlets accept only flat, two- or three-pin plugs, as illustrated.

Standard New Zealand three-pin electrical plug

DIRECTORY

EMBASSIES AND CONSULATES

Australia
72–76 Hobson St, Wellington. *Tel (04) 473 6411.*
www.australia.org.nz

Canada
Level 11, 125 The Terrace, Wellington.
Tel (04) 473 9577.

United Kindgom
44 Hill St, Wellington.
Tel (04) 924 2888.
www.britain.org.nz

USA
29 Fitzherbert Terrace, Wellington.
Tel (04) 462 6000.

TOURISM ORGANIZATIONS

Christchurch and Canterbury Tourism
Old Chief Post Office, Cathedral Square West.
Tel (03) 379 9629.
www.christchurchnz.com

Destination Rotorua Tourism Marketing
1106 Arawa St, Rotorua.
Tel (07) 348 4133.
www.rotoruanz.com

Hawkes Bay Tourism
2nd Floor Civic Court, Napier.
Tel (06) 834 1918.
www.hawkesbaynz.com

Latitude Nelson
Cnr Trafalgar and Halifax sts. *Tel (03) 546 6228.*
www.nelsonnz.com

Positively Wellington Tourism
Level 28, Grand Plimer Tower, Wellington.
Tel (04) 916 1205.
www.WellingtonNZ.com

Tourism Auckland
Auckland Viaduct, Auckland.
Tel (09) 979 7070.
www.aucklandnz.com

Tourism Dunedin
193 Princes St, Dunedin. *Tel (03) 471 8042.*
www.dunedinnz.com

Tourism New Zealand
157 Lambton Quay, Wellington.
Tel (04) 917 5400.
www.purenz.com

Tourism West Coast
26 Mackay St, Greymouth.
Tel (03) 768 6633.
www.west-coast.co.nz

DISABLED TRAVELLERS

Disability Information Centre
Tel 0800 693 342.

Personal Security and Health

OUTDOOR **SAFETY**
NEW ZEALAND
MOUNTAIN SAFETY COUNCIL

New Zealand is one of the safest countries in the world to visit. New Zea-landers have a reputation for being friendly and law-abiding, and the political and economic climate is stable. Violent crimes occur in New Zealand as in any other society, and visitors need to take sensible precautions to protect themselves and their property. The greatest risks, however, are environmental; many tourists have been caught out in the mountains, bush, or on the water with inadequate food and clothing, having underestimated the terrain and the speed with which New Zealand's weather can change.

Fire engine

Ambulance

PERSONAL SAFETY

There are few areas in New Zealand that are not suitable for tourists to visit. However, unlike large European and Asian cities, the streets are often deserted after dark and it is not advisable, particularly for women, to walk alone at night. Use common sense by avoiding parks and poorly lit, secluded places, especially in urban areas after dark. Even in the main cities there is little public transport late at night, although taxis are readily available and are safe to board.

Many tourists hitchhike, and although trouble-free in most instances, it is not recommended as a safe form of getting around the country, especially if travelling alone. Women, in particular, should never hitchhike alone.

Road accidents are a major public health issue in New Zealand, and tourists intending to drive should make themselves aware of the road rules *(see p375)*. The speed limit is 100 km/h (60 mph) on the open road and 50 km/h (30 mph) in urban areas. While most of the road network is sealed, many back roads are gravel and require extra care *(see p376)*. It is compulsory to wear seat belts in cars.

PERSONAL PROPERTY

Travellers need to take sensible precautions with their property in New Zealand. Petty crime such as theft from cars can occur, and is best avoided by making sure vehicles are locked and any items left in a vehicle remain out of view. Valuable items such as passports, credit cards and traveller's cheques should be kept in a money belt or in a hotel safe deposit box. A comprehensive travel insurance policy that covers personal property loss or theft is advisable.

LOST PROPERTY

Stolen property should be reported to the police, although the chances of recovering the goods will depend on the circumstances. The police will issue a report, which can be used to support an insurance claim, if necessary. Most shopping malls, hotels, airports, train and bus stations operate a lost property service and it is worth checking with the service in case any lost items have been handed in.

MEDICAL TREATMENT AND INSURANCE

New Zealand has excellent medical services. The telephone numbers of all general practitioners and hospitals in each area are listed near the front of each regional telephone book.

Under New Zealand's accident compensation scheme, visitors are covered for personal injury by accident, entitling them to coverage for medical and hospital expenses within New Zealand, but not for treatment or loss of earnings outside New Zealand. However, non-accident medical treatment is not free. Even though medical attention is reasonably priced, visitors are advised to make arrangements for adequate medical and dental cover before leaving home.

A doctor's prescription is necessary to obtain most forms of medication in New Zealand. Visitors bringing in a large quantity of medication should have a doctor's certificate to avoid difficulties with Customs. No vaccinations are needed to enter New Zealand.

Policewoman   **Fire officer**

PHARMACIES

New Zealand has an extensive network of pharmacies (more commonly called chemists) which offer everything from cosmetics to prescription drugs. Qualified chemists can be relied on to provide free advice but prescriptions must be written out by a doctor. Major towns have urgent pharmacies, which are open until late at night. Their telephone numbers and addresses are available in the front section of the local telephone directory.

ENVIRONMENTAL HAZARDS

With no dangerous animals including any species of snakes, and few serious contagious diseases, New Zealand poses a low risk to the visitor. Its changeable climate is probably the greatest threat, especially to people who venture into the wilderness unprepared. Hypothermia can set in quickly and be fatal, and it is vital to take warm clothing, food and drink even when going for a day's walk in the bush or mountains. Many tramps involve river crossings, and water levels can rise extremely rapidly after heavy rain. It is often necessary to take shelter and wait until rivers drop to a safe level.

New Zealand's clean air, coupled with a thinner ozone cover, means that sunburn

Pharmacy in Auckland

can occur quickly. A good hat and sun block with a rating of at least SPF 30+ are essential items in summer.

Lifeguards patrol popular beaches, and red and yellow flags indicate areas where it is safe to swim. However, the New Zealand coastline is extensive, and in areas where there are no lifeguards, there may be dangerous rips. Rivers also claim many lives, sometimes those of trampers who are too impatient to wait for flood waters to subside.

Giardia, a waterborne parasite that causes diarrhoea, stomach cramps and nausea, is present in many waterways. It is best to avoid drinking from lakes, ponds or rivers without boiling or treating water first. The water supply in most towns and cities is generally excellent and usually safe to drink.

The tiny, black, bloodsucking sandfly is the greatest environmental irritant, biting exposed skin and causing an annoying itch. They are particularly bad on the west coast of the South Island, but can usually be kept at bay with a good insect repellent.

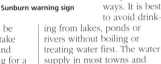
Sunburn warning sign

Surf rescue boat at Mount Maunganui (see p128)

(see p128)

DIRECTORY

EMERGENCY NUMBERS

Police, Fire and Ambulance
Free call Tel 111, 24 hours, all areas.

AA Emergency Road Service
Free call Tel 0800 500 222 24 hours, all areas.

Search and Rescue
Free call Tel 111, 24 hours, all areas.

MAJOR HOSPITALS

Auckland
Tel (09) 379 7440.

Christchurch
Tel (03) 364 0640.

Dunedin
Tel (03) 474 0890.

Wellington
Tel (04) 385 5999.

URGENT PHARMACIES

Auckland
Tel (09) 520 6634.

Christchurch
Tel (03) 366 4439.

Dunedin
Tel (03) 477 0890.

Wellington
Tel (04) 385 8810.

NATIONAL HELPLINES

Dental
For dental care, look under "Dentists" in the Yellow Pages.

Lifeline
Auckland Tel (09) 522 2999.
Christchurch Tel (03) 366 6742.
Dunedin Tel (03) 471 6208.

Samaritans of Wellington
Tel (04) 473 9739.

Poisons Centre
Urgent calls Tel 0800 764 766.
Non-urgent calls Tel (03) 479 7248.

Banking and Local Currency

A large number of banking institutions operate in New Zealand, almost all of them foreign owned. Major banking chains include the Bank of New Zealand, Westpac, National Bank, Kiwibank, ANZ and ASB. Branches of all the leading chains can be found in the central business districts of the major cities, while suburban shopping centres generally have branches of one or two banking institutions. Foreign currency can be readily exchanged at banks and private moneychangers. There is no restriction on the amount of foreign currency that can be brought in or taken out of New Zealand, although people carrying more than NZ$10,000 in cash must make a declaration to Customs.

Bank logos

BANKING

The New Zealand banking system is modern and efficient. However, electronic banking has led to a decline in the number of bank branches, and some small rural towns no longer have a local banking service. If travelling to a remote area, it is advisable to check in advance what facilities for exchanging or accessing money are available. Banks are generally open from 9am to 5pm Monday to Friday, and some also open reduced hours on Saturdays. Money changers at international airports open to coincide with incoming and outgoing flights. International exchange rates are displayed in most major banks.

TRAVELLER'S CHEQUES

Traveller's cheques are still the safest way to carry large sums of money. Thomas Cook and American Express traveller's cheques are widely accepted in New Zealand. Foreign currency cheques can be cashed for New Zealand dollars at banks, American Express and Travelex branches, and private money-changers, some of which display bureaux de change signs. Major hotels will accept traveller's cheques as payment for accommodation. Some souvenir shops in major cities and resort areas are also willing to accept traveller's cheques.

CREDIT CARDS

All major credit cards are used in New Zealand. Visa, Mastercard, Diners Club, and American Express are the most widely accepted, and can be used to book and pay for hotels, rental cars and airline tickets, as well as to pay for entry to major tourist facilities and for purchases from shops. In small shops and cafés, however, credit cards may not always be accepted, so it is wise to carry some cash. The logos of the credit cards accepted are usually clearly displayed in shops.

Withdrawing cash from an ATM in Auckland

AUTOMATIC TELLER MACHINES AND ELECTRONIC TRANSFER

ATMS (Automatic Teller Machines) are widely available in New Zealand and can be found in shopping centres and outside banks in all towns and cities. Travellers should check with their own bank before leaving home whether they can use their debit card to access cash through ATMs in New Zealand; this will differ from bank to bank depending on what international banking networks they belong to. It is possible to withdraw cash from an ATM using a credit card with an encoded PIN number: the "Plus" logo on an ATM indicates this service is available to VISA card holders, while the equivalent symbol for Mastercard holders is "Maestro".

Sign displayed by a private moneychanger

MONEYCHANGERS

Moneychangers can be found in downtown locations in the major cities and resort areas. They are generally open from 8am to 7:30 or 8pm on weekdays, and from 10am until early evening on weekends, offering an alternative after banks have closed for the day. However, their commissions and fees are higher than banks.

DIRECTORY

LOST CARDS AND TRAVELLER'S CHEQUES

American Express
Tel 0800 441 068.

Diners Club
Tel 0800 657 373.

Mastercard
Tel 0800 449 140.

Visa
Tel 0508 600 300.

LOCAL CURRENCY

The unit of currency in New Zealand is the New Zealand dollar (NZ$), divided into 100 cents (c). Since one, two and five cent coins have been taken out of circulation prices for cash purchases have been rounded up or down to the nearest ten cents. New Zealand converted to decimal currency in 1966 and now none of the old-style coins are still in use. In 2006 a set of new, smaller coins was introduced. It is important to be aware that it is quite likely you will find that small shops, cafés and taxis may not be able to provide change for $50 or $100 notes, and so it is advisable to always carry cash in $10 and $20 notes. To make it more difficult for counterfeiters to operate and to ensure notes can stay in circulation for longer, plasticized bank notes are replacing paper ones.

Bank Notes

New Zealand's bank notes are issued in denominations of $5, $10, $20, $50 and $100. Sir Edmund Hillary, the first man to climb Mount Everest (see pp19, 50) features on the $5 note, and 19th-century women's suffrage campaigner Kate Sheppard is on the $10 note.

NZ$100 note

NZ$20 note

NZ$50 note

NZ$5 note

NZ$10 note

10 cents (10c)

20 cents (20c)

50 cents (50c)

Coins

Coins currently in use in New Zealand are 10c, 20c, 50c, $1 and $2. The 10c piece features a traditional Maori carving, while the $1 coin showing the national icon, the flightless kiwi, brings reality to the colloquial term "kiwi dollar".

1 dollar (NZ$1)

2 dollars (NZ$2)

Using New Zealand's Telephones

New Zealand has a modern, sophisticated telephone system. Public payphones are operated by the major telecommunications company, Telecom, and are widely distributed on streets in towns and cities, as well as in public buildings, airports and shopping centres. Hotels charge a premium for calls from hotel rooms, so it is best to use public payphones instead. There is also an extensive mobile telephone network for those wanting the convenience of their own telephone.

PUBLIC TELEPHONES

Most New Zealand public payphones accept only prepaid phonecards and credit cards. Telephones located in well-supervised areas, such as shopping malls, may accept coins. Signs on the outside of phone boxes indicate what mode of payment is acceptable for the particular payphone. Phonecards can be purchased at supermarkets, newsagents and dairies as well as Post Shops.

Public telephone booths

Public telephone boxes have a receiver, a 12-button key pad, a set of instructions, a list of useful numbers and both white and yellow page telephone directories. A free information service number (123) enables callers to find out the likely cost of an overseas call or the cost of reversing the charges prior to making the call. There is no charge for making emergency 111 calls from a public payphone. Toll-free 0800 numbers are also free.

USING A COIN/PHONECARD OPERATED PHONE

1 Lift the receiver and wait for the dial tone.

2 Insert the coins required or a Telecom phonecard. The amount of credit remaining on your card is displayed.

3 Dial the number and wait until you are connected.

4 When your money runs out, you will hear a warning beep. Either replace with a new phonecard or supplement with coins.

5 Replace the receiver at the end of your call and retrieve your card. The display will tell you how much credit remains on the card.

Phonecards
These are available in $5, $10, $15, $20 and $50 denominations.

MOBILE TELEPHONES

Mobile telephones can be used throughout most of New Zealand, apart from remote and mountainous areas, such as some sections of the west coast of the South Island. Visitors can rent mobile phones on a short-term basis although this is an expensive option. For tourists wanting the convenience of a mobile phone, a cheaper alternative is to buy a phone that uses prepaid cards. These phones can be purchased for under NZ$100 and prepaid cards are readily available at bookshops and dairies.

HOME COUNTRY DIRECT

Visitors from about 50 selected countries can use the Home Country Direct service to make calls through a telephone company in their country of origin. The calls are billed to the caller by his/her home telephone company. Check the White Pages of the Telephone Directory for the numbers to dial.

If using a payphone to make an international call, it is cheaper to use one of the discounted Telecom prepaid cards than a credit card or phonecard. These are available at Telecom outlets, dairies and service stations.

Advertisement for E-mail and Internet services at a café

FAX AND E-MAIL SERVICES

Post shops, photocopying shops and many hotels, motels and even hostels send and receive faxes on your behalf. There is a fixed charge per page.

Cybercafés operate throughout New Zealand, providing E-mail and Internet services to travellers. Cafés will set a visitor up with an E-mail address, if necessary, but it is best to obtain an address with one of the major Internet servers before leaving home.

Visitors can also send and receive E-mails at many hotels. The Yellow Pages of the telephone directory carries the names of places offering fax and E-mail and Internet services.

TELEPHONE DIRECTORIES

Each region in New Zealand has a White Pages and a Yellow Pages. The White Pages lists residential and commercial telephone numbers in alphabetical order as well as emergency and government department numbers. The Yellow Pages lists business numbers according to industry groupings. In many regions the White Pages and Yellow Pages are contained in one directory but in the larger regions, such as Auckland, Wellington and Christchurch, they come in separate volumes.

REACHING THE RIGHT NUMBER

- For long distance within New Zealand (STD calls), dial the correct area code, then the number.
- For an international number (IDD call), dial 00 followed by the correct country code, then the area code and number.
- For local and national directory enquiries, dial **018** (50c per enquiry).
- For international directory enquiries, dial **0172** ($1.50 for two enquiries).
- For all internal operator-assisted calls, dial **010**.
- For all international operator-assisted calls (credit card collect calls), dial **0170**.
- For price-defined international calls, dial **0160** instead of 00 at the beginning of the call ($3.99). If you call the international operator on **0170**, the charge is $3.99.
- The prefixes **021, 025, 027** and **029** are mobile telephone numbers and **0800** numbers are toll free.
- See also Emergency Numbers, *p363*, or search for national numbers on **www**.whitepages.co.nz

Postal Services

New Zealand's postal service is run by New Zealand Post. Letters and parcels can be sent through Post Shops, which are either owned by or are agencies of New Zealand Post. Many Post Shops are located in bookshops. Hours of opening vary between Post Shops, but most are open at least from 9am to 5pm.

DOMESTIC AND INTERNATIONAL MAIL

There are two main classes of domestic mail: FastPost, which arrives the day after posting, and standard post, which takes two to three days. A standard post letter within New Zealand costs 50c, and FastPost costs $1.

International airmail takes a minimum of one week to reach most countries. Letters and parcels sent via the cheaper International

New Zealand postwoman

Economy mail system take three weeks. Non-urgent parcels should be sent through EconomyPost, while urgent documents and parcels will reach their destination within a few days via International Express.

A number of private courier companies also offer competitive rates for sending letters and parcels overseas.

STAMPS

Stamps can be bought at supermarkets, dairies, newsagents and Post Shop branches. New Zealand Post's Stamp Business Unit produces 12 commemorative issues a year and one to three definitive stamps.

Stamps with New Zealand outdoor themes

POSTBOXES

New Zealand uses standard and FastPost postboxes. These can be found on street corners or outside Post Shops. In busy areas they will be cleared twice daily, once at noon and once at 6pm.

Standard and FastPost boxes

POSTE RESTANTE

The main post office in each town serves as a post restante. Have mail addressed clearly: c/- (care of) "Poste Restante, Central Post Office", followed by the name of the appropriate town. Post restante mail will be held for three months. A passport or some other form of identification is needed to claim Poste Restante mail.

TRAVEL INFORMATION

The vast majority of visitors arrive in New Zealand by air. Auckland is the busiest port of entry, followed by Christchurch. Once in New Zealand, tourists generally use the domestic air network to get around, particularly to travel from resorts in the North Island to the South Island. The coach network covers most major routes in the country. The rail network is limited, but some of the major routes travel through spectacular scenery. For visitors wanting to explore New Zealand away from the main transport routes and resorts, a car is the best way to travel. The roads are in good condition, although extra care is needed on alpine routes and back country roads.

Air New Zealand's *koru* (fern) logo

ARRIVING BY AIR

Around 15 international airlines fly into New Zealand, and others, such as **British Airways**, serve the country only on a codeshare basis (using a local airline to serve their routes). The national airline, **Air New Zealand**, has an extensive international network, with either direct or codeshare links with more than 130 countries worldwide. It is particularly active in the Australian and Southern Pacific sectors.

Air New Zealand and **Qantas** fly into the United States, mostly to cities on the west coast, while **Cathay Pacific**, **Emirates**, **Singapore Airlines**, **Malaysia Airlines**, **Japan Airlines** and **Korean Air** depart from the major Asian airports for New Zealand. **Aerolineas Argentina** flies direct from Auckland to Buenos Aires.

INTERNATIONAL FLIGHTS

New Zealand is a 3-hour flight from eastern Australia, 10 hours from Pacific Rim cities such as Singapore, Hong Kong and Tokyo, and about 24 hours from Europe. Taking account of delays and transfers, a flight from Europe can be very taxing and it is a good idea to arrange a stopover en route, either in Asia, the USA or one of the Pacific Islands.

New Zealand has three main international terminals. Auckland is the major gateway, followed by Christchurch and Wellington. Auckland airport has the most direct international connections,

including links to Argentina, Canada, Chile, China, Dubai, Germany, Indonesia and Japan. Christchurch and Wellington airports have fewer direct international links and primarily service trans Tasman flights, although both have direct flights to Pacific island destinations. Christchurch also has direct links to Singapore and Dubai. It is also possible to fly direct from Australia to Hamilton, Palmerston North, Dunedin and Queenstown. By international standards, none of the airports are congested and are rarely being affected by bad weather, though snow can have an impact on Queenstown, and wind on Wellington.

AIR FARES

Because New Zealand is a relatively remote country, air fares can be expensive, particularly during the peak season from December to February when airlines charge premium rates. However, a wide variety of discounted fares is available during the low season. These can provide significant savings of up to 50 per cent off full economy fares, although they may lack flexibility and carry cancellation penalties. It is a good idea to get prices from a number of travel agents or

International signpost at Christchurch

AIRPORT	**ℂ** INFORMATION	DISTANCE FROM CITY
Auckland	(09) 275 0789	21 km (13 miles)
Wellington	(04) 385 5123	8 km (5 miles)
Christchurch	(03) 353 7777	11 km (7 miles)
Dunedin	(03) 486 2879	30 km (18 miles)

e "City of Sails" design of Auckland International Airport

rect from airlines before aking a booking. Ask about pecial promotional fares, uch as two-for-one tickets, dvance purchase excursion res, student discounts, pecial deals for senior citizens and rates for stand-by ights. Also compare the rates or "open return" tickets with xed date return tickets. heck the limitations and enalties before buying a pecial rate ticket.

N ARRIVAL

uring flights to New ealand, visitors are given ustoms declaration documents to complete. These are be handed in on arrival, ong with passports. Fresh od or plant material must e placed in bins provided efore the immigration area. eavy fines are imposed on eople who fail to declare uarantine items into the ountry (see pp.358–9). Auckland, Wellington and hristchurch airports have a ride range of shops and ostal and telecommunication ervices. Car hire firms oper-te from the airports, and

banking facilities are open to coincide with international flight arrivals (see p364). Transfer from the airports to the city centres is straightforward: taxis and shuttles (vans with trailers for carrying luggage) are available for door-to-door service, and buses run regular services to the city centres. Bookings can be made at the airports for further domestic air travel.

Airport bus

Door-to-door shuttle

Airport taxi

Auckland's domestic and international terminals are in separate buildings about 1 km (0.6 mile), or a five-minute walk, apart; a free shuttle service operates between them from 6am to 10:30pm daily. At Christchurch and Wellington, the international and domestic services are located in the same building.

TAXI FARE TO CITY	BUS TRANSFER TO CITY	SHUTTLE FARE TO CITY	TRANSFER TIME TO CITY
NZ$80	NZ$15	NZ$30	60 mins
NZ$30	NZ$5	NZ$25	30 mins
NZ$30	NZ$7	NZ$20	15 mins
NZ$70	Not available	NZ$17	30 mins

Domestic Air Travel

New Zealand has an extensive domestic air transport network, linking all of the major and provincial cities as well as many smaller towns. Although it is a small country, New Zealand's long, thin shape means that land travel between major centres, such as Auckland, Wellington and Christchurch, is time-consuming. As a result, air services play a crucial transport role. The main domestic carrier is **Air New Zealand**. Air New Zealand also owns airline companies that operate feeder services to provincial centres. A wide range of heavily discounted fares are always available, particularly on the internet or if travellers are prepared to be flexible and to book well in advance.

Air New Zealand domestic flight arriving at Wellington airport

AIR ROUTES AND AIRLINES

Air New Zealand operates a national network that connects the main cities and provincial centres, including the major tourist resorts of Rotorua and Queenstown. Some 26 towns and cities are serviced by scheduled flights. Feeder services to provincial centres are operated under the Air New Zealand Link banner, which comprises **Air Nelson**, **Mount Cook Line** and **Eagle Air**. It is also possible to fly from Invercargill to Stewart Island, from Auckland to Great Barrier Island, from Wellington to Blenheim (as an alternative to the ferry) and from Wellington to Picton on SoundsAir (16 times per day).

Jet Star, operated by **Qantas**, is a cut-price airline, which flies between Auckland, Wellington, Christchurch and Queenstown. As well as internal flights, Freedom Air also offers flights between Hamilton, Palmerston North and Dunedin in New Zealand to Brisbane, Melbourne, Sydney and Coolanagatta in Australia. Qantas offers flights between Auckland and Christchurch, and between Auckland and Wellington. It has reintroduced its Christchurch to Wellington service too.

Pacific Blue is a New Zealand subsidiary of Virgin Blue and offers low fares which must be booked over the internet. At present it only has five flights per day from Auckland to Wellington, three per day from Wellington to Christchurch and two per day from Auckland to Christchurch.

DISCOUNTS FOR OVERSEAS VISITORS

Airlines offer discounted domestic air fares as part of an international package, so it is advisable to check with a travel agent before departure. Various air passes can be bought which allow visitors to make a number of single domestic flights for a set price. Air New Zealand's "South Pacific Airpass" is a coupon-based system that allows visitors to travel within New Zealand, and also between New Zealand, Australia and some South Pacific islands.

Visitors buy a minimum of two and up to a maximum of ten coupons, which allow flights within designated "zones", and are priced according to zone. For instance, a direct flight from Auckland to Hamilton counts as zone 1, while a flight between Auckland and Christchurch counts as zone 3. The pass is only available to overseas visitors to New Zealand and can be bought in their home country in conjunction with an international air ticket. Additional coupons can be bought at Air New Zealand offices at any of the destinations and are refundable before or after departure.

FLY–DRIVE DEALS

A convenient way to travel in New Zealand is to fly to a destination and then continue by car. Arrangements can be made for different drop-off and pick-up points for hire vehicles; for example, it is possible to fly from Auckland to Queenstown, then drive from Queenstown to Christchurch. Air New Zealand and other airlines have links with the major car hire firms, which offer discounts to passengers travelling on those airlines (see p374).

A wide range of fly–drive packages operate from Auckland to the South Island during the ski season, including deals combining flights, campervan or car rental, and ski lift passes at very competitive rates. Travel agents and airlines offer a variety of special promotions and it is best to shop around for the most suitable and economical package.

Mount Cook Line ski-planes in snowy conditions at the Mount Cook Airfield

Passengers checking in at Christchurch International Airport

AIR FARES

Standard domestic fares can be expensive, but airlines allocate a variety of fares to each flight, and even people making bookings at short notice can sometimes get a good deal.

Air New Zealand, for instance, offers an Express Class of fares that represent a substantial discount over standard fares. Express Class is divided into three categories, with different conditions attached to each.

Younger passengers also qualify for discounts. Children below 2 fly for 10 per cent of the adult fare on an adult's lap, while children above two to 11 pay 75 per cent of the adult fare.

CHECKING IN

On domestic flights, air lines require passengers to check in at least 30 minutes before the flight departs. Air New Zealand has self check-in kiosks for domestic flights. It is not necessary to confirm flights, but it is a good idea to make sure they are on time.

BAGGAGE RESTRICTIONS

All passengers, including children, travelling economy class on domestic flights have a baggage allowance of 20 kg (70 lb) and a one bag limit. The maximum weight for cabin baggage is 7 kg (11 lb) and must be storable under the seat in front or in an overhead locker. Personal articles, such as an overcoat, handbag or camera, may be carried into the aircraft.

DIRECTORY

DOMESTIC AIRLINES

Air New Zealand
Tel 0800 737 000.
www.airnewzealand.co.nz

Jet Star
Tel 0800 800 995.
www.jetstar.com

Pacific Blue
www.flypacificblue.com

Qantas
Tel 0800 808 767.

SoundsAir
Tel 0800 505 005.
www.soundsair.com

PRINCIPAL DOMESTIC AIR ROUTES

Domestic flights operating between major cities, complemented by a host of connecting flights between smaller towns and tourist resorts, cover the country quite comprehensively. Flying is ideal for those with limited time to spend in the country.

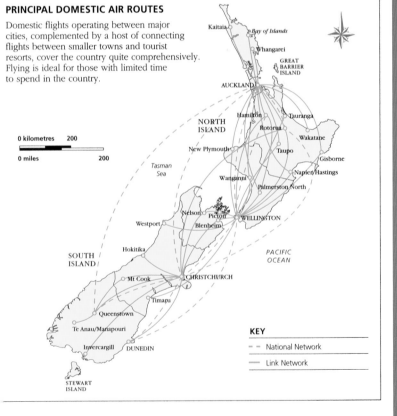

KEY

- - National Network

— Link Network

Travelling by Train, Coach and Inter-island Ferry

Although New Zealand does not have an extensive rail network, trains connect all the main cities and passenger journeys are outstanding for their breathtaking scenery, some not visible from the road. The mountainous terrain has forced railway engineers to build spectacular viaducts and long tunnels. New Zealand's coach service is extensive and efficient, connecting most points throughout the country. Coaches are a good alternative to train travel and cater for independent travellers as well as those who prefer guided tours. The North and South islands are connected by ferry with several sailings each day.

The TranzAlpine crossing Kowai Bridge near Springfield

THE NEW ZEALAND RAIL NETWORK

The New Zealand rail network is operated by a private company, **Tranz Scenic 2001 Ltd**, with choices of Tranz-Coastal, TranzAlpine and OverLander trains offering scenic rail journeys. Passenger rail services connect all the major cities as well as a number of provincial centres, including Ohakune, Palmerston North, Picton, Kaikoura and Greymouth. In the North Island, the OverLander train connects Auckland to Wellington, and vice versa.

SPECIALITY TRIPS

All the key rail routes travel through areas of scenic interest. Justifiably popular is the TranzAlpine journey from Christchurch to Greymouth, which crosses the Canterbury Plains before cutting dramatically through the Southern Alps via the Otira Tunnel (see pp242–3), and on through the rainforests of the West Coast. Many visitors return to Christchurch on the same day,

while others buy a one-way ticket and proceed by road from Greymouth to other attractions on the West Coast. The TranzCoastal, which runs between Picton and Christchurch, is also popular for the splendid scenery of the Kaikoura coast.

In Otago, there are two, privately-run excursion trains – the Taieri Gorge Railway (see p264) and the Kingston Flyer (see p279).

COACH TOURS

Coach travel is a safe, efficient and popular means of transport for tourists in

InterCity coach on State Highway 6, West Coast

New Zealand. The main operators are **InterCity Coachlines** and **Newmans Coach Lines**. Coach travellers have the option of joining a guided tour, taking regular scheduled services, or using one of the travel pass options available to independent travellers. Most New Zealand cities and towns are linked by InterCity, which has both scheduled services and three-month travel passes. Discounts of 30 per cent and 50 per cent are sometimes available on scheduled services, although these are subject to cancellation penalties.

The **Magic Bus** is another service that offers a travel pass system targetted at backpackers. Travellers buy a national coach pass, which they can use at any time within 12 months of purchase. Other coach companies also service specific routes in the various regions.

TICKETS AND BOOKINGS

Bookings for rail travel can be made through travel agents, or by calling Tranz Scenic Reservations seven days a week from 7am to 9pm

New Zealand trains do not have separate sections for different classes. However, there is a multi-tier fare structure for both rail and ferry travel, and discounts of up to 50 per cent on standard fares are often available, especially during off-peak periods. Always ask for the best possible price when making a booking.

TRAVEL PASSES

An economical and independent way to travel is to use the Tranz Scenic rail and ferry pass, similar to the date-based passes available in the United Kingdom and Europe. A choice of two passes is available, one valid for seven days travel, the other for a calendar month. The passes represent a substantial discount on standard fares. They do not, however, include coach trips.

A ship from the Interislander fleet

INTER-ISLAND FERRY SERVICES

The main inter-island ferry service between Wellington and Picton is provided by the **Interislander** fleet, which carries passengers, cars and freight. The Interislander service operates five return trips a day, taking about three hours each way. The trip is one of the most spectacular cruises in the world, offering breathtaking views, and the three ships in the fleet are all extremely comfortable, with a wide range of facilities on board, including restaurants, bars, cafés, movie theatres, children's rooms, observation decks and "quiet rooms" for business people. Travellers can book for other services when on board.

The **Bluebridge Cook Strait Ferry** runs twice daily and offers similar facilities to the Interislander ferries.

It is advisable to book in advance for the ferries, particularly during school holidays and especially if you are taking a car across the strait.

DIRECTORY

RAIL COMPANIES

Tranz Scenic 2001 Ltd
Tel 0800 872 467.
Tel 0064 4 495 0775 (overseas).
www.tranzscenic.co.nz

COACH COMPANIES

InterCity Coachlines
Tel (09) 913 6100.
www.intercitycoach.co.nz

Newmans Coach Lines
Tel (04) 499 3261.

Magic Bus
Tel (09) 358 5600.

FERRY COMPANIES

Interislander
Tel 0800 802 802.
Tel 0064 4 498 3302 (overseas).
www.interislandline.co.nz

Bluebridge Cook Strait Ferry
Tel (04) 472 3707.
www.bluebridge.co.nz

PRINCIPAL RAIL, COACH AND FERRY ROUTES

In New Zealand, travel by the national coach network, the scenic rail network and the inter-island ferry services enables visitors to cover much of the country. Local bus companies service smaller towns. Note that the following rail services do not carry passengers: Wellington to Napier, Auckland to Tauranga, Auckland to Rotorua, and Christchurch to Invercargill.

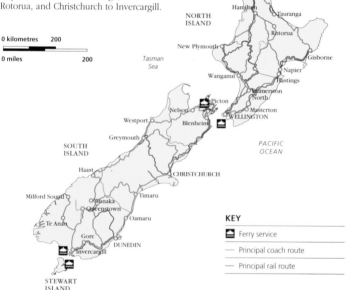

KEY

🚢 Ferry service

— Principal coach route

— Principal rail route

Travelling by Car

Motorway signboard in Auckland

Although the public transport system offers plenty of options for travelling between towns and cities, a car allows you to thoroughly explore New Zealand's scenic rural areas, and gives you the flexibility to stop at small country cafés, wineries and other points of interest, or simply pause to admire a view. Outside the main cities the roads are relatively uncongested, and in some areas virtually empty. Roads are generally in good condition, although even the major highways have many winding, hilly sections. Multi-lane motorways occur on the approaches to the main cities and between Auckland and Hamilton.

Avis rental booth at Auckland International Airport

DRIVING LICENCES

Provided you have a legal domestic or International Driving Permit, you can drive in New Zealand for up to 12 months. If your licence is not in English, take an English translation or get an International Driving Permit. All drivers, including overseas visitors, must take their licence with them when driving.

CAR RENTAL

Rental cars are readily available throughout the country with a large range of rental companies to choose from. Companies such as **Avis**, **Budget** and **Hertz** have nationwide networks.

Rates vary enormously depending on the size of car,

season and length of rental period. Off-season rates for a small car can be as low as NZ$19 a day, while a four-wheel drive vehicle at peak season rates can cost NZ$140. Rates are cheaper in the main cities than in the more remote towns, where rental companies have fewer cars available.

Some car hire firms offer fixed kilometre/mileage rentals, which are suitable for sightseeing around one of the major cities for two or three days. For longer rental periods and open road travel, it is better to choose a deal allowing you to travel an unlimited number of kilometres/miles. Fuel is not included in the rental price.

Rental companies frequently offer special promotions, such as combining car rental with

ski packages. When renting a car, discuss your travel plans with the company so that they can advise you on the most appropriate deal.

Smaller companies appear to charge less than the established ones, but they do not always include in their quotations features such as insurance. Some companies may also charge extra if you want to return the car to a depot other than the one you rented it from.

Sometimes car rental companies charge low rates for people to drive from one location to another where cars are needed, for example, from Wellington to Auckland. This is an economical way to travel, but sightseeing time may be limited as cars usually need to be delivered urgently.

Most rental companies will not hire to anyone under the age of 21. Companies prefer to be paid by credit card, and even if payment is by cash or traveller's cheque they are likely to ask for a credit card imprint as security against loss or damage.

State Highway 1 parallelling the railway line along the Kaikoura coast

OTHER VEHICLES

A popular form of transport with visitors to New Zealand is a campervan or motor-home. The largest companies, such as **Maui Rentals** and **Kea Campers**, have depots in Auckland, Christchurch and Queenstown. Campervans are available in a range of sizes, from two-berth to six-berth. All are equipped with a refrigerator and gas cooker, and some of the more luxurious have their own shower, toilet and microwave. Prices vary greatly throughout the year. In summer, a two-berth van will cost about NZ$145 a day

Maui Rentals campervan parked near Auckland waterfront

and a six-berth van about NZ$275 a day, while from May to September the same vehicles will cost about NZ$65 and NZ$170.

New Zealand is an ideal place for travelling by campervan, as camping grounds can be found in virtually every town, often in beautiful locations (*see p297*).

INSURANCE

Car and campervan rental rates usually include insurance cover for collision damage and theft from the vehicle. However, insurance policies often carry a very high excess payment, in some cases around NZ$1,500 for a car and NZ$5,000 for a campervan. Many companies offer "excess waiver" options, allowing payment of a daily rate of around NZ$10 to NZ$20 to reduce the excess to under NZ$200. Personal accident plans are available, but this risk should be covered by comprehensive travel insurance. Insurance for drivers under 25 is more expensive.

Service station selling both petrol and diesel

FUEL

The majority of New Zealand cars run on petrol, while most four-wheel drive vehicles and campervans use diesel. Petrol costs about two-thirds of the price of petrol in Europe. It is dispensed by the litre and is available in regular unleaded and premium unleaded grades. Diesel is cheaper than petrol and is easily obtained.

Fuel is bought from gas stations, commonly known as "service stations". Many city stations are open until late at night and some remain open 24 hours. Even very small settlements have a service station or shop with a petrol pump, but these are often closed in the evening and on weekends, so fill up in town to avoid running short of fuel when travelling long distances. Most service stations also sell a range of basic grocery items as well as newspapers and magazines.

Speed limit sign

ROAD RULES AND SIGNS

New Zealanders drive on the left-hand side of the road. All signposting follows standard international symbols, and all distances are in kilometres. The speed limit is 100 km/h (60 mph) on the open road and 50 km/h (30 mph) in urban areas. Excessive speed is a major hazard on New Zealand roads, and speed cameras are scattered throughout the country, both on the open road and on city streets. Cameras record the details of vehicles exceeding the speed

limit and drivers are fined on a graduated scale depending on the speed. Travelling 50 km/h (30 mph) in excess of the speed limit may result in a 28-day licence suspension. Because of New Zealand's many winding roads, signs warning motorists to slow down to a recommended speed are very common.

A broken or solid yellow line down the centre of the road means it is illegal to overtake another vehicle because of poor visibility. Main highways have passing lanes at regular intervals. When turning, drivers must give way to traffic not turning and to all traffic crossing or approaching from the right.

Drink-driving laws are strictly enforced in New Zealand. A driver may be required to give a breath screening test at any time. The legal blood alcohol level is 80 milligrams of alcohol per 100 millilitres of blood (30 milligrams for a driver under 20). Police in the countryside are every bit as vigilant as in the cities and often conduct random breath testing.

Traffic accidents involving injury must be reported to the police within 24 hours. When an accident involves another vehicle, drivers should exchange insurance company details. It is best not to accept responsibility for an accident but rather inform the police of what happened and let them decide.

It is compulsory for both drivers and passengers to wear seat belts, and babies and children under five must be put in an infant's car seat.

Drivers moving slowly past sheep on a state highway

ROAD CONDITIONS

Considering the small population and the size of the country, the quality of New Zealand's roads is excellent. However, visitors used to travelling long distances on two- or three-lane freeways with no opposing traffic need to take care. Median barriers exist only on motorways in the major cities, and on other roads the only thing separating drivers from opposing traffic is a painted centre line. Because of New Zealand's hilly terrain, stretches of winding road are common even on the major state highways. Another potential hazard are railway lines that cross main roads. Flashing lights and railway barriers are usually activated to indicate an approaching train, but these may be absent in remote areas, and it is wise to reduce speed at all railway crossing signs.

Many back roads leading to scenic areas or points of interest are unsealed, for example the road leading to the Oparara Basin north of Karamea (see p234). These roads require extreme care as they are often narrow and it is easy to lose control on the gravel surface or on verges. Winter driving is generally trouble-free, but ice and snow in the mountainous and inland areas of the South Island can cause problems.

SIGNS ALONG COUNTRY ROADS

Different road signs offer warnings and instructions for drivers. Speed limits vary depending on the conditions of the road and the amount of traffic. Notably hazardous are railway crossings, gravel roads, and one-lane bridges, where traffic moving in the direction of the large white arrow has priority. Drivers should be wary of stock or wildlife straying onto roads.

Be careful of penguins

Slippery gravel road

Beware of cows

Railway crossing ahead

Watch out for kiwis

School children crossing

Be aware of pukekos on the road

One-lane bridge ahead

AA breakdown service truck

Grit is regularly scattered on these roads to prevent cars from skidding, but it is advisable to check on road conditions with the DOC or Automobile Association before travelling over alpine routes such as Arthur's Pass (see pp242–43) and Haast Pass (see p273).

One-lane bridges are common on minor highways and back roads, particularly on the west coast of the South Island. A red arrow means you must give way to opposing traffic. Occasionally, drivers will come across combination rail-and-road bridges and it is important to heed flashing lights indicating that a train is approaching.

Rail-and-road bridge near Kumara Junction

Wandering farm stock are sometimes a problem, although generally only on minor roads. It is relatively common to be delayed by farmers shifting flocks of sheep along country roads. Drivers need to be patient and drive extremely slowly while the animals move past. Possums and other nocturnal animals often venture on to the roads at night and drivers should drive carefully in order to avoid hitting them.

ROADSIDE ASSISTANCE

Car hire companies deal with breakdowns involving their own vehicles, and will arrange to provide replacements, if necessary. The **Automobile Association** (AA) is a nationwide motoring organization providing breakdown services and information on road conditions. Other services offered include provision of detailed maps covering every area of New Zealand, guides covering all types of accommodation, from camping grounds to luxury hotels, technical advice and touring information. The AA has offices in almost every large town. Members of most overseas motoring organizations have reciprocal rights with the New Zealand AA. To get the benefit of AA services while in New Zealand, take your home motoring organization card into an AA office in New Zealand where you will be issued with a temporary membership.

AA membership entitles you to six free breakdown callouts a year, as well as discounted rates at some hotels and motels and on car rental.

INNER-CITY DRIVING

If driving in New Zealand cities, an up-to-date street map is essential, especially for spotting one-way streets. If possible, avoid the peak traffic hours of 7:30am to 9am and 4:30pm to 6pm, especially in Auckland and Wellington. Traffic reports are broadcast on local radio stations (see p361).

Parking is available in downtown areas, in metered parks, parking buildings and shopping mall car parks. Councils administer parking, and wardens issue fines to vehicles that are parked illegally or that have expired meters.

Most cities have clearway zones and during certain times vehicles parked in these areas may be towed away. If this occurs, call the local traffic authority or police to find out where your car has been impounded. Retrieving the car involves paying an on-the-spot fine.

Parking meter operated with coins, credit card or by text message

General Index

Acknowledgments

DORLING KINDERSLEY would like to thank the following people whose contributions and assistance have made the preparation of this book possible.

Contributors

Helen Corrigan is a Wellington-based writer, editor, researcher and publicist. She has a background in journalism and radio and since 2002 has been a parliamentary press secretary.

Roef Hopman is a public relations consultant and freelance writer in Auckland. Formerly Chief Editor of *Design Trends*, he organizes public relations projects for Pacific Rim countries and contributes to various publications.

Gerard Hutching is a freelance journalist who specializes in natural history and the environment. He has written several books, including *The Natural World of New Zealand* which won the 1999 Montana Book of the Year (environment).

Rebecca Macfie is an award-winning Christchurch-based journalist. She specializes in business and current affairs feature writing, and contributes to a range of New Zealand newspapers and magazines.

Geoff Mercer lives in Hastings. He has written for daily newspapers in Wellington and Hawke's Bay. He now compiles oral histories, writes and publishes biographies, and contributes articles to various publications.

Simon Noble lives in Nelson and has a long involvement in the region's natural, historic and scenic areas. He is the author of *The Treasured Pathway*, a guide to a heritage highway through northern Nelson and Marlborough.

Peter Smith is an Auckland artist, educator, writer and yachtsman, and former principal of Auckland College of Education.

Michael Ward is a chef who has worked in the food industry for some twenty years. Michael has a keen interest in promoting New Zealand food and wine.

Mark Wright is a Dunedin-based freelance writer whose work ranges from articles on travel, technology and health to classic cars. He has a background in radio and writes scripts for television and video.

Additional Contributors

Georgina Palffy; Simon Vita

For Dorling Kindersley

Publishing Manager Kate Poole
Cartographic Editors Casper Morris, David Pugh
Production Michelle Thomas
Publishing Director Gillian Allan
Revisions Editor Neil Lockley
Revisions Designers Mariana Evmolpidou, Supriya Sahai

Indexer

Kay Lyons

Additional Photography

Peter Bush, Louise Goossens, Ian O'Leary

Design and Editorial Assistance

Emma Anacootee, Lydia Baillie, Rhiannon Furbear, Jenn Hadley, Brendan Hutching, Hayley Maher, Sam Merrell, Kate Molan, Helen Partington, Marianne Petrou, Susana Smith, Conrad Van Dyk.

Special Assistance

Debbie Ameriks and Amelia Manson, Office of Treaty Settlements, Wellington; Tim Amos, Department of Conservation, Wellington; Lane Ayr, Bay of Islands Swordfish Club; Kate Banbury, Waitomo Glow Worm Caves New Zealand, Otorohanga; Jennifer Beatson, Latitude Nelson; Black's Point Museum, Reefton; Hughie Blues and Amanda Turner, Waikokopu Café, Waitangi; Julia Bradshaw, Lakes District Museum, Arrowtown; Linda Burgess, Wellington; Dennis Buurman, Ocean Wings; Elizabeth Caldwell, Arts Council of New Zealand; Cathedral Church of St Paul, Wellington; Alan Cooper, Geology Department, University of Otago, Dunedin; C.P. Group, Auckland; Croydon Aircraft Company, Gore; Jo Darby, Tourism Industry Association New Zealand; Carol Davidson, New Zealand Festival 2000; Department of Conservation Visitor Centres; Jenny Dey, Photosource New Zealand Ltd; Richard Doyle and Lisa Hoffman, Christchurch City Council; Far North Regional Museum, Kaitia; Tammy Fromont and Nineke Metz, Destination Northland Limited; Dianne Gallagher, New Zealand Mountain Safety Council Inc.; Jane Gilbert, Film New Zealand; Gillooly family, Farewell Spit Safari, Collingwood; Donna Gray, Abel Tasman National Park Enterprises; Lesley Grey and Sharon Pasco, Stewart Island Promotion Association; Frank Habicht, Paihia; Haoni Waititi Marae, Auckland; Lee Harris, Fiordland Travel Limited, Queenstown; Tania Harris, Waitangi National Trust; Christine Harvey, Whale Watch®, Kaikoura; Cameron Hill, Air New Zealand, Auckland; Hillary Commission; Barbara Hinkley and Suzanne Knight, Museum of New Zealand Te Papa Tongarewa; InterCity Coachlines; Anne Irving, City Gallery, Wellington; Peter Jackson, Blenheim; Jean Johnston, Wellington City Council; Kapiti Cheese; Kelly Tarlton's Underwater World and Antarctic Encounter, Auckland; Michael Liao, Kiwifruit Country, Te Puke; Fay Looney, New Plymouth; Peter McCleavey Gallery, Wellington; Ruth McGirr, Robert McDougall Art Gallery and Annex, Christchurch; Bill and Joan MacGregor, Lake Hawea; Robert McGregor, Art Deco Trust, Napier; Annabelle MacKenzie and Cathy Muker, New Zealand High Commission, Kuala Lumpur; Cathy Maslin, Key-Light Image Library; Heather Mathie and Betty Moss, Alexander Turnbull Library; Darryl May, Oamaru; Montana Marlborough Winery; Anita Moreira, Air New Zealand, Kuala Lumpur; Morven Hills Station, Oamaru; Museum of Caves, Waitomo; Newmans Coach Lines; New Zealand Fighter Pilots Museum, Wanaka; Okarito Nature Tours, Westland; Old Mandeville Airport, Gore; Otago Early Settlers Museum, Dunedin; security staff, Parliament House, Wellington; Libby Passau and Nick Turzynski, Hodder Moa Beckett Publishers Ltd; Jacky Payne; Penguin Place, Otago Peninsula; Meng-Chong Phang, New Zealand Tourism Board, Singapore; Clive Ralph, Napier; Rewa's Village, Kerikeri; Chris and Phil Rose, Wairau River Wines; Royal Albatross Centre, Taiaroa Head; Russell Museum; Mary Sharrock, Ansett Airways, Australia; Jenny Shipley, MP, Wellington; Stone Store, Kerikeri; Annalese Taylor, New Zealand Tourism Board, Auckland; Judith Tizard, MP; Tourism Auckland Office; Tourism Industry Association New Zealand; Tranz Rail Ltd; Tom Van der Kwast, Picton; Andrew and Jeannie Van der Putten; Visitor Information Centres; Tim Warren, Visual Impact Pictures Ltd; concert staff, Whakarewarewa Thermal Village, Rotorua; Whangarei Museum of Fishes; Dr Rodney Wilson, Auckland War Memorial Museum; Jane Wynyard, The Royal New Zealand Ballet.

Photography Permissions

The publisher would like to thank the following for their assistance and kind permission to photograph at their establishments.

Graham Abbott, Hanmer Springs Thermal Reserve; Art and Gourd Gallery, Golden Bay; Ashford Craft Village, Ashburton; Auckland International Airport; Auckland Zoological Gardens; Avis, Auckland International Airport; Babich Winery, Auckland; Grant Barron, Olveston House, Dunedin; Café de Paris, Hokitika; Canterbury House Vineyards, Waipara; Christ Church Cathedral, Christchurch; Dr Fiona Ciaran, Aigantighe Art Gallery, Timaru; Clapham Clock Museum, Whangarei; Coal Town Museum, Westport; Dargaville Maritime Museum; DFS Galleria, Auckland; Driving Creek Railway and Potteries, Coromandel; Dunedin Public Art Gallery; Dunedin Railway Station; The

Edwin Fox, Picton; Ana Foreman, Weta Shop, Coromandel; Gibbston Valley Winery, Queenstown; Lindsay Hazley, Southland Museum and Art Gallery, Invercargill; Helen and Ross Ivey, Glentanner Station; Kevin Judd, Cloudy Bay; Steve Jones, Science Centre, Manawatu Museum and Art Gallery, Palmerston North; Kauri Kingdom, Kaitaia; Stuart Landsborough's Puzzling World, Wanaka; Left Bank Art Gallery, Greymouth; Le Brun family, Blenheim; Malcolm McLaughlan and Peter Thornley, Icon Restaurant, Wellington; Maori Arts and Crafts Institute, Rotorua; Royce McGlashen, Nelson; Matakohe Kauri Museum, Dargaville; Mountain Jade Greenstone Factory, Hokitika; Mt Bruce Wildlife Centre, Wairarapa; Mountford Vineyard, Canterbury; Museum of Transport and Technology, Auckland; Museum of Wellington City and Sea; New Zealand Automobile Association; New Zealand Rugby Museum, Palmerston North; North Otago Museum, Oamaru; Nigel and Teresa Ogle, Tawhiti Museum, Hawera; Outdoor Heritage, Newmarket; Out of New Zealand, Auckland; Parnell Fire Service; Parnell Police Station; Pegasus Bay, Canterbury; Provincial Council Buildings, Christchurch; Queenstown Rafting; Rainbow's End Adventure Park, Auckland; Rippon Vineyards, Wanaka; St John's Ambulance; St Paul's Cathedral, Dunedin; Shantytown, Greymouth; Sheraton Auckland Hotel; Shotover Jet, Queenstown; Southward Car Museum, Paraparaumu; Stockton Mine, Westport; Thames School of Mines and Mineralogical Museum; Tramway Museum, Paekakariki; Waiau Waterworks, Coromandel; Waipara Springs, Canterbury; Whakarewarewa Thermal Village, Rotorua; Whale Watch®, Kaikoura; Whanganui Riverboat Centre; Zambesi, Wellington.

Picture Credits

t = top; tl = top left; tlc = top left centre; tc = top centre; trc = top right centre; tr = top right; cla = centre left above; ca = centre above; cra = centre right above; cl = centre left; c = centre; cr = centre right; clb = centre left below; crb = centre right below; cb = centre below; bl = bottom left; br = bottom right; b = bottom; bc = bottom centre; bcl = bottom centre left; bcr = bottom centre right.

The publisher would like to thank the following individuals, companies and picture libraries for permission to reproduce their photographs:

AGL AERIAL IMAGERY: 39br; AIR NEW ZEALAND: 368tc; ALAMY IMAGES: Paul Grogan 109tl; Paul Miller 11br; Paul Thomspon Images 323tl; Douglas Fisher 323cl; Jon Arnold Images 10cra; ANSETT AUSTRALIA: 368cla; ANZ NATIONAL BANK LIMITED: 364clb; ART DECO TRUST: 146bl; AUCKLAND CITY COUNCIL: 377br.

BAY OF ISLANDS SWORDFISH CLUB: 103tc, 103cla; BNZ: 364cl; BRITOMART LIMITED: 70cla; PETER BUSH: 20t, 33cr, 38clb, 38bl, 38br, 71tr, 119clb, 157bl, 347cr, 360bl.

CHRISTCHURCH CITY COUNCIL: 218; CITY GALLERY, WELLINGTON: 164tr; CORBANS WINES: 36tl; CORBIS: Peter Beck 322cl; Graham Tim 11cl; Zefa/Jose Fuste Raga 10bl; Stuart Westmorland 288tl.

DEPARTMENT OF CONSERVATION, WELLINGTON: 191tr, 219b, 238tr, 350tc; DESTINATION NORTHLAND LIMITED: 96cl, 103cra, 108bc.

GARETH EYRES, EXPOSURE: 39tl, 41bc, 42cr, 58–59, 108c, 121cr, 144–145, 186–187, 204–205c, 239cr, 271br, 283tr, 351tl, 352tl, 352b, 353t; GETTY IMAGES: Darryl Torckler 99br.

FIORDLAND TRAVEL LIMITED: 280tr, 284tr, 284cla, 284clb, 284bl, 283tl, 283cl, 283cr. HERZOG WINERY AND LUXURY RESTAURANT: 312cl; HODDER MOA BECKETT PUBLISHERS LTD: 33bl.

INTERCITY COACHLINES: 372bc; INTERISLANDER: 373tl.

KEY-LIGHT IMAGE LIBRARY: Warren Jacobs 22–23; Brian Enting Photography 23tl; Warren Jacobs 26tr; Andy Radka 26cl; Nick Servian 30br, 30–31c; Michael Pole 34tr; James White 34clb; Graham Meadows 34bc; Nick Servian 34br; Gary Bowering 37bc; Graham Radcliffe 42bl; Brian Enting Photography 47bl; Andy Belcher 64tl; Geoff Mason 64tr; Brian Enting Photography 64br; Warren Jacobs 100–101; Richard Cory-Wright 119br; Brian Enting Photography

142clb; Andy Belcher 143cr; Michael Hall 152; Nick Servian 165tr; Graham Radcliffe 173br; Peter Laurenson 183crb; Warren Jacobs 183br; Brian Chudleigh 194tr; Geoff Mason 195br; Caroline Hobbs 239tr; Nic Bishop 244bl; Geoff Mason 247cl; Tim Hawkins 252bc; Warren Jacobs 272cl; Nic Bishop 273ca; Peter Reese 290cl; Geoff Mason 350bl; Ron Redfern 351cc; Warren Jacobs 355tl; Geoff Mason 370br; Graham Radcliffe 372cl; KIWIFRUIT COUNTRY: 129tr.

LAKES DISTRICT MUSEUM: 279c; Holger Leue: 22br, 26cr, 27bl, 34cla, 34–35c, 49bc, 65cr, 65br, 68cl, 73cl, 74tl, 75bl, 77tr, 78br, 83bc, 89t, 92bl, 93tl, 103br, 113b, 120cl, 122br, 123tc, 127br, 130tr, 131crb, 138tl, 143tr, 190tr, 190cla, 192tl, 194–195c, 227br, 232tl, 238tl, 244br, 252tr, 252cl, 253tl, 254, 267c, 272br, 276tl, 277c, 278tr, 280br, 282tr, 282cr, 282bl, 283cl, 283b, 286tl, 288cl, 288bc, 289br, 297cl, 376cla, 376cra, 376bl, 377cl; Rob Lucas: 24bl, 24bc, 24br, 25tlc, 25bl, 25crb, 132tl, 244tl, 252tl, 272tl, 283cr.

ROBERT McDOUGALL ART GALLERY AND ANNEX: 32bl; DARRYL MAY: 268tl, 268cla, 268clb, 269ca, 269ca; ROD MORRIS: 1 (inset), 17tc, 24tl, 24clb, 24cb, 24crb, 25tl, 25tr, 25cla, 25cra, 25tl, 47cr, 89cl, 192tr, 192cl, 192bl, 192br, 245cr, 251cl, 266cr, 272bl, 289cr, 291tl; MUSEUM OF NEW ZEALAND TE PAPA TONGA-REWA: 29bl, 30tl, 30bl, 31tl, 31cr, 33tl, 46tr, 46bc, 47trc, 51ca, 57bl, 166tl, 166tr, 166cla, 166clb, 167tl, 167clb, 360tl.

NAPIER CITY COUNCIL: 148tr; NATIONAL PARTY OFFICE: 53bc; NELSON TASMAN TOURISM: 215tl; NEWMANS COACH LINES: 358br; NEW ZEALAND FESTIVAL 2000: 40tc, 156clb, 156–157c, 335tl; THE NEW ZEALAND HERALD: 18b, 53tr, 117bl, 157tc; NEW ZEALAND MOUNTAIN SAFETY COUNCIL INC.: www. mountainsafety.org.nz 362tl.

OFFICE OF TREATY SETTLEMENTS: 45ca, 53cl; OLVESTON HOUSE: 265tl

LLOYD PARK: 23br, 35bl, 35bc, 190–191c, 191br, 240–241, 247tc, 247cra, 247cr; PHOTOSOURCE NEW ZEALAND LTD: 2–3, 8–9, 35cl, 35cr, 35clb, 38ca, 39clb, 39bl, 40bl, 43c, 43b, 54–55, 62cl, 109cra, 119bl, 121bl, 150tl, 161cl, 176–177, 182tr, 182bl, 193tr, 194tl, 194br, 195tl, 238cl, 245tl, 253cra, 281cr, 354tl, 355cr.

THE ROYAL NEW ZEALAND BALLET: 92cr, 157br.

SCIENCE CENTRE AND MANAWATU MUSEUM: 175tr, 175br, 175bl; Sky City Auckland Limited, 74tl; STEWART ISLAND PROMOTION ASSOCIATION: 288tl; SUPERSHUTTLE: 369C.

TOURISM NEW ZEALAND: 56bl, 57br, 60tl, 95b, 97tl, 295cl, 297t, 354bl, 358tc, 375cl; ALEXANDER TURNBULL LIBRARY: 9 (inset), 18c, 30tr, 31tr, 31b, 32tl, 33br, 36cl, 44, 45bl, 46tl, 46cl, 46bl, 46cla, 47tc, 47br, 48tl, 48c, 48bl, 48br, 49br, 50tr, 50clb, 50bl, 51c, 51bc, 51br, 52tl, 52clb, 52cb, 55 (inset), 59 (inset), 62tl, 62bl, 62–63c, 63tl, 63cr, 85br, 137br, 171br, 187 (inset), 226cr, 235cl, 293 (inset), 357 (inset).

VISUAL IMPACT PICTURES LTD: 16, 26bl, 27cr, 27br, 28tr, 35cra, 35crb, 35cla, 39cra, 40cr, 78tr, 80–81, 103bl, 109crb, 112, 117cl, 123bl, 128bl, 142tr, 182tl, 190clb, 191tl, 195bl, 214tr, 246tl, 274–275, 291cr, 292–293, 296br, 356–357. WAIRAU RIVER WINES: 207cr; WAITANGI NATIONAL TRUST: 41cr, 96br, 104cl, 104bl, 105tl, 105bl; WAITOMO GLOW WORM CAVES NEW ZEALAND: 120tl; WELLINGTON CITY COUNCIL: 87br, 156br; DR KIM WESTERSKOV: 86cr, 103clb, 149br, 193tl, 193cra, 193cb, 266tl, 280tl; WESTPAC LIMITED: 354cl; WHALE WATCH®: 209cla; WOMEN'S GOLF NEW ZEALAND: 39tr.

Front Endpaper: All special photography except CHRISTCHURCH CITY COUNCIL: bc; HOLGER LEUE: br; VISUAL IMPACT PICTURES LTD: cl.

Jacket – Front: GETTY IMAGES: Image Bank/Peter Turner main image; MUSEUM OF NEW ZEALAND TE PAPA TONGAREWA: Hei tiki ornament. Maker unknown, Pounamu (greenstone). Gift of Mr W L Buller bl. Back – DK IMAGES: Peter Bush cla, clb, bl; Gerald Lopez tl. Spine – DK IMAGES: Gerald Lopez b; GETTY IMAGES: Image Bank/Peter Turner t.

Further Reading

Art and Culture

Contemporary Painting in New Zealand Dunn, M., Craftsman House, Auckland 1996.

Dream Collectors: 100 Years of Art in New Zealand Wedde, I., Walsh, J. and Johnson, A., Te Papa Press, Wellington 1998.

A History of New Zealand Architecture Shaw, P., Hodder Moa Beckett, Auckland 1998.

Looking for the Local: Architecture and the New Zealand Modern Clark, J. and Walker, P., Victoria University Press, Wellington 2000.

Mau Moko: The World of Maori Tattoo Te Awekotuku, N. & Nikora, L.W., Penguin, Auckland 2007.

New Zealand Pottery: Commercial and Collectable Henry, G., Reed Publishing, Auckland 2007.

Old New Zealand Houses 1800–1940 Salmond, J., Reed Publishing, Auckland 1998.

100 New Zealand Craft Artists Schamroth, H., Godwit, Auckland 1998.

100 New Zealand Paintings Brown, W., Godwit, Auckland 1997.

Fiction

Believers to the Bright Coast O'Sullivan, V., Penguin, Auckland 1998.

The Best of Katherine Mansfield's Short Stories Mansfield K., Random House, Auckland 1998.

The Best of Owen Marshall Marshall, O., Random House, Auckland 1997.

The Bone People Hulme, K., Picador, Auckland 1986.

Land of the Long White Cloud: Maori Myths, Tales and Legends Kanawa, K.T. and Foreman, M., Penguin Auckland, 1997.

Mister Pip Jones, L., Penguin, Auckland 2006.

The Matriarch Ihimaera, W., Reed Publishing, Auckland 1996.

Once Were Warriors Duff, A., Tandem Press, Auckland 1990.

100 New Zealand Poems Manhire, B. (ed.), Godwit, Auckland 1994.

Plumb Gee, M., Penguin, Auckland 1981.

Potiki Grace, P., Penguin, Auckland 1986.

Reconnaissance Kassabova, K., Penguin, Auckland 1999.

Season of the Jew Shadbolt, M., David Ling Publishing, Auckland 1988.

Skylark Lounge Cox, N., Victoria University Press, Wellington 2000.

Geography and Geology

Aotearoa and New Zealand: A Historical Geography Grey, A., Canterbury University Press, Christchurch 1995.

Awesome Forces: The Natural Hazards That Threaten New Zealand Campbell, H. and Hicks, G., Te Papa Press Wellington 1998.

Contemporary Atlas of New Zealand Kirkpatrick, R., David Bateman, Auckland 1999.

Historical New Zealand Atlas Malcolm McKinnon et al (eds.), David Bateman, Auckland 1997.

History and Politics

A Concise Encyclopaedia of Maori Myth and Legend Orbell, M., Canterbury University Press, Christchurch 1998.

The Discovery of Aotearoa Evans, J., Reed Publishing, Auckland 1998.

Historical Dictionary of New Zealand Jackson, K. and McRobie, A., Addison, Wesley, Longman, Auckland 1996.

Making Peoples: A History of New Zealanders from Polynesian Settlement to the End of the 19th Century Belich, J., Penguin, Auckland 1996.

New Zealand, the Story So Far: A Short History Bohan, E., Harper Collins, Auckland 1997.

The Oxford History of New Zealand Oliver W.H. (ed.), Oxford University Press, Wellington 1981.

Politics in New Zealand

Mulgan, R. Auckland University Press, Auckland 1997.

Penguin History of New Zealand, King, M., Penguin, 2003.

The Treaty of Waitangi Orange, C., Bridget Williams Books, Wellington 1991.

Natural History

A Field Guide to the Alpine Plants of New Zealand Salmon, J., Godwit, Auckland 1999.

Field Guide to the Birds of New Zealand Heather, B. and Robertson, H., Viking, Auckland 1996.

Game Animals of New Zealand Roberts, G., Shoal Bay Press, Blenheim 1998.

Ghosts of Gondwana, Gibbs, G., Craig Potton Publishing, Nelson 2006.

Kiwi: New Zealand's Remarkable Bird Peat, N., Godwit, Auckland 1999.

Native Trees of New Zealand Salmon J., Reed Publishing, Auckland 1996.

Natural History of New Zealand Bishop, N., Hodder and Stoughton, Auckland 1992.

The Natural World of New Zealand Hutching, G., Viking, Auckland 1998.

Outdoor Activities

Bird's Eye Guide: Tramping in New Zealand Barnett, S., Craig Potton Publishing, Nelson 2006.

Classic New Zealand Mountain Bike Rides Kennett, P., Kennett, S. and Kennett, J., Reed Publishing, Auckland 1998.

Classic Walks of New Zealand Potton C., Craig Potton Publishing, Nelson 1997.

New Zealand: Pure Adventure McLennan, C., David Bateman, Auckland 1999.

A Tramper's Guide to New Zealand's National Parks Burton, R. and Atkinson, M., Reed Publishing, Auckland 1998.

Glossary

CULTURE

Aotearoa: Maori name for New Zealand, literally "Land of the Long White Cloud", coined by the explorer Kupe's wife *(see p17)*

haka: war dance and song performed by males *(see p30)*

hangi: style of cooking food in an earth oven where the heat is provided by special stones or embers *(see p137)*

hongi: greeting by pressing noses together. When people *hongi*, their *hau* or life essence intermingles

iwi: tribe, people. A *hapu* is a subtribe and *whanau* an extended family

kai: food. Any word with *kai* in it relates to food, for example *kai moana* (seafood) *(see p109)*

kete: woven basket made from the fibre of flax, kiekie or pingao plants *(see p31)*

mana: authority, prestige, psychic power

maori: ordinary or usual, used by indigenous New Zealanders from the 19th century to distinguish themselves from *pakeha* (stranger or different)

Maoritanga: Maori culture

marae: gathering place, open courtyard in front of a village meeting house where important meetings, funerals and entertainment take place *(see p116)*

mere: flat greenstone war club, most highly valued of weapons *(see p200)*

moko: tattoos incised on the faces, buttocks and thighs of men and the lips and chins of women *(see p30)*

pa: fortified village or stockade *(see p50)*

pakeha: stranger, person of European descent

poi: ball made of leaves attached to a piece of string and used by women in graceful dances *(see p30–31)*

tane: man, male

tangi: funeral

taonga: treasures, cultural items such as carvings or woven cloaks passed down through the generations

tapu: holy, sacred, forbidden; taboo in English

tiki: from *heitiki*; prized greenstone figure worn around the neck. Debate continues over the origins and religious significance of this ornament *(see p30)*

wahine: woman, female

waiata: songs. There are many types, for example *waiata tangi* (laments) and *waiata aroha* (love songs)

waka: canoe. The masterpieces were elaborately carved 30-metre *waka taua* or war canoes *(see p47)*

whare: house. There are a number of different houses: *whare runanga* (meeting house) *(see p28)*; *whare whakairo* (carved house); *whare puni* (family sleeping house)

GEOGRAPHY AND NATURE

kauri: huge forest tree growing in northern New Zealand *(see p24)*

kea: uncommon but inquisitive alpine parrot whose name is derived from its call *(see p25)*

kiwi: flightless, nocturnal indigenous bird which uses its long beak to probe in the earth for worms *(see p24)*

koru: the spiral, the principal motif used in Maori carving, inspired by the unfurling fern frond or *koru*; it signifies "awakening, the process of growth, joy" *(see p24)*

kumara: sweet potato, transported from Polynesia to New Zealand where it became a staple food *(see p45)*

manuka: shrubby plant popularly known as the tea tree with proven anti-bacterial qualities, source of honey and oils *(see p24)*

paua: black coloured shellfish known elsewhere as abalone, prized for its beautiful shell which is worked into jewellery *(see p345)*

pohutukawa: large spreading coastal tree covered in scarlet flowers during early summer, hence described as the "Christmas tree" *(see p25)*

ponga: tree fern

pounamu: greenstone or jade, the most precious stone used in jewellery and weapons, found in the South Island and traded with North Island tribes *(see p 237)*

Te Ika a Maui: the fish of Maui, the North Island

Te Wai Pounamu: South Island

EVERYDAY WORDS AND PHRASES

Haere mai: Welcome

Haere ra: Goodbye (from the person staying to the one going)

E noho ra: Goodbye (from the person going to the one staying)

Ka pai: Thank you

Kia ora: Thank you, good luck, good health

Tena koe: Hello (to one person)

Tena koutou: Hello (to more than three people)

Kei te pehea koe: How are you?

Kei te pai: Very well, thank you

WORDS COMMONLY FORMING PLACE NAMES

ao: cloud

atua: spirit or gods

awa: river or valley

hau: wind

ika: fish

iti: small

kai: food

kainga: village

kare: rippling

manga: stream, tributary

manu: bird

maunga: mountain

moana: sea or lake

motu: island

nui: big

one: beach, sand or mud

papa: flat, broad slab

po: night

puke: hill

puna: water spring

rangi: sky, heavens

roa: long

roto: lake

rua: two, hole

te: the

wai: water

wero: challenge

whanga: bay or inlet

whenua: land or country

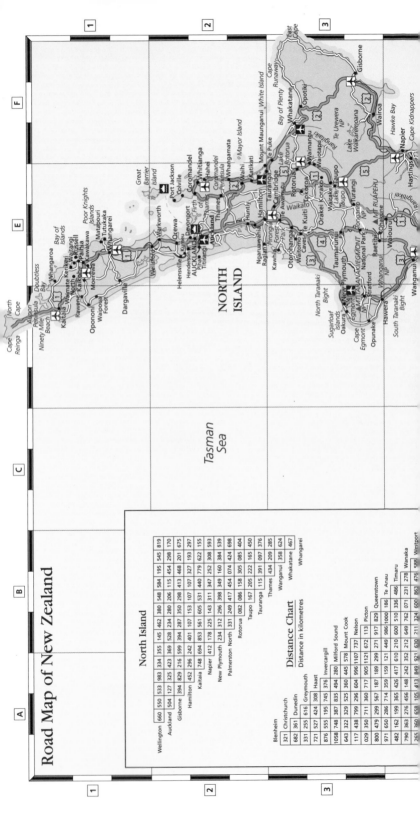

Road Map of New Zealand